OVER THE EDGE

OVER THE EDGE

Remapping the American West

EDITED BY
VALERIE J. MATSUMOTO
AND BLAKE ALLMENDINGER

Published in association with the UCLA Center for Seventeenth- and Eighteenth-Century Studies and the William Andrews Clark Memorial Library

UNIVERSITY OF CALIFORNIA PRESS
BERKELEY LOS ANGELES LONDON

University of California Press
Berkeley and Los Angeles, California

University of California Press, Ltd.
London, England

Library of Congress Cataloging-in-Publication Data

Over the edge : remapping the American West / edited by Valerie J. Matsumoto and Blake Allmendinger.
p. cm.
Includes bibliographic references and index.
ISBN 0-520-21148-0 (cloth : alk. paper).—ISBN 0-520-21149-9 (pbk. : alk. paper)
1. West (U.S.)—Civilization. 2. Regionalism—West (U.S.). 3. West (U.S.)—Ethnic relations. 4. Sex role—West (U.S.). I. Matsumoto, Valerie J. II. Allmendinger, Blake.
F591.089 1999
978—dc21 97-39311
CIP

Printed in the United States of America
9 8 7 6 5 4 3 2 1

The paper used in this publication meets the minimum requirements of American National Standards for Information Sciences—Permanence of Paper for Printed Library Materials, ANSI Z39.48-1984.

CONTENTS

Part Two: Crossing Boundaries

Part Three: Creating Community

ILLUSTRATIONS

Figures

Maps

ACKNOWLEDGMENTS

This project began when George Sanchez and I were asked to organize a program series on the U.S. West for the UCLA Center for Seventeenth- and Eighteenth-Century Studies and the William Andrews Clark Memorial Library. The result was the 1993–94 program series, "American Dreams, Western Images: Mapping the Contours of Western Experiences," which featured more than fifty scholars, writers, and poets. I am grateful to George for his creativity and grace under pressure, and thank Peter Reill, Director of the Center for Seventeenth- and Eighteenth-Century Studies, for giving us this opportunity. I am also indebted to the terrific Center staff and Clark Library staff—including Debbie Handren, Marina Romani, and Lori Stein—for their invaluable support of both the program and the resulting book.

For the richness of the program series, I thank the participants: Blake Allmendinger, Karen Anderson, Ned Blackhawk, Gordon Chang, Miroslava Chavez, Mike Davis, Arleen de Vera, William Deverell, Douglas Flamming, Chris Friday, Anne Goldman, David Gutiérrez, Ramón Gutiérrez, Yvette Huginnie, Norris C. Hundley, Louise Jeffredo-Warden, Susan Johnson, Robin D. G. Kelley, Elaine Kim, William Kittredge, Kerwin Klein, Shirley Lim, Patricia Nelson Limerick, George Lipsitz, Yolanda Lopez, Linda Maram, Jesús Martínez-Saldaña, Margo McBane, Melissa Meyer, Deborah Dash Moore, Katherine Morrissey, Mary Murphy, Peter Nabokov, Susan Rhoades Neel, John Nieto-Phillips, Brian O'Neil, Peggy Pascoe, Alicia Rodriguez, Mary Logan Rothschild, Roger Rouse, Vicki Ruíz, Ramón Saldívar, George Sanchez, Alexander Saxton, Virginia Scharff, Jill Watts, Richard White, Jo Ann Woodsum, Mitsuye Yamada, Al Young, Judy Yung, and Bernice Zamora. Blake Allmendinger, Bill Deverell, Doug Flamming, Anne Goldman, and Susan Neel also lent extra support as the Center's Ahmanson-Getty Fellows for the year.

Editing the conference volume initiated a second process for which thanks are due. One of the contributors aptly likened editing an essay collection to herding hummingbirds. I thank Blake Allmendinger for being a dauntless, efficient, and inspired hummingbird wrangler. I am immensely grateful to Marina Romani whose work has been crucial to the completion of this project. Thanks to all the contributing authors for their patience and good will.

For her guidance and vision I thank Monica McCormick, our editor at the University of California Press. I also thank Vicki Ruíz and an anonymous reader for their insightful, constructive comments on the manuscript. Kevin Mulroy and the staff of the Research Center at the Autry Museum of Western Heritage kindly helped Blake and me as we hunted for cover art. We thank Bruce Hershenson for allowing us to use the poster for "Tempest Cody Rides Wild" that graces the cover.

This endeavor has been fueled not only by exciting scholarship but also by great food. Thanks to Gerri Gilliland, whose restaurant Gilliland's wowed us all with fabulous feasts throughout the program series. The delicious meals at Nizam made Blake's and my working meetings there particularly enjoyable.

Valerie Matsumoto

I would like to thank the Center for Seventeenth- and Eighteenth-Century Studies for awarding me an Ahmanson-Getty fellowship in 1993–94; the William Andrews Clark Memorial Library, for providing access to materials and a place to do my research; Valerie Matsumoto, for inviting me to join her in producing this book; and the scholars I met during my time at the Clark, whose work has inspired me. Along with Valerie, I would like to thank Monica McCormick for her enthusiastic support of this project.

Blake Allmendinger

INTRODUCTION

Blake Allmendinger:

I like the smell of manure but can't stand the sight of it. The memory of a feedlot can make me homesick for green dung and the nostalgic whiff of ammonia. But when I go home to visit I seldom work in the stables. Walking behind a horse with a shovel reminds me why I wanted to leave home in the first place.

As a member of the English Department at UCLA, I specialize in the field of western American literature, yet I confess that many regional political issues, and even certain aspects of western history and literature, don't really interest me. Although I grew up on a ranch, I don't care much for animals. The debate between ranchers and government over the right to lease grazing land leaves me feeling sort of ho-hum. Dolly Parton's disco version of "Downtown" made me want to learn how to line-dance, but I neglected to sign up for lessons. I can never remember the date of the Homestead Act, when the transcontinental railroad was finished, or when the '49ers went West. I know the frontier ended in 1890, but only because it ended in a convenient round number. I thought Cormac McCarthy's *All the Pretty Horses* romanticized violence and stereotyped Mexicans, and groaned when I learned it was the first installment in a grandiose trilogy. But though I reject western clichés, I know that I do so while at the same time embracing pastel cow skulls, tin sheriff's badges, and politically incorrect items of clothing, including anything that wiggles fringe when it moves.

My most cherished possessions are two pairs of cowboy boots, handmade in red alligator and diamondback rattlesnake. I hope alligators and rattlesnakes aren't endangered species (and here I should say something about natural resources and our precious environment), but why not be honest? I wanted those boots, I got them, and that's all I care about. Wearing my dyed alligator boots I feel the same way that Dorothy did while wearing her ruby red slippers. I seem transported from Kansas to Oz—to the West of my fantasy.

As a gay man who grew up on a ranch where (and I'm estimating now) only 10 percent of the livestock were thought to be gay, I had few role models and no alternative culture to draw inspiration from. Feeling alienated by or bored with the West as I found it, I made up a West that was more appealing and personally relevant. It was the West of my imagination, one which questioned western ideals, mythic archetypes, tradition, and received information; one which glorified the marginal and fetishized things that were transgressive, outrageous, or camp.

All of us recognize a West whose history is represented by certain dates and hard facts; whose literary heritage is embodied by a canon of literature; whose images are communally recognized, shared, and experienced; whose geographic identity is sketched as a series of immobile boundary lines. But at the same time, each of us makes up the West for ourselves. We interpret historical facts, individually experience works of fiction and film, and transgress those seemingly immobile boundary lines in peculiar, often quite profound ways. To argue that there is one West, one frontier, or one borderland—that we know where it is and how to make sense of it—is to claim the fragile authority of the Wonderful Wizard of Oz.

Valerie Matsumoto:

During my childhood in a tiny farming community in the Imperial Valley of California, I did not think of the place I grew up in as the "West." Fields of tomatoes, squash, and melons covered the flat desert like a dusty green quilt seamed by irrigation canals. Many of the farm families—Filipino American, Japanese American, Mexican American, European American—lived in town, our small houses equipped with swamp coolers to alleviate the blistering summer heat. We all shopped at Mock Sing Gar's grocery store; the menfolk liked to hang out at the counter of the Hi-Ho Cafe on the main street. The big local event was the annual tomato festival, at which the best of the winter harvest would be as proudly displayed as crown jewels; the featured attractions included arts and crafts exhibits, prize-winning breads and pickles, carnival rides, and contests for both the Tomato Queen and the fastest packer.

The "West," as portrayed in black and white on the one television station we received from Yuma, seemed to be an entirely different place. Comic strips, advertisements, movies, and cartoons transmitted and amplified my impressions of John Wayne leading white pioneers to build a home on the frontier, dramatic cattle drives, cowboys and Indians skirmishing among the cactus. (The only Indian I had ever seen was a Sikh farmer from El Centro.) To really be a part of that West, I sensed that one had to ride a horse.

We had a dog, numerous cats, parakeets, turtles, and a pygmy marmoset, but no horse. Popular culture also conveyed the notion that the "West" belonged to a vanished past that had little connection to the people, places, or activities with which I was familiar.

Many kinds of migration traversed the landscape of "my" mundane West. Sportsmen from the cities descended upon our town in the autumn to hunt doves. Every summer many of my classmates' families headed to coastal areas with enticing names such as Riverside and Oceanside to do seasonal harvest work. When the United States and Mexico started the bracero program, workers from the South streamed into our labor camps and fields. Indeed, my family also migrated, spurred by such international developments. By the early 1960s, as more and more Mexican produce entered the United States, many of the small farmers of southern California could no longer compete with the large-scale operations of landowners in Sinaloa and Sonora. Like countless other California dreams, the Matsumoto Brothers' packing-box label "Mr. Tomato" became a relic of the past.

Moving eastward to a larger town on the U.S.-Mexico border in Arizona brought my family to a place that looked a great deal more like the popular-culture "West." The rolling hills of the high Sonora desert were studded with saguaro cacti and mesquite trees; quail, roadrunners, scorpions, and horned toads abounded. The local place names were Spanish and Indian words: Nogales, Amado, Tubac. Here traces of the past were layered with the present, in the form of Indian petroglyphs and pottery shards found on local ranch land, and missions such as the ones at Tumacacori and San Xavier del Bac.

Living on "the border" I gained a sense of boundaries—whether geographical or cultural—as powerful, arbitrary, and shifting. The city I lived in was called Nogales. Actually it is the name of two cities separated by a fence; on the Arizona side live about twenty or thirty thousand residents; on the Sonora side there are some three hundred thousand. Nogales has become a major gateway for commerce and immigration; as hopeful job-seekers and trucks filled with mangos, cucumbers, and bell peppers stream north, American tourists trek south to coastal resorts and Mayan ruins. When I was a teenager, going "across the line" into the sister city meant a day's shopping trip for ironwood carvings and pan dulce, or to get your high school yearbook photo taken at the only photographer's studio in both Nogaleses. But that line was a blurry one when the annual Cinco de Mayo parade high-stepped through both towns, or when breakages in one Nogales sewer line led to gastroenteritis for people dependent on a linked water system. A new development has even more alarmingly revealed the artificial nature of geopolitical parameters: Nogales has recently been identified as a site of disease cluster by epidemiologists who suspect that the high incidence of bone marrow cancer and lupus among longtime residents may be traced to contaminated air or water. According to the *Los Angeles Times,* although there are few indications of pollution on the Arizona side, approximately "100 U.S.-owned electronics plants and other factories, called *maquiladoras,* line the Mexican side of Nogales and emit numerous toxic chemicals into the air. The concrete-lined Nogales Wash carries a nightmarish mix of raw sewage and toxics from Mexico."[1] As signs in Nogales now read: "La Contaminación No Lleva Pasaporte"—Pollution Doesn't Carry a Passport.

The arbitrary nature of boundaries particularly struck me when I was an undergraduate at Arizona State University in Tempe, doing research for an honors thesis on Nisei women in central Arizona. At the outset of World War II Japanese Americans were uprooted from their communities in the western coastal states and the southern third of Arizona, which became a designated military zone. I then learned that the dividing line in Arizona ran along Highway 95 to Highway 60 through Wickenburg and Sun City, running through Phoenix along Grand Avenue and Van Buren Street, cutting through Tempe and bisecting Mesa. This line, drawn ostensibly to ensure the security of military installations on the south side of the highway, resulted in a bizarre situation. Half of the Japanese American community in central Arizona was taken away to the Poston internment camp; the other half remained in their homes for the duration of the war. Families on the north side watched as their neighbors across the street prepared for the uncertainties of life behind barbed wire, in cramped tar-papered barracks furnished with steel army cots. Only a few yards of dirt and asphalt determined who was dangerous and who was not, whose loyalty could be relied upon and whose not, whose way of life would be sundered and whose spared. The power of such shifting lines continues to shape the contours of the social as well as the physical landscape.

Blake:

Today, although the West may be settled, its meanings and boundaries remain unfixed and unsealed. The United States, while wanting to close its southwestern border to migrants from Mexico, at the same time, in accordance with NAFTA, wants to open its borders to allow a free-flow of sanctioned economic activity. Within the United States the continued increase in western travel and tourism has forced the national park system to question its regulations and policies. Are the invisible walls surrounding Yellowstone and Yosemite there to preserve nature for the public or to keep people out? Biosphere 2, a private park and quasi-terrarium—peopled by scientists and funded by Ed Bass, the famed Texas billionaire—in 1994 encountered a similar problem dealing with penetrable boundaries and the contamination of its pristine environment. The Arizona desert's experimental edenic utopia came to grief when alleged saboteurs "breached four of the five sealed doors to the dome . . . and smashed several glass panes."[2] The project, which had attempted to demonstrate that scientists could create and live in a state of pure nature, was based on what now seems like naive idealism.

The next frontier appears to be cyberspace, the imagined area behind one's computer screen. The concept of cyberspace as an unfenced range of computer technology, inhabited by cowboys called hackers who rustle information from forms of artificial intelligence, is a western conceit that has been fostered by William Gibson, the author of *Neuromancer* and the inventor of cyberpunk, as well as by a group of computer professionals who form the Electronic Frontier Foundation.[3] Cyberpunk explores the lack of constraints and the absence of ethical limits on the new space frontier. Video voyaging offers the advantages of bodiless anonymity and conceptual freedom of movement while raising fears about the lawlessness that exists in a world of vigilante information-acquisition and piracy.

The West is populated by conservatives who want to seal up its borders in order to protect private property, a "pure" form of life, and national and economic security, as well as by liberals who want to open up borders, welcoming an influx of "aliens" as an opportunity to shake up the old status quo. (In recognition of the fact that so many UFO sightings seem to take place in the area, the state of Nevada has just renamed an abandoned road that runs through the desert, dubbing it the Extraterrestrial Highway. "'Of course there's going to be both horizontal and vertical [road signs] so extraterrestrials can see them and land,' chuckled Tom Tait, executive director of the Nevada Commission on Tourism.")[4]

The debate that informs U.S. immigration policies and calls for economic free trade, that leads to the reassessment of park and recreation services and misadventures in amateur science, that structures the vocabulary of cyberpunk literature and computer technology, also affects the formation and interaction of departments, programs, and disciplines within academia. How is our traditional understanding of the West challenged by the Chicana/o experience? Is Asian American literature also western literature, and if so, what occurs when we juxtapose the China men of Maxine Hong Kingston with Bret Harte's "Heathen Chinee"? Is there a black or queer western history? Should western scholarship seal itself off from work being done in other fields or should it encourage intellectual interdisciplinarity?

Of the twenty contributors to this collection of essays, some, like the Native American writer Louise Jeffredo-Warden, are practicing artists and poets; some, like the culture-critic Mike Davis, teach freelance and write independently. But most of them work in various departments within academia. Their scholarship—drawing on history and literature, architecture and urban planning, gender and economic theory, race relations and legal codes, environmentalism and Catholic Church doctrine, painting and native storytelling, popular culture and film—views the West through a cockeyed kaleidoscope. Representing a motley assortment of disciplinary perspectives, filtered through the lens of more than one methodology, the essays, as separate fragments of color, combine to form patterns when seen from particular vantage points.

To put it another way, while we have solicited diverse and wide-ranging essays, at the same time we have decided, for the purposes of organization, to classify and arrange them accordingly. In order to map our terrain we have drawn up some boundary lines, dividing the essays thematically into three separate categories: "Imagining the West," "Crossing Boundaries," and "Creating Community." Like criss-crossing lines in a travel guide, these categories suggest ways of negotiating the West intellectually, and like pathbreaking trails, the essays, if they don't all arrive at the same point, at least intersect on the way. The act of imagining the West, for example, is a transformative process that involves the mental reconfiguration, and even the physical relocation, of the West on film, in art, and in literature. Dorothy reimagines the West by traveling from Kansas to Oz, and while no one in this collection travels quite so far afield, several scholars cross geographical borders, comparing the West with the biblical settings of the Middle East and the Cold-War landscape of Russia. As with the act of imagining, the process of crossing boundaries also allows one to create new or to merge existing communities. As the final group of essays in this collection will indicate, interethnic rivalries and racial hostilities surface in certain western locations when prejudicial barriers enforcing segregation begin to disintegrate and collapse. Imagining the West is a transgressive act, just as crossing or transgressing boundaries is a creative endeavor leading to the production of new configurations and hybrid communities.

Conversely, the most popular icons of westernness (for example, works by Albert Bierstadt, George Catlin, and Frederic Remington) represent a West which most of us recognize. "Imagining the West," on the other hand, argues that the West isn't necessarily what or where one might think it is. The first essay in this part, by Patricia Nelson Limerick, addresses the practice of tourism. Beginning with an autobiographical anecdote and continuing with a critical reinvestigation of history, Limerick reminds us that tourism is a problematic term and a subjective enterprise. Those of us who have felt our space invaded by tourists have also, at one time or another, been tourists ourselves. In fact western tourism, in some form, dates back to the migrations of early Native Americans and to the explorations of European "discoverers." Seeing and being seen are imaginative, reciprocal acts of conceptualization, representation, and perception which, Limerick maintains, implicate all of us.

In the two essays that follow, Blake Allmendinger and Jill Watts travel the globe, visiting the West in places as far-flung as pre-Christian Rome and

Gold Rush Alaska. Allmendinger reads *Ben-Hur* as a transplanted western, as a spiritual contest between "civilization" and "savagery." Noting that Lew Wallace wrote his best-selling novel in the 1880s while governing New Mexico, Allmendinger demonstrates that the novel pits all godless Romans against one Jew, Ben-Hur, whose religious conversion occurs at the time of Christ's crucifixion and thus corresponds with the dawning of a new Christian age. Foreshadowing the decline of decadent Rome and the resurrection (through one man) of an enlightened society, *Ben-Hur* also historically mirrors the efforts to transform New Mexico from a warring, "primitive" territory into a state "safe" for white settlement. Similarly, Watts examines the "civilizing" role that religion plays in her essay on Mae West and film. In *Klondike Annie,* West plays a woman of questionable virtue who accidentally kills her Shanghai employer, escapes to the West Coast, and finally sails for Alaska. On the last leg of her voyage she meets an evangelist named Soul Savin' Annie, and when Annie dies, West assumes her identity. The rest of the action, which takes place in Alaska, centers on West's efforts to convert the unregenerate territory in the guise of Soul Savin' Annie, while at the same time subverting Annie's message by slipping double entendres into her sermons on race, gender, and (of course!) sexuality.

Anne E. Goldman also travels back in time, revealing that nineteenth-century western texts, such as María Amparo Ruiz de Burton's *The Squatter and the Don* and Helen Hunt Jackson's *Ramona* are more than romances. Goldman exposes layers of meaning beneath the literary surfaces of these two classic works, disclosing how both novels present regional and national issues pertaining to race relations, social stability, and cultural authority. While Goldman revisits the frontier that we thought we knew, finding fresh perspectives from which to view western literature, Douglas Flamming focuses on another artist who drew inspiration from non-western sources. Flamming assesses the work of the early twentieth-century African American writer Arna Bontemps, whose move from California to New York (where he participated in the "New Negro" Renaissance), brief stay in the South, and return home were consecutive chapters in one writer's quest to discover his racial heritage and westernness. Bontemps places the West on an experiential and spatial continuum, situating it in personal and relative terms by using the West as a hyphen to signify his hybrid identity.

The essays in the next part elaborate on this notion of imagined, perceived, or constructed identity. If the West is a concept as much as a process or place, then it is a concept subject to change, as the essays in "Crossing Boundaries" suggest. Susan Lee Johnson describes Gold Rush California as a network of homosocial societies, as a cluster of mining camps in which whites and blacks, European, Mexican, and South American immigrants, and local Native Americans enacted a set of complex relationships. Because the people in these camps, like the members of many early frontier societies, were predominantly men, they performed not only the strenuous labor of mining but the domestic tasks that were traditionally considered "female" activity. What it meant to be "masculine" was therefore a concept that miners tested and sometimes revised. In a companion piece, Mary Murphy notes that westernists working in gender studies tend to focus less on men than on women. By using the biographies of two nineteenth-century men as case histories, she seeks to determine if there was a western male equivalent of the cult of true womanhood. The actions and writings of these men reveal their opinions on a wide range of issues, including male sexuality and marriage. Murphy infers from this evidence that an alternative ideal of manhood—which differed from the one popularized by Owen Wister, Remington, and Theodore Roosevelt—may have existed for some men out West.

As if in response to this article, Karen Anderson, in the following essay, critiques the concept of motherhood. She defines the white response to Changing Woman, the Navajo culture's most revered deity, as a fearful reaction to matriarchal empowerment. Using this early example of opposition to non-white female authority as the historical prologue to a more complex argument, Anderson then scrutinizes the maternalist politics of the U.S. government in the twentieth century, focusing on the impact certain policies have had on Native American and Mexican American citizens. In the West, Anderson notes, the government has tried over time to make mothers in minority families conform to an ideal of white, middle-class motherhood. Using these mothers as role models, the government has sought to encourage minority children to assimilate by relinquishing their ties to their heritage. While Anderson analyzes the role that women play in domestically grounding and culturally stabilizing western society, Virginia Scharff investigates the relationship between women and western mobility. Scharff believes we must stop "envisioning women's history as a narrative chiefly about attempts to establish geographical stability (or, what you might call 'home on the range'), and begin to accord itineracy the historical importance in western women's lives that the record suggests is necessary." Her essay traces the movement of one African American woman from the South to the West, during the Civil Rights Era, and records an important first step in this previously undocumented historical pilgrimage.

Valerie:

Boundaries of race and ethnicity have played a critical role in shaping the perceptions and representations of communities in the West, as addressed in the last four essays in Part 2. William Deverell delineates the progress of a 1924 pneumonic plague epidemic in Los Angeles, analyzing how disease, economics, and racial classification became linked in the minds of city officials. Deverell asserts that civic boosters marketed Los Angeles as a tourist mecca through the use of stereotypical imagery and language that relegated racial-ethnic people to cultural compartments more rigid than street or district divisions. The municipal response to the epidemic both revealed elite European American views of Mexican Americans and served to solidify them through the militarized enforcement of quarantine.

How racial-ethnic minority groups have developed their own collective identities and sought to represent themselves constitutes the marrow of the next essay by Arleen de Vera. The thwarted elopement in 1930 of Felix Tapia and Alice Saiki, and the resultant tensions between the Filipino American and Japanese American communities of Stockton, California, form a backdrop for her examination of how immigrant Filipinos created and re-created their ethnicity in relation to other racial-ethnic groups. This interethnic conflict and identity formation were played out within the context of the larger framework of racial hierarchy; ultimately, the Filipino Americans' attempts to distinguish themselves from the Japanese Americans did not prevent their being targeted for exclusion by whites, who still perceived Asians as "all alike" and equally undesirable as Americans—a status reified in law.

The following two essays draw attention to the impact of classifications of race and sex in legal and administrative systems. The power of such classifications is strikingly reflected in three centuries of statutes aimed at barring interracial marriage, and nowhere in the United States, Peggy Pascoe observes, were these laws more elaborately developed than in the West. Her study of anti-miscegenation laws reveals how the judicial system structured family formation and property transmission along racial dividing lines. As the 1919 Paquet case demonstrates, such laws were successfully invoked in probate cases in order to contest the right of a non-white spouse—usually a widow—to inherit an estate, thus reinforcing both white supremacy and women's dependence on men.

Notions of race and entitlement have been connected in American Indian tribal policy as well as in state and federal law. Individual tribal requirements for membership reflect not only the desire to maintain autonomy and ethnic identity but also the fact that enrollment may bring access to material resources and services in addition to acknowledgment of a shared heritage. As Melissa Meyer suggests, this has made the question of who is an American Indian—and more specifically, who can qualify for tribal enrollment—a complex one. One of the most commonly used criteria, blood quantum, like the anti-miscegenation laws, mirrors late nineteenth- and early twentieth-century scientific efforts at racial classification. Meyer's research illustrates how, in the diverse communities of the West and beyond, determining ethnic identity is an increasingly complicated—and still decidedly significant—task.

The essays in the third part illuminate the development of a range of communities in the West. Some focus on creativity and exigency, contestation and cultural adaptation; others raise timely questions regarding the relationship between humanity and the natural environment as well as the possibilities for constructing new models of collectivity.

Ramón Gutiérrez's essay on the religious organizations of Indian slaves in colonial New Mexico emphasizes adaptation and creation in the context of cultural convergence and conflict. Originally rooted in the slaves' need for mutual support in the absence of kin, confraternities such as the Hermanos Penitentes reflected the intersection of two systems of ritual practice. Over the course of three centuries, they evolved as a vehicle for the expression of ethnic solidarity and a source of grassroots political leadership. By the early twentieth century, the flocking of tourists to the Hermanos' annual rites of flagellation and crucifixion drove the group to practice in secret, deepening their sense of spiritual community.

The following two essays spotlight women's efforts to shape community dynamics. Miroslava Chavez focuses on the mediation of domestic strife in nineteenth-century Mexican California. Her examination of civil and criminal court cases in Los Angeles reveals women's appeals to judicial authority in their struggles with fathers and husbands. The rulings in these disputes—involving physical abuse, financial support, adultery, and unlawful coercion—show that ethnicity and socioeconomic circumstances proved key factors in determining how women were treated in the legal system. We return again to Los Angeles, this time in the 1930s, in my study of the array of activities through which second-generation Japanese American women supported their ethnic community. In this exploration of girls' and teenagers' work and recreation in Little Tokyo, the multiple pressures facing young women serve to underscore the importance of the vibrant peer-support networks they formed. Their adaptation and synthesis of a variety of cultural forms helped to create a lively urban Nisei world.

How racial-ethnic groups have both cooperated and competed with each other in the arena of work casts in sharp relief the contours of cultural boundaries. In tracking the struggles over union organizing in the salmon canneries of southeastern Alaska, Chris Friday maps the conflict among three overlapping communities of Native Alaskans, Asian Americans, and European Americans. The course of campaigns by rival organizations to sway worker loyalties vividly illustrates how class interests might not prove sufficient to override cultural and regional differences or work patterns that pitted local people against seasonal migrants and that privileged men's labor over women's. The trajectory of groups such as the Alaska Native Brotherhood and the Alaska Native Sisterhood also mirrored the changing focus of community concerns over time, as the contest for control of the labor force increasingly shifted to efforts to regain rights to a land base.

In the next two essays, human relationships with the natural environment take center stage in the study of community dynamics. Through a story about Coyote's fruitless attempt to outrun the River in a race, Louise Jeffredo-Warden conveys the Gabrielino Indians' understanding of the power of the natural environment and the futility of defying it. As reflected in such centuries-old lessons, the indigenous peoples of southern California held a sense of their relationship to the land as one based on reciprocity and moral obligation. Accordingly, their conception of community extended beyond human ties to include animals, plants, rocks, and streams.

The urgency of the need to repair and re-create the human relationship with the environment drives Mike Davis's essay on the military devastation of the Great Basin of California, Nevada, and Utah. In this federally designated "national sacrifice zone," nuclear weapons testing and biowar research have blasted the desert into a barren lunar landscape and inflicted cancers, neurological disorders, and genetic defects on those who live "downwind." A coalition movement—including Mormons, Paiute and Shoshone Indians, and Nevada ranchers—has coalesced to oppose further nuclear testing and toxic waste disposal; their ties to similarly affected communities in Kazakhstan and the Pacific Islands demonstrate that both ecological damage and efforts to heal it may transcend national borders.

In the final essay, Jesús Martínez-Saldaña challenges geographically and nationally bounded definitions of community membership through his examination of Mexican transnational migrants, a subject of particularly passionate debate in the U.S. West. The songs of Los Tigres del Norte, an immigrant musical group popular on both sides of the southern border, articulate the economic need that has spurred Mexican immigrants to seek work abroad and give voice to their critique of the imposition of social and political boundaries. Why, one *corrido* (ballad) asks the border, are you a line that divides people rather than uniting them regardless of color? Despite their material contributions to both the United States and Mexico, the immigrants—who number in the millions—are not treated as full members of the community in either country; Martínez-Saldaña proposes a new interpretation of them as citizens of a binational system with rights and responsibilities in two republics.

These meditations on boundary crossings and social configurations eventually lead to a broader range of imaginings of the West. As Martínez-Saldaña states, "The American West does not exist only in the collective consciousness of this country. It is also present in the imagination of people in other nations." The powerful allure of envisioned Wests continues to attract newcomers from all over the nation and the world: artists, retirees, utopians, tourists, gamblers, rebels, refugees, and workers from one end of the class scale to the other. The impact of this ongoing influx serves to advance the sense of community as a dynamic, often messy, process.

The cultural struggles and cultural synthesis generated by the confluence of peoples pulled by vast economic tides, the contestation over resources and meanings of community, a growing awareness of the intimate connection between human and natural ecosystems, although not unique to the West, have spotlighted both the urgency and the vibrant potential of reassessing and reconstructing social relations. As we move toward passage across the frontier of the twenty-first century, the mixed legacies of the past come with us, as warning ghosts, borrowed strength, weapons, tools, and toys. Sifting through and scrutinizing them, as the writers in this collection have done, provides a useful point at which to consider where we are and where we may be going.

Notes

1. Marla Cone, "Human Immune Systems May Be Pollution Victim," *Los Angeles Times* (February 3, 1996): A1, A14–15.
2. Sharon Begley et al., "In the Desert, Big Trouble Under Glass," *Newsweek* 123 (April 18, 1994): 54.
3. Raymond Gozzi, Jr., "The Cyberspace Metaphor," *ETC: A Review of General Semantics* 51 (Summer 1994): 221.
4. Carla Hall, "'Extraterrestrial Highway' Gets Green Light in Nevada," *Los Angeles Times* (February 3, 1996): A19.

Part One

IMAGINING THE WEST

1

SEEING AND BEING SEEN

Tourism in the American West

PATRICIA NELSON LIMERICK

In the summer of 1970, I undertook unintended field work in the subject of western tourism. I was attending the University of California at Santa Cruz, and that fact set certain limits on summer employment. Before Santa Cruz was a university town, it was a tourist town. Bordering on the beach and boardwalk was a jumble of motels. In the summer of 1970, I worked as a maid at the St. Charles Motel. This was pretty hard work, really an indoor version of stoop labor: stooping to strip beds, stooping to make beds, stooping to vacuum, stooping to clean toilets and scrub tubs. I was only nineteen, but every evening, my back hurt and I felt like a zombie. At the end of the day, the one point of clarity in my head was my feeling toward tourists. When the motel guests had eaten potato chips in their rooms, and ground some of those potato chips into the rug, I had particularly clear—really quite radiantly clear—feelings about tourists. When it comes to understanding the feelings of local residents about tourists, and when it comes to understanding the frustrations of the service jobs attached to tourist economies, the summer of 1970 gave me a certain intellectual and psychological advantage.

My employer at the St. Charles Motel made me wear a white uniform, with white stockings, and white shoes, and a white kerchief. With that costume, in a blizzard in Colorado, I would have been invisible. In the summer in Santa Cruz, far from blizzard conditions, I was very visible indeed; I was virtually Central Casting's archetype of The Maid. This visibility gave me one of my few occupational satisfactions. Every day at noon, I would take my sack lunch down to the Boardwalk along the beach. Then I would sit on a bench and eat my lunch, among the swirl of tourists lining up for the roller coaster and the carousel. As I sat there, I would say, nonverbally but (thanks to my uniform) still very clearly, "You are having fun, but I am the

Maid. In other words, the fact that *you* are having fun correlates directly to the fact that *I* am leading such a dreary life."

Even as I did my best to advertise my resentment of the people who made my employment possible, I believe I knew that the situation was more complicated than my emotions. I knew that when I sat, in a manner a little reminiscent of Edgar Allan Poe's reproachful raven (though opposite in color), on the Santa Cruz Boardwalk, I was not really confronting a privileged class. Santa Cruz was not Newport or Aspen; Santa Cruz was a working-class tourist town. Most of the people who were at the Santa Cruz beach would return to put on their own working-class uniforms at the end of that vacation.

I open with this story because I believe that scholars writing about western tourism can be tempted to adopt the point of view of the locals, to see the tourist from the outside, to cast the tourist as an alien, even contemptible other. In thinking about tourism one runs a constant risk of casting the tourists themselves as boorish, invasive, repellent, and insensitive. This casting of the tourist as unappealing other is, of course, exactly the skill I had mastered in 1970, when I ate my lunch at the Santa Cruz Boardwalk and, as we would say now, "performed" my victimization.

My lunches on the Santa Cruz Boardwalk call our attention to another risk in the scholarship on tourism: the risk of missing the class differences within the unit we call tourists. There have been very rich people with second homes in Aspen, Colorado, and Jackson, Wyoming. There have been much-less-rich people who have pulled their resources together for a week of vacationing in budget motels near beaches and boardwalks. Unless we watch ourselves, we fall into the habit of clumping all these people together, simply, as tourists. That clumping permits a not very accurate drawing of class lines: the outsider-tourists become the privileged middle or upper class; the insider-providers of tourist services become the working class. With that formulation, we miss the many and consequential occasions in which working-class people have been themselves tourists, a situation which fit, I think, most of the people I glowered at along the Santa Cruz Boardwalk.

In fact, if one thought of the categories, tourist versus tourist industry worker, as separate and exclusive, my own background would be an anomalous one. My heritage is very much mixed, with a line of descent on both sides. Tourism was a big element in my hometown, Banning, California. The resort town of Palm Springs was just down the road, and many people who worked there—as maids, gardeners, bellmen, waitresses—lived in Banning because they could not afford to live in Palm Springs. Travelers driving through Banning on their way to Palm Springs were also a source of income, and no one knows this better than I. My father owned and operated a date shop—a roadside store selling chocolate-covered dates and walnut-stuffed dates, date malts, and date shakes. My mother worked full-time as a legal secretary, and so my family's California Date Shop proved to be my day care center.

When I was still a toddler, my parents bought me some cowgirl clothes—a fringed vest and skirt, and the proper boots. With this purchase, we might now say, my parents took the first step in my commodification. Before I was three years old, I had been added to the resources, amenities, and attractions of the California Date Shop. Quite a number of my father's customers made regular stops at the store, and they soon took up a custom of inquiring after the "cowgirl." "How's the cowgirl?" they would say. If I now have considerable empathy for the residents of tourist towns who live in a constant muddle of authenticity and constructed identity, then early days at the California Date Shop provided my first round of experiential learning and field work in the subject of western tourism.

But my parents were also tireless tourists themselves, packing us off for an extended car trip at least once a year, with the forests of the Sierras, the beach, and the Grand Canyon as our most frequent destinations. Thus I was in childhood both the touring and the toured upon, both the subject doing the seeing and the object being seen. If we take tourism to be an example of the sin of snoopishness, as it appears in some of the critical literature, then I was indeed both sinned against and sinning. And I suspect that that mixed experience is the bedrock reason why I cannot muster the purity of outlook that other writers can bring to the subject of tourism. I do not know if I was, in the usual equation, subject or other, other or subject, or some unholy combination of the two. My vivid memories of how a motel maid's back feels at the end of the day prevent me from celebrating the fine economic opportunities of a regional shift to tourism. On the other side, I remember too clearly my pleasure in watching Indian dances in northern Arizona, or in watching waves crash on southern California beaches, to damn tourists as a kind of invasive infection, spreading the viruses and microbes of inauthenticity and commodification. Forty years ago, when I put on the uniform of the cowgirl, I gave up my claim to purity and authenticity. After spending one's formative years in the California Date Shop, one can never claim to be untainted by contact with the coins, dollars, traveler's checks, and credit cards of the tourist.

We form a larger subculture than we realize, those of us who were raised, supported, formed, and informed by western tourism. If there is accuracy in the predictions that tourism will prove to be the principal industry in many areas of the West, this is a subculture that is going to grow and grow. But where did we come from, or, more precisely, where did western tourism come from? When did western tourism begin?

North America was full of paths and trails that served the purposes of hunting, gathering, seasonal migration, and trade. One stimulant for Indian mobility was, however, curiosity: too many Indian stories tell of travels undertaken for the purposes of inquiry and adventure to suggest that Indian people traveled only for economic purposes. Every seashell, from the Atlantic or the Pacific, that ended up in the interior was its own testimony that travel has a long history on this continent. But should we call this tourism? The very question raises the matter of how much purity we are inclined to hold out for in defining what tourism is. To be a true tourist, must an individual be embedded in the emotions and economies of modern industrial, capitalistic society? Or did true tourism come to this planet before the cash economy? Here we confront an oddly inverted and yet very high standard of purity. To be a *true* tourist, one must meet high standards for impurity, for holding motives considerably more tangled and corrupted than pure curiosity, and for engaging in transactions mediated much more by paper and plastic currency than by direct human contact. In truth, the standards for impurity are set too high here. There are good reasons to look for behavior that bears some resemblance to tourism before the arrival of the cash economy, and there are also good reasons to look for motives that are not always tainted and exploitative in post-lapsarian, conventional, modern tourism. So however you think of early Indian travel, one has to recognize it as curious, active travel, and recognize in it at least a small degree of kinship with the tourism of the last century and a half. Part of that more recent travel is, after all, Indian travel to Europe and to the eastern United States, a revealing counterpoint to the travel, in the opposite direction, of Europeans and Euro-Americans visiting Indian territory.

In the first half of the nineteenth century, Anglo-American explorers-writers introduced a practice more directly connected, and, indeed, precedent-setting for what we now think of as tourism. To William Clark and Meriwether Lewis, to Zebulon Pike, to Stephen Long, to John C. Fremont, the West was the exotic place of their adventuring and self-testing. They treated their western experiences in a manner very similar to the way later Anglo-Americans would treat beaver pelts, buffalo hides, minerals, trees, grasses, and soil. The explorers extracted western experience and packed it out of the West. They then processed and refined it into the form of reports. When explorers wrote their reports, their literary activity was directly parallel to the activities of the felters and hatters who made western beaver pelts into hats, parallel to the activities of the men who refined western minerals in mills and smelters.

The explorers supplied these refined and processed parcels of experience to readers eager to learn about the Far West. These were writers of remarkable intellectual confidence. In their travels, they traced only a narrow line across the West, and yet they wrote confidently of the character of the whole region. If, over the centuries, we have taken a long time to reckon with the reality of the American West, this surely is one of the reasons: many of our ideas about the West originated in the minds of people who were just passing through, people who saw only a little and who still wrote as if they knew the whole. For these travelers, their relationship to their audience made it necessary to cast the West as that exotic place "out there." To dramatize their own daring and mark their own achievement, these explorers had to dramatize the West's strangeness, novelty, unpredictability, and general wildness. The explorers of the first half of the nineteenth century thus built the foundation for later tourism. Offering an image of the West defined by its separateness from the familiar, the explorers' reports provided a portrait of a place that was, if dangerous and threatening, also very interesting. It is important to note that none of these explorers traveled through empty or "virgin" space. All of them made frequent references to inhabitants, particularly Indians, Mexicans, and the mixed-blood families of fur traders.

Explorers may have been laying the foundation for tourism, but they were government men, federal agents, people on official business, and not exactly tourists. Sometimes accompanying them were people closer to the model of tourism: gentlemen, sometimes European aristocrats, sometimes artists or naturalists, out to see the sights in the West. Some of these fellows do give the impression of taking part in a mid-nineteenth-century anticipation of Outward Bound. My own favorite for this category has been Sir William Drummond Stewart, a Scottish nobleman who took the artist Alfred Jacob Miller along on his outing to the Rockies in the 1830s. In an archetypal moment of early tourism, Miller told the story of the party's approach to a fiercely overflowing river, with tree trunks and branches bobbing wildly in the flood. They reached the river, and Stewart plunged in. Miller plunged in after him, and, miraculously, made it to the far shore. As he fought his way up on the bank, Miller said to Stewart, "You know, sir, I do not know how to swim." "Neither do I," replied Stewart. "You know not what you can do until you have tried."[1]

I am surprised that Outward Bound has not taken this as its founding moment, surprised that Stewart's words are not the celebrated slogan for adventure tourism all around the planet. But as advertising slogans go, "You know not what you can do until you have tried," has its weaknesses. One does not have to contemplate Miller's story very long (or especially to contemplate his drawing of the fiercely flooding river) to realize that this story could easily have delivered up the opposite ending, with Miller and Stewart both drifting downstream and off the pages of history. "You know not what you *cannot* do until you have tried" is as good a moral to this story, but not a particularly affirmative way to advertise adventure tourism.

An enthusiasm for tourism on Stewart's scale of strenuosity was slow to develop. Indeed, to see the emergence of tourism on a sizable scale, one has to look to a more "facilitated" form of travel. The completion of the transcontinental railroad in 1869 and the expansion of luxury travel by palace cars and Pullman cars unleashed a tourism boom on the West. This was, of course, insulated travel, insulated both from nature and from natives. These tourists were people of means, people who wanted comfort and service, people for whom the era of conquest was a little too recent and raw. Predictably, much of the effort of recruiting these tourists rested on reassurance, repeating the promise that the West was safe now, with tame hotels, parlors, and verandas from which the wild scenery could be calmly viewed. This enterprise in promotion also played on the nineteenth-century American inferiority complex. By one common perception among intellectuals and the upper and middle classes, the United States, in comparison to Europe, was simply too new, too young, too short on history; by the same pattern of thinking, western scenery was too different, too big, too stark, too dry. Thus tourist promotion in the late nineteenth century sought legitimacy through European analogies: California was the Mediterranean, a transplanted Italy; Colorado was Switzerland, with replicas of the Alps. Western resort hotels had, by the same token, to match European luxury; for this elite and well-financed type of tourist, European-like scenery had to be accompanied by European-like buildings and services.

These mid- and late-nineteenth-century tourists had an influence and impact far beyond their numbers. Quite a number of these people had contacts and ties with publishers and editors, and thus they found a direct channel to influencing public opinion. These were journal-keepers, diarists, impression-recorders, and word-mongers, and many of them could not look out a train window at a wide open western horizon without reaching for their pens. The result of their compulsive literacy was, by 1900, a western landscape blanketed by words, covered two or three inches deep with the littered vocabulary of romantic scenery appreciation. By 1900, a place like Yellowstone had already been the scene of so much published scribbling and emotion that it was extremely difficult for anyone to have an immediate, direct response to the landscape, without a chorus of quotations going off in the head. Before the eye could take in the walls of Yosemite, the mind had already provided the caption: soaring, sublime, uplifting; grandeur, glory, and spirit. With the script of response already written, one's only remaining task was to try to feel what one already knew one was *supposed* to feel.

My own favorite example of this pattern has long been the southern Californian George Wharton James, former minister, reborn promotional writer who, at the turn of the century, unleashed a flood of words promoting everything possible in the Southwest. As a literary hired hand of the railroads and resorts, George Wharton James said, in pages of text one could measure by the pound, that everything—deserts, mountains, oases, Indians, Mexican American villagers, irrigated farms, growing towns and cities—was colorful and fun . . . and totally risk-free. No threats here, every page of James's slick and slippery prose said; the threats are all gone; it's your playground now.[2]

This enterprise was, of course, a little more complicated than it seemed at first. It was not easy to hit the balance in this constant effort of packaging and manipulating the image of the West. The West had to be cast as tame and safe, with no features that would seriously scare tourists. At the same time, it could not be so tame and safe that it went over the edge and became dull and familiar. This pressure, by the turn of the century, brought a withdrawal of many of the European analogies and a move toward a greater accent on more interesting and distinctive elements of westernness. This shift in accent appeared in the proliferation of dude ranches, and the recognition that one could sometimes make more money by herding tourists down a trail than by herding cattle. One could see the shift, as well, in the rise of rodeos as tourist entertainment, where skills once used for work now became skills used for show.

As both these examples indicate, the accenting of western distinctiveness was a very selective matter. The process worked by freezing a moment in an imagined past, disconnecting cattle-working techniques from their real-life context, and locating them instead in a timeless moment when real westerners were cowboys, when the mark of real westernness hinged, by everyone's understanding, on a certain close, cooperative, and even affectionate relationship with a horse. In much more recent times, the movie *City Slickers* reinvigorated the appeal of dude ranches. Dude ranching bookings accelerated; and the old formula—by which one is repaired from the injuries of urban, industrial civilization with an interlude of simple, rural western life—gained new force. As historian Earl Pomeroy has observed, this had long been a very illuminating choice: developers marketing western rural authenticity to urbanites chose to sell them the experience of simulated work on a cattle ranch, and not simulated work in a copper mine or on a sugar beet farm.[3]

The rise of this kind of western tourism, at the turn of the century, might well strike some historians as a watershed moment in western history, perhaps the best indicator of the end of the frontier. When places and people who were once frightening and threatening turned quaint and fun, when Indians did war dances for tourists at train stations (and skipped the attack on the invaders that might logically follow a war dance), when visitors flocked to the stores and restaurants of San Francisco's Chinatown, when painters set themselves to extracting the charm from the Indian and Hispano people of Taos, when deserts, which had terrified overland travelers, turned pretty and appealing in their colors and clear lines, then it might well seem that the frontier was over and the distribution of power clearly settled in the American West. Here, one could think, the violent history of conquest ended, and a new, tame history of buying souvenirs and taking photographs began.

To my mind, the unsettled issues of conquest did not disappear, even if tourists could not see them. But I can get a glimpse of why other historians might think that the flood of tourists into the West provided the clearest and most dramatic statement: the war was over; white people had won; the West was subdued; the West was an occupied terrain, and the tourists were the army of occupation.

With the gradual shift away from the railroad and toward the automobile as the vehicle of tourism, the flood of tourists only broadened and deepened. For the first two decades of the twentieth century, the automobile remained primarily an additional toy for the vacationing rich. But by the 1920s, the automobile was serving as the agent for the democratization of tourism, for the redefinition of western tourism as a mass experience. There were still a lot of poor people left out of this mobile festival, since one still needed the resources to afford a car, leisure, gasoline, shelter, and food. But the group on the road, from the 1920s on, was *much* broader in its origins and occupations than the nineteenth-century tourists had been. With auto camps, motels, gas stations, roadside restaurants, and commercial strips, as J. B. Jackson has argued, a new kind of landscape came to exist in support of automotive tourism.[4] Following the well-set patterns of western economic development, the federal government's role was crucial, with federal money and direction playing an important part in the construction of highways. Western tourism has been in a long phase of expansion, pressed by the power of the word "more"—more motels, more gas stations, more attractions, more communities trying to figure out how to get in on this action.

More confusion and more discontent have also been a part of this expansion. A coherent history of the resistance to and rejection of the tourist industry is a hard thing to come by, but it is an enormously rich topic. The signs of rejection are fairly widespread today. In November of 1993, the voters of the state of Colorado rejected a tax, in existence for ten years, that supported a state tourism board and a range of promotional activities. In the Northwest, the permanent residents of La Conner, Washington, recently began a campaign to institute a "tourist-free zone" in the center of their town, with a La Conner resident, the novelist Tom Robbins, also proposing that developers wear identifying tags so that they might be properly shunned. One suspects that quite a number of residents of western tourist towns understand the appeal of this idea. As a number of them have said, living in these towns is like always having houseguests, guests who may rotate but who never go away.[5]

Certainly, Edward Abbey was industrial tourism's most persistent and audible critic. Tourism, Abbey wrote in one essay, "is always and everywhere a dubious, fraudulent, distasteful, and in the long run, degrading business, enriching a few, doing the rest more harm than good," and this is one of his more moderate statements. And yet Abbey, in his vigorous and appealing writing about the southwestern deserts and especially about the Colorado Plateau's canyonlands, had a significant impact in increasing tourism in the area, putting a little-known area squarely at the center of the reading public's attention. Abbey was equally important for denouncing tourism and for recruiting more tourists, and that is only one of the many paradoxes that run through western tourism.[6]

The national parks have long represented the best documented case of the puzzles and paradoxes of tourism. From the beginnings of the National Park Service in 1916, its officials knew that they had to sell the parks. Unless they could get significant numbers of Americans to visit the parks, the parks would be without a political constituency. And so the Park Service was placed, from the beginning, at the sharp edge of the divide between the goals of "providing for the enjoyment" of the parks, and preserving the parks, in some more or less intact form, for "future generations."[7]

The sharpness of that edge has not been blunted over time, as the Park Service hops between increasing tourist access with more roads and more facilities, and regulating and restraining crowds and traffic. A 1990 survey asked national park visitors what factors governed their choice of which parks to visit. First on the list of the public's criteria was natural beauty. Second was the factor, "how crowded the park is," and there is some kind of deep and puzzling irony in the workings of this factor that I cannot begin to untangle. Spend a few hours behind a parade of Winnebagoes heading in to Yellowstone, and you might begin to think that this criterion of "crowdedness" functions in the opposite way one might expect: the more crowded the park, the more people want to go there. But third on the list of decision-making factors was the availability of restrooms, and fourth was the availability of parking.[8]

When one first contemplates it, this survey provides one of the occasions for a "Hmph!" response to western tourism. Is this the best that members of the American public can do? They are presented with the opportunity for moving and instructive encounters with nature, and their attention stays fixed on the prospect of restrooms and convenient parking spaces? But this survey also presents an opportunity to go beyond the "Hmph!" response—to recognize that a preference for comfort and convenience is, in truth, a hallmark of current times, and, further, it is an enthusiasm often shared by scholars and historians. Who, among us, has not felt some desperation in midtown Manhattan, confronting an urban wilderness with neither restrooms nor parking spaces? Just how high is the ground we can occupy in judging the crassness and baseness of the tourist mind? Should there not be a little more in the way of solidarity among philistines?

There may be nothing inherently disillusioning or disheartening about people's concern for porta-potties, but one might be more actively disheartened by the ranking, in that survey, awarded to the very last item on the list of criteria. In last place, as a reason to visit a park, came "educational program."

A few years ago, I learned an important lesson about the word "educational," thanks to Kevin Costner and *Dances with Wolves.* When *Dances with Wolves* looked like it might win some Oscars, the *Today Show* sent a camera crew out to talk to a western historian about the film. The cameraman and the reporter set up their equipment in my office, and then we started in on the interview. The two men looked increasingly cheery; this was a pretty lively professor, and their gloomy expectations of grim, tiresome, and pedantic mini-lectures were not being fulfilled. But then my moment of learning came. It was wonderful, I said, that public audiences were so interested in western history, but was it completely beyond imagination to think that a popular feature film might also be educational?

There was nothing particularly striking or insightful about what I said, but what *was* remarkable was the look on the faces of these two men, a look of disappointment and almost repulsion when they heard the word "educational." "Up until this moment," you could see them thinking, "we thought we had a pretty lively interview, and now she is going to start talking about 'education.' This interview is now plummeting down toward dreariness and we may as well shut off the camera."

But does it have to be this way? Does the word "educational" have to provoke such a powerful impulse to despair, or flight? Could not education, reconceived and redirected, make for more vigorous tourism, with more productive social consequences? I think of my childhood visits to the California missions, which were pretty, but finally quite dull. In truth, the story of the California missions, as places of forced labor and considerable human suffering, was anything but dull. I do not know what the guides are doing at the California missions today, but one hopes they are using the complexity and tragedy of the missions' history to increase the interest in—and even the *education* provided by—the tours.

And, as a part of the agenda of tourism, could we not widen the concept of sites worth seeing? I think here, especially, of the photographer Richard Misrach's work on a northern Nevada naval bombing range. This piece of the Great Basin absorbed bomb after bomb, with quite a number of them still lying unexploded on the site, and with shells and devastated bombing targets all over the place. Misrach has photographed the bombing range extensively, but his book *Bravo 20* goes beyond collecting images to suggest the creation of a Bravo 20 National Park. This would be a "unique and powerful addition to our current park system," Misrach says. "In these times of extraordinary environmental concern, it would serve as a permanent reminder of how military, government, corporate, and individual practices can harm the earth. In the spirit of Bull Run and the Vietnam Memorial, it would be a national acknowledgment of a complex and disturbing period in our history."[9]

Working with landscape architects, Misrach has drawn up the plans for this park. Like most parks, this one would have a loop road, this time called Devastation Drive; to view the somewhat risky terrain of unexploded bombs, the tourists would walk along a boardwalk, very much like the boardwalk leading through the geysers of Yellowstone, but called the Boardwalk of the Bombs. Misrach has even made plans for the gift shop, with books and videos on military and environmental issues, as well as "imprinted clothing such as camouflage-style caps, t-shirts, pants; 'Nevada Is Not a Wasteland' and 'Bombs Away' mugs, tote bags, and bumper stickers; and for the kids, Mattel models based on the most advanced, top-secret military designs—up-to-date delivery systems and Stealth bombers."[10]

It is impossible to look at Misrach's proposal without thinking that we have, as a society, been *very* limited and unimaginative in our thinking about the possibilities of tourism. I myself never took a more interesting tour than the one we had a few years ago, of the Hanford Nuclear Reservation in eastern Washington. Begun in 1943 to produce the plutonium for the Manhattan Project's bombs, Hanford now has eight retired nuclear reactors, a number of retired production facilities, and *a lot* of radioactive and chemical waste. The day at Hanford was the most memorable and unsettling day of my life as a tourist. The impact of that visit tells me that western tourism will have arrived, become mature, gained its full meaning, realized its deeper possibilities, when Hanford, the Nevada Test Site, and the northern Nevada Bravo 20 pull in as many visitors as Disneyland or Las Vegas. But, for now, we remain stuck in a mode in which a visit to an important site in western history is still supposed to mean *escape* from the world's problems, and not a way of reckoning with them.

The history of western tourism does provide the material for explaining one of the most complicated issues of historical thought today. For one example, consider the experience of the wildlife at the base of Pike's Peak. In the 1880s, in Colorado Springs, the local coyotes got the jump on postmodernist theory. General W. A. J. Palmer of the Denver and Rio Grande Railroad had planned the town of Colorado Springs as an upper-class resort, and participants at an upper-class resort had to have proper entertainment. So they had dinners and dances, and they played polo, and they rode to hounds. But if the tourists at Colorado Springs were going to play the part of British aristocrats, who would play the part of the fox? This is where the Colorado coyotes stole the march on postmodernism; in the absence of proper foxes, coyotes had to fill in.[11] And so the Colorado Springs coyotes had their chance to learn, early on, what it meant to be a part of a constructed experience, to be conscripted into someone else's act of representation, to carry the burdens of an imagined and inauthentic identity, and to suffer all the real-life, down-to-earth consequences and injuries of that burdensome construction.

This is one element that all theoretically inclined historians can celebrate in the topic of western tourism: this is the subject that makes all the abstractions of cultural theory—construction, authenticity, appropriation, identity, representation, performance—concrete and clear. Nearly everyone associated with the subject of western tourism has had moments where they looked like, acted like, talked like case studies designed for the express purpose of illustrating postmodernist theory.

As one of the best possible examples of what I mean here, consider the interesting recent mobility of the Grand Tetons. The Tetons are, usually, located right next to the site of Jackson, Wyoming. They have been in that neighborhood for some millennia. But, in the late 1980s, they hit a phase of remarkable mobility. A handsome photograph of the Tetons appeared in a brochure advertising Amtrak, which does not run through Wyoming. The Tetons appeared, as well, in an ad for a resort in Montana. And, in what seems to have irritated Wyomingites the most, the Tetons then moved south, to lend their authority and appeal to a condominium project in the Colorado Rockies. "We are more than a little miffed that our competitors continue to use our assets to promote their areas," said a spokesman for the Jackson Hole Chamber of Commerce, who went on to remark that Jackson was "seriously considering trademarking the Tetons." The ad agency that put together the brochure for the Colorado condominiums denied culpability: "It was just a case of mistaken identity," this group said. The manager of the Montana resort was more willing to admit errors of judgment: "I was totally against using the Tetons, but we had to get something out on the market immediately."[12]

"Wyoming Insists that Tetons Must Stay," said one headline in the *New York Times*.[13] In this whole episode, as in many others, western tourism delivers on its full, instructional promise. If you have a student or colleague who does not understand the meaning of appropriation of identity or the politics of representation, then let that individual contemplate the restlessness of the Tetons, and contemplate the jealous possessiveness of the Jackson Chamber of Commerce, tugging away for commercial *and* emotional control of an image.

Or consider my neighboring city of Denver. Every year or so, Denver collapses into a fit of anxious self-consciousness and worries about its image. Should it surrender the fight for sophistication and package itself as a cow town? While the smell of a feedlot is *not* a much-sought-after *experience*, tourists love many of the associations of cow towns: handsome men on horseback, rugged outdoor life, the heritage of the Wild West, the contact with lives more grounded, authentic, and real than lives in cities, offices, and industries. But just as a wave of enthusiasm for embracing the role of the cow town begins to build, then the anxieties break right behind. If Denver capitalizes on its frontier history and advertises itself as a cow town, will it not, by that act, move toward the past and away from the future, rendering itself into a backwater town, a town of the nineteenth century where no twenty-first-century high-tech company would want to locate? Every year or so, a group of consultants pitch into this problem. Poor Denver sits like a hopeful star, forgotten in the green room, overlooked and immobilized while the make-up and costume experts debate what look would best distract attention from the subject's many flaws.[14]

Or consider the example of Cheyenne, Wyoming. In 1989, the mayor of Cheyenne tried to address the problem of tourist disappointment in the city. Cheyenne is a town heavily dependent on the federal government and defense spending, and it is a town that suffered from the slump in oil and energy production. Despite its modern complexities, Cheyenne has still chosen to dramatize its Wild West identity, adopting the slogan, "Live the Legend." Once a year, during Frontier Days, Cheyenne goes all-out for Wild West imagery, with plenty of cowboys, horses, bulls, and dust. But the rest of the year, tourists pulling off the interstate experience considerable disappointment. Live the Legend? What Legend? As one young visitor said, "There's got to be some cowboys around here somewhere"; instead, there were businesspeople and secretaries, service station attendants and waitresses.[15]

To ease this disappointment, the mayor in 1989 recommended that all residents offer their visitors various signifiers of westernness. They should wear western dress and say "howdy" instead of "hello." Moreover, a troop of real estate agents, carpenters, and servicemen responded to the mayor's initiative, and pitched in to stage periodic gunfights in the street. Once again, it would take only three or four "howdies" from real estate agents dressed, perhaps more authentically than the mayor intended, as bandits and outlaws for even a very prosaic student to begin to get a firm grasp on the notion of constructed and appropriated identity, and on the contested meanings of authenticity.[16]

In Kellogg, Idaho, the rush of towns capitalizing on westernness brought forth an even more remarkable demonstration in cultural theory. Kellogg had gone into a terrible, possibly terminal, slump from the recession in mining and logging. The landscape in large areas around Kellogg spoke of those earlier industries, with large sections "deforested from acid rain and pollution from a smelter that is no longer in use." In 1989, with the inspiration provided by a $6.5 million federal grant to engineer a ski slope, Kellogg considered its image. Would the town adopt a western theme to accompany its ski resort? Too many towns in the area had already made that choice. So

Kellogg settled on "old Bavarian" as its image of choice. Not everyone was enthusiastic. "I have," said one resident in a wonderful and memorable line, "some real reservations about going Bavarian."[17]

"I have some real reservations about going Bavarian" is a sentiment to savor, but it is also a sentiment to challenge. "So you have some reservations about going Bavarian," one wants to say to the speaker from Kellogg. "Would you have any reservations about going back to mining? Isn't a bit of Alpine bric-a-brac a small price to pay compared to those earlier prices of acid rain, pollution, deforestation, and cyclical economic collapse?"

Here is the central question of western tourism, past and present. Given the instability and even decline of the conventional, rural western enterprises, given the economic troubles afflicting mining, logging, ranching, and farming, does not the lesson of history point in the direction of tourism? The lesson of western history is that extractive industries have provided a treacherous foundation for permanent and stable communities. If one looks for a different, and more reliable, kind of foundation, all roads seem to lead to tourism, to the preservation and publicizing of local natural and cultural resources, as a permanent attraction for visitors with deep pockets. Here, the theory goes, is the clean industry, the sustainable industry. By this thinking, the residents of Kellogg, Idaho, may feel a little goofy in their pinafores and lederhosen, but wearing silly clothes is a small price to pay for the escape from environmental injury and economic instability represented in the town's old smelter.

Whether one calls it the end of the frontier or not, some sort of major shift is indeed under way in the American West today. The rural extractive industries are undeniably on the ropes. The only question is whether they have one or two more rides left on the boom/bust roller coaster, or whether the whole ride is over. Under those circumstances, it is hard to find economic options other than tourism. In tourism's Third World labor arrangements, in its often terrible disparity between rich and poor in places like Aspen, in its various environmental impacts from sewage to air pollution, and in its ongoing vulnerability to the swings of the American economy, tourism may be an unappealing alternative to mining, logging, ranching, and farming. But what else is there?

At this point in my reflections, I come face to face with a powerful, if unexamined, urge among historians of my generation to steer their narratives toward some sort of happy or, at the least, promising ending. The lessons of western history, one feels certain in saying, tell us that the extractive uses of western resources come with a very definite limit in time and extent. On that count, one cannot fudge. But my own inclination to fudge evidently becomes more powerful when it comes to the appraisal of tourism as an alternative to these dead-end enterprises. I would like to believe that there are better ways to *do* tourism, ways that give greater respect to the dignity of the toured upon—or, probably more important, that give greater *wages* to the toured upon. I would like to believe that at the heart of tourism is a very understandable human curiosity, a sympathetic impulse to go beyond the limits of one's own familiar world, and to see and to learn about new places and new people. I would like to believe that this curiosity is not intrinsically damaging and degrading.

Consider, for instance, the pattern adopted by visitors to Utah and Salt Lake City before 1890. The one feature of local society, on every non-Mormon visitor's mind, was polygamy. Visitors to Salt Lake were thus the living, walking embodiments of the component of snoopishness in tourism. If visitors walked past a Mormon house and the door happened to be open, they would peer in, hoping for a glimpse of polygamy in private life.

This was tourism at its peak of snoopishness, tourism as intrusion, tourism as psychological and domestic invasion. But this is also where a suspension of the casting of the tourist as contemptible, intrusive other seems in order. Is there anyone among us who does *not* find polygamy very interesting? Jessie Embry's fine book on Mormon polygamous families is a case in point.[18] It is a well-done book in scholarly terms, but one reads it, eagerly, energetically, not simply out of admiration for its scholarship, but also for reasons not all that removed from the snoopishness of the gentile tourists of the late nineteenth century. One turns the pages of Embry's book in a spirit not entirely separate from the eagerness with which tourists hoped that a door would open and they could get a glimpse of a polygamous family at home. The curiosity that drives the historian and the curiosity that drives the tourist have a certain amount in common. The spirit of inquiry with which the historian pokes into the lives of people of the past bears a certain resemblance to the spirit of inquiry with which tourists have poked into the lives of their contemporaries. Historians had better put some effort into a sympathetic understanding of the interior world of tourists, because tourists are, in some not necessarily very agreeable way, our kinfolk.

But the relation of historians to tourists is even more tangled than this, because contemporary tourism relies heavily on the *marketing* of history. When you track the history of western American tourism, you arrive, ironically, at a branch of tourism that rests on the marketing of the romance, color, and interest of western American history. To use the term employed by professionals in this field, you confront heritage tourism, tourism that capitalizes on the attractions and interest of the past. This kind of tourism has a way of rendering western history in pastel colors, sketching a cheery and inconsequentially quaint past. And yet the messages of heritage tourism reach a much larger audience than writings of academic historians will ever reach; it does not seem entirely justifiable for historians to turn on our heels and retreat in contempt from the impurity of heritage tourism.

I am willing to go pretty far in asking for a reconsideration of tourism, and for a reconsideration of our usual portrait of the tourist as a bumbling, contemptible, invasive other. But I recognize that, even with this reconsideration, what tourists want from western history and what historians are willing to give them may be fundamentally at odds. This is a struggle not likely to dissolve in friendly, reciprocal empathy and understanding.

When art tourism hit Taos, New Mexico, early in the twentieth century, Anglo-American artists rushed in to paint Indians and Mexican Americans, producing appealing images that in turn inspired further waves of tourism. When I am starting to get too cheery and soft-headed in my appraisal of tourism, it helps to remember a story that anthropologist Sylvia Rodriguez tells in an article on the Taos Art Colony. Joseph Sandoval was a child in Taos Pueblo when art tourism hit the area. Sandoval's father served as a model for the artists, and then, at age six, Joe himself began to pose. Years later, Joseph Sandoval described his start in modeling. "When sitting as a young child for [the painter Irving] Couse, Joe remembers that he became frightened at the idea of the artist's 'catching' his image in paint and ran out of the studio down the street. However, he was soon overtaken by Mrs. Couse who brought him back, chained him around the waist to a chair within easy reach of a great bowl of luscious fruit and a tempting mound of cookies. A blanket was draped over the chain, says Joe, and Couse, without further complications, completed the painting."[19]

I end with this story to counteract any tendency toward the suspension of critical judgment that I may have shown in this essay. This image of a chained child, with a blanket placed over the chain to make the picture pretty, is part of the heritage of western tourism. As we examine the rising influence of tourism in the western economy, we return to pay attention to that chain.

Notes

1. Marvin C. Ross, ed., *The West of Alfred Jacob Miller* (Norman: University of Oklahoma Press, 1951), 119.

2. Patricia Nelson Limerick, *Desert Passages: Encounters with the American Deserts* (Albuquerque: University of New Mexico Press, 1985), 113–126.

3. Earl Pomeroy, *In Search of the Golden West: The Tourist in Western America* (New York: Alfred A. Knopf, 1957), 172.

4. J. B. Jackson, "The Stranger's Path," *Landscape* 7 (Autumn 1957): 11–15.

5. Michelle Mahoney and Steve Lipsher, "Tourist Bureau Closing," *Denver Post,* November 4, 1993; Timothy Egan, "What Attracts Tourists Repels Some Residents," *New York Times,* June 5, 1989.

6. Edward Abbey, *Abbey's Road* (New York: E. P. Dutton, 1979), 86.

7. Alfred Runte, *National Parks: The American Experience* (Lincoln: University of Nebraska Press, 1979), 104.

8. Michael deCourcy Hinds, "Anxious Armies of Vacationers Are Demanding More from Nature," *New York Times,* July 8, 1990.

9. Richard Misrach, with Myriam Weisang Misrach, *Bravo 20: The Bombing of the American West* (Baltimore: Johns Hopkins University Press, 1990), 95.

10. Ibid., 96.

11. Pomeroy, *In Search of the Golden West,* 21.

12. "Photogenic Tetons Get Around a Lot More than Wyoming Likes," *Denver Post,* December 26, 1989.

13. "Wyoming Insists that Tetons Must Stay," *New York Times,* December 27, 1989.

14. "Denver Told Image Will Lasso Tourists," *Denver Post,* March 15, 1991; "Visitors Cool on Denver," *Denver Post,* June 24, 1993.

15. "'Not-So-Wild' West Disappointing," *Denver Post,* July 2, 1989.

16. Ibid.

17. Timothy Egan, "Kellogg Journal: Mining Town Given Lift in Effort to Be a Resort," *New York Times,* July 13, 1989.

18. Jessie L. Embry, *Mormon Polygamous Families: Life in the Principle* (Salt Lake City: University of Utah Press, 1987).

19. Quoted in Sylvia Rodriguez, "Art, Tourism, and Race Relations in Taos: Toward a Sociology of the Art Colony," *Journal of Anthropological Research* 45, no. 1 (1989): 83.

2

TOGA! TOGA!

BLAKE ALLMENDINGER

In 1983, a hiker, walking among the dunes of central California, tripped over the head of a sphinx, which the windswept sands had uncovered. The artifact was something that Cecil B. DeMille—not an Egyptian ruler—had conceived long ago. Before filming his first version of *The Ten Commandments*, sixty years earlier, DeMille had constructed a series of sets in the desert. One of these sets re-created the city of Ramses the Magnificent. Twenty-four sphinxes, weighing five tons apiece, and four 35-foot-tall statues of the pharaoh, made of concrete and plaster, had been erected and photographed, then dismantled and buried. Although film historians had subsequently searched the region for years, it took decades before the sands revealed where the lost city lay. In 1993, ten years after the hiker had rediscovered the head of one sphinx, a team of experts was still slowly digging to see what else was there. "Ground radar readings confirm that materials lie below the shifting dunes," claimed one cautious reporter.[1] But whether they indicated the presence of vast secret treasures, no one would speculate.

The U.S. frontier has provided the inspiration and setting for many great epics, some of which ostensibly take place in exotic foreign locales. *Ben-Hur* (1880), one of the best-selling novels of the late nineteenth century, tells the story of one man, a Jew, who escapes Roman bondage, finding personal salvation at the foot of Christ's cross. The author, Lew Wallace, governed the New Mexico territory in the late 1870s while he was writing *Ben-Hur*. In addition to using the southwestern landscape as a substitute for the deserts of Palestine, Wallace based the action in his novel on contemporary local historical incidents. While he was working to make the recently acquired U.S. territory "safe" for white settlement, placing Indians on reservations and arbitrating range wars between bandits and cattlemen, Wallace was simultaneously narrating "civilization's" rise over "savagery." *Ben-Hur* demonstrated the hero's conversion and triumph over pagan, decadent Rome. The novel glorified the decline of a barbaric culture and the dawning of a new Christian age at the same time that U.S. imperialist policies were attempting to justify white expansion on the western frontier. However, a decided ambivalence—an identification, first with the agents of "civilization," then with the forces of "savagery"—plagued Wallace throughout his life and careers. *Ben-Hur* was the best-known but not the only example of Wallace's mixed views on the subject of empire, both at home and abroad.

Lewis Wallace was born in 1827 in Brookville, a small town on Indiana's frontier. His father, David, after training and teaching at West Point, had given up the military, returned to his home state, and gone into politics. In the early 1830s, before his father became governor and moved to the capital, Wallace's family lived in the small town of Covington. Here, near the Indiana-Illinois border, Indians had begun to wage war. The Illinois state militia, fighting on behalf of white settlers, had tried to remove native peoples from land near the border. The warrior Black Hawk, however, having rallied five tribes of Indians, had declared war on intruders. In the spring of that year, tribes had killed two settlers not far from Covington. Because of his military experience, the townspeople elected Wallace's father (whom they nicknamed "the Colonel") to train a defensive militia. Although the militiamen never faced war, they prepared for encounters with Indians in a field next to town. In his autobiography, published in 1906, Wallace recalled watching the troops and then going home, inspired by this dress rehearsal to sketch "real" battle scenes in chalk on his slate. (Wallace would later use the same materials to compose the first draft of *Ben-Hur.*) "Alexander, Caesar, Napoleon, Genghis Khan, and Tamerlane the limp-legged, were heroes in reserve," he wrote, compared to the subjects of his early battlefield drawings; "none of them—no, not all of them together—slew half the number of men I wiped from my fields of carnage in [the] course of a week."[2]

Wallace enjoyed watching and reproducing scenes of men armed for combat. The reproduced scenes, in fact, realized the bloody encounters in which Covington's men never fought. Reared on the literature of Irving and Cooper, Wallace could sympathize with the victors and with the vanquished as well. When he read about the death of Uncas, for example, it caused him "the keenest anguish," he claimed.[3] For the Indians, once they were wiped from his slate, could be remembered as noble heroes of a now extinct race.

As a child, Wallace sympathized with both sides in battle. As an adult, he demonstrated the same conflicting loyalties, both in life and in literature. In 1846 he served as a second lieutenant in Company H of the First Indiana Infantry during the Mexican War. Although he never saw action, he nevertheless supported the cause of Manifest Destiny, which claimed divine title to northern Mexico's land. But after returning to the private sector and practicing law, and after serving in the Civil War as a low-ranking general, Wallace went back to Mexico in 1865, this time joining forces with Benito Juárez. Having earlier defended the right of the U.S. to annex part of Mexico's land, Wallace now worked with a rebel Mexican army to prevent another invasion and colonization by foreigners. By ousting Archduke Maximilian of Austria, the puppet dictator whom Napoleon III had installed, Wallace hoped to prevent the expansion of the French ruler's empire.[4]

His first novel, *The Fair God*, demonstrated that Wallace could side first with the conquerors and then with the conquered in what was now Mexico. Wallace finished the first draft of the novel in 1853, after serving in the Mexican War, and published the final draft in 1873, after working with Benito Juárez. Set in the past, the epic narrates the conquest of the Aztecs by Spain. Rallied by the hero, Guatamozin, Aztec warriors attempt to fight off invading Spanish troops led by Cortés. At times Wallace seems to sympathize with the Aztec leader, whose courage and cunning in war help the Aztecs win several battles. But at times Wallace seems to identify with the Spaniards, whose triumph is destined by history. The author, sometimes referred to on the title pages of his books as "General Lew Wallace," was a military man who had fought on the winning side in two recent wars. His family, along with the rest of the nation, had also been waging an undeclared war on American Indians who refused to give up their land. For example, while he was governor, Wallace's father had ordered hundreds of Indians sent west to Kansas; traveling by a route called The Trail of Death, 150 captives had died on the way. And while Wallace was writing *The Fair God*, the U.S. was continuing to displace and eliminate its own native peoples. Spain's victory over the Aztecs, in Wallace's novel, if not intentionally justifying U.S. acts of aggression against its indigenous people, at least inaugurated a history of imperialistic conquest and settlement, one which dated from the arrival of the Spanish in Mexico to the nineteenth-century U.S. government's invasion and colonization of various western domains.[5]

The political imprint of one culture on that of another was sometimes accomplished using the stamp of religion. In 1878, President Rutherford B. Hayes appointed Wallace, a well-known war hero and loyal Republican, to govern New Mexico. Until then, the Catholic Church, led by Franciscan friars, had enjoyed only partial success in their efforts to convert Pueblo Indians. In *The Land of the Pueblos* (1888), Wallace's wife, Susan, depicted the Pueblos as a passive race, yearning for Anglo-European missionaries to rescue their souls. Perhaps because her husband was writing *Ben-Hur* at the time, she compared the Pueblos to the Jews who had been converted by Christ. Although they were as different from the white settlers as "the Jews are from the other races in Christendom," the Pueblos were one day bound to adopt the "one model" of Christ and to succumb to "the influence of the same inspiration," she prophesied.[6]

Wallace himself, however, entertained conflicting opinions about the "civilizing" role that religion should play. In a lecture entitled "Mexico and the Mexicans," delivered in 1867, Wallace blamed the Catholic Church for making the people complacent, arguing instead that the Mexican peasantry should protest against members of the landowning elite who exploited them.[7] In *The Fair God*, published just six years later, Wallace seemed almost to prefer the Aztec religion, which included disturbing elements of superstition and sacrifice, but which appeared no worse than the enslaving Christian religion that was introduced by Cortés.

While the Catholic Church was trying to convert the Pueblos, the U.S. government was attempting to confine the Apaches and Navajo.[8] During Wallace's years in New Mexico, the government made a series of efforts to contain warring tribes. In 1877, the year before Wallace arrived, 453 Apaches and Navajo were transferred to Arizona from their home reservation in Warm Springs, New Mexico. In transit, approximately three hundred Indians escaped from captivity. Although some eventually turned themselves in, the rest, led by the Apache warrior Victorio, remained at large for four years, running south into Mexico and returning periodically to attack U.S. cavalry. In 1881 Joaquín Terrazas, the cousin of the governor of Chihuahua, in league with the U.S. government, led a posse that tracked down the fugitive warrior in Mexico, killing Victorio and seventy-six fellow conspirators.[9] Wallace, who had asked the U.S. government for more money and troops to help capture the Indians, was satisfied when the warring escapees were killed, believing, as his wife claimed, that the natives were "what they were when the Spaniards found them—cunning, blood-thirsty, untamable." But during the feud, Wallace had also grudgingly admitted that he admired the chief for resisting white rule. "In some respects," he said of Victorio, "he is a wonderful man, and, commencing with a band of seventy-five warriors, he succeeded in uniting tribes always hostile to one another before, and in a few weeks he had three hundred well-armed followers. He has held his own against us from that day to this."[10]

Wallace had good reasons for respecting Victorio. By comparison, some of the white invaders who appropriated Indian land were themselves less than admirable. The recent acquisition of California and the Southwest by the U.S. had made it possible for white bankers, lawyers, cattlemen, gamblers, and bandits to move into the area. Establishing their own rings of influence, these vigilantes and entrepreneurs had murdered men, rustled cattle, and conspired in their efforts to wipe out competitors. In Lincoln County, in southeast New Mexico, during Wallace's tenure as governor two factions held sway; and in 1878, shortly after Wallace took office, violence between the two factions broke out. Wallace declared a state of insurrection and then offered amnesty, but neither his threats of force nor his promises of forgiveness stopped outlaws who would continue their depredations for the next several years. Finally, Wallace attempted to prosecute some of the worst offenders in court. As part of a program to make witnesses testify, Wallace struck a bargain with Billy the Kid, a hired gun who had worked at different times for various gangs. In exchange for his testimony, Wallace allegedly promised not to punish Billy for his own role in the war. (Billy had killed one man in Lincoln and was thought to be implicated in the deaths of at least several more victims.) But after appearing in court in 1879, Billy escaped from jail and went on a killing spree, violating the terms of his amnesty. After being captured and jailed several more times, Billy was eventually tracked down and killed in 1881 by sheriff Pat Garrett.[11]

History reveals Billy to be not a noble hero who fought selflessly for a worthwhile cause but a ruthlessly violent and pragmatic man. The facts, few though they are, cast a harsh light on Wallace as well. Some critics have argued that Wallace tricked Billy into testifying in court by promising to give Billy amnesty, and that Wallace then revoked or conveniently forgot the promise once the case was resolved. Others have contended that Wallace made the promise in earnest but that Billy's later crimes violated the terms of his amnesty. Letters exchanged between the two men suggest that both of them, being in difficult straits, tried to strike the best deal that they could. Billy, a troublemaking loner who fought for both sides but who had no stake in the feud, gave his testimony not because he cared whether justice prevailed but because he wanted to save his own neck. Wallace, a former military leader who had no experience governing disorderly citizens and a political novice who had little initial understanding of the complex rivalries of New Mexico's gangs, also seemed desperate to find a solution that worked. Negotiating with an unsavory criminal was a means to this end. The man who, when he first came to New Mexico, declared a state of insurrection and then proclaimed amnesty, again switched back and forth, threatening and conciliating Billy in letters that he wrote to the outlaw-in-hiding. In a letter dated March 15, 1879, Wallace told Billy that he had arranged for them to meet on neutral ground so that the two men could talk. "The object of the meeting at Squire Wilson's is to arrange the matter in a way to make your life safe. To do that the utmost secresy [sic] is to be used. *So come alone.*"[12] If history were as dramatically satisfying as westerns, in which heroes and villains play well-defined roles, this meeting between Billy the Kid, the West's most famous outlaw, and Lew Wallace, the territorial governor of New Mexico and the author of the epic *Ben-Hur,* would have been a momentous showdown. Instead, two men, who desperately needed each other for their own distinct purposes, came together under the cover of darkness to transact their shady business in a small frontier town. The clear-cut victories and defeats in western legend and literature gave way to a historical reality that was problematic and much more mundane.

Wallace's career as a soldier-politician was shaped by some of the most important events of the mid- and late nineteenth century: by the Black Hawk War, the Mexican War, the Civil War, various local Indian skirmishes, and the famous range wars in Lincoln County, New Mexico. Wallace's novels, however, were set in the long distant past. Writing at a time when literary realism was beginning to come into prominence, Wallace clung to romances that he had read as a boy, writing adventure tales that were situated on foreign frontiers. Having fought, Wallace could realistically describe the grisly horrors of war in his autobiography. Having governed in peacetime as well, he could chronicle the historical process of conquest and rule with the calm detachment of one who knows which side is destined to win. But in his historical fiction, looking back on the past, he tended to idealize and romanticize those who were doomed to defeat. Wallace made various careers for himself, first as a soldier, then as a politician, and finally as the author of one of the most popular historical epics in American literature. But sympathy for the losing side sometimes caused him to criticize institutions that had contributed to Wallace's success in real life. The army, the government, and even the Catholic Church could appear as instruments of oppression, used by the conquerors to impose their will on the conquered. Wallace's identification with one side, then the other, continued throughout his life and his literature. But nowhere did it play itself out more dramatically than in his famous novel, *Ben-Hur.*

Because Wallace wrote parts of *Ben-Hur* while he lived in the West, and because he based it on a conflict between "civilization" and "savagery," the novel in certain respects resembles the formula western, which was then in development. No western, no matter how representative, fulfills every requirement of the genre, and *Ben-Hur,* because it isn't a member of the genre but merely a relative, lacks certain signs of affinity. But in addition to its resemblance to the historical epic and religious conversion tale, the novel manifests three traits which John G. Cawelti claims all westerns share. According to Cawelti, one of the most influential critics to posit a formula, the typical western is characterized, first, by an action that "takes place on or near a frontier."[13] This action, occurring at "the epic moment" when "civilization" and "savagery" clash (66), loosely resembles the plot of Wallace's own epic narrative. Ben-Hur's defeat of the Romans in battle, his victory in the chariot race over his former friend and rival, Messala, and his conversion to Christianity at the end of the novel, which redeems the Jewish hero as well as his followers, mark successive stages in the dismantling of Rome's evil empire and the founding of a new holy society.

Cawelti's ideal western is also populated by three types of characters:

law-abiding "townspeople" who make up society; "savages" who inhabit the unredeemed wilderness; and a "hero" who remains poised between these two opposed spheres (46). In Wallace's novel, these three types of characters are represented by the Jews, the Romans, and Ben-Hur, respectively. The hero lives among Jews, who are destined to be converted to the new Christian faith, and among Romans, who are heathens and blasphemers. Born as a Jew in Jerusalem, Ben-Hur is later adopted by a tribune from Rome. Subscribing first to the Old Testament law of an eye for an eye, he seeks revenge against Messala and schemes to attack Rome with his troops; accommodating himself later to the New Testament teachings of Christ, he scuttles his plans for further destruction and dedicates himself instead to constructive good works. Just as the western hero performs acts that are alternately ruthless and civilized, so he finds himself attracted to women who are both morally dangerous and honorable. Simultaneously drawn to the heroine (a schoolmarm, for instance) and to the villainess (typically a saloon girl or prostitute), the hero identifies equally with characters who exist both inside and outside society. Moving back and forth between "civilization" and "savagery," Wallace's hero also finds himself drawn to two different women: Esther, a Jew, who is modest and loyal, and Iras, a Roman spy who betrays Ben-Hur while seducing him at a desert oasis.

Finally, Cawelti insists that the western be staged against the backdrop of nature (39–40). The desert or high plains, a sweeping prairie or mountain range, dramatizes the fact that pioneers could easily become stranded, dwarfed, or engulfed by the wilderness in the process of attempting to tame the frontier. In addition, the harsh extremes of the climate and the hostile "savages" who inhabit the unfriendly environment contribute to the impression that the chances for white survival are slim, that the struggles confronting a new civilization are great, even epic. Wallace modeled his Middle Eastern landscape on deserts in the southwestern U.S. While living in New Mexico, he observed that the Rio Grande Valley looked more like "the region of the Nile" than did any other place he had visited; his wife noted that scenes of "low adobe houses" and herdsmen with their flocks, gathered to drink at a stream, reminded her of illustrations of biblical stories set in far distant lands.[14]

As Cawelti's work demonstrates, westerns share many of the same characteristics on film and in literature. Reading Wallace's novel, one can understand why *Ben-Hur* was filmed more than once. Because of its depiction of exploits, crowd scenes, and spectacles, many of which exist in the reader's imagination as indelible images, the novel anticipates the later techniques of cinema. At times, Wallace's audience seems to function less as reader than as spectator, not so much processing narrative as simply witnessing scenes. (In the chariot-race scene, for example, the reader becomes one of the crowd in the Circus seats, watching and cheering Ben-Hur.) The unnamed narrator serves as an impersonal camera's eye, patiently guiding the reader-as-spectator through the excitement of the tumultuous throng. (In the race scene, again, the narrator says: "try to fancy it; . . . look down upon the arena, and see it glistening in its frame of dull-gray granite walls.")[15]

Unlike Cawelti, the critic Will Wright, limiting himself to a discussion of films, argues that westerns follow one of four basic plots. In the "vengeance" plot, the hero is a member of civilization who temporarily leaves it in order to protect it from villains. But at some point during the struggle, a member of society asks the hero to give up his quest for revenge. Only after defeating the villains, however, does the hero return to society.[16] On film, as well as in literature, Ben-Hur narrates the archetypal "vengeance" plot. The hero first seeks revenge when Messala sends Ben-Hur into slavery. While in exile he fights, as an individual and as a representative of Jewish society, against bondage to Rome. The word "vengeance" appears more frequently than just about any other word in Wallace's novel. The hero swears "vengeance" when his mother and sister are cast into prison (105); he threatens "vengeance" when he thinks that his family is dead (163); he tells Sheik Ilderim that he is racing against Messala for "vengeance," not money (225); and he spends three years training troops to fight against Rome because he craves "vengeance" in war (445). Only at the end of the book, when he witnesses Christ's death on the cross, does the hero realize that he must accept God's will and lay down his arms.[17]

Cawelti and Wright agree that the western hero moves back and forth between the worlds of his friends and his enemies. Wright claims, for example, that the hero, in his effort to befriend civilization by engaging the villains in war, becomes like the villains, realizing his latent potential to kill or do harm.[18] This seeming paradox explains one of Ben-Hur's early crucial decisions. Even before he goes off in chains to serve as a galley slave, Ben-Hur indicates that he holds a grudge against Rome. In a conversation with his mother in the Palace of Hur, he says that he has decided to beat the Romans by joining them. If he wants to train an army to conquer Rome's troops, he must learn how to fight. And since Jerusalem doesn't have an army, he must therefore leave home. Infiltrating the ranks will enable Ben-Hur to spy on his enemies, thus allowing the hero to develop his own counter-strategy. "I will fight for her," Ben-Hur says of Rome—"if, in return, she will teach me how . . . to fight against her," he promises (100).

Ben-Hur has a showdown with Rome—but not on the battlefield. On the racetrack at the Circus at Antioch, he finally conquers Messala. (Having been adopted by one of Rome's tribunes and having been given the chance to race horses enables Ben-Hur to master Rome's favorite sport. Thus, in the chariot race he beats the enemy at the enemy's game.)[19] Wallace stages the race as a shoot-out between two western gunfighters, stating that the contestants' horses burst forth from the gates "like missiles in a volley from so many great guns" (318). The fastest gun wins. The "quick report" of Ben-Hur's whip urges his horses on, causing them to pull the hero across the finish line first (327). The 1925 and 1959 films simplify the encounter between Ben-Hur and Messala, representing it as a clear-cut triumph of good over evil. But Wallace problematizes the race, suggesting that the adopted Ben-Hur, who over time has become more and more like the Romans, has also come to have few moral differences with Messala. In the 1959 film, Messala, seeking revenge, maneuvers his cart next to Ben-Hur's, using a protruding, rotating spike on one of his wheels to rip through the spokes of his competitor's wheel (see fig. 2.1). In the novel, however, Ben-Hur attacks first, driving his chariot up to Messala's, running his "inner wheel" behind the other's cart and causing his rival to crash (328). Ben-Hur's vengeful feelings match those of his enemy: they motivate the hero to commit an act of aggression and savagery. The film versions rid themselves of this disturbing complexity, reducing Ben-Hur and Messala to allegorical types. Here, the hero and villain drive white and black horses, respectively. In the novel, however, these distinctions are blurred, and the colors of each man's horses are mixed (303).

Wallace's historical epic and religious conversion tale, set overseas in the biblical past, has something in common with westerns, which originated in the late nineteenth century.[20] Wallace spent much of his life manning outposts on distant U.S. frontiers. His experiences, which influenced Wallace while he was writing his masterpiece, explain why *Ben-Hur* has some of the qualities that all westerns share. But his ambivalent feelings about those experiences make *Ben-Hur* even more problematic than most western narratives.

Wallace wrote Books 6, 7, and 8—the last three books of *Ben-Hur*—while he lived in New Mexico.[21] Book 6, which Wallace wrote shortly after assuming office as governor, opens with the announcement that a "great change" has occurred: Pontius Pilate has replaced Valerius Gratus as governor. Wallace's doubts about the benefits of empire may explain why the appointment of a new governor in the novel is represented as no cause for joy. Wallace chose to use this transitional period in history, when the U.S. government was removing New Mexico's previous territorial governor and installing Wallace instead, as the time to write about Rome's appointment of a new and even more evil tyrant. As Wallace noted, "the Jews knew the change of rulers was not for the better" (342), just as New Mexico's natives must have suspected that Wallace's tenure as governor would adversely affect their autonomy.

Wallace, the ruler, partially identified not with the Romans but with the subjugated Jews and their hero, Ben-Hur. In an essay entitled "How I Came

Figure 2.1 A still from the famous chariot-race scene: the villain, Messala, and the hero, Ben-Hur, drive horses of contrasting colors.

to Write *Ben-Hur,*" first published in 1893, Wallace alleged that a conversation with the famous agnostic Colonel Robert G. Ingersoll had inspired him to write a religious conversion tale. In a debate about the existence of God and the divinity of His Son, Jesus Christ, Wallace was forced to acknowledge his ignorance, confessing that he had spent his whole life dealing with worldly concerns and that he had previously "neither believed nor disbelieved" in the cornerstones of Christian theology.[22] Wallace converted to Christianity after resolving to study the question and make up his mind. The result was a novel, *Ben-Hur,* which tells the story of one man's religious awakening. Wallace, who stated years later that he had written the novel with a growing sense of reverence and awe, identified with the novel's protagonist, finding personal salvation while tracing Ben-Hur's road to enlightenment.

Wallace and his hero made the same holy pilgrimage. But Wallace and the Romans shared the same military and political goals: to invade, conquer, and govern their foes. Wallace's process of composing the novel was, to say the least, odd. After drafting the first version in chalk on a slate, Wallace then wrote the final version on paper in bold purple ink.[23] Deliberately or not, Wallace linked himself with the enemy in the act of writing *Ben-Hur.* For purple is the color adopted by imperial Rome. When they sweep through the streets of Jerusalem, the Romans barely touch the ground with the hems of their togas, which are trimmed in rich royal hues (97, 112). When they march on parade, they deck their horses in plush purple livery (101). When they attend sporting events, races, and games at the Circus, they sit under bright colored canopies while the spectators sweat (236).

Wallace's identification with both the Jews and the Romans explains why differences between the two groups sometimes seem blurred. In theory, *Ben-Hur,* like the formula western, dramatizes the conflict between "civilization" and "savagery." But the notion that Jews represent "civilization," and that Romans represent "savagery," is problematic at best. Can the Romans be said to represent "savagery" when their culture, even though it is now in decline, is at the same time responsible for bequeathing to western civilization numerous cultural legacies? And can the Jews, whose history reveals an equally impressive and extensive list of accomplishments, be viewed as exclusively "civilized" when Wallace characterizes them as unrefined natives who are destined to be subdued, either by Roman troops or by Christ? Like the Indians in westerns, the Jews are indigenous members of (Israelite) tribes. They are invaded by military forces representing an encroaching civilization that is looking for new land to inhabit and rule. If the Jews who defend their homeland aren't defeated by the Romans in war, they will be admonished and sweetly chastised by Christ, who will tame them by harnessing them to the yoke of religion. Like the Pueblos in the territory of New Mexico (whom Susan Wallace compared to unredeemed Jews) and, before them, the Mexicans in the New Viceroy of Spain, the Jews in *Ben-Hur* are refined only to the extent that they believe in one God; they will achieve total redemption when they come to accept that Christ is God's Son.

Ben-Hur resembles the formula western, yet, at the same time, it doesn't. The chariot race between Ben-Hur and Messala, which concludes with Ben-Hur's triumph at the end of Book 5, represents, in the defeat of his rival, Ben-Hur's symbolic resolution of his conflict with Rome. After this, the conflict remains between Ben-Hur and Christ. By meekly suffering humankind's scorn and betrayal, the Savior teaches Ben-Hur that it is better to lay down his arms and spend his life performing good works than it is to fight against Rome. Slightly more than the first half of *Ben-Hur* is concerned with the Jewish hero's adherence to Old Testament law. The principle of an eye for an eye justifies Ben-Hur's righteous wrath against Rome; as an ideology it motivates the same kind of vigilante behavior that occurs in most westerns. But the remainder of Wallace's novel addresses the hero's need to accept and put into practice the teachings of New Testament law. This part of *Ben-Hur* reads not like a western but like a tale of religious conversion, emphasizing the virtues of self-sacrifice, love, and humility.[24]

Conforming alternately to one of two different kinds of behavior, Ben-Hur appears simultaneously passive and active, meek and recklessly bold. Thus, as a hero, Ben-Hur seems like a statue in motion, a static figure whose action seems more symbolic than real. In the novel's first epic set piece, during the battle with pirates at sea, the galley slave is chained to his bench in the hull of the ship, forced to watch through the ship's porthole as the action plays out. Ben-Hur enters the chariot race, the second set piece, and wins. But his triumph, although meaningful, is mainly symbolic: the race is a game, and the win is merely a ceremonial victory over one of Rome's men. Christ's submission to his enemies not only motivates Ben-Hur's decision not to fight against Rome but justifies his inconsequential actions (or his relative inaction) in the first part of *Ben-Hur.* For the hero learns, through witnessing the crucifixion of Christ, that submission on earth leads to triumph in heaven.

As a boy, Wallace had been disappointed that the Black Hawk War had ended before his father's militia could fight. As an adult, Wallace had felt frustrated that his infantry's company hadn't participated in any significant action in the Mexican War. In the Civil War, General Ulysses S. Grant had scapegoated and martyred Wallace's troops, blaming them for arriving at Shiloh too late to help the Union side win. Later, during the range wars and Indian wars in Lincoln County, New Mexico, Wallace had pleaded in vain for more assistance from the U.S. cavalry, believing that military action would have helped restore rule. Wallace's military career, in other words, had been marked by disappointment, postponement, and failure. But his excursion into literature yielded him an escape from the frustrations that he had encountered in life. Although the hero of Wallace's novel is associated with peripheral action or with a central action that never transpires, Ben-Hur is justified by Christ in the end. His heroic status, as an advocate of peaceful resistance, is eclipsed only by Christ's shining martyrdom.

Wallace's religious experience, however, was less intense than Ben-Hur's. His admission, that he had become a believer in the process of writing his novel, piqued the interest of his readers to such an extent that Wallace eventually felt compelled to say more. At the outset of his autobiography, he attempted to satisfy his readers' profound curiosity. "In the very beginning, before distractions overtake me, I wish to say that I believe absolutely in the Christian conception of God. As far as it goes, this confession is broad and unqualified." Wallace didn't use the opening chapter of his autobiography to proselytize his readers or to proclaim his own fervent faith. He took the opportunity merely to issue a reticent statement ("As far as it goes") and to answer a seemingly tiresome question that fans of his novel, writing to him, had apparently asked more than once. Adding that "I am not a member of any church or denomination, nor have I ever been," Wallace made a profession of faith that consisted of bland generalities.[25] In addition to his conversion, another event—of more worldly importance and of more immediate interest to Wallace, perhaps—occurred shortly after the author finished writing *Ben-Hur.* Reading the novel and being impressed by the author's religious devotion, which had led Wallace to write so movingly about the last days of Christ, President James A. Garfield offered Wallace the U.S. ambassadorship to the Ottoman Empire. Willing to forget his troubles in the New Mexico territory and take a new job abroad, Wallace was also no doubt pleased to accept a position that paid approximately four times his governor's salary.[26] It would be cynical to suggest that the career benefits were more important to Wallace than the spiritual rewards for writing *Ben-Hur.* Indeed, it seems unlikely that Wallace wrote with the idea of personal advancement in mind. But Wallace's military and political promotions, as they have been chronicled by Wallace and others, seem to have played a more obvious role in his life than his religious conversion did. His conversion, in fact, on the surface, at least, seemed to help his career. For it was part of the President's plan that a devout Christian such as Wallace should be appointed to represent the U.S. in a heathen land overseas. Although Ben-Hur had been forced to choose between commanding troops on the battlefield and serving as a soldier for Christ, Wallace, professing his faith in the Gilded Age, when the gospel of wealth achieved dominance, didn't have to choose between earthly and heavenly glory. Conveniently, his well-known religious beliefs helped Wallace prosper that much more easily.

After reading *The Fair God,* an acquaintance of Wallace's remarked that Wallace wanted to be both a "conquistador" and a "Moses" in Mexico;[27] that Wallace fantasized about liberating the nation through both violent and nonviolent means. Again in *Ben-Hur,* Wallace identified with soldier-politicians and religious converts as well. His equal affinity with "civilization" and "savagery" force one to question whether those concepts represent polar extremes. Like *Ben-Hur,* the western defines "civilization" and "savagery" in relative rather than absolute terms. Through the actions of its hero, the western indicates the difficulties inherent in opposing these worlds. Moving back and forth between (moral) civilization and (spiritual) wilderness, the western hero—like Ben-Hur—exists in each sphere. Paradoxically, he defends civilization by resorting to uncivilized means, as Ben-Hur does when he wreaks havoc on Rome. In order to maintain social order he practices anarchy, claiming the vigilante's right to judge, punish, and kill, instead of leaving these decisions and actions to God. Although he fights for (Jewish) society, the individual hero has no social ties. Indeed, Ben-Hur doesn't seek revenge until he mistakenly thinks that his mother and sister are dead. (The supposed death of his family makes his rebirth as a war-hero possible.) The ambivalence that plagued Wallace throughout his life and careers resembles the dilemma that provides the tension in his novel, *Ben-Hur.* And the tension between "civilization" and "savagery" resembles the conflict that the western, through the actions of its hero, finally seeks to resolve.

Ben-Hur is a western in toga, in drag. Wallace used the conflict that motivated many formula westerns not only to work out issues that concerned the West as a region but to explicate matters that affected the U.S. as a whole. The Mexican War and the Civil War—which dealt with issues of national priority, such as sovereignty, conquest, and race—were as influential for Wallace in the process of writing *Ben-Hur* as were matters of local priority: the Black Hawk War, the removal of the southwest Apaches and Navajo, and the resolution of range wars in Lincoln County, New Mexico. The novel, which relives the conflict between Romans and Jews, also re-enacts major political and cultural struggles that were waged in the U.S. in the mid- and late nineteenth century. Ben-Hur contemplates imperialistic U.S. acts of aggression by narrating the historically and geographically distanced encounters between Rome and Jerusalem during the dawning of a new Christian age.

As a "spiritual" western, *Ben-Hur* functions as a transitional text in the history of American literature. The novel's enormous success was due to the fact that it combined characteristics of two popular genres, one of which predated and the other of which succeeded *Ben-Hur.* As a tale of Christian conversion, the novel modeled itself on the sentimental literature of the early and mid-nineteenth century. It endorsed the same brand of feeling and piety that had made *Uncle Tom's Cabin* (1852), the nineteenth century's other best-selling novel, such a triumphant success. Ministers who warned their congregations against the evils of reading fiction for pleasure made an exception and approved *Ben-Hur* because Wallace's novel was religious in emphasis. Clergymen testified to the phenomenal power that the novel exercised in converting their flocks. And some of those converts went so far as to write Wallace, claiming that *Ben-Hur* had inspired them to become missionaries and to preach overseas.[28]

As a tale of frontier adventure, *Ben-Hur* looked back to the works of Irving and Cooper, which Wallace had read as a child. It also looked forward to the genre of westerns, which would be developed in the decades to come. The theme of moral redemption, reverently explicated in the novel's contemplative passages, competes for the reader's attention with scenes of manly contests, heroic adventures, and war. And as the novel combines two different genres, so the novel's hero alternately plays two different roles. Ben-Hur is the sentimental hero(ine) whose spheres are the church and the home. In the course of the novel, he converts to Christianity, reunites with his mother and sister, and returns to his home/land, Jerusalem, where he is restored as the rightful Prince in the Palace of Hur. Wallace gives Ben-Hur soft womanly features that are intended to express extreme states of feeling: a "dimpled" mouth, "full eyes," and the rosy cheeks of a blushing young girl (71). When he asks Quintus Arrius for information about his mother and sister, Ben-Hur clasps "his hands in appeal" (126), using the same sentimental gesture that he later uses when he supplicates Christ. But passive humility gives way to anger when Ben-Hur believes that Messala has murdered his kin. The emotional change that comes over Ben-Hur is "instant," "extreme" (126). His womanly, expressive countenance becomes steely and stern. His muscles flex in rebellion, signifying Ben-Hur's intent to destroy his arch-nemesis. Immediately, Ben-Hur transforms himself into the avenger, into the vigilante hero whom fans of westerns admire.

Wallace's novel was one of the late nineteenth-century's best-selling books. It combined sentimental literature, one of the favorite genres of women, with literature of the strenuous life, for which there was a correspondingly large male readership. Like the novels of Harriet Beecher Stowe, Susan Warner, and others, *Ben-Hur* privileged the domestic and sacred spheres. (The hero's need for family and home/land is as great as his yearning for Christ.) But like the writings of Theodore Roosevelt, the works of Jack London, and early formula westerns, *Ben-Hur* glorified the adventures of men who lived on a distant mythic frontier. It became astoundingly popular, appealing to a diverse national audience by accommodating contradictory, multiple views on such subjects as race wars, religion, and Manifest Destiny, and by packaging such serious issues in an entertaining literary hybrid that incorporated the historical epic, the sentimental conversion tale, and the early formula western.

Notes

A version of this essay appeared in *Ten Most Wanted: The New Western Literature*, edited by Blake Allmendinger. Reproduced by permission of Routledge, Inc. Copyright 1998.

1. Robert Epstein, "The Search for DeMille's Lost City," *Los Angeles Times*, March 11, 1993: F12.

2. Lew Wallace, *Lew Wallace: An Autobiography* (New York: Harper, 1906), 16. A summary of the war and its effect on Wallace appears here and in Morsberger and Morsberger, *Lew Wallace*, 5.

3. Wallace, *Lew Wallace*, 188.

4. Wallace's years with the Juáristas are dealt with in detail in Irving McKee, *"Ben-Hur" Wallace: The Life of General Lew Wallace* (Berkeley: University of California Press, 1947), 90–110.

5. *The Fair God, or, the Last of the 'Tzins: A Tale of the Conquest of Mexico* (New York: James R. Osgood, 1873). My understanding of *The Fair God* is based on the reading of the novel given in Robert E. Morsberger and Katherine M. Morsberger, *Lew Wallace: Militant Romantic* (New York: McGraw-Hill, 1980), 224–37. For an account of the 1838 removal of the Potawatomi Indians, see ibid., 12.

6. Susan Wallace, *The Land of the Pueblos* (New York: Alden, 1890 rpt.), 16, 131.

7. Cited in Morsberger and Morsberger, *Lew Wallace,* 215.

8. Edward H. Spicer believes that, in the territories of Arizona and New Mexico, the U.S. "thought in terms of extermination or forcible isolation, rather than Christian conversion." The concept of the reservation, he claims, "developed out of the policy of isolation" and offered a practical alternative to killing the Indians. See *Cycles of Conquest: The Impact of Spain, Mexico, and the United States on the Indians of the Southwest, 1533–1960* (Tucson: University of Arizona Press, 1962), 344–45, 347. At the same time, the religious conversion and political containment of the Indians in the southwestern U.S. have been seen as equally controlling strategies designed to cope with the "other." One western historian argues, for instance, that General Kearney's 1846 triumphal march into New Mexico and Bishop Lamy's 1852 arrival in Santa Fe both constituted invasions, although one was sponsored by the U.S. government and one was decreed by the Church. See Howard Roberts Lamar, *The Far Southwest 1846–1912: A Territorial History* (New Haven: Yale University Press, 1966), 102–03. For information on Jean Baptiste Lamy, who was appointed to reform the Catholic Church in New Mexico, see Paul Horgan, *Lamy of Santa Fe: His Life and Times* (New York: Farrar, Straus and Giroux, 1975). Willa Cather's novel *Death Comes for the Archbishop* (1927) is a thinly disguised account of his career in New Mexico.

9. The war against Victorio is chronicled in C. L. Sonnichsen, *The Mescalero Apaches* (Norman: University of Oklahoma Press, 1958), 160–64; Dan L. Thrapp, *Victorio and the Mimbres Apaches* (Norman: University of Oklahoma Press, 1974); McKee, *"Ben-Hur" Wallace,* 155–56; and Morsberger and Morsberger, *Lew Wallace,* 282–87.

10. Morsberger and Morsberger, *Lew Wallace,* 916, 918.

11. As one would imagine, there have been numerous works written on the Lincoln County War and on Billy the Kid. For the best account of Billy's role in the feud, see Stephen Tatum, *Inventing Billy the Kid: Visions of the Outlaw in America, 1881–1981* (Albuquerque: University of New Mexico Press, 1982), 15–34; for an explanation of Wallace's role, see Morsberger and Morsberger, *Lew Wallace,* 257–81.

12. Wallace's emphasis. The complete correspondence between the two men is traced in Morsberger and Morsberger, *Lew Wallace,* 274–77.

13. John G. Cawelti, *The Six-Gun Mystique* (Bowling Green, Ohio: Bowling Green University Popular Press, 1971), 35. Subsequent references to this edition appear in the text.

14. Lew Wallace made this observation in a letter that he wrote, quoted in

Morsberger and Morsberger, *Lew Wallace,* 291. Susan Wallace commented on the western landscape in *The Land of the Pueblos,* 51.

15. Lew Wallace, *Ben-Hur: A Tale of the Christ* (New York: Grosset and Dunlap, 1922 rpt.), 319. Subsequent references to this edition appear in the text.

16. Will Wright, *Six-Guns and Society: A Structural Study of the Western* (Berkeley: University of California Press, 1975), 69.

17. Some critics feel that *Ben-Hur* is a revenge tragedy disguised as a historical religious romance. These critics, including Carl Van Doren, argue that Ben-Hur's thirst for revenge overpowers his hunger for Christ and that his thirst lingers at the end of the book, even after Christ dies. See *The American Novel 1789–1939* (New York: Macmillan, 1940), 114.

18. Wright, *Six-Guns and Society,* 156.

19. In addition, the chariot race scene, as it has been staged in the theater and later on screen, has involved a number of western directors, actors, and props. In the popular 1899 stage version, the future "cowboy" movie star William S. Hart played Messala. His expertise with horses enabled him to prevent a serious mishap in the theater on opening night, when the horses veered out of control and almost ran off the stage. In MGM's 1925 silent film version, directed by Fred Niblo and starring Ramon Novarro, the race scene was directed, not by Niblo, but by the second unit director, B. Reaves Eason, who later directed the land rush scene in *Cimarron* (1930) and the stallion scenes in *Duel in the Sun* (1946). In MGM's follow-up 1959 film version, directed by William Wyler, Charlton Heston (Ben-Hur) and Stephen Boyd (Messala)—amazingly—raced their own chariots. Professional rodeo riders drove the rest of them. For more information, see William S. Hart, *My Life East and West* (Boston: Houghton Mifflin, 1929), 149; Morsberger and Morsberger, *Lew Wallace,* 464–66, 475–76, 483.

20. For a discussion of the relationship between the historical romance and the dime novel, see Tatum, *Inventing Billy the Kid,* 43. In a retrospective review of *Ben-Hur,* written twenty-five years after the book first appeared, Hammond Lamont claimed that the book's characters and incidents "make a dime novel about bandits and beauties seem dull and lifeless. . . . Jesse James is a divinity student in a white choker when compared with Messala. . . . And for your high-souled, dauntless hero, we back Ben Hur against any combination of Old Sleuth and Crimson Dick yet presented to the world." In "The Winner in the Chariot Race," *The Nation* 80 (February 23, 1905): 148.

21. Writing from Crawfordsville, Indiana, on May 6, 1890, Wallace informed A. J. Wissler that he composed the last three books of *Ben-Hur* while he lived in New Mexico. Wallace Papers, New Mexico Records Center and Archives, Santa Fe.

22. Wallace, "How I Came to Write *Ben-Hur,*" *Youth's Companion* 66 (February 2, 1893): 57. Later the essay was reprinted in Wallace's autobiography, where it was placed near the end.

23. Wallace, *Lew Wallace,* 938.

24. It is an indication of the de-emphasis of the hero's quest for revenge in the second half of *Ben-Hur* that in the 1959 film no mention is made of the hero's attempt to gather and train Jewish troops. After the race the film concerns itself only

with Ben-Hur's reunion with his mother and sister and with his conversion to Christianity.

25. Wallace, *Lew Wallace,* 1–2.

26. Morsberger and Morsberger, *Lew Wallace,* 296.

27. As quoted in ibid., 267.

28. Morsberger and Morsberger, *Lew Wallace,* 450. Noting that the subject of religion was "one of perennial importance in the making of best sellers" in America in the middle and late nineteenth century, James D. Hart claims that Wallace's novel "combined the historical values of Scott and the moral worth of Mrs. Stowe, the two previous novelists who had battered down almost the last prejudices against fiction. *Ben-Hur* was endorsed on all sides by clergymen and leaders of public opinion." See *The Popular Book: A History of America's Literary Taste* (Berkeley: University of California Press, 1950), 163–64.

3

SACRED AND PROFANE

Mae West's (re)Presentation of Western Religion

JILL WATTS

Mae West and western religion may seem like an unlikely couple. After all, Mae, masquerading as Diamond Lil—the bowery's most famous fallen angel, epitomizes the antithesis of the west and of everything holy. An American cultural icon, she has come to symbolize the tough-talking "bad girl" of the urban slums of New York City. But despite this widespread and hard-earned reputation, the press, studio, and even Mae often exploited links between her image and popular fantasies of the west. Publicists, journalists, and her studio often used catchphrases like "the Wild West," "West is West," and "Go West, Young Man" to promote Mae and her career. Western inscriptions easily fit her for, in many ways Mae, the author of books, plays, and many of her own films, constructed herself into a western landscape, resembling the contours so well-defined by Frederick Jackson Turner. She was wild and untamed, harsh and alluring, unpredictable and challenging. While she was not virgin territory, she did beckon exploration. The imagined west resonated so well with Mae, it inspired one journalist of the 1930s to write, "West is no longer a region; it's a woman. A brand new type of 'western' has suddenly appeared—nothing to do with cowboys and the great open spaces, but wild enough for all that. Mae West is a whole wild west show in herself."[1]

Still it might be a surprise that Mae wrote and appeared in three films set in the west. And in one of these, *Klondike Annie* (1936), she even explored religion in a western context. In *Klondike Annie,* she created western space that facilitated a re-imagination of religion, allowing her to intertwine sex and religion with sin and redemption. And when West goes west, religious order triumphs through religious innovation.[2]

An evaluation of Mae's construction of the sacred west/West and her manipulation of the western genre suggests possibilities for a reinterpretation of the core and substance of her work. Mae has been the topic of academic debate for some years. In the 1960s and 1970s, feminist scholars essentially resurrected the sex goddess from obscurity, some praising her for empowering women and others criticizing her for perpetuating patriarchy and male dominance. Since then, debates over Mae West have raged on inconclusively for, as many have discovered, the ambiguities that haunt her performance make it difficult to pinpoint its definitive meanings.[3] My approach, which moves beyond an analysis based exclusively on gender, differs from these earlier assessments. In my view, an unraveling of her intentions and meanings requires a recognition of the layered and nuanced nature of her work.

Mae West was an extremely complex artist who grappled with a multiplicity of societal tensions and laced her work with a wide and conflicting assortment of messages. Much of this derived from her background. Born in 1893, she was raised in Brooklyn's turn-of-the-century working-class neighborhoods by a family subsisting on an uncertain and unstable income. As a maturing performer who became the family's breadwinner, Mae borrowed from a variety of trends present in American popular culture in the early 1900s. However, by her own account, her unique style developed most directly out of her contact with African American culture. Throughout her life, from childhood until her death in 1980, she maintained strong connections with the black community and borrowed extensively from African American culture, incorporating black music, especially the blues, and dance into her performance.[4]

Her immersion in African American culture led Mae to what is known in the black community as the tradition of signifying. Defined by literary scholar Henry Louis Gates as "black double-voicedness," signifying derives from the language games of black trickster-heroes who through innuendo, double entendre, parody, pastiche, and numerous other verbal, visual, and literary tropes, mediate between the sacred and the profane. Pitting opposing forces against each other, tricksters (signifiers) revise and reorder a disorderly world by challenging and undermining the dominant powers.[5] In signifying, Mae discovered a powerful tool of covert resistance that empowered her art and made her legendary for her double-voicedness. And she was conscious of herself as a signifier, for she often remarked, "It isn't what I do, but how I do it. It isn't what I say but how I say it and how I look when I do and say it."[6]

When Mae came to Los Angeles in 1932 to appear in her first film, she arrived prepared to signify. She immediately challenged Hollywood's power, questioned its prestige, and established herself as a rebellious presence, remarking in one of her first interviews, "I'm not a little girl from a little town making good in a big town. I'm a big girl from a big town making good in a little town." Indeed, Mae had already achieved national fame on stage, becoming widely celebrated for her distinctive style and controversial productions. As early as 1927, she had set New York City abuzz with her play *SEX*, a production that won her much publicity as well as a jail sentence for staging an immoral production. Despite continuous opposition from New York's police, censors, and moral guardians, she continued to write and produce plays focusing on some of the most contentious topics of the era, ranging from miscegenation to homosexuality. But it was the character of Diamond Lil, the wise-cracking prostitute from New York's Lower East Side, that brought Mae real fame. In 1928, after a smashingly successful run on Broadway in *Diamond Lil*, she toured the nation with the play, attracting accolades from critics and audiences across the country.[7]

By February 1936, when *Klondike Annie* premiered, Mae West reigned as one of Hollywood's brightest stars. She had made several blockbuster films and had achieved national and international recognition as America's first lady of the screen and streets. Although she had attracted a massive following of loyal fans and her films had saved Paramount from bankruptcy, her struggle with censorship had followed her west. With a little help from her studio, throughout her early years in the film industry, she continually fought off attempts to suppress and alter her work. *Klondike Annie* was no exception and embroiled her in one of the hardest fought battles of her career.[8]

The earliest versions of *Klondike Annie*, presented to the censors in an outline form, told a tale of spiritual regeneration in the west during the 1890s. Mae plays the Frisco Doll, a gambling palace "hostess" in Shanghai, who accidentally kills her Chinese employer while fighting off his advances. Fearing retribution and arrest, Doll escapes to San Francisco where she secures passage to the Klondike on a frigate. On board she meets a young female evangelist named Soul Savin' Annie. Doll "becomes intensely interested and impressed by the girl and her work." They establish a warm friendship and when Annie falls ill, Doll remains faithfully by her side. Despite Doll's efforts, Annie dies before they reach Nome.[9]

Eluding capture in Nome, Doll assumes Annie's identity. But she soon "becomes a changed woman," embracing Annie's cause, leading a religious revival from Nome's mission, and awakening the spiritual conscience of the entire settlement. In the end, her deception revealed, she resolves to stand trial for her crime, believing her faith will sustain her and that she will be exonerated on the basis of self-defense.[10]

While the original plot attempted to show the redemption of Frisco Doll (alias Diamond Lil), censors refused to permit the moral regeneration of Mae's imagined self. The proposed story flagrantly violated the Motion Picture Production Code by depicting prostitution, miscegenation, and murder. Additionally, Production Code officials branded it a "burlesque" of religion.[11] The censors went to work, busily cutting portions of the script and later of the film. They firmly excluded any hint of sexual intimacies, especially between the races. Furthermore, they prevented Mae from being either too bad or too good, forbidding her to portray either a prostitute or a missionary. The censors insisted: "We believe it to be imperative to make it clear throughout the script that Doll is *not* in any sense masquerading as a preacher or any other character known and accepted as a minister of religion ordained or otherwise. Rather her assumed character should be that of a social service worker."[12] They prohibited Mae from wearing "religious garb," handling and quoting from the Bible, singing hymns, and preaching. They demanded that she substitute a settlement house for the mission, recommending: "Shots of Doll playing games with the rough miners, teaching them Mother Goose rhymes, etc. Settlement workers make it a practice to gather children around the settlement house to cut out paper dolls or play charades. Why not have Doll giving the rough miners a bit of the same instruction?" Additionally, they suggested the inclusion of a temperance message, transforming Doll into a "sort of Carrie Nation, cleaning up the saloon."[13]

But the censors underestimated Mae's ingenuity, the studio's tenacity, and the power that Diamond Lil had over the public's imagination. Combining these forces, Mae presented, or signified, her original story. Regardless of the censors' dogged interference, the film retained most of its original content.

In the final version, Doll appears as an entertainer who sings in a San Francisco casino owned by a wealthy Chinese prince, Chan Lo. Captivated by Doll's beauty, Chan Lo keeps her virtually a prisoner. She grows restless under his obsessive attentiveness and schemes to run away. When Chan Lo attempts to stop her and punish her with torture, she stabs him to death. She flees San Francisco on a freighter bound for the gold fields of the Klondike and captures the heart of its captain, Bull Brackett.[14]

At a stopover in Vancouver, the frail and, in this version, aging Sister Annie Alden boards Brackett's ship. Bound for a settlement house in Nome, she tells Doll of her determination to "provide material and spiritual guidance" to the wild and unruly townsfolk. Sharing a room with Doll, Annie learns of Doll's sordid past and sweetly but firmly urges her to repent. "It takes courage to be good, but I know you have the courage," Annie says. "If you'd try you could resist every temptation." Doll puffs a cigarette and drawls, "What's the good of resisting temptation? There'll always be more."[15]

Annie, sensing the challenge of an unconverted soul, continues her campaign to win Doll over to her cause. She insists that Doll study a book entitled *Settlement Maxims.* Despite her reluctance, Doll accepts the book and over the course of the long voyage develops affection and respect for the fragile settlement house worker. But the trip is hard and while Doll blossoms, Annie declines, eventually suffering a serious heart attack. Compassionately, Doll nurses the failing evangelist, wiping her brow and feeding her spoonfuls of soup. As their ship pulls into Nome's harbor, Doll returns Annie's book, admitting, "I've begun to see things different now . . . you know I actually enjoyed readin' it." In her last dying breath Annie gasps, "I won't need it any more. May it keep you in the path of righteousness all the days of your life."

Doll has only a brief moment to grieve, for Nome's handsome police inspector, Jack Forrest, has boarded the vessel with a warrant for her arrest. In a state of desperation, she switches places with Annie. Slipping on Annie's bonnet and modest black dress, she convinces Forrest that the Frisco Doll died en route to Nome.[16]

Once in Nome, Doll unhappily discovers that she must continue her masquerade until Bull's ship receives clearance and they can depart. But after convincing the other settlement house workers that she is Sister Annie, guilt overcomes her. She realizes that she has benefited from Annie's death, and to repay her fallen friend, she decides to transform the struggling settlement house into an active agency of social uplift. Enthusiastically, she proclaims to her co-workers: "You people have been on the wrong track an' I'm going to steer you right. You'll never get anywhere 'cause you don't know how to wrassle the Devil. . . . You got to know him, know his tricks. I know him. And how I know him." She organizes a town meeting, invites the entire community, and solicits support from a scantily clad and tightly corseted saloon owner named Fanny Radler. When Radler balks, Doll warns her, "Listen you, I speak your language too. . . . Any time you take religion for a joke, the laugh's on you and if you know what's good for you, you'll be there."

The following Sunday night the settlement house overflows with happy celebrants and merry tunes. The crowd cheers as Doll appears on the rostrum. She sings a rousing temperance song and the auditorium grows quiet as she speaks: "You know folks, I once made the mistake of thinking that religion was only for certain kinds of people. But I found out different. I came to realize that you don't have to go around lookin' sad and wearing a long face to be good. I want to show you that you can think right and do right every day of your lives and still have a good time in this world."

Overpowered, a member of the audience rises, offers a confession, and Doll miraculously reunites him with his wife. At the end of the evening, the congregants eagerly fill the collection plate and happily recess for cake and punch served by Fanny Radler and her dance hall girls.

The entire town marvels at Doll's extraordinary talents, one settlement worker exclaiming "Sister Annie has accomplished the impossible! They're shutting down the town on Sundays and promise law and order will be restored!" Single-handedly, Doll has saved Nome and uplifted its residents. Furthermore, her love life improves. Bull waits in port hoping she will join him on the high seas. But she has also attracted the affection of Jack Forrest who, after discovering her true identity, offers to resign his post and help her escape.

What will Doll do? Choose Brackett or Forrest? Remain a saint or a sinner? "Caught between two evils," she muses, "I generally like to pick the one I've never tried before." After this reflection, Doll sheds Annie's dowdy attire and emerges in full Diamond Lil regalia. "Sister Annie," exclaims Brother Bowser, one of the settlement workers, "what is this transformation?" Towering above her brother-in-the-spirit, she announces her departure. Looking downcast, she remarks, "That's the way I do things—sudden like—or I don't do them at all." She instructs the flock to use the collection money for a new building and a large sign reading "Sister Annie Alden's Settlement House" and swaggers off screen and out of town.

The film ends with Doll aboard Bull Brackett's ship, determined to return to San Francisco and turn herself in. She tells Bull of a dream where "Annie spoke to me. I heard her say 'Go back and do the right thing.'" Certain the jury will accept her plea of self-defense, Doll explains "I've got to make up for my past." But Bull objects to her reformation and as she reclines on a couch, she takes him in her arms. "You're no oil paintin'," she purrs, "but you sure are a fascinatin' monster." The scene fades out with a passionate kiss.

Klondike Annie arrived at the theaters with much hoopla. Before the film's release, the studio began a publicity campaign that undermined the censors' efforts to eliminate religion and sex from the production. A studio synopsis identified Sister Annie as "going to Alaska to join a band of missionaries" and Doll's activities in Nome as "prayer meetings."[17] Advertising highlighted the film's sexual susurration, publicists creating slogans out of traditional Westian innuendos. "Come up and see me again fellows, thar's more gold in them thar hills," exclaimed one lobby poster. Another read "Out where the whiskers grow just a little bigger, out where the he-men are faster on the trigger, out where the gold's awaiting the digger, that's where the west begins." Additionally, a studio contest encouraged fans to submit lines for Mae written in Westian double entendres, tutoring the public to encode and decode her double meanings and to recognize when and what Mae signified.[18]

As a result most, if not all, the audience left *Klondike Annie* with the impression that they had just seen a film about sex and religion. Several reviewers understood Doll to be what one called a "prostie."[19] Despite the censors' meddling, Mae was Diamond Lil and Diamond Lil was every role she played. Mae affirmed this, declaring "the character I created in *She Done Him*

Wrong [the film version of *Diamond Lil*] is the one I'm still using and it seems to be doin' alright."[20] Many also perceived Doll and Chan Lo as engaged in an intimate relationship, signified by Mae's performance of "I'm an Occidental Woman in an Oriental Mood for Love." Furthermore, the public discerned the picture's religious content. Kindled by visual signification, viewers immediately recognized Doll's settlement house frock as that of a Salvationist; critics identified Sister Annie as a missionary and Mae as an evangelist, hearing her singing hymns and delivering sermons. Alliteration even led one reviewer to compare Mae's Sister Annie to the era's most famous and flamboyant female evangelist Sister Aimee Semple McPherson.[21] Soon the censors realized that their efforts had been thwarted, their New York boss, Will Hays, lamenting, "My worst worry is not the alleged salaciousness, but the producer's failure to avoid the impression that it is a mission house picture and the Doll is masquerading as a missionary."[22]

Objections quickly surfaced around the country. In a letter to Paramount Studios, the San Francisco Motion Picture Council complained "any picture that represents its heroine as a mistress to an Oriental, even as murderess, then a cheap imitator of a missionary jazzing religion is not in harmony with the other educational forces."[23] The Catholic Church's Legion of Decency condemned *Klondike Annie,* calling for its boycott. A postcard arrived at Paramount, addressed to both Will Hays and Mae West and bearing a scrawled message, "Shame on you."[24]

Newspaper magnate William Randolph Hearst joined the protest. In an internal memorandum to his editors, he declared the film "an affront to the decency of the public." He ordered editorials assailing the picture and its star and banned advertisements for the film from his papers. "After you have had a couple of good editorials regarding the indecency of this picture," he wrote, "then DO NOT mention Mae West in our papers again while she is on the screen." Commentary attacking Mae appeared in Hearst papers nationwide and several editors called on Congress to take action against the star.[25]

The furor actually stimulated even more public interest, drawing record crowds to see *Klondike Annie.* New York City's Paramount theater added extra showings of the film, beginning at 8:30 A.M. and ending at 2:00 in the morning. The box office returns outdistanced Mae's previous effort and ran far above the industry's average. Although the film generally received negative reviews, some critics charging that it was morally offensive and others complaining because Mae had gone "soft," attendance remained high. Mae was already an American institution and fans clamored to follow not only her career but Diamond Lil's as well.[26]

The key to Mae's appeal rested in the complexity and fluidity of her messages. Certainly, many filmgoers were drawn to *Klondike Annie* because of its promise of risqué humor and its lampooning of religion. But *Klondike*

Annie is a signifying vehicle that possesses two voices that simultaneously mock sectarians and secularists. Humorist James Thurber recognized the dualism. In an illustration accompanying his review of the film, he drew Mae with wings and halo soaring "invisibly above the bad boys and girls who she goes to Alaska to join but remains to save, or darn near."[27]

Thurber's rendering captures the central ambiguity of *Klondike Annie*—is Doll a saint or a sinner? The answer is yes. She is both Frisco Doll and Sister Annie. Playing the Doll, Mae becomes the ultimate signifier, for Doll is a doll, a plaything that is forever representational of something it is really not. Open to all roles and meanings, she becomes a conduit, channel, and mediator. As a signifier and trickster, Mae erects *Klondike Annie* as a trickster's trickster tale. Soaring on Thurber's wings, between the heavens and "the bad boys and girls," Doll transmits and translates sacred intentions to the world of the profane. In the role of the trickster/signifier, Mae creates chaos and then reorders the world, only to eventually generate chaos again.

But despite the confusing fluctuations in Mae's work, her confrontation with the signified prostitute, Fanny Radler, functions essentially as a good old western showdown with her other self, revealing the trickster's central message. Bilingual, Doll can speak in both sacred and secular voices, reminding Radler, the spectator, and even herself, "Whenever you take religion for a joke, the laugh's on you." This is the trickster's voice, signifying on hedonists and puritans who both (mis)interpret her endeavor as a travesty of religion. By reversal and revision, *Klondike Annie* transforms ridicule of religion into a morality play. And the signifier Doll's redemptive ability becomes so powerful that she converts not only a whole godless town, but its most hardened sinner, herself. "I didn't feel anywhere near as damned at this movie as I did, when I was a young man, at *Rain,*" testified James Thurber. "For in *Rain* a religious man goes sexual, and that disturbed me, but in *Klondike Annie* a sexual woman goes religious, and that gave me a sense of peace."[28] Despite everyone's efforts, Diamond Lil had been saved.

The trickster accomplishes this transfiguration by exploiting societal polarities and upsetting the normal balance of power. At the heart of signification is the issue of power. In trickster tales, the trickster (signifier) occupies a position of weakness within the community structure and gains power by initiating conflict between those who possess strength and status. In *Klondike Annie,* Doll, as a performer, is a woman who makes a living by selling her (imagined) self and thus lacks power and control over almost everything including her own body. She fights this by consistently wreaking havoc everywhere she goes, undermining all conventions and everyone's expectations and securing power by redirecting it.

By turning the world on its head, the trickster/signifier passes through three stages (or in the case of *Klondike Annie,* three acts) that closely follow the motif of a conversion tale. In the first stage (Act One), Doll appears in a state of sin. Drawing from white society's racist assumptions, Mae presents Doll in what the dominant culture of the 1930s considered a degraded state; Doll is a white woman living among the Chinese in San Francisco's notorious Chinatown, a community whites consider to be pagan and heathen. But immediately, Doll, the trickster, commences signification through inversion and reversal. Manipulating a series of polarities, Doll rebels against her powerlessness by exploiting the offensive racist stereotypes affixed to Asians by white Americans. In *Klondike Annie,* Asian characters appear as either docile, subservient, and ingratiating, or inscrutable, devious, and violent. While Mae's work reifies the racism ingrained in American society, at the same time, it also undermines at least some of its components. Verbally Doll spurns the overtures of Chan Lo, but the manner of her rendition of "I'm an Occidental Woman in an Oriental Mood for Love" implies that at some level she not only finds men of another race attractive but has engaged in intimacies with them. This enactment of a white woman who yearns for the Asian male operates as a pivotal element in *Klondike Annie,* for it scrambles the proscriptions for racial segregation and explodes the assumption that white women only involuntarily participate in interracial sex. As Doll thanks one of the Chinese men who helped her escape from Chan Lo, she murmurs, "I wish I could reward you somehow," glancing just below his waist. It is within this rupture of expectations about race, gender, and sex that the signifier first attempts to seize power by triggering binary oppositions and challenging authority.

The struggle for empowerment ensues over Mae's and Doll's attempt to control what feminist film critics have identified as "the male gaze." These scholars contend that American cinema, ruled by notions of patriarchy, is constructed to sustain and promote male supremacy and female oppression. To further this agenda, Hollywood movie moguls manufacture spectacles purposefully tailored to the male gaze, allowing men to visually identify with film heroes and through them to participate in a cinematic suppression and domination of women. Hence filmmakers construct the female character to be gazed upon and thus controlled.[29]

However, Mae, who oversaw everything from the scripting to the cinematography of her films, successfully manipulated the gaze, ultimately transforming it into a visual form of signification. As Doll performs "I'm an Occidental Woman in an Oriental Mood for Love," the camera pans over the crowd, revealing an audience of Chinese men who gaze upon her performance with desire and yearning. This serves the traditional purpose of establishing Doll as an object to be dominated by the men in both the fictional and real audience. But it is quickly countered by the next shot revealing that Doll, with equal desire and command, gazes back at the male spectator. By assuming control of the gaze, Mae/Doll successfully signifies interracial mixing.

Furthermore, while Doll's whiteness is highlighted—she is an "Occidental Woman," a "pearl of pearls," and a "white doll"—her racial identity is also covertly contested. Doll's contacts are confined to the Chinese community and she comfortably conforms to and adopts elements of that culture. She speaks Mandarin, occasionally wears Asian dress, and maintains positive relationships with the others, all Chinese, who also work for Chan Lo. Like Doll, all of those employed by Chan Lo are completely under his control and she shares more camaraderie with them than anyone else, Chinese or European American, in the film. And it was only within this western setting—turn-of-the-century San Francisco—that Mae could dream up such an amalgamation. In the west, racial identities could be somewhat destabilized and racial boundaries, although still rigid, could sometimes be crossed.

Significantly, the next stage (Act Two) of Doll's transformation, where she repents and is converted, occurs during a voyage. The ocean setting signifies references to Christian symbolism; as Doll crosses over the waters to freedom, she is liberated from Chan Lo's enslavement and reborn into a new life through a baptism on/in the waters. Again, Mae reinforces the ideology of racism; she does not begin the process of spiritual renewal until freed of all Chinese ties signaled when her maid, Fah Wong, disembarks just before Sister Annie boards.

With the arrival of Sister Annie, forces of binary opposition lock horns as Doll and Annie engage in a verbal struggle over spirituality. But, despite Doll's impervious sacrilegious surface, she signifies a positionality that belies the obvious. At one level, "what's the good of resisting temptation, there'll always be more" fatalistically rejects the notion that true spiritual purification can be sustained and that such a state of grace is even desirable. But it also signifies two other possibilities. First, Doll's response questions the assumption that goodness can be achieved only by resisting temptation. Conversely, she also invokes Sister Annie's position that the greatest goodness results from the most difficult of all challenges—the denial of all temptation. Such paradoxes characterize the vagaries of Mae's work but also create the confusion that leads to order.

In the final stage (Act Three), Doll, like most ideal communicants and/or tricksters, assumes the role of the missionary dedicated to spreading the word. But as signifier, Doll has revised the gospel and, in turn, pits tradition against convention. The settlement house workers of Nome are a joyless, lackluster bunch, a small band of odd-looking characters given to off-key singing and dull sermonizing. But, masquerading as Sister Annie, Mae revitalizes the faith espoused by her co-religionists in Nome. She excises its dreary conventionality, introducing a spiritual energy that reflects the newness of the frontier. Doll's faith is western—raucous, demonstrative, and emotional. Formality is shed and hymns sound more like barroom tunes than sacred standards. A Turnerian ghost haunts Mae's deconstruction and reconstruction of religion; she democratizes the worship process, breaking down ecclesiastical rule and leading the congregation into a more participatory worship process. This disruption of religious tradition creates a sacred space of empowerment that Doll seizes when she takes the podium to address the congregation. Posing as Sister Annie, Doll constructs a more egalitarian faith where a woman, through her connections to sacred forces, assumes the traditionally male position of religious authority and becomes the most powerful person in the community. Throughout the conversion tale, Doll has grown more powerful and it is her signifying gaze from the podium that reinvigorates the entire town's spirituality.

Not surprisingly, much of Doll's power emanates from her signification on American society's relegation of sex and religion to the polar extremes of the moral spectrum. Throughout her career, Mae agitated for Americans to accept sex as natural, healthy, and enjoyable. In the film, Doll's success as an evangelist has as much to do with her sexuality as it does with her faith. Doll is not just a sexually experienced woman but one whose liaisons have crossed racial boundaries. And as her devotion to religious work increases, so does her erotic allure. The real Sister Annie, living an existence of physical denial, lacks Doll's strength. Doll succeeds where Annie fails because she possesses the best of both the spirit and flesh. In the evangelist's voice, Mae reminds us, "You can think right and do right every day of your lives and still have a good time in this world." In Mae's re-vision, the strongest of believers is both righteous and sexual.

Still, as the story closes, Doll calls into question even her own conversion as well as the amount of power she has successfully wrested from the male-dominated society. At the end, Doll really has only two options, to surrender herself to Jack Forrest or Bull Brackett. Doll signifies on the limited possibilities for women by labeling the police inspector and the ship captain as "two evils" not only for the carnality they offer but also because they represent male authority. Clearly her choices are limited; rather than pursuing a cross-class relationship with Forrest, Doll capitulates to Brackett, a pairing more suited to her real station in life. This serves to reinforce the strict class lines in American society. However, even as she succumbs to the appropriate match, she signifies on gender restrictions. In the final scene, as Bull hungrily sizes her up, she responds, "You're no oil paintin'." And as she returns his gaze, she calls him a "monster," indicating both a desire for and a resentment against him.

The western genre provided a convenient framework for Mae's attempt to signify on power and authority in American society. Most westerns focused on a male hero who arrived in town as a stranger and through his special talents saved the community by playing good against evil.[30] This "Western" complied with the typical structure but substituted a woman in place of a man. Despite this revision, Mae in many ways reaffirmed the idealized west found both in popular culture and in the writings of Frederick Jackson

Turner. *Klondike Annie* advanced the assertion that the west functioned as a place open to religious experimentation. Such an assumption remained fully grounded in Turner's vision, implying that in the case of religion, the west was a spiritual void endowed with extraordinary democratizing potential. European Americans, like Sister Annie and/or Frisco Doll, therefore, assumed they could do three things in the west—first, misbehave (sin); second, renew spiritual commitment (convert); and third, proselytize and institute sacred authority (conquer). In this paradigm, white westerners who disregard and ignore the sacred life of indigenous peoples become immortalized as heroes in a struggle for religious freedom. As Sister Annie, Doll spreads notions of moral ascendancy and superiority in the west. From this perspective, *Klondike Annie* is a reminder of western realities, for it is not a tale of spiritual democracy but, rather, one of religious imperialism.

Mae envisioned the west as a religious tabula rasa where she could both sin and redeem. While mocking America's sacred institutions, she reinforced the necessity for religious order. As Doll, she rejected moral authority. But as the evangelist, Sister Annie, she instituted it, taming the wild west (and the wild West) with a new doctrine that seemed to make the west just a little less chaotic and a little more like the fantasied east. In *Klondike Annie,* West meets the west, offering us insight into the pervasiveness of our mythology about both the west and La West. It also reminds us of the contradictory and enigmatic qualities ascribed to the images of both the region and the star. But as *Klondike Annie* ends and Doll passionately kisses Bull Brackett, we are left with an uncomfortable sense that perhaps little has changed on this voyage from San Francisco to Nome and back. But it is nothing more than the trickster's signifying gesture that initiates the confusion that will again reestablish order.

Notes

1. Marie Beynon Ray, "Curves Ahead," *Colliers,* October 7, 1933, 21, 10; Mae West, *Way Out West,* Tower T-5028, 1964; Emanuel Cohen, prod. *Go West, Young Man* (Los Angeles: Paramount Pictures, 1936; re-released Los Angeles: MCA/Universal Video, 1993); John Cohen, "And West Is West," *New York Sun,* October 21, 1993; George Davis, "Decline of the West," *Vanity Fair,* May 1934, 46, 82; Kenneth Baker, "War Clouds in the West?" *Photoplay,* December 1933, 47, 109; Elza Schallert, "'Go West'—If You're an Adult," *Motion Picture,* May 1933, 32–33, 84; Stark Young, "Diamond Lil," *The New Republic,* June 27, 1928, 145, 146. In addition to writing all of her plays and scripts for her earliest films, West wrote several books. See Mae West, *The Constant Sinner* (New York: Macaulay, 1930); *Diamond Lil* (New York: Macaulay, 1932); *Goodness Had Nothing to Do with It* (Englewood Cliffs, N.J.: Prentice-Hall Inc., 1959); *Mae West on Sex, Health, and ESP* (London: W. H. Allen, 1975); and *The Pleasure Man* (New York: Dell Publishing, 1975).

2. William LeBaron, prod., *Klondike Annie* (Los Angeles: Paramount Pictures,

1936; re-released Los Angeles: MCA/Universal Video, 1993). For other Mae West films set in the west see *Goin' To Town* (Paramount, 1935) and *My Little Chickadee* (Universal, 1940).

3. For some recent interpretations of Mae West's work, see Carol Ward, *Mae West: A Bio-Bibliography* (New York: Greenwood Press, 1989); Ramona Curry, *Too Much of a Good Thing: Mae West as a Cultural Icon* (Minneapolis: University of Minnesota Press, 1996); Marybeth Hamilton, *"When I'm Bad, I'm Better": Mae West, Sex, and American Entertainment* (New York: HarperCollins Publishers, 1995); Marybeth Hamilton, "Mae West Live: SEX, the Drag, and 1920s Broadway," *The Drama Review* 36 (Winter 1992), 82–100; Pamela Robertson, *Guilty Pleasures: Feminist Camp from Mae West to Madonna* (Durham: Duke University Press, 1996); June Sochen, *Mae West: She Who Laughs, Lasts* (Arlington Heights, Ill.: Harlan Davidson, Inc., 1992); Molly Haskell, *From Reverence to Rape: The Treatment of Women in the Movies* (New York: Holt, Rinehart and Winston, 1973), 107, 115–119; Marjorie Rosen, *Popcorn Venus: Women, Movies, and the American Dream* (New York: Avon, 1973), 129–130, 160–164; Lea Jacobs, *The Wages of Sin: Censorship and the Fallen Woman Film, 1928–1942* (Madison: University of Wisconsin Press, 1991); Robert Allen, *Horrible Prettiness: Burlesque and American Culture* (Chapel Hill: University of North Carolina Press, 1991), 274–283.

4. For sources that document West's association with the African American community, see Richard Grupenhoff, *The Black Valentino: The Stage and Screen Career of Lorenzo Tucker* (Metuchen, N.J.: Scarecrow, 1988), 98–101, 107–108; Robert Johnson, "Mae West: Snow White Sex Queen Who Drifted," *Jet*, July 25, 1974, 40–48; George Haddad-Garcia, "Mae West, Everybody's Friend," *Black Stars,* April 1981, 62–64; West, *Goodness,* 64–65; Kevin Thomas, "Mae West, Like Rock 'n' Roll Music Is Still Deeply Rooted in Ragtime," *Washington Post,* January 1, 1967, sec. 6, p. 2; John Kobal, *People Will Talk* (New York: Alfred A. Knopf, 1986), 153–161. For biographical studies of West, see George Eells and Stanley Musgrove, *Mae West: A Biography* (New York: William Morrow and Company, 1982); Sochen, *Mae West: She Who Laughs, Lasts*; Jon Tuska, *The Complete Films of Mae West* (New York: Citadel Press, 1973); Ward, *Mae West: A Bio-Bibliography.*

5. Henry Louis Gates, Jr., *The Signifying Monkey: A Theory of African American Literary Criticism* (New York: Oxford University Press, 1988), 51–88.

6. Mae West, *The Wit and Wisdom of Mae West,* Joseph Weintraub, ed. (New York: Avon, 1967), 61.

7. West, *The Wit and Wisdom,* 27; West, *Goodness,* 79–148.

8. Eells and Musgrove, *Mae West: A Biography,* 107–110, 147–158.

9. Memorandum dated 1935 and initialed by G. S., Motion Picture Producers and Distributors Association (MPPDA), *Klondike Annie: Censor Files,* Margaret Herrick Library, Academy of Motion Picture Arts and Sciences (AMPAS). The original screenplay was intended to be a composite of one of West's original plays *Frisco Kate,* that essentially placed Diamond Lil in San Francisco, and a story by writers Marion Morgan and George B. Dowell entitled "Hallelujah, I'm a Saint or How About It Brother?" Paramount Studios, *Klondike Annie: Script File,* Paramount Collection, AMPAS.

10. Memorandum dated 1935 initialed by G. S., MPPDA, *Klondike Annie: Censor Files,* AMPAS.

11. See correspondence between censors and Paramount in MPPDA, *Klondike*

Annie: Censor Files, AMPAS; Gerald Gardner, *The Censorship Papers: Movie Censorship Letters from the Hays Office, 1934 to 1968* (New York: Dodd, Mead, and Company, 1987), 139–147; Leonard J. Leff and Jerold L. Simmons, *The Dame in the Kimono: Hollywood, Censorship, and the Production Code from the 1920s to the 1960s* (New York: Grove Weidenfeld, 1990), 53–54, 60–61. For other treatments of West and censorship, see Ramona Curry, "Mae West as a Censored Commodity: The Case of *Klondike Annie,*" *Cinema Journal* (Winter 1993), 57–84; Gregory Black, *Hollywood Censored: Morality Codes, Catholics, and the Movies* (Cambridge, Mass.: Cambridge University Press, 1994), 223–230.

12. Joseph Breen to John Hammel, letter dated September 4, 1935, MPPDA, *Klondike Annie: Censor Files,* AMPAS.

13. Ibid.

14. Although they had already given their approval of *Klondike Annie* in December, after viewing the preview screening of the film the censors recalled it, claiming that the producer had added unacceptable scenes to the final version. Censors deleted the scene showing Chan Lo preparing to torture Doll and the murder of Chan Lo. Joseph Breen to John Hammel, letter dated December 31, 1935; Joseph Breen to John Hammel, memorandum dated February 10, 1936; Joseph Breen to John Hammel, letter n.d., MPPDA, *Klondike Annie: Censor Files,* AMPAS; "Klondike Annie," *Motion Picture Herald,* February 15, 1936, 44; LeBaron, prod., *Klondike Annie.* For significant interpretations of *Klondike Annie,* see Curry, *Too Much of a Good Thing,* 57–77; and Hamilton, *"When I'm Bad,"* 218–225.

15. LeBaron, prod., *Klondike Annie.* All subsequent references to *Klondike Annie* are from the LeBaron production unless otherwise indicated.

16. The censors also edited out a scene showing Doll making up Annie to look like a prostitute. MPPDA, *Klondike Annie: Censor Files,* AMPAS; LeBaron, prod., *Klondike Annie.*

17. Paramount Studios, *Pressbook: Klondike Annie* (Los Angeles: Paramount Studios, 1936), 1, Paramount Collection, AMPAS.

18. Paramount Studios, *Pressbook: Klondike Annie,* 1, 22, 2–24, AMPAS; *Screen Book Magazine,* April 1936, "Klondike Annie: Production File-clippings," AMPAS. See back cover, *Motion Picture Herald,* February 15, 1936.

19. *Variety,* March 18, 1936; typewritten comments by social worker, MPPDA, *Klondike Annie: Censor File,* AMPAS; *Variety,* October 27, 1997, "Klondike Annie: Production File-clippings," AMPAS.

20. Paramount Studios, *Pressbook: Klondike Annie,* 28, AMPAS. In her review of *Klondike Annie,* Elizabeth Yeaman commented, "She is the same Mae West of all previous pictures." *Citizen,* February 28, 1936, "Klondike Annie: Production File-clippings," AMPAS.

21. *Pittsburgh-Sun Telegraph,* February 22, 1936; *Hollywood Reporter,* March 21, 1936; *Variety,* February 5, 1936, March 18, 1936; *MD Herald,* February 15, 1936; typewritten comments by social worker, MPPDA, *Klondike Annie: Censor Files,* AMPAS; *New York Times,* March 15, 1936, sec. 10, p. 3; March 12, 1936, 18; *Time,* March 9, 1936, 44, 46; *Citizen,* February 28, 1936; *Times,* February 28, 1936; *Evening News,* February 28, 1936, "Klondike Annie: Production File-clippings," AMPAS.

22. Will Hays to Joseph Breen, letter dated February 29, 1936, MPPDA, *Klondike Annie: Censor Files,* AMPAS.

23. Claude A. Shull, President San Francisco Motion Picture Counsel to Paramount Studios, letter dated May 1, 1936, MPPDA, *Klondike Annie: Censor Files,* AMPAS.

24. Anonymous to Will Hays and Mae West, n.d.; *Pittsburgh Catholic,* January 20, 1936, 1, MPPDA, *Klondike Annie: Censor Files,* AMPAS; *Examiner,* March 1, 1936, *Motion Picture Herald,* March 14, 1936, "Klondike Annie: Production File-clippings," AMPAS; Paul Facey, *The Legion of Decency: A Sociological Analysis of the Emergence and Development of a Social Pressure Group* (New York: Arno Press, 1974); James Skinner, *The Cross and the Cinema: The Legion of Decency and the National Catholic Office for Motion Pictures, 1933–1970* (Westport, Conn.: Praeger, 1993), 17–19, 34, 50.

25. Hearst to Koblentz and all managing editors, memorandum, n.d., MPPDA, *Klondike Annie: Censor Files,* AMPAS. The source of Hearst's animosity for West was widely debated. Although some saw it as originating from moral outrage, many speculated that it had originated from West's refusal to appear on Hearst columnist Louella Parson's radio talk show for free. *Time* intimated that West had slighted Marion Davies. West believed that her earnings, which approximated that of the newspaper magnate, made Hearst jealous. Regardless, Paramount managed to advertise *Klondike Annie* in Hearst papers by inserting advertisements urging readers to call the theater for details on a special showing. By October 1936, Hearst ended his news blackout on West and his ban on advertisements for her films. *Variety,* February 26, 1936, March 4, 1936, October 13, 1936; *Citizen,* March 14, 1936; *Illinois Daily News,* February 28, 1936; *Motion Picture Herald,* March 7, 1936, March 14, 1936; *Evening News,* March 5, 1936; *Herald,* February 25, 1936; *Examiner,* February 27–29, 1936, "Klondike Annie, Production File-clippings," AMPAS; *Time,* March 9, 1936, 44, 46; West, *Goodness,* 186.

26. *Hollywood Reporter,* March 18, 1936, March 21, 1936; *Variety,* February 5, 1936, February 26, 1936; *MD Herald,* February 15, 1936; *Pittsburgh-Sun Telegraph,* February 22, 1936, MPPDA, *Klondike Annie: Censor Files,* AMPAS; *Motion Picture Herald,* March 7, 1936, 19; March 14, 1936, 34, 78; *Hollywood Reporter,* March 4, 1936; *Evening News,* February 28, 1936; *Times,* February 28, 1936; *Citizen,* February 28, 1936, "Klondike Annie: Production File-clippings," AMPAS.

27. James Thurber, "Redemption," *Stage,* April 1936, 46–47.

28. Thurber, "Redemption," 47.

29. Laura Mulvey, "Visual Pleasure and Narrative Cinema," *Screen* (Autumn 1975), 6–18; Jill Dolan, *The Feminist Spectator as Critic* (Ann Arbor: UMI Research Press, 1988); Miriam Hansen, *Babel and Babylon: Spectatorship in American Silent Film* (Cambridge, Mass.: Harvard University Press, 1991).

30. Will Wright, in *Six-Guns and Society: A Structural Study of the Western* (Berkeley: University of California Press, 1975), outlines the elements that compose a western. He contends that westerns position the good against the bad, society against outsiders, and the strong against the weak. He also contends that westerns all follow the same pattern of a hero with special abilities arrives as a stranger in town. The hero commences a battle with those outside of society and ultimately defeats them, making the community safe and gaining acceptance within the social group. But at the end the hero surrenders or loses his (or, in *Klondike Annie*'s case, her) special place within the society.

4

"I THINK OUR ROMANCE IS SPOILED," OR, CROSSING GENRES

California History in Helen Hunt Jackson's *Ramona* and María Amparo Ruiz de Burton's *The Squatter and the Don*

ANNE E. GOLDMAN

One would sooner pray under the red-tiled roof of a Southern Pacific railroad station as see the bell tower that rises above the fake adobes of Taco Bell as a link to the history of Spanish California. Certainly, a more secular testament to the mission system would be difficult to find. Yet this commercial icon, ubiquitous along the sprawl of fast-food restaurants and gas stations that run the length of Route 82—the old El Camino Real connecting missions from San Diego to San Francisco—is but the most contemporary in a long series of visual abbreviations for the life of the missions which, a century ago, provided Anglo boosters of the newly inaugurated state with an appropriately mythic cultural legacy. Less than thirty years after the Treaty of Guadalupe Hidalgo consigned Alta California to the United States, writers for magazines like the *Century,* the *Atlantic Monthly* and the *Overland Monthly* represent the buildings of Mexican California, those most topographically distinct icons of its culture, in a manner which does justice to Shelley's "Ozymandias." Old as the pyramids, fragile as the crumbling turrets of some Far Eastern crusader's stronghold, the missions, in account after account, are the "monuments of an epoch already past," "crumbling into ruin," passing away grandly yet definitively "in the long procession of the centuries."[1]

What I would like to call attention to here, more than the striking uniformity of this kind of representation, is its tendency to hurry the passing of the elderly. Or rather, the middle-aged: for when one considers that thirty years marks our own distance from the civil rights struggles of the sixties, the three decades which interpose between the end of the Mexican–United States War and the flourishing of literature celebrating its repercussions hardly seems a long enough span to justify relegating the culture of the

Californios to some dusty museum shelf. Yet over and over again, as Cecil Robinson asserts in *With the Ears of Strangers: The Mexican in American Literature,* Mexican California is figured as an anachronism, its "Spanish" past revered but made archaic, its Mexican present "scorn[ed]" when it is not "simply ignore[d]" (67–68). In the South, plantation and local-color fiction produced after the Civil War lullabied white readers jittery over the (temporary) black political gains of Reconstruction. This literature in effect "reconstructed" the antebellum South of mansions and manor houses, celebrating their rigid social hierarchies while vilifying or obliterating the active black labor that undergirded its graceful columns and broad verandas. Narratives by and about California during this period are equally nostalgic, but if they look backwards to an apparently more harmonious past, what Robinson frames as "an ancient, dignified, and serene tradition" of aristocratic dons and humble peones equal in feudal luster to visions of the grand old South (135), they naturalize political conflict—the ongoing contest over land deeded the Californios by the Spanish Crown—by rewriting Californio history less as antebellum than as antediluvian.

I wish in this essay to concentrate on two significant exceptions to the willful amnesia that characterizes much late-nineteenth-century California literature. These narratives foreground a contemporary political problem, the "land grab" that is dispossessing the state's natives of territory, residents defined in Helen Hunt Jackson's *Ramona* (1884) and María Amparo Ruiz de Burton's *The Squatter and the Don* (1885) as, respectively, Native Americans and Californios.[2] The crumbling monuments represented in the fictions of their contemporaries mask political work-in-progress by providing the American Southwest with an antique cultural finish. By writing history as a phenomenon of the (literary) present, Jackson and Ruiz de Burton expose the larger narrative project that labors to reestablish social stability and cultural authority in a space characterized as much by ruptured lineages as by gentle breezes and burgeoning fruit trees. Their own insistence on the unfinished and contentious nature of western social life reveals how literary work at the turn of the century, even as it appears to efface history, is constantly rewriting it.[3]

Helen Hunt Jackson's perennially best-selling *Ramona* and María Amparo Ruiz de Burton's self-published *The Squatter and the Don* establish judgments at odds with the cultural teleology favored by their discursive era, which in large measure authorizes the new regime by recoloring its right of primogeniture. In accordance with the conventions of romance, both books chart the uphill progress of suitors who are forced to contend with familial prejudice and social obstacles before attaining their ends. But in keeping with the state's complicated series of colonial overlays, these twin versions of the California pastoral racialize the marriage plot. In *Ramona* and *The Squatter and the Don,* as in Gertrude Atherton's *The Californians* (1898) and the short stories of *The Splendid Idle Forties* (1902), the affianced struggle against conventions that prohibit *mestizaje* (mixed marriage) at the same time as, historically speaking, they bear witness to it.[4] Ramona, the daughter of an Indian mother and an Anglo father, is raised on the rancho of an old Californio family as the ward of Señora Moreno. Because she falls in love with Alessandro, a full-blood Indian, she is forced to leave "the privileged life of the Moreno ranch" and is "plunged into the tragedies and poverty of life among the Indians."[5] The lovers of Ruiz de Burton's narrative—Clarence Darrell, newly rich son of a squatter, and Mercedes Alamar, youngest daughter of the once wealthy Don Mariano—must overcome maternal disapproval for the union of long-established Mexicano (read "cultured") and newly arrived Anglo (read "uncouth") as well as resist the manipulations of the squatters, with the blessings of Clarence's father, to harass and humiliate the Alamar family.

While ostensibly driving the plots of *Ramona* and *The Squatter and the Don,* mixed marriage, for Jackson and Ruiz de Burton, provides the means by which a distinctly political agenda is carried out. The struggles of the suitors are not purely stylized versions of romance as much as they are representatives of an overtly historical struggle to (re)define borders, of Californio efforts to maintain their livelihood and their land amidst increasing pressure from encroaching Anglo settlers. Jackson recognizes this not only in her federally sponsored treatise on U.S. Indian policy, *A Century of Dishonor,* but in *Ramona* as well.[6] *Ramona* charts the social effects of its heroine's personal involvement, the essentially ethnographic component of what in race-blind romances would be scripted as psychic conflict. Falling in love in this book about culture clashes demands anthropological observation, not internal struggle; like Jackson herself, Ramona is swept off her feet by Native American cultures, not the charm of idiosyncrasy. Likewise, Gertrude Atherton's 1890 historical romance *Los Cerritos* justifies the U.S. conquest of Mexican land by naturalizing it as an affair of the heart.[7] The marriage of wealthy landowner Alexander Tremain and California beauty Carmelita Murieta, a mestiza who is *herself* an icon of the Spanish conquest of California, celebrates the more recent Anglo American domination of the state. Tremain's romantic conquest is also a victory for class interests, since in winning Carmelita over the protestations of Castro, the Mexican squatter who has fallen in love with her, he replays his legal triumph over the squatter community to which both Castro and Carmelita belong. Representing racial difference within the intimate locus of the private, Atherton uses mixed marriage to engage the sociopolitical configurations of post-1848 California and to dispense with them. In *The Squatter and the Don,* on the other hand, the union of Californio and Anglo we see in Elvira Alamar's marriage to George Mechlin acknowledges a political (and personal) reality to make a point about Californio culture and the relation of region to nation.[8] George works in

New York as a bank cashier, but quickly returns to California and its superior traditions: "Now, George Mechlin was making his second visit to his family. He had found New York so very dull and stupid on his return from California" (69). Like Clarence, whose voyages to the East make him long for the "flavor of the real genuine grape which our California wines have" (171), George's recognition of California's cultural superiority over the "dull and stupid" East proves that mestizaje is not a union of equals but the means by which an elite dispossessed *politically* reconfirm their superiority as a culture. Since the Californios for Ruiz de Burton are the "real genuine" California, mixed marriage in *The Squatter and the Don* redefines provincialism with a gloss that remains revisionist to this day.

As distinct from many other turn-of-the-century California fictions in which the historical reference point for plot disturbances (familial squabbles, class war, mixed marriages) is obscured rather than revealed, the insistently political arguments of both Jackson's and Ruiz de Burton's narratives suggest a turning toward, rather than a turning away, from history. And in the sense that both books politicize struggles for land (numerous passages in *Ramona* bewail the suits brought by "thieves and liars" [177]—i.e., Anglos—to dispossess Mexicans and Native Americans, while Ruiz de Burton critiques federal policy in *The Squatter and the Don* as "a settled purpose with our law-givers to drive the natives to poverty, and crowd them out of existence" [146]) it is clear that history, as much as romance, drives the narratives. Yet for all its passionate politics, Jackson's book writes a version of recent history that backdates current events, anticipating the demise of the Californios and the mission Indians and foreclosing upon any recommendations for change. Ruiz de Burton's romance develops a similar literary pathology when it invokes the "plight" of native Californians by mourning their downward slide, yet the story concludes with a call to action that provides for the possibility of a kind of textual and political behavior that is more than simply elegiac.

I will turn to *Ramona*'s negotiation of history and romance first. If the majority of Anglo American writings in the pastoral genre delineate the border between Mexico and California with as clear a sense of its divisions as a Rand-McNally map, Jackson is both less willing to grant territory to Uncle Sam and less happy to whitewash land theft as the product of a natural selection. Nor does she defuse the charge any explicit representation of political conflict carries by domesticating such violence, a displacement performed time and time again by her contemporaries. Instead, her attention to the repercussions of conquest reads as the agenda of a progressive, a woman who after being appointed Commissioner of Indian Affairs by President Chester Arthur in 1883 devoted much of the latter half of her life to Indian policy reform. In *Ramona,* she refuses to ignore the seizure of power and land that has led Anglo American readers from Eureka to San Diego to call California their own. Instead of exoneration, the "Americans" are vilified in the scornful words of Señora Moreno as "hounds . . . running up and down everywhere seeking money, like dogs with their noses to the ground" (8, 10). Jackson counsels readers not only to recognize conquest for what it is but to empathize with the sufferings of a people humiliated on their own ground, an attention to American injustice to its own citizens frequently witnessed in the Spanish-language press[9] but only rarely in Anglo American narratives, which until the last several decades celebrated the Bear Flag Rebellion as condoned by the Californio elite and translated the war itself into an "annexation":

> The people of the United States have never in the least realized that the taking possession of California was not only a conquering of Mexico, but a conquering of California as well; that the real bitterness of the surrender was not so much to the empire which gave up the country, as to the country itself which was given up. Provinces passed back and forth in that way, helpless in the hands of great powers, have all the ignominy and humiliation of defeat, with none of the dignities or compensations of the transaction. (12–13)

Oblique references to dispossession ("The Father knew the place in the olden time. He knows it's no child's play to look after the estate even now, much smaller as it is!" [5]) give way to open denunciations of injustice. For Ramona's edification Alessandro recounts a particularly telling incident in the history of labor exploitation: "One man in San Bernardino last year, when an Indian would not take a bottle of sour wine for pay for a day's work, shot him in the cheek with a pistol, and told him to mind how he was insolent any more!" (279).

Yet for all its willingness to extend sympathy to the bereaved, *Ramona*'s representation of historical grievance as inevitable tends, if not to condone despoliation, to negate the potential for redress. The despoiling of native Californians may be a tragedy, but it is authorized by "American" law, racial law, and natural law nonetheless.[10] Lamentation, not exhortation, characterizes this sunset picture of Old California, while the recognition of loss favored by the text's moral system is not the angry call for revenge voiced by the demonized Señora Moreno, whose hyperbolic language and cruel treatment of Ramona discourage readerly sympathy, but the wistful resignation articulated by Alessandro and Father Salvierderra, the novel's figures, respectively, of heroism and grace. Alessandro's response to the fact that the Americans "are going to steal all the land in this country" is simply to despair: "we might all just as well throw ourselves into the sea and let them have it" (177). This image, which echoes (if in an altered key) the triumphant westerly march from sea to shining sea, is confirmed when Alessandro loses his reason and is wrongly murdered as a horse thief. Father Salvierderra, too, bows to the results, if not the tone, of Manifest Destiny when he counsels, "'We are all alike helpless in their hands, Alessandro. They possess the country, and can make what laws they please. We can only say, "God's will be done,"' and he crossed himself devoutly, repeating the words twice" (67). The padre's litany furthers the very imperial program he decries, as he mourns the cruelty of Anglo despotism (a technique to deal with guilt) only to sanctify Manifest Destiny as God's law.[11] Framed in the language of faith, this kind of victimization furthers distinctly secular work as well, by soothing the jangled nerves of readers harried by the frenetic pace of the Gilded Age, and reconstructing, if only imaginatively, an urbane culture lost to urban sprawl in which "old mission garden" and "proud avenue" are cut up into "building lots"[12] and steel trespasses on land "tilled for two centuries" by people of the same blood.[13] Hence the appeal of Father Salvierderra as the remnant of a tattered gentility, whom Jackson characterizes using ethnography's standard of the dying savage: "He was fast becoming that most tragic yet often sublime sight, a man who had survived, not only his own time, but the ideas and ideals of it" (35–36). A Mexican Ishi, the priest's devotion is attractive by virtue of his proximity to extinction.

This kind of aestheticization of violence endangers what should by rights be an historicizing project. In his introduction, Michael Dorris notes Jackson's urgent desire to right political wrongs, citing a letter to a friend in which the author distinguishes between the strategies of *A Century of Dishonor* and *Ramona*. In the former she "had tried to attack the people's conscience directly," while in *Ramona* she had "sugared my pill, and it remains to be seen if it will go down" (xviii). Bittersweet, finally, may be the palliative that Jackson's descriptions of Mexican California provide, but, clearly, passages like the following are therapeutic for harassed visitors from the "modern" states: "It was a picturesque life, with more of sentiment and gayety in it, more also that was truly dramatic, more romance, than will ever be seen again on those sunny shores. The aroma of it all lingers there still; industries and inventions have not yet slain it; it will last out its century,—in fact, it can never be quite lost, so long as there is left standing one such house as the Señora Moreno's" (12). Jackson's image of isolated architectural grandeur recalls late-nineteenth-century European landscaping paintings in which well-dressed figures stroll through the magnificent but ruined buildings of capital cities—a visual parable of the rise and fall of civilizations. Just so are we, her readers, situated with respect to "Old California"; moralizing with the aid of hindsight upon the crumbling structures of an apparently ancient history. Dispossessed of its urgency, history is deprived of its political antidote as well.

> I hope . . . that the time will come when some faithful historian will chronicle all the deeds of daring and service these people have performed during this

struggle, and give them due credit therefor.
FRANCES HARPER, *Iola Leroy* (1892)

Anger at contemporary injustice rather than wistfulness for an idyllic but irretrievable past underwrites María Amparo Ruiz de Burton's own chronicle of Mexican California. What Lorna Dee Cervantes will characterize a century later in her "Poema para los Californios Muertos" as "the pure scent of rage"[14] is articulated in *The Squatter and the Don* in the controlled tones befitting the turn-of-the-century historical romance. Nonetheless, outrage rather than mournful complacency drives the narrative. If *Ramona* is a romance which takes place in history, then Ruiz de Burton's narrative is a history, a history spoken in several languages: of romance, to be sure, but also of the law and the political tract, as well as of a specifically feminine judgment which eludes the conventions of the romantic. What I wish to outline here is the way in which these languages, all fully historicized, allow her to voice a more far-reaching critical evaluation than is generally possible within the constrains of a genre at best politically unaccommodating, at worst prohibitive of indictments which extend beyond accounts of individual rapaciousness to testimony about systemic failure. The exoticized picture of "sunny shores" Jackson paints in *Ramona*—a geographically indistinct coastline which could as easily be Hawaiian or Cuban as Californian—mystifies regional boundaries and mystifies their relation to nationalist projects and imperial goals. The topography and topicality of *The Squatter and the Don,* on the other hand, clarify how local politics are underwritten by corporate interests themselves furthered by the federal government.

Even the chapter titles call our attention to the text's historiographic project. The opening chapter, "Squatter Darrell Reviews the Past," announces the interpretive paradigm shift the book is undertaking—Darrell is not glamorized as a sturdy "settler" making good land which lies fallow, but is instead revealed as morally compromised, willing to overlook the ethical problems posed by locating "claims on land belonging to any one else" (57). At the same time, the title gestures toward the book's revisionary agenda to reconstruct a "Past" not so much neglected as misrepresented. Succeeding chapters certainly acknowledge romance, but alternating with laments of "Shall It Be Forever?" and celebrations like "Reunited at Last," are headings which include "Pre-Empting Under the Law," "Why the Appeal was Not Dismissed," and "The Fashion of Justice in San Diego," titles relentless in their invocation of political scandal, depicting contests over land with an almost clinical legal precision.

Thus the Darrell-Alamar courtship evolves within a context of political corruption so thoroughly detailed that it competes with the narrative's romantic trials for center stage. Historical romance most often frames its political lessons as a series of digressions, however lengthy, from the movement of the suitors toward union; biographical sketches of Frederick Douglass and explanations of the three-fifths suffrage rule disrupt the story of familial reunion which unfolds in Frances Harper's *Iola Leroy* (1892), for instance, but they never succeed in usurping the reader's loyalty for the main text.[15] In *The Squatter and the Don,* laments over Mercedes's tears and Clarence's travels alternate with the Don's chronicle of dispossession. In chapter after chapter Ruiz de Burton writes a history at cross-purposes with the ethnocentric, blindly optimistic boosterism of state growth-charts like Charles Nordhoff's "forward-thinking" *California: For Health, Wealth, and Residence, a Book for Travellers and Settlers* (1872) and the ostensibly more racially inclusive backwards-glancing meditations on "Spanish California," which insist nonetheless on whitewashing conquest. Her own deglamorized historical assessment charts and graphs the ruses of a justice system which is unjust, federal complicity with state-sponsored violence, corporate manipulations of natural and industrial resources, so that the *affaire de coeur,* ostensibly the prime mover of this textual universe, is reduced to the status of an illustration of social turbulence more generally.[16] Ruiz's railroad of conservatively suited entrepreneurs is considerably less romantic than "the galloping monster" that some fifteen years later will coil its metal "tentacles" around Frank Norris's ostensibly realist narrative *The Octopus.*[17] In *The Squatter and the Don,* Norris's "iron-hearted Power" (51) is unavoidably a social phenomenon—an office occupied by a dryly ironic Leland Stanford who sits behind a desk taking the nineteenth-century equivalent of a conference call with the Big Four, aspiring not to destructive grandeur but only to "taking care of business" (318).

Where her contemporaries defuse political violence by relocating it in a domestic space defined in opposition to the social domain, Ruiz de Burton politicizes the family circle, so that home becomes the locus from which to describe national conflict. The talk of Clarence and Mercedes, then, is as often pragmatic as lyrical. Their own happiness is both inseparable from the aspirations of the social body (here, San Diego) and contingent upon the continued well-being of this public sphere: "this young couple went on discussing San Diego's chances of life or death, and their own hopes in the future" (298), Ruiz de Burton narrates. As she continues, the intimacies of romance give way, to be wholly displaced by an historical grievance: "They were not the only couple who in those days pondered over the problem of the '*to be or not to be*' of the Texas Pacific, which *never came!* . . . The monopoly triumphed, bringing poverty and distress where peace might have been!" (298). The language with which Ruiz documents political corruption plunders the vocabulary of the romance; moral fervor and impassioned plea do not remain within its province but bleed over into the political domain, with a corresponding redirection and expansion of readerly sympathy. The sorrows of the Californios as a collective enlist our attention as often as the singular difficulties of Mercedes and Clarence. The indignant righteousness with which Mercedes decries political wrongs in the following passage, for instance, matches word-for-word the vocabulary of aggravated assault with which Ruiz de Burton details her suitors' sufferings:

> I shall always lay it at the door of our legislators—that they have not only caused me to suffer many outrages, but, with those same laws, they are sapping the very life essence of public morality. They are teaching the people to lose all respect for the rights of others—to lose all respect for their national honor. Because we, *the natives* of California . . . were, at the close of the war with Mexico, left in the lap of the American nation, or, rather, huddled at her feet like motherless, helpless children, Congress thought we might as well be kicked and cuffed as treated kindly. (174)

This cleverly engineered passage speaks to the concerns of several audiences. Ruiz appeals to the hurt feelings of westerners disparaged by the rest of the nation as provincial by insisting that California's problems are not created by either Joaquín Murrieta or the San Francisco Vigilante Committee but rather are a product of federal disregard. Thus the "outrages" of one Californiana illustrate a national ill which is destructive to the "national honor" and the "people" as a whole. The segue from "my" complaint to "we, the natives" reminds Californios that the author's sufferings speak for their own, while the word "outrages" speaks volumes to readers of the Spanish-language press where it encodes a distinctly racially inflected pattern of abuses against Mexicano citizens of the U.S. Even eastern readers are brought into the fold, not only by the generalized appeal of the orphan parable but by the way self-respect and respect for others opens up to the inclusive problem of "public morality."

Despite the fact that she was publishing in English, for an interethnic audience, Ruiz de Burton is as sharply critical of federal expedience as are political editorials like the eulogy for Governor Juan Bautista Alvarado published in the Spanish-language newspaper *La República.* In this 1882 obituary, the Treaty of Guadalupe Hidalgo is framed as "cuestionable" (questionable), and the Mexicans of California are described as the "compatriotas" (compatriots) of the late governor, a community of integrity, a colony "descansaban, en vano, en las garantías ofrecidas por dicho tratado para respetan las concesiones de terrenos" (trusting in vain in the guarantees offered by said treaty to respect the conceded terrain).[18] Don Mariano's diagnosis of political ills outlines the failure of the U.S. government to honor the terms of the Treaty of Guadalupe Hidalgo as clearly as any polemical essay:

> With very unbecoming haste, Congress hurried to pass laws to legalize their despoliation of the conquered Californians. . . . Because California was expected to be filled with a population of farmers, of industrious settlers who would have votes and would want their one hundred and sixty acres each of the best land to be had. As our legislators thought that we, the Spano-American

> natives, had the best lands, and but few votes, there was nothing to be done but to despoil us, to take our lands and give them to the coming population. (175)

Rejecting the consolations of euphemism which the heroes of *Ramona* are loathe to give up, Ruiz de Burton's Don Mariano discourses upon the virtues of expediency with the urbanity of his biographical namesake, Don Mariano Guadalupe Vallejo. With assessments like these, Ruiz clarifies the racial inflections of a regional policy that is itself a product of federal venality.[19] Counterpointing the controlled rancor with which Don Mariano exposes unjust laws are the laws themselves. Ruiz de Burton does not merely borrow from the vocabulary of the justice system; she reproduces, wholesale, relevant legal documents. Reiterating her own twenty-year suit for title to land deeded her grandfather, Lieutenant Don José Manuel Ruiz in 1804, the author in her fiction recites portions of congressional proceedings and their outcome, invoking the state's language in order to expose its built-in loopholes with the practiced eye of the lawyer.[20] *Ramona* demonstrates the facility with which the law becomes an abstraction; in Jackson's critique of Gilded Age mercantilism, legality is a trope that simultaneously decries and justifies the inexorable advance of civilization. The fact that the Californios did not, "in those happy days . . . reckon land by inches" proves, for Jackson, their undoing: "It might be asked, perhaps, just how General Moreno owned all this land, and the question might not be easy to answer. It was not and could not be answered to the satisfaction of the United States Land Commission, which, after the surrender of California undertook to sift and adjust Mexican land titles; and that was the way it had come about that the Señora Moreno now called herself a poor woman" (12). Ruiz de Burton, on the other hand, refuses to rewrite the law to accord with generic convention; her protracted discussions of legal euphemism, evasion, and abstraction correspondingly tire readers expecting the pleasures of the deus ex machina rather than the pains of habeas corpus. Her insistence on mimetic fidelity makes the narrative clumsy; her refusal to grant the law a metaphorical register means that such language maintains a discursive authority independent of the literary boundaries within which it is invoked. But in giving up the aesthetic pleasures of metaphor the writer is also calling attention to its political register, critiquing and deglamorizing the (legal) euphemisms by which the state sanctions its power.

Coupled with this virtually professional exploitation of legal discourse, Ruiz uses irony to critique the euphonious abstractions of the turn-of-the-century historical romance. The "settlers" in particular feel the sting of Ruiz de Burton's literary scorn. The droll mirthlessness of the following repetition, for instance, dispatches them in two swift sentences: "Yet, this was the best that could be done, as his time was limited. But he was amiable, the ladies were amiable, and the gentlemen were amiable" (122). This phrase also critiques the linguistic "amiability" of the genre as a whole, whose mellifluous cadences mask sordid realities. The judgment Ruiz de Burton metes out below is all the more biting for its crisp austerity: "The stakes having been placed, Darrell felt satisfied. Next day he would have the claim properly filed, and in due time a surveyor would measure them. All would be done 'according to law' and in this easy way more land was taken from its legitimate owner. This certainly was a more simple way of appropriating the property of 'the conquered' than in the days of Alaric or Hannibal" (76). A very complex kind of historicizing is operating here. Clearly, the author's indictment of the squatters depends upon historical revision; rather than romanticizing conflict as the by-product of Manifest Destiny or glossing over the conflicts generated by Anglo "settlement," she focuses on the legal protocols that enable the dispossession of the Californios. But when she invokes "the days of Alaric or Hannibal" she uses "history" itself as a trope for political ends. The juxtaposition of classical history with contemporary events ensures that what her contemporaries often frame as a domestic issue be accorded an imperial register. This allusion to the Eurocentric standard for American historiography authorizes her own history of a region much disparaged by American (read: "eastern") practitioners of this field as provincial and forces readers to recognize the parallels between an uncontested version of history and her own contestatory revision of historical "truth." At the same time, she invokes empire to correct conventional definitions of imperialism as always occurring elsewhere.

This is not to argue that revising historiography ensures, a priori, effective political critique. As in Jackson's exploitation of Alessandro and Father Salvierderra as allegorical figures, character often works iconographically in *The Squatter and the Don,* as shorthand for a cultural script that forecloses upon a more complicated rendering of the relation between collective practice and individual biography. Indeed, the prolonged account of despoliation the book charts can take on the character of a timeless lament that undermines its historicizing work, the careful plotting of familial conflict contingent upon a political rubric. In the following passage, for instance, the trenchant account of land foreclosure, increasing Anglo immigration, and corporate manipulation of public policy gives way to the consolations of a more abstract elegy: "It seemed to Clarence as if the little fountain was in sympathy with the dispossessed owners, but did not dare to raise its timid voice in behalf of the vanquished, who no longer had rights in their patrimony, and must henceforth wander off disinherited, despoiled, forgotten" (85). On the one hand, the very completeness of this list of misfortunes revises official versions of the American conquest that give short shrift to the losses suffered by the Californios. On the other hand, this plaint, characteristic as well of *Ramona* and other turn-of-the-century representations of Mexican California, carries with it a paralyzing sense of closure and surfeit, so that the detailing of the loss becomes the end rather than the means.[21] Just so, Ruiz occasionally figures cultural conflict using an abstract language of deterioration and loss. As he contemplates the weddings of his son and daughter to Anglo Americans, "Don Mariano was kind and affable to all, but many days passed before he became reconciled to the fact that the marriage of his two children was not celebrated as his own had been, in the good old times of yore" (123).

But this narrative listlessness is the exception rather than the rule. Ruiz de Burton does not allow the language of mourning to monopolize her text; pathos may be the preferred convention of the historical romance, but the writer never sustains this voice for long, shifting instead to modes more suited to the polemic than the pastoral. The passage I have quoted above is followed on the next page by a sardonic voice that stills the lugubrious reverberations of the lament: "Voices calling them to dinner were now heard, and they returned to the picnic grounds. No banquet of the Iliad warriors surpassed this, showing that the settlers of Alamar had found the Don's land and the laws of Congress very good" (86). Even where the narrative is most despairing, Ruiz de Burton builds in what I can only call textual "loopholes," inflections slight enough to pass the notice of readers schooled by *Ramona* to favor the consolations of the "dying fall" but that provide a small but discernible opening for critical ears. Speaking on behalf of the Californios, Don Alamar explains to Clarence:

> I don't see any remedy *in my life-time.* I am afraid there is no help for us native Californians. We must sadly fade and pass away. The weak and the helpless are always trampled in the throng. We must sink, go under, never to rise. If the Americans had been friendly to us, and helped us with good, protective laws, our fate would have been different. But to legislate us into poverty is to legislate us into our graves. Their very contact is deadly to us. (177, emphasis added)

This remarkably searching critique refuses to indict individual instances of corruption in order to call into question the apparently impartial abstraction of the Law itself. In addition, the eulogy supplies readers with enough contradictory indices to permit multiple glosses. The verb series ("fade," "pass away," "sink," "go under") transforms the Don's pronouncement into a funeral dirge: there is no hope for rallying, only the wearying certainty of imminent demise. But these synonyms for cultural extinction are undermined by the chronological possibility indicated in the first sentence. The very temporality of "in my life-time," that is, unravels the more conventional cultural teleology of the passage. Additionally, the equation posited by the second to last line ("But to legislate us into poverty is to legislate us into our graves") underlines the fact that the Don's image of death is precisely that; a metaphor. The yawning grave is not an unequivocal fact, but merely the means by which Ruiz figures the creation of a permanent—but still living and breathing—underclass.

This temporal window gestures toward a different future. Yet the opening is narrow, and the possibility of a more forward-looking reading is correspondingly slight when you consider the interpretive energy needed to uncover it. Loopholes may not require professional training—the expertise of Ruiz de Burton's arguments demonstrates this—but they do demand close scrutiny and a skeptical disposition. How much more likely, then, for readers to be guided by eulogy than by those interpretive gestures at variance with generic expectation. Toward the close of the book Don Mariano attests, "'You see we are Clarence's vaqueros now'" (247), a pronouncement that, if ironic, certifies the more fatalistic reading by echoing how the mighty have fallen. This acknowledgment makes explicit the political inequities other writers gloss over, but within the terms of the resolutely ahistorical pastoral, the image of the conquerors conquered recalls other cycles and rehearses the rise and fall of civilizations in a manner more biblical than temporal.

I have indicated some of the rhetorical maneuvers by which Ruiz de Burton redirects the backwards glance of the historical romance—a sustained historicism that keeps current events current, an irony that encourages critical attention and cuts across the grain of the pastoral's tendency toward euphemism, a wholesale appropriation of legal and polemical languages in order to question the primacy of the lexicon of the romance. All of these strategies are successful to a degree, but they are nevertheless embedded within a narrative whose generic conventions encourage postmortem rather than prevention—a kind of critical medicine which does little to improve the health of the patient. Yet *The Squatter and the Don* is critically successful in a way that *Ramona* is not, because it calls our attention to the very generic borders its characters have difficulty transgressing. Clarence and Mercedes speak the language of romance, but Ruiz de Burton parodies their suspirations and swoons in such a way as to remind readers that *their* literary aspirations do not speak *her* mind. If pastoral conventions generally take the history out of historical romance, they are also gendered and racialized in such a way as to trivialize the work of women writers and to condescend to the writings of a people represented as romantic but idle; "good-natured," as Josephine Clifford McCrackin writes in "A Lady in Camp," but "not very deep" (222).[22] Time and time again Anglo American writers use "the shimmer of romance and poetry" (McCrackin, "Arizona Deserts," 307) as a foil for the drudgeries and commercialism of the Gilded Age, a means of enjoying the rustic pleasures of Californio life—represented, of course, at the safe remove of the past. McCrackin's "La Graciosa," whose title conjures up images of the good life, makes this point particularly emphatically. No sooner does Nora move to the San Francisco Bay Area from the East Coast than she becomes the object of Don Pedro's attentions. Gently mocking her Anglo heroine's penchant for the romantic but supportive of this rose-colored reading, McCrackin invokes a language of rapture—the same language D. H. Lawrence, Mary Austin, and Willa Cather will borrow to celebrate the Southwest with almost half a century later. Whether she is admiring the beauty of the landscape or the graciousness of Mexicano custom, Nora sighs for "the romance of it all." "Everything had a dash of romance to Nora's unbounded delight" (34), the narrator repeats for us, then, to ensure we subscribe to the same view, describes the rodeo as being "all as romantic as Nora's heart could wish" (35). Even the young woman's mercenary encouragement of the Don is simultaneously chided and justified by this appeal: "Well, was it not romantic, after all, to marry the dark-eyed Don, with the haughty bearing and the enormous wealth?" (41).

When we bear in mind that McCrackin's relentless aestheticization of a culture represented at its sunset is conventional for late nineteenth-century Anglo treatments of "the Mexican," we can read Ruiz de Burton's insistence on deglamorizing the seizure of Mexican land not only as an historiographic corrective but as a literary revision as well. Instead of maintaining with Jackson that the "picturesque life . . . can never be quite lost" (12), she insists that government corruption and illegal business practices like those which enriched Leland Stanford and the Big Four will bring "ruin and squalor and death . . . to people who never harmed you!" (319).[23] She refuses to render sublime the decline of the Californios, playing in *The Squatter and the Don* on the romantic genre itself. Sometimes this parody is broad; whenever Mercedes's brother Victoriano begins to describe Clarence's sister Alice, the object of his own attentions, his family teases him in dialogue which resembles the verbal slapstick of Laurel and Hardy or the punning confusion of a "Who's on First" routine. At other points Ruiz de Burton's satire is subtle, as in the following critique of femininity, which at once makes use of and mocks sentimental convention: "Mercedes took her hat and gloves and cloak off, and sat at the window *to enjoy* her misery in a thoroughly womanly fashion" (167). Ruiz's italicization of the verb "enjoy" insists on the virtues of parody here, as does juxtaposing this scene with other representations of feminine sensibility. Despite the fact that the heroine of Charles Stuart's *Casa Grande* (1906) is consistently described as a tomboy, for instance, she sheds tears of genteel joy that do not carry a trace of Ruiz de Burton's satire: "Once again the little room with white curtains and white bed became silent witnesses of the girl's happy tears" (109).

Nor does such attention to the limits of genre remain implicit. Mercedes's gratification upon learning that her intended is not a squatter after all, but has purchased his land from her father, allows Ruiz de Burton the opportunity to provide readers with explicit lessons in literary interpretation. "It isn't half so *romantic* to love a plain gentleman as to love a brigand, or, at least, a squatter," Mercedes's sister Elvira teases her. "Are you regretting that, after all, you cannot sacrifice to love your patrician pride by marrying a land-shark, thus proving you are a *heroine?*. . . . Really, I think our *romance* is spoiled. It would have been so fine—like a *dime novel*" (141, emphasis added). Romance, heroine, dime novel: the vocabulary here is insistently metatextual, directing readers to gloss this sisterly joke in the most literary of terms. *The Squatter and the Don,* it turns out, is more than a romance—or rather, as Elvira's negation indicates, not one at all. In place of the love story, now comically deflated, we are to substitute an expressly political history: of class conflict, racial injustice, land theft. Playing the two terms of her generic equation off of one another, Ruiz de Burton appropriates the historical romance only to use it against itself; her hero and heroine are not figures to be exploited for the entertainment of an audience nostalgic for what gets figured as a feudal paradise—ricos sampling the fruits of the California vine, peones contentedly harvesting it—but instead struggle to maintain their land and livelihood in an all-too-squalid present.

Yet her acerbic rereading of the romance has its limits. Bakhtin has argued that the ideological work of the novel is to "do the police in different voices" and we can position Ruiz de Burton's multi-pronged rhetorical strategizing within this context. Her wholesale recirculation of the law, her reproduction of historical texts like the Huntington letters, the various satirical registers with which she voices her characters' romantic tribulations—these are unsettling, undermining maneuvers, yes, but in the end they are not enough. After all is said and done in *The Squatter and the Don,* Ruiz de Burton provides us with an interpretive "key" to her story which does and says everything again—a nonfictional "Conclusion" spoken in a distinctly polemical register, from which the author exhorts readers to political action. The forward-carrying motion of this second narrative finish is clear; from its unapologetic title "Out with the Invader" to its explicit recommendations for change, this eight-page coda makes us, if not reject the critical utility of the 309-page fiction which precedes it, at least question its efficiency. Freed from the constraints of a genre enforcing plaint rather than platform, Ruiz de Burton here urges "*the people of California*" to "*take the law in their own hands,* and seize the property of those men, [the] arrogant corporation" and to "confiscate it, to reimburse the money due *the people*" (366). Nor does she keep this call general, but instead invokes specific historical figures, reinstating the Californios as the rightful heirs of the state and providing Mexicano readers with models of political behavior, albeit class-inflected, as far removed from Father Salvierderra's gracious resignation as they are from the rapaciousness of the Big Four: "The Spanish population of the State are proud of their countryman, Reginaldo del Valle, who was one of the first to take a bold stand against the monopoly. This young orator with great ability and indomitable energy, has never flagged in his eloquent denunciations of the power which has so trampled the laws of California and the rights of her children" (369).

Finally, then, Ruiz de Burton's reliance on a "Conclusion" framed as *hors du texte* asks us to reconsider the limits of genre. Under her direction, the historical romance may be elastic enough to support a plurality of voices, yet the manipulation of different registers is not enough, since the very generic frame within which she is working is itself already spoken for—not a neutral medium, but a form colored by Anglo American writers who have exploited it to romanticize the Mexican American as an anachronistic contradiction in terms, and a literary vehicle sexualized by masculine readers and critics as insufficient for the demands of a political gloss.

Notes

Thanks to Sandra Gunning for her critical comments on an earlier draft of this essay, and to Genaro Padilla, discussions with whom have shaped this essay from its outset.

1. "monuments . . . ," Elizabeth Hughes, *The California of the Padres; or, Footprints of Ancient Communism* (San Francisco: I. N. Choynski, 1875), 2; "crumbling into ruin," Helen Hunt Jackson, *Ramona* (1884; New York: Signet Classic, 1988), 35; "in the long procession . . . ," Hughes, *California of the Padres,* 2. Further page references to both books will appear in the text.

From the mid-1850s through the turn of the century, the *Overland Monthly* enjoyed a particularly authoritative status as the voice of the literary Anglo American West. See Cecil Robinson's *With the Ears of Strangers: The Mexican in American Literature* (Tucson: University of Arizona Press, 1963); and this description: "The *Overland Monthly,* which was to be Western America's answer to the *Atlantic Monthly* and which had pretensions to being a formulator of opinion in the West, carried a number of stories and articles on Mexico, most of them uncomplimentary" (73). Further page references to Robinson will appear in the text.

2. María Amparo Ruiz de Burton, *The Squatter and the Don,* ed. Rosaura Sánchez and Beatrice Pita (1885; Houston: Arte Público Press, 1993).

3. Surprisingly, despite his exhaustive survey of Anglo American literature, Cecil Robinson finds that "[t]he defeat and dispossession of the dons, an episode that had much of poignancy in it, was a tale that remained, except for a limited treatment of it by a few writers, untold at the time that it was happening" (154). My own research seeks to demonstrate that, on the contrary, beginning as early as three decades after the conquest, Anglo American writers were relentlessly engaged in reworking the story of this dispossession, as were, even more explicitly, Mexicano writers. This essay builds on the work of a number of scholars of nineteenth-century Mexican American literature, many of whom are affiliated with the Recovering the U.S. Hispanic Literary Heritage Project, and whose archival research analyzes a wealth

of material from the mid-1800s onward treating the repercussions of conquest. For writing on California in particular, see, among others, Antonia I. Castañeda, "The Political Economy of Nineteenth-Century Stereotypes of Californianas," in *Between Borders: Essays on Mexicana/Chicana History,* ed. Adelaida R. Del Castillo (Encino, CA: Floricanto Press, 1990); Douglas Monroy, "They Didn't Call Them 'Padre' for Nothing: Patriarchy in Hispanic California," in *Between Borders* and *Thrown among Strangers: The Making of Mexican Culture in Frontier California* (Berkeley: University of California Press, 1990); Lisbeth Haas, *Conquests and Historical Identities in California, 1769–1936* (Berkeley: University of California Press, 1995); Genaro Padilla, *My History, Not Yours: The Formation of Mexican American Autobiography* (Madison: University of Wisconsin Press, 1993); and Rosaura Sánchez, *Telling Identities: The Californio Testimonios* (Minneapolis: University of Minnesota Press, 1995). This essay was drafted several years ago; since the re-publication of Ruiz de Burton's 1872 novel, *Who Would Have Thought It?* in 1995 (Houston: Arte Publico Press), scholars including Jesse Alemán, José Aranda, and Amelia de la Luz Montes have begun examining her canon in ways that will undoubtedly reshape our thinking about Ruiz de Burton's relation to nineteenth-century American literature as a whole. Like my own essay, Alemán's unpublished essay "Novelizing California: History, Romance, and Novelistic Discourse in María Amparo Ruiz de Burton's *The Squatter and the Don,*" historicizes Ruiz de Burton's romance over and against Helen Hunt Jackson's *Ramona.* I look forward to its appearance in print.

4. Gertrude Atherton, *The Californians* (1898; New York: Grosset & Dunlap, 1908); *The Splendid Idle Forties: Stories of Old California* (New York: Macmillan, 1902).

5. This description of rancho life, from the back cover of the 1980's Signet Classic edition, is itself anachronistic and would not have accorded with Jackson's characterization of Californio families a century earlier, however well-to-do.

6. Helen Hunt Jackson, *A Century of Dishonor: A Sketch of the United States Government's Dealings with Some of the Indian Tribes* (Boston: Roberts Brothers, 1889).

7. Gertrude Atherton, *Los Cerritos: A Romance of the Modern Time* (1890; Ridgewood, NJ: The Gregg Press, 1968).

8. I am referring here to Ruiz's own second marriage to the Anglo military captain Henry Burton, with whom, in an autobiographical reiteration of her political arguments about region and nation, she goes to live in Washington, where she becomes the confidante of Mary Lincoln. I am indebted to Vicki Ruiz for pointing out this autobiographical link.

9. Francisco Ramírez, celebrated young editor of Los Angeles's *El Clamor Público,* often called attention to the failure of federal policy to accord with regional practice. "¿No tenemos todos los mismos derechos iguales a la proteccion de las leyes?" (Don't we have equal rights under the law?) he asked rhetorically in one edition, only to answer in the negative in another: "No se les [Mexicanos en Alta California] administra justícia, no se les repeta a su propiedád [sic], no se les deja libertad en el ejercício de su industra . . . un ataque flagrante a los princípios del derecho de gentes, una triste contradiccion con los princípios de que hace alarde el gobierno americano" (They do not administer justice to us, they do not respect our property, they do not permit us freedom in the exercise of our industry . . . a flagrant attack on the principles of peoples' rights, a sad contradiction with the principles

that the American government boasts of) ("¡Americanos! ¡Californios!," *El Clamor Público,* 21 February 1857; "Los Mexicanos en la Alta California," *El Clamor Público,* 1 August 1855). But scores of essays in newspapers throughout the country lamented the separate and unequal treatment accorded the Mexicanos made U.S. citizens in 1848.

10. See, for instance, the following description of "American law" as unjust but incontrovertible:

> The doctor said the land did not belong to Ysidro at all, but to the U.S. Government; and that he had paid the money for it to the agents in Los Angeles, and there would very soon come papers from Washington, to show that it was his. Father Gaspara had gone with Ysidro to a lawyer in San Diego, and had shown to this lawyer Ysidro's paper,—the old one from the Mexican Governor of California . . . but the lawyer had only laughed at Father Gaspara for believing that such a paper as that was good for anything. He said that was all very well when the country belonged to Mexico, but it was no good now; that the Americans owned it now; and everything was done by the American law now, not by the Mexican law anymore. (257)

11. I am indebted to Sandra Gunning for her help with this argument.

12. Josephine Clifford McCrackin, "La Graciosa," in *Overland Tales* (San Francisco: A. L. Bancroft, 1877), 30. Further page references to the stories in this volume will appear in the text.

13. "Niñita," *The Century Magazine* 23 (April 1882). Although I do not have the space to gloss it here, this story of a nameless young Mexicana who falls in love with and is finally jilted by the Anglo railroad official sent to purchase her father's land deserves fuller attention as a refiguration of land politics, cultural conflict, and the corporate interests that underlie them.

14. Lorna Dee Cervantes, "Poema para los Californios Muertos," *Emplumada* (Pittsburgh: University of Pittsburgh Press, 1981), 43.

15. Frances E. W. Harper, *Iola Leroy* (1892; Boston: Beacon Press, 1987), 130.

16. In their excellent introduction, Rosaura Sánchez and Beatrice Pita also insist on the narrative's "historicity": "*The Squatter and the Don,* like all romances, textualizes a quest which necessarily involves conflict and resolution, given here as the trials and tribulations standing in the way of the felicitous union of a romantic couple. Because the novel is also marked by its historicity, however, the quest is not merely for the love of a maiden, but also for land and justice. The narrative thus follows two tracks, one historical and one romantic, with the latter serving to frame the reconstruction of a critical period in the history of the Southwest" (5). I am indebted to their analysis; my own reading, however, subordinates the romantic plot to the historical agenda of the narrative, which I see as its major formal component and ideological work. Thus I would not characterize the text, as do Sánchez and Pita, as "two-tracked" or bifurcated in structure.

17. Frank Norris, *The Octopus* (1901; New York: Viking Penguin, 1986), 51, 12. Further page references will appear in the text.

18. Note how openly critical of the "Americanos" are writers of the Spanish-language press, and how consistently papers like San Francisco's *La República* define Mexican and American as oppositional terms, identifying the Californios as a subject Mexican colony rather than a "hyphenated" (i.e., Mexican American) community. In

this letter from Tehachape, one F. Elias writes the Editor: "recibió una carta de Colima, Mexico, de un amigo de el [el Señor W. Kuetz]. . . . y dicen que los Mexicanos tratan al extrangero [sic] y en particular al alemán con mas respeto y consideración que los Americanos" (he received a letter from Colima, Mexico, from a friend of his . . . and they said that Mexicans treat the foreigner and in particular the German with more respect and consideration than do the Americans) ("Carta de Tejachipe," *La República,* 5 August 1882). Another writer, reporting on a theatrical event, makes this swipe at the "American" press: "La prensa americana, que raras veces hace un cumplimiento a nuestra colonia, confiesa la mencionada festividad es la major que aquí se ha visto entre la raza española" (The American press, which on few occasions pays our colony a compliment, admitted that the mentioned festivity is the best that has been seen here among the Spanish race) (*La República,* 5 August 1882).

19. Counterpointing the Don's eloquent indictment is an equally clear acknowledgment, via the squatters, of the racism underlying federal legal policy: "'Those greasers ain't half crushed yet. We have to tame them like they do their mustangs, or shoot them, as we shoot their cattle,' said Mathews. 'Oh, no. No such violent means are necessary. All we have to do is to take their lands, and finish their cattle,' said Hughes, sneeringly" (73).

20. See, for instance, the analysis of an 1872 law on p. 80: "In the very first section it recited, that 'every owner *or occupant* of land, whether it is enclosed or not,' could take up cattle found in said land, etc., etc. It was not stated to be necessary that the *occupant* should have a good title. All that was required seemed to be that he should *claim to be an occupant* of land, no matter who was the owner"; or see the gloss of "settle" as framed by Congress on p. 88.

The tone and diction of the book's critique of the justice system refigures the language of Ruiz's own legal communications—perhaps providing her with the consolations of an interpretive authority denied her in court. The bitter outrage with which Don Mariano chastises Leland Stanford echoes a letter Ruiz wrote to President Benito Juárez on behalf of her own land: "the said Judge of the Frontier refused to make the survey as he was instructed to do. . . . As I could not appear to answer in person the complaint of the Judge, I had to name a proxy to represent me, and the Judge forced him to pay the sum of $190. . . . This being an extortion as arbitrary as it is shameful in the authority charged with the administration of justice, I beg you will deign to order that Judge Chacon . . . to avoid the repetition of a disobedience which has caused me so much expense and loss and injury, [and] beg also that you may explain to the Judge with all clearness the way in which he shall run the lines" ("Title of Property to the Ensenada de Todos Santos in Lower California granted to Don José Manuel Ruiz by the King of Spain in 1804," pp. 13–14, Ruiz de Burton papers, Bancroft Library, University of California, Berkeley).

21. For an example of the pathologizing of culture, consider this Anglo conflation of *la llorona* and *la malinche*: "There is a tradition that the ghost of Cortez's Indian mistress, the gentle Doña Marina, walks where the shadows are deepest in the cypress avenues. . . . What a company they would be, . . . many times greater than the daily assemblage of the living on the Alameda—if all the restless and disappointed men and women who have inhabited Chapultepec in the past should gather like the

twilight shadows in its melancholy walks, and look at each other as they passed, with dumb, wistful, reproachful, or threatening, or despairing eyes!" ("A Diligence Journey in Mexico," *The Century Magazine* 1 [November 1881]: 2.)

22. That the popularity of the historical romance for turn-of-the-century California moved men as well as women to exploit it alters neither the humble status of this form nor its feminine signature, as the dismissive comments of critics writing as late as the 1960s indicate. Cecil Robinson cites writer Harvey Fergusson as grumbling that "what ailed 'the huge and infantile body of our conventional Western romance, from Beadle's dime novels on down' was the result of its having been 'sired by Sir Walter Scott and dammed by the Genteel Tradition'" (151). For his *Casa Grande: A California Pastoral* (New York: Henry Holt, 1906), Charles Stuart's choice of "A California Pastoral," not "A California Romance," as a subtitle is probably dictated by concern that the latter would ally the book with an all-too feminine sentimentality. Or consider the anxious insistence of Josiah Royce's editor who in his introduction to *The Feud of Oakfield Creek* (1907) distinguishes this fiction by insisting it must be read not merely as "local-color" (feminine/regionalist) fiction, but also in the (presumably masculine and national) tradition of realism: "In writing the history of California," he claims, Royce "carefully stripped the romantic element from adventurers such as John Charles Frémont, from the early mining camps, and from the San Francisco vigilantes. In his novel there is a notable absence of the sentimentality that dominates Helen Hunt Jackson's *Ramona*" (xx–xxi).

Women, too, were not impervious to the critical pressure brought to bear upon the sentimental. McCrackin's essay "A Bit of 'Early California'" tries to dispel this label by suggesting "That many strange and wonderful things happened in early times in California, is so trite a saying that I hardly dare repeat it. As my story, however, is neither harrowing nor sentimental, I hope I may venture to bring it before the reader" (274).

23. Together with his business partners, Sacramento merchants Collis P. Huntington, Mark Hopkins, and Charles Crocker, Leland Stanford, founder of Stanford University, made his fortune by investing $60,000 in the Central Pacific Railroad Company and then voting himself and his associates "construction contracts that paid them $90 million for work that cost them only $32.2 million." (See Richard White, *"It's Your Misfortune and None of My Own": A New History of the American West* [Norman: University of Oklahoma Press, 1991], 249.)

5

A WESTERNER IN SEARCH OF "NEGRO-NESS"

Region and Race in the Writing of Arna Bontemps

DOUGLAS FLAMMING

In 1917, Paul Bontemps of Watts, California, sent his only son, Arna, to a boarding school in nearby Los Angeles. Arna Bontemps, destined to become one of the most prolific and versatile African American writers of the twentieth century, was not quite fifteen at the time. Before parting, the father advised his son: "'Now don't go up there acting colored.'" These were words Arna Bontemps never forgot and, in a sense, never forgave. Fifty years later he recalled his father's admonition and answered: "How dare anyone—parent, schoolteacher, or merely literary critic—tell me not to act *colored.*"[1]

What did it mean to act "colored" in the early twentieth-century West? Bontemps's own answer, negotiated during his young adulthood in California and subsequently represented in his literature, suggests the complex relationship between region and racial identity. Bontemps saw his father as a manifestation of the West, as one who had forsaken his Afro-southern roots in an effort to become colorless. He saw his great uncle, Buddy Ward, as a manifestation of the South, as one who had reluctantly migrated West and refused to surrender his Afro-southern folkways. Growing up largely isolated from the small black community in Los Angeles, Arna gradually began to question his father's view and to envy Uncle Buddy's sense of heritage. He developed a longing for what he later called "Negro-ness," which he saw as a southern, not western, quality. Throughout his high-school and college years, he grappled with the conflict between his father and Buddy, ultimately concluding that he must re-establish ties with the African American culture he felt he had lost in the West. That was why, in 1924, at the age of twenty-one, he left Los Angeles for New York's Harlem and the "New Negro" Renaissance, hoping not only to establish himself as a writer but also to discover his own identity as a black American.

Later in life, Bontemps published several autobiographical essays that examined his childhood in California and the tensions between his father and Uncle Buddy.[2] In these self-reflective pieces, Bontemps reduced the complex personalities of Paul and Buddy to their least common denominators; the two men functioned as simple metaphors for complicated realities. The autobiographies themselves were thus something akin to fiction, as Bontemps probably realized. But in the question of identity—Bontemps's identity and everyone else's—personal constructions intersect with empirical context in fascinating and instructive ways. The cultural conflict between Paul and Buddy, and more particularly Arna's understanding and reaction to that conflict, opens a window on a much-neglected topic of Afro-western history—the issue of black identity.

A recent biography of Arna Bontemps by Kirkland C. Jones bears the curious title, *Renaissance Man from Louisiana.* Bontemps was born in Louisiana, but he was not really *from* there. The only "Southland" he really knew in the 1920s was southern California; his family brought him to Los Angeles County when he was four years old and, except for his college years in northern California, he remained there until he moved to Harlem in 1924. In a symbolic sense, though, Jones's title hits the mark. It reflects Bontemps's yearning for his Louisiana "home," a longing that profoundly influenced his life and literature.[3]

Arna was born in the small town of Alexandria in 1902, the first child of Paul and Maria (Pembrooke) Bontemps. Both of his parents were from mulatto families with long, mostly free-black histories in the heavily French Creole region of central Louisiana. Maria was a schoolteacher who prized learning, purged her voice of southern accent, and longed for her children to receive good educations outside of the South. Arna's father had received formal vocational training in New Orleans and, like so many Creole men in Louisiana, had become a skilled brick mason. In his youth, Paul Bontemps was also a musician, occasionally blowing horn for Louisiana ragtime bands. Thinking back on his life in a 1965 autobiographical essay, Arna Bontemps reflected that "mine had not been a varmint-infested childhood so often the hallmark of Negro American autobiography. My parents and grandparents had been well-fed, well-clothed, and well-housed."[4]

His parents nonetheless felt compelled to leave the South in 1906, when Arna was only four. The education they wanted for Arna and his sister, Ruby, could not be had in Louisiana. And there were more immediate concerns. The Atlanta race riot of 1906 stirred racial animosities across the South and rippled through Alexandria. Paul Bontemps did not want to leave the South, but his safety and that of his family seemed increasingly imperiled.[5]

He therefore moved his own family and Maria's parents to southern California, settling just south of Los Angeles city. Paul and Maria bought a house in the small settlement of Watts. "We moved into a house in a neighborhood where we were the only colored family," Arna remembered. "The people next door and up and down the block were friendly and talkative, the weather was perfect, there wasn't a mud puddle anywhere, and my mother seemed to float about on the clean air." Maria's parents, preferring a more rural environment, bought several acres of farmland between Watts and Los Angeles, in what local residents called the "Furlough Track," where they built a substantial house and a barn.[6]

Watts and the Furlough Track were scarcely developed when the Bontemps and Pembrooke families arrived in 1906. What growth there was resulted from Henry E. Huntington's Pacific Electric streetcar line, completed in 1902, which stretched from Los Angeles to Long Beach and ran north-south through the area. Watts became an incorporated municipality not long after the Bontempses arrived, but even by 1910 the population of the town had not reached two thousand, with fewer than forty blacks. Slightly to the north of Watts, the Furlough Track was an eclectic, diverse area. A scattering of black families had settled amidst the Anglo farmers, along with a small community of Mexican families who had moved there to construct the interurban railway and then put down roots.[7]

Los Angeles city boomed in the early twentieth century, and its black population grew rapidly as well—from about 100 in 1880 to nearly 7,600 by 1910. By 1920, African Americans in Los Angeles numbered at least 15,579; ten years later the figure rose to nearly 39,000, which now included the blacks who lived in Watts, which was annexed by Los Angeles in the mid-1920s. Still, the concomitant growth of the European, Japanese, and Mexican-heritage communities meant that blacks made up only a small percentage of the local population, usually between 2 or 3 percent. The African American community in Watts, like that in nearby Pasadena, was a smaller version of the black community in Los Angeles. Throughout the towns and cities of Los Angeles county, black communities represented small minority populations that were predominantly middle class, with high rates of home ownership and political activism. In this regard, they had much in common with other African American communities that emerged in the principal Pacific Coast cities.[8]

As more blacks moved to Los Angeles and surrounding communities, Anglo resistance to blacks in "white" residential districts forced most African Americans to live in certain areas, which amounted to embryonic ghettos. But the key word is embryonic, for the Los Angeles neighborhoods "open" to people of color remained predominantly white through the 1920s, with blacks, Mexicans, Russian Jews, Japanese, and Filipinos occupying loosely defined ethnic enclaves therein. For blacks in southern California during

Arna Bontemps's childhood and young adulthood, the West offered a more open and diverse society than the Jim Crow South, whose viciously discriminatory racial system had driven Paul Bontemps westward.

For Arna's father, the move to California was more than a relocation. It was a conscious break from the past, from the South, and even, to some degree, from his race. He gave up playing jazz and committed himself to masonry and construction work. More important, he gave up the Catholicism of Creole Louisiana and led his entire family into the Seventh-Day Adventist Church, a decision that profoundly influenced Arna's life. Shortly after joining the Adventist fold, Paul Bontemps became the first black Adventist minister in the West. Eventually, he would abandon the masonry trade and devote himself full-time to the church.[9]

Paul Bontemps gave himself to the standard American vision of the West—to the idea of starting over, to the creed of a better future. His was not a frivolous undertaking. He made hard, disciplined decisions. He committed himself to his children's future. Reminiscing about Louisiana with relatives, he said: "'Sometimes I miss all that. If I was just thinking about myself, I might want to go back and try it again. But I've got the children to think about—their education.'" When Maria died of illness in 1914, leaving Arna motherless at twelve, Paul's parental duties weighed heavier and his commitment to the children's education deepened. Arna later recalled that his own education and that of his sister was "one of the things [my father] took pride in and devoted himself to."[10]

For Paul Bontemps education was one means of becoming fully American, or perhaps as he saw it, fully western. In southern California, he strove not to be a successful "black" man, but a successful man. Success, as he saw it, required a certain colorlessness, a conscious abandonment of ethnic culture. Not that he misunderstood the power of race. His masonry work in Los Angeles was curtailed in part by racist white trade unions, and the churches he pastored were all-black (by custom as much as by Adventist polity). But he saw his racial identity as something to rise above. For him, acting "colored" meant a way of thinking and behaving that kept individuals down. For him, "colored" meant aspects of Afro-southern folk culture that he and other middle-class blacks thought of as checks on middle-class respectability and economic success: loud talk, dialect speech, ostentatious dress, belief in superstition. He hoped Arna's integrated upbringing and schooling would shield him from such influences, and he sought to set an example for Arna to follow. Or so Arna perceived his father's views.

But there were other examples for Arna's observation, in particular his great-uncle, John Ward, known to the family as Buddy. In his youth, Buddy had been an urbane ladies' man with style and flash. But it was hard to maintain Creole pride in Jim Crow Louisiana, and Buddy's life eventually sank deep into a bottle. Ruined and penniless, he was institutionalized in New Orleans until he dried out. Then he moved West, joining the family (his sister was Arna's grandmother) in southern California. His arrival caused a stir. Young Arna, expecting the "young mulatto dandy with an elegant cravat and jeweled stickpin" that he has seen in a family photograph, was shocked when a terribly disheveled Buddy stumbled through the door: "he entered wearing a detachable collar without a tie and did not remove his hat. His clothes did not fit. They had been slept in for nearly a week on the train. His shoes had come unlaced. His face was pocked marked. Nothing in his appearance resembled the picture in the living room."[11]

But Uncle Buddy had an ace up his sleeve, or rather in his suitcase, which contained no clothes at all but was filled with treats and gifts from Louisiana—"jars of syrup, bags of candy my grandmother had said in her letters that she missed, pecans, plus filé for making gumbo." He talked about the South and held the family's rapt attention. As Buddy brought the Californians up-to-date on the news from back home, young Arna "became entranced" with Buddy and the South. It was a feeling he never quite lost, reinforced as it was by Buddy's ongoing presence. From 1908, when Arna's grandfather Pembrooke died, until 1917, when Arna went to boarding school, the Bontempses lived at the Pembrooke farmhouse. Buddy lived there, too, during Arna's most impressionable years.[12]

Living at the Pembrooke house, Buddy turned out to be everything Paul Bontemps sought to avoid. Buddy used the word "nigger" with a casual ease that Paul openly condemned, and he brought loud, drunken friends to the house. In Arna's estimation, "they were not bad people." But they were "what my father described as don't-care folk." And, to make matters worse for Paul, "Buddy was still crazy about the minstrel shows and minstrel talk that had been the joy of his young manhood. He loved dialect stories, preacher stories, ghost stories, slave and master stories. He half-believed in signs and charms and mumbo-jumbo, and he believed whole-heartedly in ghosts." Paul Bontemps had a word for such a person, and that word was "colored." To his distress, Buddy and Arna spent long hours together; his son loved the old man and was fascinated by his stories of the South.[13]

The conflict between Paul Bontemps and Uncle Buddy was nothing less than a struggle for young Arna's soul. It was one man's West against another man's South; it was disciplined practicality against joyful folkways. It was hope for an integrated future versus love of a racial past. And as the years passed, Arna began to understand the dynamics of that struggle. When his father sent him to the Adventist academy in the San Fernando Valley, Arna "took it that my father was still endeavoring to counter Buddy's baneful influence." There was more to it than that: Paul needed to take a well-paying masonry job outside the city, and the San Fernando Academy offered an excellent academic environment for his smart son. No doubt, though, Paul Bontemps hoped the distance between Arna and Buddy would be advantageous. Hence, his admonition to Arna: "'don't go up there acting colored.'"[14]

Through high school and college the son respected his father's wishes. Arna thrived in the Adventist schools and followed Paul Bontemps's disciplined, intellectual path. He did not act like Uncle Buddy. He worked hard, watched his manners, and excelled in his studies. Throughout his entire life, Bontemps would remain an efficient, disciplined worker. In actual fact, there was nothing "colorless" about such behavior, but Arna had come to define his world and his race in the diametrically opposed examples of Paul and Buddy. Arna mildly defied his father during his college years (at Pacific Union, an Adventist school some fifty miles northeast of San Francisco), when he abandoned the pre-med studies Paul had recommended, changed his major to English, and announced his intention of becoming a writer. Paul Bontemps voiced his disapproval but nonetheless took pride in Arna's educational achievements.[15]

Ironically, the academic world that Paul Bontemps assumed would keep Arna's Negro-ness at bay had just the opposite effect. With the exception of one colored girl in his second grade class, Arna was always the only black person in his class, from first grade through his college graduation. "I was just a lone wolf," he recalled. Despite his generally positive school experiences, and his friendships with classmates and teachers, color obviously set him apart. "Teachers always assumed that I was going to be at the bottom of the class, and when they found out I wasn't, this sort of shook 'em up a little bit." Arna laughed it off, but deep down those racial assumptions began to grate. So did the absence of black people in his history books. As early as age twelve he was frequenting the public libraries in Watts and Los Angeles looking for books about Negro life. "I was seeking a recognizable reflection of myself and my world in the collections of books available to a boy reader," he recalled. "What I found was cold comfort, to say the least."[16]

Gradually, he concluded that his schoolteachers were shielding him from a proper understanding of the African American past. Some did not know any better, he thought, but others probably did. "I began to suspect," he later wrote, "that the colossal omissions they perpetuated were more than inadvertent. They were deliberate. Many may have been vindictive." Thus, a young and bookish Arna Bontemps, surrounded in school by whites who knew nothing of black history and cared less, developed an intense longing for a meaningful racial heritage and began what his biographer has aptly called a "journey into blackness."[17]

Buddy was more than happy to help Arna make that journey, and, as a result, Arna's definition of Negro-ness would always bear a close resemblance to Buddy and his stories of the South. Buddy had said "I'd a heap rather be down home than [in California], if it wasn't for the *conditions*." Even his father, in more relaxed moments, longingly recalled Louisiana. For Arna, that only underscored the lure of the South and made the West seem increasingly colorless.[18]

One curious point here—and Bontemps himself, introspective and insightful as he was, never quite registered it—was that Los Angeles was in no way devoid of Negro-ness, however it might be defined. The vast majority of blacks in southern California were southern-born and southern-raised, and Arna had relatives from Alexandria living in Los Angeles, including his close friend and cousin, Benny.

Consider, too, Arna's experiences when he came home summers from college (usually staying in the city with cousin Benny). In 1922, while taking summer school courses at UCLA, he discovered a copy of *Harlem Shadows,* a collection of poems by the Jamaican-born writer Claude McKay. Bontemps devoured it several times over, and "then began telling everybody I knew about it." When he read McKay's poems to his black friends, Bontemps was struck by their reactions. "Nearly all of them stopped to listen," he later wrote. "There was no doubt that their blood came to a boil when they heard 'If We Must Die.' 'Harlem Dancer' brought worldly-wise looks from their eyes. McKay's poems of longing for his home island melted them visibly, and I think these responses told me something about black people and poetry that remains true."[19]

That same summer he discovered Jelly Roll Morton and jazz. Morton, from New Orleans via Chicago, would play in town until the midnight curfew, then move south of the city limits, beyond Watts to Leak's Lake pavilion and play some more. Bontemps and his cousin Benny, who played trumpet with a band at Leak's Lake, would go "and listen closely to the haunting music throughout the night." About that time, too, the messianic Back-to-Africa leader, Marcus Garvey, visited Los Angeles and packed the Trinity Auditorium, Bontemps being one in attendance.[20]

Despite the richness of these experiences and the increasing vitality of the local black community, Arna Bontemps felt that he could not truly find himself or his heritage in Los Angeles. Other observers were more impressed with the black West. Chandler Owen of Harlem, editor of the national black journal *The Messenger,* visited southern California on a speaking tour in 1922. Owen gazed upon Central Avenue and called it "a veritable little Harlem, in Los Angeles." And yet, for Bontemps, Los Angeles could never be what Harlem was, a Mecca for the black world of the twenties.[21]

"Before I finished college," he wrote, "I had begun to feel that in some large and important areas I was being miseducated, and that perhaps I should have rebelled." The Adventist schools he attended in California were academically excellent, and some of his teachers actively promoted his writing talents; in that sense, his western upbringing had given him permission to dream of being a writer. But at the same time, he felt that the West had somehow robbed him of his birthright—a personal connection to Negro life. His father's coldness for things "colored" clashed with Arna's love for Buddy and his curiosity about black history.[22]

The result was Arna's sharply bifurcated view of heritage, region, and identity. "In their opposing attitudes toward roots my father and my great uncle made me aware of a conflict in which every educated American Negro, and some who are not educated, must somehow take sides," Arna wrote in the last decade of his life. "By implication at least, one group advocates embracing the riches of the folk heritage; their opposites demand a clean break with the past and all it represents." By the time he graduated from Pacific Union, there was no possibility that he would choose the latter.[23]

"So," asked Arna Bontemps, "what did one do after concluding that for him a break with the past and the shedding of his Negro-ness were not only impossible but unthinkable?" His own answer was to go to Harlem: where the "Negro Art Renaissance," as W. E. B. Du Bois called it, was blooming; where Claude McKay had written his poems; where Langston Hughes (another young heritage-starved westerner) and other black writers were publishing verse and fiction. In 1924 Bontemps left a post-office job in Los Angeles to become a writer in the Harlem Renaissance.[24]

It was a cautious rebellion. His father was at the station to see him off. Arna already had the promise of a teaching job at the Harlem Academy, an Adventist high school. He had also received some affirmation of his talent on a national scale. Early in the summer of 1924 he received word that *Crisis* would publish one of his poems, appropriately titled "Hope." That was all the incentive he needed. His train pulled into New York in August 1924, he caught the subway to Harlem, got off at 125th Street, and walked up into what was for Arna Bontemps the most beautiful world he had ever seen.[25]

As he later described it, Harlem in 1924 "was like a foretaste of paradise. A blue haze descended at night and with it strings of fairy lights on the broad avenues. From the window of a small room in an apartment on Fifth and 129th Street I looked over the rooftops of Negrodom and tried to believe my eyes. What a city! What a world!" He went to the Harlem public library and found young black women employed at the front desk, a sight unknown back home. Better yet, the young woman who accepted his application for a library card recognized his name from his recently published poem in *Crisis.* It was a sweet beginning, and things only got better as he quickly became an accepted figure in Renaissance circles. By day, he taught at Harlem Academy. By night, he roamed with the poets. Before long he married and roamed less, but he continued to love Harlem and to write about the heritage of race.[26]

Arna Bontemps went to Harlem to explore the South or, as he might have said it, southern *Negro-ness.* The irony was that he was a westerner seeking Dixie's soul in a northern ghetto. It would be years, in fact, before he actually experienced the South first hand. In Harlem, Bontemps became part of a young generation of western writers and artists who were energizing the New Negro Renaissance. Although Harlem attracted blacks from all across the United States and from the Caribbean, most of the young mavericks of the Renaissance's explosive years—from the publication of *The New Negro* in 1925 to Wallace Thurman's *Infants of Spring* in 1932—were from the West. Besides Bontemps, blacks from the West included the well-known Langston Hughes (from Lawrence, Kansas), Aaron Douglas (from Topeka, Kansas, with a B.A. in Fine Arts from the University of Nebraska), and Wallace Thurman (from Salt Lake City, Utah, with some time spent at the University of Southern California). Like Bontemps these young people were educated in predominantly white schools. They shared his emotional need to explore black culture (especially the lower-class black culture that seemed to them unquestionably "Negro") and to express that culture in their art.[27]

Bontemps's career in Harlem evolved differently from that of the other black westerners. His work was less dramatic than that of Hughes or Douglas, and it was never explosively controversial, like that of Thurman. But he began producing award-winning poetry and short stories immediately, establishing the disciplined work habits that would mark his astonishingly productive career of nearly fifty years as a writer of novels, short stories, poetry, children's literature, memoirs, and history, and as an editor of historical and literary anthologies. Largely ignored in the standard accounts of the Renaissance, and inaccurately described by one scholar as a poet who was "struggling in Harlem," Bontemps found a comfortable niche in Harlem early on.[28]

A good day job and his marriage in 1926 to one of his students, Alberta Johnson, set him apart as an unusually settled member of the young Renaissance crowd. He was one of the few black artists of the Renaissance to marry, settle down, and have children. Family life curtailed Bontemps's appearances on Harlem's night-club circuit, but he gave no indication that he missed the bohemian scene. If his soul found comfort in Uncle Buddy's world, Arna nonetheless maintained a substantial share of his father's discipline and responsibility.

Bontemps accepted the prevailing worldview of the young generation of New Negro artists and the wealthy whites who underwrote much of their work. The basic goal was to restore "primitivism" to a soulless world. Broadly put, the new ethic ran as follows: the modern world was on the verge of disaster because the European pursuit of civilization had crushed the primitive and natural aspects of life that were critical to humanity's well being; Negroes—African and American alike—had preserved at least some of their primitivism; by presenting that primitivism in their art and letters, New Negroes might save modern civilization from its drought of soul. A resurgence of primitivism (and a romanticization of it) was not Du Bois's idea of

Renaissance, but it *was* what Hughes, Douglas, and Bontemps had in mind. In giving voice to primitivism—to what they considered the authentic and almost-extinct voice of African Americans—the black westerners sought at last to find their own true selves, to save Negro Americans from their ongoing loss of Negro-ness, and perhaps to save the soul of the nation. "The idea," Bontemps recalled, "intoxicated us."[29]

Acting colored, or rather the self-expression of "color" in literature and art, was largely the aim of Bontemps and the western contingent of the Renaissance crowd. Before long, this trend prompted a struggle between some of the "old guard" Harlem writers (led by Du Bois) and the western newcomers, a struggle that paralleled the rift between Paul Bontemps and Uncle Buddy, and a cultural schism that might best be understood as a regional fault line.

For Du Bois, black art had a specific political purpose. White racist stereotypes of black Americans seized upon promiscuous, dialect-speaking, lower-class caricatures to discredit all blacks. Respectable art by educated blacks, Du Bois reasoned, offered the best way to undermine white racist stereotypes. This dominant assumption among leading black intellectuals rendered some subjects taboo, including black promiscuity, drunkenness, and southern-style primitivism in general.

But the western blacks who dominated the post-1925 Renaissance had no desire to distance their art from the earthier aspects of African American culture. Indeed, they had moved to Harlem to close the gap between themselves and Afro-southern folk culture. Artistically, they loved jungle scenes, jazz rhythms, blues sensibilities, sensuality, thick dialect—all the things Paul Bontemps saw as "colored."

The trend could be seen in a series of works by the black western writers. Langston Hughes's first book of poems, *The Weary Blues* (1926), set the tone by plunging his verse into the world of the black masses, explicitly linking African jungle moons and tribal dances with Harlem cabarets and jazz-filled nights. That same year, Wallace Thurman's ill-fated journal *Fire!!* (it lasted only one issue) received the ire of New York's established black intellectuals for showcasing the very subjects considered inappropriate by the old guard. (Subsequently, Thurman's two successes in 1929—the Broadway hit *Harlem* and his first novel, *The Blacker the Berry* . . . —would also emphasize the bawdier aspects of black life in Harlem.) The debate over "racial" art boiled up in New York's intellectual circles, but Arna Bontemps never wavered in his belief that "colored" representations (as he and his friends defined them) were much-needed in literature.[30]

Bontemps's first novel *God Sends Sunday* (1931) underscored his commitment to racial art by presenting as its main theme the Afro-southern misadventures of Uncle Buddy.[31] Bontemps did not care to write about a westerner who moved to Harlem, as did Wallace Thurman in *The Blacker the Berry* . . .[32] Nor did he use the black West as his setting, as Langston Hughes did in his novel, *Not Without Laughter* (1930).[33] Bontemps wanted to write about the South, the region he once called "that vast everglade of black life."[34]

God Sends Sunday is all about Afro-southern folk culture. The protagonist is Buddy incarnate, thinly veiled as a jockey named Little Augie. Virtually all of the characters in the book are what Bontemps's father would have called "don't-care" folks. They are sporting men and painted women, whose earthy dialect and violent behavior flow like the Mississippi in full flood as they wander up and down between New Orleans and St. Louis. And they do not, in fact, care about anything but good times and immediate gratification. Little Augie races horses, chases women, gambles, and fights, his luck with horses and women running hot and cold until he finally hits rock bottom. Then he goes West to find his sister.

At last Augie arrives in Los Angeles, or rather in Mudtown, "the Negro neighborhood" outside of Watts. Mudtown, he discovers, "was like a tiny section of the deep south literally transplanted." With his sister, Leah, and her grandson Terry (close representations of Arna's grandmother and Arna himself), Augie plans to settle down at last—but he cannot. His restless, volatile personality leads him once again into drunkenness and trouble. In a fight over a young woman, he cuts up a neighbor—perhaps mortally—with a beet knife. Facing nothing but trouble in Mudtown, Augie flees to Mexico, hitching a ride to the border with his only possession—freedom of movement.[35]

The curious thing about *God Sends Sunday* is that it is not about the black West, which Bontemps knew best, or about the northern ghetto, which surrounded him as he wrote, but about the black South, which he had never seen. Even the part of the novel situated in southern California is really about the South, not the West. The novel's "Mudtown" is obviously based on the Furlough Track where Arna had lived for a time with his grandmother and Buddy; but the real Furlough Track, as later described by Arna himself, was nothing like a transplanted section of the Deep South.[36] Except for the different landscape and a few Mexicans in the background, Little Augie's West proves no different than his South. In an aside in the novel, Bontemps mentions that most blacks in the West live in the large metropolitan areas; but those blacks never appear in Bontemps's book. His story is about a very southernized "Mudtown," a virtually all-black, rural world, filled mostly with "don't-care" Negroes.

The novel received mixed, sometimes heated, reviews. Some critics praised it as an authentic, sensitive portrayal of Afro-southern culture. Others judged it a crude, uninspiring portrayal of the same. Uncle Buddy received a copy from Arna, celebrated with his friends, and wandered drunk onto a road where a car ran him down. Paul Bontemps, reading his copy in Watts, had less to celebrate and lived to question his son's chosen vocation.[37]

A shocked W. E. B. Du Bois hated the book. The *Crisis* editor, who had bestowed prizes on Bontemps's early poetry, now turned a sharp pen against the author. "A profound disappointment," he fumed.

> There is a certain pathetic touch to the painting of his poor little jockey hero, but nearly all else is sordid crime, drinking, gambling, whore-mongering, and murder. There is not a decent intelligent woman; not a single man with the slightest ambition or real education, scarcely more than one human child in the whole book. . . . In the "Blues" alone Bontemps sees beauty. But in brown skins, frizzled hair and full contoured faces, they are to him nothing but ugly, tawdry, hateful things, which he describes with evident caricature.[38]

Du Bois called Bontemps a race hater, but nothing could be further from the truth. Du Bois mistook Bontemps's joyful representation for hateful misrepresentation. Bontemps later said: "Du Bois did not fail to express pained displeasure—in much the same terms as my own upright father used when he read it—and I, in my exhilaration, was convinced that neither quite understood."[39] In fact they did not understand. Bontemps wrote what he did in *God Sends Sunday* not because he despised poor southern blacks but because he loved them, even envied them. He felt they still possessed what he had lost growing up out West—a culture linked to primitivism, an enduring tie to an African past, an undeniable sense of self.[40]

But Bontemps soon discovered the South first hand, and the experience affected his work. Shortly after the publication of *God Sends Sunday,* the Great Depression undercut Bontemps's job at the Harlem Academy, and he accepted a position at Oakwood College, an all-black Adventist school (with a white president) in northern Alabama. Bontemps loved the rural landscape and the ordinary black southerners he found there, but he quickly came to hate the South's suffocating racism and intolerance. "We had fled here to escape our fears in the city," Bontemps wrote, "but the terrors we encountered here were even more upsetting than the ones we had left behind." Bontemps began at last to realize what prompted his father to leave Alexandria for Los Angeles. Now it was Arna's turn to be a young black father with a family's safety and future to consider.[41]

Bontemps's Alabama years gave rise to his second novel, *Black Thunder* (1936), which offered a fundamentally different vision of Afro-southern culture. Troubled by the racism that surrounded him in northern Alabama, Arna journeyed briefly to Fisk University in Nashville, Tennessee, where some of his friends from the Harlem Renaissance had established a haven for black education and art.[42] There, Bontemps found a treasure of slave narratives and read them "almost frantically" and "began to ponder the stricken slave's will to freedom." He found the slave rebellions—"efforts at self-emancipation," he called them—especially compelling, and he decided to write his next novel on Gabriel Prosser, whose 1800 rebellion ended in failure and his execution. To Bontemps, Prosser's desire for freedom seemed like an "unmistakable equivalent of the yearning I felt and which I imagined to be general."[43]

Back at Oakwood, tensions became unbearable. Bontemps fell under suspicion, and he did not even feel free enough to tell his black colleagues about the Gabriel Prosser project. Meantime, friends from the Renaissance, including the increasingly radical Langston Hughes, kept stopping by Oakwood to visit the Bontemps family, thereby rousing more suspicions about the young black intellectual. Bontemps stayed through spring 1935, when the school's president horrified him by stating that Arna could save his position on the faculty only by publicly burning his books by Renaissance writers.[44]

Arna Bontemps kept his books and returned to the West. At the time, he perceived this move as the great failure of his early manhood.[45] In 1935, driving his family across the Southwest and marveling at the caravans of Okies, he knew his homecoming would be less than pleasant. He was broke, Alberta was expecting their third child, and all five of them would have to live with Paul Bontemps and his second wife in their small house in Watts. Upon arrival Arna sold the Ford "in the hope that what we had received for the car would buy food till I could write my book."[46]

Back in Watts, Bontemps spent half a year writing one of the strongest (yet least-appreciated) novels of the Renaissance era. Circumstances were rather strained. His father accepted the imposition with stiff politeness and once openly criticized his son for arriving at such straits. With no space for a typewriter or even a writing table, Arna "wrote the book in longhand on the top of a folded-down sewing machine." Compared to Alabama, though, southern California seemed tranquil. In the mid-1930s, class and race tensions were actually running high in Great-Depression Los Angeles; but from his writing window, Bontemps looked out on a landscape of peaceful ethnic diversity. "A Japanese truck farmer's asparagus field was just outside our back door," he recalled. And "in the vacant lot across from us on Wiegand [Avenue] a friendly Mexican neighbor grazed his milk goat." Bontemps loved the climate. "We could smell eucalyptus trees when my writing window was open and when we walked outside," he said, "and nearly always the air was like transparent gold in those days." Despite Arna's sense of failure, his family had survived the South and made it safely to the West—just as Paul Bontemps's family had done in 1906.[47]

Having now fled Dixie himself, Arna wrote about the South differently. *Black Thunder* was not about preserving folk life. It was about getting free, about harnessing the revolutionary potential of Afro-southern culture. In

Black Thunder, the slave Gabriel can no longer abide bondage. He seizes upon Old Testament promises of God's vengeance against evil and rallies his fellow slaves for freedom. They plot to kill the white people in Richmond in hopes of fostering a general black uprising. For Gabriel, the only choice was freedom or death. And in the end a betrayed Gabriel dies calmly on the gallows, "excellent in strength, the first for freedom of the blacks, savage and baffled, perplexed but unafraid, waiting for the dignity of death."[48]

From the vantage point of Little Augie's flippant escape to Mexico in *God Sends Sunday,* Bontemps had moved a very long way. His early longing for "Negro-ness" in what he perceived to be a "Negro-*less*" West had led him to Harlem and, by twists of fate, to Alabama. Profoundly disturbed by the Deep South, he returned to the relative safety of the West to write a novel whose basic theme, as Bontemps himself described it, was the "self-assertion by black men whose endurance was strained to the breaking point."[49]

Oddly, Bontemps would ultimately move back to the South and remain there until his death in 1973. With a small advance for *Black Thunder,* he moved to Chicago and remained there several years, attending graduate school and working for the federal writers program. But the northern ghetto disturbed him. Blacks were confined to the South Side, which Bontemps viewed as a hellish cauldron of poverty and crime. Nor could he return to Harlem, where the Renaissance had been devastated by the Great Depression and the riot of 1935. So, in the early 1940s, when Fisk University asked him to join the faculty and serve as Head Librarian, he accepted.[50]

Arna Bontemps thus returned to the South at the very time that hundreds of thousands of southern blacks were moving to Los Angeles to work in the war industries. The South he moved to was not quite the Alabama he had fled. Fisk University, along with the black middle-class community that surrounded it in the upper-South city of Nashville, offered his family a less threatening form of Jim Crow than they had found in Alabama and a safer middle-class environment than they had found in Chicago. And although Arna occasionally accepted visiting appointments at Yale and other universities, he would remain in Nashville until the end. But in a final testament to the power of region in shaping Bontemps's life and art, his last book of essays, published posthumously and titled *The Old South,* includes three autobiographical stories. Those stories are not about the Old South, of course, but about his coming-of-age—and his quest for identity—in the twentieth-century West.

The issue of African American identity was a matter of concern and debate among blacks throughout the United States in the first three decades of the twentieth century. The question of "acting colored" was never an exclusively "western" matter. It rattled through black middle-class households everywhere, as concerned parents pointed out local variants of Uncle Buddy and warned their children that "loud" and "lazy" were tickets to poverty. But for Arna Bontemps in California—and for the other black westerners who made their way to the Harlem Renaissance—the question of "acting colored" would always be a matter of culture that transcended class. And it was a matter of region as well.

Indeed, whenever the issue of "acting colored" arose, it reflected a regional context. In the South, where the vast majority of blacks still lived, a crushing apartheid-like system circumscribed the issue by forcing all blacks into a tightly restricted subservient caste.[51] In northern cities the African American population soared (especially beginning with the Great Black Migration of World War I), prompting a conflict between northern-born blacks and southern-born newcomers and also sparking a white backlash that resulted in the widespread ghettoization of all blacks.[52]

The West, by comparison, had the smallest black population to begin with and received fewer Afro-southerners than the North during the Great Migration. Most black western migrants moved to the growing coastal cities, which, prior to the 1890s, had only the tiniest of black communities. For that reason, it was not clear where blacks would fit into the rapidly changing society of the West Coast. Despite pervasive discrimination by whites against all people of color, black residential patterns in the West were less concentrated than in the South or North. By the 1930s, blacks would find themselves locked into highly restricted residential areas. But in the formative years of the century, there was more flux and uncertainty—all the more so because the West was a decidedly multiracial environment, and it was not clear where blacks would stand in the regional hierarchy of ethnic status and power. African Americans therefore found relatively more openness in the West than elsewhere (at least for a while), and that openness complicated the issue of black identity.[53]

Bontemps understood the power of place in shaping racial identity. For him, the openness of western society felt strangely like a severance of heritage and created in him a longing for the identifiably black aspects of African American culture. He found black culture first in the stories of Uncle Buddy, then in Harlem, and finally in the South itself. But he seems never to have found it in the West. It is not too much to say that the early-twentieth-century West turned Arna Bontemps into a cultural nationalist, albeit a soft-spoken one.[54] A disciplined, religious, hard-working family man, he lived his life much in accordance with his father's example. But his art remained close to the soul of Uncle Buddy.

From the summer of 1922, when he read African American poetry to his young friends in Los Angeles, Arna Bontemps expressed his love for black culture—for "Negro-ness." He never saw any contradiction between racial appreciation and racial integration. In matters of civil rights, he was staunchly integrationist, citing Charles S. Johnson's injunction to be engaged in "intensive minority living."[55] But Bontemps's idea of integration never included the abandonment of what he saw as black culture. He desired to be a full citizen of society *and* to celebrate the richness of his racial heritage. Bontemps's cultural journey thus presaged what remains today an important and recurrent tension in the singularly diverse society of the American West.

Notes

The author wishes to thank Blake Allmendinger, Bill Deverell, Valerie Matsumoto, Marlon Ross, and Bryant Simon for their thoughtful and timely critiques of this essay as it moved from one draft to another. Special appreciation also to Peter Reill and all the good people at the Clark Library for the wonderful "American Dreams, Western Images" program, which offered an exceptional opportunity to think long and hard about region and race.

1. Arna Bontemps, "Why I Returned," in Arna Bontemps, *The Old South: 'A Summer Tragedy' and Other Stories of the Thirties* (New York: Dodd, Mead, and Co., 1973), p. 10.

2. See especially Bontemps, "Why I Returned"; and Arna Bontemps, "The Awakening: A Memoir," in Arna Bontemps, ed., *The Harlem Renaissance Remembered* (New York: Dodd, Mead, and Co., 1972).

3. Kirkland C. Jones, *Renaissance Man from Louisiana: A Biography of Arna Wendell Bontemps* (Westport, CT: Greenwood Press, 1992). This paragraph represents my own reading, not necessarily Jones's view, of the book's title.

4. Ibid., chs. 1–2; Bontemps, "Why I Returned," p. 1.

5. Bontemps, "Why I Returned," pp. 3–5; Jones, *Renaissance Man,* pp. 26–28.

6. Bontemps, "Why I Returned," pp. 5–6; what Bontemps and other residents called the Furlough Track was officially designated by the county as the Furlong Tract; see Patricia Rae Adler, "Watts: From Suburb to Black Ghetto" (Ph.D. diss., University of Southern California, 1977), p. 280, n. 24.

7. Adler, "Watts," pp. 49–50, 101, table V.6, and ch. 4 generally.

8. Pacific Coast African American history during the early twentieth century is examined in Albert S. Broussard, *Black San Francisco: The Struggle for Racial Equality in the West, 1900–1954* (Lawrence, KA: University of Kansas Press, 1993); Lawrence P. Crouchett, et al., *The History of the East Bay Afro-American Community, 1852–1977* (Oakland: Northern California Center for Afro-American History and Life, 1989); Douglas Henry Daniels, *Pioneer Urbanites: A Social and Cultural History of Black San Francisco* (Berkeley: University of California Press, 1990); Rudolph M. Lapp, *Afro-Americans in California,* 2nd ed. (San Francisco: Boyd and Fraser Publishing, 1987); and several works by Quintard Taylor: *The Forging of a Black Community: Seattle's Central District from 1870 through the Civil Rights Era* (Seattle: University of Washington Press, 1994); "Black Communities in the Pacific Northwest," *Journal of Negro History* 64 (Fall 1979): 342–54; "Black Urban Development—Another View: Seattle's Cen-

tral District, 1910–1940," *Pacific Historical Review* 58 (November 1989): 429–48; and "Blacks and Asians in a White City: Japanese Americans and African Americans in Seattle, 1890–1940," *Western Historical Quarterly* 22 (November 1991): 401–29.

Principal works on African Americans in Los Angeles include: Adler, "Watts"; J. Max Bond, "The Negro in Los Angeles" (Ph.D. diss., University of Southern California, 1936), with population figures, p. 55, table 8; Lawrence B. de Graff, "City of Black Angels: Emergence of the Los Angeles Ghetto, 1890–1930," *Pacific Historical Review* 39 (1970): 323–52; Emory J. Tolbert, *The UNIA and Black Los Angeles* (Los Angeles: Center for Afro-American Studies, 1980); and Douglas Flamming, "African American Politics in Progressive-Era Los Angeles," in William Deverell and Tom Sitton, eds., *California Progressivism Revisited* (Berkeley: University of California Press, 1994), pp. 203–28. The author of this essay is currently at work on a book entitled *A World to Gain: African Americans and the Making of Los Angeles, 1890–1940.*

9. Arna Bontemps, *Black Thunder* (New York, 1936; reprint, with a new introduction by the author, Boston: Beacon Press, 1968), p. xxiii; Jones, *Renaissance Man,* p. 36.

10. Bontemps, "Why I Returned," p. 8; Ann Allen Shockley, interview with Arna Bontemps, July 14, 1972, Arna Bontemps Collection, Fisk University, Special Collections Library.

11. Bontemps, "Why I Returned," p. 6.

12. Ibid., pp. 6–7.

13. Ibid., p. 9.

14. Ibid., p. 10; for Arna's softer version of why he was sent to the Academy (which does not present Buddy's baneful influence as a factor in his father's decision), see his story, "3 Pennies for Luck," in Bontemps, *The Old South,* pp. 233–35.

15. Bontemps, "Why I Returned," pp. 10–12.

16. Shockley interview with Bontemps; Jones, *Renaissance Man,* p. 45.

17. Arna Bontemps, "Introduction," *Great Slave Narratives* (Boston: Beacon Press, 1969), vii, quoted in Jones, *Renaissance Man,* pp. 44–46.

18. Bontemps, "Why I Returned," pp. 8–9.

19. Bontemps, "The Awakening," p. 7.

20. Ibid., pp. 7–8.

21. Chandler Owen, "From Coast to Coast," *The Messenger* (May 1922): 409.

22. Bontemps, "Why I Returned," p. 10.

23. Ibid., p. 11.

24. Ibid., p. 12. Du Bois explained the meaning of the "Negro Art Renaissance" to Angelenos in the *Los Angeles Times* (June 14, 1925, p. 1 of the Sunday Literary section); the article also promoted his theatrical pageant, "Star of Ethiopia," which was presented in two performances at the Hollywood Bowl. By the time Du Bois's article and pageant appeared in Los Angeles, Bontemps had been in Harlem for nearly a year.

25. Jones, *Renaissance Man,* pp. 51–53.

26. Arna Bontemps, *Personals* (London: Paul Breman Limited, 1973), pp. 4–5. *Personals* is a collection of Bontemps's poetry, which includes an introduction in which he discusses the Renaissance.

27. Studies of the Harlem Renaissance, which include many excellent works,

have largely ignored the western-ness of the young Renaissance crowd. Fundamental works on the Renaissance include, Nathan Irvin Huggins, *Harlem Renaissance* (New York: Oxford, 1971); David L. Lewis, *When Harlem Was In Vogue* (New York: Knopf, 1981), and Lewis's introduction to his edited anthology, *The Portable Harlem Renaissance Reader* (New York: Viking, 1994), pp. xv–xliii; Arnold Rampersad, *The Life of Langston Hughes. Vol. I: 1902–1941, "I, Too, Sing America"* (New York: Oxford University Press, 1986); and Ann Douglas, *Terrible Honesty: Mongrel Manhattan in the 1920s* (New York: Farrar, Straus and Giroux, 1995). There were other westerners (not mentioned in the text paragraph) involved in the Renaissance: Louise Thompson, a minor Renaissance player who became an important New York Communist in the 1930s, had lived in various towns in the mountain West but grew up mainly in Sacramento, California, and received her B.A. from Berkeley; Sargent Johnson moved to San Francisco as a young adult, decided to become an artist, and emerged as one of the finest sculptors of the period (he won prizes in Harlem, but continued to live in San Francisco); finally, Carl Van Vechten, the leading white supporter of the young black writers, was, despite his cosmopolitanism and world travels, the product of Cedar Rapids, Iowa.

28. "Struggling" quote in Lewis, *Portable Harlem Renaissance Reader,* p. xxx. For Bontemps's own pleasant recollection of his early years in Harlem, see his "3 Pennies for Luck," p. 236; and "The Awakening," p. 24.

29. Bontemps, *Personals,* p. 5. The relationship between primitive Africa and modern black life is a theme in two of Bontemps's early poems: "Nocturne at Bethesda," winner of the *Crisis* poetry award for 1926; and "Golgotha is a Mountain," winner of the *Opportunity* poetry prize the same year. "Nocturne" is reprinted in *Personals,* pp. 28–29. "Golgotha" is reprinted in Lewis, *Portable Harlem Renaissance Reader,* pp. 225–26, and, with slightly different punctuation, in Bontemps, *Personals,* pp. 18–20.

30. The westerners' emphasis on "colored" art sparked a backlash. George Schuyler, a New Yorker by upbringing, debunked the racial-ness of his peers' work in "The Negro-Art Hokum," an essay appearing in *The Nation* (June 16, 1926). Langston Hughes shot back immediately with his powerful "The Negro Artist and the Racial Mountain," which appeared in the following issue of the same journal (June 23, 1926) and quickly became the New Negro manifesto, cheered by Bontemps and the other western-raised blacks. Both essays are reprinted in Lewis, *Portable Harlem Renaissance Reader,* pp. 91–99; and see Rampersad, *Life of Langston Hughes,* vol. 1, pp. 130–31, 134, 137–38. Wallace Thurman issued a powerful defense of "colored" art in his 1927 essay "Negro Artists and the Negro," *The New Republic* (August 31, 1927): 37–38. Thurman's journal has been reprinted: *Fire!! A Quarterly Devoted to the Younger Negro Artists* (Metuchen, NJ: Fire!! Press, 1982).

31. Arna Bontemps, *God Sends Sunday* (New York, 1931; reprint, New York: AMS Press Inc., 1972).

32. Wallace Thurman, *The Blacker the Berry . . . : A Novel of Negro Life* (New York, 1929; reprint, New York: Macmillan, 1970).

33. Langston Hughes, *Not Without Laughter* (New York, 1930; reprint, New York: Alfred A. Knopf, 1969). Hughes's novel (set in the small town of "Stanton" Kansas) is not so much about the black West he knew in Lawrence, Kansas, but about the black West he *wished* he had experienced there.

34. Bontemps, "The Awakening," p. 1. Bontemps even tried at first to write "au-

tobiographically" about a southern boy and his adventures in the South, a project doomed to fail, one might say, because Bontemps had no real experience living in the South and only the fewest childhood memories of the place.

35. Bontemps, *God Sends Sunday,* pp. 116, 119, 197.

36. See Bontemps's introduction to Arna Bontemps and Jack Conroy, *Any Place but Here* (New York: Hill and Wang, 1966).

37. See Robert E. Fleming, *James Weldon Johnson and Arna Wendell Bontemps: A Reference Guide* (New York: Macmillan, 1978), pp. 72–73, 79–81.

38. Du Bois quoted in James P. Draper, ed., *Black Literature Criticism: Excerpts from Criticism of the Most Significant Works of Black Authors over the Past 200 Years* (Detroit: Gale Research Inc., 1991), vol. 1, pp. 209–10, citing *Crisis* 40 (September 1931): 304. See also Bontemps, "The Awakening," pp. 25–26.

39. Bontemps, "The Awakening," p. 26.

40. Marlon Ross of the University of Michigan's English Department, whose book on the Harlem Renaissance is forthcoming, has suggested that my reading of Bontemps's "love" of Afro-southern folk culture is too simple. His alternative suggestion, oversimplified here, deserves consideration: Bontemps's "love" was tinged with self-hatred, for ultimately Lil' Augie is an impotent and pathetic character. *God Sends Sunday* is thus a novel about the death of the South and southern types; it leaves unanswered the question of what will replace these types precisely because it is a book about a past life passing into an unknown future.

41. Bontemps, *Black Thunder,* p. x. See also Rampersad, *Life of Langston Hughes,* vol. 1, pp. 227–28; and John O'Brien interview with Arna Bontemps, reprinted in Draper, ed., *Black Literature Criticism,* vol. 1, p. 222.

42. James Weldon Johnson, Charles S. Johnson, and Arthur Schomburg, all of whom Bontemps had known in Harlem, had settled in at Fisk. "All, in a sense, could have been considered as refugees living in exile," Bontemps wrote, "and the three, privately could have been dreaming of planting an oasis at Fisk where, surrounded by bleak hostility in the area, the region, and the nation, if not indeed the world, they might not only stay alive but, conceivably, keep alive a flicker of the impulse they had detected and helped to encourage in the black awakening in Renaissance Harlem." Bontemps, *Black Thunder,* p. xi.

43. Ibid., pp. xi, xii, xiii.

44. Ibid., p. xiv. Bontemps thought he might be removed from the faculty earlier than 1935. In about 1932, he wrote Hughes, "I was . . . pointed out as being favorable to the revolution and, as a result, may not be rehired. I am not really bumped, but the faculty is to be cut in half (due to depression) and I may not be on the new slate." Bontemps to Hughes c. 1932, in Charles H. Nichols, ed., *Arna Bontemps-Langston Hughes Letters, 1925–1967* (New York: Dodd, Mead and Co., 1980), pp. 18–19.

45. Bontemps had not always been so reluctant to return. In his first year at Oakwood, he wrote to Langston Hughes that if he should leave Alabama, he would "come to California and go to U.S.C. next winter—that is really what I want to do." Once back in Los Angeles, he speculated, "I could spend time in Mexico, write more children's books, finish a long delayed novel, etc. etc." Bontemps to Hughes, c. 1932, in Nichols, *Arna Bontemps-Langston Hughes Letters,* pp. 18–19.

46. Bontemps, *Black Thunder,* p. xiv.

47. Ibid., p. viii; Rampersad, *Life of Langston Hughes,* vol. 1, p. 306.

48. *Black Thunder,* pp. 69, 222. The novel won widely favorable reviews. In words that must have validated Bontemps's search for racial authenticity, the reviewer for the *New York Times* wrote: "If one were looking for a sort of prose spiritual on the Negroes themselves, quite aside from the universal dream that they bear in this story, one could not find it more movingly sung." Another reviewer stated that Bontemps had "written of the Virginia countryside as one who knows it and loves it." Quotes from *Book Review Digest, 1936,* p. 105 (all five reviews listed were graded as positive). Sales lagged far behind the reviews, however, and Bontemps made almost no money for his best work until *Black Thunder* was revived amidst the black power movement of the late 1960s. Appreciation of *Black Thunder* has now reached a high point; in 1992, Beacon Press issued a new edition of the novel with an introduction by Arnold Rampersad.

49. Bontemps, *Black Thunder,* p. xv.

50. "We had fled from the jungle of Alabama's Scottsboro era to the jungle of Chicago's crime-ridden South Side," Bontemps wrote, "and one was as terrifying as the other." Bontemps, "Why I Returned," p. 18. On his move to Fisk and his decision to remain in the South, see ibid., pp. 19–25.

51. Basic works in the enormous literature on southern race relations in the late nineteenth and early twentieth century include: J. Morgan Kousser, *The Shaping of Southern Politics: Suffrage Restriction and the Establishment of the One-Party South* (New Haven, CT: Yale University Press, 1974); Earl Lewis, *In Their Own Interests: Race, Class, and Power in Twentieth-Century Norfolk, Virginia* (Berkeley: University of California Press, 1991); Howard N. Rabinowitz, *Race Relations in the Urban South, 1865–1890* (New York: Oxford University Press, 1978); and C. Vann Woodward, *The Strange Career of Jim Crow,* 3rd rev. ed. (New York: Oxford University Press, 1974).

52. In the rapidly growing field of Great Migration studies, basic works include: Kenneth L. Kusmer, *A Ghetto Takes Shape: Black Cleveland, 1870–1930* (Urbana: University of Illinois Press, 1978); Peter Gottlieb, *Making Their Own Way: Southern Blacks' Migration to Pittsburgh, 1916–1930* (Urbana: University of Illinois Press, 1987); James Grossman, *Land of Hope: Chicago, Black Southerners, and the Great Migration* (Chicago: University of Chicago Press, 1989); Alan H. Spear, *Black Chicago: The Making of a Negro Ghetto* (Chicago: University of Chicago Press, 1967); Joe William Trotter, Jr., *Black Milwaukee: The Making of an Industrial Proletariat, 1915–1945* (Urbana: University of Illinois, 1985); Joe William Trotter, Jr., ed., *The Great Migration in Historical Perspective: New Dimensions of Race, Class, and Gender* (Bloomington: Indiana University Press, 1991).

53. On the black West, particularly the Pacific Coast, during this period, see note 8.

54. See especially Bontemps's discussion of things "colored" in "Why I Returned," pp. 10–11.

55. Ibid., p. 22.

Part Two

CROSSING BOUNDARIES

6

"DOMESTIC" LIFE IN THE DIGGINGS

The Southern Mines in the California Gold Rush

SUSAN LEE JOHNSON

In 1853, Helen Nye wrote from California to her mother in Massachusetts: "I have heard of Miners at some diggins subsisting for days on Acorns of which we have a very fine kind in this Country." Nye was a white woman whose husband was a merchant at Don Pedro's Bar, in the area known during the Gold Rush as the Southern Mines. She explained to her mother how newcomers learned to make use of the oak tree's bounty by watching native people during their autumn harvest. In general, though, Gold Rush immigrants saw the food that Indians most valued as something to be eaten only in dire circumstances. As Charles Davis explained to his daughter in Massachusetts, while acorns, grass, and wild oats abounded in the Sierra Nevada foothills, these were suitable only for "Wild Indians and Wild Animals."[1] Davis's disdain for native sustenance suggests that cooking and eating became sites of contestation in the diggings. In fact, this was the case all over the gold region, given the relative absence of women there. But it was especially true in the Southern Mines, which was both the homeland of Miwok Indians and the destination for a majority of non-Anglo American immigrants to Gold Rush California, including Mexicans, Chileans, French, Chinese, and some African Americans.[2] In the Southern Mines, culinary practices fit into a larger constellation of activities that signaled for many a world of confusion—men mending trousers and caring for the sick, Anglos dining on acorns and frijoles. As Edmund Booth complained to his wife back in Iowa, "Cal. is a world upside down—nothing like home comforts and home joys."[3]

To understand why California seemed like a world standing on its head, one must ponder the multiple meanings of such everyday practices as eating acorns, digging gold, and inhabiting a race or a gender.[4] Even in so short a time as the Gold Rush years and even in so small a place as the Southern

Mines, meanings proliferated, evolved, collided. While native people there lived in communities with roughly equal numbers of women and men, among immigrant peoples skewed sex ratios meant drastically altered divisions of labor in which men took on tasks that their womenfolk would have performed back home. Analyzing how men parceled out such work and how they thought about what they were doing tells us much about the content of gender in the Gold Rush. Crucial too are the meanings of the domestic and personal service work that the small number of non-native women did in California, and the perceptions native and immigrant peoples held of one another's ways of manufacturing material life.

Skewed sex ratios in the diggings were accompanied by an extraordinary demographic diversity: people came to California from all over the world, producing and reproducing ideas about color, culture, and nation that, on U.S. soil, often coalesced into conversations about race. Race, like gender, is a set of changing ideas about human difference and hierarchy, and a relation in which those ideas are put into practice.[5] In a time and place like Gold Rush California, its meanings pulsed through everyday life like an erratic heartbeat. For instance, the way that certain tasks, such as cooking or laundry, came to be associated with certain non-Anglo men demonstrates how constructions of race could be mapped onto constructions of gender in the diggings.

Indeed, in the boom years of the Gold Rush, relations of class were often obscured or even subsumed by the day-to-day salience of gender and race. This was in part because the means of getting gold during the initial boom was by "placer" (surface, individualized) mining rather than "quartz" (underground, industrialized) mining.[6] Placer mining required almost no capital and did not necessarily entail a hierarchy among workers—claims could be staked for free, the necessary tools were simple and easily built or acquired, and the work could be done (though it was not always done) by a small group of people who rotated tasks. Later, entrepreneurs developed "hydraulic" mining, a more capital-intensive means of exploiting surface deposits, whereby men shot powerful streams of water against hills assumed rich in "deep gravels." When hydraulic and quartz mining took hold, they were accompanied by an elaboration of class hierarchies. Class relations followed a different course in areas—like much of the Southern Mines—where insufficient water and underground deposits thwarted development of hydraulic and quartz mining. In such areas, class-making was often signaled by the growth of local water companies, whereby capitalists bought up rights to scarce water and then sold use of the water to placer miners who needed it to wash gold-bearing dirt. But all of these developments—water monopolies and hydraulic and quartz operations—came about as the initial boom, which was predicated on rich surface diggings, began to give way to a bust. In the early years of the Gold Rush—roughly 1848 to 1853—class contests and solidarities often had as much to do with immigrants' memories of class in their homelands as with actual social relations structured through divisions of labor in the mines. Gold Rush California was an unusual time and place.

This, though, is not news; historians have long noted the social peculiarities of the Gold Rush. Indeed, while not all histories of the event and its context have been self-consciously social histories, all have attended to key social dimensions of the demographic cataclysm that followed the 1848 discovery of gold in the Sierra Nevada foothills. Most have noted that "society" in the diggings was, first, mostly male and, second, significantly multiracial and multiethnic.[7] These two demographic realities, along with the initial absence of state power in the foothills, the social implications of that absence, and the suspension of some class distinctions, are among the most oft-mentioned aspects of Gold Rush California. Yet with one exception—an important new cultural history that compares arguments about the meanings of gold in both American California and Australian Victoria—twentieth-century scholarship has stressed questions of social structure over those of social meaning. Newer work, then, must build on these earlier accounts, employing interrelated modes of analysis developed in ethnic studies, feminist studies, and cultural studies. That is, to the concern with demography we must add a concern for the *content* of social categories such as gender or race.[8]

In this essay, I explore some social meanings and cultural consequences of two of the peculiarities that have interested Gold Rush historians—that is, the relative absence of women and the overwhelming presence of polyglot peoples. I do so by concentrating on what might be thought of as "domestic" life in the diggings—and especially on practices relating to cooking, serving, and eating meals.[9] Not everyone in the Southern Mines dug gold, but everyone did perform, or relied on others to perform, life-sustaining and life-enhancing tasks such as procuring provisions and preparing food. Since few could reproduce the divisions of labor that made performance of these tasks seem more or less predictable and culturally coherent back home, Gold Rush participants devised new ways to provide for their needs and wants. But all the while they wondered about what it meant that Anglo American men were down on their knees scrubbing their shirts in a stream, that Mexican women were making money hand over fist selling tortillas in the gold town of Sonora, or that French men seemed so good at creating homey cabins in the diggings.

Distinguishing between two kinds of work—domestic and personal service work, on the one hand, and work in the mines, on the other—may seem to reify categories of labor. In making such distinctions, one invokes the discursive division between home and the workplace that accompanied the growth of industrial capitalism in the nineteenth century. One also echoes more recent Marxist-feminist delineations of productive and reproductive labor, which have placed "reproductive" chores (often women's work) on a par with those "productive" chores (often men's work) assumed to constitute true economic activity.[10]

But impulses similar to those that split home life off from labor in the nineteenth century—impulses scrutinized by twentieth-century feminists—also led most Gold Rush participants to view mining as qualitatively different from and more important than their other daily tasks. This makes intuitive sense, since immigrants traveled hundreds or thousands of miles to dig gold or to profit from those who did. Yet performing this privileged economic activity required that miners pay attention to the exigencies of everyday life. Then, too, for one group in the Southern Mines—Miwok Indians—gold digging rarely became the most important, community-defining kind of labor performed. So the dichotomy drawn here between mining labor and domestic and personal service work is at once heuristic *and* grounded in some, but not all, relevant historical circumstances.

In the end, though, the distinction serves another purpose. During the 1980s, historians learned to use poststructuralist analyses of language that show how binary oppositions work—oppositions such as the one between productive and reproductive labor. In the productive/reproductive labor distinction, for example, the leading term (productive or "breadwinning" work) takes primacy, while its partner (reproductive or "domestic" work) is weaker or derivative. This hierarchical relation mirrors some social relations of dominance and subordination based on gender, and also on race.[11] So foregrounding "reproductive" or "domestic" labor in a history of a mining area, where mining labor might be assumed to take precedence, is itself a gesture toward unsettling that hierarchical relation. I begin, then, not in the mines, but in the canvas dwellings of Gold Rush participants.

Though most immigrants lived in such homes, the word "tent" actually described a wide variety of structures. Some people lived in cramped quarters, such as the Chinese men Scottish traveler J. D. Borthwick saw, who were organized "in a perfect village of small tents." But when miners stayed still for any length of time, they built more elaborate shelters. For instance, though Belgian miner Jean-Nicolas Perlot and his French companions lived at first in a small tent and a brush hut, within a year they constructed a sturdy log cabin covered with a canvas roof. In such cabins, immigrants built bedsteads and fireplaces, though some men remembered how improvised chimneys forced smoke inside instead of drawing it out. Heavy rain in the foothills could impair the draft of even a well-built fireplace, and Welsh-born Angus McIsaac noted in his diary that men living with such irritants often compared their smoky cabins to scolding wives or leaky ships.[12]

McIsaac's observation suggests how readily Gold Rush participants saw in their material world metaphoric possibilities, how easily the frustrations of camp life took on gendered meanings. McIsaac himself thought a smoky home was "ill compared" to a scolding spouse or a leaky vessel, noting, "were I compelled to take charge of either, I would on all [occasions] choose the former." While McIsaac considered a woman the most pleasing ward, he took for granted the gender hierarchy his words implied. Meanwhile, he and his neighbors took charge of their more immediate surroundings by christening their cabins with names that suggested, even celebrated, the absence of sharp-tongued spouses: Loafers' Retreat, Temperance Hole, and Jackass Tent. Like the white miners who called their camp Whooping-boys Hollow, McIsaac and friends took a certain pleasure in the canvas-covered world-without-women they created.[13]

Not all shelters in the Southern Mines bespoke the ambivalent bachelorhood of men like McIsaac. Among immigrant peoples, more Mexican men than others came to California with their womenfolk. So some Mexican communities in the diggings celebrated different social possibilities than did Whooping-boys Hollow. One observer of such communities was William Perkins, a Canadian merchant in the town of Sonora, which was founded in 1848 by miners from the state of the same name in northern Mexico. Perkins was rhapsodic in his descriptions of Mexican camp life there:

> I had never seen a more beautiful, a wilder or more romantic spot. The Camp . . . was literally embowered in the trees. The habitations were constructed of canvas, cotton cloth, or of upright unhewn sticks with green branches and leaves and vines interwoven, and decorated with gaudy hangings of silks, fancy cottons, flags, brilliant goods of every description; the many-tinted Mexican *zarape,* the rich *manga,* with its gold embroidery, Chinese scarves and shawls of the most costly quality.

For Perkins, the scene recalled "descriptions we have read of the brilliant bazaars of oriental countries." Whatever the orientalizing eyes of Perkins saw, there is no reason to doubt that Mexicans did indeed decorate their dwellings with bright flags and fabrics and *serapes.* Perkins noted that it was Mexican men who built the houses, and who, "leaving their wives and children in charge," went off during the week to dig gold. However few and far between, then, even in Gold Rush California there were eye-catching, well-tended worlds-without-men.[14]

For the most part, though, miners fended for themselves. Once they built cabins or pitched tents, inhabitants had to organize domestic labor such that all stayed well-fed and healthy. The most common type of household in the boom years of the Gold Rush was that of two to five men who constituted an economic unit: they worked together in placer claims held in common, alternating tasks and placing the gold in a fund from which they purchased provisions. This generalization holds for most white men, both North American and European, and most free African Americans during the Gold Rush. It may hold for many Mexican and Chilean and perhaps some Chinese men as well. But for those North Americans, Latin Americans, and Chinese who went to California under conditions of slavery, debt peonage, or contract labor, other domestic arrangements probably obtained. And whenever women were present in the camps or whenever men lived in or near towns with boardinghouses and restaurants, daily subsistence was a different matter.[15]

All Gold Rush households, save those of Miwoks, relied on tenuous market relations to supply most of their basic needs. Out in the camps, men traded in gold dust for supplies at the nearest store, generally a tent or cabin a fair hike from home stocked with freight hauled overland from the supply town of Stockton, in the San Joaquin Valley. Beef, pork, beans, flour, potatoes, and coffee ranked high on miners' lists of items purchased. In flush times they might also be able to buy onions, dried apples, or a head of cabbage, though fresh fruits and vegetables were the hardest items to find.[16]

Limited foodstuffs spelled monotonous meals for most, but also encouraged people to exchange cooking techniques. Men from Europe and the U.S., for example, sometimes adopted Mexican practices. Perlot and his companions, en route to the mines in 1851 and low on provisions, met up with a party of Mexicans who were eating what looked to Perlot like turnips dipped in salt and pepper, fresh tortillas, and hearty beefsteaks cooked over an open flame. The Mexican men gave Perlot some raw meat, and he returned with it to his own party, proclaiming, "Messieurs . . . in this country, this is how beefsteak is cooked." Howard Gardiner, from Long Island, was less enthusiastic about the Mexican meals he learned to prepare during lean times, such as those based around *pinole,* recalling that he and his partners lived "more like pigs than human beings." Just as Gold Rush shelters took on gendered meanings, so too could Gold Rush food become racialized in its procurement, preparation, or consumption.[17]

Among Latin Americans, men might try to appeal to one another's tastes, especially when commercial interests were at stake. Vicente Pérez Rosales, a small-time Chilean *patrón* who went to California with his brothers and five laborers, learned in mid-1849 that non-Anglos were being driven from the mines. So he turned his attention to trade, setting up a store filled with Chilean cheese and beef jerky, toasted flour, dried peaches, candied preserves, and barrels of brandy. All items sold well except the jerky, which was full of what looked like moth holes. So the Chilean merchants laid the jerky out in the sun and coated it with hot lard to fill up the apertures. Then they piled it up in a pyramid shape and doused it with Chilean hot sauce. The pungent smell caught the attention of some Mexicans, and so the traders told the customers that it was the kind of jerky "served to the aristocracy in Santiago." Pérez Rosales recalled, "We lied like experienced merchants who assure a trusting female customer that they are losing money on an item, and would not sell it at such a low price to anyone but her." Here and elsewhere Pérez Rosales turned Mexican unfamiliarity with Chilean foodstuffs to his advantage, playing on envy of aristocratic privilege and, in his own mind, making women of Mexican men, thereby underscoring Chilean manliness. Such interethnic episodes, which were charged with taken-for-granted notions of gender and tinged with class meanings, must have occurred frequently in the Southern Mines.[18]

Most immigrants, like these Mexican customers, preferred to purchase their provisions. But during the first few winters of the Gold Rush, floods and treacherously muddy roads between Stockton and the foothills brought severe shortages of supplies.[19] So many miners tried to supplement store-bought food by hunting and fishing, and a few gathered greens or planted small gardens. Not all who hunted met with success. New Englander Moses Little brought down some quail just in time for Christmas dinner in 1852, but he spent most of his shot at target practice. William Miller, also from New England, had better luck. He and his white partners were camped near a group of free black miners, and in addition to joining together to dam the river and work its bed, the two parties went out deer hunting with one another and otherwise shared provisions. Heavy rains foiled the mining plans, but the African American and Anglo American residents of the camp continued to exchange gifts of fresh venison—despite harassment from white southerners who resented the presence of free blacks. By Christmas, one of the black men, Henry Garrison (born in New York but emigrated from Hawaii), had moved into Miller's tent. All parties spent the holiday together indulging in a "Splendid Dinner" of venison and the trimmings, and dancing to the music of Garrison's fine fiddle playing. Though men were not always successful hunters—given both the inexperience of immigrants from towns and cities and the decline in foothill animal populations wrought by the Gold Rush—cultural memory of hunting as a male pursuit encouraged men to give it a try.[20]

Fewer men planted gardens or gathered greens. So visitors were astonished by Perlot's singular store of herbs and vegetables. After serving salad to an incredulous miner in the mid-1850s, Perlot took him on a stroll: "I led him a hundred paces from the house . . . where I gathered chervil; a few steps farther to a place where cress was growing well . . . ; a little farther, I found lamb's lettuce." One of Perlot's partners, the French Louvel, had planted the garden the year before. On seeing it, the newcomer exclaimed, "My God, . . . how stupid can you be! to suffer four years as I have, without having had an idea as simple as that."[21]

Still, most immigrant men suffered from the dietary deficiencies created by their ignorance of the wild plants that Miwok women gathered and their unwillingness to grow more familiar crops.[22] Perhaps they hesitated to plant vegetables because their campsites were temporary, or because kitchen gardens were generally women's responsibility back home. Whatever the reason, their reluctance made them sick. George Evans, for example, could not fathom why he was too ill to work in the mines, until doctors told him he had scurvy. So he had friends gather wild cabbage and onions, and he bought some potatoes and a bottle of lime juice. His health took a turn for the better.[23]

Evans, given his condition, was wise to eat his vegetables raw, but most miners cooked their food and had to decide among themselves how to share culinary duties. The evidence for such divisions of labor says more about Anglo men than other gold seekers, but Europeans and free blacks, at least, seem to have followed similar practices. The Belgian Perlot claimed, in fact, that most men organized cooking in like fashion: "The rule generally observed between miners in partnership . . . was to do the cooking by turns of a week." Similarly, John Doble, from rural Indiana, explained, "sometimes one does the cooking and sometimes another and one only cooks at a time and cooks for all who are in the Cabin."[24]

A man's "cook week" began on Sunday, when he prepared for the days ahead, as Moses Little recorded: "It being my week to cook I have been somewhat busy—more so than on other Sabbath—Coffee to burn A box full of nuts to fry Bread to bake & Beef to cut up & take care of." During the week, the cook continued to make large quantities of staple foods like bread and beans, in addition to getting up three meals a day. The days around New Year's, 1850, must have been the cook week of Henry Garrison, the fiddle player who lived with William Miller and his dancing partners, because Miller's journal for that period is filled with references to Garrison cooking breakfast, making apple pudding, and stirring up a "Beautiful Stew" of squirrel meat. Miller must have looked forward to Garrison's cook weeks, because at least one of his other partners had trouble even lighting a fire, say nothing of preparing meals. Domestic competence was hardly universal in the diggings, but men valued it when they found it among their comrades.[25]

While it is more difficult to determine from English-language and translated sources whether most gold seekers adopted similar divisions of labor, such sources do provide some evidence of Chinese domestic habits. Yet white observers were more apt to note how odd they found Chinese foods, cookware, and eating implements than to describe how Chinese men divided up domestic work. When J. D. Borthwick visited Chinese camps, the miners invited him to eat with them, but he declined, finding their dishes "clean" but "dubious" in appearance. He added that he much preferred "to be a spectator," a role chosen by many a white man in his dealings with Chinese miners. The spectacle Borthwick described was that of a Chinese camp at dinnertime, with men "squatted on the rocks in groups of eight or ten round a number of curious little black pots and dishes, from which they helped themselves with their chopsticks." Borthwick's word picture evoked white men's visions of the Chinese; there was something both delicate and animal-like in the circle of men with their curious cookware. While his words said as much about white visions as about Chinese practices, they did suggest that Chinese miners working in large parties broke into smaller groups who shared meals, and that they used cooking and eating utensils from their homeland.[26]

Some white men were more gracious than Borthwick when invited to join Chinese circles. John Marshall Newton was camped near five hundred Chinese miners in 1852. After helping the Chinese secure their title to a claim that had been challenged by English miners, Newton fancied himself a "hero" in his neighbors' eyes. The Chinese men did give him gifts and invite him for meals; no doubt they appreciated Newton's assistance in what often proved for them an inhospitable local world. But however much they credited his actions, they also relished making him the butt of dinnertime jokes. Invariably when Newton sat down to eat someone would hand him chopsticks. "Of course I could do nothing with them," Newton recalled, and so "the whole 500 seeing my awkwardness would burst out into loud laughter."[27]

To the Chinese miners, their neighbor must have looked a bit like an overgrown child fumbling with his food. Still, despite this momentary reversal of a dynamic in which white men disproportionately held the power and resources necessary to ensure survival in the diggings, more often Chinese men found it expedient to curry favor with whites. In a situation where white men missed more than anything "home comforts and home joys," Chinese men could turn such longings to their advantage. Howard Gardiner, for example, lived for a time by himself near a Chinese man. Sometimes Gardiner would stay late working on his claim, and when he went home, he recalled, "I found that the Celestial had preceded me and prepared supper." Gardiner's neighbor must have found some benefit in looking after the white man. Meanwhile, for Gardiner the arrangement seemed so unremarkable—so familiar—that he granted it only passing mention. In everyday events like these, where men of color performed tasks white men associated with white women, Gold Rush race relations became gender relations as well.[28]

Among some men in the diggings, such domestic practices were institutionalized. Timothy Osborn, a white man from Martha's Vineyard, lived in 1850 near a party headed by a Mississippi planter. The white planter brought four of his thirty black slaves with him from home, whom Osborn observed were "prompt in executing the commands of their master." Osborn, who did his own domestic work, remarked that the African American men "were very useful fellows about a camp . . . in cooking and keeping everything 'decently and in order.'" Northerners sometimes complained about slave labor in the mines, but, if Osborn's sentiments were at all common, the idea of having someone else prepare meals for white men and clean up around their camps had its appeal. After all, this was a culturally intelligible division of labor, even if back home it usually followed what were understood as lines of gender rather than race.[29]

Osborn did not stop to think why his black neighbors were so "prompt" in obeying their master—after all, California was admitted to the union as a "free" state as part of the Compromise of 1850. The New Englander later learned that at least one of the men had left behind a wife and children in Mississippi; this could have provided good motivation for helping the master achieve his goals as quickly as possible. Then, too, although four black men accompanied the planter to California, by the time the group left for home, only three joined the return party. Maybe one of the men had been able to buy his way out of bondage after a few months of diligent work in the diggings. This was a common occurrence in California, where the price of freedom was generally around a thousand dollars. Whatever motivated the African American men's behavior, Osborn himself could not help but look longingly at the services they provided.[30]

In still other camps, men who were not in hierarchical relationships with one another nevertheless chose divisions of labor that bore resemblance to the habits of home. When Perlot teamed up with Louvel, the Frenchman who gardened behind the cabin, the two came up with such an agreement. According to Perlot, Louvel had a "refined palate" and was a superb cook. So the men decided to forgo cooking in weekly rotations: "Louvel . . . consented to do it alone, on condition that I would go hunting every Sunday. He concocted the stew, I furnished the hare; each one found his satisfaction in this arrangement." In the long run, the plan had its costs. During the summer, both Louvel and Perlot spent their time digging a ditch for water to make it easier to wash gold-bearing dirt once the rains began. When they finished and found the skies still clear, Louvel grew restless. As Perlot recalled, Louvel "had nothing for distraction but his culinary occupations," while Perlot kept busy hunting. After weeks of inactivity, Louvel left to join a fellow countryman further north. Perlot was on his own for several months until he found a new partner, for whom he immediately prepared a welcoming feast. This partner was the fellow who was so taken by Perlot's succulent salads—so taken that the newcomer, like Louvel before him, agreed to take on cooking duties indefinitely. Perlot had a way with men.[31]

No doubt similar domestic arrangements existed elsewhere in the diggings. But most who could rely on someone to make all their meals by definition either lived in or near a boardinghouse, owned a slave, or had a wife. Thomas Thorne lived in the best of all possible Gold Rush worlds. An Anglo immigrant from Texas, Thorne came to the Southern Mines with both enslaved women and men *and* a white wife. Together Thorne's wife Mary and the enslaved Diana Caruthers and her daughters ran a boardinghouse that was renowned for delicacies such as buttermilk and fresh eggs. A few miners lived with the Thornes, while others took their meals at the cabin for a weekly fee. Neighbors like Charles Davis ate there only on occasion, as

Davis explained to his daughter: "here in California we can get . . . a great plenty of common food of every kind. . . . But no eggs, no Turkey, no Chickens no pies no doughnuts no pastry . . . unless we take a meal at Mrs. Thornes."[32]

Even when black labor helped to create such plenitude, white men associated domestic comfort largely with white women—in this case, with Mary Thorne. When Mary was ill, Davis acknowledged that there was "nobody except the Old darkey Woman & her two daughters to serve up for the boarders." But his preface of "nobody except" defined the presence of the Caruthers women as a sort of absence. Indeed, while white men might credit the usefulness of slaves for housework, it was white women's domestic abilities that most enthralled them. After eighteen months of cooking for himself, Lucius Fairchild, a future governor of Wisconsin, moved into a sturdy frame dwelling where one of the residents lived with a wife and child. The Vermont woman kept house for the men, and Fairchild was ecstatic: "You can't imagine," he wrote to his family, "how much more comfortable it is to have a good woman around." Or, as a similarly situated Anglo gold seeker put it, "A woman about a house produces a new order of things."[33]

It was not only family homes that triggered gendered and racialized imaginings. Roadside houses where white women cooked for travelers also proved good sites for conflating things culinary and things female. Consider how P. V. Fox described his stop at such an establishment: "Had beef steak, Pickled Salmon, Hash, Potatoes, Bread, biscuit, Griddle cakes & Sirrup, Tea & coffee. Pies & cakes, Peach sauce, and a chat with the land lady (The rarest dish)." It was indeed the case that meals at white women's boardinghouses were more elaborate than white miners' usual fare. In particular, where an Anglo woman served food, milk and eggs were sure to be found—not surprising, since cows and chickens had long been a special province of women in rural American divisions of labor. In California, the prospect of indulging in such items could take on the urgency of romance. On one occasion, Samuel Ward—brother of soon-to-be-famous Julia Ward Howe—was traveling to Stockton from the mines and hesitated to stop at a new wayside inn rather than the one kept by a male acquaintance on the Tuolumne River. But, he recalled, "a smiling hostess in the doorway and a tethered cow hard by tempted me." Then he completed the metaphor: "This infidelity to my friend, the landlord of the Tuolumne, was recompensed by the unusual luxury of eggs and milk, for which I felt an eager longing."[34]

As Ward's turn of phrase suggests, men's longings and men's loyalties could be confusing in California. Domestic concerns were somehow female (were they not?) and so it was only natural (was it not?) that men would prove inept at caring for themselves in the diggings. Often enough, such was the case. But for every case of scurvy, for every burnt loaf of bread, for every man who could not cook a decent meal for his partners, there were daily domestic triumphs in the diggings. When he first arrived in the mines, for example, Pennsylvanian Enos Christman complained that his flapjacks "always came out heavy doughy things" that no one could eat. But trial and error brought good results, as Christman proudly noted: "We can now get up some *fine dishes!*" What were men to make of the domestic contentment they found in the diggings? What did it mean when a New Englander sat down to his journal after a sumptuous trout dinner and wrote, "French cooks we consider are totally eclipsed and for the reestablishment of their reputation we . . . recommend a visit to our camp"?[35]

For English-speaking men to liken themselves to French cooks was no empty gesture. Anglo American and British immigrants seem to have considered exaggerated domesticity a national trait among French men. Englishman Frank Marryat was delighted to find a large French population in the town of Sonora, "for where Frenchmen are," he wrote, "a man can dine." Likewise, A. Hersey Dexter, who suffered through the hard winter of 1852–53, claimed he was saved by "the little French baker" next door who allowed neighboring miners a loaf of bread each day. Yet it was the traveler Borthwick who best elaborated this vision. Borthwick described a French dwelling in Calaveras County that bore resemblance to that of Perlot and Louvel—a "neat log cabin," behind which was a "small kitchen-garden in a high state of cultivation." Alongside stood a "diminutive fac-simile of the cabin itself," inhabited by a "knowing-looking little terrier-dog." Along with Dexter, Borthwick insisted on fashioning French men and things French as somehow dainty (small, little, diminutive)—echoing Borthwick's descriptions of Chinese men huddled around their "curious little black pots."[36]

But in French domestic lives Borthwick found nothing exotic—the cabin was neat; the garden was cultivated; even the dog had an intelligent face. Instead, Borthwick found among the French a magic ability to create a homelike atmosphere: "without really . . . taking more trouble than other men about their domestic arrangements, they did 'fix things up' with such a degree of taste . . . as to give the idea that their life of toil was mitigated by more than a usual share of ease and comfort."[37] The experience of Perlot and Louvel, of course, indicates that some French-speaking men were more inclined to "fix things up" than others. But the Anglo propensity for casting all French men as a sort of collective better half in the diggings is telling. More explicitly than back home, where gender could be mapped predictably onto bodies understood as male and female, gender in California chased shamelessly after racial and cultural markers of difference, heedless of bodily configurations.

California *was*, for many, a "world upside down." Lucius Fairchild, for example, worked for a time waiting tables and felt compelled to explain the situation to his family: "Now in the states you would think that a person . . . was broke if you saw him acting the part of *hired Girl*. . . . but here it is nothing, for all kinds of men do all kinds of work." Besides, he went on, "I can *bob around the table,* saying 'tea or Coffee Sir.' about as fast as most *hombres*." Though Fairchild insisted it meant nothing in California, his explanation suggested that it meant a great deal—white men bobbing around tables waiting on other white men. If he could act the part with such enthusiasm, did gender and race have less to do with bodies and essences than with performing tasks and gestures? No doubt Fairchild thought he could tell a "natural" hired girl from a "made-up" one. But the anxiety such situations produced could be striking.[38] Fairchild, for example, compared his own performance not to those of "real" women but to those of other "hombres"—as if the English word might not adequately insist upon his own essential manhood.

It was true that people who thought of themselves as "hombres" rather than "men" had less call to wait on or be waited on by other male gold seekers. Mexican men, as noted, arrived with their womenfolk more often than other Gold Rush immigrants. Mexican women did domestic work in California not just for husbands and brothers but often—at a price—for larger communities. Consider, for example, the party assembled in 1848 by Antonio Franco Coronel, a southern California ranchero. Coronel went to the diggings with four servants, two native men and two Sonorans, a woman and her husband, who were indebted to their *patrón* for the cost of the journey north. The Californio gave the woman a half-ounce of gold each day to buy provisions for the group. Of her own accord, she started preparing more food than her party could eat; the extra she sold. She charged a peso a plate for tortillas and frijoles, and eventually earned three or four ounces of gold (fifty dollars or more) per day.[39]

Likewise, in the town of Sonora, Mexican women made a magnificent display of their culinary talents, cooking in open-air kitchens huge quantities of wheat and corn tortillas to serve along with a *sopa* of meat cooked in chile sauce. William Perkins recalled that both Indian and Spanish Mexican women sold their wares in this manner, while native men who had once lived in Spanish missions passed through the weekend crowds carrying buckets of iced drinks on their heads and singing out "*agua fresca, agua fresca, quatro reales.*"[40] A few white women also sold food in quantity—one gold seeker met a woman from Oregon "who cooked and sold from early morn to dewy eve dried apple pies for $5.00 each." But nowhere did Anglos create the extensive commercial domestic world that Mexican women, along with Mission Indian men, set up on the streets of Sonora. It was a world that was reminiscent of Mexican cities where women supported themselves by hawking tortillas, tamales, and fresh produce. Even Hermosillo and Ures in northern

Mexico could not have produced as many willing customers for women's wares as the Gold Rush town of Sonora, however. There is no way to quantify how much gold dust passed from men's to women's hands in this domestic marketplace, but it must have been considerable.[41]

Still, as Fairchild's waitressing suggests, this commercial sphere included men who provided goods and services as well. Fairchild was not alone in serving his fellow (white) man, but more often men who did such work were not Anglo American. Helen Nye, the woman who lived at Don Pedro's Bar, was in a good position to keep track of the demand, in particular, for non-Anglo cooks. Her home was also a boardinghouse, but she did not prepare the meals. In letters to her mother and sisters, Nye explained her absence from the kitchen in a number of ways. Once she intimated that her husband had decided to hire a French cook, seemingly over her objections. On another occasion, she wrote that although she wanted to help out, "about all who hire as Cooks prefer to do the whole and have the regular price." In yet another letter, she complained that her cook Florentino had "left in a kind of sulky fit" and that his job landed in her hands. This, she wrote, "was too much as it kept me on my feet all the day."

The shifting ground of Nye's explanation suggests that she worried about what her female relatives might think of her circumstances. Still, the male cooks kept on coming. Florentino got over his fit and returned, and he was preceded and followed by others, including an African American man. And though Nye implied that her husband made hiring decisions, she once revealed her own hand in the process by writing to her sister, "I think I shall try a Chinese cook next they are generally liked." Nye's compulsion about explaining her relationship to domestic duties and her inconsistent descriptions indicate that novel divisions of labor could unsettle notions of womanliness as well as manliness. What *did* it mean for a white woman to turn over cooking to a French man, a black man, a Chinese man?[42]

It was confusing—the way that gender relations, race relations, and labor relations coursed into and out of customary channels in California, here carving gullies out of hard ground, there flowing in familiar waterways, whereby women waited on men, darker-skinned people served lighter-skinned people, and a few held control over the labor of many. Beyond food preparation, other kinds of domestic and personal service work became sites of confusion and contestation—especially laundry, sewing, and the care of convalescing men, activities that were often gendered female in immigrants' homelands.[43] Washing clothes, for example, was generally the province of individual miners in the diggings, but in more densely populated areas, women and men of color often took in laundry for a price of twenty-five to fifty cents per piece. White men's letters and diaries indicate that Mexican women, African American men, and, most especially, Chinese men all opened wash houses in the

Southern Mines. But however often white men scrubbed their own shirts or handed them over to people of color to wash, they were haunted by memories of white women who did this work back home. A bit of Gold Rush doggerel entitled "We Miss Thee, Ladies" called white men in California "a banished race," and lamented to "ladies" left behind:

> We miss thee at the washing tub,
> When our sore and blistered digits,
> Hath been compelled to weekly rub,
> Giving us blues, hysterics, figits.[44]

One of the more serious indications that life in the diggings did indeed give immigrant men "figits" about race and gender is the extent to which Gold Rush personal accounts, written primarily by Anglo Americans and Europeans, are filled with painstaking descriptions of native sexual divisions of labor. No other people's daily habits so interested white men, and no aspect of those habits proved so fascinating as the seemingly endless round of Miwok women's work. This was not a new fascination. For nearly three centuries, Europeans and then white Americans had commented on native divisions of labor, concluding that Indian women did most of the work while Indian men frittered away their time hunting and fishing. Historians have studied the actual differences between native and white divisions of labor that gave rise to such perceptions, as well as the ways in which such perceptions bolstered Euro-American ideologies of conquest. These elements infuse descriptions of California Indian practices as well.[45]

But Gold Rush accounts were written in a particular historical context—one where men far outnumbered women, where a stunningly diverse population inhabited a relatively small area, and where most turned their attention to an economic activity that offered potential (however seldom realized) for quick accumulation of capital. In this context, where differences based on maleness and femaleness, color and culture, and access to wealth and power were so pronounced and yet so unpredictable, curiosity about the habits of native peoples took on a special urgency. In particular, men who recently had assumed responsibility for much of their own domestic work now seemed preoccupied with how differently native women maintained themselves and their communities.

White men were especially interested in how Indian women procured and prepared acorns, perhaps the single most important food Miwoks ate. In 1852, for example, John Doble watched as a nearby Miwok encampment grew from three bark huts to four hundred in preparation for what he called "a big Fandango." As he approached the camp, he found a half-dozen Miwok women at work. Suddenly he realized why he had seen in the foothills so many flat stone outcrops filled with round indentations. It was on such surfaces that women sat pounding acorns with oblong rocks; the holes were created by the repeated impact of stone against stone. Once the acorns were hulled and ground, Doble observed, women leached the meal to remove the bitter-tasting tannic acid. Then they made it into bread or else boiled it, which involved dropping red-hot rocks into tightly woven baskets filled with water.[46]

Other men's descriptions of this process shared Doble's obsession with detail, an obsession matched rarely in Gold Rush personal accounts save in explanations of placer mining techniques. Even miners' own culinary efforts did not receive as much attention as those of native women. It was almost as if, in their diligent representations of the seemingly reproductive work of Miwok women and the seemingly productive work of mining men, diary and letter writers tried to reinscribe ideas about gender difference that life in the diggings had so easily unsettled. But ideas about gender difference were always already ideas about race difference, and Miwok women were not the "ladies" whose absence made white men fidget. Indeed, in California, difference piled upon difference until it was hard for Gold Rush participants to insist upon any one true order of things. After all, no one could deny that white miners also performed "reproductive" tasks. Nor could anyone deny that native women's customary chores were "productive"—or that Miwok women now panned for gold as well. Besides, there were few simple parallels between Indian women's labor and the Euro-American category of "domestic" work. Try as men might to remember the comfort of customary gender relations, discomfort and disorientation were far more common in the diggings. In response, immigrant men tried to make sense of what they saw by drawing on an older discourse that opposed native women's drudgery and native men's indolence.

It was a familiar refrain. French journalist Étienne Derbec knew the tune: "It is generally believed that the Indians live from the hunt; but, mon Dieu! they are too lazy." Derbec claimed that Indian women always struggled under heavy burdens—either baskets of seeds and nuts when out gathering or family provisions when traveling—while men carried only their bows and arrows. Enos Christman, watching Miwoks pass through Sonora, noted this too: "The women appeared to do all of the drudgery, having their baskets . . . well filled with meat." A more thoughtful diarist might have noted whose work produced the animal flesh the women carried.[47]

Friedrich Gerstäcker, a German traveler, assessed native divisions of labor differently. He acknowledged that a woman had to collect seeds, catch insects, cook meals, rear children, and bear heavy loads, while a man merely walked about "at his leisure with his light bow and arrow." But Gerstäcker thought he understood why: "though this seems unjust," he wrote, "it is necessary." He went on, "in a state of society where the lives of the family depend on the success of the hunter, he must have his arms free." Still, the seemingly contradictory impulse either to castigate native men for their sloth or to elevate their economic role to a position of dominance arose from a common, culturally specific concern about the meanings of manhood.[48]

This concern had its roots in the changing social and economic order that sent such letter, diary, and reminiscence writers off to California in the first place—one in which the transformation from a commercial to an industrial capitalism was accompanied by an increasing separation of home and workplace and by shifting distinctions between male and female spheres. White men who aspired to middle-class status were quickly caught up in this whirlwind of change, and the uncertainty of their own positions in the emerging economic system made the potential for quick riches in California all the more enticing.[49] What most found in the diggings was no short-cut to middle-class manhood, but rather a bewildering array of humanity that confounded whatever sense of a natural order of things they could find in mid-nineteenth-century Western Europe or eastern North America. They might try to reinscribe gender difference through ritual descriptions of Miwok women's "domestic" chores and their own "breadwinning" labor. But, in the selfsame gesture, that reinscription produced and reproduced race difference as well. Besides, the content of both immigrant and Indian lives in the diggings defied such easy oppositions.

Then, too, Miwok people talked back. Native women in particular looked with disbelief at how immigrant peoples organized their lives. Leonard Noyes, for example, recalled that an older Indian woman one day gave him "quite a Lecture on White Women working [too] little and Men [too] much." "She became very much excited and eloquant over it," Noyes remembered, "saying it was all wrong." In exchanges like these, Gold Rush contests over the meanings of gender and race—always close to the surface of everyday life—were articulated emphatically.[50]

And Miwok sexual divisions of labor were not unchanging; they were dynamic constructions that shifted according to the exigencies of local economies impinged upon by market forces. At times native people resisted the changes, continuing older practices to an extent that bewildered immigrant observers. As Timothy Osborn exclaimed, "so long as a fish or a squirrel can be found . . . they will not make any exertions towards supplying themselves with any of the luxuries so indispensable to the white man!" He watched as Miwok women gathered acorns, and wondered why they did so, "while with the same labor expended in mining they could realize gold enough to keep them supplied with flour and provisions for the entire winter!"[51]

Elsewhere, immigrants saw different strategies. Friedrich Gerstäcker noted, "the gold discovery has altered [Indians'] mode of life materially." On the one hand, he thought, "they have learned to want more necessaries," while on the other, "the means of subsistence diminishes." More and more, Miwoks supplemented customary ways of getting food with gold mining in order to buy nourishment. Perlot recalled that in 1854 he regularly saw Indian women traveling to immigrant towns in Tuolumne and Mariposa counties to purchase flour with gold they had dug. At Belt's Ferry on the Merced River, where Samuel Ward lived, Miwoks probably spent *more* time mining than they did gathering and hunting. Following an Indian-immigrant conflict in 1851 known as the Mariposa War, merchant George Belt received a federal license to trade with local Miwoks as well as a contract to furnish them with flour and beef in order to keep the peace. Ward watched over Belt's ferry and store, and got to know native people who felt their best chance for survival lay in setting up camp near an Indian trader. Mining, performed by both women and men, supplied the gold they used to buy goods at the store. Still, problems multiplied in the contract for provisions, and even goods for purchase failed to appear on the shelves. So Miwok women frequently fanned out in search of seeds and nuts, and Miwok men watched for salmon runs or headed down to the San Joaquin Valley to hunt for wild horses.[52]

The more things stayed the same, the more they changed. Miwok men watched for salmon, but found the fish had been waylaid by dams built downstream. Miwok women gathered, but just as their menfolk had added horse-raiding to hunting duties decades before, so might women now pan for gold as often as they collected acorns. White men looked for women to wash their clothes, but instead of wives or mothers, they found a mart for laundry dominated by Chinese men. White women, few in number, set up housekeeping in California, but learned that there were plenty of men for hire to help lighten the burdens of everyday life. African Americans who came to the mines enslaved worked as hard as ever, but found, too, that the Gold Rush opened up new possibilities for freedom. Mexican women sold tortillas on the street, just as they had in Sonoran towns and cities, but discovered that in California the market for their products seemed as if it could not be glutted. And Chilean, French, and Mexican men engaged in one more strategy to help themselves and their families out of precarious situations back home. Given racial and ethnic tensions in the mines and Anglo American efforts to assert dominance in California, some such men were not lucky enough to escape with their lives. If they did, though, they learned that mining the white miners—with their incomparable nostalgia for "home comforts and home joys" and their sense of entitlement to the same—was both safer and more lucrative than washing gold-bearing dirt.

Still, as often as Anglo men patronized a commercial domestic sphere peopled largely by non-Anglos, they also turned inward to create for themselves the comforts and joys of home. Some men reveled in what one man called the "fellow-feeling" that grew out of shared domestic tasks.[53] Many more bemoaned the absence of white women—for whom household chores increasingly were considered not only a responsibility but a natural vocation—and belittled their own, often manifest, abilities to sustain life.[54] Indeed, in the diggings, the process of idealizing the home and woman's place in it was uncomplicated by the day-to-day tensions of actual family households. Thus, gold or no gold, newly married Moses Little could write confidently that there were "riches far richer" back home with his "companion in Domestic Happiness." Benjamin Kendrick was similarly emphatic in his recommendation: "I would not advise a single person that has a comfortable home in New England to leave its comforts and pleasures for any place such as California with all its gold mines." But New Yorker A. W. Genung went farthest in giving the gold country's missing quality—domestic comfort—an explicit gender and, implicitly, a race. Acknowledging its advantageous physiography, fine climate, and economic potential, Genung nonetheless was adamant about California's chief deficiency: "The country cannot be a great country nor the people a happy people unblessed by woman's society and woman's love." The society of Miwok or Mexican women did not figure in Genung's equation; the woman whose love California lacked was white. For men such as these, the more things changed, the more things stayed the same.[55]

For many, then, the gold boom created what seemed an unnatural state of affairs—even so, a state of affairs to which they were ineluctably drawn. Benjamin Kendrick might not advise a single person to leave an eastern home, but he and thousands upon thousands of men did just that. While Gold Rush California was an unusual time and place, it was a time and place of its historical moment and geopolitical position. Thus New Englander Kendrick no less than Californio Antonio Franco Coronel and Belgian Jean-Nicolas Perlot felt compelled to risk the journey. The U.S. had just achieved continental breadth when gold was "discovered" in the Sierra Nevada foothills—that is, not just when someone saw it in a sawmill's tailrace, but when it took on meaning in an expanding nation and an imminent industrial capitalist world order. The representatives of this emerging order were busy sending tentacles out about the globe, linking peoples, places, and products to each other in their pursuit of wealth. In this world of commerce and now of industry, gold was money, or wealth, that could be turned with human labor and tools of manufacture into capital. Not all who rushed for gold were capitalists—far from it—but all had been touched by capitalism's dynamic tendencies. Some sought gold to create capital; others to ward off that dynamism and its habit of turning human energy into labor power.[56]

Those who sought gold, however, discovered much more than buried treasure. They discovered a world upside down. It was not just the white men who boasted about feather-light flapjacks, or the Mexican women who managed a domestic market, or the French men who tidied their tasteful cabins, or the Miwok women who panned for gold; it was a world turned by a spasmodic fiasco of meanings. As time went by in the Southern Mines, Anglo American men—and their womenfolk, who arrived in large numbers only after the initial boom—found more reliable ways to assert dominance in the diggings. As even more time went by, and as the Gold Rush passed into popular memory, Anglo Americans, and particularly Anglo American men, found ways to claim the event as a past that was entirely their own.[57] In so doing, they buried a past in which paroxysms of gender and race brought daily discomfort to participants, but also glimpses of whole new worlds of possibility. If we are to find in the Gold Rush a usable past at this present time, when changing relations of race and gender so bewilder those accustomed to power, we must dig deeply in the meanings as well as the structures of the "world upside down" that Edmund Booth described to his wife in 1850.[58] We must understand a time and place wherein white men wept when they thought about what they believed they had left behind.

Consider an episode Enos Christman recorded in his diary in 1852. One night, two Mexican women happened by a group of Anglo miners who were settling into their blankets at Cherokee Camp, near Sonora. The traveling musicians produced guitars and a tambourine, and the men set aside their bedding, listened to the serenade, and then got up to dance with each other. As the night wore on, the music's tempo slowed, until finally the women started strumming the chords of "Home, Sweet Home." They did not intone the lyrics; these women had watched Anglo miners long enough to know that the familiar tune alone would evoke the desired reaction. The men responded apace: "Suddenly a sob was heard, followed by another, and yet another, and tears flowed freely down the cheeks of the gold diggers." The musicians walked away, their tambourine filled with pieces of gold.[59]

Notes

1. Helen Nye to Mother, January 6, 1853, Helen Nye Letters, Beinecke Library, Yale University, New Haven, Connecticut; Charles Davis to Daughter, January 1, 1852, Charles Davis Letters, Beinecke Library. I use the term "immigrant" to refer to all newcomers in the Sierra Nevada foothills, including those from the eastern U.S.

2. For elaboration, see Susan Lee Johnson, "'The gold she gathered': Difference, Domination, and California's Southern Mines, 1848–1853" (Ph.D. diss., Yale University, 1993). See also Rodman Paul, *California Gold: The Beginning of Mining in the Far West* (1947; Lincoln: University of Nebraska Press, 1965), esp. pp. 91–115.

3. Edmund Booth, *Edmund Booth, Forty-Niner: The Life Story of a Deaf Pioneer* (Stockton, Calif.: San Joaquin Pioneer and Historical Society, 1953), p. 31.

4. Conceptually, I have been helped here by Denise Riley, *"Am I That Name?" Feminism and the Category of "Women" in History* (Minneapolis: University of Minnesota Press, 1988), esp. p. 6; and Evelyn Brooks Higginbotham, "African-American Women's History and the Metalanguage of Race," *Signs* 17, no. 2 (Winter 1992): 251–74, esp. 253–56.

5. Much of the important scholarship on this and related points is summarized and critiqued in Thomas C. Holt, "Marking: Race, Race-Making, and the Writing of History," *American Historical Review* 100, no. 1 (February 1995): 1–20. See esp. Barbara Jeanne Fields, "Race and Ideology in American History," in *Region, Race, and Reconstruction: Essays in Honor of C. Vann Woodward,* ed. J. Morgan Kousser and James M. McPherson (New York: Oxford University Press, 1982).

6. For years, the best overview of California mining has been Paul, *California Gold,* and of western mining more generally, Rodman Paul, *Mining Frontiers of the Far West, 1848–1880* (1963; Albuquerque: University of New Mexico Press, 1974). Just as this article was going to press, a wonderful new overview appeared: Malcolm J. Rohrbough, *Days of Gold: The California Gold Rush and the American Nation* (Berkeley: University of California Press, 1997). Scholarship on industrialized mining in the Far West has burgeoned of late, while work on placer mining has lagged behind. On hardrock mining, see, e.g., David M. Emmons, *The Butte Irish: Class and Ethnicity in an American Mining Town, 1875–1925* (Urbana: University of Illinois Press, 1989); A. Yvette Huginnie, "'Mexican Labor' in a 'White Man's Town': Race, Class, and Copper in Arizona, 1840–1925" (book manuscript, forthcoming); Elizabeth Jameson, *All That Glitters: Class, Culture, and Community in Cripple Creek* (Urbana: University of Illinois Press, forthcoming); Mary Murphy, *Mining Cultures: Men, Women, and Leisure in Butte, 1914–1941* (Urbana: University of Illinois Press, 1997). A work that will shed light on the impact of placer mining regionally is Elliot West, *Visions of Power: The Colorado Gold Rush and the Transformation of the Great Plains* (Lawrence: University Press of Kansas, forthcoming). On changes over time in class relations in California's Southern Mines, see Johnson, "'The gold she gathered,'" esp. pp. 382–412. I have elaborated on the assertions made therein in the book version of this study, which is forthcoming from W. W. Norton.

7. For a discussion of the meanings of "the social" in this historical context, see Susan Lee Johnson, "Bulls, Bears, and Dancing Boys: Race, Gender, and Leisure in the California Gold Rush," *Radical History Review* 60 (Fall 1994): 4–37.

8. The earliest scholarly work on the Gold Rush appeared in the 1880s: Charles Howard Shinn, *Mining Camps: A Study in American Frontier Government,* ed. Rodman Wilson Paul (1884; Gloucester, Mass.: Peter Smith, 1970); and Josiah Royce, *California from the Conquest in 1846 to the Second Vigilance Committee in San Francisco, A Study of American Character* (1886; Santa Barbara, Calif.: Peregrine, 1970). Shinn's was a happy account of the special genius of Anglo-Saxons for self-government. Royce took a darker view, indicting Gold Rush participants for their "social irresponsibility" and their "diseased local exaggeration of [Americans'] common national feeling toward foreigners." The 1940s brought two more key publications—Paul, *California Gold;* and John Walton Caughey, *The California Gold Rush* [formerly *Gold Is the Cornerstone*] (1948; Berkeley: University of California Press, 1975)—of which Paul's proved most enduring. Paul, too, rejected Shinn's notion of "race-instinct," and saw the managerial talents of white miners as something that developed over time, particularly as placer mining gave way to hydraulic and quartz mining. Starting in the 1960s, another group of historians began to situate the Gold Rush in larger narratives of racial domination, racial resistance, and race- and class-making in California, thereby centering the experiences of ethnic Mexicans, native peoples, Chinese immigrants,

and African Americans in stories of mining and community formation that had long represented them as marginal characters: see Leonard Pitt, *The Decline of the Californios: A Social History of the Spanish-Speaking Californians, 1846–1890* (Berkeley: University of California Press, 1966); Alexander Saxton, *The Indispensable Enemy: Labor and the Anti-Chinese Movement in California* (Berkeley: University of California Press, 1971); Rudolph M. Lapp, *Blacks in Gold Rush California* (New Haven, Conn.: Yale University Press, 1977); Albert L. Hurtado, *Indian Survival on the California Frontier* (New Haven, Conn.: Yale University Press, 1988); Ronald Takaki, *Strangers from a Different Shore: A History of Asian Americans* (Boston: Little, Brown, 1989); Sucheng Chan, *Asian Americans: An Interpretive History* (Boston: Twayne, 1991); Tomás Almaguer, *Racial Fault Lines: The Historical Origins of White Supremacy in California* (Berkeley: University of California Press, 1994). The classic "new social history" of the Gold Rush is Ralph Mann's study of two towns in the Northern Mines: *After the Gold Rush: Society in Grass Valley and Nevada City, California, 1849–1870* (Stanford, Calif.: Stanford University Press, 1982). For Mann, the absence of women, the abundance of foreign-born peoples, and the emergence of clear class hierarchies come to life in the analysis of quantifiable data. Mann demonstrates the process by which Nevada City became a center of Anglo-American commerce and county government, while Grass Valley became a community of working-class Cornish and Irish miners. For a more recent account of social and religious themes in the Gold Rush period, see Laurie F. Maffly-Kipp, *Religion and Society in Frontier California* (New Haven, Conn.: Yale University Press, 1994). Along with Rohrbough, *Days of Gold,* the most important new work on the Gold Rush to appear in over a decade is David Goodman, *Gold Seeking: Victoria and California in the 1850s* (Stanford, Calif.: Stanford University Press, 1994). Goodman's is a history of ideas about wealth, republicanism, order, agrarianism, the pastoral, domesticity, and excitement, and the ways in which those ideas helped people make sense of their participation in the Australian and American gold rushes.

9. See Johnson, "'The gold she gathered,'" esp. chap. 3, for full consideration of these and other "domestic" tasks, including laundry, sewing, and care of the sick. For a trenchant analysis of related themes among cowboys, see Blake Allmendinger, *The Cowboy: Representations of Labor in an American Work Culture* (New York: Oxford University Press, 1992), esp. pp. 50–59. For helpful, but different, accounts of "domestic" concerns in Gold Rush California, see Goodman, esp. pp. 149–87, and Maffly-Kipp, esp. pp. 148–80, both of whom emphasize gender over race and ethnicity in their analyses of "domesticity."

10. Analyses of productive vs. reproductive labor particularly characterized Marxist-feminist thought of the 1970s and 1980s. A culminating explication and critique appears in Joan Kelly, "The Doubled Vision of Feminist Theory," in *Women, History and Theory* (Chicago: University of Chicago Press, 1984). See also the essays collected in Zillah Eisenstein, ed., *Capitalist Patriarchy and the Case for Socialist Feminism* (New York: Monthly Review Press, 1979); and Heidi Hartmann, "The Family as the Locus of Gender, Class, and Political Struggle: The Example of Housework," *Signs* 6, no. 3 (Spring 1981): 366–94.

11. See Evelyn Nakano Glenn, "From Servitude to Service Work: Historical Continuities in the Racial Division of Paid Reproductive Labor," *Signs* 18, no. 1 (Fall 1992): 1–43; and Joan Scott, "Deconstructing Equality-versus-Difference: Or, the

Uses of Poststructuralist Theory for Feminism," *Feminist Studies* 14, no. 1 (Spring 1988): 33–50.

12. J. D. Borthwick, *The Gold Hunters* (1857; Oyster Bay, N.Y.: Nelson Doubleday, 1917), p. 252, and see pp. 143, 302; Jean-Nicolas Perlot, *Gold Seeker: Adventures of a Belgian Argonaut during the Gold Rush Years,* trans. Helen Harding Bretnor, ed. Howard R. Lamar (New Haven, Conn.: Yale University Press, 1985), pp. 100–101, 153; Journal entry, December 18, 1852, Angus McIsaac Journal, Beinecke Library.

13. Journal entry, December 18, 1852, McIsaac Journal; Jesse R. Smith to Sister Helen, December 23, 1852, Lura and Jesse R. Smith Correspondence, Huntington Library, San Marino, California.

14. William Perkins, *Three Years in California: William Perkins' Journal of Life at Sonora, 1849–1852,* ed. Dale L. Morgan and James R. Scobie (Berkeley: University of California Press, 1964), pp. 101, 103. On Orientalism, see Edward W. Said, *Orientalism* (New York: Pantheon, 1978).

15. These generalizations are based on wide reading in Gold Rush personal accounts that describe household organization; an adequate citation of the evidence would run several pages. But see, e.g., Moses F. Little Journals, Beinecke Library, items 12 and 14, passim; John Amos Chaffee and Jason Palmer Chamberlain Papers, Bancroft Library, University of California, Berkeley, Chamberlain Journals 1 and 2, passim; Alfred Doten, *The Journals of Alfred Doten, 1849–1903,* 3 vols., ed. Walter Van Tilburg Clark (Reno: University of Nevada Press, 1973), 1: 91–250, passim; Perlot, pp. 89–292, passim. Secondary accounts that address such issues include Paul, *California Gold,* pp. 72–73; Caughey, pp. 177–201; Mann, p. 17. While I have not undertaken a full statistical analysis of the 1850 census, even a spot check through the microfilm reels for Calaveras, Tuolumne, and Mariposa counties supports my contentions about household size. See U.S. Bureau of the Census, Seventh Federal Population Census, 1850, National Archives and Records Service, RG-29, N. 432, reels 33, 35, 36 [hereafter cited as 1850 Census].

16. See, e.g., John Doble, *John Doble's Journal and Letters from the Mines: Mokelumne Hill, Jackson, Volcano and San Francisco, 1851–1865,* ed. Charles L. Camp (Denver: Old West Publishing, 1962), pp. 38–39, 58; Doten, 1: 115–27 (Doten kept a store in Calaveras County, and these pages record the patronage of Chinese, Mexicans, and Chileans); Helen Nye to Mother, January 6, 1853, Nye Letters (Nye's husband was a merchant at Don Pedro's Bar in Tuolumne County); Account book entries, 1852–53, Little Journals, item 13; Charles Davis to Daughter, January 5 [1852], Davis Letters; Perlot, pp. 153, 154, 159–60; Howard C. Gardiner, *In Pursuit of the Golden Dream: Reminiscences of San Francisco and the Northern and Southern Mines, 1849–1857,* ed. Dale L. Morgan (Stoughton, Mass.: Western Hemisphere, 1970), pp. 95, 107, 164–65.

17. Perlot, pp. 56–57; cf. George W. B. Evans, *Mexican Gold Rush Trail: The Journal of a Forty-Niner,* ed. Glenn S. Dumke (San Marino, Calif.: Huntington Library, 1945), p. 200. Gardiner, p. 95; cf. Perkins, p. 106.

18. Vicente Pérez Rosales, "Diary of a Journey to California," in *We Were 49ers! Chilean Accounts of the California Gold Rush,* trans. and ed. Edwin A. Beilharz and Carlos U. López (Pasadena, Calif.: Ward Ritchie Press, 1976), pp. 3–99, esp. 70–77. This event actually took place in Sacramento, entrepôt for the Northern Mines and some camps in the northern part of the Southern Mines.

19. See, e.g., Journal entries, October 20, November 15, and December 19, 1852, Little Journals, item 12; Perlot, pp. 155–60; A. Hersey Dexter, *Early Days in California* (Denver: Tribune-Republican Press, 1886), pp. 20–26.

20. Journal entries, December 21, 24, and 25, 1852, Little Journals, item 12; Journal entries, November 25 and 27, 1851, Timothy C. Osborn Journal, Bancroft Library; Journal entries, October 13–December 25, 1849, passim, William W. Miller Journal, Beinecke Library; Perlot, p. 272.

21. Perlot, p. 272. And see Journal entry, November 26, 1849, Miller Journal; Doten, 1: 85, 147–48, 151; Doble, p. 94.

22. On Miwok women's gathering, see Richard Levy, "Eastern Miwok," in *Handbook of North American Indians,* vol. 8, *California,* ed. Robert F. Heizer (Washington, D.C.: Smithsonian Institution, 1978), pp. 398–413, esp. 402–05.

23. Evans, pp. 260–61. Cf. Perkins, p. 262; Borthwick, p. 57; Doble, p. 58; Journal entries, August 12–24, 1851, Chamberlain Journal no. 1; Benjamin Butler Harris, *The Gila Trial: The Texas Argonauts and the California Gold Rush,* ed. Richard H. Dillon (Norman: University of Oklahoma Press, 1960), p. 123 (on scurvy among Mexican miners); Étienne Derbec, *A French Journalist in the California Gold Rush: The Letters of Étienne Derbec* (Georgetown, Calif.: Talisman Press, 1964), pp. 121–22, 40–41.

24. Perlot, p. 260; Doble, p. 245. See also Journal entries, August 24 and September 6, 1852, Little Journals, item 12.

25. Journal entries, October 24, November 22 and 24, 1852, Little Journals, item 12; Journal entries, December 22 and 30, 1849, January 1, 4, and 5, 1850, Miller Journal. And see Journal entries, July 14, 1850, January 12 and February 9, 1851, George W. Allen Journals, Beinecke Library.

26. Borthwick, pp. 255–56, 302–03.

27. John Marshall Newton, *Memoirs of John Marshall Newton* (n.p.: John M. Stevenson, 1913), pp. 48–50.

28. Gardiner, p. 166. Although Gardiner spent most of his time in the Southern Mines, this actually took place in the Northern Mines.

29. Journal entries, July 26 and August 23, 1850, Osborn Journal. See also Josiah Foster Flagg to Mother, March 9, 1851, Josiah Foster Flagg Letters, Beinecke Library.

30. Journal entries, July 26 and August 23, 1850, Osborn Journal. For background on slavery in the diggings, see Lapp, esp. pp. 64–77; Johnson, "'The gold she gathered,'" chaps. 2 and 5.

31. Perlot, pp. 258–71, esp. 259–60, 271.

32. Census 1850, reel 35; Samuel Ward, *Sam Ward in the Gold Rush,* ed. Carvel Collins (Stanford, Calif.: Stanford University Press, 1949), pp. 28, 149–52, 167; Charles Davis to Daughter, January 5 [1852], and January 6, 1854, Davis Letters.

33. Charles Davis to Daughter, January 5 [1852], and January 6, 1854, Davis Letters; Lucius Fairchild, *California Letters of Lucius Fairchild,* ed. Joseph Schafer (Madison: State Historical Society of Wisconsin, 1931), pp. 48, 63; Enos Christman, *One Man's Gold: The Letters and Journal of a Forty-Niner,* ed. Florence Morrow Christman (New York: Whittlesey House, McGraw-Hill, 1930), esp. p. 187.

34. Journal entry, April 18, 1852, P. V. Fox Journals, Beinecke Library; Ward, p. 168 (Julia Ward Howe would become a prominent participant in the U.S. wom-

en's movement and the author of "Battle Hymn of the Republic"). See also Journal entry, July 3, 1850, Osborn Journal; Journal entry, March 30, 1851, Allen Journals; Mrs. Lee Whipple-Haslam, *Early Days in California: Scenes and Events of the '50s as I Remember Them* (Jamestown, Calif.: Mother Lode Magnet [c. 1924]), p. 11. On women in dairy and poultry production, see, e.g., Joan M. Jensen, *Loosening the Bonds: Mid-Atlantic Farm Women, 1750–1850* (New Haven, Conn.: Yale University Press, 1986), and "Cloth, Butter and Boarders: Women's Household Production for the Market," *Review of Radical Political Economics* 12, no. 2 (Summer 1980): 14–24; John Mack Faragher, *Women and Men on the Overland Trail* (New Haven, Conn.: Yale University Press, 1979), esp. p. 51, and *Sugar Creek: Life on the Illinois Prairie* (New Haven, Conn.: Yale University Press, 1986), esp. pp. 101–05.

35. On domestic failures, see, e.g., Journal entry, December 22, 1849, Miller Journal; Doble, p. 54. For the triumphs, see Christman, p. 126; Journal entry, July 12, 1850, Osborn Journal.

36. Frank Marryat, *Mountains and Molehills; or, Recollections of a Burnt Journal* (1855; Philadelphia: J. B. Lippincott, 1962), p. 136; Dexter, pp. 23–24; Borthwick, pp. 342–44.

37. Borthwick, pp. 342–44.

38. Fairchild, p. 139. On gender as performative, see Judith Butler, *Gender Trouble: Feminism and the Subversion of Identity* (New York: Routledge, 1990), esp. pp. 24–25, 33, 134–41, and *Bodies That Matter: On the Discursive Limits of "Sex"* (New York: Routledge, 1993), esp. pp. 1–23, 223–42.

39. Antonio Franco Coronel, "Cosas de California," trans. and ed. Richard Henry Morefield, in *The Mexican Adaptation in American California, 1846–1875* (1955; San Francisco: R & E Research Associates, 1971), pp. 76–96, esp. 93–94. And see Derbec, p. 128. Coronel may have exaggerated his cook's profits, but even if he doubled the amount she took in each day, her earnings would have been greater than those of the average miner in 1848. See "Appendix B: Wages in the California Gold Mines," in Paul, *California Gold,* pp. 349–50.

40. Perkins, pp. 105–06.

41. Harris, p. 124; Silvia Marina Arrom, *The Women of Mexico City, 1790–1857* (Stanford, Calif.: Stanford University Press, 1985), pp. 158–59, 192–93.

42. Helen Nye to Sister Mary, December 26, 1852, February 8 and March 14, 1853, May 20, 1855, Nye Letters.

43. For elaboration, see Johnson, "'The gold she gathered,'" pp. 179–96.

44. Doble, p. 58; Derbec, p. 142; Christman, p. 132; Gardiner, pp. 69, 188–89; Perkins, pp. 157–58; Friedrich W. C. Gerstäcker, *Narrative of a Journey Around the World* (New York: Harper and Row, 1853), p. 225; Borthwick, pp. 82, 361. On Chinese laundry workers, see Takaki, pp. 92–94; Paul Ong, "An Ethnic Trade: The Chinese Laundries in Early California," *Journal of Ethnic Studies* 8, no. 4 (Winter 1981): 95–113. For the poem, see "The Miners' Lamentations," California Lettersheet Facsimiles, Huntington Library.

45. See, e.g., William Cronon, *Changes in the Land: Indians, Colonists, and the Ecology of New England* (New York: Hill and Wang, 1983), pp. 52–58, 92; Glenda Riley, *Women and Indians on the Frontier, 1825–1915* (Albuquerque: University of New Mexico Press, 1984), esp. pp. 76–81.

46. Doble, pp. 42–50. See also Journal entries, November 16 and 17, 1852, Little Journals, item 12; Ward, p. 136; Derbec, pp. 154–56; Gerstäcker, pp. 210–11; Doten, 1: 212.

47. Derbec, p. 155; Christman, p. 180.

48. Gerstäcker, p. 217

49. See, e.g., Mary Ryan, *Cradle of the Middle Class: The Family in Oneida County, New York, 1790–1865* (Cambridge: Cambridge University Press, 1981); Charles E. Rosenberg, "Sexuality, Class, and Role in Nineteenth-Century America," *American Quarterly* 35 (May 1973): 131–53; E. Anthony Rotundo, *American Manhood: Transformations in Masculinity from the Revolution to the Modern Era* (New York: Basic Books, 1993); Mark C. Carnes and Clyde Griffen, eds., *Meanings for Manhood: Constructions of Masculinity in Victorian America* (Chicago: University of Chicago Press, 1990); J. A. Mangan and James Walvin, eds., *Manliness and Morality: Middle-Class Masculinity in Britain and America, 1800–1940* (Manchester: Manchester University Press, 1987).

50. Leonard Withington Noyes Reminiscences, Essex Institute, Salem, Massachusetts, transcription at Calaveras County Museum and Archives, San Andreas, California, p. 75.

51. Journal entry, October 20, 1849, Osborn Journal.

52. Gerstäcker, pp. 217–18; Perlot, p. 181; Ward, pp. 51–52, 111, 125, 126–27, 136–37. On the Mariposa War, see Johnson, "'The gold she gathered,'" chap. 5.

53. William McCollum, *California As I Saw It. Pencillings by the Way of Its Gold and Gold Diggers. And Incidents of Travel by Land and Water,* ed. Dale L. Morgan (1850; Los Gatos, Calif.: Talisman Press, 1960), pp. 160–61. Cf. Harris, pp. 113, 123, 132–34, 136.

54. On vocational domesticity, see, e.g., Nancy F. Cott, *The Bonds of Womanhood: "Woman's Sphere" in New England, 1780–1835* (New Haven, Conn.: Yale University Press, 1977), esp. p. 74. Catharine Beecher popularized the idea in her *Treatise on Domestic Economy* (1841), which was in its ninth printing at the time of the Gold Rush; see Kathryn Kish Sklar, *Catharine Beecher: A Study in American Domesticity* (New York: W. W. Norton, 1976), pp. 151–67.

55. Journal entry, August 31, 1852, Little Journals, item 12; Benjamin Kendrick to Father, September 25, 1849, Benjamin Franklin Kendrick Letters, Beinecke Library; A. W. Genung to Mr. and Mrs. Thomas, February 14, 1852, A. W. Genung Letters, Beinecke Library.

56. For elaboration of these themes, see Johnson, "'The gold she gathered,'" chap. 2.

57. For discussion of collective memory of the Gold Rush, see ibid., chap. 1 and Epilogue; and Susan Lee Johnson, "History, Memory, and the California Gold Rush," paper presented at the Power of Ethnic Identities in the Southwest Conference, Huntington Library, San Marino, California, September 23, 1994, and the American Historical Association Annual Meeting, Chicago, January 8, 1995.

58. I completed this essay at the historical moment (during the summer of 1995) when affirmative action policies came under unprecedented attack across the U.S., but especially in the State of California.

59. Christman, pp. 204–05.

7

MAKING MEN IN THE WEST

The Coming of Age of Miles Cavanaugh and Martin Frank Dunham

MARY MURPHY

The field of western women's history began as a response to the fact that the majority of academic and popular histories of the North American West portrayed an overwhelmingly masculine world—a world in which Anglo-American men blazed trails, fought Indians, trapped beaver, herded cattle, plowed fields, drank, gambled, and whored. Then—if they survived all that—they settled down with good women and fathered a bunch of native westerners. Susan Armitage aptly called this approach narrating the history of "Hisland."[1] Over the past two decades, historians of women have sought to revise that portrayal, first by peopling Hisland with women, then by rewriting western history as it would have been seen through women's eyes, creating a complementary "Herland." The most recent wave of women's history uses gender as a category of analysis, rather than a topic of study, a shift beyond work that conflates the term "gender" with women. But if we truly want to employ gender as a category of analysis, then we need to examine categories of both female and male and the ways in which ideal systems of womanhood and manhood influenced the beliefs and actions of women and men. In other words, we need to begin writing the history of the West as a history of "Theirland."[2]

We know what the gender ideal for white, middle-class, Anglo-American womanhood was in Victorian North America: the prescriptions laid down by ministers, reformers, and *Godey's Lady's Book,* encapsulated in the "cult of true womanhood." We also know a good deal about how women lived according to those ideals—or deviated from them—through hundreds of examinations of women's lives in every region of the country. The construction of womanhood revolved around women's relationships to men—as daughters, sisters, wives, mothers. However, we know little of what men thought manhood should be or what ordinary fathers, husbands, sons, and brothers thought about women. As Anthony Rotundo has pointed out, "Nearly everything we know about human behavior in the past concerns men and yet it is equally—and ironically—true that we know far more about womanhood and the female role than we know about masculinity or the man's role."[3] For instance, did men really believe in the cult of true womanhood? Did men think about women as "good" or "bad"? If so, what kinds of relationships did they want with each? And how did they reconcile them? What exactly did a man want in a wife? And what did he think a husband was supposed to be? How did a good father behave? Within the boundaries of the gender system of North America's dominant culture in the late nineteenth and early twentieth centuries, how did men themselves define manliness, and what role did their relationships with women have in shaping that definition? To paraphrase Ava Baron, *knowing* that gender, race, and ethnicity matter tells us little about *how* the categories of gender, race, or ethnicity develop, change, or operate in society. What we need to do is to historicize those concepts in our particular studies.[4]

This essay offers a preliminary exploration of these questions through the lives of two men, Miles J. Cavanaugh, Jr., and Martin Frank Dunham, one born in the West, the other an immigrant to it. Cavanaugh and Dunham left behind intriguing, sometimes frustrating documents that reveal glimpses of what they thought about women, about coming of age, about what being a man in the West meant. Martin Frank Dunham journeyed to Edmonton, Alberta, in 1908, corresponding regularly with his fiancee, Edith Sander, in Berlin, Ontario. Dunham's letters cover the news, hopes, and disappointments of three and a half years. He kept writing because he kept postponing the wedding. He hadn't yet proved himself; he hadn't made his fortune in the great western land of opportunity; he wasn't yet man enough to take a wife. He was sure Edith would understand. Miles J. Cavanaugh, Jr., a Montana pioneer, lawyer, legislator, and poet, wrote an autobiographical essay shortly before his death in 1935, which recounts his life from childhood to his early twenties. The bulk of the document deals with three years Cavanaugh spent in a Montana mining camp. He was a naive eighteen-year-old youth when he arrived, an experienced twenty-one-year-old man when he left. His account is fondly sentimental, dominated by romantic and sexual escapades, and shaped by the conventions of western storytelling with which he was familiar. These documents present the voices of two men informing us about their coming of age, their first jobs, their first serious courtships, and, in one case, his first experience with sex.[5]

Miles J. Cavanaugh, Jr., was born in Denver in 1865 while his father sought his fortune in Montana's first gold rush at Alder Gulch. Cavanaugh Sr. returned to Denver to claim his son and wife and brought them to Montana in 1866. A victim of wanderlust, Cavanaugh kept the family moving in search of his main chance. At one point the Cavanaughs settled in Butte long enough for Miles to complete school in 1882 as a member of Butte High School's first graduating class of three.[6]

The following year, at the age of eighteen, Miles accompanied his father to the Comet mine near Wickes, Montana, thirty-five miles northeast of Butte. He worked as a hoisting engineer and bookkeeper and lived with other single men in the town's boardinghouse. When the new schoolteacher, Isabelle, arrived, Miles "was immediately smitten" and sought to monopolize her company. He became Isabelle's regular escort at all dances and community social events, and took her riding and walking. Miles, however, did not spend all his free time with the schoolteacher, for he had also discovered, in back of the cluster of town residences, "a four roomed frame house, comfortably tho not elaborately furnished, with a seeming surplus of bedrooms." The house was owned by a saloonkeeper and occupied by a quiet, comely brunette of about twenty-four years known only as Nellie.[7]

Late one summer night Miles "stealthly" paid a call on Nellie. During previous conversations in the saloon he had been struck by her intelligence. This night she told him of her past tainted by an early marriage "to a man who had abused and afterwards deserted her, of her vain struggle with life in the city, and of drifting later into her present way of life." Miles was infused with sympathy, "and somehow, tho I never sensed just how and why it happened we repaired to her bedroom and retired. For the first time in my life I became conscious of the warmth and softness of a womans body in contact with my own. This new experience with its delirious sensation and subsequent languorous relaxation left nothing to be desired, and when just before dawn, I left for my own sleeping room my mind and body were filled with wonderment at this new phase of life that had been opened to me."[8]

Miles visited Nellie on other occasions, "but never again did I experience the wild joy, the inexplicable delight of that new and entirely strange biological experiment." During this entire period, Miles continued to court Isabelle, to take her riding and for moonlight walks, never hinting of his dalliance with Nellie, nor seemingly moved to engage in similar activity with his schoolteacher sweetheart. In fact, "never a kiss nor caress was exchanged between us to excite desire. I just adored her. I never thot of her as a woman in the sense that Nellie was."[9]

As two other stories from the autobiography demonstrate, Miles was not as innocent as his recollections of Nellie imply. In describing the social entertainments of the camp, for example, he recalled one masqued ball, during which he had assumed "the guise of an elegantly, if scantily attired young lady," a costume he procured from a traveling prostitute who regularly visited the camp around paydays. When he left the dance intending to cross the street for a drink at the saloon, he was followed by an eager male admirer. Determined not to betray his masquerade, he tried to elude his suitor by weaving through the town, but finally, too chilled to continue, he sought refuge in his own house, thus starting the rumor mills grinding. His pursuer returned to the dance and reported "that he had run the painted lady to cover" in Cavanaugh's sleeping apartment, and, as Miles wrote, "another scandal was started on swiftly widening waves among the prudes of the village."[10]

A page or two later Miles related another incident of sexual pursuit, this in the genre of western tall-tale telling. A prospector returned to camp and released his three burros, including a female named Jennie. Shortly thereafter another miner arrived in camp and unloaded his weary male burro. Burro pheromones took over: although tired and hungry, the new arrival "no sooner saw Jennie loitering near, than in his mind thoughts of rest and food were displaced by visions of sexual conquest, and to effect his purpose he unsheathed a very formidable weapon for the attack." Miss Jennie was not interested, and she, too, led her suitor on a race through the camp, at one point into the kitchen of the local boardinghouse. By this time, the chase of asses had drawn quite a crowd, including "many timid housewives peer[ing] thru curtained windows to witness the deflorations of virginity." Jennie finally leapt onto the roof of a dugout, but alas was trapped, and there "in the presence of the interested spectators his fell purpose was accomplished while tears streamed from poor Jennie's eyes." The lesson to be drawn from this incident, Miles concluded, was "that ultimate success depends on ruthless persistent aggressiveness."[11]

In yet another tale of sexual derring-do, Miles again acted as the object of desire, in a play scripted by his father. Cavanaugh Sr. had been in Bannack developing a gold mine and boarding with its owners, Mr. Sheehan, a seventy-four-year-old gentleman and his wife, a blond beauty of twenty-five. Sensing that the May-December match might not last, Cavanaugh Sr. sought to insinuate his son into Mrs. Sheehan's good graces and arranged to have Miles visit. While Cavanaugh occupied Mr. Sheehan with the mine, Mrs. Sheehan became quite taken with Miles, who "was twenty now, and strong healthy and not repulsive in looks or manners and of a very sensitive and sympathetic disposition." One morning while he was in the library, she appeared and suddenly asked, "'Do you mind if I kiss you?'" He replied, "'I should say not' whereupon she gave me such a kiss as almost took my breath." Miles claimed to be terrified and as soon as he could, he returned to Comet and his chaste, "adored Isabelle." Mrs. Sheehan later reappeared in the narrative as a rich divorcee, but having been rejected by Miles, she in turn scorned him.[12]

Late in 1886 the mine at Comet began to fail and the camp to disband. Miles went on to study law. And what of Isabelle and Nellie? In one sentence Miles reported that Isabelle married a miner and moved to a distant camp. Nellie, in the fashion of hundreds of western prostitutes, simply disappeared.

The young Miles Cavanaugh was confused about women and what to do with them. His stories about himself reveal a search for the appropriate role he should play in the quest for romance and sex. Should he hunt the objects of his desire with "ruthless persistent aggressiveness"? Should *he* become the object of pursuit? Could he steer some middle course? When chased, he retreated in terror, and unlike poor Jennie, escaped inviolate except for one kiss. When he wooed ardently it was without eroticism; his courtship of Isabelle was on an ethereal plane. The result seemed to be that she married someone else. His liaisons with Nellie were hardly the result of an aggressive campaign. Miles wants us to believe that it was an almost unconscious, accidental course that brought him to the prostitute's bed.

Miles Cavanaugh liked all the women he wrote about. Nevertheless, he sorted them and his relationships with them into categories shaped by late Victorian sexual ideology, which limited his ability to respond to any of them as a full human being who combined the intellectual, spiritual, and erotic. Isabelle was the lady: pious, pure, educated. She came to the mining camp as the symbol and instrument of civilization. Isabelle was Molly Wood to Miles's Virginian. Nellie was the whore with the heart of gold. Mrs. Sheehan became the dramatized version of the gold digger and western divorcee, a relatively unexplored stereotype of western women. She is the woman who comes west not as a bearer of civilization and not as a prostitute, but as a person looking for her main chance. As we will see in the examination of Frank Dunham, such women made men very uncomfortable.[13] Miles Cavanaugh's autobiography reveals his affection for women and his delight in their company, but he portrays them as virtual caricatures. None possesses the complex personality of an interesting person nor the many-hued emotional palette of fears, desires, and curiosity that Miles himself did.

Martin Frank Dunham was nearly twenty years older than Cavanaugh and an immigrant to the West, yet the two had much in common. Born in Ontario in 1882 into a family of devout farmers, Frank signed the pledge not to drink or smoke at the age of eighteen, and as a young man in Edmonton he occasionally felt hampered by his inability to dance. Nevertheless, his religious upbringing brought him comfort and imbued him with a strong sense of morality. Although he irregularly attended church in Edmonton and later Camrose, he enjoyed himself at Methodist socials which echoed his life in Ontario. In the West, however, he broke his pledge, regularly smoking cigars and occasionally taking a drink.[14]

Frank apparently had no desire to be a farmer. He attended Normal School, for two years taught in Berlin (the town name was changed to Kitchener during World War I), and in 1904 was accepted at the University of Toronto. In order to earn money for school he spent two summers in England selling stereoscopic views. In 1904 he also met Edith Lillian Sander, daughter of Solomon Sander, a successful Berlin merchant. They began corresponding when Frank went to England in the summer of 1904. In 1907 Frank graduated from the university and started work as a reporter for the *Toronto Daily Star.* A year later he headed west having accepted a job on the *Edmonton Bulletin,* founded by Frank Oliver to promote regional agriculture. In route he stopped in Chicago where Edith was studying music and painting and presented her with an engagement ring.

Frank was twenty-six when he arrived in Edmonton, and ready to take advantage of any opportunities the West offered him. Edmonton was a bustling prairie city. Originating as a Hudson's Bay Company fort, Edmonton had boomed as a launching point for the Klondike gold rush in 1897–98. In 1906 Edmonton became the capital of the recently formed province of Alberta. By 1908 the city had over eighteen thousand residents and Strathcona, the community situated on the bluffs across the North Saskatchewan River, another forty-five hundred. It was a market city, with grain elevators, flour mills, lumber- and brickyards, a pork packing plant, and the commercial businesses necessary to support a regional economy of coal mining and agriculture.[15]

Frank Dunham was an unadulterated optimist. On his first day in Edmonton he wrote to Edith that he was "simply delighted with the West. To come out here is the best move I ever made and after being here only one day I can almost say that I never want to live East again." For all the time he remained in the West he never changed that point of view. Time after time, he told Edith that the West was a land of opportunity, a great country, a place where an ambitious and hard-working man could make his fortune: "The longer I live out West the more hope I have in this country and the brighter I see my chances for success. I have some big schemes in my mind at the present time, which I must not mention further, but which will mean great things somewhere in the future if I can carry them out." When a visitor from the East reminded him of the West's lack of music, culture, and art, he momentarily regretted the possibilities of the life he had abandoned in Toronto. Nevertheless, he was ever optimistic that these amenities would soon arrive in Edmonton. He agreed with his visitor that westerners seemed to think of very little but "the race for wealth," but he was content to be one of them, "to remain in the west where a great country is being built up and where I feel that I am sort of getting in on the ground floor."[16]

Frank chronicled with personal satisfaction the completion of a streetcar system in Edmonton, negotiations for a railroad bridge across the North Saskatchewan River, the laying of the cornerstone for the provincial legislature building, the arrival of a new steamer for outings on the river, and the performance of every visiting artist to the city—all of whom received favorable reviews from him in the pages of the *Bulletin.* Frank was a booster. His job required him to travel throughout Alberta reporting on the state of agriculture and the growth of communities. When he took charge of the *Camrose Canadian* in 1910, he also readily assumed the job of publicity commissioner for the town and produced an immigration bulletin designed to lure settlers to the area.

Newspaper reporting was hardly the most lucrative of jobs; although Frank made steady improvements in his position, from reporter for the *Bulletin* to managing editor of the *Canadian*, he saw his real economic opportunity in real estate. He plowed all of his savings into city lots, first in Strathcona and then in Camrose. He eagerly took on the job of publicity commissioner in Camrose, figuring that when immigrants contacted him about opportunities, he would be able to sell them his land. Frank did turn a profit, but apparently never as much as he hoped. At one point he sold two lots in Strathcona and reported that had he waited a week he could have made considerably more. On the eve of his marriage he informed Edith that he was not doing as well as some, although he had improved his assets, and she need not worry about being provided for.

For Frank, manhood was achieved through comradeship with his male friends ("I never aspired to be popular with the ladies but I always covet the respect and good will of my own sex"), respect earned from his boss and co-workers, and ability to provide for a wife. Frank did not become part of the cult of physicality that Anthony Rotundo describes as part of the "the Masculine Primitive," the ideal of manhood that was coalescing in the last half of the nineteenth century. Quite matter-of-factly, Frank recounted riding and walking miles across the Alberta countryside in the course of his daily work and relaxing on Sunday by skating and playing hockey. Frank loved sports and admired sportsmen, but he was not enamored of competition and drew no particular attention to his physical accomplishments. Most often he would write about skating parties, amateur hockey, and organizing baseball games and contests as part of agricultural fairs designed to boost Alberta. In 1911 Frank told Edith that he had met a man whom he would like to emulate. This was the Methodist minister, Reverend Robert Pearson, whom Frank had known in Toronto and who was now evangelizing in the West. Frank felt Pearson, by example more than by his preaching, set the model for manhood: "In his college days he was a great rugby player and has continued to be a great lover of sport while preaching the gospel. His life exemplifies the manly man, the man who knows the temptations of life and yet who instead of shunning the world mingles with the world and does what he can to make it better."[17] Frank, too, embraced his world and presented himself to Edith as a man always on the go, hard pressed to carve out time on Sunday to write to her.[18] He was always making contacts who, he assured her, would prove useful in the future, and he kept an eye out for his golden opportunity. He seemed to relish just about everything he did.

But what did he think about women, about Edith, and about how she would fit into his life? Frank Dunham was a man who believed that a woman's place was in the home, the church choir, and the ladies' club. He disparaged a spinster he met as "single and fair fat and forty." One evening in 1910 he planned to go to a Methodist service where the advertised sermon was "the ideal wife." "No doubt," he wrote, "there will be a large gathering of the fair sex there to attempt to divine the reason why they have not as yet worked their charms on men." Noting an apparently large number of single women in Edmonton, he confessed he did not understand why they had come there: "They occupy positions as stenographers in business places and the government offices and cannot help but lose more and more their power of being home makers." Frank acknowledged women's struggle to meet the expenses of city life, and pitied them, but he seemed to have no understanding that perhaps women also hoped Edmonton would be their place of opportunity. In fact, Frank seemed to think that the women who came west were of dubious character. In a discussion of unsuccessful marriages, he noted, "I have seen several cases lately where young men have picked up with western girls whom they know very little and have been sorry for it, or at least I had better say that I have been heartily sorry for them." In his mind the problem was not with western men, but with western women: "the girls down East are far superior to the majority that can be found out here." Frank may only have been trying to reassure Edith that he was not attracted to any of the women he met in Edmonton, yet his comments betray a deeper uneasiness. What seemed to disturb Frank was not a migration of "unsuitable" women, but the fact that women who came west to find work or husbands, who independently and aggressively pursued their futures—as he was—were not behaving as he thought women should.[19]

For Frank, women who did not choose a life of domesticity were deeply flawed. In one of the many letters to Edith anticipating their future together, he attested, "I know . . . that the instincts of home are strong in you and mean more to you than all the foolish vanities which so many girls are engaging their paltry brains in these days. You have a better conception of a true woman's career, Edith, than any girl I ever met, and I love you for that." He looked forward to the day when they could set up housekeeping for he believed "that the home life is the only life and that no man is truly happy and fortified against temptations until he is a married man." Frank respected Edith's good influence, her kindness, her sense of Christian duty, and her common sense. He treasured these qualities and, since he continued to postpone their wedding, he relied upon them to keep in her good graces.[20]

Frank delayed their marriage because he had not yet met his standards of what he believed necessary to take a wife. Edith was at home surrounded by friends and family, who apparently kept wondering when Frank was going to come and marry her. He did not see the public side of their engagement; he interpreted friends' interest as inappropriate inquisitiveness. Frank offered Edith sympathy, but he was not about to be rushed. In the first letter in which he addressed this issue he wrote, "I have only been out of college a year and a half and in that time I do not think I have as yet a sufficiently firm grip on this old world to launch on the sea of matrimony." He summed up, "I do not feel that as yet I have made good." Frank confessed he needed more time to convince the people of Edmonton that he had "the right stuff." Again in May 1909, after accompanying a newly married friend to look for an apartment, he told Edith that he would not consider a flat a suitable home for her. Since she had been raised in a beautiful house, he would not ask her to begin life "at the bottom of the ladder." In 1909 he canceled a trip to see her in order to take a new job as city editor for a new paper, the *Daily Capital,* and in 1911 he delayed his scheduled departure for his wedding several times because he wanted to take advantage of situations which he believed would advance his position. Edith was disappointed, and probably angry, but she kept her anger well hidden, perhaps because the one time she expressed it, Frank's response was so unsatisfactory.[21]

Only once in more than three years of correspondence did Edith reveal her ire concerning Frank's behavior. She had not heard from him in several weeks and must have expressed her displeasure strongly. Frank apologized but also patronized: "I do not blame you for feeling the way you do, but are there not other ways of curing a man of a bad habit other than giving expression to your anger? Explosions of this kind do ease one's sense of injustice I know but they really do not look well on paper. Good nature in a girl is everything." Frank postponed their marriage because he believed he had not yet proved his manhood, either to Edith or to his peers. Yet, while caught up in his own efforts to construct his identity, he found time to give Edith advice on how to hone her femininity—mainly by acquiescing to his decisions.[22]

Still, with a few exceptions—when Frank felt Edith was pressing him to come home or write more frequently—he had nothing but praise for her nature and her activities. Frank approved of Edith's participation in women's clubs and in fact hoped that when she arrived in Camrose, she would breathe some spirit into the women's clubs of that town. However, he had a limited vision of appropriate public activity and was confident she agreed: "You would make a fine militant suffragette with all your physical strength and auburn hair," he wrote in 1910, "but I know it would be useless to have anyone solicit your active interest. You know the value of the women at the fireside too well for that."[23]

During the time that Frank was in Alberta, he often escorted young women to recitals, house parties, church socials. Yet he apparently always acted in the most platonic and brotherly fashion. According to his letters, Edith was the only woman whom he ever courted, and in some ways the only woman to whom he ever paid any real attention. On the eve of his departure to marry her he penned, "Believe me Edith there never at any time has been any thought in my mind but that you are the only girl I have ever met that I would want to marry. This has often had the effect of my being very independent towards women an attitude which I believe I have carried too far for my own good." Interestingly, he assumed marriage would change his attitude toward all women: "when we get together around our own fireside I must be taught to respect the wishes of yourself and women in general much more than I have done. It will take me some time to do it Edith but you will find me a willing student for I realize what a man loses by shunning too much the society of women." According to the record he left, Frank had shunned sexual activity as well as the companionship of women. In this same letter, which he used to allay any fears Edith might have about what kind of bargain she was making, he testified, "I know what you expect of me in the way of purity of life and conduct and I am glad to say Edith, that I do not expect to have to make any apology to you in this respect." (Of course, Miles may have said the same thing to Isabelle.)[24]

What happened to Cavanaugh and Dunham after they completed their apprenticeships as men? Miles read law with Senator Thomas Carter, was admitted to the bar in 1891, and returned to Butte in 1894. He served two terms in the state legislature, one term as assistant city attorney, and on the city school board. Sometime in the early 1890s he married Alphonsine Milot, who bore him two daughters, and presumably died, for there is no record of divorce and Miles remarried in 1897. He was active in Butte civic clubs and in the Society of Montana Pioneers. He also wrote poetry, hundreds of verses over the course of his life, and short stories. Miles Cavanaugh's passing made the front page of both Butte newspapers. He died in 1935 at the age of seventy and was lauded as a scholar, poet, and citizen. His wish that a volume of his poetry be published was never fulfilled, although individual poems were. None of his stories or autobiographical writings ever saw print but were included in a vast collection of Montana history and memorabilia collected by his son-in-law and donated by his daughter to Montana State University.[25]

Frank Dunham left the West much sooner than he had anticipated. He did bring Edith back to Camrose after their wedding in 1911, seven years after they began courting. She did host tea parties and join the church choir. Their first child was born the day before their first wedding anniversary, another daughter sixteen months later. When World War I broke out Frank moved his family back to Ontario. If he was called overseas he wanted Edith close to her family. But he spent the war years working for a newspaper in Stratford, Ontario. He died in 1948 at the age of sixty-six; Edith lived for another seven years.[26]

Dunham and Cavanaugh, one son of the East, one of the West. These are, of course, only two men, a small and perhaps unrepresentative sample. So can their voices, autobiographical and intimate, tell us anything about late nineteenth- and early twentieth-century ideologies of masculinity? Miles and Frank had much in common. Although born almost twenty years apart, their life courses paralleled in many respects. Both were ambitious. Not satisfied with the work they obtained after high school, they went on to college. Both graduated at age twenty-five and then spent several years establishing themselves in their respective fields—law and journalism—before they married, Frank at age twenty-nine, Miles also in his twenties, and for the second time at age thirty-two. But what of their attitudes toward women, their ideas of marriage, their sexual behavior? Do they share anything here as well? Does Frank's eastern Methodist upbringing shape him to be a different man than Miles, son of western wanderlust?

Frank held the nineteenth-century middle-class view that a man's life was incomplete without marriage, that in fact a dwelling place only became a home when it was the locus of a wedded couple. He believed that a true woman like Edith would be a morally uplifting influence, that she would temper his overweening materialism, polish his rough edges, gently incorporate him into a social life he had shunned. And all this would be to the good. Frank had put Edith on a pedestal. He measured all women he met against her and found them wanting. Surely his words of praise and love must have pleased her. However, it was a daunting task to live up to Frank's ideal. On those few occasions when Edith got angry or expressed impatience or disappointment, Frank reacted with some sympathy, but with greater defensiveness and condescension. Frank was lonely and working hard in order to bring Edith west and make her his wife. Indeed, he saw Edith as his reward for years of work and loneliness. He seemed unaware of the inequality of their relationship or the powerlessness that Edith must have felt. Edith, in the prime of her life, was waiting at home to take up her career while Frank was busily consolidating his.

Miles shared Frank's view of marriage. In a wedding toast in 1888, he proposed, "He has not lived who never had a wife, nor she who never had a husband. The happiest phase of man's existence is born of the very ceremony we witness here tonight." Miles revealed more of his sexual behavior and attitudes about sexuality than did Frank. What he discloses are ideas also documented by Anthony Rotundo in his study of hundreds of middle-class men in the Northeast. Miles's sexual experimentation and attitudes were not unique to western men. Miles made distinctions between "good" and "bad" women, or more accurately between asexual and sexual females. Female sexuality was alluring, comforting, dangerous, and disreputable. We do not have enough information about Miles's wives to know anything about them, but odds are they were both more like Isabelle than like Nellie or Mrs. Sheehan. Miles came of age in Comet. He lived independently of his family and had his first steady work. He fell in love, and he lost his virginity, quite significantly with different women.[27]

Dunham and Cavanaugh's presentations of themselves suggest the strong persistence of a core of values that defined Anglo-American middle-class manhood from the early nineteenth century perhaps to the norm-shattering days of World War I. These included a commitment to work as the defining attribute of identity and a conviction that youthful work should result in a professional career; a belief that marriage was the validation of mature manhood and that an appropriate mate embodied the tenets of the cult of true womanhood; and a sexual ideology that could and did divorce love from eroticism.

One problem in assessing the stories of Dunham and Cavanaugh is that we lack a context for the examination of western-bred men. Just as women's history was born in the cradle of New England, historians' first studies of manliness, manhood, and masculinity are coming out of the Northeast and Midwest. And just as historians of western women first had to break down lingering stereotypes of gentle tamers, pioneer drudges, and whores with hearts of gold, historians of western men will have to humanize even more deeply entrenched icons of rugged mountain men, stoic braves, and romantic cowboys. Attention to the experiences of Teddy Roosevelt, Owen Wister, and Frederic Remington has created a West that served as a spa for the restoration of masculinity eroded by the pressures of industrialization, incorporation, and urbanization—a spa whose therapeutic retreat prepared men to return to the fray of eastern life. If anything, Dunham and Cavanaugh's stories show that the West was home, not way station. White, middle-class, well-educated though they were, Cavanaugh and Dunham were not caught up in the clutches of the masculine primitive ideal that apparently gripped so many eastern men of the late nineteenth century.[28]

Pursuing this difference may be a fruitful avenue of further research in regional variations of gender ideology. Were men like Cavanaugh and Dunham, who were born in the West or who came, stayed, worked, and married there, more secure in their ability to deal with the "primitive"? Dunham and Cavanaugh accessed the western environment through daily work. Did the vigorous life become so much a part of everyday life that it negated a compulsion to impose continuous physical challenges to prove one's manhood? The stories of Miles Cavanaugh and Frank Dunham tell us that much is yet to be learned about men's response to the West. They remind us that work and family were at the heart of men's daily lives as well as women's, and that men as well as women shaped themselves in the mirror of each other's eyes. Only by recovering and analyzing the intimate stories of men's and women's relationships with the western experience will we be able to write a truly gendered and truly human history of the region.

Notes

My thanks for their generous criticism of this essay to Dale Martin, Susan Rhoades Neel, Anastatia Sims, and the members of the "American Dreams, Western Images" seminar.

1. Susan Armitage, "Through Women's Eyes: A New View of the West," in Susan Armitage and Elizabeth Jameson, eds., *The Women's West* (Norman: University of Oklahoma Press, 1987), 9.

2. The beginning of western women's history as a coherent field can be marked by the publication of Joan M. Jensen and Darlis A. Miller's historiographical essay, "The Gentle Tamers Revisited: New Approaches to the History of Women in the American West," *Pacific Historical Review* 49 (May 1980): 173–213. Since then the field has so proliferated it is difficult to keep abreast of the many monographs, articles, edited diaries, and oral histories documenting and analyzing the lives of women in the North American West. For an overview of the range of issues studied by western women's historians, see essays in Armitage and Jameson, eds., *The Women's West;* Lillian Schlissel, Vicki L. Ruiz, and Janice Monk, eds., *Western Women: Their Land, Their Lives* (Albuquerque: University of New Mexico Press, 1988); and Elizabeth Jameson and Susan Armitage, eds., *Writing the Range: Race, Class and Gender in the Women's West* (Norman: University of Oklahoma Press, 1997).

3. E. Anthony Rotundo, "Learning About Manhood: Gender Ideals and the Middle-Class Family in Nineteenth-Century America," in J. A. Mangan and James Walvin, eds., *Manliness and Morality: Middle-Class Masculinity in Britain and America, 1800–1940* (New York: St. Martin's Press, 1987), 35.

4. Ava Baron, "Gender and Labor History: Learning from the Past, Looking to the Future," in Baron, ed., *Work Engendered: Toward a New History of American Labor* (Ithaca: Cornell University Press, 1991), 8.

Peter Filene reviewed the literature on men's history up to the mid-1980s in "The Secrets of Men's History," in Harry Brod, ed., *The Making of Masculinities: The New Men's Studies* (Boston: Allen & Unwin, 1987). More recent works exploring the construction of masculinity include Gail Bederman, *Manliness and Civilization: A Cultural History of Gender and Race in the United States, 1880–1917* (Chicago: University of Chicago Press, 1995); Lisa Bloom, *Gender on Ice: American Ideologies of Polar Expeditions* (Minneapolis: University of Minnesota Press, 1993); Nancy K. Bristow, *Making Men Moral: Social Engineering during the Great War* (New York: New York University Press, 1996); Robert L. Griswold, *Fatherhood in America: A History* (New York: Basic Books, 1993); Karen V. Hansen, "'Helped Put in a Quilt': Men's Work and

Male Intimacy in Nineteenth-Century New England," *Gender and Society* 3 (September 1989): 334–354; Amy Kaplan, "Romancing the Empire: The Embodiment of American Masculinity in the Popular Historical Novel of the 1890s," *American Literary History* 2, no. 4 (1990): 659–690; Michael S. Kimmel, "Baseball and the Reconstitution of American Masculinity, 1880–1920," *Baseball History* 1 (1989): 98–112; Margaret Marsh, "Suburban Men and Masculine Domesticity, 1870–1915," *American Quarterly* 40 (June 1988): 165–186; David Morgan, "Masculinity, Autobiography and History," *Gender and History* 2 (Spring 1990): 34–39; and E. Anthony Rotundo, *American Manhood: Transformations in Masculinity from the Revolution to the Modern Era* (New York: Basic Books, 1993).

5. The Miles J. Cavanaugh, Jr., Papers are in the Merrill G. Burlingame Special Collections at Montana State University, Bozeman. The Martin Frank Dunham Papers are in the Provincial Archives of Alberta at Edmonton.

We have only half the correspondence of Edith Sander and Frank Dunham. Edith kept Frank's letters; Frank apparently did not keep hers. Frank's letters demonstrate very clearly the pattern of Victorian courtship described by Karen Lystra in *Searching the Heart: Women, Men and Romantic Love in Nineteenth-Century America* (New York: Oxford University Press, 1989). When Dunham's daughter, Mrs. E. Cleghorn, donated the letters to the archives, she included a short biographical essay about her father, "Memoirs of a Newspaper Man," that she had written and which is filed with the collection's accession records. It mentions that Edith kept a diary from 1906 to 1912, encompassing the period of their courtship and the first year of marriage. But that document has not come to light. Miles Cavanaugh's autobiography stops when he began practicing law, before his marriage. Thus how Dunham and Cavanaugh followed through on what they learned about being men and being husbands remains a mystery, as does what the women in their lives thought about them.

6. Unless otherwise noted, all biographical information on Cavanaugh is drawn from his typescript "Autobiography" in his papers. There are also brief biographical sketches of him in Tom Stout, ed., *Montana: Its Story and Biography,* vol. 2 (Chicago: American Historical Society, 1921); and Robert G. Raymer, ed., *Montana: The Land and the People,* vol. 3 (Chicago: Lewis Publishing Co., 1930).

7. Miles J. Cavanaugh, Jr., "Autobiography," 21, 27–28.

8. Ibid., 28–29.

9. Ibid., 29.

10. Ibid., 23–24.

11. Ibid., 25–27.

12. Ibid., 30–31.

13. Ibid., 29–30.

14. All biographical information on Martin Frank Dunham is drawn either from his letters or from Cleghorn, "Memoirs of a Newspaper Man" (see note 5).

15. On the development of Edmonton, see Carl Frederick Betke, "The Development of an Urban Community in Prairie Canada: Edmonton, 1918–1921," (Ph.D. diss., University of Alberta, 1981); Helen Boyd, "Growing Up Privileged in Edmonton," *Alberta History* 30 (Winter 1982): 1–10; and J. G. MacGregor, *Edmonton: A History,* 2nd ed. (Edmonton: M. G. Hurtig Publishers, 1975). On Strathcona, see John Gilpin, "The Development of Strathcona," *Alberta History* 42 (Summer 1994): 15–22.

16. Dunham to Sander, May 8, 1908; October 17, 1908; December 12, 1908; and December 23, 1908.

17. Dunham to Sander, January 16, 1910. See also Carl Betke, "Sports Promotion in the Western Canadian City: The Example of Early Edmonton," *Urban History Review* 12 (October 1983): 47–56.

18. Dunham uses an enormous amount of letter space apologizing for not writing; he tried to write once a week, and sometimes wrote more frequently, but often two to three weeks passed between letters.

19. Dunham to Sander, September 18, 1911; January 16, 1910; and January 10, 1909.

20. Dunham to Sander, March 17, 1910.

21. Dunham to Sander, January 16, 1909; and May 1, 1909.

22. Dunham to Sander, October 20, 1910.

23. Dunham to Sander, November 24, 1910.

24. Dunham to Sander, September 3, 1911.

25. *Butte Daily Post,* August 3, 1935, p. 1; and *Montana Standard,* August 3, 1935, p. 1. Cavanaugh's will suggests that his second wife, Cora, was a widow with a son when she and Miles married. Miles J. Cavanaugh will, No. 10226, Clerk of the Court, Silver Bow County Courthouse, Butte, Montana.

26. Cleghorn, "Memoirs of a Newspaper Man."

27. Miles J. Cavanaugh, Jr., "At a Wedding Dinner, Oct. 30, 1888," Cavanaugh papers.

28. On the West as a therapeutic place, see G. Edward White, *The Eastern Establishment and the Western Experience: The West of Frederic Remington, Theodore Roosevelt, and Owen Wister* (New Haven: Yale University Press, 1968); and Jane Tompkins, *West of Everything: The Inner Life of Westerns* (New York: Oxford University Press, 1992).

8

CHANGING WOMAN

Maternalist Politics and "Racial Rehabilitation" in the U.S. West

KAREN ANDERSON

As those familiar with Navajo culture realize, Changing Woman was its most revered deity, a figure whose beneficence and wisdom left an enduring cultural heritage. A symbol of cyclical change and continuity, for Navajos she represented a maternal power of great benefit to family and community. For whites, however, she and other American Indian spiritual figures represented a subversive "superstition" that sustained a dangerous communalism and a disorderly system of gender relations.[1]

As Bettina Aptheker has observed, "cultural heritage is an instrument for holding family and community together—a task that is often seen as women's work." Because women have a major role in the socialization of the next generation and because they work to create the emotional milieu in which identity is formed and experienced, the politics of gender, culture, and identity are emotionally and politically freighted. Examining women's roles and actions in processes of cultural reproduction and their meanings for the construction of gender, race, and class relations is one goal of my study of racial ethnic women in modern America.[2]

Dominant groups have often sought to regulate the roles and activities of women in order to reproduce or reconstruct race, class, or gender relations in a changing context. Under these circumstances, women become the object and vehicle for change—changing "woman," thus, becomes a policy concern. In the period under consideration here, the early decades of the twentieth century, the potential subversiveness of women as mothers made the regulation of maternity a critical component of the construction of race, class, and gender relations in the United States.

The relationship between maternity and the state is a topic of increasing interest to feminist scholars. Most historical studies of the politics of maternalism in the United States in this period have focused on the eastern states, emphasizing the creation of mothers' pensions and of infant and maternal health policies as the most significant expressions of state welfare and intervention for women, and examining the racial dimension of state maternalism only with reference to African Americans. Although some note the surveillance and regulation of the lives of working class and racial ethnic mothers that accompanied state provisions for them, most scholars regard the mothers' pensions and related programs as generally beneficial and empowering for women.[3]

An important critic of that view is Gwendolyn Mink, whose article on the race and gender politics of welfare provision points to the contradictions of the welfare state and its meanings in an increasingly heterogeneous culture. Mink concludes that the formative influence on the American welfare state was "the clash between racial diversity and an idealized American citizenship." The idealized citizen was decidedly masculine; he was economically self-supporting and, thus, assumed to be invulnerable to political corruptions. The conflation of racial differences and impoverishment in the minds of middle-class white Americans heightened their "concerns about the compatibility of democracy and diversity."[4]

For female and male reformers in this period, gender became the mechanism for mediating these tensions. Middle-class women were to model good motherhood and monitor the conditions and practices of motherhood among immigrants, racial minorities, and the poor in order to ensure the reproduction of capitalist workers and democratic citizens. This project of "racial rehabilitation" required a politics of assimilation linked to the surveillance and regulation of motherhood. According to Mink, mothers' pensions in particular "more directly and more rigidly policed and prescribed the moral qualities of motherhood."[5]

Turning our attention to the West reveals important and overlooked dimensions to these dynamics by extending our analytic purview to policies aimed at American Indians, Mexican Americans, and others. This reveals that the gendered politics of race and citizenship were formulated and implemented as public policy prior to the mothers' pension movement of the 1910s and included various forms of exclusion and maternal dispossession as well as maternal regulation. Indeed, many Americans, then and now, have imagined the West as the locus for the enactment of an ongoing struggle between "civilization" and "savagery" whose gendered dynamics have received scant attention.[6]

That struggle entailed the policing of a shifting system of "internal frontiers" that were simultaneously imagined and institutionalized. According to Ann Stoler, "a frontier locates both a site of enclosure and contact, of observed passage and exchange." The permeability of boundaries—whether geographical, political, or cultural—invests their maintenance with inordinate significance. In the American West, those boundaries were supposed to contain a particularly dense tangle of intersecting and overlapping interests and identities. Indeed, as Patricia Limerick has noted, the racial/ethnic "diversity of the West put a strain on the simpler varieties of racism." When combined with highly contested notions of gender, Mink's "clash between racial diversity and an idealized American citizenship" assumed forms in the West that were complex and nationally salient.[7]

Relations between American Indians and European Americans provide the most and least obvious case of this proposition. This is so because, until recently, these relations have occupied the center of historical scholarship on race relations in the West while their connections to gender have received scant attention. The symbolic and material roles of women in cultural reproduction provide the links between the two systems.[8]

For many, motherhood was the most central of those roles, particularly for policy-makers. As Ann Stoler has noted regarding imperial relations, colonial officials feared that metis children would remain sentimentally bound to the cultures of their indigenous mothers. The recognition that women were critical to the assimilationist agenda contributed to whites' anxiety and vigilance regarding women's relationships to "civilization." The centrality of racial ethnic women in shaping the loyalties and competencies of their children was a source of power and danger for them—it positioned them to resist some of the impositions of whites while making them vulnerable to drastic interventions in their families.[9]

This places women who are not from the dominant culture in ambiguous positions. As mothers, they inevitably have to mediate between two cultures, often with contradictory meanings for themselves, their children, and their husbands. Because cultural identity has frequently been defined in terms of traditional family organization and associated with activities often carried out by women, including food preparation, child socialization, and religious observance, the problem of adapting to the dominant culture and its institutions has automatically involved a challenge to gender roles and relationships. As such, it has sometimes promoted gender and intergenerational conflict as women and men define their roles in the process of adaptation and/or resistance to the dominant culture.

Despite apparent similarities in the motives of those who would reshape motherhood to white, middle-class specifications, the importance and form of maternalist interventions varied from group to group and over time. I will briefly compare their expressions regarding Mexican American and American Indian women from the 1910s through the 1930s.

Maternalist policies toward Mexican Americans were contradictory, deriving in part from the role of immigration in shaping the relationship of all people of Mexican descent to the U.S. government. As George Sanchez has documented, gender-based assimilationist policies directed at Mexicanas were an important expression of state interest in producing compliant citizens and workers for democratic capitalism. At the same time, state support for Americanization programs waned in the 1920s, in part because officials assumed that many immigrants would remain Mexican nationals and in part because women resisted these efforts. Sanchez, however, fails to explain that resistance, adopting an implicit binary model of culture (American vs. Mexican) and taking women's defense of traditional culture for granted even though his evidence reveals a generational conflict among women over cultural meanings and gender.[10]

The acculturative pressures of the dominant society had contradictory effects on Mexican American women's family roles and power. They diminished women's maternal power by socializing their children to new values and promoting changes which made maternal experience an inadequate guide to effective behavior in a new cultural setting. At the same time, however, they sometimes prompted women to revise the gender basis for parental authority in their families. Because they experienced the liabilities of patriarchal family structures along with their children and because they often identified with the concerns and goals of their second-generation children, Mexican women often subverted the traditional family order. They, thus, found themselves experiencing conflicts with their husbands over parental decisions and roles and over the implications of cultural adaptation for the interrelated politics of gender and ethnic identity.

At the same time, however, the circumstances of the American immigrant experience necessitated a strong familial orientation, especially for women. The social isolation of some Mexican farm households in the Southwest and the migratory nature of much Mexican work enhanced the importance of kin networks. Poverty and prejudice increased the need to maintain family ties in order to ensure economic security and to provide emotional support in the face of an often hostile Anglo society. For Mexican women, the family often served as a buffer against the vicissitudes of American life. The complicated interconnections of emotional and practical dependency, however, created particular difficulties for women as they sought a measure of self-definition and autonomy in their lives.

In an urban context, social controls loosened, particularly in relation to young women. For many Mexican mothers, the "new Woman" symbolized social license and increased women's vulnerability to various forms of sexual exploitation. One such mother complained as follows:

> It is because they can run around so much and be so free, that our Mexican girls do not know how to act. So many girls run away and get married. This terrible freedom in this United States. The Mexican girls seeing American girls

> with freedom, they want it too, so they go where they like. They do not mind their parents; this terrible freedom. But what can the Mexican mothers do? It is the custom, and we cannot change it, but it is bad.[11]

The threat to motherhood as a central source of power and a mainstay of dignity for women posed by Anglo middle-class institutions and values made many Mexican women wary of the dominant culture's influence in their lives and, especially, those of their children. Some tried to take their daughters to Mexico to secure husbands and avert American social relations. Others sought to impose rules to diminish their daughters' contacts with American institutions, fearing that those contacts would pose a threat to religious values and maternal authority.[12]

In the 1920s, the perception that the flapper represented a substantial challenge to Mexican values was quite accurate and was expressed in a large number of *corridos* (ballads) written about the threat she posed. In "El Enganchado," or "the hooked one," the singer laments that "the girls go about almost naked" and "even my old woman has changed on me—she wears a bob-tailed dress of silk, goes about painted like a *pinata* and goes at night to the dancing hall." He concludes that he is returning to Michoacan and "as a parting memory I leave the old woman to see if someone else wants to burden himself." These ballads consistently link Mexicanas' adoption of the fashionable femininity symbolized by the flapper with a neglect of domestic responsibilities and an abandonment of the language, food, and gender systems of Mexican culture. By virtue of her independent sexuality, the subversive *agringada* (flapper) disrupted the entire moral order and threatened a political capitulation to the dominant class/ethnic order.[13]

The idea of woman as traitor, as old as the legends of Eve and Malinche, signifies women's anomalous position within culture—responsible for its maintenance and reproduction, but expected to acquiesce in men's control over its definitions, and thus, over its political relations. As Micaela di Leonardo has observed, "ethnicity itself is seen to belong to men: they arrogate to themselves (and identify with) those ethnic characteristics maintained by women to whom they are connected." In situations of cross-cultural contact, especially when economic, social, and political hegemony is at stake, cultural definitions themselves become contested terrain—within and outside of the group. As a result, the terms of assimilation/resistance to the dominant culture frequently created significant divisions between Mexican men and women. Moreover, as Maria Herrera Sobek concludes, the fact that Mexican women could exercise power through their cultural roles in order to claim and sometimes establish new definitions of Mexican American culture indicates the strength of their commitment to some forms of change.[14]

In California and elsewhere, Mexican women were excluded from some of the benefits and regulations of the welfare state, but not from institutional actions and dynamics that extended beyond those of the state. In this period, discrimination against Hispanics in public welfare laws reinforced women's dependence on their families for support in the absence of a male breadwinner. Under state and federal laws, various provisions and practices operated to exclude Hispanics from eligibility and to discriminate in the level of support provided. In Arizona, for example, the mother's pension law made assistance available only to citizen widows whose husbands had been citizens, thus excluding most Mexican women from coverage. The denial of agricultural workers and the imposition of residency and citizenship requirements under Social Security disqualified many Hispanics from later Aid to Families with Dependent Children and other programs. In Graham County, Arizona, the relief administrator reported the case of a woman (who was an American citizen married to a Mexican national) who had applied for welfare after her husband had been "repatriated" to Mexico. She, along with many others in similar circumstances, was refused assistance.[15]

For Native Americans, maternalist interventions were much more drastic and absolutely central to fundamental policies in the early decades of the century. Acculturative pressures on Indians increased dramatically, supported by the forced education of a growing number of Indian children in institutions run by whites and by the swelling presence of missionaries, field matrons, Bureau of Indian Affairs officials, traders, and other agents of white culture on or near the reservations. Many of these officials believed that the reconstruction of Indian family and gender relations was critical to the goal of assimilation.

White policy-makers believed that assimilation required the imposition of individual property ownership, through a process of land allotment, and the construction of the gender relations they thought would ensure the integration of men into a system of private property and wage work and women into a family structure based on monogamous marriage and the nuclear family. The Dawes Act of 1887 was passed in order to secure the former goal, and numerous ad hoc policies were devised to achieve the latter. Although the Dawes Act was not applied to all Indian nations, it reflected the core assumptions driving assimilation and had devastating effects for the large numbers of Indians forced to abandon communal economies and their subsistence practices in favor of private ownership of small and often unproductive plots of land.[16]

In order to enable the construction of the "free" Indian male citizen, white policy-makers insisted on the simultaneous creation of a dependent and subordinated Indian woman. His "independence" required her labor—domestic, reproductive, emotional, and productive. As wives, women were supposed to enact the domestic values that were normative among middle-class whites. They were to ensure the health and well-being of their families through a frugal domesticity, maintain stable families through their emotional work, and restrict their public activities to some civic improvements.

To create such "normative" family relations, white officials intervened directly and frequently in Indian families. Their regulatory impulses focused particularly on women's sexuality, marriage practices, and childrearing. Because parental practices were critical to the socialization of children, agents of white culture believed that assimilation would only occur when the authority of Indian parents over their children had been subordinated to or replaced by that of white officials.

For women, that meant an attack on their most important social role and identity. Government-mandated boarding school policies removed their daughters and sons from them, sometimes for years at a time. Moreover, acculturative pressures were designed to create a cultural divide between mothers and children. Not surprisingly, many women resisted these assaults on their most cherished roles, values, and relationships.[17]

No area of policy in the early twentieth century pitted Indian women's (and men's) interests against the U.S. government more systematically than the effort to promote education for "civilization." Native American resistance grew as more schools were opened and white officials made more systematic efforts to enforce mandatory school attendance policies. Indian parents routinely hid their children from reservation officials, and federal agents responded with "roundups" of truant children and attempts to coerce parents into turning over their children.[18]

More importantly, the partial success of the schools in inculcating Native American students with contempt for traditional beliefs and practices introduced profound tensions into many families and communities. As the Meriam Report noted in 1928, the home had become "the place of conflict between the old and the new." Polingaysi Qoyawayma's return to the Hopi mesas in the 1910s after an extended boarding school stay illustrates the painful struggles that sometimes ensued when daughters' internalization of different values undermined maternal authority and roles.[19]

Viewing her home through white eyes, Polingaysi saw only the difficulty and privations of Hopi life: "The poverty of the scene made her heartsick. This life was not for her." She demanded that her father make a bed and table for her and insisted on demonstrating the cooking skills she had learned at Riverside, however inappropriate they were for Hopi resources and traditions. Sevenka, her mother, wondered: "What shall I do with my daughter, who is now my mother?"[20]

At the same time, Polingaysi would not grind corn with her mother, insisting that Sevenka use a grinding mill. More significantly, she refused to marry as custom dictated, rejecting the Hopi womanhood her mother symbolized and valued. Instead Polingaysi vowed that "for no man . . . would she grind corn on her knees." Such labor for her mother, however, carried deep moral significance. She lectured her daughter:

> Mother Corn has fed you, as she has fed all Hopi people since the long, long ago when she was no larger than my thumb. Mother Corn is a promise of food and life. I grind with gratitude for the richness of our harvest, not with cross feelings of working too hard. As I kneel at my grinding stone, I bow my head in prayer, thanking the great forces for provision. I have received much. I am willing to give much in return. . . . It is sad that the white man's way has caused you to forget the Hopi way.[21]

Polingaysi Qoyawayma's wholesale adoption of white culture did not typify the response of most Native American girls to the Indian education program in this period. Most former students returned to the reservations or their communities and resumed many of their traditional activities and roles, whether out of choice, necessity, or both. The lack of fit between their training and the conditions at home made it virtually impossible for most young Native American women to enact the domestic roles their education had encouraged.[22]

This "return to the blanket" occasioned much white criticism of educational policies, of Indian cultures, and, particularly, of Indian women. Indian women's failure to support change would endanger the whole project, undermining men's motivations and abilities to participate as responsible citizens, providers, and protectors and jeopardizing their children's progression from wards of the United States to citizens.

Those who represented white culture to Native Americans were not all of one opinion on these matters, however. Jane Gay's observations of the Nez Perce allotment process prompted her to conclude that "civilization has been built up largely upon the altruism of the woman, at the cost of her independence and is still an expensive luxury to her." Gay's feminism reveals that the politics of the dominant society were neither monolithic nor static. Among whites themselves, the meanings of "civilization" and its gender relations were also subject to dispute.[23]

Transformations in the American economy and in social relations had intensified power conflicts in the late nineteenth and early twentieth centuries. The growth and increasing militancy of the working class posed challenges to capitalist dominance. Ethnic and religious heterogeneity threatened white, Protestant control over politics, the economy, and culture. Women's increasing participation in education, employment, politics, and the "cheap amusements" of city life challenged men's authority at home and in public life.[24]

The instability and heterogeneity of cultural values among whites of all classes threatened the identification of "whiteness" with a particular package of beliefs and practices. This posed serious dilemmas for white officials promoting Indian assimilation. If Indians were to become like whites, precisely which whites should they be emulating? How should cross-cultural contacts between whites and Indians be institutionalized and regulated? Official insistence on rigid gender roles for American Indians heightened as conflicts among whites jeopardized the conflation of race and culture at the heart of the assimilationist enterprise.

A simple social control model that assumes a monolithic and homogeneous white culture and state imposing an always damaging program of economic and social change on equally homogeneous Indian or Mexican American cultures also distorts our understandings of the history of women from these groups. Some of the competencies and technologies offered to them by whites offered a means to improve their circumstances in a changing cultural and economic context. Moreover, Native American and Mexican American women's selective and situated appropriations and transformations of white cultural practices in the areas of family, sexuality, and economy reveal their cultural agency in historical practices.

What the histories of racial ethnic women demonstrate is that imposed subordination was often difficult to achieve, in part because women themselves are agents as well as objects of change. The actions and experiences of racial ethnic women were and are critical in forging the connections between the social relations of everyday life and the gendered construction of the public world in the United States. Because it served as a critical site for the project of gendered "racial rehabilitation" described by Mink, the U.S. West was and is especially important to an understanding of the role of women and gender in the politics of cultural reproduction and the politics of race, class, and gender.

Notes

1. Ruth Roessel, *Women in Navajo Society* (Rough Rock, Ariz.: Navajo Resource Center, 1981).

2. Karen Anderson, *Changing Woman: A History of Racial Ethnic Women in Modern America* (New York: Oxford University Press, 1996); Bettina Aptheker, *Tapestries of Life: Women's Work, Women's Consciousness, and the Meaning of Daily Experience* (Amherst: University of Massachusetts Press, 1989), p. 228.

3. Theda Skocpol, *Protecting Soldiers and Mothers: The Political Origins of Social Policy in the United States* (Cambridge, Mass.: Harvard University Press, 1992); Linda Gordon, ed., *Women, the State, and Welfare* (Madison: University of Wisconsin Press, 1990); Kathryn Kish Sklar, "The Historical Foundations of Women's Power in the Creation of the American Welfare State, 1830–1930," in Seth Koven and Sonya Michel, eds., *Mothers of a New World: Maternalist Politics and the Origins of Welfare States*

(New York: Routledge, 1993), pp. 43–93; Molly Ladd-Taylor, "'My Work Came Out of Agony and Grief': Mothers and the Making of the Sheppard-Towner Act," in Koven and Michel, eds., *Mothers of a New World,* pp. 321–343. Gwendolyn Mink, Eileen Boris, and Sonya Michel particularly notice the contradictory meanings of the welfare state for poor and racial ethnic women. Gwendolyn Mink, "The Lady and the Tramp: Gender, Race, and the Origins of the American Welfare State," in Gordon, ed., *Women, the State, and Welfare,* pp. 92–122; Eileen Boris, "The Power of Motherhood: Black and White Activist Women Redefine the 'Political,'" in Koven and Michel, eds., *Mothers of a New World,* pp. 213–245; Sonya Michel, "The Limits of Maternalism: Policies toward American Wage-Earning Mothers during the Progressive Era," in Koven and Michel, eds., *Mothers of a New World,* pp. 277–320.

4. Mink, "The Lady and the Tramp," pp. 92, 105.

5. Ibid., p. 110.

6. Maureen Fitzgerald's examination of Protestant policies toward Irish Catholic and Jewish families in New York City in the nineteenth century achieves a similar extension. Her work reveals that mothers' pensions evolved in reaction to the establishment of Catholic and Jewish institutions outside the regulatory grasp of Protestant reformers. Maureen Fitzgerald, "Irish-Catholic Nuns and the Development of New York City's Welfare System, 1845–1903," (Ph.D. diss., University of Wisconsin, 1992). Dolores Janiewski, "Learning to Live 'Just Like White Folks': Gender, Ethnicity and the State in the Inland Northwest," in Dorothy O. Helly and Susan M. Reberby, eds., *Gendered Domains: Rethinking Public and Private in Women's History* (Ithaca: Cornell University Press, 1991), pp. 167–180. Indeed, Frederick Jackson Turner saw the frontier as "the meeting point between savagery and civilization." Frederick Jackson Turner, *The Significance of the Frontier in American History,* ed. Harold P. Simonson (New York: Frederick Ungar Publishing Co., 1963), p. 28.

7. Ann Stoler, "Sexual Affronts and Racial Frontiers: European Identities and the Cultural Politics of Exclusion in Colonial Southeast Asia," *Comparative Studies in Society and History* (July 1992): 514–551. Patricia Limerick's call to close the frontier as an analytic tool for western history may be premature. Patricia Nelson Limerick, *The Legacy of Conquest: The Unbroken Past of the American West* (New York: W. W. Norton and Company, 1987), pp. 17–32, 260.

8. Mary E. Young, "Women, Civilization, and the Indian Question," in Virginia Purdy, ed., *Clio Was a Woman: Studies in the History of American Women* (Washington, D.C.: Howard University Press, 1980), pp. 98–110; Janiewski, "Learning to Live 'Just Like White Folks.'"

9. Young, "Women, Civilization, and the Indian Question"; Ann Laura Stoler, "Sexual Affronts and Racial Frontiers: European Identities and the Cultural Politics of Exclusion in Colonial Southeast Asia," in Frederick Cooper and Ann Laura Stoler, eds., *Tensions of Empire: Colonial Cultures in a Bourgeois World* (Berkeley: University of California Press, 1997), pp. 198–237; George J. Sanchez, "'Go After the Women': Americanization and the Mexican Immigrant Woman," in Ellen Carol DuBois and Vicki L. Ruiz, eds., *Unequal Sisters: A Multi-Cultural Reader in U.S. Women's History* (New York: Routledge, 1990), pp. 250–263.

10. Sanchez, "'Go After the Women,'" pp. 250–263.

11. Emory Bogardus, *The Mexican in the United States* (New York: Arno Press and the *New York Times,* 1970, reprint of 1934 edition), p. 28.

12. Ibid.; Mario Garcia, *Desert Immigrants: The Mexicans of El Paso, 1880–1920* (New Haven: Yale University Press, 1981), pp. 200–201; Beatrice Griffith, *American Me* (Boston: Houghton Mifflin Company, 1948), pp. 76–80. Obviously, familial control of young girls also gave parents some control over a daughter's choice of a husband by allowing for relaxed vigilance when an acceptable suitor appeared.

13. William Chafe, *The Paradox of Change: The American Woman in the Twentieth Century* (New York: Oxford University Press, 1991); Mary Ryan, *Womanhood in America from Colonial Times to the Present,* 3rd ed. (New York: J. Watts, 1983), pp. 167–252; Sheila Rothman, *Woman's Proper Place: A History of Changing Ideals and Practices, 1870 to the Present* (New York: Basic Books, Inc., 1978); "El Enganchado" from Paul S. Taylor, *Mexican Labor in the United States: Chicago and the Calumet Region* (Berkeley: University of California Press, 1932), pp. vi–vii; Manuel Gamio, *Mexican Immigration to the United States* (New York: Dover Publications, 1971); Maria Herrera-Sobek, "The Acculturation Process of the Chicana in the *Corrido,*" *De Colores* 6 (1982): 7–16. The fear of maternal power characteristic of modern American gender ideology derives also from women's successful use of maternal rhetoric and role performance to increase women's social and political power.

14. Micaela di Leonardo, *The Varieties of Ethnic Experience: Kinship, Class, and Gender among California Italian-Americans* (Ithaca: Cornell University Press, 1984), p. 221; Herrera-Sobek, "The Acculturation Process of the Chicana." These conflicts were also expressed in folk tales. William Jones Wallrich, "Some Variants of the 'Demon Dancer,'" *Western Folklore* 9 (April 1950): 144–146.

15. Mary Kidder Rak, "A Social Survey of Arizona," University of Arizona Bulletin No. 111 (Tucson, Ariz.: University Extension Division, 1921), pp. 37–38; Letter, J. C. Brodie to B. B. Moeur, September 4, 1934, Governor's Papers, Box 6, Arizona State Archives; Letter, Valente Soto et al. to B. B. Moeur, August 13, 1934, Governor's Papers, Box 6, Arizona State Archives; Winifred Bell, *Aid to Dependent Children* (New York: Columbia Universty Press, 1965); Letter, Karl H. McBride to W. C. Ferguson, November 15, 1938, Governor's Papers, Box 10, Arizona State Archives; Selden C. Menefee and Orin C. Cassmore, *The Pecan Shellers of San Antonio* (Westport, Conn.: Greenwood Press, 1978, reprint of 1940 edition), pp. 37–43; Migratory Labor, July 1940, Records of the Department of Health, Education, and Welfare, Record Group 47, Box 34, National Archives; Norman D. Humphrey, "Employment Patterns of Mexicans in Detroit," *Monthly Labor Review* 61 (November 1945): 913–923.

16. David H. Getches, Daniel M. Rosenfelt, and Charles F. Wilkinson, *Federal Indian Law: Cases and Materials* (St. Paul, Minn.: West Publishing Company, 1978), pp. 69–77; Leonard A. Carlson, *Indians, Bureaucrats, and Land: The Dawes Act and the Decline of Indian Farming* (Westport, Conn.: Greenwood Press, 1981), pp. 115–162; Janet A. McDonnell, *The Dispossession of the American Indian, 1887–1934* (Bloomington: Indiana University Press, 1991).

17. Frank Knox, "Report on the Ute Indians of Utah and Colorado," October 15, 1915, Special Reports, Board of Indian Commissioners, Papers of the Bureau of Indian Affairs, RG 75, National Archives, vol. 1 [hereafter cited as BIA].

18. Margaret Connell Szasz, *Education and the American Indian: The Road to Self-Determination since 1928*, 2nd ed. (Albuquerque: University of New Mexico Press,

1977), pp. 10–11, 22; Hearings before a Subcommittee of the Committee on Indian Affairs of the U.S. Senate, 71st Congress, 3rd Sess., 1930, pp. 4481–4483; Fran Leeper Buss, ed., *Dignity: Lower Income Women Tell of Their Lives and Struggles* (Ann Arbor: University of Michigan Press, 1985), pp. 150–168; interview with Irene Mack Pyawasit, Fran Buss Oral History Collection, Special Collections, University of Arizona Library [hereafter cited as UA]; Testimony of As-ton-pia at St. Michaels Mission, Arizona, September 6, 1932 [?], Paper of the Franciscans, St. Michaels, Arizona, UA.

19. Brookings Institution, Institute for Government Research, *The Problem of Indian Administration* (Baltimore: Johns Hopkins University Press, 1928), p. 567; Polingaysi Qoyawayma, *No Turning Back* (Albuquerque: University of New Mexico Press, 1964), p. 69; Robert A. Trennert, *The Phoenix Indian School: Forced Assimilation in Arizona, 1891–1935* (Norman: University of Oklahoma, 1988), pp. 56, 145–146.

20. Qoyawayma, *No Turning Back,* pp. 67–76; quotes on p. 69.

21. Ibid., pp. 67–76.

22. Flora Warren Seymour, "Report on the Mescalero Indian Reservation, New Mexico," June 6, 1932, BIA, vol. 10; Flora Warren Seymour, "Indian Service Educational Activities in the Southwest," July 28, 1932, BIA, vol. 10; William Ketcham, "Report on the Eufala Boarding School, Eufala, Oklahoma," February 20, 1917, BIA, vol. 1.

23. Frederick E. Hoxie and Joan T. Mark, eds., *With the Nez Perces: Alice Fletcher in the Field, 1889–1892* (Lincoln: University of Nebraska Press, 1981), p. 35; Estelle Aubrey Brown, *Stubborn Fool: A Narrative* (Caldwell, Idaho: Caxton Printers, Ltd., 1952); Janiewski, "Learning to Live 'Just Like White Folks.'"

24. Peggy Pascoe, *Relations of Rescue* (New York: Oxford University Press, 1990); Kathy Peiss, *Cheap Amusements: Working Women and Leisure in Turn-of-the-Century New York* (Philadelphia: Temple University Press, 1986); Ryan, *Womanhood in America*; Elizabeth Ewen, *Immigrant Women in the Land of Dollars: Life and Culture on the Lower East Side, 1890–1925* (New York: Monthly Review Press, 1985); Carroll Smith-Rosenberg, *Disorderly Conduct: Visions of Gender in Victorian America* (New York: Oxford University Press, 1985), pp. 245–296.

9

MOBILITY, WOMEN, AND THE WEST

VIRGINIA SCHARFF

One day in April of 1984, a historian named David Garrow awaited the arrival of a sixty-eight-year-old Los Angeles woman he had never met. She was divorced, a retired college professor, an African American. He had contacted her by telephone, offering to come to see her, but she insisted on driving to the place he was staying, picking him up, and taking him to her home. There, she showed him a typescript, more than two hundred pages long, detailing her recollections of momentous events some thirty years earlier. Her name was Jo Ann Gibson Robinson, and as president of the Montgomery, Alabama, Women's Political Council, she had, in 1955, helped to set events in motion for the public transportation struggle that sparked the black freedom movement in the American South.[1]

I argue here that both western and women's history must begin to take seriously the significance of geographical mobility.[2] Feminist geographers and historians have for more than a decade asked how gender is implicated in, and reconstituted by, the organization of space.[3] Historians have also documented movement of women into, through, and around the trans-Mississippi region. Numerous studies of women on the Overland Trail trace changes, and continuity, in gender patterns among westering European Americans.[4] But there are many other examples of scholarship dealing with women on the move, including work on changes in the lives of indigenous women in groups that moved from the Midwest onto the Great Plains, or from the Great Basin of Nevada onto reservations. We also see women in motion in Mexican migration to the United States, in Asian immigration and Japanese American relocation, among migrant farmworkers and military wives, on the part of cowgirls and women in wild west shows, in the African American exodus to the Plains after the Civil War, and among middle class women drivers.[5] Still, spatial mobility as a category of analysis in western women's history has yet to be theorized fully or employed systematically.

I think it is time we stopped envisioning women's history as a narrative chiefly about attempts to establish geographical stability (what might be called "home on the range"), and begin to accord itineracy the historical importance in western women's lives that the record suggests is necessary.[6] At the most mundane level, for an endless and turbulent stream of reasons, women move around more than they stay put. Geographical mobility, or limitation of such mobility is, I argue, a significant factor in all history, including women's history, western history, and western women's history. And, dialectically, gender often acts as a force structuring mobility.[7]

In an effort to drive home (ahem) the significance of geographical mobility to history in general, and to western women's history in particular, I want to tell a story about a woman whose mobile personal history makes the whole category of "western women" suspect. I will take some analytical cues from theorists who have been interested in exploring the significance of space and time to history, from Martin Heidegger to Anthony Giddens. I see geographical mobility as one form of space-time relations in a larger set of possible reconfigurations of human presence and absence, a set of relations implicated not only in the movement of bodies in space, but also in such things as the publication of autobiographical writing, the electronic reproduction of words, sounds, and images, and variously mediated dramatic reenactments of life stories.[8]

I want to call attention to the politics implicit in what I do. I tell this story, of course, not as an objective observer, but in order to highlight the significance of physical motion in women's lives. I recognize that, in talking about travels, impediments to mobility, and transformations of presence and absence in the life of Jo Ann Gibson Robinson, I lay claim to some kind of relationship with the woman whose words I write down and interpret. I initiate a very one-sided relationship, given the fact that I am physically present, at the moment of writing, and she is physically absent—not here to answer back, retelling her own story in her own way.[9] I am the author of this article. I'm white; she is black, and my senior by nearly four decades. Marking our differences, I insist that we have something complicated, but important, in common, as persons gendered female, moving through late twentieth-century American space. Invoking her presence by citing and interpreting her words, I tread today what Donna Haraway has called a "very fine line between the appropriation of another's (never innocent) experience and the delicate construction of the just-barely-possible affinities, the just-barely-possible connections that might actually make a difference in local and global histories."[10] With the intent to recognize the commonalities and connections a world of humans in motion hides, but makes possible, I will tell and speculate about the story of a twentieth-century woman, an

African American, an activist, and, maybe or maybe not, a western woman. Significantly, the story begins outside the West, in the heart of the American South.

Personal mobility can be considered a hallmark of Jo Ann Gibson Robinson's life. Born to landowning black farmers in Culloden, Georgia, in 1916, the youngest of twelve children, Robinson graduated from Fort Valley State College and moved to Macon to take a teaching job. There, she was married briefly to a man named Wilbur Robinson. Five years later, she moved by herself to Atlanta to enter the graduate program in English at Atlanta University, and upon earning her M.A. took another job at Mary Allen College in Crockett, Texas. A year later, she received a better offer from Alabama State, a historically black public college, and moved to Montgomery in 1949, at the age of thirty-three.[11]

Like many academics with out-of-town family, Robinson planned to spend Christmas break that year with relatives, in this case, in Cleveland, Ohio. Few Americans traveled by air in 1949, but Robinson was a notably mobile woman. Unlike most African Americans of the time, she owned and drove her own car. She was, moreover, willing to go to rather elaborate lengths to make sure that her automobile was safely stored while also managing to get herself and her baggage to the airport on time. "One of the men students loaded my suitcases in my car for me," she recalled, "and I drove at a leisurely pace out to the airport, checked my luggage for a trip to the East, then returned to the college campus, locked my car in a garage, made my way to the nearest bus stop, and waited for the short ride to a friend's home. We were all going to the airport together. I had never felt freer or happier."[12]

Racism has always structured American space, although space has never imbibed race in a rational or orderly way. Most African Americans did not then, and still do not, take for granted the freedom to move unimpeded through space, let alone the right to enjoy public support of personal mobility. Still, learning the racial ways of space requires substantial local knowledge. The more African Americans moved from one place to another in the United States, the more arbitrary, esoteric, and varied the forms of racial rules that they would encounter. Segregation practices also changed over time. In Mobile, during the 1940s and 1950s, passengers were seated on a first-come, first-serve basis. In Macon, Georgia, and elsewhere, blacks were expected to seat themselves from the rear of the bus forward, while whites were to sit from the front toward the rear until all seats were taken. At one point in the Montgomery struggle, white leaders proposed that buses have "flexible" whites only sections to be designated by a moveable sign saying "white" on one side and "colored" on another, a practice abandoned in the city decades earlier.[13]

That winter morning in 1949, Jo Ann Gibson Robinson got a rude awakening. The Montgomery city bus she planned to ride had only two passengers on it as she boarded—a white woman sitting in the third row from the front, and a black man near the back. Lost in thoughts of the holiday to come, and unaware that local conventions of transit segregation in Montgomery called for the first ten rows to be reserved for whites, Robinson took a seat in the fifth row.[14] The driver leaped to his feet and hustled back to confront Robinson. "He was standing over me saying, 'Get up from there! Get up from there!' with his hand drawn back. . . . I felt like a dog," she wrote. She stumbled off the bus in tears, and cried, she said, "all the way to Cleveland." Then she got mad. When she returned from her vacation, she called a meeting of the Montgomery Women's Political Council.[15]

Historians have demonstrated that African American women faced down discrimination on public transportation from the moment such transit systems first appeared in the United States. Interestingly, the first reported incident of black women's resistance to unfair treatment occurred in San Francisco in 1866, when the wealthy abolitionist Mary Ellen Pleasant sued the city's trolley company after she had been denied a ride.[16] The Montgomery Women's Political Council, an organization of black professional women, had been founded in 1946, when the local chapter of the League of Women Voters refused to integrate. The WPC was already well aware of incidents of harassment by Montgomery bus drivers against black passengers, especially women. By 1953, the WPC had collected some thirty complaints against the bus company. Between 1950 and 1955, Robinson and other WPC members met regularly with the mayor of Montgomery, persistently protesting a pattern of abusive behavior ranging from obscene language and general rudeness on drivers' part toward black patrons, to buses that stopped at every block in white neighborhoods but only every two blocks in black areas, to drivers who made blacks pay at the front, then get off the bus to re-enter at the back door, often leaving before the black passenger was back on board. Worst of all, since 70 percent of passengers were black, reserving some ten double-seats for whites often meant that black passengers were standing over empty seats. Over several years, a host of black civil rights and civic groups repeatedly brought their concerns to the mayor and city government, but got nowhere. By 1955, the mayor told a delegation from the Women's Political Council that if bus patrons "were not satisfied, they could always drive their own cars!"[17]

Little did Mayor W. A. Gayle dream of becoming a prophet. On December 1, 1955, Montgomery civil rights activist Rosa Parks, riding home on a city bus with a full bag of groceries, defied local segregation ordinances by refusing to give up her bus seat to a white man. Parks was, of course, not the first African American in Montgomery to challenge either the legal or the social practice of bus segregation; she was acting on behalf of a community of civil rights activists who had for some years sought the "right" person to test the segregation ordinance. As a middle-aged, professionally skilled, prominent African American woman, her gender, age, and class figured, alongside race, in the decision to make hers the test case. Jo Ann Robinson noted the significance of gender when she invoked Parks's right to be treated like a lady: she "was a woman, and the person waiting was a man."[18]

On the night of Parks's arrest, Robinson and others went, about midnight, to their offices at Alabama State (a perilous move, considering the general notion that black women should not go about alone at night in southern towns).[19] There, they drafted a letter of protest, calling for a city-wide one-day boycott of the bus lines. They mimeographed tens of thousands of notices of the proposed December 5 action, invoking the notion of feminine dignity insulted, and also making themselves present where they had not before been, with the printed declaration, "Another Negro woman has been arrested and thrown in jail. . . . The next time it may be you, or your daughter, or your mother."[20]

They delivered their leaflets (by private car) all over town, to "schools, businesses, beauty parlors, beer halls, factories." On December 5, 1955, black taxi drivers charged passengers only ten cents a ride, and some two hundred private automobiles joined forces to transport Montgomery's black bus riders. In a mass action "comparable in precision to a military operation," 90 percent of Montgomery's bus riders stayed off the city line. This would prove to be only the first day in thirteen months of stalwart protest, confrontation, negotiation, and perhaps most unusual of all, independent, alternative volunteer mass transit. Operating out of forty-three dispatch and forty-two pick-up stations, 325 private automobiles arrived every ten minutes between the hours of 5 and 10 A.M. and 1 and 8 P.M., with hourly pick-ups during the rest of the day. Many Montgomery residents, black and white, also gave rides on a more haphazard basis. As contributions arrived from around the nation, the newly formed Montgomery Improvement Association and local churches purchased station wagons, hired drivers, and bought gasoline.[21]

The Montgomery Bus Boycott blasted the first hole in the wall of *de jure* racism in the American South. Jo Ann Robinson was there every mile of every day, editing the MIA newsletter, organizing car pools on an unprecedented scale, preparing the defense of those ride pools when segregationist officials tried to prohibit them, herself offering rides to boycotters day after day. When, a year into the boycott, the Montgomery Police Commissioner joined the White Citizens' Council, Robinson re-dedicated herself to the struggle in a highly symbolic way: "I put my car in the garage and walked. . . . I suffered with my colleagues and peers."[22]

The car (a Chrysler) suffered too. One night, the police came by her house and threw acid on it, and Robinson experienced the automotive body damage as a kind of combat wound, proof of valor to be displayed with pride. "I kept that car . . . until 1960, after I had resigned from Alabama State. It had become the most beautiful car in the world to me. I turned it in for a new one only when I moved to California, for I did not think the Chrysler would hold up through the deserts I had to cross."[23]

In 1960, segregationists in the Alabama legislature launched an investigation of "subversives" and forced a dozen of Alabama State's most outspoken faculty to resign.[24] Robinson taught briefly at Grambling, but soon decided to move to be near friends in Los Angeles. She was wise to buy a new car, since she made the journey across the Great American Desert long before the interstate highway system had made reliable roads commonplace in the South and West. And though the move to Los Angeles took her further than she had ventured before, it was certainly in character for a woman who had already made a living in four states—Georgia, Texas, Alabama, and Louisiana. Robinson had again and again seized the opportunity to move from one place to another, to get away from a bad situation, and seek a better one. But just as surely, she did not take mobility for granted. If her experience in the bus boycott had taught her the importance of contesting geographical constraints based on race, she also knew the ways in which gender, as an economic, occupational, and intellectual structure, impeded women's power to move. She avowed that her professional achievements, something women didn't generally have, gave her courage to leave. As she recalled, "I had been less afraid than most women, because I knew I could get teaching positions elsewhere." Robinson taught English in the Los Angeles public schools, where she worked until her retirement in 1976, remaining active in civic and social work. After she retired, she did what good Angelenos at least aspire to do, investing successfully in real estate.[25]

Jo Ann Robinson started out life as a southerner, but a notably mobile citizen of that region. She became involved in the cause that, in her words, "gave me courage" as a middle-aged professional, contributing to the Montgomery Bus Boycott struggle her eloquence as well as her political savvy and energy. The story of her life, thus, can be read as a dramatic narrative that crests in the 1950s, in the southern United States. During the period of her life deemed most significant by historians, she was at the center of a conflict that, more than virtually any other in American history, demonstrated the race, class, and gender politics of the interconnected domains of public space, personal mobility, and human dignity.

But lives do not hold still, waiting for their stories to be written as dramas. Ironically, the role she played in organizing the boycott, and in seeing it through to its successful conclusion, made it impossible for her to stay in Montgomery. Neither did the significance of her participation become apparent to most students of the struggle until her memoir was published in

1987. By that time she was more than seventy years old, retired, and living quietly on the Pacific Coast, far from the place of her birth.[26] Even after retirement, she remained active in a variety of civic organizations, including the League of Women Voters and Black Women's Alliance, gave one day a week of free service to the Los Angeles city government, worked in a child care center and in senior citizens' assistance, and played contract bridge.[27]

For more than thirty years, Jo Ann Robinson lived at the Pacific edge of the trans-Mississippi West, and it was from the West that her voice rang across the wire to David Garrow, offering to give him a ride. Wondering how western women's history might come to terms with such a reflective, moving subject forces us to recognize, once again, that lives like Jo Ann Robinson's persist beyond the borders of political events and burst the boundaries of region, demanding respect on their own complex terms.[28]

Can we call Robinson a "western woman"? Certainly, in some senses, we can. After all, the literature of "western women's history" is full of individuals who moved into the West from some other region, many of whom spent far less time in the West, and contributed less of consequence to any western community than Robinson has. Annie Oakley came from Ohio and never actually lived in the West. Isabella Bird, always an Englishwoman, headed into the West by coming east from Hawaii, had her Rocky Mountain adventure, and left the country. Esther Morris, the vaunted "mother of woman suffrage," was a native of New York.[29] Jo Ann Robinson is surely as much a part of "western women's history" as are these canonical figures, and her memoirs can be read as an affirmation of the not yet entirely moribund theme that the West is the place to make a new start.

Still, to claim her entirely for the subfield of western women's history would be to appropriate her life in a cynical and even pathetic bid for scholarly legitimacy; it wouldn't be, in any responsible sense, true. What Robinson's story reminds us is that nobody is only one thing, a statement that is by now a postmodern bromide. More pertinent to my point today, Robinson's picaresque tale returns us to the insights of Chicana and Chicano scholars and others who have argued that the term "West" is itself a totalizing and value-laden example of the link between power and knowledge.[30] Listening to Robinson's story teaches us the particular lesson that female mobility renders suspect the very category of "western women's history." When women move, region may not always be a useful way of classifying or analyzing their lives.

When people of either sex move, moreover, what seems most stable in their identities may be reconfigured. The most salient component of Jo Ann Robinson's identity in 1950s Alabama was her racial status, then termed "Negro" or "colored." I don't wish to argue the silly position that race didn't or doesn't matter in the West, but the significance of migration to African American history, and to transformations of African American identity, is certainly well known. It is, moreover, a commonplace of western history, as currently practiced, and of United States women's history, as a consequence of the gradual acceptance of work on western women into the canon of American women's history, that conceptualizing of race relations in dualistic, black/ white terms distorts the multicultural historical experience of American women.[31] While historians have devoted the most attention to black migration from the Southeast to Northeast in the period between 1920 and 1960, Robinson's story suggests that movement to and through the West offers a fertile field of inquiry for historians of African Americans as well as western historians, as the work of Quintard Taylor, Gretchen Lemke-Santangelo, Shirley Ann Moore, Douglas Flamming, and others demonstrates.[32]

Western history, women's history, and African American history as scholarly endeavors help us understand Jo Ann Gibson Robinson's life. But Robinson's is a story of a woman in motion, and taking mobility seriously forces us to question the stability of our most cherished historical categories of analysis. As we think about the person, Jo Ann Gibson Robinson, moving bodily through space, and about her words, reproduced and available to people who will never meet her, who may be born long after she is gone, reacting in unforeseeable ways to her disembodied presence in their lives, we must ask whether the time has come to imagine history anew. David Hollinger has responded to the radical potential of postmodern theory, and the political challenges of multiculturalism, with a call for "postethnic history."[33] Is it perhaps time, as well, for a *postwestern history*? Jo Ann Gibson Robinson's story, southern and western but not exclusively or wholly either, is remarkable, but in so many ways, far from unique. People who aren't supposed to get around—African Americans, or women, who for whatever reason are supposed to know their place—somehow find room to move. Coming to terms with surprisingly mobile people like Robinson makes me, as a sometime historian of the American West, suddenly conscious of the weight of the western frame, suddenly alert, edgy, and restless.

Notes

1. David J. Garrow, "Foreword," to Jo Ann Gibson Robinson, *The Montgomery Bus Boycott and the Women Who Started It* (Knoxville: University of Tennessee Press, 1987), pp. viii–xv.

2. On the significance of mobility in American history, see George W. Pierson, "The M-Factor in American History," *American Quarterly* 14, no. 2 (Summer 1962): 275–289. For an example of an extended attempt to understand geographical mobility in feminist terms, see Virginia Scharff, *Taking the Wheel: Women and the Coming of the Motor Age* (New York: Free Press, 1991).

3. For critical reviews of feminist geography literature, see L. Bondi and M. Domosh, "Other Figures in Other Places: On Feminism, Postmodernism, and Geography," *Environment and Planning D: Society and Space* 10 (1992): 199–221; Linda

McDowell, "Space, Place, and Gender Relations: Part I. Feminist Empiricism and the Geography of Social Relations," *Progress in Human Geography* 17, no. 2 (1993): 157–179; Linda McDowell, "Space, Place, and Gender Relations: Part II. Identity, Difference, Feminist Geometries and Geographies," *Progress in Human Geography* 17, no. 3 (1993): 305–308. A pioneering work analyzing the spatial implications of American women's history is Dolores Hayden, *Redesigning the American Dream: The Future of Housing, Work, and Family Life* (New York: W. W. Norton and Company, 1986). The most ambitious example of new work in feminist historical geography is Daphne Spain, *Gendered Spaces* (Chapel Hill: University of North Carolina Press, 1992).

4. Johnny Faragher and Christine Stansell, "Women and Their Families on the Overland Trail to California and Oregon, 1842–1867," *Feminist Studies* 2 (Fall 1975): 150–166; John Mack Faragher, *Women and Men on the Overland Trail* (New Haven: Yale University Press, 1979); Julie Roy Jeffrey, *Frontier Women: The Trans-Mississippi West, 1840–1880* (New York: Hill and Wang, 1979); Sandra Myres, *Westering Women and the Frontier Experience* (Albuquerque: University of New Mexico Press, 1982); Byrd Gibbens, *This Is a Strange Country: Letters of a Westering Family, 1880–1906* (Albuquerque: University of New Mexico Press, 1988); Glenda Riley, *The Female Frontier: A Comparative View of Women on the Prairie and the Plains* (Lawrence: University Press of Kansas, 1988); Lillian Schlissel, *Women's Diaries of the Westward Journey* (New York: Schocken Books, 1982); Lillian Schlissel, Byrd Gibbens, and Elizabeth Hampsten, *Far from Home: Families of the Westward Journey* (New York: Schocken Books, 1989).

5. On Native women, see Margot Liberty, "Hell Came with Horses: Plains Indian Women in the Equestrian Era," *Montana, The Magazine of Western History* 32, no. 3 (Summer 1982): 14–15; Margot Liberty, "Plains Indian Women through Time: A Preliminary Overview," in Leslie B. Davis, ed., *Lifeways of Intermontane and Plains Montana Indians: In Honor of J. Verne Dusenberry*, Occasional Papers of the Museum of the Rockies, no. 1 (Bozeman: Montana State University, 1979), pp. 138–141; Elliott West, *The Way to the West* (Albuquerque: University of New Mexico Press, forthcoming); Rebecca Bales, "Changing Gender Roles and Sexuality in the Modoc Tribe of Northeastern California," paper presented to the Western History Association, New Haven, Connecticut, October, 1992. On Mexican migration, see Rosalinda Melendez Gonzalez, "Distinctions in Western Women's Experience: Ethnicity, Class, and Social Change," in Susan Armitage and Elizabeth Jameson, eds., *The Women's West* (Norman: University of Oklahoma Press, 1988), pp. 237–251; Vicki L. Ruiz and Susan Tiano, eds., *Women on the United States–Mexico Border: Responses to Change* (Boston: Allen and Unwin, Inc., 1987); George Sanchez, *Becoming Mexican American: Ethnicity, Culture and Identity in Chicano Los Angeles, 1900–1945* (New York: Oxford University Press, 1993). On Asian immigration and relocation, see Evelyn Nakano Glenn, *Issei, Nisei, War Bride: Three Generations of Japanese American Women in Domestic Service* (Philadelphia: Temple University Press, 1986); Valerie Matsumoto, "Japanese American Women during World War II," *Frontiers* 8, no. 1 (1984): 6–14. On migrant farmworkers, see Fran Leeper Buss, *Forjada Bajo el Sur: Forged under the Sun: The Life of Maria Elena Lucas* (Ann Arbor: University of Michigan Press, 1993); James N. Gregory, *American Exodus: The Dust Bowl Migration and Okie Culture in California* (New York: Oxford University Press, 1989). On cowgirls and women in wild west shows, see Dee Brown, *The Gentle Tamers: Women of the Old Wild West* (Lincoln:

University of Nebraska Press, 1993); Teresa Jordan, *Cowgirls: Women of the American West* (Lincoln: University of Nebraska Press, 1993). On African American migrants to the Plains, see Nell Irvin Painter, *Exodusters: Black Migration to Kansas after Reconstruction* (Lawrence: University Press of Kansas, 1976). On middle class women drivers, see Virginia Scharff, "Of Parking Spaces and Women's Places: The Los Angeles Parking Ban of 1920," *NWSA Journal* 1, no. 1 (Fall 1988): 37–51; and Scharff, *Taking the Wheel;* Sandra Rosenbloom, "Why Working Families Need a Car," in Martin Wachs and Margaret Crawford, eds., *The Car and the City: The Automobile, the Built Environment, and Daily Urban Life* (Ann Arbor: University of Michigan Press, 1992). For a more comprehensive bibliography of sources, see J. Etulain and P. Devejian, *Women and Family in the American West* (Albuquerque: Center for the American West, 1991). Thanks also to Elliott West for help with citations on Native American women.

6. I have made a similar argument in Virginia Scharff, "Gender and Western History: Is Anybody Home on the Range?" *Montana: The Magazine of Western History* 41, no. 2 (Spring 1991): 62–65. For a suggestive example of the possibility of such analysis, see Sarah Deutsch, *No Separate Refuge: Culture, Class, and Gender on an Anglo-Hispanic Frontier in the American Southwest, 1880–1940* (New York: Oxford University Press, 1987).

7. For a model of this form of dialectical analysis, see Belinda Bozzoli, "Marxism, Feminism, and South African Studies," *Journal of Southern African Studies* 9, no. 2 (April 1983): 137–171.

8. On space-time relations, see Anthony Giddens, *A Contemporary Critique of Historical Materialism* (New York: Macmillan, 1981); William H. Sewell, Jr., "A Theory of Structure: Duality, Agency, and Transformation," *American Journal of Sociology* 98, no. 1 (July 1992): 1–29.

9. On the problem of univocality, interpretation, and appropriation in the social sciences, see James Clifford, *The Predicament of Culture: Twentieth-Century Ethnography, Literature, and Art* (Cambridge: Harvard University Press, 1988); James Clifford and George E. Marcus, eds., *Writing Culture: The Poetics and Politics of Ethnography* (Berkeley: University of California Press, 1986); Renato Rosaldo, *Culture and Truth: The Remaking of Social Analysis* (Boston: Beacon Press, 1989); D. Gordon et al., "Feminism and the Critique of Colonial Discourse," *Inscriptions* nos. 3 and 4 (1988); Frances E. Mascia-Lees et al., "The Postmodernist Turn in Anthropology: Cautions from a Feminist Perspective," *SIGNS: Journal of Women in Culture and Society* 15, no. 1 (Fall 1989): 7–33.

10. Donna Haraway, "Reading Buchi Emecheta: Contests for Women's Experience in Women's Studies," *Women: A Cultural Review* 1 (1990): 243.

11. Robinson, *Montgomery Bus Boycott,* pp. xii, 9–10.

12. Ibid., p. 15.

13. Ibid., pp. 79, 90. For a detailed account of the rise of segregation practices, see Howard N. Rabinowitz, *Race Relations in the Urban South, 1865–1890* (New York: Oxford University Press, 1978).

14. Robinson, *Montgomery Bus Boycott,* p. 79.

15. Ibid., pp. xiii, 15–16.

16. Pleasant succeeded in forcing the company to transport black passengers. Helen Holdredge, *Mammy Pleasant* (New York: G. P. Putnam's Sons, 1953), p. 62.

Paula Giddings details a history of black women's opposition to discrimination in transportation in *When and Where I Enter: The Impact of Black Women on Race and Sex in America* (New York: William Morrow and Co., 1984), pp. 261–270; see also Barbara Y. Welke, "When All the Women Were White, and All the Blacks Were Men: Gender, Class, Race, and the Road to *Plessy,* 1855–1914," *Law and History Review* 13, no. 2 (Fall 1995): 261–316; Robin D. G. Kelley, "'We Are Not What We Seem': Rethinking Black Working-Class Opposition in the Jim Crow South," *Journal of American History* 80, no. 1 (June 1993): 75–112.

17. Robinson, *Montgomery Bus Boycott,* pp. 22, 31–2.

18. Ibid., p. 43; Giddings, *When and Where I Enter,* pp. 262–264.

19. Taylor Branch, *Parting the Waters: America in the King Years, 1954–1963* (New York: Simon and Schuster, 1988), p. 131.

20. Robinson, *Montgomery Bus Boycott,* pp. 45–46.

21. Ibid., pp. 92–94.

22. Ibid., pp. 39–74, 115.

23. Ibid., p. 140.

24. Branch, *Parting the Waters,* p. 312.

25. Robinson, *Montgomery Bus Boycott,* pp. 169–171. Kelley, "'We Are Not What We Seem,'" p. 95, notes that "Central to black working-class politics was mobility, for it afforded workers relative freedom to escape oppressive living and working conditions and power to negotiate better working conditions."

26. Robinson, *Montgomery Bus Boycott,* pp. xii, xv.

27. Ibid., pp. 171–172.

28. Robin Kelley uses the term "infrapolitics" to approach the political meaning of black working class opposition in the South, and acknowledges a scholarly tradition examining the meaning of everyday life ranging from the work of anthropologist James C. Scott, to theorist Michel de Certeau, to labor historian E. P. Thompson; Kelley, p. 77 fn. 9. Kelley, however, fails to acknowledge a long, global, and sophisticated tradition of feminist theoretical analysis of sexual and personal politics, including the work of, among many others, Mary Wollstonecraft, Alexandra Kollontai, Simone de Beauvoir, Kate Millett, and Joan Wallach Scott.

29. Glenda Riley, *The Life and Legacy of Annie Oakley* (Norman: University of Oklahoma Press, 1994); Isabella Bird, *A Lady's Life in the Rocky Mountains* (Norman: University of Oklahoma Press, 1960); T. A. Larson, *History of Wyoming* (Lincoln: University of Nebraska Press, 1978), pp. 84–94.

30. David Gutierrez, "Significant to Whom? Mexican Americans and the History of the American West," *The Western Historical Quarterly* 24, no. 4 (November 1993): 519–539, offers a powerful analysis of the significance of the literature of Chicano history. See also Antonia I. Castaneda, "Women of Color and the Rewriting of Western History: The Discourse, Politics, and Decolonization of History," *Pacific Historical Review* 61, no. 4 (November 1992): 501–534; Virginia Scharff, "Else Surely We Shall all Hange Separately: The Politics of Western Women's History," *Pacific Historical Review* 61, no. 4 (November 1992): 535–556.

31. Ellen Carol DuBois and Vicki L. Ruiz, "Introduction," DuBois and Ruiz, eds., *Unequal Sisters: A Multicultural Reader in U.S. Women's History* (New York: Routledge, 1991), p. xii; Scharff, "Else Surely We Shall all Hange Separately," p. 546.

32. Quintard Taylor, *The Forging of a Black Community: Seattle's Central District, from 1870 through the Civil Rights Era* (Seattle: University of Washington Press, 1994); Gretchen Lemke-Santangelo, *Abiding Courage: African American Women and the East Bay Community* (Chapel Hill: University of North Carolina Press, 1996); Shirley Ann Moore, "Getting There, Being There: African American Migration to Richmond, California, 1910–1945," in Joe William Trotter, ed., *The Great Migration in Historical Perspective: New Dimensions of Race, Class, and Gender* (Bloomington: Indiana University Press, 1991), pp. 111, 118–120; Douglas Flamming, essay in this volume.

33. David A. Hollinger, "Postethnic America," *Contention: Debates in Society, Culture, and Science* 2, no. 1 (Fall 1992): 79–96; David A. Hollinger, "How Wide the Circle of the 'We'? American Intellectuals and the Problem of the Ethnos since World War II," *American Historical Review* 98, no. 2 (April 1993): 317–337.

10

PLAGUE IN LOS ANGELES, 1924

Ethnicity and Typicality

WILLIAM DEVERELL

Anglo Saxon civilization must climax in the generations to come. . . . The Los Angeles of Tomorrow will be the center of this climax.

CLARENCE MATSON, "THE LOS ANGELES OF TOMORROW," IN *SOUTHERN CALIFORNIA BUSINESS*, NOVEMBER 1924

Turn-of-the-century booster marketing of Los Angeles rested upon simple images and symbols. Neatly tended gardens, attractive boulevards, and lovely homes: all could be represented as common, even prosaic, sights in the promised "Sunny Southland." Without doubt, regional climate occupied a special and iconic place in the creed of boosterism. Characterized especially by year-round warmth and aridity, weather proved an irresistible touristic lure. Boosters needed little convincing that climate merited a central role in their sophisticated selling of a "semi-tropic" city. Such reliance can easily be discerned in the myriad references to sunshine and health in such promotional vehicles as *Land of Sunshine* or the Southern Pacific's *Sunset.*[1] A wider embrace of nature's beauty and good health was exhibited by the hugely successful public relations firm known as the Los Angeles Chamber of Commerce which adopted the catchphrase "Los Angeles—Nature's Workshop" as one of its regional mottoes.[2]

Inherent to this campaign which sold a new commodity (the city itself) was a particular method, that of incessant reference to typicality and "the typical" (see figs. 10.1, 10.2). Image-making relied on repetition and sameness, on typicality, and this theme exists as backdrop in nearly every organized campaign of advertising Los Angeles from the railroad era of the 1870s and 1880s forward through the 1920s. The marketing was hardly as complex as it was merely brilliantly redundant, what with lithographic or photographic reproduction of the same neighborhoods, the same homes,

Figure 10.1 Typical southern California residence. Courtesy of the Huntington Library.

Figure 10.2 Typical park in California. Courtesy of the Huntington Library.

the same palm trees, the same bungalows, typical street scenes, typical vegetation, typical orange groves (with those ever-present snow-capped San Gabriels in the background). Postcards—little more than mass-produced and mass-distributed images of representativeness—blanketed the nation with images of Los Angeles life and landscapes. What may seem like caricature today was critical repetition then, the visual construction of regional idioms explicitly designed to encourage capital investment, tourism, and settlement. Stock images of life in Los Angeles were designed around the simple notion of representing the representative, over and over again.[3] But is there more to this story of wishful and pretty sameness?

Now look at these images (see figs. 10.3, 10.4), also from the mid-1920s, also from Los Angeles: disorderly, not neat, not beautiful. Yet the claim is that these views are also somehow "typical," apparently trustworthy representations of what Mexican Los Angeles looks like, what Mexican Los Angeles *is* like. The concern in this essay is to examine that assertion and the darker dimensions of the booster project surrounding "typicality." Behind the careful repetition of every ostensibly benign representation of the typical this and the typical that lay uglier assumptions, assumptions less about gardens, trees, or bungalows than about people, especially people of color.[4]

A plague epidemic, like that which struck Los Angeles in the fall of 1924, is a decidedly atypical event. But the municipal response to this public health crisis was refracted through a prism of stereotype, a civic tendency to render ethnic (in this case Mexican) lives, culture, and behavior as somehow "typical." To be sure, this story of plague is also about terrifying disease and family tragedy.

On October 2, 1924, Dr. Giles Porter, of the Los Angeles City Health Department, answered a call at the home of Jesus Lajun at 700 Clara Street. A day laborer for the Los Angeles Railway, Mr. Lajun was clearly ill, but Porter suspected nothing remarkable about the flu-like symptoms or Lajun's swollen and tender groin. Like her father, Francisca Concha Lajun, aged fifteen, seemed to be suffering from a bad case of the flu. She complained of a headache and a sore throat, and she had a temperature. Francisca did not get any better the next day, and a neighbor, Luciana Samarano, dropped by to help care for her. On October 4, now desperately ill, Francisca was taken to the hospital, but she died on the way there. Cause of death was listed as "double pneumonia."

Weeks passed. Meantime, infection careened virtually unseen through neighborhoods, homes, and bodies. At the end of October, physician George Stevens called Los Angeles General Hospital to report his suspicion that some highly contagious disease was whipping through the same neighborhood

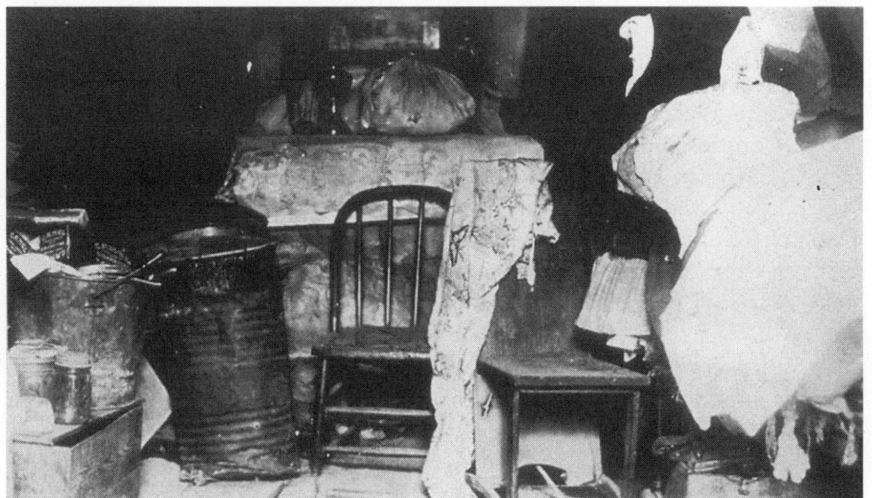

Figure 10.3 Typical interior of Mexican home. Courtesy of the Huntington Library.

Figure 10.4 Typical backyard. Courtesy of the Huntington Library.

where the Lajun family lived. He and another doctor, Elmer Anderson, had recently seen patients over there, all of whom complained of similar symptoms: chest pain, backache, fever. Stevens requested that a quarantine ward be set up to receive patients.

On October 29, an ambulance accompanied by Dr. Emil Bogen, resident physician of Los Angeles General Hospital, was sent over to the predominantly Mexican (and overwhelmingly poor) district. Bogen and the attendants found a group of people clustered around the front porch of a little house. In the house's only room, an old Mexican woman lay crying on a large double bed. Her cries were regularly broken by hacking coughs. A young Mexican man of about thirty lay on a couch against the wall; he did not cry, but he was clearly "restless and feverish." Several other people were in the room; one man agreed to translate discussion. Bogen found out that the man had gotten sick the day before, that he had a pain down his spine, and that he was running a dangerously high fever of about 104 degrees. He had red spots on his chest. The old woman had been coughing for two full days. She spit up blood. The ambulance took these two people away, to General Hospital.[5]

At another house nearby, a man, his wife, and their young daughter complained of the same aches and pains. They, too, exhibited disturbing symptoms. They appeared extremely anxious, their corneas were cloudy, and their faces had a sickly blue tinge. Four boys, brothers, were sick at yet a third house. Bogen learned that their mother and father had already died of what was thought to be pneumonia. Others were sick nearby, the interpreter said. Authorities took the boys to the hospital.

This house at 742 Clara Street, where the boys had gotten sick, would become the death house.[6] Before it was all over it must have seemed as if the house was possessed by evil, which, in a way, it was. In addition to the boys, others at 742 Clara complained of lingering sickness that day. Physicians took cultures from two of the sick adults, and they inoculated a guinea pig with the cell samples. The animal would soon die, as would the two people. Health investigators at General Hospital began piecing together information about those who had already died, including the parents of the sick, now-orphaned, boys. Original diagnoses of the sick people, which ran the gamut from meningitis, influenza, pneumonia, and typhus, began to be reconsidered.

"Lucena [it seems likely that her name was actually Luciana] Samarano, age 39, female, Mexican, 742 Clara Street," is how the medical inspection began which described the boys' mother. Luciana had fallen ill in the middle of October, just at the time she began to care for Francisca Lajun, and died within five days at the tiny house where she, her family, and a handful of roomers lived. Six months pregnant when she first fell ill, Luciana delivered a stillborn infant shortly before dying.[7] Doctors first ascribed her death to heart disease. Family members held a wake at the Clara Street house which was attended by many family members and friends. Burial followed at the Municipal Cemetery.

Luciana's husband, Guadalupe, had gotten sick a few days after his wife died. So had Jessie Flores, a family friend and next-door neighbor who had nursed Luciana during her illness. Guadalupe went downhill very fast, and a Spanish priest, Father Medardo Brualla from Our Lady, Queen of the Angels Church in the nearby plaza, had been summoned. The situation looked hopeless, but it was decided to send Jessie and Guadalupe to the hospital anyway. Father Brualla administered last rites. Jessie Flores and Guadalupe Samarano were dead within days. So, too, was Father Brualla.[8]

Unsuspecting health officials released Guadalupe Samarano's body to remaining family members so that they might hold funeral services at 742 Clara Street, just as they had been held for his wife, Luciana. Horace Gutierrez, Luciana's young cousin, was the next to get sick, and it was his illness and eventual death that really confirmed the presence of an epidemic. As Horace lay dying in the hospital, Dr. George Maner, the hospital pathologist, happened to engage in a conversation with several of the younger physicians who expressed confusion over the symptoms of several critically ill patients, Gutierrez and Guadalupe's brother Victor among them. At first facetiously, Dr. Maner suggested that perhaps the patients were suffering from plague; he had just finished reading about plague in Manchuria. But when he found evidence of just that beneath his microscope after performing an autopsy on Horace's body, the physician no longer joked. He sought the advice of a colleague, who, upon seeing the distinctive, unmistakable microscopic representation of *Yersinia pestis,* supposedly exclaimed, "Beautiful but damned."[9] An ancient disease, the Black Death, had arrived in the city of tomorrow.

The four Samarano brothers tried to fight off the intruder trying to kill them. Ten-year-old Roberto had gotten sick the same day as his mother's cousin. And like Horace Gutierrez, he died on October 30. Soon all the boys were deathly ill in the general hospital. Gilberto died next, then Victor. Little Raul hung on (see fig. 10.5). Horace Gutierrez's sixteen-year-old brother Arthur died. Fred Ortega, a boarder at 742 Clara Street, died. Joe Bagnola, another boarder, died. Alfredo Burnett, Luciana Samarano's son from an earlier marriage, was admitted to the hospital at the end of October along with all the others, exhibiting "weakness, fever, irritability, and stupor." He died on November 11.

Many more people would sicken and die, especially those who harbored the plague infection in their chests (where it could easily migrate, person to person). People who had visited 742 Clara Street to help with chores got sick and died. Luciana Samarano's sixty-three-year-old mother, who lived at

Figure 10.5 Plague survivor Raul Samarano, c. 1925. Courtesy of the Huntington Library.

342 Carmelita Street, developed a cough and a fever and died in a matter of days. Samarano relatives at 741 Clara Street died. Guadalupe Valenzuela, fifty-two years old, from Marianna Street in Belvedere Gardens, just across the city line, could not fight off the disease. Neither did her son, Jesus, and her daughter, Maria. Jesus and Maria were cousins of Guadalupe Samarano. At least one of them had been to Luciana Samarano's funeral in the middle of October. Jesus died first, at home, on October 31. Health officials learned from Maria that relatives were expected from New Mexico; guards rushed to meet them on the train station platform and prevent them from coming to the house.[10]

Throughout the first week of November, now a month after the first victim had died, the body count rose. Fear and rumor spread through the neighborhood. The Jimenez brothers had lived at 742 Clara Street, but when everyone in the house started getting sick and dying, they had quickly moved to nearby Date Street. But they did not move quick enough. One day after moving, Mike Jimenez got sick. Then his brother Jose fell ill with fever, aches and pains; both brothers died within days. Eulogio Peralta, twenty-two, from Bauchet Street, died. A credit slip found among his effects was from the Fox Outfitting Company on South Broadway in downtown where Eulogio worked. It showed Peralta's address as 742 Clara Street. Like the Jimenez brothers, Eulogio Peralta had tried to outwit and outrun the plague by moving away when people started getting sick and dying. Like the Jimenez brothers, it was too little, too late, and the disease caught him and killed him.

Thomas Vera, a young man who lived in a shack out back of 712 ½ Clara Street with three other adults and two children, died. He had been a friend of the Jimenez brothers, Mike and Jose. Hanging out with them probably killed him. Emmett McLauthlin died. With his brother Frank, Emmett ran an ambulance service from where he lived on Hope Street. He had helped move Guadalupe Samarano from 742 Clara Street to the county hospital at the end of October.

Thirty-two-year-old Mary Costello almost died. She had been the attending nurse to Guadalupe Samarano in late October. Complaining of headache, backache, chills, pains in her chest, and exhibiting "marked general malaise," Costello was hospitalized in an isolation ward at the end of the month. By Halloween she was spitting up blood. Doctors hooked her up to an intravenous injection of a Mercurochrome solution, a combination germicide and herbicide. This did not kill nurse Costello; neither did the plague. After a week, she had improved slightly; by month's end, still exhibiting the symptoms and characteristic weariness of a bout with pneumonic plague, Mary Costello had seemingly beaten the disease. Little Raul Samarano also fought off the pneumonia consistent with this strain of plague bacillus. As such, he was the only member of his family to escape death.[11]

The 1924 plague outbreak in Los Angeles was the last major outbreak of the disease in the United States. More than thirty people died, most all of whom had been connected by networks of kin or neighborhood. Ninety percent of those killed by the disease were of Mexican descent.

The situation calls for drastic action.

DR. WALTER DICKIE TO WILLIAM LACY, PRESIDENT OF THE LOS ANGELES CHAMBER OF COMMERCE, NOVEMBER 15, 1924

Plague is a mysterious and especially frightening disease. Its arrival in Los Angeles in the mid-twenties, in a poor neighborhood within sight of downtown, elicited a powerful response from the city's leaders. In an era (and city) rife with Americanization programs, many of which were explicitly concerned with "purity" and "hygiene," there can be little doubt that plague represented an apex of "uncleanliness" and demanded sometimes desperate cleansing measures.[12] The intravenous injections of Mercurochrome which Mary Costello endured, for instance, were thought to be a way of sterilizing the body's infected blood and other fluids.

A similar activity took place in particular Los Angeles neighborhoods, where authorities attempted cleansings as well, often with agents no less fierce than Mercurochrome. Not unlike an isolation ward at the county hospital, these neighborhoods underwent physical isolation, quarantined by force and heavy rope. Ironically enough, many had already been virtually quarantined by the restrictions imposed upon populations socially and politically ostracized due to ethnicity and class. Plague simply presented another method by which to enforce isolation of Mexican neighborhoods and Mexican people. And in ordering and describing this work, city authorities let suggestions of ethnocentric blame creep into their reasoning and their documents, not to mention assertions of white supremacy over and above supposed Mexican typicality. To turn our view in that direction, we must follow the city's response to the plague, in facets medical, political, and military.

Dr. Walter Dickie, Los Angeles resident, secretary of the California Board of Health, and the man who would take charge of medical affairs surrounding the outbreak, apparently first read about the epidemic in his morning newspaper at the end of October or beginning of November. The as-yet-unnamed disease had taken nine lives, the paper said, and seemed to be a kind of especially virulent pneumonia. Dickie wired an official of the city health department, inquiring as to the cause of death of Luciana Samarano. The reply read simply: "Death L. S. caused by Bacillus pestis."[13]

Word began to spread, in both official circles and the infected neighborhood. Benjamin Brown, a surgeon attached to the United States Public Health Service, wired the U.S. Surgeon General of the gravity of the situation in early November. His telegram was encoded for secrecy. "Eighteen cases ekkil [pneumonic plague]. Three suspects. Ten begos [deaths]. Ethos [situation bad]. Recommend federal aid." The Surgeon General responded by immediately sending a senior surgeon to Los Angeles to monitor the situation and make regular reports.[14]

Acting on the basis of their own diagnosis, the city health department ordered a quarantine of the so-called "Mexican district," a downtown section of small homes and industrial sites around Macy Street. The quarantine was to begin at midnight on October 31. Patrol of the roped-off area, which housed an estimated 1,800 to 2,500 people, was left to the Los Angeles Police Department and guards employed by the health department.

With rope supplied by the Los Angeles Fire Department, the authorities shut down the Macy Street neighborhood. In-and-out traffic was forbidden; guards were placed at both the front and back of any home known to house (or have housed) a plague victim. Health authorities urged residents to clean their homes inside and out; people were also told to wear thick clothing (especially underwear) at all times. The everyday activities of people ceased, and "gatherings of all nature" were prevented. Children were to stay home from school and keep away from movie houses. Pacific Electric trolley conductors, running their cars down Macy Street, shouted to riders that no one was to get on or off the cars at any of the regular stops.[15]

Los Angeles city government also responded. Mayor George Cryer called an emergency meeting for Monday afternoon, November 3. Present were various medical personnel representing federal, state, and local agencies, as well as others less versed in the particulars of infectious disease transmission or prevention: "members of the Board of Directors of the Chamber of Commerce, the local publishers and the business and financial interests of the city." These civic and commercial leaders understood that the plague outbreak might make the city a victim as well. The hastily convened committee of "experts," which constituted nothing less than the ruling oligarchy of the city, would meet more than once during the scary weeks of the epidemic's virulent phase.[16]

All medical and preventive work in connection with the epidemic was placed under the direction of Dickie of the Board of Health. He suggested that the city adopt or continue various emergency procedures. All cases of possible plague were to be sent to the county hospital, and a laboratory was to be set up immediately; "all undertakers [were] instructed not to embalm any bodies of Mexicans or others dying suddenly or of undetermined causes until the bodies [could] be examined by a representative of the State or City Health Department"; and rodent trappings would begin immediately in order to establish the boundaries of the epidemic.[17]

The quarantine continued and grew to include other neighborhoods. Rumors spread that a hundred, two hundred, Mexicans were dead and dying. Between residents and the police powers stepped the Los Angeles County Charities, trying to ensure "cubicle isolation" of homes. Parents were told to prepare a mixture of hot water, salt, and lime juice for their children to gargle several times a day. Charities' staff made a card index of every member of every home, and they delivered packages of food and bottles of milk to each house.[18] The Catholic Board of Charities sent into the field a priest and a social worker who spoke Spanish. Physicians and nurses began daily house-to-house tours, hailing occupants (who by public health standards of the day were called "inmates") from streets and sidewalks to determine if anyone within had fallen sick. People caught outside their homes or neighborhoods had to sleep in the Baptist Mission Church at the corner of Bauchet and Avila streets because the authorities would not let them pass through the ropes.

The quarantine, which lasted two weeks, would eventually stretch to include five urban districts. And there can be little doubt, given the way in which these neighborhoods were described (by language and perimeter), that there existed a perceived overlap between ethnicity and disease. The aim was to ensure that both large and small congregations of Mexican people be snared within the net. The quarantine included: the Macy Street district, largest of the five and including the Clara Street address; South Hill Street district, which included "one large apartment house, occupied by Mexicans"; the Marengo Street district, "including several isolated Mexican homes;" the Pomeroy Street district, including "two isolated Mexican homes"; and the Belvedere Gardens district, just outside city boundaries, where an unknown, though considerable, number of Mexicans lived.[19]

Records from the Belvedere Gardens describe the perimeter established by Carmelita Street, Brooklyn Avenue, a ravine just off Marianna Street, and Grandview Street. Like the city's efforts, the county quarantine was highly militarized. Health authorities later boasted that the epidemic ended so quickly precisely because the county's eventual four hundred quarantine guards and support personnel "were placed on a military basis and the organization was perfected." Some quarantine guards, most of whom were paid five dollars a day (except those working in closest proximity to the plague contagion, who were paid more), had been soldiers in the First World War; some even had wartime quarantine experience.[20]

Although they were dealing with an extraordinary situation, county officials gave the quarantine careful thought. The plans reveal ethnic as well as epidemiological attitudes. The Belvedere quarantine operation was placed in the hands of county health chief J. L. Pomeroy, a man with significant quarantine experience who believed that special guard details were "the only effective method of quarantining Mexicans." Pomeroy worried that Belevedere residents might disrupt quarantine procedures: he and his men "worked quietly" throughout the day of November 1 "so as not to unduly alarm the Mexicans." Pomeroy wondered about "a general stampede" and admitted that "we feared [the Mexicans] would scatter." The quarantine went up and around the neighborhood with stealth. "We waited until midnight so as to give them all a chance to get in. . . . then the quarantine was absolute."[21]

Guards, sworn in and issued badges, took up patrol "in the field" on one of three eight-hour shifts. Shifts had captains as well as quartermasters, guards "walked post," and surplus military and armory equipment provided the materiel of guard camps. Guards complained of run-of-the-mill soldiers' ailments: one burned himself when a coffee pot blew its top, another rushed to get a dose of "lockjaw preventive serum" when he stomped on a nail.

Guards did more than prevent the daily comings and goings of people in the neighborhood. Despite "general orders" which listed rule number one as "No Shooting," guards spent a good deal of time killing stray cats and dogs, a handful of chickens, a donkey or two, even a goat. They also damaged or destroyed a considerable amount of property within the militarized perimeter. Mrs. Pasquale Moreno, for instance, seems to have had her sewing machine requisitioned by quarantine guards, who broke it. Firewood, at least in the early days of the quarantine, proved scarce, and quarantine guards, trying to stay warm under chilly November skies, looted the neighborhood. Mr. L. S. Camacho, who lived on Brooklyn Avenue, later sought damages from health authorities for the destruction of a house he owned on San Pablo Court. There quarantine guards in search of combustibles ripped off plaster boards, an entire door, and even stole a stepladder—all of which they promptly burned. Neighbors swore that they had seen the guards attack the little house. In a later investigation of the claim, the County Health Department's special agent agreed that "half of the rear of the house was torn out by the guards." Mr. Camacho was granted his compensation request of fifteen dollars.[22]

We do not know what came of Benigno Guerrero's claim for damages in the amount of sixty dollars for the Mexican food destroyed at his business (which he translated as "Quality Tamales Home") in Belvedere. But we do know that he wrote a letter to health officer Pomeroy:

> My dear Dr. Pomeroy,
>
> Enclosed you will find the bill of food that I have being forced to destroy. That food was my only capital to keep my business going and I am sorry not to possess your language to impress you with the idea, than such small amount of money was the only means to provied [sic] food for my family, wife and four children, 8, 6, 3 and 1½, years old. Bring your attention to that situation, my dear Dr. Pomeroy and you will grant than the bill be payed.
>
> Sincerely very truly yours,
> B. Guerrero[23]

Most of the property destruction was by plague-fighting design, however, and not the result of individual action by quarantine guards. The overall plan, borrowed from San Francisco's program of plague eradication in the earlier part of the century, was a combination of slash and burn destruction and a campaign to lift structures well off the ground with blocks so that cats and dogs (those lucky enough to escape execution as strays) could run under the buildings in hunting rats. In the words of Walter Dickie: "The quickest and cheapest [method], the one we are adopting, is to take everything off the ground in the blocks infected and raise it 18 in. above the ground and take the siding off all sides of the house except the front so dogs and cats can go under, so when you get through, you can see all under." Accordingly, various "sanitary details" in both the city and county ripped the siding from homes, especially at the foundation level, buried garbage, and burned spare lumber, old furniture, clothing and bedding, even entire shacks. Workers sprayed houses and other buildings with petroleum or sulphur, and they scattered lime and rat poison everywhere. Some squads utilized "hydrocyanic" gas, a cyanide mixture; others rigged hoses to truck exhaust pipes and pumped carbon monoxide into buildings. By the end of 1924, quarantine guards had performed well over ten thousand plague "abatements" of greater and lesser destruction.[24]

The destruction of these homes and shacks without compensation was likewise part of the overall plan. In conversations with the City Council and Board of Directors of the Los Angeles Chamber of Commerce (which had quickly established its own health and sanitation committee), Dickie had advised that the structures to be "cleansed" first be declared nuisances, which meant that no compensation would need to be paid to property owners. "I wouldn't advise any compensation at all," said Dickie. Council members wondered aloud about the legality of such a move, but once assured by Dickie that "no compensation" was the way to go, they assented. Nor were destroyed houses or buildings replaced. An official report, issued less than a year after the plague outbreak, stated that over a thousand shacks and old houses, "housing Mexican wage earners mostly," had been destroyed and that, all told, roughly 2,500 buildings had been destroyed in the months from November 1924 to June 1925.[25]

Not only would buildings have to be destroyed. Rats would have to be killed, thousands and thousands and thousands of them. The Chamber of Commerce appointed a committee of its own to explore, in conjunction with the City Council and medical personnel, ways to raise money to kill plague-carrying rats and squirrels. The City Council would eventually grant the extraordinary sum of $250,000 for November 1924 through July 1925 (and twice that for the next twelve months) to be used primarily in rodent eradication programs. An entirely new city department arose *sui generis* to wrestle with the rat problem. Like some sort of latter-day Hudson's Bay Company, the department hired hunters and placed one dollar bounties on dead rats and ground squirrels. The staccato "pop" "pop" "pop" of small caliber weapons could be heard throughout the city day and night, and rodent poison appeared everywhere. The poison, a thick syrup containing phosphorous or arsenic, was spread on little squares of bread and cast about throughout entire neighborhoods, both quarantined and not. Its resemblance to molasses apparently caused rat killers some concern that the poison atop "dainty poison croutons" would find its way into the mouths of children (later, the officials of the federal Public Health Service would discontinue the practice for just this reason). Once the city began killing rats, Mexicans in the infected neighborhoods (who had been kept in the dark about what was killing them) knew that the epidemic had a name: plague.[26]

The rat-proofing work took on the appearance of a desperate fire-fighting operation as the city tried to extinguish both *Yersinia pestis* and the urban rat. Squads worked their way (and their spray) through entire neighborhoods in lock-step formation, attacking rats and structures (and unfortunate stray animals) house by house, block by block.[27] The effort was not entirely limited to ethnic neighborhoods: "It is important to remember," this same report noted, "that the danger from infected rats exists . . . even in residence districts occupied by native Americans, and these must be dealt with as definitely as the foreign districts." Be that as it may (apparently inhabitants of "foreign districts" could not, by definition, be "native Americans"), rat eradication work tended toward particular confluences of ethnicity and poverty. The program would work best "in the Mexican, Russian, Chinese and Japanese quarters by the destruction of all structures not worth rat proofing."[28]

The carcasses of countless rats stacked up at an emergency laboratory established in the Baptist Mission at Bauchet and Avila, where people rendered homeless by the quarantine sought shelter. Later moved to a more permanent location on Eighth Street, the lab (or "ratatorium") acted as headquarters for the ambitious rat-killing, rat-counting, and rat-testing operation.

Back at the county hospital, hospital personnel tried to ward off the chance of infection. Anyone suspected of either having plague or coming into contact with a plague victim had been immediately shuttled from quarantine to the county hospital. There, in isolation at the recently completed contagious disease building, they were labeled with red tickets to distinguish them from other patients. Physicians unaccustomed to wearing gloves during autopsy procedures took up the habit. Hospital workers wore gowns, rubber gloves, caps, and gauze masks. When that protection was deemed insufficient, they took to wearing a full face mask made from a pillowcase, eye holes cut out and covered over with clear celluloid. Physicians later noted that "procuring and working in these masks was a matter of considerable exertion, and also of considerable comment and divertissement."[29]

The Perils of Bad Publicity

> The thing that interests us and probably you more than this list of fatalities is what is the cause of this outbreak.
>
> DR. WALTER DICKIE BEFORE THE BOARD OF DIRECTORS, LOS ANGELES CHAMBER OF COMMERCE, NOVEMBER 6, 1924

By the middle of November, although occasional plague deaths would continue through the new year, the epidemic was believed to have ended.[30] By Thanksgiving, the Chamber of Commerce had received a signed statement from Dickie that the plague was over, a document which the organization deemed "just the thing to be good publicity."[31] Damage control, already under way by then, accelerated. The *Los Angeles Realtor* in its December 1924 issue, for instance, ran a feature by Chamber President William Lacy. Entitled "The Truth About Los Angeles," the article urged readers not to believe all that they had heard about the city's recent problems. Hysterical talk about "a slight drought," a power shortage, a foot and mouth epidemic, and "a slight epidemic of pneumonic plague" ought not deter people from visiting or investing in Los Angeles. It was a credit to the people of the city, Lacy continued, that concerted and cooperative work stamped out "the few cases of pneumonic plague."[32]

Commercial figures such as Lacy found themselves in a propaganda war with the East, mostly of their own making. For years, as eastern papers and publications pointed out, Los Angeles boosters crowed about the unique symbols of southern California living. Sunshine, fat oranges, pretty little bungalows, palm trees: boosters bombarded eastern cities and eastern folk with these ever-so-familiar images. But now, as Los Angeles found itself in a public relations tight spot, competitors and critics seized the opportunity to point out the limits of booster hubris in the City of Angels. Even typicality had its limits, if not its opponents.

For instance, in a hard-hitting piece for *The Nation,* former editor of the *Los Angeles Daily News* William Boardman Knox took the Los Angeles Chamber of Commerce to task for keeping the plague epidemic (as well as other health problems) under journalistic wraps. According to Knox, the plague and resulting quarantine provoked a mass exodus from the city as well as an economic collapse: "land values dropped 50 percent; bankruptcy courts were flooded with yesterday's millionaires; bank clearings were cut in half." In other words, Knox intimated, "don't believe all you hear (or *see*) about Los Angeles." The "typical" might be self-serving artifice, less than what met the eye.[33]

The city's commercial elite attempted to combat the rash of unfavorable publicity: at stake was the sheer viability of the campaign to establish the yardstick of typical Los Angeles places, diversions, scenes. Worse, winter tourism from East to West was threatened. But Chamber of Commerce stalwarts were, if anything, masters of spin. Even before the plague epidemic had become widely known, the organization had pledged to redouble its efforts at selling Los Angeles after being chastised by one of its leaders for not doing enough. "I think the Chamber is in the most dangerous moment in its career," Paul Hoffman told his fellow Chamber directors (exactly one day before the plague epidemic became known to public health officials). "We have got to impress the people of Los Angeles with the fact that we are going on to bigger things—If we go on as we have been doing, I don't think that is enough."[34]

Such a necessity apparently became all the more imperative in the wake of the epidemic. The Chamber's Publicity Committee, as Knox intimated in his *Nation* essay, was not about to let unfavorable news get in the way of advertising Los Angeles. And they had certainly kept bad news about the city's health record quiet before; already that year, the Chamber had wrestled with news about a smallpox outbreak in the city. At the beginning of the year, Chamber directors exchanged fears about what widespread knowledge of smallpox would mean. "It would be a black eye we couldn't get over for years," said one. Another added that "it is my personal feeling to suppress publicity."[35] All through November Chamber directors reiterated the desperate need to counteract eastern news of trouble in the Southland, even to the point of agreeing to print up special postcards (what else?) which every Chamber member could then rush east.

The local press stood by ready and willing to help—help through omission as opposed to commission. George Young, managing editor of the *Examiner,* eased the minds of the Chamber's Board of Directors when he assured them (with specific reference to the plague) that editors all along the Hearst chain "would print nothing we didn't think was in the interest of the city." Indeed, one teenaged resident of Los Angeles, who would grow up to be a local physician, remembers the plague as "a big hush up." Even his father, who owned a suitcase factory on Los Angeles Street, within walking distance of the Macy Street quarantine, knew little if anything of the outbreak.[36]

The Spanish-language paper *El Heraldo de Mexico,* which generally supported the plague suppression efforts, referred to "the hermetic silence in which authorities have locked themselves." News of the plague dominated *El Heraldo*'s headlines for days and days in November.[37] *Examiner* Editor Young, backed up by Harry Chandler of the *Los Angeles Times,* even thought that a virtue could be made of "the close squeeze we just had." Once the rat eradication program did its work, "we could then advertise Los Angeles as the ratless port."[38]

Faced with a medieval problem like Black Death in their "Los Angeles of Tomorrow," nervous boosters from the Chamber sought out health officials for briefings throughout the month, even after the various quarantines had been lifted. For instance, at a Saturday meeting on November 15, Walter Dickie spoke at length about the plague in front of directors of the Chamber of Commerce and the Los Angeles City Council.

Standing before a map of greater Los Angeles, Dickie pointed out that the black pins jabbed into the map "are pneumonic plague cases." His few yellow pins were bubonic cases. Though the assembled civic leaders certainly knew it, Dickie nonetheless pointed out that the epidemic, and the rats which helped spread it, were "not only a health problem but an economic problem." In this, Dickie made explicit reference to the port of Los Angeles. "I realize that the dream of Los Angeles and the dream of officials and the Chamber of Commerce is the harbor. Your dream will never come true as long as plague exists in Los Angeles and as long as there is any question of doubt in reference to the harbor." Unless the harbor received a clean bill of health, as soon as possible, Dickie warned, "half of the commerce of your harbor will quickly vanish. . . . No disease known," Dickie stated ominously, "has such an effect upon the business world as the plague." Chamber leaders and councilmen must have blanched.[39]

The situation was desperate, Dickie warned. Even if the determination of plague foci (or origins of each case) looked to be complete, no one could be sure about much of anything, at the harbor or anywhere else. The proximity of the Macy Street quarter to downtown Los Angeles and important industrial sites made the problem all the more acute. Dickie did not want any rats from the Mexican quarter chased into downtown. "You are not a great way off from [the] Baker building," he pointed out, obviously gesturing to his map and the city's commercial district.

Nor did people relish the thought of Mexicans from the district coming into downtown, as they did every single day for work or shopping. Cafe, restaurant, and hotel workers who lived in the Macy Street district lost their downtown jobs, as did others characterized simply as Mexican, therefore dangerous. The Biltmore Hotel, for instance, fired its entire Mexican labor force of 150, regardless of the home addresses of these men and women. A delegation of Mexican governmental officials and journalists met with the Chamber of Commerce to protest the action; they were met by Clarence Matson, whose 1924 prophecy about the city's Anglo-Saxon future opens this essay. The Chamber promised to look into the matter.[40]

Dr. Dickie wanted more laboratory support, more manpower for rat-killing and rat-proofing, and he wanted more medical teams for autopsy work. The latter request was "so that all Mexicans that die and all suspicious deaths that come into the Bureau of Vital Statistics shall be examined." The association of disease with ethnicity could not have been made more grimly explicit: "If it is not a general rule to autopsy all Mexicans that die of acute illness and are suspicious, many foci are going to be overlooked." In other words, this plague outbreak had become (indeed had been since the beginning) peculiarly Mexicanized.[41]

Dickie had overseen the placing of thousands of rat traps and would need thousands more. But he admitted that the Macy Street district—where 90 percent of the plague victims had encountered the disease—had not received as much attention, for instance, as the harbor. In a remarkable admission (and plea for help), Dickie implored his audience of elite Anglo businessmen: "I wish you gentlemen would go down to the Macy St. district. We haven't done anything because it is a question whether that area is worth the money you will have to put on it to clean it up and after you clean it, whether it will pay the property owner to put it into shape for human habitation. That is something [that] should be considered by the city."[42]

Dr. Dickie did not mean that *nothing* had been done in the Macy Street quarter; after all, the houses and structures there had been attacked by the sanitary squads who sprayed, burned, knocked down, and lifted up. But he did mean to ask the Council and Chamber whether or not they would see to it that the area be, essentially, razed and rebuilt. "All [of the area's little shacks and homes have] to be gutted out and destroyed and go back to the original structures and each original structure must have the ground area all exposed so that there can be no place for harboring rats."[43] Those assembled assured the physician that they well understood his warnings ("We are thoroughly alive to the situation") and would support cleanup efforts even if they cost a half million dollars.

Dickie ended his comments before the assemblage by arguing that the city must do more about the housing conditions of "the foreign population." "There is no reason why these Mexicans shouldn't be housed in sanitary quarters in the environment they are used to living in," he pointed out. Otherwise, the city risked epidemics (of smallpox, plague, typhus) of far greater proportion than the current crisis. Dickie chastised the city's elite: "As long as you have the foreign population, Mexicans, Russians, and various nationalities, you have to take care of them." City/county boundaries did not make any difference. The situation in Belvedere Gardens was just as bad, if not worse, than that within Los Angeles itself: "I haven't seen anything in my life to equal it," Dickie said, whereupon councilman Boyle Workman piped in that houses in Belvedere Gardens were "built out of piano boxes."[44]

Destruction would have to take place before construction, an activity that the city and county officials apparently pursued with some enthusiasm.[45] Furthermore, the publicity problem occupied a great deal of time as well, and this seemed to take precedence over any committed plans for renewal. Even health officials got into the act. In his report describing the city's health care response to the plague, City Health Commissioner George Parrish listed the name and address of each plague victim, hoping in some way to combat what he called "the grossly exaggerated reports published in the Eastern newspapers, with the evident intention of stopping the ceaseless migration of tourists to this wonderful city."[46]

Officials also engaged in a congratulatory discussion of their own in explaining why this had been but a "slight epidemic."[47] For one, it seemed as if the plague had limited foci, with at least ten cases, including most of those in the county, traced directly to 742 Clara Street. The alacrity with which Angelenos began killing rats was also fortunate. And lastly, officials thought that they had been lucky in another respect, again couched in terms of supposed ethnic typicality. "The Mexican," read one contemporary report, "unlike the Oriental, does not attempt to hide his sick or dead. Being a Catholic people, they always, when ill, call the Priest, and generally are prompt in securing medical aid." This Catholic practice was seen in marked distinction to the Chinese and their response to the deadly plague outbreak in San Francisco's Chinatown earlier in the century.[48]

Revelation of such cultural practices, and, more important, revelation of the concomitant tendency of the dominant culture to stereotype such practice as "characteristic" or "typical," encourages us to read the reaction to the plague epidemic of 1924 as part of the typifying project which elites participated in during the period. Knowing how those inside the various quarantines felt or acted in the face of organized, even militarized, public health or police authority is a difficult task. Outside of official pleas for reparations, there is little information or documentation in quarantine or political records. It is equally if not more difficult to know what the epidemic and fear of disease meant to these thousands of people caught behind the quarantine ropes.[49] But if our analysis of the plague is contextualized within a broader social and cultural landscape, we may see reaction to it on the part of Anglo authority as an important part of a veritable public relations campaign to validate the booster paradigm of "typical Los Angeles."

Conventional reduction of things, events, landscape features, and individuals to archetypal representation both created and reinforced cultural tendencies toward ethnic stereotype.[50] For instance, in attempting to determine how certain plague victims encountered the disease, officials relied upon reflexive assumptions about traditional, that is, typical, Mexican behavior and Mexican attitudes. How did teenaged Francisca Lajun, who lived down the street from 742 Clara Street, contract the plague which quickly killed her? The answer was unclear, but ethnic stereotype supposedly could explain a great deal. As such, "Mexican-ness," or simply "being Mexican," created an environment which could foster disease.

"That evidence could not be obtained to connect these two cases [Francisca Lajun and anyone at 742 Clara Street] may be explained by the reluctance of the Mexican to impart information, especially when he does not fully comprehend the reason. If the tendency of the Mexican to visit relatives and friends during their illness is recalled, the explosive nature of this outbreak, limited to friends and relatives, is partly explained."[51]

Similarly, Chamber of Commerce leaders declared before health personnel that they knew about the living conditions of Mexicans, or at least enough to understand the transmission of the disease (even though it is clear that most had never been into the largely Mexican Macy Street quarter before). By their reckoning, this knowledge alone could rightly be substituted for epidemiological expertise. Experience as capitalists and paternalists, and even as tourists, provided the necessary skills and reference points.

"I am not only familiar with the housing conditions of our Mexicans," Director William Lacy said, "but familiar with the Mexican peon's way of living in Mexico." There, fifteen years previous, Lacy had witnessed an outbreak of plague on the west coast in which, he said, the "Mexican population died like fleas." The only recourse had been to "blast practically half the city down and drive the people into the country in order to clean up the city." Los Angeles had better not repeat that history. On the contrary, the aim was to keep the population quarantined both in "their" and "a" place: "as we are bound to have that population, we must assume the responsibility of providing them a place to live peaceably." Lacy seemed not to realize the odd juxtaposition of "peaceableness" with health; it was as if the plague had made the "docile" Mexicans of Los Angeles unruly.[52]

But of course that was true; the plague had rendered Mexicans unusually dangerous in the eyes of many whites, not only because Mexicans seemed to have the disease but also, I suspect, because the disease was seen to be peculiarly Mexican. Perhaps Anglo anxiety in this chicken-and-egg manner helps explain the even more interesting language of some of William Lacy's colleagues. D. F. McGarry closed one discussion by pointing out that the city's Mexican population could not easily be dislodged from the poor districts. "In many instances they are there because of cheap rent contiguous to their work. They cannot afford to live in quarters that would be acceptable to us or as should be for the ordinary citizens."

The assumption that Mexicans were not somehow "ordinary" is interesting enough (i.e., they existed in some category reserved for them as *Mexicans*), but McGarry followed this remark with a fascinating slip, by averring to "this particular plan of eradicating them from those districts, which is highly proper and wise." Rat-killing and potential solutions to a "Mexican problem" merged: eradication as verb, if not action, of choice.[53] Perhaps it was just too difficult for the councilman to think about where to put *them* once the quarantines, be they social, economic, or medical, were lifted.

There is little doubt that the cross-over of words and concepts between rats and Mexicans occurred. Recall Dr. Pomeroy's fear that the Mexican population in Belvedere "would scatter" or "stampede" if they knew of the plague or of quarantine plans. Even the militarized response to the plague—best expressed by the quarantine and sanitary details—had as its purpose a goal of aggressive cleanliness aimed at both rats and Mexicans. Just as Mercurochrome was thought to be a cleanser for the plague's internal manifestations, so too with "petroleum spray" and chloride of lime aimed, not surprisingly, at the lives of those people who existed at the confluence of poverty and ethnicity, effectively "quarantined" well before the epidemic hit.

This is not to suggest that, given the epidemiological history of the 1924 plague outbreak, the *specifics* of such associations had no validity whatsoever. Certain links of sociability, ethnicity, neighborhood, and kin obviously contributed to the pattern of plague distribution. But it is in the *generality* of elite Anglo comment and point of view, the instinctive, reflexive reach to such phrases as "the Mexican" that we recognize the broader implications regarding assumptions of ethnic and racial typicality.

The most obvious expressions of Anglo categorization in this regard were also the simplest and most graphic. Illustrations (reproduced in this essay) which accompanied the contemporary public health document describing the plague outbreak noted such environments as the "typical interior of [a] Mexican home" and a "typical backyard." It is as if the photographer—in this case more than likely a public health official—had merely wandered over from his Chamber of Commerce assignment of shooting "typical factories" or "typical palm trees" to taking pictures of "typical Mexicans" (although the absence of people in the photographs is interesting). So-called typical images of Mexican lives and homes, homes far removed from the stock bungalow images, no doubt served to relieve a fair amount of anxiety in the health or civic community. Reaction to such images might accomplish two related tasks. One, if the plague rendered Mexicans something other than "peaceable," photographs which repositioned them into their usual, "typical" spaces and places might serve to render them less unruly in the minds of elite Anglos. And two, "typical" images of degradation and filth could seemingly help solder the perceived connections between plague transmission and ethnicity; any of these photographs would inevitably commingle disease with poverty, poverty with ethnicity, ethnicity with disease. It was, after all, typical.[54]

Descriptions of the districts, really nothing more than extended captions to the images, confirmed patterns of seeing and believing. Quarantined neighborhoods, bulging under an "ever increasing Mexican population," exhibited the "*usual number* of over-crowded rooming houses and temporary shacks on the back lots." Even the cumulative collection of typical Mexicans could create a homogeneous group: "the unobstructed and uncontrolled immigration from Mexico tends yearly to increase *this class* of inhabitants."[55]

The practice of assigning ethnic Mexicans to rigid cultural containers, boxes even more rigid than those created by street or district boundaries, encouraged Anglos to look at Mexicans in certain, particular ways. And plague in 1924 offered a kind of proof to the essentialist theorem. In other words, if the dominant view tended toward an image of all ethnic Mexicans as a class of equally degraded, poverty-stricken laborers living in rat-infested congregations, what could offer greater affirmation than a nasty outbreak of pneumonic plague which killed mostly Mexicans? It isn't difficult to discern the outlines of the ugly circular logic.

The 1924 plague epidemic in Los Angeles killed people in a few distinct neighborhoods; it killed people who came into contact with one another, and the dead were nearly all ethnic Mexicans. These were not mutually exclusive categories. But neither were they part of an essentialist triangle, where the one category (place, culture, ethnicity) naturally led to the other. Yet an examination of the reaction to the plague reveals a tendency on the part of the dominant culture to view and to explain the plague epidemic along such lines, lines of familiarity and lines of typicality.

Such a response could do little to break down conventional understandings of ethnic life and culture in Los Angeles. On the contrary, contemporary language helped reinforce ideas about "the typical Mexican" and restricted laborer space in the industrial economy. Having embarked upon a booster city-building journey which demanded iconic images and symbols, Anglo Los Angeles produced an ambitious glossary of "the typical," a project which, alongside obvious socio-economic stratification, effectively snared ethnic Mexicans and held them fast. Just as Anglos in Los Angeles felt certain that they understood the bungalow and the palm tree, so too did they self-consciously assert that they understood this Mexican, frozen in time and quarantined in space.

Notes

This essay is part of a larger book project examining ethnic relations, particularly between Anglos and Mexicans, in Los Angeles history. Much of the thinking and research on this essay came out of the time I spent as an Ahmanson-Getty Fellow at the Clark Library and Center for Seventeenth- and Eighteenth-Century Studies during the "American Dreams, Western Images" year-long investigation. I would like to thank the Ahmanson Foundation and Getty Trust, as well as the other fellows and participants for their encouragement and support. Special thanks to George Sanchez, Valerie Matsumoto, and Blake Allmendinger; my appreciation as well to Peter Reill, Marina Romani, Dace Taube, Alan Jutzi, Jennifer Watts, Bryant Simon, Diana Barkan, Dr. Shirley Fannin, Clark Davis, Mike Davis, Tom Sitton, Jane Apostol, and Martin Ridge. My deep gratitude to Doug Flamming, my Ahmanson-Getty partner in 1993–94.

1. Charles Dwight Willard, booster extraordinaire, started the *Land of Sunshine* in 1894; the journal eventually became less boosterish in tone and content, especially once Charles Fletcher Lummis took over the editorial duties full-time and changed the magazine's name to *Out West.* In its earlier life, however, the journal was little more than a Chamber of Commerce publication.

2. "Facts About Industrial Los Angeles, Nature's Workshop" (Los Angeles: Los Angeles Chamber of Commerce, 1926). For insightful readings of regional boosterism in the period, see, among others, Norman M. Klein and Martin J. Schiesl, eds.,

20th-Century Los Angeles: Power, Promotion and Social Conflict (Claremont, CA: Regina Books, 1990), esp. chap. 1; Clark Davis, "From Oasis to Metropolis: Southern California and the Changing Context of American Leisure," *Pacific Historical Review* 61 (August 1992): 357–386; Kevin Starr, *Inventing the Dream: California through the Progressive Era* (New York: Oxford University Press, 1985); Kevin Starr, *Material Dreams: Southern California through the 1920s* (New York: Oxford University Press, 1990), esp. chap. 5; Robert Fogelson, *The Fragmented Metropolis: Los Angeles 1850–1930* (Berkeley: University of California Press, 1993); Mike Davis, *City of Quartz* (London: Verso Press, 1990), esp. chaps. 1 and 2; see also William Deverell, "Privileging the Mission over the Mexican: The Rise of Regional Consciousness in Southern California," in Michael Steiner and David Wrobel, eds., *Many Wests: Place, Culture, and Regional Identity* (Lawrence: University Press of Kansas, 1997).

3. Some sense of the degree to which "typicality" informed the ways in which Los Angeles constructed and understood all kinds of cultural categories can be gained even by examination of non-Anglo promotional vehicles. The "typicality trope" crossed racial bounds, and it was present as well amongst the African American community. For instance, the proud pamphlet *Western Progress,* published in 1928 by two African American entrepreneurs, highlighted the "economic and social advancement in Los Angeles" through these now-familiar images. Businesses, homes, sunshine, flowers, and so on were all exhibited as representative images of African American life in the city. The Conner-Johnson Funeral Home, for instance, "typifies so well the progressive west" and Nickerson's Drug Store stood as "an excellent example of the new idea in western business." See Louis Tenette and B. B. Bratton, *Western Progress: A Pictorial Story of Economic and Social Advancement in Los Angeles, California* (Los Angeles: Tenette & Bratton, 1928). African American boosterism, and its relationship to Anglo boosterism, has been discussed in William Deverell and Douglas Flamming, "Race, Rhetoric, and Regional Identity," in *Power and Place in the American West* (Seattle: University of Washington Press, forthcoming). For an earlier depiction of the reflex, see *Los Angeles California, Queen City of the Angels* (Los Angeles: M. Rieder, ca. 1907), with its pamphlet depictions of the city's "typical Mission residence" and "typical cottage house" (both extremely large).

4. This reflex could be found at work even within the progressive reform community. See, for instance, John Kienle, "Housing Conditions among the Mexican Population of Los Angeles," M.A. thesis, University of California, 1912; Kienle, who would soon run the city's housing commission, noted that "the idea was not to have the investigations confined to one locality or any particular type of construction, but to cover the vast area dotted with Mexican homes, thus endeavoring to select those in each community, which, in my judgment, were typical of the rest" (p. 2). Kienle had opened his discussion with an apparent nod to diversity amongst the Mexican population in Los Angeles, pointing out that "there are many Mexicans in Los Angeles, who are divided into different classes." Two pages later, however, he admits that "there are three classes of Mexicans."

5. Details about the plague outbreak and its victims are drawn largely from "Plague in Los Angeles, 1924–25," bound manuscript produced by the California State Board of Health, copy in the Huntington Library, subchap. 1 [of 12], p. 49. Hereafter cited as "Plague in Los Angeles." Other sources I have found helpful in

this project include James H. Jones, *Bad Blood: The Tuskegee Syphilis Experiment* (New York: Free Press, 1981), esp. chap. 2; Hans Zinsser, *Rats, Lice and History: The Biography of a Bacillus* (Boston: Little, Brown, 1934); Alan Brandt, *No Magic Bullet: A Social History of Venereal Disease in the United States since 1880* (New York: Oxford University Press, 1987).

6. Clara Street is directly behind the Terminal Annex Post Office on Alameda Street (not yet built in 1924), within sight of downtown Los Angeles. The little bit of Clara Street still in existence today is dominated by a penal complex.

7. See Helen Martin, *The History of the Los Angeles County Hospital (1878–1968) and the Los Angeles County-University of Southern California Medical Center (1968–1978)* (Los Angeles: University of Southern California Press, 1979), chap. 15: "The Plague Epidemic." Years later, a Los Angeles physician tracked down Luciana Samarano's midwife (who had not contracted plague); the midwife verified that Luciana had delivered a stillborn child on the very day that she died. See John Emmett to Alexander Langmuir, July 17, 1952, in miscellaneous correspondence files, Communicable Disease Division, City and County of Los Angeles Health Services Department.

8. Bruella's first name may have been Medrano. He is buried in the clergy burial plot at the San Gabriel Mission.

9. Martin, *History of the Los Angeles County Hospital,* p. 68.

10. Maria Valenzuela was sent to the county hospital on October 31, just as the Belvedere Gardens quarantine was getting under way. Her mother, however, was not; one of the county physicians wrote that Guadalupe Valenzuela, along with her son and another daughter, were "appreciably under the influence of liquor" and that he "was not concerned regarding her condition." She died on November 3. See the narrative of the county plague response, "Plague," in miscellaneous correspondence files, Health Services. The author of this document is probably county public health officer Dr. J. L. Pomeroy.

11. It is difficult to determine how old Raul Samarano was at the time of the epidemic. Some texts (e.g., Martin, 1979) argue that Raul was the fourteen-month-old son of Luciana and Guadalupe. Some eyewitness accounts suggest that he was older, somewhere between six and nine years old. A photograph in "Plague in Los Angeles" seems to indicate that Raul was a very young boy, and he himself suggested this years later. A 1960 story in the *Los Angeles Examiner* about the plague brought about an impromptu reunion of Raul Samareno (his last name now changed) and Dr. Elmer Anderson, one of the physicians who had first responded to the Macy Street quarter illnesses. After the epidemic rendered him an orphan, Raul lived with relatives, became a ward of the state in foster homes, worked for the Civilian Conservation Corps in the thirties, joined the Navy, and ended up with a position in the Army Corps of Engineers in Los Angeles County. See *Los Angeles Examiner,* March 14, 1960.

The death grip of disease was actually the work of two different forms of plague: most of the cases were diagnosed as the more deadly and contagious pneumonic plague, a few others were identified as bubonic plague. According to a graph in California State Board of Health, *Special Bulletin No. 46, Pneumonic Plague: Report of an Outbreak at Los Angeles, California, October–November, 1924* (Sacramento: State Printing Office, 1925), the plague outbreak (both forms) killed the following thirty-three individuals (spelling maintained as printed): Francisca Lujon, Lucena Samarano, Guadalupe Samarano, Jessie Flores, Ruth San Ramon, Josephe Christenson, Peter Hernandez, Roberto Samarano, Gilberto Samarano, Victor Samarano, Marie Samarano, Alfredo Burnett, Father Brualla, Urbano Hurtado, Joe Bagnolio, Juliano Herrera, Fred Ortega, Arthur Gutierrez, Horace Gutierrez, Efren Herrera, Jesus Valenzuela, Juana Moreno, Refugio Ruiz, Guadalupe Valenzuello, John McLoughlin, Mike Jimenez, Jose Jimenez, Tomasa Vera, Lujo Peralta, Frank Perinlo, Maria Rodriguez, Mercedo Rodriguez, and Martin Hernandez [Abedannio]. In some cases, I have checked spellings in the 1924 Los Angeles City Directory; in others I have relied on the documentation within "Plague in Los Angeles." All plague victims except for ambulance driver McLauthlin died at General Hospital. McLauthlin died at St. Vincent's. There remains some confusion as to the identity of the four Samarano brothers; I suspect that one of them was named Victor (Raul, Roberto, Gilberto, and Victor). This would mean that two Victor Samaranos were killed by the disease: the young boy and his uncle. The other, equally plausible scenario given the poor record-keeping surrounding the plague, is that there were actually only three Samarano brothers, not four as the eyewitness accounts suggest.

12. As historian George Sanchez has noted, with particular reference to Los Angeles, "Americanization programs are an important window for looking at the assumptions made about both Mexican and American culture by progressive Californians during the 1920s." George Sanchez, *Becoming Mexican American: Ethnicity, Culture and Identity in Chicano Los Angeles, 1900–1945* (New York: Oxford University Press, 1993), p. 106. For studies of local Progressive reform, see Mary Odem, *Delinquent Daughters: Protecting and Policing Adolescent Female Sexuality in the United States, 1885–1920* (Chapel Hill: University of North Carolina Press, 1995); William Deverell and Tom Sitton, eds., *California Progressivism Revisited* (Berkeley: University of California Press, 1994); Sanchez, *Becoming Mexican American*, esp. chap. 4.

13. Quoted in Arthur Viseltear, "The Pneumonic Plague Epidemic of 1924 in Los Angeles," *Yale Journal of Biology and Medicine* 47 (March 1974): 40–54; quoted at p. 41.

14. Ibid. Viseltear also notes that both the *New York Times* and the *Washington Post* quickly picked up the story.

15. "Plague in Los Angeles," at subchap. 12, p. 11. Retired Los Angeles physician Edward Shapiro remembers riding the Pacific Electric to his weekly violin lesson and hearing the conductor yell for everyone to stay on the train. Phone interview with Edward Shapiro, August 7, 1996.

16. "Plague in Los Angeles," at subchap. 12, p. 7. An informed discussion of the Los Angeles civic and commercial elite can be found in Starr, *Material Dreams*, chap. 6; see also Davis, *City of Quartz*, esp. chaps. 1 and 2; and Frederic Jaher, *The Urban Establishment* (Urbana: University of Illinois Press, 1982).

17. "Plague in Los Angeles," at subchap. 1, p. 27.

18. Delivery of food proved absolutely critical, as some families, caught as they were in the quarantine nets, ran out of food very quickly. See *El Heraldo de Mexico*, November 4, 1924.

19. "Plague in Los Angeles," at subchap. 12, p. 6, listed Belvedere's Mexican population caught in the quarantine as five hundred. But, at other times, health officials

admitted that the entire Mexican population of Belvedere ranged from seven to twenty thousand.

20. One guard, evidently seeking a promotion, pointed out that he had been in charge of the "general cleanliness + disinfection of a German Prisoner of War camp in France." See E. Teasdale to Carl Williams, November 9, 1924, in "Applications" file, Health Services. The five-dollar-a-day wage would have made guards amongst the highest paid people within the quarantine boundaries. See Sanchez, *Becoming Mexican American,* chap. 3.

21. Pomeroy admitted that he had gone home before establishing much of the quarantine perimeter on October 31 because "the hour was late." Of yet another quarantining incident, he wrote that, despite "considerable resistance from the Mexicans. . . . military quarantine soon brought them to terms." See J. L. Pomeroy's report for 1924 in miscellaneous correspondence files, Health Services. See also the narrative description of the county response, "Plague," in miscellaneous correspondence files. While it is most likely that the author of this latter document was county health chief Pomeroy, there is a slight chance that it was one of the quarantine's other physicians, a Dr. Roth.

22. See "Claims—Damages, etc." file, Health Services.

23. Benigno Guerrero to Pomeroy, November 11, 1924; Guerrero to Los Angeles County Board of Health, n.d.; "Claims—Damages, etc." file, Health Services. The food, which, presumably, quarantine guards either ate or threw away, included hundreds of large and small tamales, ninety pounds of chili, and seventy-five pounds of mixtamel [sic].

24. Walter Dickie, transcription of remarks before the City Council of Los Angeles and Board of Directors, Los Angeles Chamber of Commerce, November 15, 1924, in City Council petition no. 7340, City Archives of Los Angeles. Hereafter cited as Dickie transcription. Cyanide and monoxide treatments may have come into use primarily once the United States Public Health Service took over much of the rat-killing in the summer of 1925. See the *Annual Report of the Surgeon General of the Public Health Service of the United States, 1926* (Washington, D.C.: Government Printing Office, 1926), pp. 80–81. I cannot find anyone who suggested that this might not be the best idea in earthquake country. San Francisco public health authorities seem to have pioneered this idea. See the photograph on page 37 of Frank Morton Todd, *Eradicating Plague from San Francisco: Report of the Citizens' Health Committee and an Account of Its Work* (San Francisco, ca. 1909). See also Guenter B. Risse, "'A Long Pull, A Strong Pull, and All Together': San Francisco and Bubonic Plague, 1907–1908," *Bulletin of the History of Medicine* 66 (Summer 1992): 260–286; *Annual Report of the Los Angeles County Department of Health, 1924* (Los Angeles: County Department of Health, 1925).

25. [George Parrish], *Annual Report of Department of Health of the City of Los Angeles California for the Year Ended June 30, 1925* (Los Angeles, 1925), p. 60. Hereafter cited as Annual Report 1925. See Dickie transcription, November 15, 1924. That little, or nothing, was done to replace the hundreds, even thousands, of structures destroyed in the quarantined districts was made clear in the 1925 report of the city health department. The department's Bureau of Housing and Sanitation bluntly declared that "no new construction has been undertaken to house the people thus

dispossessed, [and] they have been scattered to other parts of the city and county, many of them into other houses or quarters that are unfit for home habitation, a menace to the city at large and a barrier to the progress of the life and character of the persons living in them" (Annual Report 1925, p. 60).

26. In one month alone, apparently, 600,000 pieces of poisoned bait were distributed in the industrial and commercial district down by the Los Angeles River. Charles Stewart, one of the foremen of a rat-killing detail, remembered years later that he "couldn't sleep at night. . . . Small children in the district often attempted to eat our 'rat sandwiches.' More than once I slapped a piece of poisoned bread out of a kid's hand." Stewart said no children ingested any of the poison, an assertion somewhat difficult to believe given the sheer amount of "rat molasses" spread around the various neighborhoods. See City of Los Angeles Health Department press release (marking Stewart's retirement), October 17, 1958, in "Plague Reference" file, Health Services; see also Ben Zinser, "City in Nightmare: How L.A. Battled Plague," in "Plague Reference" file. The "dainty poison crouton" label comes from San Francisco; see Todd, *Eradicating Plague from San Francisco*; see also *Annual Report of the Public Health Service of the United States, 1926.*

27. By May of 1925, the number of rats killed by the program was estimated to be over 100,000. Of these, 182 had tested positive for plague.

28. See "L.A. Tenement Problem and the Bubonic-Pneumonic Plagues: Report of Survey by Representatives of Nine Leading Organizations," *Municipal League of Los Angeles Bulletin* 7 (February 1925): 2–6. On the tendency of the dominant culture to create dichotomies between "native Americans" and "Mexicans," see the insightful discussion in Lisbeth Haas, *Conquests and Historical Identities in California, 1769–1936* (Berkeley: University of California Press, 1995), chap. 5.

29. "Plague in Los Angeles," at subchap. 1, p. 52.

30. Health officials nonetheless declared the Los Angeles harbor "plague infected" at the end of the year, despite the fact that no disease-laden rodent had been discovered there. See Viseltear, "Pneumonic Plague Epidemic," pp. 49–51.

31. See Stenographer's Reports, Board of Directors meeting, Los Angeles Chamber of Commerce, Regional History Center, University of Southern California, November 26, 1924. Hereafter cited as Stenographer's Reports. The Chamber of Commerce had earlier appointed a new health and sanitation committee, composed of "physicians, health officers, business men, city editors and local publishers and charity and school organizations." "Plague in Los Angeles," at subchap. 12, p. 8.

32. *Los Angeles Realtor* (December 1924): 7.

33. W. B. Knox, "Los Angeles' Campaign of Silence," *The Nation* 121 (1925): 646–647. Of the alleged cover-up of an outbreak of polio, Knox wrote: "What are a few broken children, probably of people who don't count anyway, compared to the welfare and prosperity of a great metropolis?" A later *Nation* article regretted Knox's hyperbole but stood by the assertion of a concerted public relations' campaign to mask the true details of public health problems in Los Angeles. See "Los Angeles and Its News," *The Nation* 122 (1926): 272.

34. See Stenographer's Reports, October 30, 1924.

35. In the first weeks of 1924, the city faced a serious smallpox outbreak, which members of the Board of Directors of the Chamber of Commerce wanted kept

quiet. See Stenographer's Reports, January 9, 1924; quotes from meeting of January 31, 1924 (quoting Directors Hill and Pridham).

36. See Minutes of the Board of Directors, Los Angeles Chamber of Commerce, November 13, 1924; telephone interview with Edward Shapiro, August 7, 1996. Mr. Shapiro remembers his father as a regular reader of the *Los Angeles Times* as well.

37. *El Heraldo de Mexico,* November 4, 1924. Robert McLean, in his reformist tract *That Mexican!* chastised the white press for publishing news of the plague outbreak "in the columns on the back pages of the newspapers—columns which are reserved for the stories of the earthquakes." Robert N. McLean, *That Mexican! As He Really Is, North and South of the Rio Grande* (New York: Fleming H. Revell Company, 1928), p. 150.

38. Minutes of the Board of Directors, Los Angeles Chamber of Commerce, November 13, 1924.

39. Dickie transcription.

40. Mexican consul Almeda registered protests with the city and the Chamber of Commerce over these dismissals. The Chamber of Commerce agreed to work toward the reinstatement of those workers who did not live within the quarantined districts; those that did were out of luck.

41. Dickie transcription, November 15, 1924. It is illustrative, for instance, that despite earlier concerns about other poor and predominantly ethnic neighborhoods housing Russians, Asians, and others, Dickie's explicit reference regarding autopsies is to Mexicans, and only to Mexicans. The suggestion is, I think, that plague transmission had become a vector of ethnicity and not of class.

42. Ibid.

43. Ibid.

44. Ibid.

45. In later months, when the United States Public Health Service took over some of the plague suppression activities, it was noted that the policy of destroying homes willy-nilly was "expensive, time consuming, and devoid of any great benefits." See *Annual Report of the Public Health Service of the United States, 1926,* p. 80.

46. Annual Report 1925.

47. In a small pamphlet published about a year after the outbreak, the Los Angeles County Medical Association celebrated both "the limited number of deaths" and absence of "a money loss, which, while running into the millions, could have been, five, or ten or twenty times as great!" Los Angeles County Medical Association, *The Bubonic and Pneumonic Plague: Some Questions and Answers in Regard Thereto* (Los Angeles, [County Medical Association, 1926?]).

48. "Plague in Los Angeles," at subchap. 12, p. 4. The Chinatown plague of 1900, according to one physician who studied it, was "one of the darkest pages in the history of North American medicine" in that an effort was made by the city's business and political leaders to cover up the outbreak and silence medical personnel. In addition, some city physicians refused to endorse the findings of plague by others. The outbreak arguably lasted four years. See Silvio J. Onesti, Jr., "Plague, Press, and Politics," *Stanford Medical Bulletin* 13 (February 1955): 1–10, quoted at p. 1; see also Henry Harris, *California's Medical Story* (San Francisco: Grabhorn Press and J. W. Stacey, Inc., 1932). Harris notes succinctly, in reference to the Chinatown outbreak,

that "such news was bad, for business and capital, always timid and jumpy, were fearful of sick rats and Chinamen." See also Risse, "'A Long Pull, A Strong Pull.'"

49. There is one tantalizing mention of rebellion by the "inmates" of the Macy Street quarantine within the newspaper record. The unsubstantiated story, which appeared decades after the outbreak, mentions LAPD officers wielding shotguns at angry residents who demand that the quarantine be broken. See Zinser, "City in Nightmare."

50. I found several helpful sources in this regard: Mark Reisler, "Always the Laborer, Never the Citizen: Anglo Perceptions of the Mexican Immigrant during the 1920s," *Pacific Historical Review* 45 (May 1976): 231–254; and, for a particular study of Los Angeles, Douglas Monroy, "Like Swallows at the Old Mission: Mexicans and the Racial Politics of Growth in Los Angeles in the Interwar Period," *Western Historical Quarterly* 14 (October 1991): 435–458. See also Carey McWilliams, *Southern California Country: An Island on the Land* (New York: Duell, Sloan and Pearce, 1946), esp. chap. 15; David Gutierrez, *Walls and Mirrors: Mexican Americans, Mexican Immigrants, and the Politics of Ethnicity* (Berkeley: University of California Press, 1995), esp. chap. 3; Haas, *Conquests and Historical Identities,* esp. chap. 5; and Sanchez, *Becoming Mexican American.*

51. "Plague in Los Angeles," at subchap. 12, p. 43.

52. See remarks of William Lacy, Stenographer's Reports, November 6, 1924.

53. Stenographer's Reports, November 6, 1924. A still-useful study of the "Mexican problem" can be found in Carey McWilliams, *North from Mexico: The Spanish-Speaking People of the United States* (New York: Lippincott, 1949), chap. 11.

54. Such association was by no means new nor limited to Los Angeles. Assumptions about ethnicity's role in disease susceptibility and transmission had long been staples of American medical, not to mention political, thought. For a representative version of this ideology, albeit slightly later, see Benjamin Goldberg, "Tuberculosis in Racial Types with Spanish Reference to Mexicans," *American Journal of Public Health* 19 (March 1929): 274–286. "We seem, throughout the United States," Goldberg wrote (with specific reference to Chicago), "to be asleep to the menace of the immigrant Mexican" (p. 274). It is especially intriguing that Goldberg distinguished the health risks posed by urban African Americans from Mexicans. The former, he argued, had a more legitimate claim upon citizenship and its benefits (including, presumably, health care) than the latter. I am grateful to David Gutierrez for bringing this article to my attention.

55. "Plague in Los Angeles," at subchap. 12, pp. 19 and 29 (italics added).

11

THE TAPIA-SAIKI INCIDENT

Interethnic Conflict and Filipino Responses to the Anti-Filipino Exclusion Movement

ARLEEN DE VERA

"I now pronounce you man and wife." With these words, Justice of the Peace H. P. Andrews, County of Sacramento, State of California, on February 3, 1930, formally declared Felisberto Suarez Tapia and Alice Chiyoko Saiki married, and set the seal on a madcap elopement. Tapia, twenty-three, a Filipino box maker employed at the Stockton Box Factory, and Saiki, eighteen, a second-generation Japanese American, had met at Alice's father's pool hall in Stockton.[1] Immediately after the marriage, the happy couple set about making their plans. Alice would return to her parents' home in Stockton, where Felix would later join her. Just two nights apart, and then with the marriage certificate in hand, they could begin their new life together as husband and wife.[2]

But instead of a happy ending, their joining was to lead to tragedy and conflict. The next day, when Felix appeared at the Saiki home, his in-laws flatly refused his requests to see his wife.[3] Believing that his father-in-law had coerced Alice into leaving for Japan, an anguished Felix turned to local Filipino community leaders, who then called for a sympathy boycott and picket of Japanese-owned businesses. In retaliation, local Japanese labor contractors threatened a boycott of their own: to pass over several hundred Filipino farm laborers for work during the upcoming grape and asparagus seasons.[4] Rather than a personal family matter between a recalcitrant father, an absent wife, and an anguished groom, the Filipino and Japanese communities were polarized, ready to come to blows, while European American residents and the police kept a wary eye on both groups.

That local European American residents viewed these developments with such concern spoke volumes about the state of race relations. During the first month of 1930, minor tensions between Filipinos and Japanese in Stockton were overshadowed by the racial violence then engulfing California. Just days after an anti-Filipino race riot in Watsonville in which one Filipino was killed, a bomb exploded in the Stockton headquarters of the Filipino Federation of America, causing heavy damage. Shocked at the turn of events, one thousand Filipinos gathered at a Stockton mass meeting and voted to hold a major demonstration and parade for Philippine independence through Stockton on Saturday, February 8, to be held in conjunction with other public demonstrations in New York, Philadelphia, Chicago, and elsewhere.[5] In response, nativists seized the opportunity to call for an end to Filipino immigration to the United States.

This essay is a preliminary exploration of one way Filipinos responded to the anti-Filipino exclusion movement: by asserting a Filipino identity, an identity which in the process was continuously questioned, modified, and reaffirmed. As Michael M. J. Fischer has noted, groups act not upon a single, undifferentiated identity, but upon multiple identities, which are situational and, at times, contradictory. As Fischer notes: "Ethnicity is not something that is simply passed on from generation to generation, taught and learned; it is something dynamic. . . . Insofar as ethnicity is a deeply rooted emotional component of identity, it is often transmitted less through cognitive language or learning . . . than through processes analogous to the dreaming and transference of psychoanalytic encounters."[6] Most historical studies have chosen to focus on European American perceptions toward Filipinos and Japanese, often as groups with common characteristics.[7] In this context, the Tapia-Saiki incident offers an interesting point of departure. How did Filipinos view their relationship to European Americans and Japanese? Did these perceptions change with the rise of the anti-Filipino exclusion movement? How did Filipinos assert their identity when the anti-Filipino exclusion movement lumped them together with Chinese and Japanese as "cheap Oriental labor"? In short, this essay is a preliminary exploration of a much larger question: the process by which a group comes to self-identify and create and re-create its ethnic identity in relation to other racial groups.

This essay will also draw upon two concepts, culture and projection. By "culture," I mean those ideas, views, images, norms, and values a group shares, including racial attitudes and assumptions about human behavior and society. All these elements together constitute culture, by which means order and meaning can be imparted to people's lives. But culture is not static: culture is itself shaped *by* material conditions, even as it influences people's responses *to* material conditions.[8] As for "projection," I refer to the psychological act of transferring blame and responsibility for one's fears and condition onto another, in this case, another racial group.[9]

Filipino Migration and Japanese Settlement

The origins of Filipino immigration to the United States date back to 1898. Following Spain's defeat in the Spanish-American War, the Philippines became a colonial possession of the United States, and its people American "nationals"—an ambiguous legal status that meant neither citizen nor alien.[10] Beginning in the early 1910s, several thousand young Filipino men and women came to the United States to further their college educations. Educated, Westernized, and English-speaking, these "pensionados," as they were called, made a favorable impression on the American public. Most returned home to become the Philippines' professional elite.[11] Others also came to try their luck. Inspired by the stories of their American teachers, and by the pensionados' letters home, Filipinos arrived by the thousands in the port cities of San Francisco, Los Angeles, and Seattle during the 1920s. From less wealthy and educated backgrounds than the pensionados, many hoped to become self-made men and planned to attend school while working. Others hoped to earn enough to return home and purchase land or pay for their siblings' education. By 1930, more than thirty thousand Filipinos had settled in California, with most finding work in agriculture and service.[12]

Stockton's Filipino community mirrored these general trends. Every February, just before the asparagus season was to begin, Filipino Town came alive: some two thousand Filipino laborers streamed in, joining the town's one thousand permanent Filipino residents. Among the latter were a small group of Filipino entrepreneurs, owning among themselves a grocery store, a photo studio, the lone Filipino newspaper, and a tailor shop.[13]

These businessmen often doubled as the leaders of local Filipino community organizations. Teofilo Suarez, who owned the tailor shop, was also the president of a local fraternal organization.[14] Damiano Marcuelo, a former pensionado and the editor and publisher of the newspaper *The Three Stars,* was also the head of the Filipino Workers' and Business Men's Protective Association. In all, these businessmen, along with a few labor contractors and professionals, formed a fledgling business and intellectual grouping that spoke for the Filipino community of Stockton.[15] Their leadership would be tested in the following months during the rise of the anti-Filipino exclusion movement in 1930.

Stockton's Japanese community was centered around agriculture as well, though small business played a larger role in this community. A 1930s survey of occupations revealed that close to half of the town's 1,400 Japanese residents were farmers.[16] Another significant occupation was labor contractors, who provided and controlled the supply of agricultural labor, labor provided mostly by Filipinos.[17]

The beginning of 1930, though, raised new concerns about the role and place of Japanese in American society. Before 1930, the Issei, the first-generation Japanese immigrants, had guided their community through the difficult years of the anti-Japanese movement, which had led to racial violence and exclusionary laws barring land ownership, intermarriage with European Americans and Japanese immigration. By 1930, however, second-generation Japanese Americans, or Nisei, made up the majority of Japanese communities on the mainland.[18] Worried that this generation would be lost to them, community leaders consciously appealed to "racial" and parental loyalty to discourage Nisei interracial dating and marriage.[19]

Anti-Japanese/Anti-"Oriental" Sentiment and the Boycott Controversy

In January 1930, a columnist for the *Manila Sunday Tribune* wrote on a paradox facing Filipinos in the United States. Though Filipinos were defined as American nationals, it was Chinese and Japanese aliens who benefited politically:

> Once an alien is admitted, his advantages over a Filipino are by far the greater. In case of trouble the alien has his consul to go to for assistance. He is protected by his home government. The Filipino has no consul to whom to appeal for any injustice done to him. . . . it must not be forgotten that [the Filipino] is not entitled to all the rights and privileges of an American citizen, because he is not, and cannot be one.[20]

That their expectations of the United States could be so at odds with the realities was a painful shock. Their treatment as a second-class group violated the principles of liberty and equality and the Christian example of brotherhood they had been taught back home. Typical was the comment of the secretary of a central California Chamber of Commerce:

> It must be realized that the Filipino is just the same to us as the manure that we put on the land—just the same. He is not our "little brown brother." He is no brother at all! He is not our social equal! And we don't propose to make him that or pretend that he is. Why the Filipino should be greatly appreciative of the little that we have given him. . . . We have got to have the Filipino to do that work. . . . [T]hat's his place in *this* society.[21]

Thus, though Filipinos saw themselves as clearly different from both Chinese and Japanese, some European Americans saw them only as yet another wave of cheap "Oriental" labor. At King's Employment Agency in Stockton, one employer saw little social difference between the two groups, saying "[O]f all this cheap labor the Jap has always been the best. The Filipino is the *same kind of trash* but you get worse labor for the dollar."[22]

Another source of tension, expressed by both Filipino workers and small business owners, was economic. Filipino farm laborers filed complaints against some Japanese contractors who they claimed had swindled them out of their wages;[23] likewise, Japanese grocers filed complaints with local authorities, alleging that Filipinos had skipped town without paying their grocery bill accounts in full.[24] Some Filipino businessmen in Stockton also viewed the Chinese and Japanese with suspicion, as they were economic competitors for Filipino patronage. One contemporary observer wrote: "Filipino businessmen complain that their paisanos are disloyal, 'unpatriotic,' patronizing non-Filipino shops when Filipino shops are just as accessible and satisfactory. . . . Encouragement of paisanos to be loyal to their businessmen compatriots is seen in the following advertisement from a Filipino newspaper: 'When you come to town see us and patronize your people.'"[25]

For some Filipinos, this tension was at least in part due to historical factors. Under Spanish rule, Filipinos had been excluded from small business positions by law. Though these laws were later lifted in the nineteenth century, the prejudices and stereotypes persisted.[26] That these tensions continued was confirmed by sociologist Bruno Lasker, who noted in 1931 that Filipinos had "a hostile attitude" toward Chinese, resulting from "trade competition."[27] Just as Chinese in the Philippines had been cast in an unfavorable light, so Filipinos viewed both Chinese and Japanese in Stockton in the same way.

U.S.-Japan relations also played into Filipino attitudes toward the Japanese in the United States. Fears that Japan would challenge the United States for domination of the Pacific had worried American military experts stationed in the Philippines for years, since Japan's 1905 victory in the Russo-Japanese War.[28] So widespread was Japan's image as aggressor to both American and Philippine interests that one Filipino fruit worker in Stockton told an interviewer in February 1930 that while he favored independence, he thought it best for the Philippines to remain under some form of U.S. protection against the "threat" Japan posed.[29] Others were simply surprised to discover Japanese living in the United States. One twenty-four-year-old Filipino going into a hotel to rent a room on his first night in Seattle was astonished to find it was owned by a Japanese family. He mused, "Now I was in America and I was discovering that not all Americans were white."[30]

But while some disdained the Chinese and Japanese, others, like newspaper editor Damiano Marcuelo, held them up as role models of business acumen. Though acknowledging that Filipino businessmen and farmers had made relatively little progress, Marcuelo asserted that their economic future could still be prosperous, if they copied the Chinese and Japanese collective model of business enterprise:

> The Chinese and Japanese people in this state ought to be admired rather than looked upon with suspicion. Laboring under a peculiar legal disadvantage,

> they succeed in getting to the top of progress, so that today we see them with zealous eyes, building chains of hotels, stores, banks, grocery and other business houses. It is perseverance, thrift, and tact in them that insure their success. But the greatest of these is ORGANIZATION and CO-OPERATION.[31]

By encouraging owners not to duplicate services and businesses, Marcuelo believed Filipino businessmen could achieve prestige and stability in the United States.

Against this backdrop of increasing tensions, racial violence, and the organized anti-Filipino exclusion movement, Felix Tapia came forward on February 6 with the news of his marriage and his bride's disappearance.[32] Convinced that Mr. Saiki's actions were an expression of racial prejudice against Filipinos, the leaders decided on a boycott. In dramatic fashion, on Saturday, February 8, in front of two thousand Filipinos congregating for Philippine independence, Teofilo Suarez declared a "sympathy boycott" of all Japanese-owned small businesses in Stockton. Suarez explained the issues behind Felix's marriage and the reasoning behind the boycott. His remarks struck a chord, for one observer noted that subsequent speakers "vociferated in dialect at great length, casting aspersions at the Japanese and urging their compatriots to support the boycott."[33] Though emotions ran high, Filipino leaders urged all to remain calm and reaffirmed their admiration of American "altruistic and humanitarian achievements."[34] Left out was any mention of "calmness and order" toward the Japanese.

The increasing frustrations, anger, and fear expressed by Filipinos found a ready outlet in the boycott. That night, under Tapia's direction, "large numbers" of pickets appeared just outside all the Japanese-owned "restaurants, pool halls and shops."[35] Amid the pickets swirled rumors that the local Japanese Association of Stockton had supported the Saikis' actions because they felt that Filipinos were "an inferior people."[36] These rumors were repeated over and over as new picketers joined the lines and as word of the boycott spread. Though economic self-interest may have played a role in the business leaders' calls to nationalism, the allegations of "racial prejudice" struck a chord with Filipinos.

With tensions escalating between their communities Filipino and Japanese leaders quickly recognized the need to take immediate action. Alarmed at reports that the businesses were losing "thousands of dollars a day," and concerned that the Japanese labor contractors' threatened retaliation could lead to increased violence,[37] a meeting between the local Japanese Association of Stockton and the Filipino Safety Committee was hastily arranged for Sunday night, February 9.[38] But at that meeting, though the Japanese Association assured all present that the rumors of racial prejudice were unfounded, and though the Filipino Safety Committee added that they "deplored" the boycott and would do all they could to resolve the situation, in the end, both sides were forced to adjourn.[39]

Without any set plans for resolution, the boycott continued. By Tuesday, February 11, several restaurants and pool halls had closed.[40] And though disruptive, the boycott had resulted in no disturbances according to police reports; still, police patrols were increased, as "the feeling is very tense."[41]

The next day, things heated up again. Leo Cinco, former president of the Filipino Contractors and Laborers Association, issued a statement deploring the Japanese role in agriculture, and charged that the Japanese undercut Filipino wages. The tensions, he maintained, were due to racial prejudice and unfair economic practices of long standing:

> The principal cause of the whole situation was when the heads of a certain Japanese organization declared they did not like Filipinos and do not want them. This information was given us by Alice Saiki, the bride of Felix Tapia.
>
> Secondly, the Japanese farmers and laborers make the wages lower. Americans pay 40 cents an hour, but the Japanese pay only 25 cents. Sometimes Filipinos have to accept 25 cents an hour from the Japanese when they cannot find work. American growers, when they come to know this, also reduce the wages and as a result wages in the farm regions are getting lower and lower.

Cinco also alleged that Japanese contractors coerced Filipinos to buy supplies "from the Japanese only," and cited cases of Japanese farmers failing to pay wages to Filipino laborers and contractors.[42]

The charges elicited a strong response. Speaking on behalf of the Japanese Association of Stockton, Secretary Hikida denied reports that the marital separation was due to racial prejudice: "The bride's father acted as he did because the marriage was the outcome of an elopement and contrary to all Japanese traditions, which demand arrangements of a marriage by the parents of the bride. It was because of violation of this tradition, and not because he is a Filipino that Saiki forced separation of Tapia and his daughter."[43]

Hikida also emphasized that dealings between Filipino workers and Japanese farmers had been fair: "The Japanese farmers have been paying good wages and have been treating their Filipino employees as members of their own families, housing and boarding them in their own homes."[44]

By February 19, two weeks after its inception, support for the boycott began to flag as the pickets lessened, then began to subside.[45] The conclusion to the Tapia-Saiki incident came the next month, when Tapia lost his civil lawsuit against the Saiki family in court.[46] With no further recourse, the matter was dropped. In the end, the controversy lasted but a few weeks.

The larger significance of the boycott controversy lay in its foreshadowing of the public debate over Filipino racial classification, a debate that became supremely important with the rise of the struggle for Philippine independence and the anti-Filipino exclusion movement. Around the same time of the Tapia trial, a Los Angeles Superior Court judge ruled in a case involving Filipino and European American intermarriage that Filipinos were

"Mongolians" and thus prohibited by law from marrying European American women. The ruling immediately plunged the community into controversy again.[47] And again, the response was a distancing from Chinese and Japanese. The Filipino Federation of America issued an editorial decrying the reclassification: "the Filipino has been classed as belonging to the Mongolian or yellow race. This ruling was made for the purpose of restricting Filipinos to the same racial laws as apply to the Japanese and Chinese. . . . We do not protest because we are denied the privilege of marrying white girls but because *as a distinct race* we wish to be recognized as such." While acknowledging the presence of racially mixed Filipinos, particularly Chinese-Filipino mestizos, the paper insisted on the Filipino belonging to the Malay race, and not the "Oriental."[48]

Other arguments were put forth to bolster the Filipino's place based upon his Westernization. Another *Filipino Nation* editorial argued that the Filipino was not an Oriental, since he was Christian, Westernized, and easily assimilable to American culture and institutions: "The Japanese, Chinese and Hindus are genuine [o]rientals in family life, religion, ideals, customs, superstitions and civilization, while the Filipino has western customs, ideals, family life, religious, government and civilization."[49] In these contradictory ways, the place of the Filipino was thought to be enhanced.

Despite these efforts, the exclusion movement gained momentum as even those sympathetic to the Filipinos' status viewed them as indistinguishable from Chinese and Japanese. One advocate for Philippine independence, Democratic Senator Harry B. Hawes of Missouri, saw cause to remark on the "basic" differences between European Americans and Filipinos:

> The people are orientals, of Malay stock. We will never be able to change their thoughts, their characteristics, their minds or their national aspirations, any more than we can change the color of their hair, the texture of their skin, or their physical characteristics. Over 300 years of Spanish rule did not bring about racial changes. We can not expect them, now or in the future, to conform their thoughts and emotions to our own, or their mental processes to operate as do ours.[50]

Growing anti-Filipino sentiment reached its high mark with the passage of the Tydings-McDuffie Act in 1934. While providing for Philippine independence in ten years, the act also reclassified the legal status of Filipinos to aliens, thus excluding Filipinos from U.S. citizenship, and set the annual limit of Filipinos who could immigrate to the United States at fifty persons. But unlike previous restrictions on the Chinese and Japanese, this act had no loopholes that allowed for the immigration of merchants, or of wives and dependents of those already here.[51] The solution to the "Filipino problem," just as it had been for the "Chinese problem" and the "Japanese problem," was exclusion.

Conclusion

As time passed, however, tensions between the Filipino and Japanese communities in Stockton eased, and occasionally points of consensus did occur, particularly between the second generation. During the summer of 1938, a group of boys, among them, Richard Nunez, a twelve-year-old Filipino, and Masao Nishimura, an eleven-year-old Japanese American, went fishing along the Stockton channel. The boys were gathering their things together to go home when Nishimura, who could not swim, fell into the water. Nunez dove in and grasped him, but together, the pair were unable to climb the slippery cement banks of the channel. One of the boys, Darrel Hazelbaker, thrust his hands out to Nunez, who grabbed and held on for a brief second, then slipped. The pair thrashed about until, exhausted but holding on to each other, they sank and disappeared beneath the murky water. Though local authorities quickly pulled them out, efforts to revive the two were in vain.

Their deaths elicited an outpouring of grief and pride within the two communities. The local Filipino community newspaper eulogized Richard Nunez as a hero and an exemplary leader who was tragically lost to the community. Conspicuous among the mourners at his funeral was Mrs. Nishimura, along with representatives of the Japanese Association of Stockton. Also present was Teofilo Suarez, Nunez's uncle and the same Teofilo Suarez who along with Felix Tapia and others had led the boycott of Japanese-owned businesses eight years before.[52]

Such a show of solidarity at that time was extraordinary. The outbreak of the Sino-Japanese War the year before had caused some local Filipino community leaders to fear the possibility of a Japanese invasion of the Philippines.[53] Some of that concern was carried over to the Stockton Japanese community as well. Issei nationalism had been heightened by the 1937 war, and local Japanese leaders had raised funds for Japan's war effort and distributed pamphlets explaining Japan's side in the conflict.[54] Despite the potential for conflict engendered in international relations and economic envy, that a bond of sympathy could be forged suggests some capacity for consensus.

As the Tapia-Saiki incident indicates, Filipino thinking on race was complex and contradictory. Filipino actions in the boycott controversy and their responses to the anti-Filipino movement suggest that the reconciliation of Filipinos to their inferior status in the United States was predicated upon an "othering" of both Chinese and Japanese as "less civilized, Oriental" groups, based on historical prejudices and/or dominant notions of "assimilability." Angered by the incidents of racial violence and the growing anti-Filipino exclusion movement, and frustrated at their absence of power, Filipinos publicly projected these emotions onto Japanese for the duration of the boycott. But despite Filipinos' efforts to prove themselves different from the Chinese and the Japanese, in the end the exclusion movement viewed Filipinos as the latest wave of "undesirable and unassimilable Orientals." The timing of Japanese settlement and Filipino migration may have led to different economic niches for the two groups, but what they shared was a common status as "other" forced on them by European Americans.

Notes

I would like to acknowledge the valuable critiques and suggestions offered by Professors Valerie Matsumoto, George Sanchez, Steffi San Buenaventura, Yuji Ichioka, Gordon Chang, and David Yoo; and by fellow students Brian O'Neil, Sunny Lee, Shirley Lim, Joan Johnson, August Espiritu, Ned Blackhawk, Jo Ann Woodsum, and Glen Kitayama.

1. *Nichi-Bei* (Japanese American News), February 20, 1930, p. 1; Unpublished Field Notes, James Earl Wood Collection, Folder 3, "Field Notes Relating to Filipinos," Bancroft Library, University of California, Berkeley. Hereafter cited as Field Notes.

2. Superior Court, Case No. 23367, Complaint, *Filisberto S. Tapia* [sic] *vs. Yasaburo Saiki,* February 18, 1930, County of San Joaquin, State of California.

3. Ibid.

4. *Stockton Daily Independent,* February 12, 1930, p. 12.

5. *Sacramento Bee,* February 3, 1930, p. 1; February 5, 1930, p. 1. There were general reports that Filipino organizations in the U.S. passed resolutions condemning the race riots and calling for Philippine independence. See *The Philippine Republic,* February 1930, p. 14.

6. Michael M. J. Fischer, "Ethnicity and the Post-Modern Arts of Memory," in *Writing Culture: The Poetics and Politics of Ethnography,* James Clifford and George E. Marcus, eds. (Berkeley: University of California Press, 1986), pp. 195–196. See also George J. Sanchez, *Becoming Mexican American: Ethnicity, Culture and Identity in Chicano Los Angeles, 1900–1945* (New York: Oxford University Press, 1993), pp. 10–21.

7. The best accounts of the anti-Japanese and anti-Filipino movements remain Roger Daniels, *The Politics of Prejudice: The Anti-Japanese Movement in California and the Struggle for Japanese Exclusion* (Berkeley: University of California Press, 1962) and Howard A. DeWitt, *Anti-Filipino Movements in California: A History, Bibliography and Study Guide* (San Francisco: R and E Research Associates, 1976). For more comprehensive accounts of both movements as anti-Asian racism, see Ronald Takaki, *Strangers from a Different Shore* (Boston: Little, Brown and Company, 1989) and Sucheng Chan, *Asian Americans: An Interpretive History* (Boston: Twayne Publishers, 1991).

8. This view of culture is based upon Antonio Gramsci's concept of cultural hegemony: "an order in which a certain way of life and thought is dominant, in which one concept of reality is diffused throughout society in all its institutional and private manifestations, informing with its spirit all taste, morality, customs, religious and political principles, and all social relations, particularly in their intellectual

and moral connotation." As quoted by Ronald Takaki, *Iron Cages: Race and Culture in Nineteenth-Century America* (New York: Alfred A. Knopf, Inc., 1979), pp. xiv–xv.

9. See David Roediger, *The Wages of Whiteness: Race and the Making of the American Working Class* (New York: Verso Press, 1991), pp. 152–153. This psychoanalytic concept and its relevance for the development of racial attitudes was first utilized by Winthrop Jordan in his landmark study, *White Over Black: American Attitudes Toward the Negro, 1550–1812* (Chapel Hill: University of North Carolina Press, 1968). Jordan referred to it as "projection."

10. Luzviminda Francisco, "The First Vietnam: The Philippine-American War, 1899–1902," in *Letters in Exile,* Jesse Quinsaat, ed. (Los Angeles: Resource Development and Publications, UCLA Asian American Studies Center, 1976), pp. 1–22; Chan, *Asian Americans,* p. 17. For a perspective on the Spanish-American War from the viewpoint of African American soldiers, see Willard B. Gatewood, Jr., *Smoked Yankees and the Struggle for Empire: Letters Home from Negro Soldiers, 1899–1902* (Urbana: University of Illinois Press, 1971).

11. Their tuition was paid by the United States government, or by the colleges and universities they attended. See Takaki, *Strangers,* p. 58; Chan, *Asian Americans,* p. 75; Dorothy Cordova, "Voices from the Past: Why They Came," in *Making Waves,* Asian Women United of California, ed. (Boston: Beacon Press, 1989), pp. 42–49.

12. C. M. Goethe, "Filipino Immigration Viewed as Peril," *Current History* (June 1931): 353–356; Casiano Pagdilao Coloma, "A Study of the Filipino Repatriation Movement," master's thesis, University of Southern California, 1939, pp. 6–7.

13. *The Philippines Free Press,* March 27, 1926, p. 13, as quoted by Larry Lawcock, "Filipino Students in the United States and the Philippine Independence Movement: 1900–1935," Ph.D. diss., University of California, Berkeley, 1975, p. 514.

14. *The Three Stars,* June 1929, p. 4. Suarez was also an officer in the Filipino Business Association of California, formed in February 1930. See *The Three Stars,* February 15, 1930, p. 3.

15. Field Notes, Folder 3, "Field Notes Relating to Filipinos."

16. A total of 208 surveys were completed by Japanese pupils enrolled in Stockton area schools. The actual numbers for the top three categories were: farmers, 90; hotel keepers, 31; and merchants, 18. Miscellaneous came in at 24. It is somewhat curious that "labor contractors" were not listed. It is possible that a separate category for labor contractors was not established on the questionnaire itself. Unfortunately, a copy of the questionnaire was left out of the thesis. See Horace F. Chansler, "The Assimilation of Japanese in and around Stockton," master's thesis, College of the Pacific, 1932, pp. 34–35.

17. Two scholars state that the majority of contractors for Filipino seasonal labor during this time were Japanese. See Bruno Lasker, *Filipino Immigration to the Continental United States and Hawaii* (Chicago: University of Chicago Press, 1931; reprinted, New York: Arno Press, 1969), p. 89; and Carol Hemminger, "Little Manila: The Filipino in Stockton Prior to World War II, Part I," *The Pacific Historian* 24, no. 1 (Spring 1980): 25.

18. Takaki, *Strangers,* p. 214.

19. Paul Spickard, *Mixed Blood: Intermarriage and Ethnic Identity in Twentieth-Century America* (Madison: University of Wisconsin Press, 1989), pp. 98–106, 118–119.

Spickard says that for Nisei, intermarriage was "resolutely opposed," particularly with Filipinos and the latter groups. Though the Japanese also rationalized their second-class status at times by projecting their anger onto Filipinos, that is a topic for a future study.

20. *Manila Sunday Tribune,* January 12, 1930, as quoted in the *Filipino Nation,* March 1930, p. 47. Though uncredited, the author is probably Maximo C. Manzon, a New York City writer. Filipinos, as U.S. nationals, often had passports stamped "American citizen." See *Filipino Student Bulletin,* "Are the Filipinos in the U.S. in as Good a Position as Aliens?" November 1929, p.1.

21. Field Notes, Folder 10, "Miscellaneous Notes Concerning Filipinos in California."

22. Field Notes, Folder 3, "Field Notes Relating to Filipinos," emphasis mine.

23. Field Notes, Folder 3, "Field Notes Relating to Filipinos." One example from Damiano Marcuelo's cases was Albert N. Kawasaki, described as an unscrupulous local Japanese labor contractor.

24. *The Philippine Republic,* March 15, 1929, p. 16.

25. Field Notes, Folder 6, "Materials Relating to Filipino Labor in California, Wages, Hours, etc."

26. See Victor Purcell, *The Chinese in Southeast Asia* (London: Oxford University Press, 1965); Edgar Wickberg, *The Chinese in Philippine Life* (New Haven: Yale University Press, 1965). While these colonial influences had also fostered the development of Filipino attitudes toward other races, regional groups, and national minorities living in the Philippines, the literature has focused primarily on the Chinese presence in the Philippines. By comparison, the numbers of Japanese were thought to be much smaller.

27. Lasker, *Filipino Immigration,* p. 10.

28. Stanley Karnow, *In Our Image: America's Empire in the Philippines* (New York: Ballantine Books, 1989) pp. 263–265.

29. Field Notes, Folder 3, "Field Notes Relating to Filipinos." This interview was with Benito Abenis.

30. Craig Scharlin and Lilia V. Villanueva, *Philip Vera Cruz, A Personal History of Filipino Immigrants and the Farmworkers Movement* (Los Angeles: UCLA Labor Center, Institute of Industrial Relations & UCLA Asian American Studies Center, 1992), p. 53.

31. *The Philippine Republic,* March 15, 1928, p. 16. Marcuelo is a little-known but important figure in Filipino American history. After his role in the Stockton Japanese boycott controversy, Marcuelo later moved to Salinas, where he became the president of the Filipino Labor Union and, along with Rufo Canete, led the 1934 lettuce strike. See Howard DeWitt, "The Filipino Labor Union: The Salinas Lettuce Strike of 1934," *Amerasia Journal* 5, no. 2 (1978): 1–22.

32. The topic of Filipino and Japanese interracial dating and marriage is one covered in fiction and in a few works. See Hisaye Yamamoto, "Yoneko's Earthquake," in *Seventeen Syllables and Other Stories* (Latham, N.Y.: Kitchen Table: Women of Color Press, 1988) pp. 46–56; John Fante, "Mary Osaka, I Love You," *Good Housekeeping,* October 1942, pp. 40, 167–179; Eiichiro Azuma, *Walnut Grove: Japanese Farm Community in the Sacramento River Delta, 1892–1942,* master's thesis, University of

California, Los Angeles, 1992; and David Yoo, "'Read All About It': Race, Generation, and the Japanese American Press, 1925–1941," unpublished paper.

33. Field Notes, Folder 9, "Miscellaneous Notes Concerning Filipinos in California." *Nichi-Bei* reported the boycott as a general boycott of all Japanese stores. See February 13, 1930, p. 1.

34. The resolution committee of Damiano L. Marcuelo, Primo Villaruz, Teofilo Suarez, Primo Umanos, and J. Billones also sent copies to Philippine Resident Commissioners Pedro Guevara and Camilo Osias. *Stockton Daily Independent,* February 11, 1930, pp. 1, 2; *Sacramento Bee,* February 11, 1930, p. 7; *The Three Stars,* February 15, 1930, p. 1.

35. Lasker, *Filipino Immigration,* p. 17; *Berkeley Gazette,* February 12, 1930, pp. 1, 13; *San Francisco Chronicle,* February 12, 1930, p. 9. The Saikis' pool hall was closed, as it had been since February 6. Field Notes, Folder 3, "Field Notes Relating to Filipinos."

36. *The Three Stars,* February 15, 1930, p. 1.

37. *Stockton Daily Independent,* February 12, 1930, p. 12.

38. *The Three Stars,* February 15, 1930, p. 1; *Nichi-Bei,* February 13, 1930, p. 1, February 20, 1930, p. 1.

39. *The Three Stars,* February 15, 1930, p. 1, p. 5; *San Francisco Chronicle,* February 12, 1930, p. 9.

40. *The Three Stars,* February 15, 1930, p. 5.

41. *The Three Stars,* February 15, 1930, p. 5; *San Francisco Chronicle,* February 12, 1930, p. 9. By comparison, other cities and counties that experienced anti-Filipino violence, such as Monterey County and San Jose, did not increase their local patrols until February 18. See *Sacramento Bee,* February 18, 1930, p. 12.

42. Newspaper clipping, *Stockton Record,* February 12, 1930, James Earl Wood Collection, Folder 4, "Miscellaneous Clippings Relating to the Filipinos in California," Bancroft Library, University of California, Berkeley.

43. Newspaper clipping, *Stockton Daily Evening Record,* February 13, 1930, James Earl Wood Collection, Folder 4, "Miscellaneous Clippings Relating to the Filipinos in California," Bancroft Library, University of California, Berkeley.

44. Ibid.

45. *Nichi-Bei,* February 20, 1930, p. 1. Bruno Lasker reported that some slight damage had occurred to Japanese property, although he does not say specifically when. See Lasker, *Filipino Immigration,* p. 17.

46. *Stockton Daily Independent,* March 25, 1930, p. 8.

47. Staff, "Anti-Miscegenation Laws and the Pilipino," in *Letters in Exile: An Introductory Reader on the History of the Pilipinos in America,* Jesse Quinsaat, ed. (Los Angeles: Resource Development and Publications, UCLA Asian American Studies Center, 1976) p. 67. For a more comprehensive treatment of the anti-miscegenation laws affecting Chinese, Japanese, and Filipinos in California and other states, see Megumi Dick Osumi, "Asians and California's Anti-Miscegenation Laws," in Nobuya Tsuchida, ed., *Asian and Pacific American Experiences: Women's Perspectives* (Minneapolis: Asian/Pacific American Learning Resource Center and General College, University of Minnesota, 1982), pp. 1–37.

48. Editorial, "We Are Malayans," *Filipino Nation,* March 1930, p. 12, emphasis

mine. This view of Filipinos as part of the "brown" or Malayan race had been a central tenet of the Filipino Federation of America from the early years. The 1927 maiden issue of the *Filipino Nation* lists among its principles "Malaysia—United."

49. *Filipino Nation,* June 1930, p. 12.

50. Hawes favored Philippine independence early in 1930. See Karnow, *In Our Image,* p. 253; *Filipino Nation,* June 1930, p. 13.

51. This restriction was further exacerbated by the revising of the anti-miscegenation laws in California in 1933 to include Filipinos on the list of those forbidden to marry European Americans. See "Anti-Miscegenation Laws and the Filipino," by the staff, in *Letters in Exile,* pp. 63–71. One study has estimated that the formation of a visible second generation of Filipino Americans in California did not occur until the 1960s. See Amado Cabezas, Larry Shinagawa, and Gary Kawaguchi, "New Inquiries into the Socioeconomic Status of Pilipino Americans in California," *Amerasia Journal* 13, no. 1 (1986–87): 5–6. In states outside California which lacked anti-miscegenation laws, there were numbers, albeit small, of second generation, often multiracial Filipino Americans. See Barbara Posadas, "Crossed Boundaries in Interracial Chicago: Pilipino American Families since 1925," *Amerasia Journal* 8, no. 2 (1981): 13–52.

52. *Filipino Pioneer,* August 5, 1938, pp. 1, 4. In one example of the generally good relations between the first generation, in August 1929, on the occasion of the Third Annual Convention of the Filipino Federation of America, held that year in Stockton, the local "Japanese Business Association" [sic] sent a "basket of beautiful flowers" to Cornelio Clenuar, manager of the Federation's Stockton branch. See picture and item, *Filipino Nation,* August 1929, p. 13.

53. Late in 1930, Manila politicians began to voice fears that the growing presence of Japanese in the southern part of the Philippines could be "encroaching" upon Philippine business opportunities. See "Japanization of Davao a Problem," *The Philippine Republic,* September 1930, p. 13. Toward the end of the decade, this "economic envy" began to shift toward fears of the "Japanese colony" in Davao becoming a potential "fifth column" that would endanger Philippine national security. See Karnow, *In Our Image,* p. 279. In another ironic twist demonstrating the ambivalence of the relationship between the two communities, the *Filipino Pioneer,* the local Filipino newspaper, in a front page story just below Nunez's obituary, mentioned Philippine Commonwealth President Manuel L. Quezon's unease at having to deal with "Japs." See "Quezon Denies Jap Agreement," *Filipino Pioneer,* August 5, 1938, p. 1.

54. The emergence of Issei nationalism as a result of the Sino-Japanese War of 1937 was not new, as nationalism had also peaked with previous conflicts in the first Sino-Japanese War of 1894–95, the 1904–05 Russo-Japanese War, and the First World War. Historian Yuji Ichioka says that given the legal, social, and economic barriers to American citizenship and basic rights, the Issei's identification with Japan must be viewed as a psychological expression of dissatisfaction with their second-class status here. Yuji Ichioka, "Japanese Immigrant Nationalism: The Issei and the Sino-Japanese War, 1937–1941," *California History* 69, no. 3 (Fall 1990): 260–275.

12

RACE, GENDER, AND THE PRIVILEGES OF PROPERTY

On the Significance of Miscegenation Law in the U.S. West

PEGGY PASCOE

Like a growing number of feminist scholars, I spend most of my time trying to understand the history of relationships between race and gender. These days, that is a pretty hot topic. For some time now, the best, and most sophisticated, work in this area has put race and gender relations in the context of what has come to be known as the "powers of desire"; in other words, it traces the connections between race, gender, and sexuality.[1] To mention only a few examples, I think of Hazel Carby's revealing study of the sexual politics of women's blues, of Antonia Castañeda's incisive critique of sexual violence in the Spanish Mexican conquest of California, or of Jacquelyn Dowd Hall's brilliant essay on rape and lynching.[2] When studies like these are combined with a remarkable constellation of recent disciplinary developments—the dynamic emergence of lesbian and gay studies, the coming of age of the history of sexuality, and the current poststructuralist preoccupation with the politics of "bodies"—the study of sex and sexuality suddenly seems to be everywhere.[3]

My own topic, the history of miscegenation law, would seem to be a prime candidate for interpretation along these lines.[4] Whenever and wherever I talk about my work, I encounter people who think that miscegenation laws were significant primarily because they reflected the ultimate American sexual taboo—that against sex between white women and black men.

There is, of course, no question that such a taboo has been pervasive in American society.[5] Certainly its power is threaded through the history of miscegenation laws. Although most experts agree that the overwhelming majority of interracial sexual relationships occurred between white men and African American or American Indian women, miscegenation laws were clearly designed to control the behavior of white women.[6] One of the very first laws, passed in 1664 in Maryland, said so explicitly: it targeted relationships between two groups the lawmakers identified as "freeborn English women" and "Negro slaves."[7] Although most later miscegenation laws referred to "whites" in general rather than to white women in particular, they, too, were most likely to pass in the wake of scandals over the participation of white women in interracial relationships. Statistics on arrests and convictions are hard to come by, but, if the several dozen criminal cases which eventually reached appeals courts are any indication, the majority of couples dragged into criminal courts for violating miscegenation laws followed this same pattern: they were made up of white women and black men.[8]

And yet, the more I study the history of miscegenation law, the more intrigued I am with the parts of the story that have so far attracted much less attention than the American obsession with controlling the sexual behavior of white women.[9] The story I want to tell in this paper focuses more on marriage and property relations than on sex and sexuality, and more on white men and women of color than on white women and black men. And, perhaps just as important for the history of race and sex classification in American law, my story takes place not in the South, the region that has for so long stood as *the* paradigm for the study of race in America, but in the West, where the existence of a multicultural population provided both unprecedented opportunities for—and unprecedented challenges to—legal racial classifications. As historians Vicki Ruiz and Ellen DuBois have pointed out in another context, paying more attention to the history of the U.S. West is one way to move feminist scholarship beyond the limitations of its usual uniracial or bi-racial analyses.[10] In these few short pages, I'll need to be more suggestive than definitive: I'll briefly outline the structure of miscegenation laws, offer as a sample one case to consider, and merely mention some historical and contemporary variations on my theme.

Let me begin by outlining the laws. Although miscegenation laws are usually remembered (when they are remembered at all) as a southern regional development aimed at African Americans, they were actually a much broader phenomenon. Adopted in both the North and the South beginning in the colonial period, miscegenation laws grew up with slavery. They did not, however, reach maturity until after the Civil War, for it was only when slavery had been abandoned that miscegenation laws came to form the crucial "bottom line" of the system of white supremacy later embodied in segregation. Miscegenation laws gained this newfound importance just at the time that they were being extended to newly formed western states.

Although the laws were in many respects a national phenomenon, it was in the West, not the South, that they reached their most elaborate, even labyrinthine, development, covering the broadest list of racial categories. Thus, while the earliest miscegenation laws, passed in the South, forbade whites to marry African Americans, later laws, developed mostly in western states, expanded the list of groups prohibited from marrying whites by adding first American Indians, then Chinese and Japanese (both often referred to by the catchall term "Mongolians"), and then "Malays" (or Filipinos). And even this didn't exhaust the list. Oregon prohibited whites from marrying "Kanakas" (or native Hawaiians); South Dakota proscribed "Coreans"; Arizona singled out Hindus. The first western miscegenation law was passed by Texas in 1837, the last more than a century later, by Utah in 1939. By the 1920s, southern states like Virginia and Georgia were expanding their laws to include categories first listed by western states.[11]

To keep pace with this multiplication of racial categories, some states packed their laws with quasi-mathematical definitions of "race." Oregon, for example, declared that "it shall not be lawful within this state for any white person, male or female, to intermarry with any negro, Chinese, or any person having one fourth or more negro, Chinese, or Kanaka blood, or any person having more than one half Indian blood."[12] Altogether, miscegenation laws covered forty-one states and colonies. They spanned three centuries of American history: the first ones were enacted in the 1660s, and the last ones were not declared unconstitutional until 1967.[13]

Although it is their sexual taboos that attract attention today, the structure and function of miscegenation laws were, I think, more fundamentally related to the institution of marriage than to sexual behavior itself.[14] In sheer numbers, many more laws prohibited interracial marriage than interracial sex.[15] And in an even deeper sense, all miscegenation laws were designed to privilege marriage as a social and economic unit. Couples who challenged the laws knew that the right to marry translated into social respectability and economic benefits, including inheritance rights and legitimacy for children, that were denied to sexual liaisons outside marriage.

Miscegenation laws were designed to patrol this border by making so-called "miscegenous marriage" a legal impossibility. Thus criminal courts treated offenders as if they had never been married at all; that is, prosecutors charged interracial couples with the moral offense of fornication or some other illicit sex crime, then denied them the use of marriage as a defense. Civil courts guarded the junction between marriage and economic privilege. From Reconstruction to the 1930s, most miscegenation cases heard in civil courts were *ex post facto* attempts to invalidate relationships that had already lasted for a long time. They were brought by relatives or, sometimes, by the state, after the death of one partner, almost always a white man. Many of them were specifically designed to take property or inheritances away from the surviving partner, almost always an African American or American Indian woman.[16]

By looking at civil lawsuits like these (which were, at least in appeals court records, more common than criminal cases), we can begin to trace the links between white patriarchal privilege and property that sustained miscegenation laws. Let me illustrate the point by describing just one case, *In re Paquet's Estate,* decided by the Oregon Supreme Court in 1921.[17] The Paquet case, like most of the civil miscegenation cases of this period, was fought over the estate of a white man. The man in question, Fred Paquet, died in 1919, survived by his sixty-three-year-old Tillamook Indian wife, named Ophelia. The Paquet estate included twenty-two acres of land, some farm animals, tools, and a buggy, altogether worth perhaps $2,500.[18] Fred and Ophelia's relationship had a long history. In the 1880s, Fred had already begun to visit Ophelia frequently and openly enough that he had become one of many targets of a local grand jury that periodically threatened to indict white men who lived with Indian women.[19] Seeking to formalize the relationship—and, presumably, to end this harassment—Fred consulted a lawyer, who advised him to make sure to hold a ceremony that would meet the legal requirements for an "Indian custom" marriage. Accordingly, in 1889, Fred not only reached the customary agreement with Ophelia's Tillamook relatives, paying them fifty dollars in gifts, but also sought the formal sanction of Tillamook tribal chief Betsy Fuller (who was herself married to a white man); Fuller arranged for a tribal council to consider and confirm the marriage.[20] Fred and Ophelia lived together for more than thirty years, until his death. Fred clearly considered Ophelia his wife, and his neighbors, too, recognized their relationship, but because Fred died without leaving a formal will, administration of the estate was subject to state laws which provided for the distribution of property to surviving family members.

When Fred Paquet died, the county court recognized Ophelia as his widow and promptly appointed her administrator of the estate. Because the couple had no children, all the property, including the land, which Ophelia lived on and the Paquets had owned for more than two decades, would ordinarily have gone to her. Two days later, though, Fred's brother John came forward to contest Ophelia for control of the property.[21] John Paquet had little to recommend him to the court. Some of his neighbors accused him of raping native women, and he had such an unsavory reputation in the community that at one point the county judge declared him "a man of immoral habits . . . incompetent to transact ordinary business affairs and generally untrustworthy."[22] He was, however, a "white" man, and under Oregon's miscegenation law, that was enough to ensure that he won his case against Ophelia, an Indian woman.

The case eventually ended up in the Oregon Supreme Court. In making its decision, the key issue for the court was whether or not to recognize Fred and Ophelia's marriage, which violated Oregon's miscegenation law.[23] The court listened to—and then dismissed—Ophelia's argument that the marriage met the requirements for an Indian custom marriage and so should have been recognized as valid out of routine courtesy to the authority of another jurisdiction (that of the Tillamook tribe).[24] The court also heard and dismissed Ophelia's claim that Oregon's miscegenation law discriminated against Indians and was therefore an unconstitutional denial of the Fourteenth Amendment guarantee of equal protection. The court ingenuously explained its reasoning; it held that the Oregon miscegenation law did not discriminate because it "applied alike to all persons, either white, negroes, Chinese, Kanaka, or Indians."[25] Following this logic, the court declared Fred and Ophelia's marriage void because it violated Oregon's miscegenation law; it ordered that the estate and all its property be transferred to "the only relative in the state," John Paquet, to be distributed among him, his siblings and their heirs.[26]

As the Paquet case demonstrates, miscegenation law did not always prevent the formation of interracial relationships, sexual or otherwise. Fred and Ophelia had, after all, lived together for more than thirty years and had apparently won recognition as a couple from many of those around them; their perseverance had even allowed them to elude grand jury crackdowns. They did not, however, manage to escape the really crucial power of miscegenation law: the role it played in connecting white supremacy to the transmission of property. In American law, marriage provided the glue that set the transmission of property from husbands to wives and their children; miscegenation law kept property within racial boundaries by invalidating marriages between white men and women of color whenever ancillary white relatives like John Paquet contested them.[27]

The Paquet case, then, illustrates the significance of property in miscegenation cases. The next step is to understand that property, so often described in legal sources as simple economic assets (like land and capital) is actually a much more expansive phenomenon, one which took various forms and structured crucial relationships. Let me mention just three of the property relationships that appear and reappear in civil miscegenation cases. The first was suggested to me by the work of critical race theorists, who are nowadays arguing that race is in and of itself a kind of property.[28] As Derrick Bell, the scholar who has made this argument most explicitly, explains, most whites did—and still do—"expect the society to recognize an unspoken but no less vested property right in their 'whiteness.'" "This right," Bell maintains, "is recognized and upheld by courts and the society like all property rights under a government created and sustained primarily for that purpose."[29]

As applied to the Paquet case, this theme is easy to trace, for, in a sense, the victorious John Paquet had turned his "whiteness" (the best, and perhaps the only, asset he had) into property, and did so at Ophelia's expense.

This transformation happened not once but repeatedly. One instance occurred shortly after the county judge had branded John Paquet immoral and unreliable. Dismissing these charges as the opinions of "a few scalawags and Garibaldi Indians," John Paquet's lawyers rallied enough white witnesses who would speak in his defense to mount an appeal which convinced a circuit court judge to declare Paquet competent to administer the estate.[30] Another example of the transformation of "whiteness" into property came when the Oregon Supreme Court ruled that Ophelia Paquet's "Indianness" disqualified her from legal marriage to a white man; with Ophelia thus out of the way, John and his siblings won the right to inherit the property.

The second property relationship I want to mention was illuminated for me by Nancy Cott, who was kind enough to share with me a work in progress in which she points out the etymological connection between the words "property" and "propriety."[31] Miscegenation law played on this connection by drawing a sharp line between "legitimate marriage" on the one hand and "illicit sex" on the other, then defining all interracial relationships as illicit sex. The distinction was a crucial one, for husbands were legally obligated to provide for legitimate wives and children, but men owed nothing to "mere" sexual partners: neither inheritance rights nor the legitimacy of children accompanied illicit relationships.

By defining all interracial relationships as illicit, miscegenation law did not so much prohibit or punish illicit sex as it did create and reproduce it. Conditioned by stereotypes which associated women of color with hypersexuality, judges routinely branded long-term settled relationships as "mere" sex rather than marriage. Lawyers played to these assumptions by reducing interracial relationships to interracial sex, then distinguishing interracial sex from marriage by associating it with prostitution. Describing the relationship between Fred and Ophelia Paquet, for example, John Paquet's lawyers claimed that "the alleged 'marriage' was a mere commercial affair" that did not deserve legal recognition because "the relations were entirely meretricious from their inception."[32]

It was all but impossible for women of color to escape the legacy of these associations. Ophelia Paquet's lawyers tried to find a way out by changing the subject. Rather than refuting the association between women of color and illicit sexuality, they highlighted its flip side, the supposed connection between white women and legitimate marriage. Ophelia Paquet, they told the judge, "had been to the man as good a wife as any white woman could have been."[33] In its final decision, the Oregon Supreme Court came as close as any court of that time did to accepting this line of argument. Taking the unusual step of admitting that "the record is conclusive that [Ophelia] lived with [Fred] as a good and faithful wife for more than 30 years," the judges admitted that they felt some sympathy for Ophelia, enough to recommend—but not require—that John Paquet offer her what they called "a fair and reasonable settlement."[34] But in the Paquet case, as in other miscegenation cases, sexual morality, important as it was, was nonetheless still subordinate to channeling the transmission of property along racial dividing lines. Ophelia got a judicial pat on the head for good behavior, but John and his siblings got the property.

Which brings me to the third form of property relationship structured by miscegenation laws—and, for that matter, marriage laws in general—and that is women's economic dependence on men. Here the problems started long before the final decision gave John Paquet control of the Paquet estate. One of the most intriguing facts about the Paquet case is that everyone acted as if the estate in question belonged solely to Fred Paquet. In fact, however, throughout the Paquet marriage, Fred had whiled away most of his time; it was Ophelia's basket-making, fruit-picking, milk-selling, and wage work that had provided the income they needed to sustain themselves. And although the deed to their land was made out in Fred Paquet's name, the couple had used Ophelia's earnings, combined with her proceeds from government payments to Tillamook tribal members, to purchase the property and to pay the yearly taxes on it. It is significant, I think, that, although lawyers on both sides of the case knew this, neither they nor the Oregon Supreme Court judges considered it a key issue at the trial in which Ophelia lost all legal right to what the courts considered "Fred's" estate.

Indeed, Ophelia's economic contribution might never have been taken into account if it were not for the fact that in the wake of the Oregon Supreme Court decision, United States Indian officials found themselves responsible for the care of the now impoverished Ophelia. Apparently hoping both to defend Ophelia and to relieve themselves of the burden of her support, they sued John Paquet on Ophelia's behalf. Working through the federal courts that covered Indian relations and equity claims, rather than the state courts that enforced miscegenation laws, they eventually won a partial settlement. Yet their argument, too, reflected the assumption that men were better suited than women to the ownership of what the legal system referred to as "real" property. Although their brief claimed that "Fred Paquet had practically no income aside from the income he received through the labor and efforts of the said Ophelia Paquet," they asked the court to grant Ophelia the right to only half of the Paquet land.[35] In the end, the court ordered that Ophelia should receive a cash settlement (the amount was figured at half the value of the land), but only if she agreed to make her award contingent on its sale.[36] To get any settlement at all, Ophelia Paquet had to relinquish all claims to actual ownership of the land, although such a claim might have given her legal grounds to prevent its sale and so allow her to spend her final years on the property. It is not even clear that she ever received payment on the settlement ordered by the court. As late as 1928,

John Paquet's major creditor complained to a judge that Paquet had repeatedly turned down acceptable offers to sell the land; perhaps he had chosen to live on it himself.[37]

Like any single example, the Paquet case captures miscegenation law as it stood at one moment, and a very particular moment at that, one that might be considered the high-water mark of American courts' determination to structure both family formation and property transmission along racial dividing lines.[38] There is, of course, more to the story than that, so with the Paquet case now firmly in mind, let me range rather widely across time and space to mention a few historical and contemporary variations on its themes of race, gender, patriarchal privilege, and property.[39]

Consider, for example, that if the Paquet case had been argued fifty years earlier, in the early 1870s, its outcome might well have been different, for during Reconstruction, several state legislatures repealed their miscegenation laws, and, in a remarkable handful of cases heard in Alabama, Louisiana, and Texas, judges declared others inoperative.[40] The reasoning behind these decisions shows both the potential Reconstruction held for challenging white supremacy and the continuing influence of the gendered powers of traditional patriarchs. Having just lost the traditional system of social control embodied in slavery law (in which courts guarded the rights of white patriarchs as slaveowners), a few judges tried, I think, to fill the gap by reinforcing the system of social control embodied in marriage law (in which courts guarded the rights of white patriarchs as husbands); the result was that a few courts extended formal legal recognition to marriages between white men and newly freed black women.

Revealing as these decisions of the early 1870s were, however, they were also quite exceptional. Between 1875 and the 1920s, miscegenation laws found such firm footing in the courts that even the patriarchal powers of husbands were overwhelmed by the rise of the newly definitive racial classifications of the segregation era. Outside miscegenation courts, too, traditional white patriarchy was in the process of being replaced by a new form of male dominance.[41] The extent of the erosion of traditional white patriarchy can be seen in the fact that by the 1930s, the most significant civil challenges to miscegenation law came from an unprecedented source in a new type of case: lawsuits in which couples made up of white women and men of color went to court to win the formal right to marry.[42] These couples were, in effect, relying on a new—and less racially exclusive—definition of the role of husband to help them challenge the racial classifications at the core of miscegenation law.

It may well be significant (and, given the sheer range of miscegenation laws in the U.S. West, it is certainly ironic) that these challenges to miscegenation laws found their firmest footholds in western state courts. The cases that would eventually set precedents for invalidating miscegenation laws first reached courts in the 1930s, and began to carry real force in 1948, when California declared its state miscegenation law unconstitutional.[43] After 1967, when the U.S. Supreme Court held that miscegenation laws violated the Fourteenth Amendment, racial categories were erased from marriage law, and miscegenation laws became a thing of the past.[44] By the 1970s, then, fifty years after Ophelia Paquet ended up in court, the decision rendered in the Paquet case no longer made legal sense.

Today, most Americans have trouble remembering that miscegenation laws ever existed. The audiences I speak to are incredulous at the injustice and the arbitrariness of the racial classifications that stand out in the cases I tell them about; they express considerable relief that those "bad old days" are now over. I share their outrage, but I also find it intriguing that so few modern listeners notice that one of the themes raised in the Paquet case—the significance of marriage in channeling property transmission—not only remains alive and well, but has, in fact, outlived both the erosion of traditional patriarchy and the rise and fall of racial classifications in marriage law.

More than a generation after the demise of miscegenation laws (and despite repeated feminist reforms of marriage laws), the drawing of exclusionary lines around marriage is still going strong. Today the most prominent—though hardly the only—victims are lesbian and gay couples, who point out that the sexual classifications currently embedded in marriage law operate in much the same way that the racial classifications embedded in miscegenation laws once did: that is, they allow courts to categorize same-sex relationships as illicit sex rather than legitimate marriage and they allow courts to exclude same-sex couples from the property benefits of marriage, which now include everything from tax advantages to medical insurance coverage.[45]

These modern legal battles and the earlier ones fought by couples like Fred and Ophelia Paquet both suggest, I think, that focusing on the historical connections between property and the political economy of marriage in the U.S. West offers a revealing window on the form and power of race and sex classifications in American law and race and gender hierarchies in American history.

Notes

A slightly different version of this paper was presented at the 50th Anniversary Conference of the Arthur and Elizabeth Schlesinger Library on the History of Women in America and published in pamphlet form in Susan Ware, ed., *New Viewpoints in Women's History: Working Papers from the Schlesinger Library 50th Anniversary Conference, March 4–5, 1994* (Cambridge: Schlesinger Library, 1994).

I am grateful to Valerie Matsumoto and Blake Allmendinger for accepting this substitute for the paper I originally presented at the Clark Library conference on

"American Dreams, Western Images," and for their suggestions for refocusing it to fit into this volume.

1. The phrase comes from Ann Snitow, Christine Stansell, and Sharon Thompson, eds., *Powers of Desire: The Politics of Sexuality* (New York: Monthly Review Press, 1983).

2. Hazel V. Carby, "'It Jus Be's Dat Way Sometime': The Sexual Politics of Women's Blues," in Ellen Carol DuBois and Vicki L. Ruiz, eds., *Unequal Sisters: A Multicultural Reader in U.S. Women's History* (New York: Routledge, 1990), 238–249; Antonia I. Castañeda, "Sexual Violence in the Politics and Policies of Conquest: Amerindian Women and the Spanish Conquest of Alta California," in Adela de la Torre and Beatríz Pesquera, eds., *Building with Our Own Hands: New Directions in Chicana Scholarship* (Berkeley: University of California Press, 1993), 15–33; Jacquelyn Dowd Hall, "'The Mind That Burns in Each Body': Women, Rape, and Racial Violence," in *Powers of Desire,* 328–349. For additional collections including work of this kind, see John C. Fout and Maura Shaw Tantillo, eds., *American Sexual Politics: Sex, Gender, and Race since the Civil War* (Chicago: University of Chicago Press, 1993); and Carol S. Vance, ed., *Pleasure and Danger: Exploring Female Sexuality* (Boston: Routledge & Kegan Paul, 1984).

3. There is now an enormous literature in these areas. Among the best starting points are the following surveys and collections: Henry Abelove, Michele Aina Barale, and David M. Halperin, eds., *The Lesbian and Gay Studies Reader* (New York: Routledge, 1993); Martin Bauml Duberman, Martha Vicinus, and George Chauncey, Jr., eds., *Hidden from History: Reclaiming the Gay and Lesbian Past* (New York: Meridian, 1989); John D'Emilio and Estelle B. Freedman, *Intimate Matters: A History of Sexuality in America* (New York: Harper and Row, 1988); and Thomas Laqueur, *Making Sex: Body and Gender from the Greeks to Freud* (Cambridge: Harvard University Press, 1990).

4. A word is in order about my use of the term "miscegenation." It is, I know, now customary for scholars to try to avoid the embarrassingly biological connotations of this term, which dates to the 1860s and means "race mixing," by referring to "cross-cultural" or "interracial" marriages. Those terms, which work just fine for describing actual marriages, are inaccurate as characterizations of miscegenation laws, for the laws did not prohibit marriages between, say, Chinese immigrants and African Americans, but only marriages between groups designated as "white" and groups designated, in effect, as not "white." In this sense, the laws served as deliberate handmaidens of a particular form of American white supremacy. In order to remind us that the laws were intended to reflect these notions, I will retain the term "miscegenation" when referring to the laws, using it in favor of the other major alternative, "anti-miscegenation," which seems to me to grant a certain legitimacy to the concept, as if the laws were aimed at a real biological phenomenon.

5. The most interesting recent work on this taboo explores shifts in its power and structure in different time periods. See especially Martha Hodes, *White Women, Black Men: Illicit Sex in the Nineteenth-Century South* (New Haven: Yale University Press, 1997); Hodes, "The Sexualization of Reconstruction Politics: White Women and Black Men in the South after the Civil War," in *American Sexual Politics,* 59–74; Robyn Weigman, "The Anatomy of Lynching," in *American Sexual Politics,* 223–245; and Hall, "Women, Rape, and Racial Violence."

6. On relationships between white men and women of color, see D'Emilio and Freedman, *Intimate Matters,* 85–108; Deborah Gray White, *Arn't I A Woman: Female Slaves in the Plantation South* (New York: Norton, 1985); Thelma Jennings, "'Us Colored Women Had to Go Through a Plenty': Sexual Exploitation of African-American Slave Women," *Journal of Women's History* 1 (Winter 1990), 45–74; Sylvia Van Kirk, *"Many Tender Ties": Women in Fur Trade Society, 1670–1870* (Norman: University of Oklahoma Press, 1980); and the essays by Johnny Faragher, Deena González, and Sylvia Van Kirk in Lillian Schlissel, Vicki L. Ruiz, and Janice Monk, eds., *Western Women: Their Land, Their Lives* (Albuquerque: University of New Mexico Press, 1988), 197–226. On white women as the special objects of miscegenation laws, see Karen Getman, "Sexual Control in the Slaveholding South: The Implementation and Maintenance of a Racial Caste System," *Harvard Women's Law Journal* 7 (Spring 1984), 114–152; A. Leon Higginbotham, Jr., and Barbara K. Kopytoff, "Racial Purity and Interracial Sex in the Law of Colonial and Antebellum Virginia," *Georgetown Law Journal* 77 (August 1989), 1994–2000; George M. Fredrickson, *White Supremacy: A Comparative Study in American and South African History* (New York: Oxford University Press, 1981), 103–105; Peter W. Bardaglio, *Reconstructing the Household: Families, Sex, and the Law in the Nineteenth-Century South* (Chapel Hill: University of North Carolina Press, 1995), 52–55; David H. Fowler, *Northern Attitudes towards Interracial Marriage: Legislation and Public Opinion in the Middle Atlantic and the States of the Old Northwest, 1780–1930* (1963; New York: Garland, 1987), 150–153, 166; and Peggy Pascoe, "Race, Gender, and Intercultural Relations: The Case of Interracial Marriage," *Frontiers* 12, no. 1 (1991), 6–7.

7. William H. Browne, ed., *Archives of Maryland,* vol. 1 (Baltimore: Maryland Historical Society, 1883), 533–534, cited in Fowler, *Northern Attitudes,* appendix, 381. As Barbara J. Fields points out, the fact that the law refers to freeborn English women rather than "white" women suggests that the law did not so much reflect racial categories already in place as show "society in the act of inventing race." Barbara J. Fields, "Slavery, Race, and Ideology in the United States of America," *New Left Review,* no. 181 (May–June 1990), 107.

8. My search of U.S. appeals court cases involving miscegenation law between 1867 and 1947 shows that 61 percent of the seventy-seven criminal cases for which racial designations were listed involved pairings between white women and nonwhite men. Appeals cases are, of course, a very special—and in some respects, very limited—kind of source; for a longer discussion of their advantages and disadvantages, see note 18 below.

9. This paper is part of a larger project, my book in progress on the history of miscegenation law, tentatively entitled "What Comes Naturally: Race, Sex, and Marriage Law, 1870 to the Present." In addition to the studies listed above, the following works are essential reading for those interested in the history of theoretical relationships between race and gender: Evelyn Brooks Higginbotham, "African-American Women's History and the Metalanguage of Race," *Signs* 17 (Winter 1992), 251–274; Tessie Liu, "Teaching the Differences among Women from a Historical Perspective: Rethinking Race and Gender as Social Categories," *Women's Studies International Forum* 14, no. 4 (1991), 265–276; and Ann Stoler, "Making Empire Respectable: The Politics of Race and Sexual Morality in Twentieth-Century Colonial Cultures," *American Ethnologist* 16 (November 1989), 634–660.

10. "Introduction" to *Unequal Sisters,* xii.

11. The most complete list of state miscegenation laws can be found in Fowler, *Northern Attitudes,* appendix, 336–439. To those familiar with late twentieth-century U.S. "racial" groupings (or, for that matter, the structure of racial oppression in the nineteenth-century American West), there is a notable omission from the list of those prohibited from marrying whites, and that is Spanish/Mexicans. The fact that Spanish/Mexicans were not listed in the laws, however, did not always mean that they fell on the "white" side of the racial divide. In terms of legal theory, individual Spanish/Mexicans were categorized as racially "Caucasian" unless it could be proven that they had "native" or "African" "blood," in which case they came under the jurisdiction of miscegenation laws targeting American Indians and African Americans. In terms of actual practice, it appears that many couples made up of whites and Spanish/Mexicans believed that their marriages would be prohibited by miscegenation law and, in fact, officials often refused to issue them licenses.

12. Oregon Codes and Stats., 1901, Chap. 8, Sec. 1999 (1866).

13. The overall development of the laws can be followed in Robert J. Sickels, *Race, Marriage, and the Law* (Albuquerque: University of New Mexico Press, 1972); Byron Curti Martyn, "Racism in the United States: A History of the Anti-Miscegenation Legislation and Litigation" (Ph.D. diss., University of Southern California, 1979); and Fowler, *Northern Attitudes.* The U.S. Supreme Court decision which declared miscegenation laws unconstitutional is *Loving v. Virginia,* 388 U.S. 1 (1967).

14. One of the first scholars to recognize this was Mary Frances Berry; see her fine discussion of the structure of miscegenation laws in "Judging Morality: Sexual Behavior and Legal Consequences in the Late Nineteenth-Century South," *Journal of American History* 78 (December 1991), 838–839. For this reason, I find the work of scholars who have explored the outlines of marriage as a social structure especially helpful in thinking through my topic. See especially Berry, "Judging Morality"; Nancy F. Cott, "Giving Character to Our Whole Civil Polity: Marriage and the Public Order in the Late Nineteenth Century," in Linda K. Kerber, Alice Kessler-Harris, and Kathryn Kish Sklar, eds., *U.S. History as Women's History: New Feminist Essays* (Chapel Hill: University of North Carolina Press, 1995), 107–121; Ramón Gutiérrez, *When Jesus Came, the Corn Mothers Went Away: Marriage, Sexuality, and Power in New Mexico, 1500–1846* (Stanford: Stanford University Press, 1991); and Verena Martinez-Alier, *Marriage, Class, and Colour in Nineteenth-Century Cuba: A Study of Racial Attitudes and Sexual Values in a Slave Society* (Cambridge: Cambridge University Press, 1974).

15. According to the list in Fowler, *Northern Attitudes,* appendix, forty-one states and colonies prohibited interracial marriage, twenty-two of which also prohibited one form or another of interracial sex, variously described as "adultery," "bastardy," "concubinage," "cohabitation," "illicit cohabitation," "fornication," "cohabiting in fornication," "illicit carnal intercourse," "sexual intercourse," or "sexual relations." Only one colony (New York) prohibited interracial sex ("adulterous intercourse") without also prohibiting interracial marriage, bringing the total number of jurisdictions which prohibited interracial sex to twenty-three.

16. My count of U.S. appeals court cases involving miscegenation law between 1867 and 1947 shows that 81.8 percent of the eighty-eight civil cases for which racial designations are listed involved pairings between white men and non-white

women. Although I have offered totals like these here and in note 9 above, readers should keep in mind that appeals court cases are not representative in any simple numerical sense; indeed, the reason cases end up in appeals courts in the first place is that they are in some respect unusual. There remains a pressing need for research into the numbers of lower-court cases, especially the statistics on criminal arrests and convictions and the frequency with which miscegenation law was invoked in civil cases involving property relations.

17. I have selected the Paquet case from my working database of appeals court decisions, which includes every decision involving the interpretation of a miscegenation law issued by an appeals court and recorded in state, regional, or federal court reporters from 1860 through 1967. Appeals court decisions are both enticing and extremely tricky historical sources. Although cases that reach appeals courts are by definition somewhat atypical, they hold considerable significance for historians because the decisions reached in them set general policies later followed in more routine cases and because the texts of the decisions provide important clues to the ways judges thought through particular legal problems. I have relied on them here not only because of these interpretive advantages, but also for two more directly practical reasons. First, because appeals court decisions are published and indexed, it is possible to compile a list of them comprehensive enough to ensure maximum coverage. In the case of miscegenation law, ensuring coverage can be a considerable challenge. Because marriage was generally considered a matter of state rather than federal jurisdiction, the vast majority of cases came up in state courts, and finding them requires painstaking state-by-state or regional research. I was considerably aided in this process by Byron Curti Martyn's encyclopedic dissertation, "Racism in the United States: A History of the Anti-Miscegenation Legislation and Litigation," the bibliography of which includes references to many cases that did not appear in the usual legal reference sources. Second, the process of making an appeal often requires that documents that might otherwise be routinely discarded after a set period of time (such as legal briefs and court reporters' trial notes) are transcribed, typed or printed, and saved, allowing historians additional clues to the relationship between the specific local context and the larger legal issues. The Paquet case, for example, can be followed not only by reading the text of the appeals court decision, *In re Paquet's Estate,* 200 P. 911 (Oregon 1921); but also in the following archival case files: *Paquet v. Paquet,* file No. 4268, Oregon Supreme Court, 1920; *Paquet v. Henkle,* file No. 4267, Oregon Supreme Court, 1920; and Tillamook County Probate file No. 605, all in the Oregon State Archives; and in *U.S. v. John B. Paquet,* Judgment Roll 11409, Register No. 8–8665, March 1925, National Archives and Records Administration, Pacific Northwest Branch.

18. Initial estimates of the value of the estate were much higher, ranging from $4,500 to $12,500. I have relied on the figure of $2,528.50 provided by court-appointed assessors. See Tillamook County Probate file No. 605, Inventory and Appraisement, June 15, 1920.

19. *Paquet v. Paquet,* Respondent's Brief, November 1, 1920, pp. 2–5.

20. Tillamook County Probate file No. 605, Judge A. M. Hare, Findings of Facts and Conclusions of Law, February 3, 1920; *Paquet v. Paquet,* Appellants Abstract of Record, September 3, 1920, pp. 10–16.

21. *Paquet v. Paquet*, Appellants Abstract of Record, September 3, 1920, p. 3.

22. Tillamook County Probate file No. 605, Judge A. M. Hare, Findings of Fact and Conclusions of Law, February 3, 1920.

23. Court records identify Fred Paquet as being of French Canadian origin. Both sides agreed that Fred was a "pure" or "full-blooded" "white" man and Ophelia was a "pure" or "full-blooded" "Indian" woman. *Paquet v. Paquet*, Appellant's First Brief, October 8, 1920, p. 1; *Paquet v. Paquet*; Respondent's Brief, November 1, 1920, p. 2.

24. The question of legal jurisdiction over Indian tribes was—and is—a very thorny issue. Relations with Indians were generally a responsibility of the U.S. federal government, which, although it advocated shaping Indian families to fit white middle-class molds, had little practical choice but to grant general recognition to tribal marriages performed according to Indian custom. In the U.S. legal system, however, jurisdiction over marriage rested with the states rather than the federal government. States could, therefore, use their control over marriage as a wedge to exert some power over Indians by claiming that Indian-white marriages, especially those performed outside recognized reservations, were subject to state rather than federal jurisdiction. In the Paquet case, for example, the court insisted that, because the Tillamook had never been assigned to a reservation and because Fred and Ophelia lived in a mixed settlement, Ophelia could not be considered part of a recognized tribe nor a "ward" of the federal government. As events would later show, both contentions were inaccurate: Ophelia was an enrolled member of the Tillamook tribe, which was under the supervision of the Siletz Indian Agency; the federal government claimed her as "a ward of the United States." See *U.S. v. John B. Paquet*, Bill of Complaint in Equity, September 21, 1923, p. 3.

25. *In re Paquet's Estate*, 200 P. 911 at 913 (Oregon 1921).

26. *In re Paquet's Estate*, 200 P. 911 at 914 (Oregon 1921).

27. Although the issue did not come up in *Paquet*, children, in addition to the wife, could lose their legal standing in miscegenation cases, for one effect of invalidating an interracial marriage was to make the children technically illegitimate. According to the law of most states, illegitimate children automatically inherited from their mothers, but they could inherit from their fathers only if their father had taken legal steps to formally recognize or adopt them. Since plaintiffs could rarely convince judges that fathers had done so, the children of interracial marriages were often disinherited along with their mothers. A classic example is the case of Juana Walker, decided in Arizona in 1896, in which Walker was declared illegitimate and thereby disinherited after the court decided that no legal marriage could have existed between her father John Walker, a "white" man, and his Pima Indian wife Churga. The chief beneficiaries of this decision were John Walker's brother William and his siblings. See *In re Walker's Estate*, 46 P. 67 (Arizona 1896). For a discussion of the Walker case, see Roger D. Hardaway, "Unlawful Love: A History of Miscegenation Law," *Journal of Arizona History* 27, no. 4 (1986), 378–379.

28. For introductions to critical race theory, see Kimberlé Crenshaw et al., eds., *Critical Race Theory: The Key Writings that Formed the Movement* (New York: New Press, 1995) and Richard Delgado and Jean Stefancic, "Critical Race Theory: An Annotated Bibliography," *Virginia Law Review* 79 (March 1993), 461–516. For particularly suggestive accounts of the relationships between "race" and property, see Derrick

Bell, "Remembrances of Racism Past," in Herbert Hill and James E. Jones, eds., *Race in America: The Struggle for Equality* (Madison: University of Wisconsin Press, 1992), 73–82; Cheryl I. Harris, "Whiteness as Property," *Harvard Law Review* 106 (June 1993), 1707–1791; George Lipsitz, "The Possessive Investment in Whiteness: Racialized Social Democracy and the 'White Problem' in American Studies," *American Quarterly* 47 (September 1995), 369–387; Eva Saks, "Representing Miscegenation Law,"*Raritan* 8 (Fall 1988), 39–69; and Patricia J. Williams, "Fetal Fictions: An Exploration of Property Archetypes in Racial and Gendered Contexts," in Hill and Jones, *Race in America*, 73–82.

29. Bell, "Remembrances of Racism Past," 78. See also Bell, "White Superiority in America: Its Legal Legacy, Its Economic Costs," *Villanova Law Review* 33 (1988), 767–779.

30. *Paquet v. Henkle*, Respondent's Brief, March 14, 1920, p. 6, Index to Transcript, August 25, 1920, p. 3. As is often the case in legal matters, the process itself was a convoluted one. The county court initially—and apparently automatically—granted Ophelia Paquet the right to administer the estate. After John Paquet objected to her appointment and challenged the validity of her marriage, the county judge removed Ophelia in favor of John Paquet. At that point R. N. Henkle, a creditor of the estate and a man said by John Paquet's lawyers to be acting for Ophelia, persuaded the county judge that John Paquet was unfit to carry out his duties; Henkle won appointment in his stead. John Paquet then appealed to the circuit court, which removed Henkle and reappointed John Paquet, who remained administrator of the estate while the marriage issue was being settled in the Oregon Supreme Court and thereafter.

31. Nancy F. Cott, "A Map of Marriage in the Public Order in the Late Nineteenth-Century United States" (unpublished paper, August 1993), p. 5. See also Cott, "Giving Character to Our Whole Civil Polity."

32. *Paquet v. Paquet*, Respondent's Brief, November 1, 1920, p. 7. Using typical imagery, they added that the Paquet relationship was "a case where a white man and a full blooded Indian woman have chosen to cohabit together illictly [sic], to agree to a relation of concubinage, which is not only a violation of the law of Oregon, but a transgression against the law of morality and the law of nature" (16).

33. *Paquet v. Paquet*, Appellant's First Brief, October 8, 1920, p. 2.

34. *In re Paquet's Estate*, 200 P. 911 at 914 (Oregon 1921).

35. *U.S. v. John B. Paquet*, Bill of Complaint in Equity, September 21, 1923, pp. 4, 6–7.

36. *U.S. v. John B. Paquet*, Stipulation, Decree, June 2, 1924.

37. Tillamook County Probate file No. 605, J. S. Cole, Petition, June 7, 1928. Cole was president of the Tillamook-Lincoln County Credit Association.

38. For a particularly insightful analysis of the historical connections between concepts of "race" and "family," see Liu, "Teaching the Differences among Women."

39. For a more extended discussion of twentieth-century developments, see Peggy Pascoe, "Miscegenation Law, Court Cases, and Ideologies of 'Race' in Twentieth-Century America,"*Journal of American History* 83 (June 1996), 44–69.

40. Between 1866 and 1877, Arkansas, Florida, Illinois, Louisiana, Mississippi, New Mexico, South Carolina, and Washington state either repealed their laws or

omitted them from state code compilations, though several would reenact them only a few years later. See Fowler, *Northern Attitudes,* appendix. Courts in Alabama, Louisiana, and Texas upheld particular marriages in *Burns v. State,* 17 Am. Rep. 34 (Alabama 1872); *Honey v. Clark,* 37 Tex. 686 (Texas 1873); *Hart v. Hoss,* 26 La. Ann. 90 (Louisiana 1874); *State v. Webb,* 4 Cent. L. J. 588 (Texas 1877); *Ex parte Brown,* 5 Cent. L. J. 149 (Texas 1877).

41. The most suggestive account I know of this redefinition of male dominance is Linda Gordon, *Heroes of Their Own Lives: The Politics and History of Family Violence* (New York: Viking, 1988), 56–57. On related topics, see Gail Bederman, *Manliness and Civilization: A Cultural History of Gender and Race in the United States, 1880–1917* (Chicago: University of Chicago Press, 1995); Michael Grossberg, *Governing the Hearth: Law and the Family in Nineteenth-Century America* (Chapel Hill: University of North Carolina Press, 1985); Elaine Tyler May, *Great Expectations: Marriage and Divorce in Post-Victorian America* (Chicago: University of Chicago Press, 1980); and Margaret Marsh, "Suburban Men and Masculine Domesticity, 1870–1915," *American Quarterly* 40 (June 1988), 165–186.

42. *Roldan v. Los Angeles County,* 129 Ca. App. 267 (California 1933); *Perez v. Lippold,* 198 P. 2d 17 (California 1948); *Oyama v. O'Neill,* 5 Race Relations Law Reporter 136 (Arizona 1959); *Davis v. Gately,* 269 F. Supp. 996 (1967).

43. *Perez v. Lippold,* 198 P. 2d 17 (California 1948).

44. *Loving v. Virginia,* 388 U.S. 1 (1967). Given that so many twentieth-century challenges to miscegenation law had been taken to court by couples made up of white women and men of color, it is striking that the Loving case involved the criminal conviction of a white man and a black woman.

45. Court cases on the issue of same-sex marriage include *Anonymous v. Anonymous,* 325 N.Y.S. 2d 499 (New York 1971); *Baker v. Nelson,* 191 N.W. 2d 185 (Minnesota 1971); *Jones v. Hallahan,* 501 S.W. 2d (Kentucky 1973); *Singer v. Hara,* 522 P. 2d 1187 (Washington 1974); *De Santo v. Barnsley,* 476 A. 2d 952 (Pennsylvania 1984); *Dean v. District of Columbia,* 18 FLR 1141 and 1387 (1991–92); *Baehr v. Lewin,* 852 P. 2d 44 (Hawaii 1993). For legal commentary on the analogy between sex and race classification in marriage laws, see Mark Strasser, "Family, Definitions, and the Constitution: On the Antimiscegenation Analogy," *Suffolk University Law Review* 25 (Winter 1991), 981–1034; James Trosino, "American Wedding: Same-Sex Marriage and the Miscegenation Analogy," *Boston University Law Review* 73 (January 1993), 93–120; Andrew Koppelman, "The Miscegenation Analogy: Sodomy Law as Sex Discrimination," *Yale Law Journal* 98 (November 1988), 145–164; and Koppelman, "Why Discrimination against Lesbians and Gays is Sex Discrimination," *NYU Law Review* 69 (May 1994), 197–287. For a particularly fine analysis of the significance of sex classifications in contemporary marriage law, see Nan D. Hunter, "Marriage, Law, and Gender: A Feminist Inquiry," *Law and Equality* 1 (Summer 1991), 9–30.

13

AMERICAN INDIAN BLOOD QUANTUM REQUIREMENTS

Blood Is Thicker than Family

MELISSA L. MEYER

American Indians must be enrolled in one of more than three hundred federally recognized tribes to receive most benefits from the federal government. To be enrolled, they must meet various criteria that vary from tribe to tribe and are set forth in tribal constitutions. Upon meeting such criteria, members are issued cards and numbers that identify their special status vis-à-vis their tribe and the U.S. government via the Bureau of Indian Affairs.[1] Members of no other ethnic or racial group in the U.S. maintain formal affiliations between themselves or with the federal government in this fashion. American Indians are unique.

That no one has explored in serious scholarly fashion how the enrollment process evolved or how "blood quantum" or degree of Indian "blood" came to be one of the most important criteria used first by federal policymakers and then by tribes themselves to establish tribal membership seems curious given the centrality of these issues to native people in the past and today.[2] Tribal enrollment has been and still is intrinsically linked to entitlement to property and other material benefits in addition to the ethnic bonds that tribal members feel. Furthermore, *everyone*—past and present, native and non-native—employed folk understandings of the metaphorical term "blood" to the point of overwhelming all common sense. The belief that blood literally or symbolically transmitted the essential qualities of the group is, perhaps, one of the few things that all of the actors in this tortuous history have shared.

Prior to their involvement with European nations, native groups determined their membership through a myriad of kinship systems that demarcated lineages of relatives. Simply distinguishing between matrilineal and patrilineal methods of reckoning descent hardly does justice to the complex forms that kinship systems might take. It is beyond the scope of this essay to elaborate on these various means of determining lineage, only to emphasize that *family* considerations, however construed, were paramount. Ironically, native notions of family lineage come closer to the origins of the term "blood" than current physiological meanings.

The historical roots of tribal enrollment extend back to the early nineteenth century when treaties with the U.S. government began to establish entitlement to specific rights, privileges, goods, services, and money. The practice of creating lists of tribal members and eventually formal censuses evolved to ensure the most accurate and equitable distribution of benefits possible. Surprisingly, the very first names to be recorded were those of individuals of mixed descent (early on referred to as "half-breeds" and then "mixed bloods"). Instead of enumerating all tribal members, U.S. policymakers relied on native leaders to distribute goods and money among their constituents. The first lists of names related to distributions of land to be held as private property. Many reasons underlay the policy of allocating plots of land to people of mixed descent. Policymakers rationalized that "half-breed" landowners would serve as a "civilizing" example to other Indians. Sometimes influential traders of mixed descent succeeded in having real or inflated "debts" covered by treaty money or land parcels. Often, federal personnel insisted that those who accepted plots of land sever their tribal affiliations, thereby fulfilling policymakers' dreams of native assimilation and hopes for reducing financial responsibilities.[3] Discovering that people of mixed descent were the first to be enumerated was surprising, but it makes sense that such record-keeping would be tied to allocations of private property. Further elaborations of the enrollment process would also revolve around distributions of land.

The 1887 General Allotment Act, or Dawes Act, heralded the most important period in the evolution of tribal enrollment. As part of the U.S. government's forced assimilation campaign, reservations across the country were divided into parcels of from 40 to 160 acres and assigned to individuals. Policymakers believed that owning private property would magically transform the collective values of most Indians and hasten their assimilation when nothing else had succeeded. Official censuses would determine those eligible to receive what came to be called "allotments" at each reservation. "Enrollment commissions" often compiled official tribal "rolls" that codified each individual's status as a member of their specific tribe. The commissions sometimes made decisions regarding individuals' fractional degree of Indian "blood" and otherwise determined whether people met eligibility requirements. Sometimes tribal members were given the opportunity to voice objections to these decisions, but not always. The long-term impact of official codification was not then apparent, so that concerns that would later be voiced about the legitimacy of enrollees' claims were not raised at the time. Native people often resisted being enumerated, believing that the whole policy aimed at dispossessing them of their land, which was the long-term consequence.[4] A substantial body of case law developed contesting the actions of the federal government in making these enrollment decisions.[5] Today, most native people must reckon their blood quantum by reference to the lists codified at this time, despite widespread stories of miscalculation. Again, tribal enrollment revolved around distributions of private property.

Despite policymakers' efforts to undermine tribal governments and political leaders, native groups maintained or created formal tribal governments and began regulating their own membership, especially in regard to land allotments, royalties from the sale of resources, distributions of tribal funds, residence, and voting. Since 1905 in the precedent setting *Waldron v. United States,* U.S. courts have upheld tribal rights to determine membership based on their own laws and customs.[6]

In 1934, Congress passed the Wheeler-Howard Act or Indian Reorganization Act (IRA) to foster economic development to relieve the poverty brought about by ill-conceived allotment policies. A central IRA feature encouraged the establishment of U.S.-sanctioned tribal governments patterned after corporations. Bureau of Indian Affairs representatives encouraged leaders from reservations that voted to accept the IRA to adopt formal tribal constitutions based on a U.S. model. In addition to making decisions regarding economic development, these tribal governments also codified enrollment requirements in their constitutions and ruled on individuals' eligibility. The IRA gave long-overdue support to Indian political organizations, but at the expense of indigenous forms and practices. Critics argue that elective IRA governments supplanted consensus governmental structures, created a permanent, voiceless, conservative minority, and were dominated by a capitalistically oriented reservation elite. Predictably, more case law developed contesting the decisions of these tribal governments. In line with established precedents, however, the courts have upheld the right of IRA governments over any contesting parties to determine eligibility for enrollment.[7]

Complicating matters further, in the twentieth century the U.S. government established its own eligibility criteria for benefits like educational aid and health care. These requirements do not interfere with tribal membership practices. Instead, they add yet another layer to the increasingly complicated question of "Who is an Indian"?

Many criteria can be used to delimit a population. Residence, cultural affiliation, language, recognition by a community, genealogical lines of descent, self-identification, and degree of "blood" have all been used at some point in the past to define American Indian populations. However, each measure produces a different sized population. For example, in 1990 the U.S. federal census enumerated 1.8 million self-identified American Indians, but only around 1 million were actually enrolled in one of the 304 federally recognized tribes. In other words, about 60 percent of all self-identified Indians in the 1990 census were enrolled. Which variables are ultimately employed is an arbitrary decision, but the implications for American Indians can be enormous.[8]

As absurd as it sounds on the surface, "Who is an Indian?" has been an important question since the mid-nineteenth century. Commissioners of Indian Affairs have regularly grappled with it in their annual reports. Judges have repeatedly defined Indian identity in regard to property and entitlement, tribal membership, and criminal and civil jurisdictional conflicts among tribes, states, and the federal government. Sociologist C. Matthew Snipp identified three separate categories of American Indian identity evident in the 1980 federal census: American Indians (those who identified as Indian for both racial and ethnic categories); American Indians of multiple ancestry (those who identify racially as Indians, but list other ancestry as part of their ethnic background); and Americans of Indian descent (those who do not list Indian as their race, but include it in their ethnic background).[9] Given such complexity, it is obvious that tribal enrollment provides only a partial answer to the question, "Who is an Indian?"

Among the most common criteria used both by tribal governments, to establish membership, and by the U.S. government, to determine who is an American Indian, is degree of Indian blood or "blood quantum." The amount necessary for enrollment can vary from 1/16 for the Eastern Band of Cherokee to 1/2 for the Hopi Nation. Some tribes, like the Cherokee Nation of Oklahoma, specify no blood quantum but require individuals to trace genealogical descent from a direct ancestor included on the Dawes Roll codified in 1907. The federal government maintains a 1/4 blood requirement for most of its benefits. Obviously, requiring a greater proportion of American Indian "blood" limits the eligible population more than a smaller percentage does.

Measuring Indian "blood" is a curious phenomenon that merits examination in its own right. It is incorrect to assume that the term "blood" is and always has been simply a metaphoric reference to genetic composition. Especially before knowledge of genetics, blood seemed the very stuff of life. The weakening effects of the loss of a great deal of blood—producing even death—cannot have been lost on the earliest humans. Among most band level people, blood has been and is regarded as a very powerful element. From the earliest times it has been regarded as the quintessential substance which carries and transmits the special qualities of the stock. Ancient Greeks linked blood to beliefs about human reproduction. Some believed that the mother's blood seeped into the fetus or that the testes separated blood from seed rendering semen a distillation of blood. Herodotus thought that African semen was black, and it took Aristotle to set the record straight. (What lively reading his field notes must be!) These beliefs concerning blood are probably among the oldest surviving ideas from the earliest days of humankind. They are widely distributed among the peoples of the world in much the same form.[10]

Ideally, understanding native conceptions of blood and transmission of group qualities should form a crucial aspect of this project. Pre-contact native groups determined membership through kinship systems. Understanding how groups that formerly determined membership by kinship came to measure blood themselves is more difficult. United States policymakers set the precedent, but tribes maintained the practice. Why?

The historical record complicates exploring native ideas about blood's properties. Intermediaries like explorers, missionaries, agents, or ethnographers produced the most documents. They generally adopted language that conflated blood and peoplehood and did not render native conceptions. Native language dictionaries tend to translate in an abrupt, matter-of-fact style ill-equipped to convey subtle, nuanced cross-cultural meanings. The Human Relations Area Files, a compilation of ethnographic information for cultures across the world, contain nothing specific to any group nor anything which might support generalizations across tribal lines. Scholars have not had these questions in mind.

Anecdotal ethnographic material concerning beliefs about menstrual blood, ritual torture (and its connection to adoption) and sacrifice, and ingesting internal organs of humans and animals confirms that some native cultures regarded blood as very powerful. But findings will not apply across tribal lines. For a larger study, delving into a few illustrative case studies where the data are better might be most productive. Interviewing native people about blood in today's volatile atmosphere would not yield results applicable to the past.

The etymological roots of the term "blood" extend deep into the Anglo-Saxon tribal psyche. In Old English, "blot" denotes blood spilled in sacrifice, a ritual intended partially to ensure continuity of the familial or tribal lineage. In Middle English the connection with sacrifice is obscured except for Christian associations with the Eucharist. By 1200, "blood" increasingly connotes lineage, descent, and ancestry in association with royal claims to property and power and presages modern conceptions of "race." Associations with intermarriage and discussions of whole- and half-blood appear. By the early eighteenth century, modern physiological meanings take the fore and "race" begins to displace the connotations of lineage and ancestry formerly attributed to "blood."[11]

In 1911, William Whitney's *Century Dictionary* turns to metaphorical meanings of "blood" in the fourth definition: "Persons of any specified race, nationality, or family, considered collectively." A citation from *Popular Science Monthly* illustrates the point: "Indian blood, thus far in the history of this country, has tended decidedly toward extinction."[12] This concise, paradigmatic phrase closely approximates ramblings about kinship and descent in popular and legal discourse.

Whitney assumes that the physiological meaning of "blood" preceded its metaphorical extensions, but the evidence suggests otherwise. Anglo-Saxons lacked "modern, or even classical Greek conceptions of physiology and biology. . . . The close relation of blod with blot, sacrifice, suggests that it may have originated in 'metaphorical' usage and only later, especially in the seventeenth and eighteenth centuries, picked up the varied but narrow biological meanings which the editors take for granted and believe are primary." Indeed, it seems more likely that the metaphorical connection of blood with lineage, descent, and ancestry preceded its literal physiological use.[13] Pre-contact indigenous peoples of the Americas could easily have related to this understanding.

European beliefs about the relationship between "blood" and peoplehood infused into the Americas from two different but related directions. Spanish and Portuguese precedents on the Iberian peninsula left their mark on the first colonizing efforts. Subsequent English ventures encountered this legacy and contributed their own distinctive ideas about superior Anglo-Saxon institutions and, eventually, bloodlines. These European ideologies left distinctive imprints on the social relationships that evolved from region to region in the Americas.

For seven hundred years prior to 1492 the Iberian peninsula witnessed increasing ethnic heterogeneity as "Iberians, Celts, Phoenicians, Greeks, Carthaginians, Romans, Visigoths, Jews, Arabs, Berbers, Gypsies, and medieval slaves of different origins" interacted and intermixed.[14] Although Jews and Moors came to be persecuted and exiled, they also contributed much to Spanish and Portuguese culture, including their genes. Some have suggested that Spanish and Portuguese success as colonizers can be attributed to their heritage of miscibility. Did this fact coupled with their idealization of the dark skinned "Moorish enchantress" and the Muslim tradition of polygyny foster intimate relationships with native women? Magnus Morner suggests that scholars need to know much more about this heritage to assess its influence on the colonization of Latin America. Even so, some similarities are apparent. Interactions on both sides of the Atlantic were characterized by "the same kind of strange mixture between savage warfare and pacific exchange, including miscegenation, between intolerance and tolerance in interethnic relations."[15] The chronicler of conquest Bernal Diaz wrote that the Spaniards raped, robbed, and pillaged, "as if they were in Moorish country." A long history thus sustained Spanish and Portuguese notions of their own cultural superiority and enabled them to rationalize the conquest, freely enter into intimate relations with native women, and define the evolving social and labor systems by reference to color and, eventually, racial and caste designators.[16]

People of English descent had their own ideas about "blood" and peoplehood. The roots of the concept of a distinct, superior Anglo-Saxon race extend back at least to the sixteenth and seventeenth centuries. The English people who conquered the eastern shores of North America brought with them a myth glorifying a "pure" English Anglo-Saxon church as part of their religious heritage. The English Reformation stimulated research designed to prove that the church was returning to supposedly purer practices that existed before 1066; they were cleansing the church of corruption. This helped to justify their break with Rome. By the American Revolution, Euroamericans believed themselves the beneficiaries of a long tradition in which the Anglo-Saxon English had enjoyed unprecedented freedoms that had been polluted by the Norman Conquest. The emphasis was on *institutions* rather than race.

In the late eighteenth and early nineteenth centuries, the emphasis changed from celebrating superior institutions to celebrating innate racial strengths. Two movements—a burst of German nationalism and a growing European interest in the history of German peoples—helped to inspire the English and Americans to celebrate Anglo-Saxons as superior people competent to create institutions capable of ruling the world. In this view, high-minded, freedom-loving German people had migrated from their simple, pure life in the forests to infuse France and England with their excellent characteristics. European Romanticism's stress on the uniqueness of individuals and peoples helped to shift the emphasis from institutions to the continuity of innate racial strengths. English-speaking people in particular fastened on the idea of each nation possessing its own *Volkgeist,* or special national spirit. It helped them to explain their success in the modern era.

The Romantic emphasis on feelings, imagination, and emotions also helped to sustain the blurry thinking necessary to rationalize some of the more extreme manifestations of racial Anglo-Saxonism. From these origins in German Romanticism, the English and, eventually, Americans were to combine race, nation, and language in a confused jumble of "rampant, racial nationalism." The new Romantic image that emerged glorified Anglo-Saxons as "adventurous, brave, and respectful toward women" as well as the "originators of trial by jury and parliamentary institutions."

However, it is one thing to celebrate a heritage and another to attack other people and nations for their inferiority. Scientific inquiry in the late eighteenth and early nineteenth centuries provided the fodder for an elaboration of the inferiority of others as the final ingredient necessary for rabid, racial, Anglo-Saxonism. Natural scientists focused on observation, measurement, and classification. They were fascinated with anthropometry, especially physiognomy, craniology, and phrenology. Linnaeus and others applied modern scientific methodology to earlier categorization schemes like the Great Chain of Being. However, comparisons that were used in the eighteenth century to emphasize the unity of mankind were in the nineteenth century used to demonstrate fundamental human differences.

Great Britain, with its colonizing endeavors in Africa, the Americas, and the Pacific, was especially fertile ground for theories of racial hierarchy. English people, particularly, with their pronounced belief in the superiority of English Anglo-Saxon bloodlines and institutions were quite anxious to separate themselves from the "savages" they had encountered who were typically of darker complexion.[17]

From the thirteenth through the early sixteenth century, terms like *pardo, loro, negro, olivastre,* and *berretino* were employed in Europe to distinguish people with darker skin. Significantly, they denoted *color* differences, not racial or caste differences. In the European colonies, as conquest of Native Americans, Africans, and Asians progressed, terms like *mestizo* and *mulatto,* denoting hybrids of any sort, evolved. Increasingly, Euroamerican colonists emphasized biological or racial categorization of people of mixed descent. Cultural factors retained greater prominence in Spanish and Portuguese social systems, but all areas witnessed this transformation of color codes to racial ones. As interracial relationships produced progeny of increasingly diverse parentage, classificatory terms became broader and more general to accommodate this growing heterogeneity. The finely tuned lists of designators of every imaginable interracial mixture (*mestizo, castizo,* Spaniard, *mulatto, morisco, albino, torna atras, lobo, zambaigo, cambujo, albarazado, barcino, coyote, chamiso, coyote mestizo, ahi te estas, cuarteron de mestizo, quinteron, requinteron de mestizo, quarteron de mulato*) reflected the concerns of elite thinkers and later scholars more than the social reality of the time.[18]

The term "half-breed" originated in English common law to distinguish between siblings who were not descended from exactly the same two biological parents. It had nothing to do with race. When it appeared in colonial laws and discourse it could refer to any person of mixed descent.[19] However, the term became ensconced in the language of the North American fur trade as people of mixed descent proliferated throughout the St. Lawrence Seaway and Great Lakes watershed and came to form a separate ethnic group.[20] Wherever trade relationships persisted, people of mixed descent proliferated. That the terms employed in early treaties would reflect fur trade social realities should not be surprising. Land cessions, often accomplished through treaties, followed closely on the heels of the denouement of the regional fur trade. Fur trade personnel, many of them of mixed descent, served as intermediaries in treaty negotiations, sometimes wrangling special considerations (like "half-breed scrip") for members of their social group. Traders, treaty negotiators, and native people alike conflated their understandings of "blood" and peoplehood. The terms had meaning for all participants and from this entry point would continue to infiltrate and permeate the language of U.S. Indian policy.

In the language of colonial racial politics and evolving scientific racism, fused notions of blood and peoplehood were also ordered hierarchically into superior and inferior stocks. "White blood" might uplift darker "blood," but not as quickly as "tainted blood" polluted. And the stain of degeneracy attached to all those of mixed descent for those of the dominant order. It was a contest that might be won only through phenotype and cultural behavior. Color lines drawn in the racial caste system remained impermeable unless an individual looked lighter and associated with and behaved like those of "purer blood."

These understandings pervaded U.S. Indian policy. From the beginning, policymakers believed that, despite their irredeemable hybrid stock, those of mixed descent would serve as a "civilizing" force and pave the way for the success of assimilation programs. There was some truth to this logic as people of mixed descent tended toward biculturalism if they existed in sufficient numbers.[21] But the reasoning was carried to absurd extremes until even land policies rested on a foundation of "blood." People of mixed descent, in general, had greater opportunity to acquire plots of land than native people. "Half-breeds" or "mixed bloods" were supposed to sever their tribal ties when they accepted land scrip, but they often did not.[22] Their tendency toward biculturalism also meant that they were more likely to accept the commodification of land, to understand the workings of the market, and to be among the first to claim further allotments of land and distributions of tribal funds. At the turn of the twentieth century, policymakers reasoned that people of mixed descent were more competent to manage real estate and removed protective restrictions designed to prevent the alienation of privately held reservation land by unscrupulous corporate interests. So firmly entrenched were these ideas that in 1917 the Commissioner of Indian Affairs literally forced all tribal people of half or more white "blood" to accept unrestricted title to their land. This meant that they were liable to pay property taxes. Small wonder that tax forfeiture emerged as the primary way in which individual Indian landowners lost land in the early twentieth century.[23]

At the White Earth Reservation in northwestern Minnesota, policymakers went to outrageous lengths in their efforts to equate white "blood" with comprehension of land in a capitalistic market. In 1907, Congress passed a law allowing "mixed bloods" of the White Earth Reservation to sell their land allotments. Failing to define "mixed blood," the law created a quagmire of uncertainty that spilled over into complex land fraud claims. In 1914 the

U.S. Supreme Court essentially applied the "one-drop rule," establishing that any amount of white "blood," no matter how minute, made an Indian a mixed blood, thus settling a complicated, nuanced issue in concrete, simplistic terms that only the judicial system can achieve.[24] Armed with their Supreme Court definition, policymakers needed only to identify the mixed bloods to settle contested land claims. Nonetheless, it seemed that only physical anthropologists could provide the information that everyone involved with White Earth land claims eagerly awaited.

Ales Hrdlička of the Smithsonian Institution and Albert Jenks of the University of Minnesota Anthropology Department put their heads together to devise and apply physical tests to the White Earth people to ferret out the mixed bloods. Phenotypic characteristics were of greatest diagnostic significance to them; they even hoped to construct a racial typology based on hair using the Pima as their pure baseline standard. When the micrometer they used to do cross-sectional analysis of hairs produced ambiguous results, the two scientists puzzled over their data. A baffled Jenks reported, "Both Hrdlička and myself have hair of most typical negro type, and the Scandinavians have hair more circular in cross section than our pure blood Pima Indians." Perplexed, Jenks was forced to conclude that, "Dr. Hrdlička and I are related to the negro, and the Scandinavians are simply bleached out Mongolians."[25] Mired in confusion, the anthropologists had to admit that classifying human races by hair texture was proving to be a far more problematic undertaking than they had initially imagined. Nevertheless, the scientists felt sure enough of their observations to go beyond identifying what they believed to be general racial characteristics to testify as to individuals' "blood" status. Through spurious methods of this sort, Hrdlička and Jenks lent their professional, "scientific" expertise to attempts to identify White Earth mixed bloods. Their efforts legalized the largest possible number of land transfers and directly contributed to the codification of White Earth enrollment lists. Outright racism received the imprimatur of academia. The cross-cultural faux pas would be humorous had it not, in reality, been so tragic.[26]

Given the destructive nature of past policies and social structures that rested on racial (and "blood") distinctions, it seems surprising that native groups would adopt the same sorts of categorizations when they codified their requirements for tribal membership. Granted, they inherited a tangled mess of property and enrollment decisions based on blood quantum, but the push for greater native sovereignty and self-determination in the mid-twentieth century nonetheless seems like a lost opportunity.[27]

Native people understood that past policies had differentiated between them on the basis of descent—specifically on the basis of intermarriage with Euroamericans. Often this meant that people of mixed descent enjoyed greater individual freedom and acquired greater amounts of what had once been collectively owned property. Under the U.S. government's allotment programs, most supported the restriction that exempted allotted landholdings from taxation. But that was the *only* restriction that native people welcomed. No one foresaw or approved the massive intrusion of the federal government into individual and tribal affairs; it was forced upon them without notice. As policymakers sought some means by which they might lift restrictions from people who clearly were proficient in the workings of the market, they fastened on "blood" as a marker of capabilities. People of mixed descent were far more likely to be deemed "competent" and given the freedom to manage their land and bank accounts as they saw fit. It is true that tribal groups suffered widespread dispossession under allotment policies, but it does not follow that native people supported all restrictions on their individual resources. More often they yearned for freedom from government regulation and resented the selective lifting of property restrictions from those of mixed descent. As they saw it, those with white "blood" were unfairly rewarded.[28]

One fact is obvious from examining tribal membership requirements. Native people established tribal policies that rewarded greater amounts of Indian "blood" rather than white "blood." Few scholars would argue that all of U.S. Indian policy amounted to genocide, but long-term demographic trends certainly point to a holocaust. Genocide has ideological as well as demographic consequences; defending and celebrating race is probably among them. In their purest form, blood quantum requirements amount to a celebration of race. But turning the tables in this fashion, though it may have accorded to some degree with their own notions of "blood" and lineage, would not spare tribes or individuals from the destructive consequences of basing policies on racial criteria.[29]

The Indians who populate the American popular imagination bear absolutely no relationship to real native people either in the past or in the present. The imagery allows Americans and people over the world to sustain highly romanticized notions of Indianness.[30] It encourages people with little or no cultural affiliation to claim Indian identity. People yearn to document descent from some relative lost in the past to enhance their chances of acquiring educational funds and gaining admittance to prestigious universities. Native people know this better than anyone. Never-before-seen "relatives" emerge as claimants every time any tribal group receives a court settlement or royalties from economic development. Such exploitation pierces as a thorn in the side of legitimate tribal members.

Given this history, it should come as no surprise that tribes with greater assets have more restrictive membership requirements. In fact, there is a correlation between more exclusive blood quantum requirements and the maintenance of reservation land bases (see tables 13.1 and 13.2). Tribes

TABLE 13.1
Blood Quantum Requirements of American Indian Tribes

Blood Quantum	*Number of Tribes*
5/8	1
1/2	19
3/8	1
1/4	147
1/8	27
1/16	9
No min. req.	98
Not avail.	17

SOURCE: Melissa L. Meyer and Russell Thornton, "American Indian Tribal Enrollment: The Blood Quantum Quandary," paper presented at Pacific Coast Branch, American Historical Association Annual Conference, Kona, Hawaii, 1991.

TABLE 13.2
Percentage by Blood Quantum That Are Reservation-based

Blood Quantum	*% Reservation-based*	*N*
1/2 or more[a]	85.7	21
1/4 or less	83.1	183
No min. req.	63.9	98

SOURCE: Melissa L. Meyer and Russell Thornton, "American Indian Tribal Enrollment: The Blood Quantum Quandary," paper presented at Pacific Coast Branch, American Historical Association Annual Conference, Kona, Hawaii, 1991.

[a]This category includes the three-eighths blood quantum.

without reservation land, like those of Oklahoma and California, tend to have more inclusive blood quantum requirements that underscore a concern with demographic survival. In this sense, enrollment criteria can be said to have both economic and demographic bases.

That claimants unrecognizable to reservation residents can and do successfully enroll carries a meaning beyond exploitation that contemporary scholars are wont to recognize. Assimilation on some level does occur, at least to the extent that descendants leave the tribal group and become unrecognizable to many of their "relatives" over the course of time. It is not easy to become enrolled even in a tribe with minimal blood quantum requirements. Countless would-be relatives are turned away every year. That so-called distant relatives actually achieve enrollment should give tribes cause to reevaluate exactly what they hope to achieve by specific enrollment criteria.

Clearly, most tribes desire that enrollment reflect some sort of valid *cultural* affiliation. The assumption is that higher proportions of Indian "blood" increase the odds that this will be the case. Everyone knows that it does not guarantee it, just as they know that some with legitimate cultural ties will be eliminated due to their inability to meet blood quantum requirements. Carrying this logic to its extreme, anthropologist John Moore has boned up on combinatorial statistics to compare the actual distribution of blood quantum in the Creek Nation to ideal distributions. He hopes ultimately to show the probabilities of a legal "half-blood" having "Indian" chromosomes for each number in the range, from zero to forty-six.[31] Whereas such a study has value in terms of tracing group descent, interracial marriage patterns, and health-related issues, it does not take much prescience to foresee some unintended and potentially disastrous uses to which it might be put. Imagine being required to produce a genetic, DNA analysis for purposes of tribal enrollment and receiving a card with a double helix hologram instead of a fractional delineation!

Many unenrolled people who claim Indian descent do not have exploitation on their minds; they are the victims of racist policies. Intermarriage across both tribal and racial lines means that blood quantums are ever-decreasing. It takes almost no time for a one-half blood requirement to exclude from tribal enrollment people who are enmeshed in family networks and actively participate in living cultures. Many people exist today who identify as 100 percent Indian, but cannot meet the enrollment criteria of any tribe. It still remains to be explained how people who value family so dearly rationalize tribal enrollment criteria that operate to exclude so many family members.[32]

Tribal enrollment policies and blood quantum requirements in particular represent a transformation in the way native people construe group membership. Indian identity has become increasingly racialized in the twentieth century. The pain engendered by such accusations of illegitimacy on this contested terrain of Indian identity has fractured Indian country and individuals' senses of themselves. Can a one-half blood quantum requirement be interpreted as anything other than a policy statement that "purity of blood" is more important than acknowledging and embracing family members? The Cherokee bear the brunt of many jokes and much criticism in Indian country; people among them who reflect European and African phenotypes bear testimony to their history of liberal interracial marriages. Oddly enough (aside from deviating from its matrilineal tradition), the Cherokee Nation of Oklahoma, with its requirement simply to trace direct familial descent to the Dawes Roll, more closely approximates the ways in which pre-contact native groups would have defined family and kin. The Hopi one-half blood quantum requirement hardly reflects "traditional" Hopi values. Measuring fractions of blood and excluding relatives from tribal membership reflects the combined influence of Euroamerican scientific racism and conflated ideas about "blood" and peoplehood.

Notes

1. U.S. Bureau of Indian Affairs, *Tribal Enrollment* (Phoenix: U.S. Bureau of Indian Affairs, 1979); Charles Park, "Enrollment: Procedures and Consequences," *American Indian Law Review* 3 (1975): 109–113. The precise number of federally recognized tribes is likely to continue to increase as groups pursue the difficult process of petitioning the U.S. government for federal recognition.

2. For a recent effort toward this end, see Pauline Turner Strong and Barrik Van Winkle, "Indian Blood: Reflections on the Reckoning and Refiguring of Native North American Identity (Resisting Identities)," *Cultural Anthropology* 11 (1996): 547–577. Terry Wilson's discussion of blood quantum requirements in "Blood Quantum: Native American Mixed Bloods," in Maria P. P. Root, ed., *Racially Mixed People in America* (Newbury Park, Calif.: Sage Publications, 1992) raises important questions regarding native people of mixed descent and notes some historical precedents, but does not carefully trace the history of tribal enrollment or the evolution of blood quantum requirements.

3. It is beyond the scope of this essay to list all treaties and statutes with provisions directed at "half-breeds" or "mixed bloods." See Felix S. Cohen, *Handbook of Federal Indian Law* (Washington, D.C.: U.S. Government Printing Office, 1942); Charles J. Kappler, comp., *Indian Affairs: Laws and Treaties,* 5 vols. (Washington, D.C.: U.S. Government Printing Office, 1942); "Chippewa Half-Breeds of Lake Superior," House Executive Documents 1513, no. 193, 42d Cong., 2d sess.

4. Loring Benson Priest, *Uncle Sam's Stepchildren: The Reformation of U.S. Indian Policy, 1865–1887* (New Brunswick, N.J.: Rutgers University Press, 1942); Robert A. Trennert, Jr., *Alternative to Extinction: Federal Indian Policy and the Beginnings of the Reservation System, 1846–1851* (Philadelphia: Temple University Press, 1975); Frederick E. Hoxie, *A Final Promise: The Campaign to Assimilate the Indians, 1880–1920* (Lincoln: University of Nebraska Press, 1984); D. S. Otis, *The Dawes Act and the Allotment of Indian Lands,* Francis Paul Prucha, ed. (Norman: University of Oklahoma Press, 1973); Francis Paul Prucha, *American Indian Policy in Crisis: Christian Reformers and the Indian, 1865–1900* (Norman: University of Oklahoma Press, 1976); Henry E. Fritz, *The Movement for Indian Assimilation, 1860–1890* (Philadelphia: University of Pennsylvania Press, 1963); Robert Mardock, *The Reformers and the American Indian* (Columbia: University of Missouri Press, 1971); Leonard Carlson, *Indians, Bureaucrats, and Land: The Dawes Act and the Decline of Indian Farming* (Westport, Conn.: Greenwood Press, 1981); H. Craig Miner, *The Corporation and the Indian: Tribal Sovereignty and Industrial Civilization in Indian Territory, 1865–1907* (Columbia: University of Missouri Press, 1976); Janet A. McDonnell, "Competency Commissions and Indian Land Policy, 1913–1920," *South Dakota History* 11 (1980): 21–34; Janet

A. McDonnell, "The Disintegration of the Indian Estate: Indian Land Policy, 1913–1929," Ph.D. diss., Marquette University, 1980; Janet A. McDonnell, *The Dispossession of the American Indian, 1887–1934* (Bloomington: Indiana University Press, 1991).

5. Jo Ann Woodsum provided invaluable research assistance in compiling all federal court cases dealing with enrollment or blood quantum requirements in any fashion. It is beyond the scope of this essay to provide more than the most general descriptive reference to these court cases.

6. *Waldron v. United States* (C.C. S.D. 1905) 143 Fed. 413. See also: (1888) 19 Op. Atty. Gen. 109; *Western Cherokee Indians v. United States* (1891) 27 Ct. Cl. 1; (1894) 20 Op. Atty. Gen. 711, 712; *Roff v. Burney*, 168 U.S. 218 (1897); (C.C.A. 8th Cir. 1897) 83 Fed. 721; *Nofire v. United States* (1897) 164 U.S. 647, 17 Sup. Ct. 212, 41 L. Ed. 588; *Hy-yu-tse-mil-kin v. Smith* (1904) 194 U.S. 401, 24 Sup. Ct. 676, 48 L. Ed. 1039; *United States v. Hefron* (2 cases), (C.C. Mont. 1905) 138 Fed. 964, 968; *Cherokee Intermarriage Cases* (1906) 203 U.S. 76, 27 Sup. Ct. 29, 51 L. Ed. 96; (1927) 245 N.Y. 433, 157 N. E. 734; *Santa Clara Pueblo v. Martinez*, 436 U.S. 49 (1978); *Chapoose v. Clark*, 607 F. Supp. 1027 (D. Utah 1985), aff'd, 831 F. 2nd 931 (10th Cir. 1987).

7. Vine Deloria, Jr., and Clifford Lytle, *The Nations Within: The Past and Future of American Indian Sovereignty* (New York: Pantheon Books, 1984); Vine Deloria, Jr., and Clifford Lytle, *American Indians, American Justice* (Austin: University of Texas Press, 1983).

8. *Census of Population, Vol. II, Subject Reports. American Indians, Eskimos and Aleuts on Identified Reservations and in the Historic Areas of Oklahoma (Excluding Urbanized Areas).* Document no. PC80-2-ID, pt. 1 (Washington, D.C.: U.S. Government Printing Office, 1985); Edna L. Paisano, comp. *We the . . . First Americans* (Washington, D.C.: U.S. Department of Commerce, Economics, and Statistics Administration, Bureau of the Census, September 1993); 1990 Federal Census of Population, unpublished data, U.S. Bureau of the Census, contact person, Edna Paisano; information about unpublished Bureau of Indian Affairs population figures are in the possession of Russell Thornton and Melissa Meyer.

9. C. Matthew Snipp, "Who Are American Indians? Some Observations about the Perils and Pitfalls of Data for Race and Ethnicity," *Population Research and Policy Review* 5 (1986): 237–252. See also: Russell Thornton, "Tribal Membership Requirements and the Demography of 'Old' and 'New' Native Americans," *Population Research and Policy Review* 7 (1997): 1–10; Russell Thornton, *American Indian Holocaust and Survival: A Population History since 1492* (Norman: University of Oklahoma Press, 1987); Russell Thornton, *The Cherokees: A Population History* (Lincoln: University of Nebraska Press, 1990); C. Matthew Snipp, *American Indians: The First of This Land* (New York: Russell Sage Foundation, 1989); William T. Hagan, "Full Blood, Mixed Blood, Generic, and Ersatz: The Problem of Indian Identity," *Arizona and the West* 27 (1985): 309–326; Fred M. Owl, "Who and What Is an Indian?" *Ethnohistory* 9 (1962): 265–284; Ronald L. Trosper, "Native American Boundary Maintenance: The Flathead Indian Reservation, Montana, 1860–1970," *Ethnicity* 3 (1976): 256–274; Susan Greenbaum, "What's in a Label: Identity Problems of Southern Indian Tribes," *Journal of Ethnic Studies* 19 (1991): 107–126; Alexandra Harmon, "When Is an Indian Not an Indian: The Friends of the Indian and the Problems of Indian Identity," *Journal of Ethnic Studies* 18 (1990): 95–123.

10. Bernard Seeman, *The River of Life: The Story of Man's Blood, from Magic to Science* (New York: Norton, 1961); Ashley Montague, *Man's Most Dangerous Myth* (Cleveland: World Publishing Company, 1964); Ashley Montague, "The Myth of Blood," *Psychiatry* 6, no. 1 (February 1943): 17; Nancy B. Jay, *Throughout Your Generations Forever: Sacrifice, Religion, and Paternity* (Chicago: University of Chicago Press, 1992).

11. See Arthur R. Borden, Jr., *A Comprehensive Old-English Dictionary* (Washington, D.C.: University Press of America, 1982), 188–189; T. Northcote Toller, ed., *An Anglo-Saxon Dictionary Based on the Manuscript Collections of the Late Joseph Bosworth* (Oxford: Oxford University Press, 1898), 111; Hans Krath and Sherman M. Kuhn, eds., *Middle English Dictionary* (Ann Arbor: Michigan University Press, 1956), 985–989; Keith Spaulding, *An Historical Dictionary of German Figurative Usage, Fascicle 1* (Oxford: Basil Blackwell, 1952), 358–362; John Kersey, *A New English Dictionary (1702)* (reprint, Menston, England: Scolar Press, 1969); Thomas Dyche and William Pardon, *A New General English Dictionary* (London: G. Ware, 1758); Thomas Sheridan, *A General Dictionary of the English Language (1780)*, vol. 1 (reprint, Menston, England: Scolar Press, 1967); John Walker, *A Critical Pronouncing Dictionary and Expositor of the English Language* (Edinburgh: Peter Brown and Thomas Nelson, 1835); John Ogilvie, *The Imperial Dictionary* (Glasgow: Blackie and Son, 1850).

12. William Dwight Whitney with Benjamin E. Smith, *The Century Dictionary: An Encyclopedic Lexicon of the English Language* (New York: The Century Company, 1911); *Popular Science Monthly* 26: 233.

13. The quotation is drawn from my research assistant Kerwin L. Klein's research notes.

14. Magnus Morner, *Race Mixture in the History of Latin America* (Boston: Little, Brown and Company, 1967), 13.

15. Ibid., 14.

16. Quotation from Bernal Diaz del Castillo, *Historia verdadera de la conquista de la Nueva Espana*, vol. 2 (Mexico City: Ediciones Mexicanas, 1955), 113, as quoted in ibid. See also Marvin Harris, *Patterns of Race in the Americas* (New York: Walker, 1964); James Lockhart and Stuart B. Schwartz, *Early Latin America: A History of Colonial Spanish America and Brazil* (Cambridge: Cambridge University Press, 1983); Peter Gow, *Of Mixed Blood: Kinship and History in Peruvian Amazonia* (Oxford: Oxford University Press, 1991); John Hemming, *Red Gold: The Destruction of the Brazilian Indians, 1500–1760* (Cambridge: Harvard University Press, 1978); J. I. Israel, *Race, Class, and Politics in Colonial Mexico, 1610–1670* (Oxford: Oxford University Press, 1975); C. E. Marshall, "The Birth of the Mestizo in New Spain," *Hispanic American Historical Review* 43 (1963): 161–184; Anthony Pagden, "Identity Formation in Spanish America," in Nicholas Canny and Anthony Pagden, eds., *Colonial Identity in the Atlantic World, 1500–1800* (Princeton: Princeton University Press, 1987), 51–94; Stuart Schwartz, "The Formation of a Colonial Identity in Brazil," in Canny and Pagden, *Colonial Identity in the Atlantic World*, 15–50; Stuart Schwartz, "New World Nobility: Social Aspirations and Mobility in the Conquest and Colonization of Spanish America," in Miriam Usher Chrisman and Otto Grundler, eds., *Social Groups and Religious Ideas in the Sixteenth Century* (Kalamazoo, Mich.: Medieval Institute, Western Michigan University, 1978), 23–37.

17. Reginald Horsman, *Race and Manifest Destiny: The Origins of American Racial Anglo-Saxonism* (Cambridge: Harvard University Press, 1981). Quotations are from pp. 26 and 30. See also Winthrop D. Jordan, *White over Black: American Attitudes toward the Negro, 1550–1812* (Chapel Hill: University of North Carolina Press, 1968); Edmund Morgan, *American Slavery, American Freedom: The Ordeal of Colonial Virginia* (New York: W. W. Norton, 1975); Ronald T. Takaki, *Iron Cages: Race and Culture in Nineteenth-Century America* (New York: Knopf, 1979); G. E. Thomas, "Puritans, Indians, and the Concept of Race," *New England Quarterly* 48 (1975): 3–27; David Smits, "Abominable Mixture: The Repudiation of Anglo-Indian Intermarriage in 17th-Century Virginia," *The Virginia Magazine of History and Biography* 95 (1987): 157–192; David Smits, "'We Are Not to Grow Wild': Seventeenth-Century New England's Repudiation of Anglo-Indian Intermarriage," *American Indian Culture and Research Journal* 11 (1987): 1–31; David Smits, "'Squaw Men,' 'Half-Breeds,' and Amalgamators: Late Nineteenth Century Anglo-American Attitudes toward Indian-White Race-Mixing," *American Indian Culture and Research Journal* 15 (1991): 29–61; Ronald Sanders, *Lost Tribes and Promised Lands: The Origins of American Racism* (New York: Little, Brown and Co., 1978).

18. The list of terms is drawn from Morner, *Race Mixture*, 58–59. Here, I am following the argument of Jack D. Forbes in *Africans and Native Americans: The Language of Race and the Evolution of Red-Black Peoples* (Chicago: University of Illinois Press, 1993). His research into colonial laws and etymology has convincingly shown that major scholars of American race relations have drawn only a "black-white" picture of social relations where native people should have been included as major players. See also J. Leitch Wright, Jr., *The Only Land They Knew: The Tragic Story of the American Indians in the Old South* (New York: Free Press, 1981); James H. Merrell, *The Indians' New World: Catawbas and Their Neighbors from European Contact through the Era of Removal* (Chapel Hill: University of North Carolina Press, 1989); James H. Merrell, "The Racial Education of Catawba Indians," *Journal of Southern History* 50 (1984): 363–384. The literature on the history of racism and miscegenation in relation to American slavery is far too vast to be cited here. See especially Jordan, *White over Black;* Morgan, *American Slavery, American Freedom;* and George M. Frederickson, *White Supremacy: A Comparative Study in American and South African History* (Oxford: Oxford University Press, 1981). See also Joel Williamson, *New People: Miscegenation and Mulattoes in the United States* (New York: Free Press, 1980); Everett V. Stonequist, "Race Mixture and the Mulatto," in Edgar T. Thompson, ed., *Race Relations and the Race Problem: A Definition and an Analysis* (Durham, N.C.: Duke University Press, 1939).

19. Morner, *Race Mixture;* Forbes, *Africans and Native Americans.*

20. Jennifer S. H. Brown, "Linguistic Solitudes in the Fur Trade: Some Changing Social Categories and Their Implications," in Carol M. Judd and Arthur J. Ray, eds., *Old Trails and New Directions: Papers of the Third North American Fur Trade Conference* (Toronto: University of Toronto Press, 1980), 147–159; Jennifer S. H. Brown, "Fur Traders, Racial Categories, and Kinship Networks," in William Cowan, ed., *Papers of the Sixth Algonquian Conference* (Ottawa: Museum of Man, 1975), 209–222; Robert E. Bieder, *Science Encounters the Indian, 1820–1880* (Norman: University of Oklahoma, 1986); Robert E. Bieder, "Scientific Attitudes toward Indian Mixed-Bloods in Early Nineteenth-Century America," *Journal of Ethnic Studies* 8 (1980): 17–30; Vincent

Havard, "The French Half-Breeds of the Northwest," *Smithsonian Institution Reports* (1879): 309–327; Anthony Pagden, *The Fall of Natural Man: The American Indian and the Origins of Comparative Ethnology* (Cambridge: Cambridge University Press, 1982); Salme Pekkala, Marian B. Hamilton, and Wiley Alford, "Some Words and Terms Designating, or Relating to, Racially Mixed Persons or Groups," in Edgar T. Thompson and Everett C. Hughes, eds., *Race: Individual and Collective Behavior* (Glencoe, Ill.: Free Press, 1958), 52–57; William J. Scheick, *The Half-Blood: A Cultural Symbol in Nineteenth Century American Fiction* (Lexington: University Press of Kentucky, 1979); William Stanton, *The Leopard's Spots: Scientific Attitudes toward Race in America* (Chicago: University of Chicago Press, 1960).

21. James Clifton, ed., *Being and Becoming Indian: Biographical Studies of North American Frontiers* (Chicago: Dorsey Press, 1989).

22. See "Chippewa Half-Breeds of Lake Superior," House Executive Documents 1513, no. 193, 42d Cong., 2d sess.

23. McDonnell, *Dispossession of the American Indian*; Janet A. McDonnell, "Competency Commissions and Indian Land Policy, 1913–1920," *South Dakota History* 11 (1980): 21–34.

24. *United States v. First National Bank* 234 U.S. 245 (1914).

25. Both quotes from A. E. Jenks to R. J. Powell, 21 March 1917, Ransom J. Powell Papers, Box 1, Minnesota Historical Society Archives.

26. Ales Hrdlička, "Trip to Chippewa Indians of Minnesota," *Smithsonian Miscellaneous Collections* 66, no. 3 (1915): 73; Ales Hrdlička, "Anthropology of the Chippewa," in F. W. Hodge, ed., *Holmes Anniversary Volume: Anthropological Essays* (Washington, D.C.: U.S. Government Printing Office, 1916), 202–203; Ales Hrdlička, "Physical Anthropology in America: An Historical Sketch," *American Anthropologist* n.s., 16 (1914): 508–554; Ales Hrdlička, "Anthropological Work among the Sioux and Chippewa," *Smithsonian Miscellaneous Collections* 66, no. 17 (1915); Albert E. Jenks, *Indian White Amalgamation: An Anthropometric Study,* Studies in the Social Sciences no. 6 (Minneapolis: University of Minnesota Press, 1916); David L. Beaulieu, "Curly Hair and Big Feet: Physical Anthropology and Land Allotment on the White Earth Chippewa Reservation," *American Indian Quarterly* 8 (1984): 281–314; Melissa L. Meyer, *The White Earth Tragedy: Ethnicity and Dispossession at a Minnesota Anishinaabe Reservation, 1889–1920* (Lincoln: University of Nebraska Press, 1994). For a critique of anthropometry, see Stephen Jay Gould, *The Mismeasure of Man* (New York: W. W. Norton and Co., 1981).

27. See M. Annette Jaimes, "Federal Indian Identification Policy: A Usurpation of Indigenous Sovereignty in North America," in Fremont J. Lyden and Lyman H. Legters, eds., *Native Americans and Public Policy* (Pittsburgh: University of Pittsburgh Press, 1992), 113–135, for a polemical account which completely absolves tribal nations from any responsibility in maintaining blood quantum requirements once granted the authority to determine their own membership.

28. Meyer, *The White Earth Tragedy;* William E. Unrau, *Mixed-Bloods and Tribal Dissolution: Charles Curtis and the Quest for Indian Identity* (Lawrence: University Press of Kansas, 1989).

29. Historians of the Shoah struggle with the narrative legacy of the Holocaust, and scholars have solidified the terms "holocaust" (the larger story) and "geno-

cide" (specific episodes within the larger story) within American Indian Studies. See Kerwin L. Klein, *Frontiers of Historical Imagination: Narrating the European Conquest of Native America, 1890–1990* (Berkeley: University of California Press, 1996) for the original elaboration of this insight. For a recent work directly exploring this issue, see Aaron Hass, *The Aftermath: Living with the Holocaust* (Cambridge: Cambridge University Press, 1995). For an introductory sampling of Holocaust studies, see especially Saul Friedlander, ed., *Probing the Limits of Representation: Nazism and the Final Solution* (Cambridge, Mass.: Harvard University Press, 1992); Peter Baldwin, *Reworking the Past: Hitler, the Holocaust, and the Historian's Debate* (Boston: Beacon, 1990); John K. Roth and Michael Berenbaum, eds., *Holocaust: Religious and Philosophical Implications* (New York: Paragon House, 1989); Charles Maier, *The Unmasterable Past: History, Holocaust, and German National Identity* (Cambridge, Mass.: Harvard University Press, 1988); James E. Young, *Writing and Rewriting the Holocaust: Narrative and the Consequences of Interpretation* (Bloomington: University of Indiana Press, 1988); Gerd Korman, "The Holocaust in American Historical Writing," *Societas* 2 (Summer 1972): 250–270. And though applying the term "holocaust," even with a lowercase *h*, to anything other than the Shoah draws much censure from Holocaust scholars, many in American Indian Studies have fixed on "holocaust" and "genocide" as the descriptors of choice. See especially Russell Thornton, *American Indian Holocaust and Survival;* David Stannard, *American Holocaust: Columbus and the Conquest of the New World* (New York: Oxford University Press, 1992); Jack Norton, *Genocide in Northwestern California: When Our Worlds Cried* (San Francisco: Indian Historian Press, 1979); Estle Beard, *Genocide and Vendetta: The Round Valley Wars of Northern California* (Norman: University of Oklahoma Press, 1981); Seena B. Kohl, "Ethnocide and Ethnogenesis: A Case Study of the Mississippi Band of the Choctaw, A Genocide Avoided," *Holocaust and Genocide Studies* 1 (1986): 91–100; Rupert Costo and Jeanette Costo, eds., *The Missions of California: A Legacy of Genocide* (San Francisco: Indian Historian Press, 1987); Ward Churchill, *Indians Are Us? Culture and Genocide in Native North America* (Monroe, Maine: Common Courage Press, 1994). Beyond these titles which make specific reference to "holocaust" and "genocide," further allusions to dramatic, traumatic population decline are too numerous to cite.

30. Roy Harvey Pearce, *Savagism and Civilization: A Study of the Indian and the American Mind* (Berkeley: University of California Press, 1988); Robert F. Berkhofer, Jr., *The White Man's Indian: Images of the American Indian from Columbus to the Present* (New York: Vintage, 1979); Raymond Stedman, *Shadows of the Indian: Stereotypes in American Culture* (Norman: University of Oklahoma Press, 1982).

31. Personal communication, John Moore to Melissa Meyer, 27 November 1990.

32. Ron Andrade, "Are Tribes Too Exclusive?" *American Indian Journal* (1980): 12–13; Henry Zentner, *The Indian Identity Crisis: Inquiries into the Problems and Prospects of Societal Development among Native Peoples* (Calgary: Strayer Publications Limited, 1973); Rob Williams, "Documents of Barbarism: The Contemporary Legacy of European Racism and Colonialism in the Narrative Traditions of Federal Indian Law," *Arizona Law Review* 31 (1989): 237–278. In addition follow the online "Native Network" (natchat@gnosys.svle.ma.us) and *Indian Country Today* for ongoing accusations and debates about Indian identity. Two absolute certainties emerge: 1) this issue is of great importance to many native people, and 2) the pain is palpable.

Part Three

CREATING COMMUNITY

14

CRUCIFIXION, SLAVERY, AND DEATH

The Hermanos Penitentes of the Southwest

RAMÓN A. GUTIÉRREZ

There is in the remote mountain villages of northern New Mexico and southern Colorado a penitential confraternity known as La Fraternidad Piadosa de Nuestro Padre Jesús Nazareno, the Pious Confraternity of Our Lord Jesus Nazarene, popularly known as the Hermanos Penitentes. The group's devotion to the passion and death of Christ, still commemorated with rituals of crucifixion on Good Friday, has long fascinated believers and disbelievers, promoters and detractors of Hispano culture in the Southwest. Since 1833 when Josiah Gregg first described the penitential rituals he observed during Holy Week at Tomé, in his much-read book *Commerce of the Prairies,* wells of ink have been spent recounting the activities of the Hermanos Penitentes.[1] Protestant authors in the nineteenth century focused on the brutality and barbarity of the bloody flagellants and their crucifixion rite to validate Anglo-American presuppositions about New Mexican Hispano Catholicism—namely, that centuries of Roman Catholic rule in what became the U.S. Southwest had bred a backward, primitive, and savage piety that hampered the civilizing mission of the Anglo capitalist gospel.[2]

At the end of the nineteenth century, a host of pundits, visionaries, and pop-historians, individuals who as a group lacked the linguistic tools and cultural sensitivity to study much less understand the activities of the Hermanos Penitentes, focused a voyeuristic gaze on the group. "Orientalizing" the Upper Rio Grande Valley for touristic purposes, they painted pictures of a primitive, simple landscape and populace in the Southwest that resembled Egypt and offered a potential escape from the decadent industrial northeastern United States. In this frame of reference, even sympathetic advocates of the brotherhood depicted it as one of the "last vestiges of medievalism in America," as "mired in webs of iconographic confusion," and locked "in a time-warp oblivious to history."[3]

This essay on the history of the Pious Confraternity of Our Lord Jesus Nazarene forms part of a larger research project on the history of Indian slavery in New Mexico. Much of the extant scholarship on slavery in the Americas has focused on the African experience. Reams have been written on the Atlantic passage, on the African slave experience in various plantation economies, and on the process of manumission, the meaning of freedom, and the stigma and meanings of color for these former slaves throughout the hemisphere. But except for Silvio Zavala's 1967 documentary history, *Indian Slaves in New Spain,* little attention has been given to the role of Indian thralls in the hacienda and ranch economies of the hemisphere.[4] My goal here is to begin to fill this lacuna, if only very partially, by studying the cultural history of *genízaros,* as Indian slaves were known in New Mexico, focusing in this essay on their religious organizations and rituals.

Membership in the Pious Confraternity of the Our Lord Jesus Nazarene, even to this day, is considered a fundamental way of life. The confraternity offers its members a code for living that is marked by a year-long calendar of pious acts, a regimen of prayer, fasting, mortification, and social works of mercy. Confraternity activities reach a high pitch during Holy Week, when Christ's passion and death on the cross are commemorated. From Palm Sunday until Holy Saturday, members of the brotherhood reenact the Way of the Cross, which according to some late-nineteenth-century accounts, actually culminated in the death of the surrogate Christ.

To understand the historical and cultural meanings of the daily, weekly, and Holy Week rituals of the La Fraternidad Piadosa de Nuestro Padre Jesús Nazareno, one must approach their rituals like one approaches the careful analysis of an onion, peeling away layer after layer. The organizational form the brotherhood takes is the *cofradía,* or confraternity. The words *confraternity* and *cofradía* both derive from the Latin word *confrater,* which literally means a "co-brother." A confraternity was a group of persons who lived together like brothers in a larger fictive or mystical family. Confraternities had their origin in Europe during the twelfth century as voluntary associations of the Christian faithful committed to the performance of acts of charity. In an era before social services were provided by the state, the pressing social needs created by poverty and vagrancy accelerated the formation of religious brotherhoods. Victims of catastrophe, disease, or unemployment found their basic needs met through the works of mercy performed by confraternities. Members of confraternities, by performing such acts, gained grace and indulgences, which were deemed sure routes to sanctity and personal salvation.[5]

Confraternities dedicated themselves to the promotion of particular devotions to Christ, to the Virgin Mary, and to various saints. They required episcopal sanction for formation and were governed by statutes that contained their rule, their prescribed ritual practices, their required works of piety, and festival days of observance. Despite great differences in devotional practices, the common thread that bound brotherhoods was their obligation to lead model lives of Christian virtue, to care for the physical welfare of the locality's needy, to bury the dead, and to pray for the salvation of departed souls.[6]

The familial language that confraternities employed made them vibrant organizational forms for the expression of broader social affinities. As equal members of the mystical body of Christ joined in spiritual brotherhood, for purposes of larger social good, residents of a community could momentarily put aside the enmities and distrust that typically marked the daily interactions of families, households, and clans. Indeed, through the creation of religious associations of co-brothers who were united in the mystical body of Christ with God as father and the Church as mother, Catholic prelates and theologians explicitly critiqued the secular, biological theory of family that had existed in Western Europe since the second century A.D.[7]

Nowadays, when we speak of *familia,* or family, we equate it with our immediate blood kin. That which is within the family is intimate, within the private walls of the home, and devoid of strangers. But if we focus carefully on the historical genealogy of the word *familia,* on its antique meanings, it was tied neither to kinship nor to a specific private space or house. Rather, what constituted *familia* was the relationship of authority that one person exercised over another, and more specifically, *familia* was imagined as the authority relationship of a master over slaves. The etymological root of the Spanish word *familia* is the Latin word *familia.* According to historian David Herlihy, Roman grammarians believed that the word had entered Latin as a borrowing from the Oscan language. In Oscan *famel* meant "slave"; the Latin word for slave was *famulus.* "We are accustomed to call staffs of slaves families. . . . we call a family the several persons who by nature of law are placed under the authority of a single person," explained Ulpian, the second century A.D. Roman jurist. Family was initially that hierarchical authority relationship that one person exercised over others, most notably slaves, but in time, also over a wife, children, and retainers.[8]

It was to temper this authority that a master exercised over his slaves or family that the Church elaborated the relationship of spiritual fraternity that was born of baptism. Through the sacrament of baptism one was born again a child of God, thus defining the person both as a natural and a spiritual being, with loyalties both to biological natural parents and to spiritual parents as well. For slaves, who often had no natural or genealogical relationships in a town, the confraternity served as an alternative kinship network morally obligated to offer protection and succor in times of need.[9]

In every town and village, in both Europe and the Americas, vertical and horizontal confraternities existed side by side.[10] The vertical confraternities integrated a locality's social groups, joining the rich and the poor, Spaniards and Indians, the slave and free. By emphasizing mutual aid and ritually obliterating local status distinctions and social hierarchy, vertical confraternities diffused latent social tensions into less dangerous forms of conflict. In place of overt class antagonism, parish confraternities squabbled over displays of material wealth, the splendor of celebrations, and the precedence due each group.

If vertical brotherhoods integrated a town's various classes, horizontal confraternities mirrored a locale's segmentation, marking organizationally status inequalities, be they based on race, honor, property ownership, or other material and symbolic goods. Relationships of domination and subordination were often articulated through confraternity rivalries and their symbolic opposition throughout the yearly cycle of sacred rites. The social supremacy of the Spanish gentry, for example, was expressed through their opulent confraternity rituals and celebrations to various saints. Dominated groups such as Indians and slaves also expressed their dignity and their collective identity with acts of piety that rivaled those of their oppressors.

Such horizontal separation of social groups is clearly apparent in the symbolic opposition that has existed in Santa Fe, New Mexico, from the eighteenth century to the present, between the Confraternity of Our Lady of Light and the Confraternity of Our Lord Jesus Nazarene, popularly known as the Brothers of Darkness. During the colonial period, noted Fray José de Vera, the population of the Kingdom of New Mexico was divided into "three groups . . . superior, middle and infamous."[11] The superior class consisted of noble men of honor, the conquistadors of the province. Below them were the landed peasants, who were primarily of mestizo or mixed ancestry but who considered themselves Spaniards to differentiate themselves from the Indians. At the bottom of the social hierarchy were the "infamous" genízaros who were dishonored by their slave status.

The Confraternity of Our Lady of Light, founded in Santa Fe in 1760, was largely composed of members of Santa Fe's Spanish nobility. The confraternity owned a private chapel, which by eighteenth-century standards was the most ornate in town, and had furnishings that were considered sumptuous, rich vestuaries, and a large endowment of land and livestock. On the feast days that commemorated Our Lady of Light's conception, purification, nativity, and assumption, her devotees carried her bejeweled image through the streets of Santa Fe accompanied by the royal garrison firing salvos, and ending in celebrations marked with dances, dramas, and bullfights.[12]

Symbolically counterpoised to the co-brothers of Our Lady of Light were the Brothers of Darkness, whose devotion was to Christ's passion and death. The members of the Confraternity of Our Lord Jesus Nazarene were primarily genízaros. The Brothers of Darkness displayed their piety through acts of mortification, flagellation, cross-bearing, and the Good Friday crucifixion of one of its members. "The body of this Order is composed of members so dry that all its juice consists chiefly of misfortunes," wrote Fray Francisco Atanasio Domínguez, describing the confraternity's poverty in 1776. They had neither membership records, accounts, nor an endowment, and frequently had to borrow ceremonial paraphernalia from other confraternities for their services.[13]

Between 1693 and 1846, approximately 3,500 Indians slaves entered New Mexican households as domestic servants, captured as prisoners of a "just war."[14] As defeated enemies living in Spanish towns, these slaves were considered permanent outsiders who had to submit to the moral and cultural superiority of their conquerors. In addition to these slaves captured in warfare, throughout the eighteenth and nineteenth centuries New Mexico's slave population swelled to about ten thousand, out of a total Spanish population of thirty thousand, through the purchase of Indian slaves from the Apaches and Comanches, and through the incorporation into New Mexican villages of Pueblo Indian outcasts from their native towns.[15]

Genízaro slaves residing in Spanish households and towns were convenient targets for Spanish racial hatreds. As captives and outcasts, the genízaros were considered infamous, dishonored, and socially and symbolically dead in the eyes of the Christian community. Though they lived in Christian households, they lacked genealogical ties to a kinship group, and had legal personalities primarily through their owners. The only public form of sociability open to them to express their common plight as slaves, and eventually to express their ethnic solidarity, were the confraternity rituals of the Catholic Church, which bound them as co-brothers in the mystical body of Christ.[16]

With only few notable exceptions, scholars in the past have usually depicted the Fraternidad Piadosa de Nuestro Padre Jesús Nazareno in a rather static and timeless fashion. The documentary and material evidence clearly suggests various periods of development, transformation, and florescence, periods that are never easy to establish with precision and can only be considered rough approximations.

The confraternity's first period, difficult to recuperate given the paucity of oral and historical sources, begins with the colonization of the Kingdom of New Mexico in 1598 and extends roughly into the 1790s. Many of the ritual forms of the fraternidad were undoubtedly introduced in New Mexico by the Franciscan friars as part of their project to Christianize the indigenous population. Given the fear that the Franciscans had of imparting heretical understandings of the sacraments to the Indians, their Christianization project became that of teaching through paraliturgies, rites of sowing and harvest, didactic dramas, devotional practices tied to cosmological phenomena, and various Franciscan devotions to the Crucified Christ, such as the Way of the Cross. The cross was a symbol that many Indians had long given special importance in their iconography, albeit because it represented the six directions of the cosmos. Ritual flagellation too was commonly practiced by Mesoamerican Indians as a purificatory rite for contact with the sacred.[17] What occurred in colonial New Mexico under the rubric of Christianization was a process of cultural convergence between two systems of ritual practice; Franciscan Holy Week rituals substituted well for the Indians' warfare and masculine rituals of power, which under Spanish rule were prohibited. Historian William B. Taylor maintains that the great continuity and convergence between Christianity and Mesoamerican religions was in the ways of representing religious power, in the ways of conjuring the supernatural, in the substances that were deemed holy and polluting, in the ways of creating and entering sacred spaces, and in the ways of anchoring and linking the natural and supernatural to very specific localities.[18]

The laws regulating slavery in New Mexico stipulated that thralls could only be kept in bondage for a period of ten to twenty years. In many cases slaves were freed upon a master's death.[19] The manumission of slaves in New Mexican society produced a peculiar problem in terms of symbolic logic. How could a person considered socially dead and dangerous be given life again as a free and integral member of the community of Christians? The solution was to negate the negation of life—that is, to negate the slave's social death through a second ritual death.

I have long suspected that the rituals of the hermandad were initially rituals of slave manumission; and here I am offering nothing more than an educated hunch. The theology of Christ's crucifixion was a particularly appropriate metaphor for manumission as a death to the state of human bondage, for in it were the ideas of death and renewal. Just as Christ had died because of our slavery to sin and so had given us eternal life anew, so too the genízaro slave's social death was negated through a ritual death, bringing the person back to life. Christ's death brought us redemption. The word "redemption" means to ransom one from the bondage of slavery through the martyrdom of a sacrificial victim. Similarly, through Christ's death we atoned for our sins, and those separated by sin were brought back together. Here again, genízaros, who were outsiders and intruders in Spanish society, were reintegrated into the community.[20] The crucifixion of Christ theologically represented a series of status elevations that paralleled the status changes that accompanied a genízaro's manumission: from spiritual slavery to freedom, from spiritual death to life, from social separation to social integration.

The rather fragmentary evidence seems to suggest that in the community's religious division of labor, the Franciscan friars localized the need for corporal penance on the genízaros, thereby gaining the genízaros' redemption from sin and their reincorporation into the community through manumission. Much of the symbolism of the Hermanos Penitentes' ritual is one of status elevation; being led out of darkness to the light, brothers of darkness in time become brothers of light. Here again we have the Franciscan mystical formula for spiritual perfection. One kills the body to have mystical union with the father of light. Physical purgation prepares the soul for illumination, which, in turn, readies the soul for its mystical marriage with Christ.[21]

A clearly distinct second period for the confraternity dates from approximately 1790 to the 1820s. In these years genízaros in New Mexico develop as a distinct ethnic group. Fray Francisco Atanasio Domínguez noted in 1776, "Although the genízaros are servants among our people they are not fluent in speaking or understanding Castilian perfectly, for however much they may talk or learn the language, they do not wholly understand it or speak it without twisting it somewhat."[22] Fray Carlos Delgado observed in 1744 that the genízaros "live in great unity as if they were a nation." Delgado added that genízaros practiced marriage-class endogamy for "they marry women of their own status and nature."[23]

Genízaros were stigmatized by their slave and ex-slave status. Fray Francisco Atanasio Domínguez reported that genízaros were "weak, gamblers, liars, cheats and petty thieves."[24] When New Mexicans today say "No seas genízaro" (Don't be a genízaro), they mean, don't be a liar.[25]

The threat Hispanos felt at having increasing numbers of members of the enemy group living within their towns led to the residential segregation and spatial marginalization of genízaros. In Santa Fe the genízaros lived in the Analco district, situated strategically across the Santa Fe River in a suburb established to protect the town's eastern approach from Apache attacks. By the mid-eighteenth century, manumitted genízaros were congregated into settlements along Apache, Navajo, and Comanche raiding routes into the settlements of the Rio Grande drainage. Belén and Tomé were established in 1740 to protect the southern approach, Abiquiu and Ojo Caliente both were founded in 1754 to protect the northwest, and San Miguel del Vado in 1794 to protect the northeast.[26]

By around 1790, genízaros were perceived as a distinct ethnic group. Spanish society viewed them as marginal persons because of their slave and former slave status. They spoke a distinctive form of Spanish, married endogamously, and shared a corporate identity, living together as if they were a nation. And their liminality between the world of the Pueblo Indians and that of the Spaniards was marked through residential segregation and congregation in autonomous settlements. Membership in the Pious Confraternity of Our Lord Jesus Nazarene became an expression of ethnic solidarity. The position of this confraternity in the Church's horizontal system of pious organizations reflected their place at the bottom of the social order.

The third period of the confraternity's history roughly begins in the 1820s and continues with some modifications to the present. What is unique about this period is the confraternity's evolution into autonomous political and economic organizations, which were eventually repudiated by the Catholic Church hierarchy. In the early years of this period we increasingly see the nominal Christian veneer in the ritual and ideological system of the hermandad being supplanted by cosmological beliefs and practices, as well as the development of the confraternity into a civic political body.[27]

The first change observed in this movement toward political autonomy is the redefinition of the confraternity's sacral topography. Fray Francisco Atanasio Domínguez in 1776 reported that there were separate altars to Jesus Nazarene in the churches at Santa Fe, Santa Cruz, Albuquerque, Tomé, and Abiquiu.[28] By 1814 the altar at Santa Fe's *parroquia* (parish) was replaced by a free-standing chapel in the church's courtyard.[29] And by 1821 this chapel had been moved off church land and established as an independent *morada,* or penitente chapel, on private property.[30] These moradas were maintained by the confraternity without any form of ecclesiastical supervision.

Starting in 1836, the Bishop of Durango (in charge of New Mexico until 1848), continually tried to assert his authority over the confraternity by imposing the rule of the Third Order of St. Francis. The bishop's hope was to regain control over branches of the confraternity that were increasingly aloof to clerical supervision, or so he asserted.[31] In 1830 José de la Peña expressed succinctly why the Church hierarchy found the Hermanos Penitentes so subversive. Peña wrote: "They have a constitution somewhat resembling that of the Third Order, but entirely suited to their own political views. In fact, they have but self-constituted superiors and as a group do as they please."[32] Fifty years later, in 1888, Jean Baptiste Salpointe, Archbishop of Santa Fe Archdiocese, similarly observed: "This society, though perhaps legitimate and religious in its beginning, has so greatly degenerated many years ago that it has no longer fixed rules, but is governed in everything according to the pleasure of the director of every locality; and in many cases it is nothing else but a political society."[33]

Archbishop Salpointe was quite correct in seeing the confraternity as the corporate political body of genízaro communities. The ritual leader of the confraternity, the *hermano mayor* or the "eldest brother," was also quite frequently the town's civic leader. He administered justice, managed the locality's economic resources, and cared for the social welfare needs of the place. Of course, one should not minimize the organization's religious functions, which continued to thrive, particularly after the secularization of New Mexico's Franciscan missions between 1830 and 1850. Devoid of priest and access to the sacraments, the Hermanos Penitentes elaborated and evolved their own rites and routes to the sacred. According to anthropologist Munro Edmonson, the ritual calendar in genízaro villages did not correspond to the Christian one.[34] The themes articulated in the *alabados,* the penitential hymns members of the brotherhood chanted in their rites, also changed over time. Rather than the themes of death and darkness as a way to salvation, metaphors and symbols of illumination, which in American Indian religious thought signify utopia, started to figure more prominently.[35] Similarly, the first report of a man actually dying on the cross on Good Friday comes from the 1890s.[36] The mystery and legitimacy of Christianity comes from the fact that Christ descended to earth and was crucified for the sins of humanity. In the absence of priests, might the crucifixion of a Penitente similarly have given legitimacy to the confraternity's devotions and served as a symbol for their own resistance to outside domination? Perhaps.

What we do know for sure is that in the late 1880s and 1890s knowledge of the Hermanos Penitentes was widely disseminated throughout the United States to a broad reading public. The development of an integrated national market criss-crossed by railways and highways, and interpolated by print journalism, made it at last possible to imagine the nation on a continental scale and to travel to its remotest corners to see the odd customs of its exotics and view the most picturesque scenes imaginable.[37] American nationalism produced and fed both the production and consumption of travel literature, and ultimately the touristic marketing of New Mexico.[38]

At the end of the nineteenth century many luminaries, writers, artists, alienated intellectuals and social misfits came to New Mexico seeking a salubrious refuge from the machine age. In the quaint villages of what was to become the "Land of Enchantment" and in its prehistoric sites was a preindustrial America, a vestige from the past that offered mystical and romantic repose.

Charles Fletcher Lummis, the man who coined the slogan "See America First," was the individual most responsible for the initial marketing of New Mexico's cultures. It was Lummis who constructed the Pious Confraternity of Our Lord Jesus Nazarene as the savage and fanatic "Penitent Brothers" for the Anglo touristic gaze, simultaneously fixing for his readers the most enduring Anglo-American representations of the Pueblo Indians, the Navajo, the Apache, and especially of the New Mexican landscape.

Lummis came to New Mexico and the American West in 1881, seeking a cure for the "brain fever" he had developed at Harvard preparing for the ministry. In the West he found health and the city editorship of the *Los Angeles Times,* and it was from there, with extended forays to New Mexico, that he penned and preached about the corruption and decadence of Anglo-Saxon New England and the vigor and salubrity of the multi-ethnic West.[39] Writing such well received and popular books as *A New Mexico David* (1891), *Pueblo Indian Folk Tales* (1891), *A Tramp Across the Continent* (1892), *Some Strange Corners of Our Country* (1892), *The Land of Poco Tiempo* (1893), *The Spanish Pioneers* (1893), *The Enchanted Burro* (1897), and *The King of the Broncos* (1897), Lummis took his readers on an "orientalist" adventure to New

Mexico through fantasies and hallucinations of Egypt, Babylon, Assyria, and deepest, darkest Africa.[40] In *The Land of Poco Tiempo* Lummis writes:

> The brown or gray adobe hamlets [of New Mexico] . . . the strange terraced towns . . . the abrupt mountains, the echoing, rock-walled cañons, the sunburnt mesas, the streams bankrupt by their own shylock sands, the gaunt, brown, treeless plains, the ardent sky, all harmonize with unearthly unanimity. . . . It is a land of quaint, swart faces, of Oriental dress and unspelled speech; a land where distance is lost, and eye is a liar; a land of ineffable lights and sudden shadows; of polytheism and superstition, where the rattlesnake is a demigod, and the cigarette a means of grace, and where Christians mangle and crucify themselves—the heart of Africa beating against the ribs of the Rockies. (4–5)

In chapter after chapter, in description after description, New Mexico was Egypt. Describing the unique light on New Mexico, Lummis wrote: "Under that ineffable alchemy of the sky, mud turns ethereal, and the desert is a revelation. It is Egypt, with every rock a sphinx, every peak a pyramid" (9). The residents of Acoma Pueblo were "plain, industrious farmers, strongly Egyptian in their methods" (69). The Indian pueblos at Taos, Zuni, and Acoma, had been built in the shape of "pyramid" blocks (51–52). Pueblo girls cloaked themselves in "modest, artistic Oriental dress" (53). The Indian pony-tail was "The Egyptian queue in which both sexes dress their hair" (111). In the wind-eroded sand sculpture of the desert, Lummis saw an "insistent suggestion of Assyrian sculpture. . . . One might fancy it a giant Babylon" (61). The Apache were the "Bedouin of the New World," and the land they inhabited, a "Sahara, thirsty as death on the battlefield" (175–76). The Penitent Brothers whipped themselves like "the ancient Egyptians flogged themselves in honor of Isis" (80).

When Lummis described New Mexico as Egypt and employed Orientalist tropes, he was mimicking what was standard fare in Anglo-American travel writing from the eighteenth century forward. Such images were employed to give readers unfamiliar with a particular place some readily identifiable imaginary markers drawn from their own colonial histories, from travels to the Holy Land by their compatriots, and from their own readings of the Bible.[41] But equally important, writes Mary Louise Pratt, Egypt offered "one powerful model for the archeological rediscovery of America. There, too, Europeans were reconstructing a lost history through, and as, 'rediscovered' monuments and ruins." By reviving indigenous history and culture as archaeology, the locals who occupied those sites were being revived as dead.[42]

What evoked the sights, sounds and smells of Egypt in New Mexico for Lummis were the women who carried clay water jars on their heads, the cool mud (adobe) houses that dotted the landscape, the donkey beasts of burden, the two-wheeled carts, the desert sun, light, and heat, and the presence of sedentary and nomadic "primitives" amidst the ruins and abandoned architectural vestiges of former grand civilizations.

Lummis introduced the Penitent Brothers in *The Land of Poco Tiempo,* noting:

> [S]o late as 1891 a procession of flagellants took place within the limits of the United States. A procession in which voters of this Republic shredded their naked backs with savage whips, staggered beneath huge crosses, and hugged the maddening needles of the cactus; a procession which culminated in the flesh-and-blood crucifixion of an unworthy representative of the Redeemer. Nor was this an isolated horror. Every Good Friday, for many generations, it has been a staple custom to hold these barbarous rites in parts of New Mexico. (79)

Lummis asserted that the brotherhood consisted largely of "petty larcenists, horse-thieves, and assassins" (106). The brotherhood was widely feared because it controlled political power in northern New Mexico. "No one likes—and few dare—to offend them; and there have been men of liberal education who have joined them to gain political influence" (106), Lummis attested.

The Penitente discourse Charles Lummis constructed was followed almost verbatim by most Anglo-American writers who described the brotherhood from 1890 on. The gaze he focused on the flagellation, the bloodletting, the use of cacti for mortification, the shrill of the *pito,* and the nature and extent of crucifixion framed numerous "eye-witness" accounts that are difficult to accept as such primarily because the descriptions so closely ape those written by Lummis. Lummis took the first, and one of the only, sets of photographs of a Penitente procession and crucifixion, and this visual record may also account for the linguistic framing of what subsequent "outsiders" saw.

Interestingly, Lummis narrates the taking of these photographs as if on a safari hunting large game animals with his camera as his gun. "Woe to him if in seeing he shall be seen. . . . But let him stalk his game, and with safety to his own hide he may see havoc to the hides of others" (85). Lummis recounts how he waited anxiously for Holy Week to arrive so that he could photograph the impossible—the Penitentes. "No photographer has ever caught the Penitentes with his sun-lasso, and I was assured of death in various unattractive forms at the first hint of an attempt" (87). But on hearing the shrill of the pito, his prudence gave way to enthusiasm and he set himself up waiting for what he called the "shot." Though the Hermanos protested, "well-armed friends . . . held back the evil-faced mob, with the instantaneous plates were being snapped at the strange scene below" (91).

Photographs of this barbaric rite were necessary, explained Lummis, because Mexicans were "fast losing their pictorial possibilities" (8–9). What Lummis failed to explain, but what did not elude the diary of Adolph Bandelier, was that Lummis and Amado Chaves had held up the Hermanos at gun point, to get these "shots."

The political subtext of Lummis's Penitente photographs and textual descriptions was a critique of New Mexican despotism and of religious fanaticism that had no place in a republic governed by Anglo Protestants. Like the Israelites who had been led out of the darkness and idolatry of their Egyptian captivity, so too the peoples of New Mexico had to be freed from their "paganism" (read Roman Catholicism) (5).

What Lummis did by hunting Penitentes, cunningly stalking his prey like game animals, trying to capture on film that which was sacred, was to begin the process of desacralization that was to mark the history of the Hermanos and their Fraternidad from 1888 to the 1950s. The Good Friday rituals of the Hermanos at the turn of the century became touristic spectacles for Anglo New Mexicans. According to Gabriel Melendez, it was not uncommon for outsiders to sit in their cars waiting for the Hermanos to emerge from their moradas. As soon as they did, a flood of auto headlights would illuminate their activities.[43]

Once the rituals and processions of the fraternidad had been desacralized, their religious icons and statues soon suffered a similar fate. Mabel Dodge Luhan, in her autobiography, *Edge of Taos Desert: An Escape to Reality*, recounts how she and her friend Andrew Dasburg created the market for the religious icons that had once adorned moradas.

> Andrew had started hunting, an instinct that awakened in him every once in a while, made him breathless, eyes darkened, fully engaged. He hunted the old Santos painted on hand-hewn boards that we had discovered soon after we came to Taos. No one had ever noticed them except to laugh, but here was an authentic primitive art, quite unexploited. We were, I do believe, the first people who ever bought them from the Mexicans, and they were so used to them and valued them so little, they sold them to us for small sums, varying from a quarter to a dollar; on a rare occasion, a finer specimen brought a dollar and a half, but this was infrequent. . . . Andrew was soon absorbed in saint-hunting. . . . he went all around the valley looking for them. He became ruthless and determined, and he bullied the simple Mexicans into selling their saints, sometimes when they didn't want to. He grew more and more excited by the chase, so that the hunt thrilled him more than what he found; and he always needed more money to buy new Santos. . . . It was Andrew who started a market for them, and people began to want them and buy them; and I was always giving one or two away to friends who took them east where they looked forlorn and insignificant in sophisticated houses. People always thought they wanted them, though, and soon the stores had a demand for

> them. Stephen Bourgeois finally had a fine exhibition of them in his gallery. All this makes them cost seventy-five, a hundred, or two hundred dollars today.[44]

The *bultos, santos,* and the various religious icons and statues that adorned home altars and moradas slowly were commercialized, deconsecrated, robbed, and placed on display in museums.

A class of alienated Anglo-American intellectuals, writers, artists, and financiers packed their belongings and headed to northern New Mexico at the end of the nineteenth century and in increasing numbers after World War I. They came rejecting the tastes, aspirations, and pretensions of the "Blue Bloods" who mimicked European aristocracy. And by so doing they started to imagine a national culture that was rooted, not in Europe, but on this continent in the cultures of New Mexico.[45]

The preservation of the simple authentic cultures these easterners found in New Mexico, and their implicit critique of the industrial age, was clear in such acts as the 1925 creation of the Spanish Colonial Arts Society by Mary Austin and Frank Applegate. They aestheticized religious expressions and revalorized colonial artifacts as commercial art best enjoyed by connoisseurs. The process of appropriation reached its greatest extreme when the Santuario de Chimayo, the religious pilgrimage site in northern New Mexico, was purchased by the Spanish Colonial Arts Society in 1929 in order to protect it from the local ignorant folk.

In Spanish colonial art products, in religious icons and handicrafts, Anglos imagined the possibility and romance of non-alienating labor. Such artifacts were not mass-produced and appeared to stand frozen in isolation, defying the principles of global capitalism.[46] Mabel Dodge Luhan captured this flight from modernity to the cultural pluralism (read classless society) of New Mexico well when she instructed her son, "Remember, it is ugly in America. . . . we have left everything worthwhile behind us. America is all machinery and money-making and factories . . . ugly, ugly, ugly."[47]

A whole generation of Anglo-Americans, under the influence of pied-piper Charles Fletcher Lummis, were lured to New Mexico hoping there to resist industrial capital, to preserve the quaint picturesque cultures they found, and to market Pueblo and Hispano handicrafts as an authentic American art that offered a solution to national alienation. We see these sentiments expressed very well in the very first page of Roland F. Dickey's *New Mexico Village Arts* (1949). "This book does not recount famous names and urbane schools of art. It tells of ordinary men and women who worked with their hands to create a satisfying way of life in the Spanish villages of New Mexico." Waxing lyrical for over two hundred pages, Dickey concludes: "Today it is possible to escape from the commonplaceness of the machine world by furnishing an adobe house in what is reputed to be the Hispanic manner. . . . Beautiful things made by hand provide a relief from the systematic lines and textures of machine manufacture, and keep awake sensitivities that are dulled by standardization."[48]

The fraternidad responded to the commercialization of their religious expressions and to their transformation into safari tour spectacles by going underground, seeking anonymity, placing a premium on secrecy, and eventually retreating into New Mexico's hinterlands. There they developed a deep spiritual and mystical sense of community. In interviews, conversations, and a recent conference on the Penitent Brotherhood, the Hermanos have consistently noted that the essence of the brotherhood is mysticism and faith. Hermano Larry Torres of Taos recently stated that to be an Hermano was to devote one's life to prayer, penitence, and sacrifice. Torres cited the Song of Songs and the life of St. Bernard of Clairvaux as his two models for reaching spiritual perfection. The two alabados, or prayers that captured the nature of his faith, were: *Un ardiente deseo,* which tells of lovers yearning for the beloved and the sweetness of their embrace, and *Por ser mi divina luz,* which describes how Christ is the beacon leading one from darkness to the light.[49] Hermano Floyd Trujillo described his duties and commitments as follows: "When one becomes an hermano it is like the bond of sacred matrimony. . . . we know the role we accept and, like Christ, we take the cross and follow him. We help the people. We help those that need help. . . . We never say no. We see the needs of the community and we take care of them. We are the leaders of the community."[50]

The Hermanos take this leadership role very seriously. Hermano Gabriel Melendez has explained that the role of the hermano is that of a mediator who makes reconciliation possible. To mediate conflicts between Hermanos, between husbands and wives, between the Church and the Brotherhood, between the saints and the local morada. It is only through such activities of mediation that social peace and reconciliation can occur.[51]

One of the most eloquent members of the hermandad, Felipe Ortega, the master of novices at La Madera, New Mexico, clearly sees the fraternidad and the morada as an anti-hierarchical organization and sacred space for the experience of Christ and the community, that stands outside and in juxtaposition to the Catholic Church. Ortega notes that when members of a morada sing their penitential hymns or alabados in a cantor/response mode, a "unison is created, one spirit, one mind, one heart." Within the morada, people stand facing each other, rather than oriented toward a priest and altar, further inscribing the egalitarian sense of community among morada members. And when the Hermanos come together to celebrate rituals, they in fact create the very sacraments. For when the Hermanos sing "Venid. Venid. Venid a la mesa divina" (Come. Come. Come to the divine table), members of the brotherhood are called to feed their souls and their bodies in a common union, at a veritable communion, through the sharing of food.[52]

I realize that this essay is both tentative and speculative, and perhaps devoid of the chronological precision one commonly finds in historical tracts. My main theoretical concern in this research has been to understand the dynamics of cultural systems of reckoning and relatedness that are imagined and spoken with the same language we use to describe biogenetic ties, but which are often deemed "fictive." Since the late nineteenth century our anthropological and historical understanding of kinship has been dominated by studies of kinship terms, componential analysis, and household structures. Simply knowing who is biologically related to whom, who co-resides, and who gave birth to whom tells us very little about how relationships are imagined and kinship obligations animated in any society. Kinship theory has been too tightly constrained by our own modern preoccupation with biology and the salience of biogenetic principles of descent. If we are to understand the meaning of kinship in the early modern period, we have to approach the topic culturally, sketching the parameter of thought by studying prescriptive literature and then exploring instances where thought was concretely negotiated in practice. Herein I have tried to show how Indian slaves or genízaros, individuals who had no kinship ties to the community of Christians in New Mexico, forged ties of affinity through the Catholic Church's structure of confraternities that were just as real, important, and vibrant as any biological link ever has been or can be.

My second explicit aim has been to focus intensively on religious thought and expression as a window into local politics. Perhaps because we live in a secular age, we often relegate religion and its rituals to the domain of magic and superstition. I have tried to show that if one is going to take politics seriously in the early modern period and to study the origins of political forms, one has to turn to religion, the idiom through which politics was expressed until quite recently. One cannot, for example, understand the appeal of the New Mexican 1960s land radical, Reyes López Tijerina, unless one understands the religious qua political organization of the villagers to whom he was appealing for help in reclaiming lands fraudulently stolen from Hispano villages in the 1850s. Reyes was the king, and he took New Mexicans, who prior to the 1960s had lived in darkness, into the light.[53]

Finally, the Hermanos Penitentes teach us how deeply notions of ethnicity and kinship are intertwined. Whether one is a child of Abraham (as a Jew), a child of Malinche (as a Chicano), or a brother of Jesus Christ (as a genízaro), ethnic identity is tied to cultural conceptions of family. At a time when our civic fabric seems frayed beyond repair, when women are reinscribed as subordinates in patriarchal thinking, and single mothers are seen as pathologies in the body politic, we must reinvent new models of relatedness, based not on hierarchy but on egalitarian principles. This is the model for a better tomorrow that I think the Pious Confraternity of Our Lord Jesus Nazarene offers us all.

Notes

Much of the research for this essay was underwritten by fellowships from the Cushwa Center for the Study of American Catholicism at Notre Dame University and the Getty Center for the History of Art and the Humanities in Santa Monica, California. I thank both institutions for their generous support.

1. Josiah Gregg, *Commerce of the Prairies* (New York, 1844; reprinted Norman: University of Oklahoma Press, 1954), pp. 181–82.

2. See the writings of Charles Fletcher Lummis, especially *The Land of Poco Tiempo* (New York, 1893; reprinted Albuquerque: University of New Mexico Press, 1952).

3. Elizabeth Boyd, *Popular Arts of Spanish New Mexico* (Santa Fe: Museum of New Mexico Press, 1974), p. 464; Lorayne Ann Horka-Follick, *Los Hermanos Penitentes: A Vestige of Medievalism in the Southwestern United States* (Los Angeles: Westernlore Press, 1969).

4. Silvio Zavala, *Los esclavos indios en Nueva España* (Mexico City: Colegio Nacional, 1967).

5. The history of confraternities can be found in my essay, "Family Structures," in *Encyclopedia of the North American Colonies* (New York: Scribner's, 1993), vol. 2, pp. 672–82; José Bermejo y Carballo, *Glorias religiosas de Sevilla* (Seville: Imprenta y Librería del Salvador, 1882), pp. 2–5.

6. George M. Foster, "Cofradía and Compadrazgo in Spain and Spanish America," *Southwestern Journal of Anthropology* 9 (1953): 1–28.

7. Stephen Gudeman, "The Compadrazgo as a Reflection of the Natural and Spiritual Person," in *Proceedings of the Royal Anthropological Institute of Great Britain and Ireland* (1971), pp. 43–49; and "Spiritual Relationships and Selecting a Godparent," *Man* 10 (1975): 221–37; George M. Foster, "Godparents and Social Networks in Tzintzuntzan," *Southwestern Journal of Anthropology* 25 (1969): 261–78; Sidney Mintz and Eric R. Wolf, "An Analysis of Ritual Co-parenthood (Compadrazgo)," *Southwestern Journal of Anthropology* 6 (1950): 341–68.

8. David Herlihy, "Family," *American Historical Review* 96 (1991): 2–35.

9. Ramón A. Gutiérrez, *When Jesus Came, the Corn Mothers Went Away: Marriage, Sexuality, and Power in New Mexico, 1500–1846* (Stanford: Stanford University Press, 1991), pp. 181–84; Stephen Gudeman and Stuart B. Schwartz, "Baptismal Godparents in Slavery: Cleansing Original Sin in Eighteenth-Century Bahia," in Raymond T. Smith, ed., *Interpreting Kinship Ideology and Practice in Latin America* (Chapel Hill: University of North Carolina Press, 1984), pp. 35–58.

10. This distinction between vertical and horizontal confraternities is more fully elaborated in Isidoro Moreno Navarro, *Las Hermandades Andaluzas: Una aproximación desde la antropología* (Sevilla: Publicaciones de la Universidad de Sevilla, 1974); and Julio Caro Baroja, *Razas, pueblos y linajes* (Madrid: Revista del Occidente, 1957), pp. 287–88.

11. Fray José de Vera quoted in Archives of the Archdiocese of Santa Fe, Loose Documents, 1813, microfilm reel 53, frame 789.

12. Eleanor B. Adams, "The Chapel and Cofradía of Our Lady of Light in Santa Fe," *New Mexico Historical Review* 22 (1947): 327–41; A. Von Wuthenau, "The Span-

ish Military Chapels in Santa Fe and the Reredos of Our Lady of the Light," *New Mexico Historical Review* 10 (1935): 175–94.

13. Eleanor B. Adams and Fray Angélico Chávez, eds. and trans., *The Missions of New Mexico, 1776: A Description by Fray Atanasio Domínguez* (Albuquerque: University of New Mexico Press, 1975), p. 18.

14. Gutiérrez, *When Jesus Came, the Corn Mothers Went Away,* pp. 150–56, 180–90. For a detailed analysis of the Catholic Church records on these slaves, see David M. Brugge, *Navajos in the Catholic Church Records of New Mexico 1694–1875* (Tsaile, Ariz.: Navajo Community College Press, 1985).

15. Gutiérrez, *When Jesus Came, the Corn Mothers Went Away,* pp. 176–80.

16. On the history of Genízaros in New Mexico, see Brugge, *Navajos in the Catholic Church Records*; Fray Angélico Chávez, "Genízaros," in *Handbook of North American Indians,* ed. Alfonso Ortiz (Washington, D.C.: Smithsonian Institution Press, 1979), vol. 9, pp. 198–200; Steven M. Horvath, "The Social and Political Organization of the Genízaros of Plaza de Nuestra Señora de Los Dolores de Belén, 1740–1812" (Ph.D. diss., Brown University, 1979); Frances Leon Swadesh, *Los Primeros Pobladores: Hispanic Americans of the Ute Frontier* (Notre Dame: University of Notre Dame Press, 1974).

17. Elsie Clew Parsons, *Pueblo Indian Religion* (Chicago: University of Chicago Press, 1939), pp. 543, 896. The Christianization of America's Indians is studied in Robert Ricard, *The Spiritual Conquest of Mexico* (Berkeley: University of California Press, 1966); Pedro Borges, *Métodos misionales en la cristianización de América, siglo XVI* (Madrid: Consejo Superior de Investigaciones Científicas, Departmento de Misionología Española, 1960); Pius J. Barth, *Franciscan Education and the Social Order in Spanish North America, 1502–1821* (Chicago: Academy of American Franciscan History, 1950); Lino Gómez Canedo, *Evangelización y conquista: Experiencia Franciscana en Hispanoamérica* (Mexico City: Editorial Porrua, 1977).

18. William B. Taylor, "Magistrates of the Sacred: Parish Priests and Indian Parishioners in Eighteenth-Century Mexico" (unpublished manuscript).

19. On the prohibition of Indian slavery in the New Laws, see Zavala, *Los esclavos indios en la Nueva España,* pp. 107–14, 179–92, 223. The 1680 Compilation of the Law of the Indies' restrictions on Indian slavery are in Laws 1 (Title 2), 12, 13, 14, and 16 of Book 6, *Recopilación de leyes de los reynos de las Indias* (Madrid, 1681).

20. Orlando Patterson, *Slavery and Social Death: A Comparative Study* (Cambridge, Mass.: Harvard University Press, 1982), p. 64.

21. In Franciscan mystical thought, one reaches spiritual perfection by traversing a tripartite route through purgation, illumination, and union. On Franciscan mysticism, see John Moorman, *A History of the Franciscan Order from its Origins to the Year 1517* (Oxford: Clarendon Press, 1968); Randolph E. Daniel, *The Franciscan Concept of Mission in the High Middle Ages* (Lexington: University Press of Kentucky, 1975).

22. Adams and Chávez, *The Missions of New Mexico,* p. 42.

23. Archivo General de la Nación (Mexico City), Historia 25–25:229.

24. Adams and Chávez, *The Missions of New Mexico,* p. 259.

25. Gutiérrez, *When Jesus Came, the Corn Mothers Went Away,* p. 189.

26. Olen E. Leonard, *The Role of the Land Grant in the Social Organization and*

Social Processes of a Spanish American Village in New Mexico (Albuquerque: University of New Mexico Press, 1970), pp. 92–109.

27. Dorothy Woodward, *The Penitentes of New Mexico* (New York: Arno Press, 1974), pp. 266–67; Horka-Follick, *Los Hermanos Penitentes,* pp. 130–33.

28. Adams and Chávez, *The Missions of New Mexico,* pp. 29, 80, 150.

29. Spanish Archives of New Mexico, microfilm reel 21, frame 686; Marta Weigle, *Brothers of Light, Brothers of Blood: The Penitentes of the Southwest* (Albuquerque: University of New Mexico Press, 1976), p. 44.

30. Richard E. Ahlborn, *The Penitente Moradas of Abiquiu* (Washington, D.C.: Smithsonian Institution Press, 1968); Bainbridge Bunting et al., "Penitente Brotherhood Moradas and Their Architecture," in Marta Weigle, ed., *Hispanic Arts and Ethnohistory in the Southwest* (Albuquerque: University of New Mexico Press, 1983), pp. 31–80.

31. Weigle, *Brothers of Light, Brothers of Blood,* p. 33; Boyd, *Popular Arts of Spanish New Mexico,* p. 449.

32. Peña quoted in Jean Baptiste Salpointe, *Soldiers of the Cross: Notes on the Ecclesiastical History of New Mexico, Arizona and Colorado* (Banning, Calif.: St. Boniface's Industrial School Press, 1898), p. 161.

33. Salpointe quoted in Laurence Lee, "Los Hermanos Penitentes," *El Palacio* 8 (1920): 5.

34. Munro Edmonson, *Los Manitos: A Study of Institutional Values* (New Orleans: Tulane University, Middle American Research Institute, 1957), pp. 33–35.

35. Juan B. Rael, *The New Mexican "Alabado"* (Stanford: Stanford University Press, 1951).

36. As far as I can surmise, Charles Fletcher Lummis was the first person to imply that the surrogate Christ in Good Friday Penitente rituals actually died on the cross. See Lummis, *The Land of Poco Tiempo,* p. 79. Subsequent references to this work appear in text.

37. On the relationship between print capitalism and nationalism, see Benedict Anderson, *Imagined Communities: Reflections on the Origin and Spread of Nationalism* (London: Verso, 1983).

38. Sylvia Rodríguez, "Art, Tourism, and Race Relations in Taos: Toward a Sociology of the Art Colony," *Journal of Anthropological Research* 45 (1989): 77–99; and "Land, Water, and Ethnic Identity in Taos," in Charles Briggs and John Van Ness, eds., *Land, Water and Culture: New Perspectives on Hispanic Land Grants* (Albuquerque: University of New Mexico Press, 1988), pp. 313–403.

39. Edwin R. Bingham, *Charles F. Lummis* (San Marino, Calif.: Huntington Library Publication, 1955).

40. Edward W. Said, *Orientalism* (New York: Vintage Books, 1979).

41. William B. Taylor, "Mexico as Oriental: Early Thoughts on a History of American and British Representations since 1821" (unpublished paper, 1990).

42. Mary Louise Pratt, *Imperial Eyes: Travel Writing and Transculturation* (New York: Routledge, 1992), p. 134.

43. Personal conversation with Gabriel Melendez, November 1994. Melendez is currently a member of the fraternidad and is the son of M. Santos Melendez, who for many years was the Hermano Supremo Arzobispal of the Concilio Supremo Arzobispal de la Fraternidad Piadosa de Nuestro Padre Jesús Nazareno.

44. Mabel Dodge Luhan, *Edge of Taos Desert: An Escape to Reality* (New York: Harcourt, Brace and Co, 1937), pp. 125–27.

45. Molly H. Mullin, "The Patronage of Difference: Making Indian Art 'Art,' Not Ethnology," *Cultural Anthropology* 7 (November 1992): 395–424; Warren Susman, *Culture and Commitment, 1929–1945* (New York: George Braziller, 1973), pp. 2–8; and *Culture as History: The Transformation of American Society in the Twentieth Century* (New York: Pantheon, 1984), pp. 153–54.

46. Mullin, "The Patronage of Difference," p. 400.

47. Quoted in ibid., p. 412.

48. Roland F. Dickey, *New Mexico Village Arts* (Albuquerque: University of New Mexico Press, 1949), pp. vii, 251–52.

49. Larry Torres, "Brief History of the Penitente Brotherhood," speech given at The Penitente Brotherhood: Art, Architecture and Ritual Conference, Albuquerque, New Mexico, September 10, 1994.

50. Floyd Trujillo, "The Morada within the Village," speech given at The Penitente Brotherhood: Art, Architecture and Ritual Conference, Albuquerque, New Mexico, September 10, 1994.

51. Gabriel Melendez, comments given at The Penitente Brotherhood: Art, Architecture and Ritual Conference, Albuquerque, New Mexico, September 10, 1994.

52. Felipe Ortega, "Morada Music and Ritual," speech given at The Penitente Brotherhood: Art, Architecture and Ritual Conference, Albuquerque, New Mexico, September 10, 1994.

53. See Peter Nabokov, *Tijerina and the Courthouse Raid* (Albuquerque: University of New Mexico Press, 1960); Michael Jenkinson, *Tijerina* (Albuquerque: Paisano Press, 1968).

15

"PONGO MI DEMANDA"

Challenging Patriarchy in Mexican Los Angeles, 1830–1850

MIROSLAVA CHAVEZ

In 1850, Gregoria Romero went before the Los Angeles justice of the peace to ask that criminal charges be filed against her husband Manuel Valencia for abusing her physically and verbally. He "gives me a *mala vida,*" she told the judge, "mistreats me with beatings, defames me, . . . threatens me with death at every step, denies me indispensable nourishment, . . . and instead of giving good advice and sustenance as a husband should do, he gives me a distressing and miserable life. I request a separation." The judge took the case under submission, but before he could render a decision, Romero reappeared in court two days later with her husband at her side. "My husband has promised me that, in the future, he will treat me well and provide me with the considerations a wife deserves," she stated. "I retract my [criminal] charge, forgiving the mistreatment he has previously inflicted." Romero's husband affirmed that he had changed his ways. "Never, for my part, will there be cause for fights," he declared, "nor anger between us." He promised to "follow a straight path and subject [him]self to scrutiny by the civil authorities." The judge, already predisposed to salvaging marriages, agreed to Romero's request and dropped the charges against her husband.[1]

By going to the judge with her complaint Romero had boldly indicated her unwillingness to tolerate her husband's repeated abuses. However, by later recanting her charges solely on his promise to reform, she revealed not only faith in the sincerity of her husband's pledges but also Mexican society's high regard for the inviolability of marriage and the husband's place as master of the home.[2] Mexican and, earlier, Spanish legal and social norms were steeped in patriarchal ideology that recognized men as the heads of the households to whom wives and children owed their obedience. Those same norms also placed restrictions and responsibilities on men: they had to provide food, clothing, and shelter for their families and were forbidden to use excessive force in guiding and instructing their wives, children, and household servants. The Los Angeles court records, as in the case of Gregoria Romero, reveal that men sometimes abused their authority, and women, when necessary, invoked the law to protect themselves and check errant husbands and fathers. The records also indicate that justice could elude women and that the courts often interpreted the law in ways that reflected deeply rooted gender biases.

In exploring women's experiences with the judicial system in Mexican California, this study relies on extant civil and criminal court cases that came before Los Angeles's Court of First Instance between 1830 and 1850. Though the tribunal existed prior to 1830, no earlier records have survived. In 1850 the court ceased to exist as a result of the ratification of California's state constitution and the introduction of the American court system. These records, which total 502 court cases, include 78 cases involving women in civil and criminal matters.[3] Of these, 47 have been selected for study because they reflect the ways in which women of different ethnic and socioeconomic backgrounds dealt with husbands, fathers, and men in the larger community who violated their authority by physically abusing them, neglecting to provide for them, or unlawfully coercing them. These cases also illustrate how local leaders handled individuals who transgressed standards of propriety. Cases involving women's property disputes and other civil matters, while equally significant in elucidating their experiences with patriarchy in Los Angeles, are not treated in this discussion because of space limitations and because they deserve a paper of their own. The focus here is on those women who appeared in the civil and criminal *conciliation* courts (usually as the plaintiff but sometimes as the defendant). Though these women constitute a distinct minority (approximately 9 percent of the 665 women who resided in Los Angeles during the 1830s and 1840s), they represent a cross-section of *gente de razón* (non-Indian) women (500) and Indian adult females (165).[4] They include married, widowed, and single women from impoverished, middling, and elite backgrounds.

Though recent historians have greatly enriched our understanding of the daily lives of women in Spanish and Mexican California, none has utilized court records with their abundance of first-person testimonies from women.[5] Scholars have, with success, drawn on the narratives collected by Hubert Howe Bancroft and his assistants, but these accounts describe events long after they occurred and lack the immediacy of oral testimony describing life as it was being lived.[6]

Drawing on sources such as court cases, which focus on adversarial relations, clearly skews our view of male and female interactions, and may suggest an inclination for men and women to engage in violent confrontations. Placing the material within its proper cultural context, however, allows for a more nuanced understanding of how and why gender relations turned sour as well as the ways in which the community handled such strife. And, more importantly, the evidence reveals not only women's anxieties, expectations, and attitudes but also how women of different circumstances—gente de razón (non-Indians or, literally, "people of reason"), *neófitos* (baptized California Indians), and *gentiles* (unbaptized California Indians) fared in the legal system and in the broader society.[7]

The discussion that follows begins with an examination of the gente de razón's understanding of marriage and the family, and then shows how women used local institutions to deal with heads of households who exceeded their paternal authority. The principal reasons women went to court—physical abuse, inadequate support, adultery, and unlawful coercion—receive close attention here. The essay also explores how women of different ethnicities and socioeconomic levels contended with men in the larger community who abused them, and the ways in which men responded to women's grievances. Finally, the discussion analyzes women's use of extralegal means to escape their troubled households, and shows how figures of authority sought to maintain their power.

Mexicans inherited from Spain strong convictions about the centrality of marriage and the family to the survival of civilized Catholic society. These convictions seemed self-evident to the residents of Los Angeles, a precarious and small community on the northern frontier whose gente de razón and Indian populations together barely numbered 2,300 as late as 1844.[8] At the most elemental level, stable marriages and families produced the children who would secure the future and also ensure continuity in cultural and moral values as well as in the inheritance and transfer of property.[9] To the clergy, marriage was a sacrament, a bond sanctified by Christ for the procreation and education of children as well as companionship. Except through death or a church-sanctioned annulment, marriages, preached the *padres,* remained indissoluble, even when one spouse was extremely cruel to the other.[10] The clergy, in their goal to keep marriages intact, frequently sought the help of civil authorities and sometimes publicly berated them and went over their heads to higher officials if their support was not forthcoming.

Most local officials lacked formal legal training, but they familiarized themselves with the relevant civil codes on marriage and the family, most of them derived from Spanish laws and decrees.[11] Permeating that law was the widely held tenet of paternal authority (*patria potestas*) that came from deep in the Iberian past and was embedded in *Las Siete Partidas* and *Leyes de Toro,* thirteenth- and sixteenth-century compilations of law that located familial authority in male heads of household—fathers and husbands—the assumption being that such delegation of power ensured a well-ordered family and stable society. A man had virtually complete authority over his dependents—wife, children, and any servants in the household—who, in turn, owed him their obedience. Qualifying a man's authority was his obligation to support, protect, and guide his dependents. The law and social mores also required a husband to respect a wife's person, but it conceded him the right to dole out mild punishment—the meaning of which varied with time, locale, and circumstance—to her and his other dependents as a way of guiding or teaching them. The ideal home (*casa de honor*) was a place where husband and wife, regardless of socioeconomic status or racial and cultural identity, treated each other well, supported their dependents, practiced their religion, remained faithful to one another, and otherwise set a good example for their children.[12] Men who abandoned or neglected the well-being of their households or engaged in excessive punishment violated not only the law but also the norms of the community.[13]

As members of the community, women had the right to hold men responsible for neglecting to fulfill their obligations or for exceeding their power and authority as heads of households. To deal with such men, women sometimes felt compelled to turn to the Court of First Instance. Depending on the matter at issue, the tribunal convened a civil or criminal trial in the first court (*juzgado primero*), presided over by the alcalde, or a conciliation trial (*juicio de concilio*) in the second court (*segundo juzgado*), presided over by the justice of the peace, or *juez de paz*. In particularly violent and abusive relationships, the alcalde—with the consent of the individual issuing the complaint, usually the woman—would order a criminal trial, treating the physical violence in the home as a crime punishable by possible imprisonment or banishment. In matters that involved so-called "light" (*leve*) crimes of physical abuse or some other transgression the court considered mild, justices ordered a civil trial or conciliation hearing, in which the aggrieved and defending parties each appointed his or her *hombre bueno*, or good man, who served as an advisor to the court. The goal of these sessions, which were common throughout Mexico and its possessions, was to reconcile the disputing couple, thus preserving the marriage for the good of the family and social stability.[14] In the case of an unmarried couple living together, the purpose was to separate them.[15] In many instances, women found that these sessions functioned only as "quick fixes" that failed to restrain a consistently violent husband. Women wanting legal separations or annulments usually received a hearing in the civil branch of the court, though the clergy preferred to handle such matters through ecclesiastical channels.

In the criminal, civil, and conciliation courts, women voiced a host of complaints against heads of households. Married women complained about husbands who physically abused them, failed to support them and their children, and otherwise set a bad example in the household. Luisa Domínguez's troubles with her spouse are representative. In 1843, she went to the conciliation court, complaining to the justice of the peace about her husband Ángel Pollorena. "My husband's treatment is insufferable," she told the judge and the hombres buenos. "At every moment he beats me [and] I ask for a separation." To prove how badly she had been abused, she exposed her body to the court, revealing the scars left from the wounds. Pollorena, also present in the court, responded, "my wife is a bad woman." "The fight began after I punished one of her children," he explained, "and, as she has [already] had three children outside of our marriage, she wants to return to the same [behavior]." "I have had two children outside of the marriage," Domínguez admitted, but "now that I am with him he does not support me."

The judge and hombres buenos believed that the marriage could be saved and ordered the couple to attempt a reconciliation. "I agree to reunite with my husband," replied Domínguez, but "with the condition that he treat me well, not punish excessively my children, or give them a bad example." Pollorena accepted her demands, though he, too, set a condition. "I promise to educate the children, comply with my obligations, and forget the past as long as she [is] prudent." To ensure that Pollorena kept his promise to Domínguez, the judge appointed several men to keep close watch over his behavior.[16]

Complaints like those of Luisa Domínguez often accompanied accusations of infidelity from women as well as men. Adultery, which the authorities treated as a criminal act and flagrant threat to marriage and the family, prompted women to appeal to the conciliation court and, if they felt especially wronged, to file civil or criminal charges against their husbands. Sometimes they even asked for the indictment of his accomplice on the grounds that the other woman had provoked the marital troubles. In 1844, Francisca Pérez accused her husband and his lover (*amasia*) of adultery, telling the judge that the other woman had "caused my husband's infidelity and refusal to give me sustenance."[17] Marina García likewise informed a judge in 1845 that she had a "bad life with my husband Francisco Limón because of Manuela Villa, who is living" with him.[18] To ensure an end to these relations, wives demanded the banishment of such women. "Having caught my husband *in flagrante delicto* with Nicolasa Careaga," Marta Reyes told the justice of the peace in 1843, "I ask that [the court] punish him and banish her from the town." When Reyes's husband admitted that he was "at fault" and "put himself at the court's disposal," the judge, with the agreement of the hombres buenos, ordered him to "treat his wife well" and sent Careaga to an undisclosed destination.[19]

A woman's decision to file a formal complaint against her spouse for abuse or adultery did not come quickly or easily. In most instances, women turned to the courts only after a prolonged period of contentious relations. Their testimony is usually filled with numerous examples of earlier abuse. Typical were Ramona Vejar and Luz Figueroa, who, in the criminal court, described years of mistreatment. "My husband Tomás Urquides," Vejar stated to the alcalde in 1842, "hits me because of Dolores Valenzuela [with whom he] has been living . . . for more than two years. . . . He has hit me so many times with a rope or whatever else he can find that I can not recall the exact number." Witnesses verified Vejar's account and also testified that Urquides had fathered a child with Valenzuela. Urquides admitted knowing Valenzuela but denied having an affair with her. He also acknowledged hitting his wife, though he said he did so in order to correct her insolence. "One day, she came to my mother's house," he informed the court, "looking for someone, and when I asked her what or whom she wanted, she responded, 'I am looking for that [sexually promiscuous woman] who is your friend and your mother who is an *alcahueta* [a mediator between lovers].' . . . I only hit her when she gives me cause to do so," he insisted, "not because [Valenzuela] tells me to do so; I do so when she neglects the children or leaves without my permission."

When Valenzuela was called to testify and admitted to a long affair with Urquides, the judge moved quickly to end the relationship. He ordered Valenzuela's banishment: she had to live at least ten leagues (thirty-five miles) from the town in a casa de honor where she and her children would be watched. Urquides, on the other hand, received only a reprimand for "correcting" his wife and a fine of ten pesos for his sexual misconduct. Within six months, Vejar was back in court complaining that Urquides had returned to his old habits. "I ran to take shelter [from him] in a nearby home," she told the judge, "but he pulled me out, beat me, and then tied me up with a rope." Before the authorities could apprehend him, Urquides fled from the town, forcing the authorities to drop the case until he could be located.[20]

Like Ramona Vejar, Luz Figueroa experienced years of abuse from her husband, Juan Riera. Figueroa's problems, however, lasted more than a decade, culminating in 1849 with flight from her husband and an appeal for help from the local priest. "What should I do?" she asked him. His response: "return to your husband." Dutifully, she returned to the household only to be beaten again by her husband. This time she turned to the court for help, describing for the judge her husband's years of abuse and his latest attack. He "picked up a leather rope and he struck me once in the face, and did so repeatedly on my back," she stated. "Luckily I was able to escape . . . and found help in a nearby house. But soon my husband found me, and pulled me from the house, dragging me through the streets and telling me to follow him or else he would kill me with the knife he pulled out of his pants." She showed the judge the scars that the many beatings had left on her body. "What [punishment] do you request for your husband for having beaten and publicly humiliated you?" asked the judge. "I request his banishment from this city because I fear that a grave injury may happen to me. He has always given me a miserable life, and in the twelve years I have been married to this man, there have been numerous relapses into his bad habits."[21] The judge ordered the arrest of Riera whom he questioned and then imprisoned pending a full criminal investigation. What that investigation revealed is unknown, since the surviving records indicate only that Riera was freed but not the reasons why. What is clear was Luz Figueroa's attempt to have him removed from her life.

Women challenged not only abusive and unfaithful husbands but also coercive fathers. Though fewer women issued complaints against fathers than husbands, those who did so frequently won the support of local authorities. In 1842, for instance, Casilda Sepúlveda complained to the judge in the civil court that her father, Enrique Sepúlveda, with the support of her stepmother Matilda Trujillo and the local priest, had forced her to marry Antonio Teodoro Trujillo. She asked the judge "for the protection of the law against such an attack on my personal liberty" and to grant her an annulment. The judge examined witnesses and found that, indeed, she had been married against her will, and he nullified the marriage. The judge then informed the local priest at Mission San Gabriel, Tomás Estenaga, of his actions, prompting Estenaga, in turn, to notify Francisco García Diego y Moreno, the bishop of both Alta and Baja California, about what had occurred. The bishop, convinced that the judge had exceeded his authority by interfering in a religious matter, reacted angrily. "Judging the validity or nullity of marriage is absolutely reserved to the ecclesiastical domain," the bishop wrote to Santiago Argüello, head of the *prefectura*, or prefecture, the highest civil authority in southern California directly responsible to the governor.[22] Bishop García then ordered Estenaga to speak privately with Sepúlveda and urge her to reconcile with Trujillo. If she refused to do so, then she and her relatives should go to Santa Barbara, the current residence of the bishop, and plead her case before the ecclesiastical tribunal there. At first, she balked at going, preferring to "present her reasons, in writing, to the Bishop," but under the prodding of Father Estenaga, she finally consented to go.

The hearing in Santa Barbara concluded with the bishop announcing that the marriage had been forced and annulling it. Sepúlveda's success in attaining an annulment, a rare occurrence in California and Mexico, was a triumph over paternal authority and her family's insistence that she marry a man whom she had refused as a husband.[23] Her victory, however, did not come without consequences. Shortly after returning to Los Angeles, she was again in court complaining that her father had retaliated against her. "I don't want to return to my father's house," she declared, for "he refuses to support me[,] refuses to recognize me as his daughter[, and] wants to disinherit me. What shall I do?" The judge's response and her long-term relationship with her father and family are unknown, since the record ends abruptly. But even if the alienation from her family was short-lived, it reveals the risk that women in this frontier community took when they challenged patriarchal authority.[24]

Sepúlveda, like all the women who used the courts to challenge male heads of households, identified herself as a member of the gente de razón. The extant court records involving Indian women—a total of nine cases—provide no instance of a neófita (baptized Indian woman) or gentil (unbaptized Indian woman) bringing a complaint against a spouse or father. Perhaps the neófitas took their complaints against family members to the priests or governors who exercised greater direct authority over their lives than other non-Indians did. Similarly, the gentiles may have avoided the courts in favor of tribal customs when it came to similar problems. The evidence indicates, however, that Indian women did use local institutions in dealing with non-family members, both Mexican and Indian, who committed depredations against them.

Vitalacia, a married Indian woman who resided at San Gabriel Mission, was the only neófita to bring a complaint to the local court, in this case the criminal court. In 1841, she told the judge that Asención Alipas, a Mexican man who was not her husband, had "maimed and cut [her] with a knife." "Last week," she informed the court, "I was at the mission gathering wheat when Lorena [an Indian woman who worked at the mission] informed me that Alipas had arrived." With a knife in hand, he "approached me and in a derisive tone asked, 'why do you no longer want to be with me?' When I told him [again] that I didn't want to be with him anymore, he took the knife and cut my hand and my braid." Alipas told the judge, "I have been having relations with Vitalacia for about four or five years past, and have sacrificed the earnings of my work in supporting her." When "I arrived at . . . the mission . . . I saw a behavior in Vitalacia that I disliked, [and] I became violent and grabbed her, cutting her hair with a knife." The cut on her hand was of her own doing, he insisted. In "trying to take the knife away from me, she grabbed the blade, and because she refused to let go of it, I pulled on it, and she cut her fingers."[25]

What angered the judge was their extramarital relationship. "What do you have to say about using a married woman?" he asked Alipas. "It is true," he responded. "I recognize my crime, but an offended man becomes violent." Puzzled, the judge pressed his inquiry. "What offense did she commit against you; she is not your wife." Alipas attributed his anger to Vitalacia's disregard for her obligations to him, particularly the sexual services that she owed him for his economic support. "She never appreciated that," he stated. The judge was unsympathetic. He found Alipas guilty of adultery and injuring Vitalacia and sentenced him to labor on public works. He urged Vitalacia, whom he also found guilty of adultery, to stay away from Alipas. Vitalacia's case is significant because it reveals that, although occupying a subordinate position in relation to the community of gente de razón, she used the court successfully to extricate herself from the grip of Alipas, whose gender and ethnic status would have normally placed him in a dominant position.

Women, whether neófitas, gentiles, or de razón, often had the assistance of their immediate families when they turned to the courts or other civil or religious authorities in dealing with men in the larger community. At times, family members, especially fathers or brothers, represented the women, particularly in instances of sexual assaults.[26] The socially and politically prominent gente de razón viewed rape not only as a grave offense against a woman's reputation, or honor, but also as a stain on the family's honor. Hispanic law reflected this attitude, as it allowed male family members to kill a perpetrator who was caught in the act of rape.[27] The threat that rape posed to elite females and their families emerged sharply in 1840 in a criminal complaint filed by María Ygnacia Elizalde, wife of the prominent José María Aguilar, a former local government official in Los Angeles who continued to have political influence.[28] She accused Cornelio López with attempting to rape her. "López broke into my house and entered my room," she told the judge, "with the intent of wanting to use my person in the [sexual] act when he saw me alone. . . . With much struggle I managed to resist the force with which he surprised me. [It was not] until Raimundo Alanis arrived that López separated himself from me, giving me the freedom and opportunity to come [to the court] to report this."

The judge ordered a full investigation followed by a trial at which Elizalde repeated her charges. López, she testified, "tried to force me to have a [sexual act] with him, but I absolutely denied him. He told me, 'why do you not want to have relations with me? Have you not already been with others?' But I continued to resist and, eventually, he relented, but only momentarily. At that moment, he looked out the [bedroom] door to see if anyone else was around, and then returned to my bed to try and force me [to have relations]. He remained an hour, after which time he left, no doubt [because] he saw Alanis sitting outside the door. I then proceeded immediately to complain to the authorities so that they would restrain him."

When López took the stand, he denied forcing her to have sex with him. On an earlier occasion, he stated, she had promised to have relations with him, but, now, when he asked her to comply, she refused, causing him to become incensed. Making him even angrier, he declared, was the extramarital affair that she was having with another man, José Avila.

Presenting the case for the prosecution was Elizalde's husband, Aguilar. The court typically either appointed a prosecutor or asked the aggrieved parties to select one, family member or not. And, usually, those selected were socially or politically prominent in the community. "During my absence," Aguilar began, "in which I had to travel to Santa Barbara, Cornelio López took advantage of my wife's solitude, and with a bold move he profaned the home of an honorable citizen." He continued, "on the morning of the nineteenth of the past month, my wife was resting in her bed from her domestic work, when suddenly Cornelio López appeared and, as if possessed with the devil and with the most obscene words, attempted to force my wife to have carnal relations; my wife, who was surprised to see this man, heroically resisted . . . this treacherous man, who . . . attempted to use her for his pleasure." López's attack, he argued, "disregarded the respect that [was] due to the institution of marriage and [that was among] the duties of a man in society." Upset about the effect of the attack on his social standing in the community, Aguilar declared that "López has made me look like a common *alcahueta* in public . . . and [has] offended my honor." Furthermore, he told the court, López's "immorality" had not only threatened his marriage, but also that of José Avila. To redeem the "offended honor of [my] wife and family," Aguilar asked the court to banish López for five years to the presidio (military garrison) of Sonoma "where work and reclusion," he continued, "will teach him not to commit such excesses and to respect the society in which he lives; and perhaps then he will be an honorable citizen."

The defense, headed by Juan Cristobal Vejar, argued that Elizalde's gender was to blame for López's behavior. "Man is susceptible to the inclinations of the female sex," Vejar argued. "That the defendant approached an honorable woman is not a crime." López's behavior may have been improper but not criminal. On the other hand, acknowledged Vejar, Aguilar had every right to be angry with López, for his anger is "founded on the insult that López caused by approaching his wife and disrespecting her [married] state." But, Vejar emphasized again, an insult is not a crime.

Before rendering a verdict, the judge waited for the authorities in Monterey to convene the first appellate court. Recent legislation, enacted in Mexico in 1837, required verdicts and sentences in criminal courts, including those in California, to be reviewed by a higher court.[29] (Earlier, appeals had gone to the governor.) The Los Angeles judge waited more than two years for creation of the Superior Tribunal, composed of three justices. Following that action, the judge at last rendered a verdict on López, who all the while had been incarcerated, finding him guilty of the attempted rape of Elizalde. "For having wanted to use with violence a married woman . . . I condemn him for the public satisfaction of José María Aguilar so that the honor of this man's wife is free from damage." Since López had been jailed for nearly three years, however, the judge believed he had served his sentence and so he set him free. The case then went on appeal to the Superior Tribunal, which responded with mixed approval to the courtroom proceedings as well as the sentence: "since the [court] proceedings lack the formal prerequisites that are necessary in overseeing personal injury cases . . . and given the time that Cornelio López has suffered in prison, the judge's decision to free López is approved." López deserved freedom, the Superior Tribunal continued, "not because of the [need for] public satisfaction" of

José María Aguilar, but because the Los Angeles judge had committed a procedural error that mandated López's release. To the tribunal in Monterey, the law took precedence over redeeming the honor of Aguilar and Elizalde.[30]

While sexual assaults by Mexican men on Mexican women were considered an affront to the honor of the women and their families, similar attacks on unbaptized Indian women brought dishonor only to the Mexican men and their relatives. Indian women were seen as lesser beings possessing no honor or esteem that could be insulted. This was the message of a rape case involving an Indian woman in 1844. That year a gentil named Anacleto accused two Los Angeles residents, Domingo Olivas, an assistant of the court, and Ygnacio Varelas, a friend of Olivas, of raping his wife at their ranchería near San Bernardino. Anacleto filed his charges with the local judge in San Bernardino, José del Carmen Lugo, who gathered additional evidence and then persuaded a Los Angeles judge to hold a criminal hearing at which Lugo presented his findings. According to Anacleto and other witnesses, Lugo informed the judge, the incident occurred shortly after Olivas and Varelas arrived at the ranchería with the intent of taking Anacleto to the court in Los Angeles (for reasons that do not appear in the public record). They found Anacleto, who was blind, and his wife inside their home. The two then "took the woman," Lugo told the judge, "and used her by force, threatening her with a knife and saying they wanted to kill them both." About this time, "some Indians and a Mexican approached" whom Varelas threatened with the knife." When the "men warned Varelas that they were going to inform the local authorities about what had occurred, he fled the scene."[31]

Varelas challenged Lugo's testimony, insisting that he and Olivas had not sexually assaulted the woman. Rather, they had offered her money for sexual relations, and she had consented. When Olivas testified, however, he contradicted Varelas and admitted to the crime which he attributed to drunkenness. Prior to the incident, he and Varelas had drunk *aguardiente* (locally brewed alcohol) that blurred their senses and led to the "lewd acts." He begged that the crime not be made public. "In view of my remorse and frank confession, please consider that I am married and have children, and I live in good harmony with my family. Therefore, I ask and beg you that this situation not be made public." He also pleaded with the judge for "a punishment that is prudent and discreet."

The judge was moved by Olivas's appeal. "The confession and guilt of Olivas and Varelas have been established," the judge ruled. "The former has violated a woman by force and the latter was his accomplice. I should condemn Olivas to service in public works," he declared, "but in order not to disrupt his marriage [or] . . . harm . . . his minor children . . . I order Olivas to pay a fine of twenty pesos and his accomplice to pay ten." The judge made no effort to compensate the Indian woman for her (or her family's) loss of honor, nor did he, in fact, make any reference to a dishonored household. He obviously placed greater value on Olivas's public reputation and family life than on the crime committed against a gentil woman or on her reputation. Clearly, gender along with ethnic and class biases influenced the court's decision in this matter. How often the court demonstrated such prejudices is unclear, since the extant records are incomplete and this is the only surviving case illustrating such biases. Further research in other materials, including the legal records of communities elsewhere, should shed additional light on this important issue.

Beyond dispute is the evidence showing that both Mexican women and neófitas devised extralegal means to contend with figures of authority whose abuses were not effectively checked by local authorities. Some women simply fled from violent households. In 1845, María Presentación Navarro, a single Mexican woman, left her home in Los Angeles because she feared the wrath of her angry father. Earlier that year, she and Antonio Reina, a married Indian man who befriended her father and family, had engaged in sexual relations that resulted in her becoming pregnant. Frightened of her father's reaction, she asked Reina to "help me escape from my father's side. . . . I fear that he will kill me." Reina took her to Rosarito in Baja California. Learning of their flight, her father asked the authorities to apprehend them and to punish Reina who, he believed, "has forcibly pulled her away from her family."[32]

The couple were captured and returned to Los Angeles where a full investigation and trial soon got under way. During the trial, the judge not only learned about the reasons for their flight but also about the tense relations between Navarro and her father. Recognizing Navarro's physical danger as well as the possibility that, in her emotional distress, she or perhaps even her father might kill the child, the judge ordered her "put in reclusion [in a casa de honor] . . . under the care of the owners of the house, [who] will oversee her pregnancy so that an infanticide will not be committed." Keeping her from the public's view would also lessen her and her family's dishonor in the larger community. As for Reina who had impregnated Navarro, the judge "banished [him] to the port of San Diego until Navarro reaches *estado* [twenty-five years of age] or leaves the municipality."

While the majority of flights involved Mexican women, neófitas also ran away from abusive households. And they, too, had to deal with disapproving male figures of authority, particularly husbands. In 1841, Manuela, a married neófita, left Los Angeles and fled to her mother's home at Las Flores ranchería because of prolonged mistreatment by her husband, a Mexican man. She employed a ruse to escape, asking him for permission to go to the center of town and then hiding in a nearby house, waiting for an opportunity to leave the pueblo. When two men approached on horseback, she asked them to take her to her mother's home at Las Flores. They agreed, but in the meantime her husband alerted the authorities, who apprehended her at Las Flores and took her back to Los Angeles where she was brought before the judge. When asked why she had left her household, Manuela explained that her husband "always hits me and has me locked up." The judge refused to believe her, concluding that the two men had seduced and then coerced her into leaving her spouse. He ordered Manuela to return to her husband, found the two men guilty of abducting a married woman, and sentenced them to labor several months on public works. Though the court thwarted Manuela's effort to flee her abusive husband, she had nonetheless been willing to chance an escape.[33]

Some women took even more drastic measures to get away from an unsafe environment. Rather than fleeing Los Angeles, they took up with other men in the town. By cohabiting with these men, they brought down on their heads the wrath not only of their husbands but also of religious and civil authorities and the entire community. Petra Varela's decision to leave her spouse for another man in 1847 resulted in her husband, Esteban López, bringing charges of illegal cohabitation and adultery against her and Antonio Valencia, a former employee of the household. "I found my wife and Antonio Valencia locked up in a bedroom," López reported to the criminal court, "and while I overlooked this incident, since then they have continued with their relations. I finally decided to leave the household," he continued, "and yet Valencia remained living there, giving a bad example to the family." When the judge questioned Varela about her behavior, she denied the charges. Valencia "is my servant," she told him. "Since the day he arrived he has consulted only with me; everything [in the household] belongs to me." Though she initially denied having relations with Valencia, under closer questioning she finally admitted to cohabiting with him. Her explanation: "my husband is disinterested and doesn't work . . . and fails to support me." Witnesses corroborated her complaints, testifying that her husband had not supported her for years, forcing her to work in order to pay household expenses, including the wages of several laborers. Even then, she had fallen into debt. López's failure to fulfill his obligations, she argued, had absolved her of any sexual obligations to him and freed her to live with Valencia. The judge held otherwise. "Petra Varela must reunite with her husband and carry out her obligations of matrimony," he ordered. As for her husband López, he "must [meet his obligations] because there are indications that he does not fulfill [his duties]." To guard against a reoccurrence of the incident, the judge banished Valencia to the port of Loreto in Baja California.[34]

Religious authorities also vigorously condemned sexual improprieties like those of Varela and Valencia. When Juana Gómez left her husband in 1837 for another man, the clergy, as was their custom, denounced the couple and used the occasion to preach about the moral evils of adultery. Gómez had abandoned her unhappy marriage in Sonora and gone north to live with Manuel Arzaga in Los Angeles, taking her two children with her. When Tomás Estenaga, the same Mission San Gabriel priest who had been involved in the Casilda Sepúlveda case, discovered that the couple were living as "husband" and "wife," he went to Narciso Durán, head of the ecclesiastical tribunal in Santa Barbara, and obtained permission to ask the civil authorities to end the scandalous relationship. "Arzaga is living with a Sonoran woman named Juana . . . and cohabits with her as if she is his proper wife," Estenaga wrote to Gil Ybarra, a local judge, whom he urged to apprehend the woman and confine her at San Gabriel Mission until her husband could take her home. Ybarra promptly approved the request.

With Gómez under the watch of the priest at San Gabriel, Ybarra traveled there to ascertain the reasons for her behavior. "Who is your spouse? Please state his name and where you were married." "I am a married woman," she responded. "They say I married in Sonora and [that] my husband is there, but it is false. . . . I consider Manuel Arzaga to be my husband. Since the first time we have been together, he has supported and maintained me and I have lived with him." Her explanation did nothing to change the civil and religious authorities' view that she and Arzaga had committed adultery. Durán declared them to be "sacrilegious profaners of holy sacraments," and recommended that she "be restored to the authority of her legitimate husband who will either forgive her or demand that she receive the appropriate punishment, which shall be best, as it will serve as a lesson to all." Judge Ybarra accepted Durán's recommendation, ordering Gómez to return to her husband and banishing Arzaga to San Diego, forbidding him to have contact with her.[35]

Attempts to leave households sometimes led to violence. This was the experience of Ysabel, an orphaned Navajo woman, who, in 1843, attempted to depart from the family that had adopted her in infancy and raised her to be a servant. Ysabel was considered a *genízara,* or detribalized Christian Indian. In Abiquiu, New Mexico, the family's point of origin, genízaros were captured Indians, most often Navajo and Apache, whom Spanish raiders sold or exchanged for payments in cash or in kind. As spoils of war, they were pressed into domestic service and, for all practical purposes, were slaves.[36]

After toiling nearly her entire life for Guadalupe Trujillo and her family in New Mexico and, later, San Gabriel, Ysabel made plans to leave. The first sign of her intention was her refusal one day in 1843 to complete her household chores. Trujillo reacted angrily to the disobedience. "Why do you refuse to do what I say? Since you haven't cooked the meal, why don't you go and complete the wash," she demanded. "I don't want to, I don't want to be with you any longer, I want to go wherever I please," Ysabel declared in defiance. "Why is it that the Indian women from the mission work less than

I do and [they] have skirts made of indianilla [presumably a fine cloth]? I am leaving the household." "You are not free to go anywhere because I have raised you since you were a child," Trujillo retorted. "I am too free," Ysabel countered. At that instant, Ysabel ran and grabbed a knife from the kitchen and threatened to use it. Alarmed, Trujillo asked, "what are you doing with that knife?" "You'll see," Ysabel responded. Trujillo then tried to take the knife away, and in the ensuing struggle Ysabel's throat was slashed and she fell to the floor, dying a short time later. The Los Angeles court, while not finding Trujillo guilty of murder, nonetheless concluded that she had unnecessarily contributed to Ysabel's death and banished her to Sonoma for three years. On appeal, the Superior Tribunal agreed that Trujillo had committed a crime but it believed that mitigating circumstances called for a different sentence. "It has been proven that Guadalupe Trujillo killed her servant, and for such an act deserves punishment; but as the [punishment] should fit the crime and as the crime Trujillo committed was a homicide done in self defense . . . [we] revoke the sentence of three years of seclusion." Instead, the tribunal ordered her to the port of San Diego for one year, allowing her to remain in proximity to her family in the San Gabriel-Los Angeles region.[37]

The evidence adduced in this paper from the court records of Mexican Los Angeles show that women—Mexican, neófita, and gentil—suffered from discrimination. That same evidence, however, reveals that the discrimination faced by women of different ethnicities and socioeconomic levels did not prevent them from challenging and sometimes checking patriarchal authority whether manifested in the law, government, church, or family. The court cases demonstrate that women took legal and, sometimes, extralegal measures to protect themselves from men who abused them, neglected to provide for them, or unlawfully coerced them. While some women turned to the civil, criminal, and ecclesiastical courts for help, others took matters into their own hands and fled from intolerable lives at home even at the risk of severe punishment by secular and religious officials as well as family members. Despite frequently oppressive laws and cultural norms, there were women—Mexican and Native American—who boldly sought a better life for themselves and their families.

Notes

A grant from the Institute of American Cultures, University of California, Los Angeles, made the research for this paper possible. I would like to thank Dr. Janet Fireman, curator and chief of history, Natural History Museum of Los Angeles County, and her staff for giving me access to the collections at the Seaver Center for Western History.

1. Romero's case is contained in the *Alcalde Court Records* (hereafter cited as *ACR*), Seaver Center for Western History, Natural History Museum of Los Angeles County, Los Angeles, California, vol. 7, pp. 1028–1033 (1850).

2. Romero's decision to retract her charges was not an uncommon choice. Other women also brought and then rescinded criminal complaints after their husbands agreed to their demands. For such cases, see, for example, *ACR*, vol. 3, pp. 690–712 (1842), vol. 4, pp. 892–914 (1844).

3. These figures come from my own investigation and tabulation of records contained in the *ACR*. The 502 cases consist of 229 criminal, 18 civil, and 255 civil and criminal conciliation trials. The cases involving women total 78, or approximately 15 percent of the total, and include 36 criminal, 7 civil, and 35 civil and criminal conciliation trials.

4. The percentage here is only a rough estimate based on the total number of women who appeared in court between 1830 and 1850 (57) and the approximate number of adult females in Los Angeles in the 1830s and 1840s (665). The 1836 and 1844 censuses are found in the *Los Angeles City Archives* (hereafter cited as *LACA*), vol. 3, pp. 666–801, City of Los Angeles, Records Management Division, C. Erwin Piper Technical Bldg., Los Angeles, California. The censuses identify *mujeres*, or adult Mexican women, as those over the age of eleven, and sometimes ten, and *niñas* as those ten or under. The censuses identify Indians differently, recording their first names, ages, professions, residences, and places of origin. The figure of 165 adult Indian females comes from my tabulation of *indias* over the age of ten years listed in the 1844 census. The 1844 census in Marie E. Northrop's "The Los Angeles Padrón of 1844, as Copied from the Los Angeles City Archives," *Historical Society of Southern California Quarterly* 42 (December 1960): 360–417, is incomplete and does not include figures for Indian men and women. It excludes, among other things, the Indian female and male population enumerated in the original census.

5. Recent studies on women in Spanish and Mexican California include Antonia I. Castañeda, "The Political Economy of Nineteenth-Century Stereotypes of Californianas," in *Between Borders: Essays on Mexicana/Chicana History*, ed. Adelaida R. Del Castillo (Encino, Calif.: Floricanto Press, 1990), 213–236; Castañeda, "Presidarias y Pobladoras: Spanish-Mexican Women in Frontier Monterey, Alta California, 1777–1821" (Ph.D. diss., Stanford University, 1990); Castañeda, "Sexual Violence in the Politics of Conquest: Amerindian Women and the Spanish Conquest of Alta California," in *Building with Our Hands: New Directions in Chicana Studies*, ed. Adela de la Torre and Beatriz M. Pesquera (Berkeley: University of California Press, 1993), 15–33; Gloria Miranda, "Racial and Cultural Dimensions of *Gente de Razón* Status in Spanish and Mexican California," *Southern California Quarterly* 70 (Fall 1988): 265–272; Miranda, "*Gente de Razón* Marriage Patterns in Spanish and Mexican California: A Case Study of Santa Barbara and Los Angeles," *Southern California Quarterly* 63 (Spring 1981): 1–21; Miranda, "Hispano-Mexican Childrearing Practices in Pre-American Santa Barbara," *Southern California Quarterly* 65 (Winter 1983): 307–320; Salome Hernández, "No Settlement without Women: Three Spanish California Settlement Schemes, 1790–1800," *Southern California Quarterly* 72 (Fall 1990): 203–233; and Douglas Monroy, "They Didn't Call Them 'Padre' for Nothing: Patriarchy in Hispanic California," in *Between Borders*, 433–446.

For studies of Mexican women in other regions that do make use of court records, see, for example, Deena J. González, "The Spanish-Mexican Women of Santa Fe: Patterns of Their Resistance and Accommodation" (Ph.D. diss., University of California, Berkeley, 1986); González, "The Widowed Women of Santa Fe: Assessments of the Lives of an Unmarried Population, 1850–1880," in *On Their Own: Widows and Widowhood in the American Southwest, 1848–1939*, ed. Arlene Scadron (Urbana: University of Illinois Press, 1988), 65–90; Ramón Gutiérrez, *When Jesus Came, the Corn Mothers Went Away: Marriage, Sexuality, and Power in New Mexico, 1500–1846* (Stanford: Stanford University Press, 1991); Sylvia Marina Arrom, *The Women of Mexico City, 1790–1857* (Stanford: Stanford University Press, 1985); Asunción Lavrin, ed., *Sexuality and Marriage in Colonial Latin America* (Lincoln: University of Nebraska Press, 1989); Lavrin, ed., *Latin American Women: Historical Perspectives* (Westport, Conn.: Greenwood, 1978); and Steve J. Stern, *The Secret History of Gender: Women, Men, and Power in Late Colonial Mexico* (Chapel Hill: University of North Carolina Press, 1995).

6. Recent historical studies that use the californio narratives to discuss women include Castañeda, "Presidarias y Pobladoras"; Douglas Monroy, *Thrown among Strangers: The Making of Mexican Culture in Frontier California* (Berkeley: University of California Press, 1990); and Richard Griswold del Castillo, "Neither Activists nor Victims: Mexican Women's Historical Discourse—The Case of San Diego, 1820–1850," *California History* 74 (Fall 1995): 230–243. For literary studies that draw upon the narratives, see Genaro Padilla, *My History, Not Yours: The Formation of Mexican American Autobiography* (Madison: University of Wisconsin Press, 1993); and Rosaura Sánchez, *Telling Identities: The Californio Testimonios* (Minneapolis: University of Minnesota Press, 1995).

7. George Harwood Phillips, "Indians in Los Angeles, 1781–1875: Economic Integration, Social Disintegration," *Pacific Historical Review* 49 (August 1980): 430; Sánchez, *Telling Identities*, 56–61; Lisbeth Haas, *Conquests and Historical Identities in California, 1769–1936* (Berkeley: University of California Press, 1995), 29–32; David J. Weber, *The Spanish Frontier in North America* (New Haven: Yale University Press, 1992), 327–329.

8. *LACA*, vol. 3, pp. 731–801. The Mexican men, women, and children numbered approximately 1,650, while the population of Indian men, women, and children was 650.

9. Arrom, *Women of Mexico City*, 57–77.

10. For official ecclesiastical statements regarding marriage and the family in the Californias, see Francisco García Diego y Moreno, *The Writings of Francisco García Diego y Moreno, Obispo de Ambas Californias*, trans. and ed. Francis J. Weber (Los Angeles, 1976). *ACR* and *Los Angeles Prefecture Records* (hereafter cited as *LAPR*) also contain religious decrees. For a summary of the church's views on marriage, annulment, and divorce in colonial Mexico, which applied in Alta California, see Arrom, *Women of Mexico City*, 65–66, 206–258; and Lavrin, "Introduction," *Sexuality and Marriage*, 1–43.

11. This observation results from my reading of the primary sources examined for this paper. Those sources contain numerous references to the *Laws of the Indies*, a seventeenth-century compilation of laws for governing New Spain, as well as to or-

dinances and decrees issued by the governors of Alta California. Historian Charles R. Cutter and legal scholar Joseph W. McKnight have noted similar findings for colonial New Mexico and Texas, respectively. Cutter, *The Legal Culture of Northern New Spain, 1700–1810* (Albuquerque: University of New Mexico Press, 1995), 34–43, 83–99; McKnight, "Law Books on the Hispanic Frontier," *Journal of the West* 27 (July 1988): 74–84; and McKnight, "Law without Lawyers on the Hispano-Mexican Frontier," *West Texas Historical Association Year Book* 66 (1990): 51–65.

12. This meaning of a *casa de honor* derives from my reading of the sources for this paper. See especially *ACR*, vol. 4, pp. 557–698, 892–914 (1844), vol. 5, pp. 1–20 (1845); and *LAPR*, book 2, part 2, pp. 572–577 (1847).

13. Stern, *Secret History of Gender*, 14–21; Arrom, *Women of Mexico City*, 65–70; and Lavrin, "Introduction," in *Sexuality and Marriage*, 6–21.

14. For more on the Court of First Instance, see Theodore Grivas, "Alcalde Rule: The Nature of Local Government in Spanish and Mexican California," *California Historical Society Quarterly* 40 (March 1961): 11–19; and Colin M. MacLachlan, *Criminal Justice in Eighteenth-Century Mexico: A Study of the Tribunal of the Acordada* (Berkeley: University of California Press, 1974). Another work, David J. Langum, *Law and Community on the Mexican California Frontier: Anglo-American Expatriates and the Clash of Legal Traditions, 1821–1846* (Norman: University of Oklahoma Press, 1987), especially chapters 2, 3, and 4, provides useful material on the tribunal system in California. Caution must be used when consulting this study, however, since Langum erroneously believes that judges ruled with little knowledge of the law or of social and community values. For more on conciliation trials in colonial Mexico, see Arrom, *Women of Mexico City*, 211.

15. See, for example, *ACR*, vol. 1, pp. 914–917 (1843), vol. 6, p. 178 (1844).

16. For Domínguez's complaint in the conciliation court, see *ACR*, vol. 1, pp. 900–902 (1843); for similar complaints made by other Mexican women in the conciliation court, see *ACR*, vol. 1, pp. 914–1917 (1843); and *ACR*, vol. 6, pp. 66–70 (1846); for those complaints heard in the criminal court, see *ACR*, vol. 4, pp. 892–914 (1844), vol. 3, pp. 168–179 (1842), vol. 7, pp. 465–492 (1849).

17. For Pérez's complaint of adultery in the conciliation court, see *ACR*, vol. 4, pp. 892–914 (1844).

18. For García's complaint of adultery in the criminal court, see *ACR*, vol. 5, pp. 20–34 (1845).

19. For Reyes's complaint of adultery in the conciliation court, see *ACR*, vol. 1, pp. 893–895 (1843); for other complaints of adultery in the criminal court, see *ACR*, vol. 3, pp. 127–167, 690–712 (1842).

20. For the second and third incidents between Vejar and Urquides, see *ACR*, vol. 3, pp. 127–167, 690–712 (1842). No record of the first incident is extant, but in Vejar's second complaint, she and the judge summarize the earlier court appearance.

21. *ACR*, vol. 7, pp. 465–492 (1849).

22. Following the ascendancy to power of the Centralists in Mexico, the national government in 1837 established prefecturas in local jurisdictions as a means of extending federal authority over local affairs. For more on the prefectura, see Langum, *Law and Community on the Mexican California Frontier*, 35–55.

23. Arrom, *Women of Mexico City*, 208.

24. Sepúlveda's case is contained in *ACR*, vol. 9, pp. 146–151 (1842); and *LAPR*, book 1, part 2, pp. 465–467, 632, 635, 650, 654, 685 (1842). Also, see Francisco García Diego y Moreno to Santiago Argüello, May 3, 1842, in *The Writings*, 120; García Diego y Moreno to Argüello, May 18, 1842, ibid.; García Diego y Moreno to Argüello, August 22, 1842, ibid., 121; García Diego y Moreno to Tomás Estenega, May 3, 1842, ibid., 122; García Diego y Moreno to Estenaga, May 21, 1842, ibid., 123; and García Diego y Moreno to Estenaga, August 22, 1842, ibid., 124. The original record of Casilda Sepúlveda's last appearance in court is not extant in the *ACR*, but a reproduced copy of her complaint is found in *California Archives* [hereafter cited as *CA*], vol. 35, p. 245 (1842), which is housed at the Bancroft Library, University of California, Berkeley. For other instances when priests intervened in women's marital troubles, see *ACR*, vol. 4, pp. 142–148 (1843), vol. 5, pp. 1–20 (1845), and vol. 7, pp. 465–492 (1849).

25. *ACR*, vol. 2, pp. 659–678 (1841). Most other cases of violence involving neófitas and gentiles were reported by family members or local officials. For those instances of abuse brought to the attention to the court by local officials, see *ACR*, vol. 2, pp. 499–530 (1841), vol. 5, pp. 303–331 (1845), vol. 6, pp. 448–473 (1837), vol. 7, pp. 411–436 (1849).

26. For cases where family members bring Mexican and Native American women's complaints to the court on their behalf, see, for example, *ACR*, vol. 2, pp. 1172–1176 (1842), vol. 4, pp. 299–348 (1843), and vol. 6, pp. 36–38 (1846); and *CA*, vol. 35, pp. 172–173 (1841).

27. Arrom, *Women of Mexico City*, 63.

28. Hubert Howe Bancroft, *History of California* (San Francisco: History Company, 1886), vol. 2, p. 688.

29. Langum, *Law and Community on the Mexican California Frontier*, 57–58.

30. The case can be found in *ACR*, vol. 1, pp. 506–562 (1840).

31. *ACR*, vol. 4, pp. 1170–1188 (1844).

32. *ACR*, vol. 5, pp. 1–20 (1845).

33. *ACR*, vol. 2, pp. 531–565 (1841).

34. *ACR*, vol. 7, pp. 763–793 (1847).

35. *ACR*, vol. 6, pp. 541–583 (1837).

36. On genízaros in New Mexico, see Gutiérrez, *When Jesus Came, the Corn Mothers Went Away*, 149–156, 176–194.

37. The case can be found in *ACR*, vol. 1, pp. 1014–1113 (1843). For other examples of cases involving women who sought to escape from their households, see *ACR*, vol. 1, pp. 810–837 (1842), vol. 1, pp. 906–908 (1843).

16

JAPANESE AMERICAN WOMEN AND THE CREATION OF URBAN NISEI CULTURE IN THE 1930s

VALERIE J. MATSUMOTO

Poring over pictures of Shirley Temple and Marlene Dietrich in the newspapers, listening to Cab Calloway, and dreaming of dashing suitors and romantic evenings, young urban Nisei women of the 1930s were enthusiastic participants in popular youth culture, ingeniously coping with the limitations imposed by depression-era economics and West Coast racial barriers. They formed Girl Scout troops and baseball teams; they sent their poems to the ethnic newspapers and waltzed at Nisei club dances. For most of the twentieth century, historians and social scientists would have interpreted this behavior as part of a debate about whether or not ethnic Americans wanted to "assimilate" into the dominant society. More recently, scholars such as Vicki Ruíz and Judy Yung have reinterpreted the activities of second-generation women as a process of drawing from many possible models in creating their own cultural forms; Ruíz has termed the process "cultural coalescence."[1] This essay examines the ways in which Japanese American women in 1930s Los Angeles engaged in cultural coalescence, giving rise to a vibrant urban, generational culture. To understand girls' and women's engagement in the creation of an urban Nisei world, it is necessary to study their impressive array of peer networks. The importance of such peer support emerges in sharp relief from young women's negotiation of the multiple pressures and influences they faced in the arenas of work, recreation, courtship, and ethnic cultural activities.

Women played energetic roles in pre–World War II Japanese American communities of the West Coast, where the majority of Issei immigrants had settled. The largest of these enclaves was Little Tokyo in Los Angeles, the focus of my research. The English-language sections of the Los Angeles Japanese American newspapers vividly reveal the variety of Nisei women's involvement in urban ethnic culture. The *Kashu Mainichi* (Japan-California

Daily News), one of the two largest Japanese American newspapers in southern California, was particularly noted for its extensive literary section, in which the Nisei found a welcoming forum for their poetry, fiction, and essays. Edited by Nisei, the English-language section itself constituted a kind of peer network, announcing milestones and club meetings, and facilitating discourse on a range of topics relevant to the second generation. The ongoing discussion of women's roles generated particularly lively, sometimes heated, reader response.

In the early twentieth century, gender role shifts stirred debate within ethnic communities as well as in the larger society over appropriate female activities. Vigorous club movements proliferated among black and white women, as middle-class matrons moved assertively into the public sphere, taking leading roles in Progressive reform. The "New Woman" emerged, hailed with pride and hope by feminists and viewed with alarm by conservatives who predicted the disintegration of the family and the American character. Yet both feminists and conservatives were disconcerted by the most flamboyant and youthful embodiment of the New Woman, the flapper, who seemed to combine personal independence and income with consumerism, lack of social responsibility, and overt sexuality. While probably only a fraction of middle-class European American women truly matched public expectations or fears about the "Jazz Baby," some of the attributes of the New Woman filtered across class and racial lines.

My research on Japanese American women, like Yung's and Ruíz's findings about Chinese American women and Mexican American women, reveals that a considerable number bobbed their hair and rebelled against parentally proscribed gender-role strictures. While remaining steadfast contributors to the family economy, they also hoped to choose their own spouses, enjoyed mainstream entertainment, and organized a variety of Nisei girls' and women's clubs. Their synthesis of interwar notions of "modern" femininity was, of course, complicated by racial discrimination in the larger society and by their ethnic community's own views with regard to female behavior. Nowhere did their efforts to come to terms with differing sets of expectations become more evident than in the urban setting of Little Tokyo.

Little Tokyo in Los Angeles served as a major cultural hub for the Issei and Nisei in southern California, growing rapidly in the two decades before World War II. Japantowns emerged in San Francisco, Seattle, Sacramento, Tacoma, and Salt Lake City, but Los Angeles boasted the largest. In 1910 the Census Bureau recorded 8,641 Japanese Americans living in Los Angeles County. By 1930 the number had swelled to 35,000, of whom half were American-born Nisei. The majority of these Nikkei (or persons of Japanese descent) resided in the area known as "Lil' Tokio," clustered around First and San Pedro Streets not far from City Hall. They ran shops and restaurants, and worked at the heart of the produce business, the City Market at

Ninth and San Pedro. The prospect of living in this bustling, vigorous community thrilled Nisei newcomer Mary Korenaga, who initially viewed California—and Los Angeles more specifically—as "the land of opportunity and fortune, the land of eternal sunshine and flower, and the land where the eyes of the Nisei are focused."[2]

To Korenaga and many of her peers, city life glittered with the allure of modernity and excitement. Indeed, Nisei Ellen Tanna revealed in a prose-poem her identification with the urban ethnic enclave, likening it to a young woman, perhaps the sort of woman she envisioned herself to be: "Little Tokio stands poised, a modern maid . . . her arms flung wide to life and the world . . . eager, facing the sun . . . alive to the encompassing occidental sophistication . . . aware and youthfully impatient of aged traditions and hovering elders. . . . "[3] In personifying Little Tokyo as a feminine gypsy, jeweled with light, serenaded, "the happiness of her own pulsing and sensuous . . . ," Tanna also wove a lively and romantic image of urban Nisei womanhood.

In contrast to Japanese American farm women, whose lives Evelyn Nakano Glenn characterizes as having retained "traditional peasant values," urban Nisei daughters had more comfortable, less arduous childhoods.[4] Like their rural counterparts, they helped out in the home and family business, but they were more likely to have free time and, like the urban Mexican American women Ruíz has studied, greater access to commercialized leisure.[5] As Mei Nakano suggests, the prewar period could be "a heady time for urban Nisei females, filled with the scent of gardenias, and the excitement of romance and dating."[6] Certainly the packed social calendar of the Los Angeles *Kashu Mainichi* reflected their opportunities to engage in a range of cultural, recreational, athletic, and social service activities within the ethnic community.

By and large, the Nisei were a very young group. In 1930, the bulk of the second generation in Los Angeles County were under twenty-one years old. In 1934, a journalist reported that the majority of the Nisei in the United States were between the ages of fifteen and eighteen.[7] Regardless of their youth, most Nisei did not lack responsibilities.

The labor of second-generation girls and adolescents proved essential to the support of the family wage economy and the ethnic community. City girls often helped clean and operate family businesses within the Japanese American enclave, sweeping a tofu shop, waiting on restaurant customers, or stocking the shelves of a grocery store. Girls' chores also included housework, from which their brothers were exempt, in addition to the supervision of younger siblings.

As adults, many Nisei women—like other racial-ethnic and working-class women—faced limited job prospects made grimmer by the fact that work outside the home was rarely a choice and more often a necessity. In the prewar period, three narrow paths led urban Japanese American women to jobs inside the ethnic community, work outside the enclave, or—for a small minority—the pursuit of opportunities in Japan. One writer termed them, "Three Roads and None Easy."[8]

Because of racial barriers and the Great Depression, full-time employment opportunities were limited, both within and outside Little Tokyo. Like their Chinese American peers, most Nisei found that in the larger job market, factors of race (and in the case of women, gender) outweighed their education and English proficiency.[9] Educated women and men alike faced a discouraging paucity of jobs. "The chief problem of every nisei grad is that of vocation," asserted T. Roku Sugahara in a 1935 article. Although he believed it was not impossible to "find an opening in the greater community," he aimed to persuade the second generation to consider the "wonderful opportunities" in agriculture and fishing, or in revitalizing the flower markets and other businesses of Little Tokyo.[10] The dearth of options led to a competitive scramble for the more desirable positions in the ethnic enclave.

A small number of Nisei women filled the needs of ethnic professionals and merchants for secretaries and clerks. Women coveted such positions, as Monica Sone recalled from her youth in Seattle: "I knew that the Nisei girls competed fiercely among themselves for white-collar jobs in the Mitsui and Mitsubishi branch firms downtown, local newspaper establishments, Japanese banks, shipping offices and small export and import firms."[11] Some women, like Yoshiko Hosoi Sakurai, channeled their skills into a family business: after graduation from high school, she worked with her parents to operate Mansei An, a popular Little Tokyo udon (noodles) and sushi shop.[12] Others worked as teachers, nurses, seamstresses, and beauticians within the ethnic community.

Domestic work proved the most readily available work outside the urban Japanese American enclave. As Evelyn Nakano Glenn found, domestic work constituted the primary area of nonagricultural wage-paid labor for Issei and Nisei women. In 1941, the Japanese YWCA in San Francisco estimated that two out of every five young women worked in domestic service.[13] This pattern persisted: during the war, the greatest number of jobs advertised in the internment camps were domestic positions recently vacated by black and white women flocking to better-paid defense and industrial work.

It is difficult to estimate how many Nisei women and men decided to seek their fortunes in Japan. Judy Yung notes that more second-generation Chinese Americans than Mexican Americans or Japanese Americans set their sights on working in their parents' homeland.[14] The ongoing discussion of opportunities abroad in the Japanese American newspapers of Los Angeles and San Francisco suggests that at least some gave it serious consideration. A 1926 interview with a Nisei collegian specializing in secretarial work underscores the limitations of the U.S. job market. She said, "After I graduate, what can I do here? No American firm will employ me. All I can hope to become here is a bookkeeper in one of the little Japanese dry goods stores in the Little Tokyo section of Los Angeles, or else become a stenographer to the Japanese lawyer here."[15] Instead she planned to go to Japan where a job in a large shipping company awaited her. Two of her Nisei women friends also intended to journey to Japan to teach English.

The smallest, yet most visible group of Nisei to turn their ambitions toward Japan were those pursuing careers in entertainment and the performing arts. Thwarted by racial barriers in the United States, some found a warm reception abroad. In 1932 the *Kashu Mainichi* reported that singer Agnes Miyakawa, violinist Alice Katayama, and pianist Lillian Katayama were "creating a sensational hit in the winter musical debut," and that Kyoko Inoue had gotten a role in a Japanese movie. Concluded the editor, "Japan is indeed the land of opportunity for the second generation who are talented in some special line of endeavor."[16] The large majority of Nisei women and men, however, cast their economic lot with the land of their birth.

Because Nisei women not only brought wages into the family but also notions of how they might be spent, consumerism constituted a second expression of their significance in creating urban ethnic culture. Since the rise of advertising and mass media in the early twentieth century, women have been targeted for the sale of appliances, cosmetics, movies, clothing, home furnishings, and food. The reach of mainstream newspapers, magazines, radio, and film in the 1920s and 1930s made the latest consumer goods and popular icons appealing and familiar to a national audience, including Nisei girls like the protagonist of a Hisaye Yamamoto short story, "A Day in Little Tokyo." When a family beach outing is preempted by a sumo tournament, thirteen-year-old Chisato Kushida kills time in Little Tokyo by buying a newspaper, reading the "funnies," and poring over pictures of Marion Davies and Jeannette McDonald. Chisato wishes she had stayed home to listen to "the weekly fairy tale from New York City [on the radio], with kids like Billy and Florence Halop and Albert Alley always perfect in every story."[17] Finally she begins to sing the Cream of Wheat advertising jingle, which she knows by heart.

Urban Nisei women, within their means, tried to keep abreast of current fashions in clothing and cosmetics. In Little Tokyo, a number of beauty salons competed for their patronage. In 1934, the Ginza Beauty Salon lured customers with "specials on shampoo and finger waves every Wednesday" and proudly announced, "The salon, to assure perfect service, now has with them another Nisei operator Miss Marion Miyamoto, who has attended the Paramount Beauty College."[18] In addition, for those desiring instruction, a Miss Brain (who appears to have been a European American consultant) would demonstrate "fine cosmetics" and give makeup analyses.

Nisei discussions about cosmetics, as well as fads like gum chewing and cigarette smoking, reflect more than the second-generation women's participation in popular trends; they also show their staging of the debate over the boundaries of sanctioned female behavior and appearance among their peers. For example, in a newspaper column on lipstick, Alice Suzuki invoked and poked fun at romantic imagery: "In olden times ladies used their ring for the seal of true love, but modern women leave their red lip-prints on the cheeks of the gallant knights—which have caused many heartbreaks and trips to Reno." Although she warned against the excessive use of "loud" red, she concluded by asserting women's right to employ cosmetic enhancement: "it is imperative that ladies must have lip-sticks and indulge in them."[19]

Suzuki's writing reveals some ambivalence, even as she stakes claims to broader parameters of acceptable behavior for "modern women," including practices considered the purview of men. Utilizing and dismissing imagery often applied stereotypically to Asian and Asian American women, she notes, "In this day and age when women are no longer the dainty little creatures that used to flutter about like butterflies, it is not surprising to see them acquiring the habits of the male in landslide fashion. Take smoking, for example. . . . What is good for the men should be good for the women." She concludes, however, by declaring, "And now that we have granted the point that it is all right for women to smoke, may we suggest that they try smoking Havana cigars and be real, real men, or try a pipe—and smell like one."[20] Her words convey the sense of smoking as unfeminine, a prevailing sentiment within the prewar Japanese American community. Another Nisei columnist commented that a "[m]ajority of the [Japanese American] homes have a 'tabu' on women smoking."[21] Playwright Wakako Yamauchi has remarked that smoking was one of the things that "nice girls" didn't do.[22] Perhaps because of this, fewer Nisei women than men became regular smokers.

As Vicki Ruíz has skillfully delineated, female participation in popular culture was complicated for non-white women by the multiple pressures they faced within the family, the ethnic community, and the larger society.[23] At times, Nisei daughters, like their Mexican American sisters, felt torn between powerful mainstream notions of modernity and romance on one hand, and the feminine ideals inculcated by strict parents reared in another country (in this case, Meiji-Era Japan) on the other. As they struggled to integrate popular and parental values, they introduced a range of gender-role issues into the Japanese American community.

The tensions between competing notions of womanhood emerged most clearly in the discourse over romance and marriage—a discourse in which Nisei women took a vocal role. Like their mothers and most U.S. women then, they expected a future centering around marriage and family. In contrast to Issei women, they expected their marital relations to be based on romantic attraction and individual choice—the hallmarks of mainstream ideals—as well as duty. Their preoccupation with "love" reflected the influence of popular literature, songs, and movies. As Lucille Morimoto wrote:

> To-night
> I want to feel your nearness,
> To hear your husky voice fade into a whisper,
> To me they will be like the sweetness of honey,
> The cool breeze on my feverish face.[24]

Margaret Uchiyamada likewise yearned and burned in cinematic style, as she lamented in a 1933 verse:

> There's a reason why I cry at night
> And writhe with pain in my heart,
> While I curse the intervening miles
> That relentlessly keep us apart.
> I know that it's foolish to lie here and dream.
> And wipe eyes that will not be dry,
> But memories are all that I have left
> Since the night we kissed good-bye.[25]

Yet even while testifying to the popularity of heterosexual romantic ideals, one Los Angeles columnist, "Mme. Yamato Nadeshiko," deplored their impact. Her diatribe also underscored the effectiveness of mainstream media as a vehicle for these rosy notions. She felt that "seeing too many movies" and "reading too many novels" had caused Nisei women to harbor unrealistic dreams of "tall stalwart sons of men, bronzed by desert's noonday heat and whipped by bitter rain and hail. Hearts of gold, strength of steel, romantic Romeos." She warned women not to wait for a "Sir Galahad" but to recognize the "everyday heroes [who] exist all about us."[26] Another columnist who identified herself as "a deb" similarly mused, "The trouble with us is—we build too many air castles. And we pick on a man, the dream of our 'teens as the 'one and only'—who not only seems sincere, but can do no wrong. But that's being over romantic and over idealized. Sort of dangerous, don't you think?" She advised her peers "to be hardboiled towards love" because "we're just bound to undergo some of its misfortunes."[27] Her admonition transmitted not only caution about, but also an expectation of, romantic love.

Given these aims, it is not surprising that second-generation women increasingly challenged the practice of arranged marriage in favor of "love marriage." As Nakano Glenn states, "With the loosening of traditional family controls, the urban nisei had moved toward the ideal of 'free marriage' by the mid 1930s."[28] Nisei women, who had far less veto power over the choice of marital partners than Nisei men, wrote frequently to Nisei advice columnist "Deirdre" to rail against arranged matches.[29] Extensive and heated dialogues among readers often raged for weeks in the popular San Francisco newspaper column. In a 1934 article in the Los Angeles *Kashu Mainichi,* Mary Korenaga passionately decried such unions, asking rhetorically if Nisei should allow themselves to "become a breeding machine to which we are forced by the third party merely for the purpose of keeping the world populated? Are we to lose emotions which we have harbored merely to become a human mechanism on the order of the common ant?" "No!" she declared. "A thousand times, No!"[30] The priority Korenaga placed on individual choice and romantic love mirrors the Nisei's embrace of mainstream ideals of companionate marriage.

Wedding announcements also revealed the adoption of mainstream female rituals: The *Kashu Mainichi* reported in 1932 that Masao Oshima, who would soon "middle-aisle it with Mr. Eddie Izumi . . . was honored at a linen shower" hosted by her friends.[31] In the same year, Yaeno Sakai was feted with a china shower given by "her feminine acquaintances."[32] The ethnic newspapers also began to take note of honeymoons, as in the case of newlyweds Shigeo and Florence Kato who planned to go to the Grand Canyon.[33] By the 1930s, the honeymoon was another mainstream middle-class practice followed by the second generation, or at least by those who were affluent enough.

Ironically, the dominant society not only broadened but also constrained Nisei marital choices, which were made within the framework established by state codification of racial discrimination, strikingly embodied in the anti-miscegenation laws that Peggy Pascoe examines. Like their mothers, Nisei women retained values of duty and obligation and expected to marry men of their own racial-ethnic group. This stemmed not only from the strong preference of the Japanese American community, but also from the even stronger opposition of the dominant society. In 1880 California's anti-miscegenation law was amended to include Asians. The marriage of a white person to a "Negro, mulatto, Mongolian or Malay" was illegal until the overturn of the law in 1948. By the 1930s, fourteen states—including Arizona, California, Idaho, Montana, Nebraska, Nevada, Oregon, Utah, and Wyoming—had anti-miscegenation laws aimed at Asian immigrants and their children.[34] In the arena of marital choice, as in other social and economic arenas, the Nisei remained highly conscious of the boundaries of race and gender.

Nisei women played a significant if sometimes stereotypical role as representatives of ethnic culture, both within and outside the Japanese American community. Kimono-clad young women and girls became a vivid image to other Nisei as well as to non-Japanese American schoolmates. As wartime events would subsequently show, European Americans on the whole viewed the Nisei as foreigners garbed in exotic robes. Ironically, unless they were learning traditional dance, most Nisei were unaccustomed to wearing kimonos, pulled out on rare occasions from mothball-filled trunks. Novelist

Yoshiko Uchida wove this situation into a scene in which an Issei mother helps her daughter and two other Nisei girls dress in kimonos for an International Club program at the daughter's high school:

> The girls gasped for breath as Hana tightened the *obi* around their chests and tried to ease the pressure with their fingers. They stumbled clumsily about the room as the thongs of the *zori* dug at the flesh between their toes. Hana smiled at their awkwardness. Although wrapped in silken grace, their unaccustomed bodies resisted, and at least in Hana's eyes, they did not look like anything other than foreigners in Japanese dress.[35]

To Hana, an Issei, the Japanese kimono in fact reveals the Nisei's "Americanness."

The teenaged Nisei protagonist of Yamamoto's story also retains a striking image of girls in kimono. Remembering a program of traditional Japanese dance performed in Little Tokyo, Chisato feels envious of "the child dancers with their faces painted dead white, their blackened eyebrows and bright red bee-stung lips. They seemed a world apart in their brilliant silken kimonos, in their gliding movements to the plucked music and wailing song, in their convoluted wigs adangle with chains of cherry blossoms."[36] While Chisato considers them "privileged" to take odori lessons, it is also clear that she regards them as inhabiting "a world apart" from her in their elaborate costumes and makeup, as they dance to a "wailing" music quite different in rhythm and key from the Cream of Wheat song that she had memorized. From Chisato's point of view, becoming a performer of traditional dance seems glamorous and means receiving approving applause from the ethnic community; but it also appears somewhat alien.

To some Issei parents, the proper wearing of a kimono and the study of traditional dance became intertwined with socializing their daughters to behave with modest feminine grace. Ko Wakatsuki, the father of Jeanne Wakatsuki Houston, co-author of *Farewell to Manzanar,* fell into this camp. He became furious when he learned that Jeanne, dressed in a Dorothy Lamour-style sarong, had been voted the high school carnival queen of 1947. In desperation he tried to bargain with her, saying, "You want to be a carnival queen? I tell you what. I'll make a deal with you. You can be the queen if you start odori lessons at the Buddhist Church as soon as school is out."[37] Both Jeanne and her father knew, however, that it was too late for these classes to have the effect on her that her father desired.

Issei parents like Ko Wakatsuki worried about the impression their daughters would make not only on European American society but also within the ethnic enclave. In addition to being viewed by non-Japanese Americans as representatives of their ethnic group,[38] Nisei women met the scrutiny of sharp-eyed Issei elders as representatives of their families. Community surveillance exerted great pressure on some young women, as reflected by the case of one Nisei who suffered from uterine hemorrhaging. As Dana Takagi has related, the woman's mother waited for months to seek medical treatment for her, fearing that the family would be stigmatized if the Japanese American community found out about her disease.[39] Ironically, because the mother insisted that the daughter's radiation treatment be kept secret, the ethnic community gossiped about the possible reasons for her regular trips to the hospital. Later she discovered that people believed she was sexually promiscuous and routinely going for abortions. While this may be an extreme example, it provides an illustration of the kinds of familial and community pressure with which single young Nisei women lived.

Less dramatic, more mundane pressures were familiar to most second-generation girls. Like Monica Sone, they found that Issei teachers and community leaders wished to mold them into "an ideal Japanese *o-joh-san,* a refined young maiden who is quiet, pure in thought, polite, serene, and self-controlled."[40] As Sone remembered, this meant that children "must not laugh out loud and show our teeth, or chatter in front of guests, or interrupt adult conversation, or cross our knees while seated, or ask for a piece of candy, or squirm in our seats."[41]

Adolescents and young women felt even more keenly the weight of expectations of proper female behavior. In 1934, one rebellious high school student in San Francisco bemoaned the limitations of "Girls who walk the usual tread of life all planned by society and family" and described a dreary round of domesticity, concluding that for women, "Life is a matter of surpressing [sic]."[42] She made it clear that fear of community scrutiny enforced compliance: "We do our darnest [sic] to keep our self free from gossip. Anything different even in a form of an experiment will cause a riot among the sneeking [sic], whispering gossip-front."[43] Although her outspoken defiance may have been unusual, her awareness of social pressure was not.

Once she reached her twenties, a second-generation woman faced increasing pressure to marry. Parental expectations were reinforced by those of the other Issei elders. A writer for the San Francisco *Hokubei Asahi* related the "typical case" of a twenty-four-year-old college-educated Nisei woman who had "staved off four proposals to her father by 'friends' of comparatively unknown or personally repulsive men." According to the author, "The matter becomes worse because of the girl's age, which is a terrible age for an unmarried Japanese daughter to be still on her father's hand—people are already beginning to ask what is the matter with her that she cannot secure a husband." He added, "She is not alone—there are hundreds like her in the same situation."[44]

Given such pressures, Nisei girls and single women found much-needed camaraderie and peer-group understanding in a wide array of urban Japanese American organizations. As Harry H. L. Kitano states, "It would be difficult to overlook the vast network of services and opportunities available to the Japanese youth."[45] There they also gained leadership training and built networks that would aid them in the trying years of wartime incarceration and postwar resettlement. Indeed, as Nakano Glenn suggests, women have "emerged over time as prime movers in the organizational life" of the ethnic community.[46]

Southern California was rich in Nisei organizations; Mei Nakano has reported that more than four hundred could be counted in Los Angeles by 1938.[47] Throughout the decade before World War II, the Nisei social calendars of the *Kashu Mainichi* and other newspapers bristled with meetings and events hosted by a burgeoning array of young women's clubs. In May of 1932, an annual Junior Girl Reserves conference drew members of at least seventeen clubs, ranging from Buddhist and Christian church-sponsored groups, YWCA affiliates, and Girl Scouts.[48] Although clubs abounded for every age cohort, adolescents and college-age single women constituted the majority of those involved in Nisei female organizations. Full-time jobs and marriage no doubt cut into the leisure time of older Nisei women in addition to drawing them into different social arenas.

The youth groups served a variety of functions. According to Kitano, they were a means of social control and socialization: "During early and late adolescence, Nisei generally were controlled by organizations within the community. These often took the form of leagues and clubs . . . " Control of these organizations was often exercised by peers rather than parents; Kitano notes that "although the Issei periodically attempted to control them," the groups were "usually guided by the Nisei themselves. The youngsters were left pretty much alone, to make mistakes, to try new things, and to translate their understanding of large community models in ways that could be of use to them."[49] For young Nisei women, who, like their Mexican American sisters "sought to reconcile parental expectations with the excitement of experimentation,"[50] youth clubs afforded a heady opportunity.

These groups provided an important alternative for Japanese American children excluded from European American clubs or unable to assume leading positions in them. "If we hadn't had these ethnic organizations to join," Yoshiko Uchida writes, "I think few Nisei would have had the opportunity to hold positions of leadership or responsibility. At one time I was president of the campus Japanese Women's Student Club, a post I know I would not have held in a non-Japanese campus organization."[51] Within their own organizations, Nisei members received reinforcement of generational and ethnic identification, often finding role models in more senior Nisei advisers. Both Christian and Buddhist churches fostered girls' and boys' clubs, although YWCA-sponsored activities were particularly extensive. The Nisei women who attended college established another tier of organizations, such as the Blue Triangles and the Chi Alpha Delta sorority in Los Angeles. Women forged lifetime friendships in these clubs. The continued meetings of some groups, fifty years later, underscore their significance for the Nisei.

Women's organizations provided socialization in both mainstream and ethnic culture. Some, like the Sumire Kai, a junior women's club, met to learn about the history of Japan and the intricacies of Japanese etiquette.[52] A similar group, the Shira-yuri (white lily) club formed in Long Beach, vowing to speak only Japanese at their meetings.[53] Other organizations provided a forum in which to explore peer-group and intergenerational issues, as well as to participate in a range of activities common to groups like the Girl Scouts of America. For example, the Junior Girl Reserves conference in 1932 included in its schedule swimming, hiking, handicrafts, nature study, music, and outdoor sports. The featured topics of discussion reflected the influence of popular culture: "What the Boy Friend Thinks?" "What is 'It'?" and "What We All Think of Dancing?"[54] The leaders also hoped to facilitate intergenerational understanding by offering discussions of mother-daughter relations.

The reportage of club events reveals how such organizations established and sometimes gently pushed the boundaries of socially sanctioned activities for Japanese American girls, from charitable endeavors to recreation. The growing popularity of dances throughout the prewar years provides an example of changing cultural mores. In this respect, generally speaking, city youth had greater latitude than their rural peers, women as well as men. Indeed, women took the initiative in planning, regulating, and maybe even attending dances, as a stern admonition to southern California gate-crashers indicated in 1931: "Men and women who walked in without invites at the last Blue Triangle dance are getting into hot water and the sooner their crusts melt away the better."[55]

Leap Year dances planned by the Blue Triangles and Chi Alpha Delta received special notice from the *Kashu Mainichi* in January 1932: "Already two dances are scheduled in February for the benefit of the supposed-to-be stronger sex by the weaker sex."[56] The Cherry Blossom and Nadeshiko Clubs of nearby Gardena, California, also planned to sponsor jointly a Leap Year dance. The repeated mention that dances would be "strictly invitational" suggests their success in attracting Nisei youth eager to "glide to the strains of Jack Gary's 8-piece Masonic orchestra" and other ensembles.[57] Such heterosexual couples-dancing would have been unheard-of for the Nisei's immigrant parents and still incurred the disapproval of rural Issei.

Many of the clubs had a social-service component. The first act of the newly formed girls' Calrose Club was to make a gift of a box of apples to a children's organization.[58] Even recreational activities like dances provided opportunities for community service. Of the five spring dances announced in the *Kashu Mainichi* in 1932, three were "benefit dances." Admission to the

Savings Association Dance required "the presentation of the invitation cards and three large cans of food, preferably Japanese."[59] Later in May, the Blue Triangles lured the light of foot to their "cabaret style" benefit dance with the promise of waltz and fox-trot contests and live music to be furnished by Dave Sato's Wanderer Orchestra.[60] Through such measures, the Nisei responded to community needs while enjoying "the excitement of experimentation." As they maintained peer-regulated activities and developed their own forums for entertainment, exercise, creative expression, and leadership training, a rich Nisei social world coalesced.

In the decade before the Second World War, young Nisei women played important roles in shaping and sustaining urban ethnic culture, while developing a strong generational consciousness that still continues to permeate Japanese American organizations. Participation in a range of youth groups gave urban Nisei girls and single women high visibility in the ethnic community, which reinforced their position as cultural negotiators. Through service projects, social occasions, athletic events, and a range of cultural arts performances, second-generation women interacted with both the Issei generation and Nisei men, as well as with members of surrounding communities. And, as their poems, short stories, essays, and letters in the Japanese American newspapers testify, the process of defining a position in society engaged and challenged them from early adolescence. In this process they remained mindful of family responsibilities and cultivated ethnic pride, while striving to piece together a kind of modern womanhood appropriate to their dreams and circumstances.

World War II internment not only dashed many Nisei dreams and shattered Japanese American communities; it has, in the historical literature, overshadowed the vibrancy of Little Tokyo and other prewar ethnic enclaves. Researching Nisei women's writings and organizations in the 1930s reveals the complexity of the second generation's negotiation of roles within the urban ethnic community. Their labor materially supported their families through the Great Depression, during World War II, and in the critical period of postwar rebuilding. They have acted as primary conduits of gender-role debate into Japanese American enclaves. And they have earned reputations within the ethnic group for being its premier grassroots organizers.[61] In the process of integrating the worlds of their parents and peers since the prewar period, urban Nisei women have created networks that continue to shape and sustain Japanese American communities today.

Notes

A version of this paper was presented at the 50th Anniversary Conference of the Arthur and Elizabeth Schlesinger Library on the History of Women in America and published in pamphlet form in Susan Ware, ed., *New Viewpoints in Women's History: Working Papers from the Schlesinger Library 50th Anniversary Conference, March 4–5, 1994* (Cambridge: Schlesinger Library, 1994).

For their insightful comments on this paper I thank Blake Allmendinger, Estelle Freedman, Peggy Pascoe, Vicki Ruíz, and Judy Yung.

1. Vicki L. Ruíz, "The Flapper and the Chaperone: Historical Memory among Mexican-American Women," *Seeking Common Ground: Multidisciplinary Studies of Immigrant Women in the United States,* ed. Donna Gabaccia (Westport, CT: Greenwood Press, 1992), p.151; see also her article "'La Malinche Tortilla Factory': Negotiating the Iconography of Americanization, 1920–1950," *Privileging Positions: The Sites of Asian American Studies,* ed. Gary Y. Okihiro et al. (Pullman: Washington State University Press, 1995), pp. 201–15. See also Judy Yung, *Unbound Feet: A Social History of Chinese Women in San Francisco* (Berkeley: University of California Press, 1995); George Sanchez, *Becoming Mexican American: Ethnicity, Culture and Identity in Chicano Los Angeles, 1900–1945* (New York: Oxford University Press, 1993); Mei Nakano, *Japanese American Women: Three Generations, 1890–1990* (Berkeley: Mina Press Publishing/San Francisco: National Japanese American Historical Society, 1990). Eileen Tamura's study *Americanization, Acculturation and Ethnic Identity: The Nisei Generation in Hawaii* (Urbana: University of Illinois Press, 1994) provides a richly detailed examination of the Nisei's education, work, and cultural shifts in Hawaii. Dissertations by David K. Yoo and Lon Y. Kurashige provide valuable windows into the history of second-generation Japanese Americans on the U.S. mainland: see Yoo, "Growing Up Nisei: Second Generation Japanese-Americans of California, 1921–1945," Yale University, Ph.D., 1994; and Kurashige, "Made in Little Tokyo: Politics of Ethnic Identity and Festival in Southern California, 1934–1994," University of Wisconsin, Ph.D., 1994.

2. *Kashu Mainichi,* January 5, 1936.

3. *Kashu Mainichi,* October 2, 1932. This excerpt contains no deletions; the ellipses are Tanna's own punctuation.

4. Evelyn Nakano Glenn, *Issei, Nisei, War Bride: Three Generations of Japanese American Women in Domestic Service* (Philadelphia: Temple University Press, 1986), p. 55.

5. Ruíz, "The Flapper and the Chaperone," p. 146.

6. Mei Nakano, p. 120.

7. *Kashu Mainichi,* May 20, 1934.

8. Kazuo Kawai, "Three Roads and None Easy," *Survey Graphic* 9, no. 2 (May 1926), p. 165.

9. Yung, p. 134.

10. *Kashu Mainichi,* June 23, 1935.

11. Monica Sone, *Nisei Daughter* (Seattle: University of Washington Press, 1953), p. 133.

12. Yoshiko Hosoi Sakurai interview, Los Angeles, California, August 28–29, 1996.

13. Gene Gohara, "Domestic Employment," *Current Life* (June 1941): 6.

14. Yung, p. 157.

15. Kawai, p. 165.

16. *Kashu Mainichi,* January 20, 1932.

17. Hisaye Yamamoto, "A Day in Little Tokyo," in *Seventeen Syllables and Other Stories* (Latham, NY: Kitchen Table: Women of Color Press, 1988), p. 119.

18. *Kashu Mainichi,* September 16, 1934.
19. *Kashu Mainichi,* October 30, 1932.
20. Ibid.
21. *Hokubei Asahi,* October 12, 1934.
22. Wakako Yamauchi interview, Gardena, California, October 3, 1995.
23. Ruíz, "The Flapper and the Chaperone," pp. 141–58.
24. From "Three Thoughts," *Kashu Mainichi,* May 22, 1932.
25. From "heartache," *Kashu Mainichi,* August 26, 1933.
26. *Kashu Mainichi,* July 10, 1932.
27. From "Feminine Interest," *Kashu Mainichi,* October 6, 1935.
28. Nakano Glenn, p. 57.
29. I discuss Nisei women's views of love and marriage, and focus on the "I'm Telling You Deirdre" column, in "Redefining Expectations: Nisei Women in the 1930s," *California History* (Spring 1994): 44–53, 88. For more information on "Deirdre"—Mary Oyama Mittwer—see my article, "Desperately Seeking 'Deirdre': Gender Roles, Multicultural Relations, and Nisei Women Writers of the 1930s," *Frontiers* 12, no. 1 (1991): 19–32.
30. *Kashu Mainichi,* March 4, 1934.
31. *Kashu Mainichi,* January 8, 1932.
32. *Kashu Mainichi,* June 4, 1932.
33. *Kashu Mainichi,* December 2, 1931.
34. Peggy Pascoe's work on anti-miscegenation law is especially useful; see her articles: "Race, Gender, and the Privileges of Property: On the Significance of Miscegenation Law in the U.S. West," in this volume; "Miscegenation Law, Court Cases, and Ideologies of 'Race' in Twentieth-Century America," *Journal of American History* 83, no. 1 (June 1996): 44–69; and "Race, Gender, and Intercultural Relations: The Case of Interracial Marriage," *Frontiers* 12, no. 1 (1991): 5–18. For a detailed discussion of anti-miscegenation laws and their application to Asian Americans, see Megumi Dick Osumi, "Asians and California's Anti-Miscegenation Laws," in *Asian and Pacific American Experiences: Women's Perspectives,* ed. Nobuya Tsuchida (Minneapolis: Asian/Pacific American Learning Resource Center and General College, University of Minnesota, 1982), pp. 1–37.
35. Yoshiko Uchida, *Picture Bride* (New York: Simon and Schuster, Inc., 1987), p. 134.
36. Yamamoto, p. 116.
37. Jeanne Wakatsuki Houston and James D. Houston, *Farewell to Manzanar* (New York: Bantam Books, Inc., 1974), p. 127.
38. The Japanese American community was highly conscious of outside scrutiny and responded, in Harry H. L. Kitano's words, with "appeals to all individuals to behave in a manner that would reflect to the benefit of all Japanese." Kitano, *Japanese Americans: The Evolution of a Subculture,* 2nd ed. (Englewood Cliffs, NJ: Prentice-Hall, Inc., 1976), p. 36.
39. Dana Y. Takagi, "Personality and History: Hostile Nisei Women," *Reflections on Shattered Windows: Promises and Prospects for Asian American Studies,* ed. Gary Y. Okihiro et al. (Pullman: Washington State University Press, 1988), p. 187.
40. Sone, p. 28.
41. Sone, p. 27.

42. *Hokubei Asahi,* October 11, 1934.

43. Ibid.

44. *Hokubei Asahi,* November 5, 1934.

45. Kitano, p. 60.

46. Nakano Glenn, p. 38.

47. Mei Nakano, p. 120.

48. *Kashu Mainichi,* May 22, 1932.

49. Kitano, *Japanese Americans,* p. 50.

50. Ruíz, "The Flapper and the Chaperone," p. 151.

51. Yoshiko Uchida, *Desert Exile, The Uprooting of a Japanese American Family* (Seattle: University of Washington Press, 1982), p. 44.

52. *Kashu Mainichi,* April 16, 1932.

53. *Kashu Mainichi,* June 9 and 17, 1932.

54. *Kashu Mainichi,* April 15 and May 22, 1932. The Junior Girl Reserves discussion of "It" was doubtless a legacy of Clara Bow, the "It Girl," and the promotion of "sex appeal" in the 1920s.

55. *Kashu Mainichi,* November 17, 1931.

56. *Kashu Mainichi,* January 5, 1932.

57. *Kashu Mainichi,* November 28, 1931.

58. *Kashu Mainichi,* November 19, 1931.

59. *Kashu Mainichi,* March 29, 1932.

60. *Kashu Mainichi,* May 6, 1932.

61. A good illustration of Nisei women's roles as community organizers can be found in the successful political movement to seek redress and reparations for World War II internment. See Alice Yang Murray's dissertation, "'Silence, No More': The Japanese American Redress Movement, 1942–1992," Stanford University, Ph.D., 1995.

17

COMPETING COMMUNITIES AT WORK

Asian Americans, European Americans, and Native Alaskans in the Pacific Northwest, 1938–1947

CHRIS FRIDAY

In 1932, Edward R. Ridley of Ketchikan noted: "There are more than enough 'local residents' right here in this town without hav[ing] to import [workers] from other places."[1] He emphasized to salmon canning companies operating in the town that his was no personal conjecture, but was the general opinion "of our people nowadays." By "our people" Ridley meant Native Alaskans—largely Tlingits—of southeast Alaska, and as the vice president of the Alaska Native Brotherhood (ANB), he did indeed have insights into the concerns and needs of Native Alaskans.[2] Ridley believed Asian American[3] contractors not only mistreated Native Alaskan workers but also severely limited Tlingit employment opportunities in the midst of the Depression.[4] In addition to arguing that canners might hire Native Alaskans more cheaply than Asian American crews, Ridley hinted strongly that the ANB might consider some form of collective action. Indeed, in the late 1930s, the ANB began to organize among Alaskans and it sought the federal government's approval to act as a union for Native men who fished and Native women who worked in the canneries.[5] The presence of competing Congress of Industrial Organizations (CIO) and American Federation of Labor (AFL) locals, whose respective memberships were largely Asian Americans—especially Chinese, Japanese, and Filipinos—and European American residents of Alaska, complicated the situation.[6] Through 1946, the jockeying among the ANB, CIO locals, and AFL locals to represent the residents of southeast Alaska who worked in canneries reveals how the members of these "communities" defined themselves, how they vied for jobs, and how they found fleeting possibilities for cooperation amidst that tremendous competition.

This story of intergroup rivalries and union affiliations is not some strange, exceptional story that played itself out in isolated Alaska, or one purely driven by competition from the national headquarters of the CIO and the AFL. It is a quintessentially western story in which a multicultural populace leaned heavily on the federal government for resolution of its racial and class problems.[7] It is also western in the sense that it illustrates how populist sentiments, or grassroots politics, make strange bedfellows, for in this region where party machines had at best a weak hold, institutions like unions and ethnic or fraternal brotherhoods carried much weight.[8]

The very construction of the communities under consideration here also made them part of the Pacific Northwest, even the U.S. West, and not just Alaska. Asian immigrant and Asian American workers traveled in regular seasonal migration patterns through central and northern California, Oregon, and Washington on their ways to and from Alaska canneries; canning companies had their headquarters in San Francisco, Portland, Astoria, and Seattle, while their markets were global; and especially after the Jones Act of 1920, the territory was virtually a colony of Washington state. It is all too easy to isolate Alaska as some huge, underdeveloped behemoth to the north that is "outside" U.S. history, even the history of the U.S. West.

Rather than constituting an isolated, non-western case in which local labor stood against "outsiders," these three "western" communities, though different in type and constituency, overlapped in the salmon canneries of southeast Alaska. Asian American cannery hands, whom most in the industry referred to as "China gangs" or "outside crews," formed the bulk of those about whom Ridley complained. Recruited up to the mid-1930s by co-ethnic labor contractors, by 1938 these workers found representation in the CIO locals, often drawing upon a "community of association" held together by semipermanent co-ethnic residents in towns along the seasonal work cycle that many of the laborers followed in the U.S. West.[9] In southeast Alaska, the resident Asian Americans, particularly the Filipinos, provided entrée into organizing "resident" and Native Alaskans for the "outside" unions.[10]

Tlingit, as well as Tsimshan and Haida people living in southeast Alaska, in contrast to the outside crews, were important to the industry as a local source of labor.[11] The men served largely as fishermen, the women in the canneries. Their participation represented an adaptation of precapitalist seasonal fishing and fish preparation activities to industrial wage labor conditions, replete with the older gender division of labor.[12] Unlike Native Americans in Oregon and Washington, who by the beginning of the twentieth century had been marginalized in the political economy of those states, Native Alaskans played a central role.[13] Largely through the auspices of the ANB and its parallel organization the Alaska Native Sisterhood (ANS), as well as through the often competing AFL unions, Native Alaskans gained institutional representatives in the struggle to control jobs. Especially among the Tlingit, who predominated in the region, the community base was an ethnic/clan/national one with separate village divisions, alliances, and loyalties.[14]

Like Native Alaskans, resident Alaskans—European Americans who had migrated to southeast Alaska towns—formed a local labor pool. Highly dependent on salmon canneries and related enterprises for their incomes, their competition for jobs with Asian Americans and Native Alaskans contributed to a common sense of shared "white" ethnicity as "Alaskans." They also developed strong populist-like resentments of the outside financial control represented by cannery companies headquartered in the lower forty-eight states and by outside political resentment epitomized by the Jones Act of 1920, which gave Washington, especially Seattle, a virtual stranglehold on Alaskan shipping.[15]

The culmination of two separate organizational thrusts brought these three communities into conflict. The first was the 1938 government-mediated decision that gave the outside, Asian American–led CIO locals the right to represent cannery workers. Having secured a foothold, Asian American unionists then moved to organize Alaska to protect against AFL counter-attacks and to strengthen workers' solidarity against cannery owners. They ran headlong into the second development, the ANB and ANS efforts to establish greater political representation for Native Alaskans. By the late 1930s, that included, as Ridley had indicated, a drive for recognition of the combined ANB and ANS as the collective bargaining agent for Native peoples in southeast Alaska. A few studies have begun to explore ANB/ANS activities in voting rights, school desegregation, and land claims, but scant attention has been paid to its collective bargaining role in spite of the importance to Native Alaskan livelihoods.[16]

The ANB came together first in 1912, created by mostly Tlingit men under the influence of Presbyterian and Russian Orthodox missionaries in the territory who had organized church-based societies bent on providing vehicles for "civilizing" and "assimilating" Native Alaskans. Similarly, in 1915, various "Women's Village Improvement Societies" reorganized to form the ANS. In the 1920s and 1930s, the organizations moved from their earlier focus on assimilation and temperance programs to take up an extensive agenda for Alaska's native peoples that they pursued for the next half-century.[17] While voting rights and other civil rights issues as well as land claims promised to provide long-term benefits, the question of collective bargaining promised more immediate returns.

Members of the ANB and ANS resented political and economic control held by "outsiders" to the territory and promoted the slogan "Alaska for Alaskans."[18] In doing so, ANB and ANS members found that they had much in common with European American residents, but not enough to bridge racial divides. Through those organizations Native Alaskans used New Deal policies—Alaska's version of the Wheeler-Howard Act, the Alaska Reorganization Act of 1936, and the Wagner Act—to regain some measure of independence in the twentieth century.[19]

ANB and ANS members tried to convince salmon canners, the federal government, and labor unions that their organization had the right to represent its members and bargain collectively for them. The *Alaska Native Brotherhood,* the organization's mouthpiece, told readers late in 1938: "The final opinion of the [delegates at the 1938 ANB Grand Camp] Convention was that the ANB can do everything that other unions can do. If we are in the majority, we can still keep our identity and collect our dues exactly as do the CIO and the AFL where these unions are in the majority. In many cases, the officers of the ANB and the local union are the SAME PEOPLE, only that the money goes to San Francisco."[20] As early as 1937 the ANB/ANS had entered into collective bargaining arrangements in Sitka, and by 1938 a number of the ANB/ANS camps (nearly each small town in southeast Alaska had one) sought to use the ANB to represent the interests of Indian purse seiners and cannery workers.[21] By 1939, ANB and ANS activities as a bargaining agent for Native Alaskans were in full swing.

Native Alaskans used the ANB and ANS to express a strong strain of ethnic pride that merged into racialism at times. Native Alaskan Frank Johnson worked as an organizer and official of the AFL-affiliated fishermen's and cannery workers' locals.[22] Along with the outside CIO locals, Johnson represented a significant competitor to ANB and ANS plans for labor organization. In 1940, Louis F. Paul, an important force in the ANB, confronted Johnson in a letter to the Ketchikan *Alaska Fishing News* arguing that he had "permitted the ANB to be used as a vehicle to increase [AFL union] membership."[23] Paul warned Johnson:

> You cannot be brown and white at the same time. . . . [F]undamentally it is impossible for the white people to overcome their racial prejudice; it is impossible for them to favor Indians over their own kind. . . . They will use you and when they are through, they will abuse you. And in the end you will come back to your own people even as our sisters have come back to us in their shame with their unfathered children.[24]

Louis Paul thus signaled to Native Alaskans that they could not expect fair treatment by "outside," "white" unions. His allusion to unfathered children seemingly played on long-standing resentments about the conduct of the outside crews and the strong Christian element in the ANB and ANS as well as a not too veiled reference to what he believed the unions would do to Johnson.

Louis's brother William L. Paul did not mince words either. In an argument supporting the ANB and ANS as a bargaining agent he stated:

> The unions will never take up the scope of activity of the ANB for our people. We will challenge any organization in the territory to show that they care enough for our people to step up and attempt to do even a small portion of the ANB work. It is not in the cards. No white man will take the punishment for his efforts.[25]

William L. Paul believed that only the ANB had the interests of Native Alaskans at heart. In 1938, he explained to Wrangell ANB Camp President Frank Desmond that "the ANB was organized to give Indians an equal chance to make a living—to put bread and butter on the table for our women and children."[26] Later, in 1942, he reportedly told Craig ANB Camp members: "Tell our young people to be proud of their race, do not be ashamed of it. We are Indians, we are not white people, and the white leaders of the CIO and . . . [AFL] do not work for the benefit of the Indians."[27]

While William L. Paul and others in the ANB raged about outside control and white racism, they focused their concerns almost solely on fishing to the virtual exclusion of cannery work and women's employment.[28] ANS members got involved in the organization of cannery workers, but when they took action, ANS members usually did so in concert with, or in support of, the fishermen. Fish prices and the status of traps, usually owned by canning companies, were the typical concerns of the ANB. The ANS was also very active in the movement to regulate and abolish traps in the territory. ANS leaders wrote letters to local and regional newspapers and to federal officers urging that traps be eliminated to "give fish and fishermen a chance!"[29] The ANS and ANB often relied on the argument that traps hurt entire families, explaining that "most of us have families to feed."[30]

When it came to organizing the women into a union, however, Native Alaskan patterns of work caused problems. Those patterns in the twentieth century were in part a continuation of long-standing practices in which women undertook a variety of seasonal tasks, of which the fish harvests were only one, and canning company strategies of using Native American women largely as a reserve labor pool to supplement the outside crews.[31] Conrad Espe, business agent for the CIO cannery workers' local in Seattle, took advantage of those employment features and warned that neither the industry nor the unions could tolerate women's part-time work. Espe declared that

> in the days of old there were whole families which . . . worked in the canneries from the 12-year-old youngster up to the grandmother. I don't think modern Industry can function along these lines. I don't think modern labor relations should be built so as to provide equal conditions for the entire family. . . . [It] must bring out the quality of the work; parity and equality of work must go hand in hand with the parity of ability to perform it. . . . A person who is a resident cannot continue, as has been done in the past in many instances, where they want to work if they feel like it and not work when they don't feel like it. . . . [T]here must be a stable work force.[32]

Espe was right: Tlingit women and indeed Native American women generally, well into the twentieth century, continued to mix subsistence activities with wage labor. For example, Sally Hopkins, born in Sitka in 1877 and later resident of Dundas Bay and Juneau, worked in salmon canneries most of her life. During the canning season, she and her children picked berries to be preserved between shifts and on off days.[33] Indeed, nineteenth-century canners had long complained about the "irregularity" of Indian women as workers.[34] They, like Espe, had wanted the women available at all times, but Native Alaskans were not willing to forego necessary and even fulfilling seasonal cycles for the sake of the canners. The ANS, however, tried to sponsor childcare facilities for families employed by the canneries during 1943 and 1944, but it was not enough to counter Espe's implications that outside crews provided a more stable work force than Native Alaskans.[35]

When the ANS acted outside the camps, however, its leaders tended to use the organization to lobby alongside the ANB for civil rights. As a case in point, ANS Grand Camp President Elizabeth Wanamaker Peratrovich's 1945 speech before the Alaska Territorial Senate is generally considered to have been the telling factor in the passage of Alaska's anti-discrimination legislation. Moreover, ANS involvement in land claims was an essential part of that long struggle.[36] Locally, in each camp, ANS activities centered around fund-raising, "mostly through Bingo games" and the sale of foodstuffs or arts and crafts; the money often went to build or maintain ANB halls or to support the civil rights issues. The ANS also embraced moral suasion harkening back to the ANS roots in the village improvement societies.[37] Labor issues took a back seat in the ANS. When Native women in southeast Alaska chose to throw themselves into the field of labor organization, they tended to do so through established labor organizations—the various AFL or CIO locals—and that meant fostering cooperation with people from the other communities of workers.

The membership of the AFL locals consisted of Native Alaskans and resident Alaskans, fishers and cannery hands alike. These organizations also made greater efforts to represent cannery workers' interests than the ANB and ANS. Like the ANB, the AFL cannery workers' and fishermen's locals took up the slogan "Alaska for Alaskans." The cannery workers' leaders claimed that their members thought that "their jobs are menaced by . . . the CIO unions," that the CIO dues paid by Alaskans financed the "CIO drive to replace residents . . . [with] outside workers."[38] Officials of the AFL locals also declared that they had "no quarrel with [the ANB] as a fraternal organization."[39] They believed, however, that "certain self-seeking, power-hungry individuals in the ANB [are] seeking to pervert that organization, to reduce it to a union smashing weapon, a tool of the employers, and through the medium of the ANB launch a vicious slanderous attack upon the bona-fide resident labor unions of Alaska."[40] The AFL cannery workers tried to paint their locals as the true defenders of Native Alaskan women and their employment. In 1939, the AFL locals publicized a case in which five women, "all Natives" and CIO members, were prevented from gaining employment in a plant where they had worked for eight years. "Most of the women have children," the leaders explained, "and the cannery work they depend upon helps to support them the rest of the year."[41] The women thus quit the CIO local "in disgust" and "joined immediately" with the AFL local. The latter also countered a CIO media blitz in local newspapers and Ketchikan radio station KGBU, with the caution that it was only an attempt on the part of the CIO "to stem the ever increasing flow of cannery workers into the fold of the [AFL] Cannery Workers Auxiliary Union."[42]

If it was accurate in its membership accounting, the AFL cannery workers' locals controlled a sizable portion of the resident workers in the region. After the 1939 season, the local claimed to have 1,300 of the approximately 4,500 resident workers on its rolls at virtually every southeastern cannery town, including Metlakatlah, Craig, Klawok, Hydaburg, Wrangell, Petersburg, Kake, Sitka, Hoonah, Angoon, and Ketchikan.[43] When the CIO cannery workers' locals petitioned in 1939 for a National Labor Relations Board (NLRB) certification election—the key instrument of federal involvement in this case—in southeastern Alaska, Marie Murphy, president of AFL cannery workers' local in Ketchikan explained that her organization "expect[s] to be the bargaining agency for Southeastern Alaska by the right of majority rule."[44] It took until 1946 for the NLRB to begin to sort out representation for Alaskan cannery workers, and in the meantime the CIO locals began a concerted effort to organize Native Alaskans and Alaska residents.[45]

As the ANB/ANS and AFL positions indicate, the CIO locals had to buck a strong tide of anti-Asian and anti-"outsider" sentiments. To counter that image, the CIO drew upon people in three areas: Resident Alaskan (European American) women, Native Alaskan women, and Filipinos residing in Alaska. Among the resident Alaskans were the handful of women in towns such as Ketchikan. Elizabeth Del Fierro, for example, was the daughter of an Italian American fisherman.[46] She lived in Ketchikan and worked in a salmon cannery there, but unlike women and girls in other canning regions who developed work cultures that fostered pan-ethnic alliances among women and assisted in organizational attempts,[47] Elizabeth Del Fierro and other women in southeast Alaska also worked with significant numbers of men. The work culture that developed there enabled men and women from diverse ethnic backgrounds to come together. Elizabeth, for example, married Salvador Del Fierro, a staunch supporter of the CIO locals and central figure as a local linchpin in Ketchikan of the "community of association" for Filipinos, with connections reaching to Seattle, Portland, and Stockton. Indeed, like the Fierros, a great many of the officers in Ketchikan's CIO local were married couples—European American wives and Filipino husbands.[48]

The Seattle and San Francisco CIO locals began their organizing efforts among Ketchikan residents in 1937, but the NLRB certification election struggles between the 1937 and 1938 seasons distracted the stateside locals from that effort.[49] Beginning late in the canning season of 1938 and continuing into 1939, the Seattle and San Francisco locals renewed their efforts to bring Alaska residents under their umbrella. First, union leaders tried to blame canners for the "Alaska for Alaskans" sentiments.[50] Fearful of an AFL counterattack on the newly won jurisdiction, the CIO locals also blamed the AFL for the popularity of the slogan. Publicist for the Seattle CIO local and prominent Nisei labor leader Dyke Miyagawa declared that the AFL created "a false race issue" in its organizing message to Alaskan residents. He claimed the AFL told "resident whites" that "the Filipinos, Japs and Chinks are trying to take everything away. . . . 'To protect yourself,' the resident organizers have been saying to the residents, 'you've got to drive out the Orientals—save Alaska for the Alaskans.'"[51]

Early in 1939, Filipino immigrant Salvador Del Fierro, "the progressive leader of cannery workers in Ketchikan," reported that "considerable headway has been made to bring about greater cooperation and unity between the workers in the Territory and those in the states." Leaders of the CIO locals agreed that in order to organize Alaskan residents as well as Native Alaskans it needed to "equalize the status" of the two groups and to bring their wages up to those "enjoyed by the cannery workers of Seattle, Portland, and San Francisco."[52] In spite of the rhetoric, the stateside CIO locals placed Alaska organizing at the bottom of their priorities. In the Seattle local's list of five proposed actions for 1939, for example, cooperation with Alaskan locals stood in fifth place.[53] When it did attempt to organize, the CIO sent men to the region and as a distant second alternative relied on people like Salvador Del Fierro to work in concert with their wives.[54]

CIO locals made headway with resident workers, however, because they used the examples of Salvador and Elizabeth Del Fierro to argue that they represented resident interests. The ability of Ketchikan's Local 237 to make public its program through KGBU radio also won it some local recognition.[55] Most telling, though, was the CIO's ability to deliver. Unlike the ANB and ANS, or the AFL locals, the CIO locals had a strong position with the canners because of the 1938 certification among "outside" workers who constituted the bulk of the workforce. The locals used that as leverage to negotiate minimum wage guarantees for Alaskan workers (resident and Native Alaskan alike).[56]

During 1942, and even more so in 1943, wartime exigencies stalled the struggles between the three communities and created a brief and uneasy coexistence. The outside crews lost approximately seven hundred members when the U.S. government interned people of Japanese ancestry, and several hundred more (especially Filipinos) to the military service, to shipyards, and to other related war industries. Internal realignments and competition preoccupied the stateside CIO locals. Resident Alaskans, too, volunteered for the military and migrated to Seattle, Portland, or other cities for wartime jobs, but because canners had negotiated contracts with the government to supply tins of salmon to the troops, those employed in the industry earned exemption from military service if they so chose, and many remained in Alaska. Unlike in the Alaska peninsula or Bristol Bay, where military concerns placed severe limits on salmon production, in southeast Alaska the war brought an intensification of the reliance on Native Alaskan employment as cannery hands and fishermen. Wartime travel restrictions further limited Native Alaskan movements, making them all the more dependent on wage labor in southeast Alaskan canneries than they might otherwise have been. For all three groups, the War Labor Board temporarily reduced competition over wages. Finally, a patriotic fervor encouraged people to set aside their differences for the national good.[57]

Late in 1943 and early in 1944, the communities began to jostle for position again through the competing unions. They did so in anticipation of renewed negotiations at the war's end, but more immediately, in October 1943, the ANB/ANS publicized the possibility that it might entertain a merger with one of the other two labor organizations.[58] Ironically, part of the pressure to merge was a result of earlier government pressure to expand ANB/ANS membership. In order to gain status as a bona fide labor organization, the NLRB required the ANB and ANS to admit non-Indians to their ranks, but they did so only as "associate members" with status as beneficiaries of any labor agreements and with no voting rights on other ANB or ANS matters. In the 1939 ANB convention, though, the ANB created the Central Council of the Tlingit and Haida Indian Tribes of Alaska (also known as the Tlingit and Haida Central Council) at least in part to distinguish itself from the mixed membership of the ANB and ANS and to pursue the land claims issue separately from the organizations' roles as bargaining agents.[59] The conflicting directives from various government agencies ultimately weakened the ANB/ANS position as a separate union and contributed to talk of a merger with one of the other unions. That news prompted unprecedented action on the part of the CIO locals—the dispatching of a woman to Alaska as a key organizer. In spring 1944, Rose Dellama went north from San Francisco to recruit resident and Native Alaskans into her union.[60]

Dellama had grown up in the "Italian tenements" of Oakland, California, and had first come to labor concerns after having been fired in the 1934 newspaper strikes of the Bay Area. She subsequently joined the Communist Party and by 1937 had found a position as secretary for the San Francisco Alaska Cannery Workers Union, which shortly thereafter became a CIO local. The stateside struggle among cannery workers to gain certification had steeled her in the politics of union organizing. Upon her arrival in Alaska, she joined up with Marguerite Hansen, the business agent of Ketchikan's CIO local, and for the entire negotiating and canning season the two stumped throughout southeast Alaska, especially in Ketchikan, Juneau, Hoonah, and Petersburg.[61]

Dellama's leftist politics, experience with the San Francisco local, and Italian American background put her in good stead with certain portions of the resident population in Alaska. For example, Elizabeth Del Fierro, an Italian American married to a Filipino, had much in common with Dellama. While she no doubt drew upon these connections, Dellama also took great pains to reach out to Native Alaskans. "They all beamed," she recalled of her first arrival in Alaska, when she used the broken Tlingit she had learned to say, "I'm very happy to be here with you."[62]

Dellama proved able to find ways to reach Native Alaskan women in particular. She explained, "These women expected the CIO to represent them in all sorts of things," including a ruling that no U.S. military personnel could associate with Native Alaskan women. Dellama approached the union leaders in Alaska about protesting the ruling, but, complained: "I couldn't get the bastards to do anything." Not content to accept the men's refusal to acknowledge women's concerns, Dellama managed to plead her case to Alaska governor Earnest Greunig. When the order was rescinded shortly thereafter, Dellama earned a reputation "as the CIO lady who got that thing repealed." While Dellama's account reveals no recognition of the substantial campaign against the order mounted by the ANB and ANS, her stance on the issue differed markedly from the CIO's male organizers who had preceded her.[63]

While Dellama and Hansen negotiated for wage improvement in the form of higher seasonal guarantees and better hourly wages as had earlier male organizers, they added efforts to overcome the twin barriers of sexism and racism. They urged the locals to give dances, to hold bingo games, and to sponsor activities to raise funds for organizing in the region. By these means they hoped to link up with the type of activities that the ANS regularly conducted to generate interest in the union through channels that might appeal to women and that would be in relatively neutral social settings.[64]

Dellama and Hansen, joined by the Del Fierros and others long familiar with organizing in the region, also made a special effort to publicize the efforts of Native Alaskans in the CIO locals. In May 1944, the national union newspaper for CIO cannery and agricultural workers, the *UCAPAWA News,* ran a picture of six Native Alaskans, five of them women, on a page of articles about the organizing campaign. The newspaper stressed the prominent role the women played in the union and the fact that the locals supported a family economy. "SUSAN BROWN," one caption read, "is an Alaskan native and has helped . . . [the CIO locals] win the benefits the workers now enjoy." Another lauded Ruth Hayes, whose mother, father, husband, and children toiled in the canneries, to indicate her long-standing association with native labor. "Sister Hayes," explained the paper, "has been largely instrumental in organizing her Local and has been its Business Agent for the past 5 years." The paper presented Margaret Wanamaker as the centerpiece, touting her as "Vice-Pres[ident] of Local 269 in Juneau, . . . [and] secretary of the Alaska Native Sisterhood of Juneau."[65] The pictures and captions reinforced the image that the CIO unions worked against discrimination, supported "bona fide" resident cannery workers, and, in doing so, helped foster the well-being of Native Alaskans.[66]

In spite of the tremendous efforts by the international union, outside organizers like Dellama, and locals like Hansen, recruiting Native Alaskans was difficult because of the activities of the ANB and ANS. According to Dellama, the "Indians were interested in unions," but the ANB/ANS was "a big problem" because it attempted to spread "all kinds of rumors" about her. She complained that while she might sign workers in a particular village on one day, on the next day, "when the Native Brotherhood organizers came to the village they would all sign up with him [sic], too. Then I would have to go back to that village and organize all over again."[67]

Dellama also had to confront cultural assumptions over which she and other non-Native Alaskans had little control. In June 1944, a dry summer, a tremendous storm, and a house fire started a conflagration that leveled the town of Hoonah, killing one and resulting in the loss of many ceremonial and personal items. Hoonah's residents were "staunch Alaska Native Brotherhood people," but Dellama had been "making headway" until an investigation of the fire pointed to its origin in the home of a "known CIO man" where Dellama and other organizers had lodged. "Suddenly it was the CIO's fault," she recalled, and "people wouldn't speak to me."[68]

After six months of organizing in Alaska, Dellama returned to San Francisco. "When I left, I told the Indians I'd be back in six months, but then I learned that the union wasn't going back. . . . The union never went back."[69] That was unfortunate for the CIO, because Dellama's presence and the CIO's media campaigns tapered off just as the battle for certification as the bargaining agent for the region began to heat up again. During the 1945 canning season, the NLRB polled resident cannery workers, Native and non-Native, on their choice for union representation. In the NLRB tally the ANB/ANS earned 364 votes as the appropriate bargaining agent for southeast Alaska while the CIO and AFL registered 357 and 301 votes respectively.[70] While the ANB/ANS achieved a plurality of the votes, NLRB officials believed the election was "not decisive" because no party had earned a simple majority. At the requests of the ANB/ANS and the CIO locals, the NLRB ordered a run-off to be completed by September 1, 1946.[71]

In the interim, the ANB/ANS and AFL became much closer partners. By the November 1945 ANB Grand Camp Convention the die was cast. Louise Collier, one of three "fraternal" AFL delegates attending the ANB convention, told the assembled conventioneers:

> Providing work is a matter of native politics. I pledge myself to fight for Indians. As my personal message, if cannery workers joined [the] CIO there would be no social work. . . . The AFL has more to offer as an affiliation. The CIO has no interest in social affairs and decisions are governed by the pocketbook. Alaska needs an all-Alaska union. AFL is for Alaskan workers. ANB is for placing natives in work first. The CIO doesn't care about placing anyone on a job [except outside workers]. What they do makes evil thoughts come.[72]

A majority of the delegates approved the proposal to merge with the AFL cannery workers' locals. The AFL promise of "complete autonomy" for the local at each small town in the region—a cornerstone of the ANB—must have helped a great deal for it allowed each ANB/ANS camp to determine how to balance the concerns of its members and other non-Indian resident workers. Nonetheless, a third of the delegates either voted against AFL affiliation or were absent.[73] A significant proportion thus balked at any alliance with the AFL.

That reluctance delayed the merger between the ANB/ANS and AFL, and showed in the NLRB election results. The new combined organization, the Alaska Marine Workers Union, struggled to keep its membership's divergent interests in check and ultimately joined with the AFL-affiliated Seafarers International Union, which provided some administrative assistance, but in spite of the merger and outside support, it garnered 465 votes to the CIO's 485 votes.[74] The election came late in the year and although the NLRB made its decision in December 1945, as late as the end of January 1947 neither the CIO nor the AFL locals seemed to know with any certainty which party had won the election.[75] By late March 1947, head of the Seafarers International Union Harry Lundeberg protested to Paul Herzog, chairman of the NLRB, that a "true election" among southeast Alaska resident workers, not one peppered with "outside" voters, would give his union a majority.[76] In attacking the Asian American–led "outside" CIO union, Lundeberg connected the Seafarers' own anti-Asian and anti-CIO campaigns with those of some Alaskan workers.[77] While the AFL contested several of the 1946 votes on these grounds, NLRB officials sustained the CIO locals as the bargaining agent.[78]

With that decision, the joint ANB/ANS and AFL activity lost its currency and the organization's leader, William Lewis Paul, bitterly accused "whites" of "deserting" Native Alaskans while the union "silently folded up and died."[79] In addition, the growing concern over communist infiltration in labor organizations, reorganizations of the internationals, and the continued struggle between the AFL and CIO once more distracted the larger stateside locals.[80] The possibility that one labor organization might represent the entirety of Alaskan salmon cannery workers again disintegrated into its component parts. By that time, however, the ANB and ANS had moved beyond labor issues to a wholesale attempt to regain rights to a land base.[81] Filipinos struggled to maintain their positions against a growing corps of college students hired by canners, the continued attacks on them as "foreigners" and radicals, and the old standby that they were "outside" workers. Efforts to accommodate Native Alaskans, Asian immigrants and Asian Americans, European Americans, and men and women never truly took hold.

In spite of the tremendous competition among these three "communities" for employment and the attending racialism and friction, some opportunities emerged for building bridges between groups. Filipino residents of Alaska not only served as loci for the geographically diffuse community of co-ethnic migrant laborers, but also as links to local communities through marriage and labor organizing. Many "white" resident Alaskans played upon the image of Asian American "outsiders" to defend their positions, but ironically found themselves allied with Native Alaskans. Native Alaskans, especially women, played a central role as an important element in the economy and politics of Alaska and developed bridges to other groups.

Labor organizations and the federal government played significant roles, too. While the CIO's racially inclusive policies have been amply demonstrated,[82] in this case the AFL's support of racial minorities is instructive.[83] It occurred during a window of opportunity that opened in the late 1930s when it began to compete with the CIO for members and as the federal government ensconced itself as a permanent player in labor arbitration. Up to the mid-1940s, as Kevin Leonard has demonstrated for Los Angeles,[84] that window remained open and the AFL continued to embrace a new racial consciousness. The onslaught of the anti-communist drives of the late 1940s and early 1950s slammed that window shut. In the meantime, both Native Alaskans and the AFL had used the opportunity to push forward their own separate, but conjoined, agendas.

The swirling tides of "community" cooperation and conflict in southeast Alaska confirm the centrality of cultural frontiers to the nineteenth- and twentieth-century West. How the people in those communities came to define themselves, sometimes in the context of discrimination, shifted over time. The ANB/ANS, for example, began as an assimilationist temperance organization, but then began to take up civil rights issues in the 1920s, combined those with labor programs beginning in the 1930s, and then transformed again in the postwar years to focus on land claims and camp-level activities. When different communities came into contact with each other at various historical moments the result was as often conflict as cooperation. Alliances were brief but promising. Maintaining them, sometimes quite literally against storms and fires, was never easy, particularly in the West with its multiplicity of active racialized peoples who were not just outsiders in the region's history.[85]

Unlike the South or the unmarked North (or East), the U.S. West's narrative and rhetoric of race up to the mid-twentieth century was not calculated as a black-white binary.[86] Instead, it held room for many players, who, though they operated under a system dominated by historically constructed "whites," struggled with each other for positions in the racial hierarchy. Social theorists Michael Omi and Howard Winant argue that such a "war of position" (though perhaps war*s* is a better term) marked a transition from an earlier epoch when racialized peoples were excluded from the political system to one in which they gained access but not control.[87] In the West, the federal government's presence and control of property (resources and land) and labor was far greater than in other regions. When shifts in federal policy occurred, such as the rights of workers to organize and bargain collectively with representatives of their own choosing, racialized peoples seized the moment to press their agendas. Yet in places where no "majority" truly existed—as was the case in Alaska and throughout much of the West—these competing communities sometimes set aside the long history of divisive struggle at their places of work to create moments of cooperation. Their grassroots political concerns as "Alaskan" and/or "workers" sometimes overrode "Tlingit," "Indian," or "Filipino" issues. The story of the competition and cooperation among Asian Americans, Native Alaskans, and European American Alaska residents thus becomes part of the West's larger story, one that goes beyond isolated ethnic enclaves and embraces the "cultural frontiers" of the interactions among peoples.[88] The West's complicated social relations force us to develop a narrative that refuses to essentialize racial, class, or gender categories. We need to dream of the shifting currents inside and between each. We also need to recognize that this is much more than a small vignette played out in distant Alaska or the U.S. West: it encompasses issues of interethnic relations that reach far beyond the region; it reveals how world markets shuffled people and resources around the globe; and more importantly, it demonstrates how people struggled at individual and community levels to make a reasonable life for themselves in the face of much larger constraints. If "western," this story is one of a cultural frontier fraught with competition and conflict often driven by national and even international market forces. Western visions thus cannot be narrow, exceptionalist explanations.[89]

Notes

1. Edward R. Ridley to Fidalgo Island Packing Company, January 11, 1932, Fidalgo Island Packing Company Records, Anacortes Museum of History and Art, Anacortes, Washington.

2. The Grand Camp, or umbrella organization, was in Ketchikan on a permanent basis. Each major village in southeast Alaska had its own designation as a

"camp" and held representation within the Grand Camp. For the standard review of the organizations, see Philip Drucker, *The Native Brotherhoods: Modern Intertribal Organizations on the Northwest Coast,* Smithsonian Institution Bureau of American Ethnology Bulletin 168 (Washington, D.C.: Government Printing Office, 1958).

3. At the risk of oversimplifying categories, I have used the term Asian American in this paper to indicate any person of Chinese, Japanese, or Filipino ancestry, immigrant or American-born. For a more detailed analysis of their activities in the industry, see Chris Friday, *Organizing Asian American Labor: The Pacific Coast Canned-Salmon Industry, 1870–1942* (Philadelphia: Temple University Press, 1994).

4. For a discussion of this issue see Fidalgo Island Packing Company to Seid G. Back, Mar. 9, 1933, Fidalgo Island Packing Company Records.

5. William L. Paul to Frank Desmond, January 16, 1938, 1938 file, box 1, William L. Paul Papers, accession no. 1885-5, Manuscripts Division, University of Washington Libraries, Seattle, Washington. Hereafter cited as Paul Papers.

6. United Cannery, Agricultural, Packinghouse, and Allied Workers of America (UCAPAWA) locals, affiliated with the CIO, won a National Labor Relations Board Certification Election in May 1938, which awarded locals in San Francisco, Portland, and Seattle the right to represent outside workers who were largely the same Asian American crews that had formerly worked in the industry under co-ethnic labor contractors. For more information on the CIO locals, see Friday, *Organizing Asian American Labor.* For information regarding the AFL locals, see *Ketchikan Daily News,* July 16, 1946, Paul Papers.

7. Patricia Nelson Limerick, *Legacy of Conquest: The Unbroken Past of the American West* (New York: W. W. Norton, 1987), argues that the West's multiculturalism was one of its defining features as people competed in the region for control of profits and property. Richard White, "Race Relations in the American West," *American Quarterly* 38, no. 3 (1986): 396–416, has argued that the West's race relations have been distinctive because of the diversity of the peoples, the territorial claim certain groups have to lands, the international components of race relations in the manner in which various groups can be associated with or draw upon foreign governments, the racial stratification of wage labor in the region, and the consistent presence of the federal government as a "regulator of racial relations." While some debate the exceptionalism of the West's racial diversity and the notion of regional exceptionalism itself (for example, see the thoughtful but brief essay by Nancy Shoemaker, "Regions as Categories of Analysis," *Perspectives* 34, no. 8 [1996]: 7–8, 10), I argue in "'In Due Time': Engaging the Narratives of Race and Place in the Twentieth-Century American West," in *Race and Racism: Toward the 21st Century,* ed. Paul Wong et al. (Boulder, Colo.: Westview Press, forthcoming), that while the West was not particularly different in its diversity, it did have a different narrative about its racial composition that allowed for a more graded and contested racial hierarchy than other regions.

8. The historiography on Populism is immense as is Populism's influence on western politics. I have been most influenced in my thinking about the weakness of party politics and the role of "populist" or grassroots organizing by Paul Kleppner, "Politics without Parties: The Western States, 1900–1984," in *The Twentieth-Century West: Historical Interpretations,* ed. Gerald D. Nash and Richard W. Etulain (Albuquerque: University of New Mexico Press, 1989), 295–338; and Michael Kazin,

"The Grass-Roots Right: New Histories of U.S. Conservatism in the Twentieth Century," *American Historical Review* 97, no. 1 (1992): 136–155.

9. Others have noted the role of individuals in rural communities as important factors in the maintenance of far-flung networks of associations among Asian Americans. For examples, see Sucheng Chan, *This Bittersweet Soil: The Chinese in California Agriculture* (Los Angeles and Berkeley: University of California Press, 1986); and Gail Nomura, "Interpreting Historical Evidence," in *Frontiers of Asian American Studies,* ed. Gail Nomura et al. (Pullman, Wash.: Washington State University Press, 1989), 1–5.

Sarah Deutsch, *No Separate Refuge: Culture, Class, and Gender on an Anglo-Hispanic Frontier in the American Southwest, 1880–1940* (New York: Oxford University Press, 1987), 9–12, discusses how kith and kin ties to those residents assisted in gaining employment. In many respects their community of association was like the "regional community" that Deutsch has described among Chicanos and Chicanas in the Southwest between 1880 and 1940. Gunther W. Peck, "Mobilizing Ethnicity: Immigrant Diasporas in the Intermountain West, 1900–1920," paper presented at the Power and Place in the North American West Symposium, Seattle, Washington, November 5, 1994, does much the same for Greeks in the Utah mining districts, but pays special attention to the manner in which class and ethnicity interact given specific historical and contextual circumstances. I have explored these ideas, too, relative to Asian Americans in "The West as East: The Crossroads of Asian Immigrant and Asian American History and the U.S. West," paper presented at the Center for the American West, University of New Mexico, Albuquerque, January 29, 1993.

10. Nora Marks Dauenhauer and Richard Dauenhauer, eds., *Haa Kusteeyi, Our Culture: Tlingit Life Stories* (Seattle: University of Washington, and Juneau: Sealaska Heritage Foundation, 1994), 275, note that during the 1930s and 1940s many Filipino men married Tlingit women.

11. For far too long, scholars have relegated Native American labor to the corners of their studies. For a strong critique of this tendency, see Martha C. Knack and Alice Littlefield, "Native American Labor: Retrieving History, Rethinking Theory," in *Native Americans and Wage Labor: Ethnohistorical Perspectives,* ed. Alice Littlefield and Martha C. Knack (Norman: University of Oklahoma Press, 1996), 3–44, as well as the other essays in the volume.

12. Victoria Wyatt, "Alaskan Indian Wage Earners in the 19th Century: Economic Choices and Ethnic Identity on Southeast Alaska's Frontier," *Pacific Northwest Quarterly* 78, nos. 1–2 (1987): 43–50; and Dauenhauer and Dauenhauer, *Our Culture,* 135, 152–155, 272, 395, 435.

13. Daniel Boxberger, *To Fish in Common: The Ethnohistory of Lummi Salmon Fishing* (Lincoln: University of Nebraska Press, 1989).

14. For examples, see Kenneth D. Tollefson, "From Localized Clans to Regional Corporation," *The Western Canadian Journal of Anthropology* 8, no. 1 (1978): 1–20; and Laura Frances Klein, "Tlingit Women and Town Politics," Ph.D. diss., New York University, 1975. Stephen Haycox, "William Lewis Paul," in *Our Culture,* ed. Dauenhauer and Dauenhauer, esp. 506–520, provides a good, succinct overview of ANB activities.

15. Claus-M. Naske, "Alaska's Long and Sometimes Painful Relationship with

the Lower Forty-eight," in *The Changing Pacific Northwest: Interpreting its Past,* ed. David H. Stratton and George A. Frykman (Pullman, Wash.: Washington State University Press, 1988), 55–76. For a discussion of the creation of whiteness in general, see David A. Roediger, *The Wages of Whiteness: Race and the Making of the American Working Class* (London: Verso Press, 1991); and Alexander P. Saxton, *The Rise and Fall of the White Republic: Class, Politics, and Mass Culture in Nineteenth-Century America* (London: Verso Press, 1990). These authors point to the need to examine such notions on a regional scale and though Carlos A. Schwantes, "Protest in a Promised Land: Unemployment, Disinheritance, and the Origin of Labor Militancy in the Pacific Northwest, 1885–1886," *Western Historical Quarterly* 13 (1982): 373–390, comes the closest to this, he does not squarely address the issue. I have examined the subject in "Asian American Labor and Historical Interpretation," *Labor History* 35 (1994): 524–546.

16. The best discussion of ANB activities is in Haycox, "William Lewis Paul," but even that essay points to the need to determine more about the ANB and ANS activities as a bargaining agent.

17. Dauenhauer and Dauenhauer, *Our Culture,* 76–88; Haycox, "William Lewis Paul," in ibid., esp. 503–504; and Drucker, *Native Brotherhoods,* 16–40.

18. *The Alaska Fisherman,* July 1930, p. 1. The sporadic issues of *The Alaska Fisherman* between 1928 and 1931 available in the Paul Papers carry the phrase "Our Platform: Alaska for Alaskans" in the paper's masthead.

19. Kenneth R. Philp, "The New Deal and Alaskan Natives, 1936–1945," *Pacific Historical Review* 50, no. 3 (1981): 309–327.

20. *Alaska Native Brotherhood,* November 25, 1938, Paul Papers.

21. William L. Paul to Frank Desmond, January 16, 1938; William L. Paul, Jr., to Charles A. Wheeler, July 13, 1942, Paul Papers. The ANB and ANS had separate, autonomous "camps" at each settlement in southeast Alaska. These, in turn, were united in the organization under the Grand Camp in Ketchikan. In this present study, I have only been able to investigate the activities of the Grand Camp in any detail. A camp-by-camp analysis is still pending. Nonetheless, there are hints that significant tensions existed within and between the camps and that some of these manifest themselves in the struggles among the ANB-ANS camps, CIO locals, and AFL branches. The records of the ANB-ANS in general, though, do indicate some of the key features of the situation.

22. See Dauenhauer and Dauenhauer, *Our Culture,* 311–313, for a brief biography of Frank G. Johnson. The fishermen organized as Alaska Salmon Purse Seiners Union (ASPSU) and the women as the Cannery Workers Auxiliary Union (CWAU). The latter was tightly affiliated with the former.

23. *Alaska Fishing News,* April 15, 1940, p. 6.

24. Ibid. This forceful statement is rather surprising given that Louis Paul is generally regarded by those who knew him as a more diplomatic person than his brother William. A Tlingit contemporary of the Pauls, Judson Brown, recalled that Louis was "inspiring" and "for the people" while William "would get side-tracked arguing with people." See Dauenhauer and Dauenhauer, *Our Culture,* 146. Haycox, "William Lewis Paul," 503–524, also notes that William Paul's style was rather abrasive at times.

25. William L. Paul to [?], n.d., Paul Papers.

26. Paul to Desmond, January 16, 1938, Paul Papers.

27. *Alaska Fishing News,* June 26, 1942, p. 6.

28. Susan H. Koester and Emma Widmark, "'By the Words of the Mouth Let Thee Be Judged': The Alaska Native Sisterhood Speaks," *Journal of the West* 27, no. 2 (1988): 36.

29. Ibid., 38.

30. *Alaska Fishing News,* November 27, 1939, p. 6.

31. For men's and women's roles, see Klein, "Tlingit Women."

32. [CIO] *Local 7 News,* March 1945, p. 4.

33. Dauenhauer and Dauenhauer, *Our Culture,* 272. The biographies of nearly every Tlingit woman in *Our Culture* confirm this mixed subsistence pattern.

34. Friday, *Organizing Asian American Labor,* 88–89.

35. *Alaska Fishing News,* November 29, 1943, p. 3.

36. Dauenhauer and Dauenhauer, *Our Culture,* 538; and Koester and Widmark, "Alaska Native Sisterhood."

37. Frederica de Laguna to Chris Friday, January 31, 1995, in possession of author; and Dauenhauer and Dauenhauer, *Our Culture,* 76, 265.

38. *Alaska Fishing News, Harvest Edition,* September 1939, sect. 3, p. 8; *Alaska Fishing News,* July 12, 1939, p. 3; May 6, 1940, p. 3; May 27, 1940, p. 3.

39. *Alaska Fishing News,* March 27, 1940, p. 7.

40. Ibid., March 25, 1940, p. 7.

41. Ibid., July 17, 1939, p. 2.

42. Ibid., July 12, 1939, p. 5.

43. *Alaska Fishing News, Harvest Edition,* September 1939, sect. 3, p. 8. These were the very sites of many strong ANB/ANS camps. Metlakatlah, though, had a history of independent action and the CIO local in Ketchikan wielded more power than the CWAU there. U.S. Bureau of Fisheries, *Alaska Fishery and Fur-Seal Industries* (Washington, D.C.: Government Printing Office, 1940), 143, lists 4,436 "native" and "white" "shoresmen" in southeast Alaska. These figures include European American engineers, machinists, radio operators, trapmen, and other skilled and semi-skilled cannery workers, some of whom shipped up from San Francisco, Portland, and Seattle. The estimate of 4,500 should only be taken as a rough figure.

44. *Alaska Fishing News,* June 5, 1939, p. 4; July 19, 1939, p. 1.

45. Minutes, Wrangell Alaska Native Brotherhood Grand Camp Convention, November 12, 1946, 3–5, William L. Paul Microfilm, roll 2, accession no. 2076–2, Manuscripts Division, University of Washington Libraries.

46. Salvador Del Fierro, Sr., interview, Washington State Oral/Aural History Project, 1974–1977, microfiche accession no. FIL-KING 75-29ck.

47. Vicki Ruiz, *Cannery Women, Cannery Lives: Mexican Women, Unionization, and the California Food Processing Industry, 1930–1950* (Albuquerque: University of New Mexico Press, 1987) argues that women's shared work experiences assisted in the formation and maintenance of unions. Patricia Zavella, *Women's Work and Chicano Families: Cannery Workers of the Santa Clara Valley* (Ithaca, N.Y.: Cornell University Press, 1987), though, demonstrates how work cultures in the same industry eventually fragmented the workforce and worked against union concerns.

In *Organizing Asian American Labor,* I have dealt with women's work cultures in the canned-salmon industry to some extent. For primary materials, see the interviews of women in the Skagit County Oral History Preservation Project at the Skagit County Historical Museum in LaConner, Washington.

48. The *Alaska Fishing News* carried regular stories of Filipino events in Ketchikan, usually with a list of participants. Those names closely correspond to the roster of Local 237 officers in the same paper. For example, see *Alaska Fishing News,* July 29, 1942, p. 4; and August 23, 1942, p. 8.

49. *Voice of the Federation,* March 20, 1937, p. 7; April 22, 1937, p. 8; November 1937, p. 2; January 19, 1939, p. 3.

50. Ibid., January 19, 1939, p. 3.

51. Ibid., July 7, 1938, p. 6.

52. Ibid., January 19, 1939, p. 3; February 2, 1939, p. 1.

53. Ibid., March 2, 1939, p. 6.

54. Ibid., June 29, 1939, p. 3.

55. Ibid., December 22, 1938, p. 3.

56. Ibid., July 7, 1939, p. 5; and August 17, 1939, p. 3.

57. *Alaska Fishing News,* October 29, 1943, p. 3; Friday, *Organizing Asian American Labor,* 187–190; and Dauenhauer and Dauenhauer, *Our Culture,* 434.

58. *Alaska Fishing News,* October 29, 1943, p. 3.

59. The origins of the Tlingit and Haida Central Council are unclear. Dauenhauer and Dauenhauer, *Our Culture,* 97, indicate that its formation came purely from pursuit of the land claims. Yet in their biography of Tlingit Jimmy George, Dauenhauer and Dauenhauer hold that Undersecretary of the Interior John Carver insisted that the ANB was too heterogeneous and "suggested that they [sic] form a political organization more limited in ethnicity. From this concept developed the Central Council of the Tlingit and Haida" (202). Haycox, "William Lewis Paul," in *Our Culture,* 517, argues that the Tlingit and Haida Central Council was created separately from the ANB in part to reduce the influence that Paul might have over the land claims cases. Indeed, in Paul's arguments before the U.S. Supreme Court in *Tee-Hit-Ton v. U.S.* (1959), he held that there was no basis for an entity such as the Tlingit and Haida Central Council and that individual camps, on the order of the ANB camps, should be allowed to file separately for their land claims. Paul's simultaneous moves to ensconce the ANB/ANS as a bargaining unit and his activities in land claims appear to be linked to his efforts at a comeback after a loss of status when in 1937 he was disbarred in Alaska on charges of defrauding his legal clients. In this context, the ANB/ANS bargaining agency might appear as a short-term measure to gain a position and the land claims as an effort to secure long-term status. For Haycox's discussion of the disbarring and the Supreme Court case, see "William Lewis Paul," in *Our Culture,* 516–519. I am grateful to Stephen Haycox for freely discussing this material with me on several occasions in 1994.

60. *Washington State CIO Labor News,* March 1944, pp. 1, 3.

61. Rose Dellama, interview by Vicki Ruiz, August 22, 1980, interview notes courtesy of Vicki Ruiz; and *UCAPAWA News,* April 15, 1944, p. 4.

62. Dellama interview.

63. Ibid.; Dauenhauer and Dauenhauer, *Our Culture,* 533.

64. *UCAPAWA News,* May 15, 1944, p. 4; *Alaska Fishing News,* March 3, 1941, p. 6; and Dauenhauer and Dauenhauer, *Our Culture,* pp. 265, 315.

65. *UCAPAWA News,* May 1, 1944, p. 3. Koester and Widmark, "Alaska Native Sisterhood," also discuss Hayes's and Wanamaker's activities in the ANS.

66. The CIO locals also supported resident Alaskans and Native Alaskans in claims of discrimination on the part of canneries and federal contractors. See *UCAPAWA News,* May 15, 1944, p. 4; July 1, 1944, p. 7.

67. Dellama interview.

68. Ibid. The biographies of Hoonah residents in Dauenhauer and Dauenhauer, *Our Culture,* 155, 318, reveal the cultural havoc the fire wrought but do not indicate the origins of the blaze.

69. Dellama interview.

70. Russell R. Miller to Essie G. Hanson, August 7, 1945, case 19-R-1268, box 5305, National Labor Relations Board, Record Group 25 (hereafter cited as NLRB, RG 25), National Archives and Records Administration, Suitland, Maryland. Minutes, ANB Grand Camp Convention, November 12, 1945, p. 4, roll 1, Paul Microfilm, confirm these figures and NLRB activities.

71. Oscar S. Smith to Thomas P. Graham, August 27, 1945, case 19-R-1268, box 5305, NLRB, RG 25; William L. Paul, Jr., to Russell Miller, August 14, 1945, ibid.; and Conrad Espe to Thomas P. Graham, Jr., n.d., ibid. By this point UCAPAWA had disintegrated and reformed as the Food, Tobacco and Allied Workers Union.

72. Minutes, ANB Grand Camp Convention, November 13, 1945, p. 11, roll 1, Paul Microfilm.

73. Minutes, ANB Grand Camp Convention, Resolution no. 28, roll 1, Paul Microfilm; Miscellaneous notes on 1945 convention, 3 pp., Paul Papers.

74. Paul M. Herzog and John M. Houston, Second Supplemental Decision and Direction, case 19-R-1268, December 13, 1946, case 19-R-1268, box 5305, NLRB, RG 25; and Wendell B. Phillips, Jr., to NLRB, January 6, 1947, ibid.

75. Leslie H. Grove to NLRB, January 30, 1947, case 19-R-1268, Alaska Salmon Industry Inc., folder 2, box 5306, NLRB, RG 25; and NLRB to Grove, January 31, 1947, ibid.

76. Harry Lundeberg to Paul Herzog, March 21, 1947, case 19-R-1268, folder 2, box 5306, NLRB, RG 25.

77. I have explored this question in "The Marine Cooks and Stewards Union on a Narrowing Path: Race, Gender, Work, and Politics in the Cold War Epoch," prepared as a paper for the 1996 Organization of American Historians Annual Meeting and expanded as a public lecture for the Northwest Center for Comparative American Cultures and Race Relations, Rockefeller Humanities Lecture Series, Pullman, Washington, April 1996. Sailors' unions on the West Coast had, since the nineteenth century, been a driving anti-Asian force. When the Chinese Exclusion Act barred immigration to U.S. territories, it did nothing to prevent Chinese from sailing on American vessels, nor ships of other nations, and landing in U.S. ports. The Sailors Union of the Pacific led the way in trying to push Chinese off the ships and then extended its program in the twentieth century to include Japanese, Filipinos, and East Indians. As a result, while onshore unions tended to drop anti-Asian programs as soon as exclusionary legislation became permanent for a given group, the

Sailors Union of the Pacific and its parent organization, the Seafarers International Union, remained actively and virulently anti-Asian. I have dealt with this topic in "A Dialogue about Race and Ethnicity in the Twentieth Century: From a Multi-Racial to a Black-and-White Perspective," Rockefeller Program in Comparative American Cultures and Race Relations, Washington State University, November 1995. Both these papers form portions of chapters in my work-in-progress on race, Pacific maritime labor, and the Marine Cooks and Stewards Union.

78. Clara M. Martin, Order Denying Motion, April 1, 1947, case 19-R-1268, folder 2, box 5306, NLRB, RG 25.

79. William Lewis Paul, "For the Good of the Order," June 22, 1949, p. 6, roll 1, Paul Microfilm; and *Ketchikan Daily News,* July 16, 1946, clipping, Paul Papers.

80. *FTA News,* December 1948, p. 3. See also Arleen De Vera, "Without Parallel: The Local 7 Deportation Cases, 1949–1955," *Amerasia Journal* 20, no. 2 (1994): 1–25.

81. *Alaska Fishing News,* September 18, 1944, p. 1, and stories in subsequent weeks and months, illustrate the intensity with which the ANB and ANS pursued their efforts to regain portions of their aboriginal land base.

82. For selective discussions, see Friday, *Organizing Asian American Labor;* and Steve Rosswurm, ed., *The CIO's Left-Led Unions* (New Brunswick, N.J.: Rutgers University Press, 1992).

83. Labor historians, in particular, have been rather romantic about the CIO's racial record and have gone to great lengths to vilify the AFL. For a critique of that romanticism, see Herbert Hill, "The Problem of Race in American Labor History," *Reviews in American History* 24, no. 2 (1996): 189–208. Hill's major criticism is that labor historians have made class a primary and immutable category of analysis, thereby relegating questions of race to ideological and transitory realms. In his own way, however, Hill has essentialized race in a fashion not dissimilar from those he criticizes. For an attempt to develop a "middle ground" between the two analyses, see Marshall F. Stevenson, "'It Will Take More than Official Pronouncement': The American Federation of Labor and the Black Worker, 1935–1955, a Reconsideration," paper presented at the 1996 Annual Association for the Study of Afro-American Life and History, Charleston, South Carolina, September 13–15.

84. Kevin Allen Leonard, "Years of Hope, Days of Fear: The Impact of World War II on Race Relations in Los Angeles," Ph.D. diss., University of California, Davis, 1992, esp. 276 ff.

85. I use the term "racialized" to suggest a process influenced by unequal power relations based on the creation and application of "otherness." It is always a shifting and contested construction and is therefore not as static as the notion of "race." I use it, too, instead of the more amorphous "racial/ethnic" because it better captures the power relationships inherent in the exercise of "race" in a stark contrast to "ethnicity." The former is frequently a tool of oppression, the latter a signifier of the assertion of an "identity," though that, too, comes with its own privileging, its own oppressive tendencies.

86. I address this issue in much greater depth and length in "'In Due Time.'" It is important to note that the binary rhetoric of race in the "North" and the "South" has obscured those regions' own multiracial and multiethnic pasts in particularly

distorting and damaging ways. Only in the contemporary setting have the popular and scholarly images of those regions begun to change.

87. Michael Omi and Howard Winant, *Racial Formations in the United States from the 1960s to the 1980s,* 2nd ed. (New York: Routledge, 1991), 87.

88. By this I mean the type of frontier described by Peggy Pascoe, "Western Women at the Cultural Crossroads," in *Trails: Toward a New Western History,* ed. Patricia Nelson Limerick, Clyde A. Milner II, and Charles E. Rankin (Lawrence: University Press of Kansas, 1991), 40–58; and Limerick, *Legacy of Conquest.*

89. Among the strongest statements of this position are Virginia Scharff, "Getting Out: What Does Mobility Mean for Women?" and Kerwin Lee Klein, "Reclaiming the 'F' Word: or, Being and Becoming Postwestern," papers presented as part of the "American Dreams, Western Images" program at the William Andrews Clark Memorial Library, 1993–94.

18

PERCEIVING, EXPERIENCING, AND EXPRESSING THE SACRED

An Indigenous Southern Californian View

LOUISE V. JEFFREDO-WARDEN

As an indigenous southern Californian I have been asked to convey to you, in the next twenty minutes or so, something of my feelings for the sacred. What this means to me is that I will also be conveying to you something of my peoples' interactions with, and membership within, the natural world.[1]

I would like to begin by discussing the actions of one of my antecedents, a young Shoshonean woman named Toypurina who on the evening of October 25, 1785, led a revolt against the priests and soldiers of Misión San Gabriel Arcángel.

Attest my elders: at that time, the mission was in a state of fluctuation and vulnerable to attack. Its oldest structures (established in 1771) were located at the outskirts of what is now Montebello. To some extent supervision of this site was maintained (structures of the mission were damaged or washed out by floodings along a segment of the San Gabriel River, but economic activities continued there) while its newest structures, located at the present-day site of the San Gabriel Mission, were still under construction (in 1774–75, the Spaniards moved their mission to what is now the city of San Gabriel, but construction on some of the principal structures there did not begin until 1790).[2]

It would take much more time than I have here today to tell you what we know of Toypurina's life and this event.[3] I will just summarize by saying that Toypurina, sister to a hereditary chief, was viewed by the Interior "Gabrielinos" as the wisest member of an elite stratum of persons known for their knowledge, power, and extraordinary intellectual and spiritual abilities.[4] Though only twenty-four years of age at the time, Toypurina, with the assistance of ex-neophyte Nicolas José, organized an attack on Mission San Gabriel in which several lineages and villages of indigenous southern Californians participated. In so doing, Toypurina earned the distinction of becoming the only Native American woman in the colonial records of Alta California said to have led a revolt against the Spanish mission system.[5]

By all accounts, Toypurina's actions in this event have been described as unsuccessful because she and her associates did not succeed in overthrowing the mission; nor did she manage, even, to escape capture by the Spaniards (she and ten others were seized on the night of the attack).[6]

Yet historical sources (both written and verbal) relate that Toypurina was an extremely intelligent and gifted individual—one surely capable of deducing the risks (cannons and muskets, for one) involved in attempting to overthrow the mission.[7] Toypurina was also an individual with great personal power and social distinction.[8] What this means to those of us with knowledge regarding particular roles and statuses in traditional Shoshonean societies is that Toypurina likely had social, moral, and religious obligations that far outweighed those of the common individual of her time—or of our time, for that matter.

Let me ask you, each one of you: Would you risk your life for an oak flat or river?

In January of 1786, Toypurina essentially stated during an interrogation for her supposed crimes that she had done as much, having fought for her traditional homeland. When asked, under the very real threat of torture,[9] why she had organized a revolt against the Spaniards, Toypurina replied "... for I hate the padres and all of you, for living here on my native soil ... for trespassing upon the land of my forefathers and despoiling our tribal domains."[10]

Perhaps I should not attempt to envision Toypurina's beliefs surrounding the chances of her revolt succeeding, but I do—each and every time I visit the locales she sought to protect. And just as I was told, I tell my daughter: I do not think Toypurina actually believed she could win this battle, one of many waged against the mission since its establishment. Rather, I believe—as perhaps other Native Southern Californians with a knowledge of their traditional religions would—that Toypurina perceived this battle to be one for which she had an inescapable spiritual and moral responsibility to undertake. Indeed, even after her capture and interrogation Toypurina continued to fight to the best of her ability, enduring solitary confinement until she was baptized in 1787 and forever exiled by the Spanish from her homeland, probably in the year 1788.[11]

I have summarized these features of Toypurina's story—long preserved through the folklore of indigenous and Spanish descendants alike—because I feel Toypurina's actions speak volumes regarding our views of the sacred, of the relationship, traditionally, that indigenous southern Californians had, and to some extent still have, with the natural environment.[12] I have also related portions of Toypurina's story to emphasize the fact that for hundreds of years now, Interior and Island "Gabrielino" peoples have been decrying and battling ecological destruction at the hands of invaders to our traditional homelands, on the offshore islands now called Santa Barbara, San Nicolas, Santa Catalina, and San Clemente, and in the regions presently contained in what are now called Los Angeles, Orange, and (parts of) San Bernardino and Riverside counties.[13]

I spent the first eight years of my life in Montebello, being raised but a hop and a skip from the original site of the San Gabriel Mission, next door to an adobe that had once belonged to my great-great-grandfather, Don Juan Matias Sanchez. The former rancho where this adobe (now a museum) is located was called La Merced, and a good portion of the Río Hondo (a tributary of the Los Angeles River, the provider for life in the region) flowed through it.

I played in that river's wash—what was left of it—when I was a child. Sometimes, my father would try to tell me how much the river had changed since he was a child and had played there, too. But the pain engendered in my father by those discussions seemed so great that I understood, even then, when his voice trailed off and he dropped the subject altogether.

The subject of the River. The subject of the Sacred.

There is a seriousness and power in talking publicly about this subject, about our relationship with the natural world, that generally overwhelms me. *How* can I possibly explain to you something my own elders, my own father, could not explain to me?

When I was a child, I don't think a day passed that my father did not admonish me to feel, to become aware of, my nativeness. That blood in me, he would constantly remind, was special. Like many other indigenous persons, he believed that with it would come a certain sensitivity and sensibility, the very thing that, despite my lightness, would distinguish me from the majority; would empower me in ways I would grow to recognize. So many times was I to hear this that, one day impatient for this knowledge, I put my father to the test. "So *explain* to me what's so special about being Indian," I insisted. "Teach me, tell me, all the great things *you've* learned from your Indianness!"

I watched my father search himself. Seriously, and I think with a little sadness at my ignorance, he looked at me, just quietly looked at me. When he did decide to speak he said, "I can't explain it to you, Louise. It's not something anyone can explain. One day you'll feel it; one day you'll understand." Pointing to the southern California soil beneath our feet, he again reminded me, "It's just good to know this is *home,* and has been so for thousands of years."

By this time my immediate family had moved to a very rural area of north San Diego County, to the outskirts of Fallbrook (located within the traditional territory of some of my grandmother's ancestors, the "Luiseños"). I had trouble acclimating myself to Fallbrook, so different was life there from my days in Montebello. But at the age of fourteen or so, I stopped to look out over a small ravine that forever changed me. It was a place that, over the years, I had passed practically every day.

When I was small—and against the wishes of my parents—I liked to play there, exploring the intricate coyote trails, looking to spy wood rats high in the trees rimming the creek's edge, listening carefully for snakes. There, while admiring the soft hues and pungent aromas of the pale summer brush, while playfully tracing Coyote's distant trails with my finger, I was suddenly stopped by the question: "Who, before me, also stood here to contemplate this place?"

That must have been the jackpot question, the one the First Ones found acceptable before revealing themselves to me, for that connectedness my father so often spoke of, that power *in being and in being one home in one's homeland,* suddenly rushed my senses. Now my grandmothers and grandfathers were all about me, I could feel them all about me—in the sand, in the brush, in the rocks among the brush. Now there was not only beauty, but sheer, overwhelming *sense* in that ravine—in all its components, both physical and spiritual. The ravine, as well as my place within it and within this world, I was beginning to understand. But the beginning to that understanding did not come without my first achieving a greater recognition of and appreciation for the subtleties in the every day, in the environment of my every day.

There is a Native Southern Californian story, which I think appropriate to tell here, about Coyote's flagrant immaturity and egoistic belief that he was the most superior of beings—just the handsomest, strongest, cleverest, fleetest of all:

> Coyote liked to hound River for a race, so much so that River finally gave in one day. "Okay," she said, "We'll race." So Coyote took off and he ran, and he ran, and he ran, and he ran until he couldn't run any more, and he stumbled and he stopped and he fell. And when he turned to look at River, he saw that she was still running.[14]

So you see, Coyote didn't understand his place in relation to everyone and everything else. He learned that, no matter how hard you run that race, you can't beat the natural order. There's just no getting around fundamental ecological principles.

Although this is a Gabrielino story in origin, I believe its sentiments are such that it could have originated among any one of the Native Southern Californian nations: Chumash, Island "Gabrielino," Juaneño, Luiseño, Cupeño, Diegueño, or Cahuilla, to name but a few.

Understanding one's place in relation to the physical and spiritual world of which we are a part necessarily entails understanding the interconnectedness of *all* beings, of *all* life and matter, inanimate and animate. It entails nurturing a holistic way of thinking about and seeing this world, a way in which seemingly unrelated factors and relationships are effectively brought together in experience and thought.[15]

This way of experiencing, thinking and seeing our world is, of course, well evidenced in indigenous southern Californian religious traditions. In particular, Luiseño songs contain metaphoric elements which have been referred to as "ceremonial couplings." A ceremonial coupling is a pair of words that, when spoken or sung together, evoke or reference particular reciprocal relationships, often ecological or co-evolutionary in nature. For example, the cyclic coupling *Ṡuukat Kwiila*—the Luiseño words for deer and Black Oak acorn—at once symbolizes our spiritual and material relationship to these First Ones (for both deer and acorn were favored, principal foods for us), as well as *Ṡuukat*'s relationship to *Kwiila* (for acorn is also a favored food of deer). Like the elements of any ecosystem, the words of a coupling are viewed as inseparably interconnected; they therefore cannot, appropriately, be sung apart. As the late Luiseño elder Villiana C. Hyde often explained to me, to separate a coupling means "you're not making *sense.*"

That underlying sense I believe our elders often refer to—and that I have briefly addressed beginning to discover in my own story about the ravine—is also evidenced in the everyday topics and organization of our discourse. I am thinking about how my elders generally refrain from telling about their lives in a linear or sequential fashion, and often relate incidents back to back that may not initially seem to share a relatedness. But I have learned to contemplate such story pairings in much the same way as I have the ceremonial couplings in our songs: as metaphoric avenues through which our elders articulate, teach, and reinforce the balance and cyclical interrelationship in power and being, in elements—aged and young, human and non-human, female and male, spiritual and material—of this world.

Each time I hear my elders' stories, I find new lessons in them. That is because the poetry of our elders, when taken to heart, when planted and nourished within, grows. In the myriad circumstances of our lives, new meanings and understandings continually branch and blossom. There are times when these branches are sharp, startling lessons, and there are times when these branches meander a while before making their point, or their connections to other branches, known to us.

Yet in the indigenous southern Californian community, we do not learn from our human antecedents alone. We learn, as well, from those who came before us all, from the First People: the insects, animals, mountains, hills, valleys, rocks, minerals, plants, trees, sands, soils, and waters. When our behavior is improper, greedy, or destructive, the First Ones teach us, ultimately, by not assisting us in our efforts to meet our needs: by decreasing the short- and long-term resources available to us all.

Long before Europeans had a scientific inkling regarding the beginnings of human life on this earth, my ancestors knew we were not the first to inhabit this planet. Given that they often referred to mountains and other geological formations produced over thousands and thousands of years as their ancestors or elders, my ancestors probably also had an accurate feeling for the relatively short time, in comparison to many other entities, human beings have inhabited this earth.

Only in this century has the dominant Western world begun to investigate what our oral traditions attest my ancestors, thousands of years ago, had a complex understanding of: the ultimate relatedness of all life on earth, and the indissoluble energy continually creating, constituting, and flowing through the universe, all life, and all systems of life support.

More than two centuries have passed since Toypurina confronted the Spanish for torturing her relatives—the *land* and *all* of its inhabitants, including her people. I hope when you consider the life choices that she made, you will bear in mind that many of the species and ecosystems she fought to protect are either gone or gravely threatened today.

Although "California is home to more plant and animal species than any other state," writes Sally Smith, it is also "the epicenter of extinction in the continental United States, with more than twice the number of federally listed endangered species as any other western state."[16] And as Tim Palmer has noted: "It seems that the plunder of almost everything in California's natural world is up in the 80 percent or 90 percent bracket: Pacific Flyway wetlands, 96 percent gone; native grasslands, 99 percent gone; wilderness, 80 percent gone; riparian woodlands, 89 percent gone; salmon and steelhead, 90 percent to 100 percent gone; valley oaks, 98 percent gone; and all major rivers but one dammed at least once."[17]

You have asked me to speak about my feelings for the sacred. In return, I urge each one of you to consider these statistics, and to ask yourself: Will the majority of Americans continue to crazily run, as did Coyote against River, or will they heed the lessons of our elders, the lessons of the First Ones? Will they collectively catch their breath long enough to start making *sense*?

Notes

1. The terms "Gabrielino" and "Luiseño," although currently employed by the federal government to specify my Native Californian descent, are monikers of the Spanish mission era. I prefer to describe and think about a portion of my indigenous

ethnicity using a Luiseño term, *Payomkawish.* The term, translatable as "Westerner," was originally employed in Luiseño territory to describe an individual residing in proximity to the coast. Both my grandmother, a Maritime Shoshone/Luiseño, and my late grandfather, a Maritime Shoshone, descend from island and coastal peoples. However, it is through my grandmother's (inland) Luiseño lineage that I am a member of the Temecula Band of Luiseños (Pechanga Reservation, Riverside County, California). My grandfather's nation (Maritime Shoshone, or, Island Gabrielino) was not granted a reservation land base, but was declared "extinct" by the federal government. For more information on the Gabrielinos and Luiseños, see Alfred L. Kroeber, *Handbook of the Indians of California* (Washington, D.C.: U.S. Government Printing Office, 1925); and Bernice E. Johnston, *California's Gabrielino Indians* (Los Angeles: Southwest Museum, 1962).

2. The construction of the present church, for example, took many years to complete and probably did not begin until 1790. Johnston, p. 129.

3. For more detailed information, see Thomas Workman Temple II, "Toypurina the Witch and the Indian Uprising at San Gabriel," *Masterkey* 32, no. 5 (1958): 136–54. Though I do not recommend this essay as unbiased or inoffensive reading (it is incredibly Euro-centered), it was authored by an individual of English and Spanish descent (in fact a relation of my Spanish great-grandmother) who, like myself, spent his youth at the original site of Mission San Gabriel (La Misión Vieja), and was informed by his family's folklore of the region. The stories he heard about Toypurina as a child made him determined to learn more about her, and to remember her in his research and writing. The essay's chronology of events runs closely to the folklore I heard as a child, from both my European and Native Californian elders.

4. Temple, who translated from the Spanish the principal documents associated with this revolt, states Toypurina was "reputed and feared as the wisest sorceress among the Gabrielinos." Ibid., p. 147. (In the Luiseño language, one term for such a wise and spiritually gifted individual is *puula.*)

5. Ibid., p. 136. Not that other native women in southern California did not lead protests or revolts against the Spanish colonial order (there are many strong, successful women leaders in our pasts and presents as native peoples), but that its imposers apparently felt Toypurina's power and her actions to be particularly threatening, not historically erasable.

6. Ibid., pp. 139, 141. It is also stated elsewhere (Hubert Howe Bancroft, *The Works of Hubert Howe Bancroft, Volume XVIII, History of California, Vol. I, 1542–1800* [San Francisco: A. L. Bancroft and Company, 1884], p. 460) that twenty prisoners were seized.

7. Temple, pp. 147–48; see also note 8, below. Toypurina probably also had knowledge of the fates of others leading attacks against the priests and soldiers of Mission San Gabriel. In fact, it was only within days of its establishment—when the Spanish, victorious in a first revolt, decapitated a local chief and drove his head onto a stake of the newly constructed willow stockade—that the kinds of consequences the people could expect to incur by revolting against their hideous acts (in this case, the mission's soldiers had lassoed and raped the dead chief's wife) were made horrifically clear. Johnston, p. 130.

8. In Toypurina's person, two traditions of leadership met and overlapped: that

of the hereditary chief (as was customary among the "Gabrielino" peoples, Toypurina stood in a position to inherit this role of village leadership from her brother); and that of the intellectually and spiritually elite of her people, among whom she held the most prominent and powerful role.

9. The threat of flogging and other forms of torture is repeatedly expressed by Temple, pp. 141, 143, 144, and 146. Moreover, many of Toypurina's captured associates had already endured severe lashings for their part in the attack. Hugo Reid (an early essayist of Gabrielino history, life, and culture who was married to a Gabrielino woman) records that the type of rawhide scourge routinely used at Mission San Gabriel was "immense . . . about ten feet in length, plaited to the thickness of an ordinary man's wrist!" (*The Indians of Los Angeles County: Hugo Reid's Letters of 1852*, ed. Robert F. Heizer [Los Angeles: Southwest Museum, 1968], p. 85). At Mission San Gabriel, no indigenous man, woman, or child was exempt from such torture, meted out on a daily basis. Listen, for example, to what Reid, by way of his wife, Bartolomea, recounts was the fate of women miscarrying at the mission: "when a woman had the misfortune to bring forth a still-born child, she was punished. The penalty inflicted was, shaving the head, flogging for fifteen subsequent days, iron on the feet for three months, and having to appear every Sunday in church, on the steps leading up to the alter, with a hideous painted wooden child in her arms!" (p. 87). Reid also records that individuals holding elite social positions such as Toypurina's were kept "chained together . . . and well flogged . . . and so they worked, two above and two below in the pit" (ibid.).

10. Though Temple (p. 148) emphasizes these are Toypurina's "exact words," it is evident he incorporates his family's folklore into his translation, or telling, of the original Spanish text of this trial, a public record in the Archivo General de la Nación, Mexico City (Ramo de Provincias Internas, volume 20, pp. 31–47). Having some knowledge and understanding of my native language (and given that Toypurina's statement here is a translation of a translation), "exact sentiments" would have been a more accurate expression for Temple to use. But to offer a picture of the type of ecosystem Toypurina was seeking to protect, I quote Reid (p. 72) in reference to the mission site established at San Gabriel:

> at the conquest of this country . . . [this site was] a complete forest of oaks, with considerable underwood. . . . The water, which now composes the lagoon of the mill (one mile and a half distant) being free, like everything else, to wander and meander where it pleased, came down into the hollow nearest to the Mission, on the Angeles road. This hollow was a complete thicket, formed of sycamores, cotton-wood, larch, ash and willows; besides, brambles, nettles, palma cristi, wild roses and wild grape-vines lent a hand to make it impassable, except where foot paths had rendered entrance to its barriers a matter more easy of accomplishment. This hollow, cleared of all encumbrance, served to raise the first crops ever produced at the Mission, and although now a washed waste of gravel and sand, nevertheless, at that time it rejoiced in a rich black soil.

11. Temple, pp. 150–51; Bancroft, p. 460. It is said the conditions of Toypurina's release from solitary confinement were that she "convert" to Christianity and submit herself to being baptized, an act from which, the Spaniards knew, she would not be able to recover her religious, political, and personal power among her people. Toy-

purina was not a mission neophyte at the time of her revolt; she said she revolted "to give courage" to those within the system "who would have the heart to fight." (Translation, Dr. Rosamel Benavides, Humboldt University; my thanks to Sarah Supahan for sharing this valuable translation of Toypurina's testimony with me. From it I sense she also revolted to retain her power as a religious leader—power the invading mission system was adversely affecting by the forced removal of native peoples from their home communities and the imposition of Christianity and slavery upon them.) Given Toypurina's influence and her people's views surrounding baptism, the Spaniards stood to gain much by making an example of her—"converting" her by way of torture, then banishing her to labor at distant missions. Here is Reid (pp. 74–75) on the subject as it relates to Mission San Gabriel: "Baptism as performed, and the recital of a few words not understood, can hardly be said to be conversion; nevertheless, it was productive of great advantage to the Missionaries, because once baptized they lost 'caste' with their people. . . . Baptism was called by them *soyna*, 'being bathed,' and strange to say, was looked upon, although such a simple ceremony, as being ignominious and degrading."

12. Toypurina's actions also speak volumes regarding women's rights and roles in indigenous southern Californian communities. Note that Toypurina achieved something few women, regardless of ethnicity or color, were able to achieve during the eighteenth century: she successfully forced an audience of some of the most influential European men residing in Alta California (Governor Don Pedro Fages, for instance) to hear, by way of her revolt and interrogation, the grievances of her people. Though a Native American woman living in an era in which both women and indigenous peoples were viewed by the Spanish as inferior, Toypurina produced disconcert and awe in her inquisitors, who elected to spare her life (in fear of escalating the situation further and incurring more attacks upon the mission?). Writes Temple (p. 148): "If looks could kill . . . her inquisitors would have dropped like autumn leaves. She was proud and headstrong alright—a commanding personality, then 24, and really attractive. Here was no wild animal at bay, for her arrogant face and almost queenly stance despite her bonds, soon dispelled any such comparison to the tough and hardbitten veterans who faced her. They were properly impressed."

13. That is, those Interior and Island Gabrielinos whose families survived generations of slavery and genocide—not an easy feat, considering that the enslavement and genocide of native peoples in southern California occurred well into the American period of California's colonial history. Once likely the most populous nations in indigenous California, totaling perhaps as many as 15,000 to 20,000 individuals, Interior and Island "Gabrielino" peoples were reduced to near extinction by the year 1910 (Kroeber, p. 883). Many other indigenous Californian nations suffered the same fate. Though the region of present-day California is considered to have been very densely populated—perhaps more densely populated than any other region of North America—its indigenous Californian population, "perhaps approaching 705,000," was reduced "to about 260,000 at the beginning of the nineteenth century, then to only 15,000 to 20,000 at the beginning of the twentieth century" (Russell Thornton, *American Indian Holocaust and Survival: A Population History since 1492* [Norman: University of Oklahoma Press, 1987], p. 200).

14. My family has long told this version of this story to its children. For another, see Reid, p. 54.

15. See Gloria Anzaldúa's *Borderlands/La Frontera* (San Francisco: Spinsters/*aunt lute,* 1987) for her discerning views and writing on the use of, and movement between, holistic and other modes of thought.

16. Sally W. Smith, "Wildlife and Endangered Species: In Precipitous Decline," in *California's Threatened Environment: Restoring the Dream,* ed. Tim Palmer (Washington, D.C.: Island Press, 1993), pp. 226, 227.

17. Tim Palmer, "The Abundance and the Remains," in *California's Threatened Environment,* p. 9.

19

DEAD WEST

Ecocide in Marlboro Country

MIKE DAVIS

Was the Cold War the Earth's worst eco-disaster in the last ten thousand years? The time has come to weigh the environmental costs of the great "twilight struggle" and its attendant nuclear arms race. Until recently, most ecologists have underestimated the impact of warfare and arms production on natural history.[1] Yet there is implacable evidence that huge areas of Eurasia and North America, particularly the militarized deserts of Central Asia and the Great Basin, have become unfit for human habitation, perhaps for thousands of years, as a direct result of weapons testing (conventional, nuclear, and biological) by the Soviet Union, China, and the United States.

These "national sacrifice zones,"[2] now barely recognizable as parts of the biosphere, are also the homelands of indigenous cultures (Kazakh, Paiute, Shoshone, among others) whose peoples may have suffered irreparable genetic damage. Millions of others—soldiers, armament workers, and "downwind" civilians—have become the silent casualties of atomic plagues. If, at the end of the old superpower era, a global nuclear apocalypse was finally averted, it was only at the cost of these secret holocausts.[3]

Part One: Portraits of Hell

Secret Holocausts

This hidden history has come unraveled most dramatically in the ex-Soviet Union where environmental and anti-nuclear activism, first stimulated by Chernobyl in 1986, emerged massively during the crisis of 1990–91. Grassroots protests by miners, schoolchildren, health-care workers and indigenous peoples forced official disclosures that confirmed the sensational accusations by earlier *samizdat* writers like Zhores Medvedev and Boris Komarov

(Ze'ev Wolfson). *Izvestiya* finally printed chilling accounts of the 1957 nuclear catastrophe in the secret military city of Chelyabinsk–40, as well as the poisoning of Lake Baikal by a military factory complex. Even the glacial wall of silence around radiation accidents at the Semipalatinsk "Polygon," the chief Soviet nuclear test range in Kazakhstan, began to melt.[4]

As a result, the (ex-)Soviet public now has a more ample and honest view than their American or British counterparts of the ecological and human costs of the Cold War. Indeed, the Russian Academy of Sciences has compiled an extraordinary map that shows environmental degradation of "irreparable, catastrophic proportions" in forty-five different areas, comprising no less than 3.3 percent of the surface area of the former USSR. Not surprisingly, much of the devastation is concentrated in those parts of the southern Urals and Central Asia that were the geographical core of the USSR's nuclear military-industrial complex.[5]

Veteran kremlinologists, in slightly uncomfortable green disguises, have fastened on these revelations to write scathing epitaphs for the USSR. According to Radio Liberty and Rand researcher D. J. Peterson, "the destruction of nature had come to serve as a solemn metaphor for the decline of a nation."[6] For Lord Carrington's ex-advisor Murray Feshbach, and his literary sidekick Al Friendly (ex-*Newsweek* bureau chief in Moscow), on the other hand, the relationship between ecological cataclysm and the disintegration of the USSR is more than metaphor: "When historians finally conduct an autopsy on the Soviet Union and Soviet Communism, they may reach the verdict of death by ecocide."[7]

Peterson's *Troubled Lands* and especially Feshbach and Friendly's *Ecocide in the USSR* have received spectacular publicity in the American media. Exploiting the new, uncensored wealth of Russian-language sources, they describe an environmental crisis of biblical proportions. The former Land of the Soviets is portrayed as a dystopia of polluted lakes, poisoned crops, toxic cities, and sick children. What Stalinist heavy industry and mindless cotton monoculture have not ruined, the Soviet military has managed to bomb or irradiate. For Peterson, this "ecological terrorism" is conclusive proof of the irrationality of a society lacking a market mechanism to properly "value" nature. Weighing the chances of any environmental cleanup, he holds out only the grim hope that economic collapse and radical de-industrialization may rid Russia and the Ukraine of their worst polluters.[8]

Pentagon eco-freaks Feshbach and Friendly are even more unsparing. Bolshevism, it seems, has been a deliberate conspiracy against Gaia, as well as against humanity. "Ecocide in the USSR stems from the force, not the failure, of utopian ambitions." It is the "ultimate expression of the Revolution's physical and spiritual brutality." With Old Testament righteousness, they repeat the opinion that "there is no worse ecological situation on the planet."[9]

Obviously Feshbach and Friendly have never been to Nevada or western Utah.[10] The environmental horrors of Chelyabinsk–40 and the Semipalatinsk Polygon have their eerie counterparts in the poisoned, terminal landscapes of Marlboro Country.

Misrach's Inferno

A horse head extrudes from a haphazardly bulldozed mass grave. A dead colt—its forelegs raised gracefully as in a gallop—lies in the embrace of its mother. Albino tumbleweed are strewn randomly atop a tangled pyramid of rotting cattle, sheep, horses, and wild mustangs. Bloated by decay, the whole cadaverous mass seems to be struggling to rise. A Minoan bull pokes its eyeless head from the sand. A weird, almost Jurassic skeleton—except for a hoof, it might be the remains of a pterosaur—is sprawled next to a rusty pool of unspeakable vileness. The desert reeks of putrefication.

Photographer Richard Misrach shot this sequence of 8 x 10 color photographs in 1985–87 at various dead-animal disposal sites located near reputed plutonium "hot spots" and military toxic dumps in Nevada (see fig. 19.1). As a short text explains, it is commonplace for local livestock to die mysteriously, or give birth to monstrous offspring. Ranchers are officially encouraged to dump the cadavers, no questions asked, in unmarked, county-run pits. Misrach originally heard of this "Boschlike" landscape from a Paiute poet. When he asked for directions, he was advised to drive into the desert and watch for flocks of crows. The carrion birds feast on the eyes of dead livestock.[11]

"The Pit" has been compared to Picasso's *Guernica.* It is certainly a nightmare reconfiguration of traditional cowboy clichés. The lush photographs are repellent, elegiac, and hypnotic at the same time. Indeed Misrach may have produced the single most disturbing image of the American West since ethnologist James Mooney countered Frederic Remington's popular paintings of heroic cavalry charges with stark photographs of the frozen corpses of Indian women and children slaughtered by the Seventh Cavalry's Hotchkiss guns at Wounded Knee in 1890.[12]

But this holocaust of beasts is only one installment ("canto VI") in a huge mural of forbidden visions called *Desert Cantos.* Misrach is a connoisseur of trespass who, since the late 1970s, has penetrated some of the most secretive spaces of the Pentagon Desert in California, Nevada, and Utah. Each of his fourteen completed cantos (the work is still in progress) builds drama around a "found metaphor" that dissolves the boundary between documentary and allegory. Invariably there is an unsettling tension between the violence of the images and the elegance of their composition.

The earliest cantos (his "desert noir" period?) were formal aesthetic experiments influenced by readings in various cabalistic sources. They are

Figure 19.1 Richard Misrach, *Dead Animals #327*, 1987. Copyright Richard Misrach.

mysterious phantasmagorias detached from any explicit sociopolitical context: the desert on fire, a drowned gazebo in the Salton Sea, a palm being swallowed by a sinister sand dune, and so on.[13] By the mid-1980s, however, Misrach put aside Blake and Castaneda, and began to produce politically engaged exposés of the Cold War's impact upon the American West. Focusing on Nevada, where the military controls 4 million acres of land and 70 percent of the airspace, he was fascinated by the strange stories told by angry ranchers: "night raids . . . by Navy helicopters, laser-burned cows, the bombing of historic towns, and unbearable supersonic flights." With the help of two improbable anti-Pentagon activists, a small-town physician named Doc Bargen and a gritty bush pilot named Dick Holmes, Misrach spent eighteen months photographing a huge tract of public land in central Nevada that had been bombed, illegally and continuously, for almost forty years. To the Navy this landscape of almost incomprehensible devastation, sown with live ammo and unexploded warheads, is simply "Bravo 20." To Misrach, on the other hand, it is "the epicenter . . . the heart of the apocalypse":

Figure 19.2 Richard Misrach, *Bombs, Destroyed Vehicles, and Lone Rock,* 1987. Copyright Richard Misrach.

> It was the most graphically ravaged environment I had ever seen. . . . I wandered for hours amongst the craters. There were thousands of them. Some were small, shallow pits the size of a bathtub, others were gargantuan excavations as large as a suburban two-car garage. Some were bone dry, with walls of "traumatized earth" splatterings, others were eerie pools of blood-red or emerald-green water. Some had crystallized into strange salt formations. Some were decorated with the remains of blown-up jeeps, tanks, and trucks.[14]

Although Misrach's photographs of the pulverized public domain, published in 1990, riveted national attention on the bombing of the West, it was a bittersweet achievement. His pilot friend Dick Holmes, whom he had photographed raising the American flag over a lunarized hill in a delicious parody on the Apollo astronauts, was killed in an inexplicable plane crash. The Bush administration, meanwhile, accelerated the modernization of bombing ranges in Nevada, Utah, and Idaho. Huge swathes of the remote West, including Bravo 20, have been updated into electronically scored, multi-target

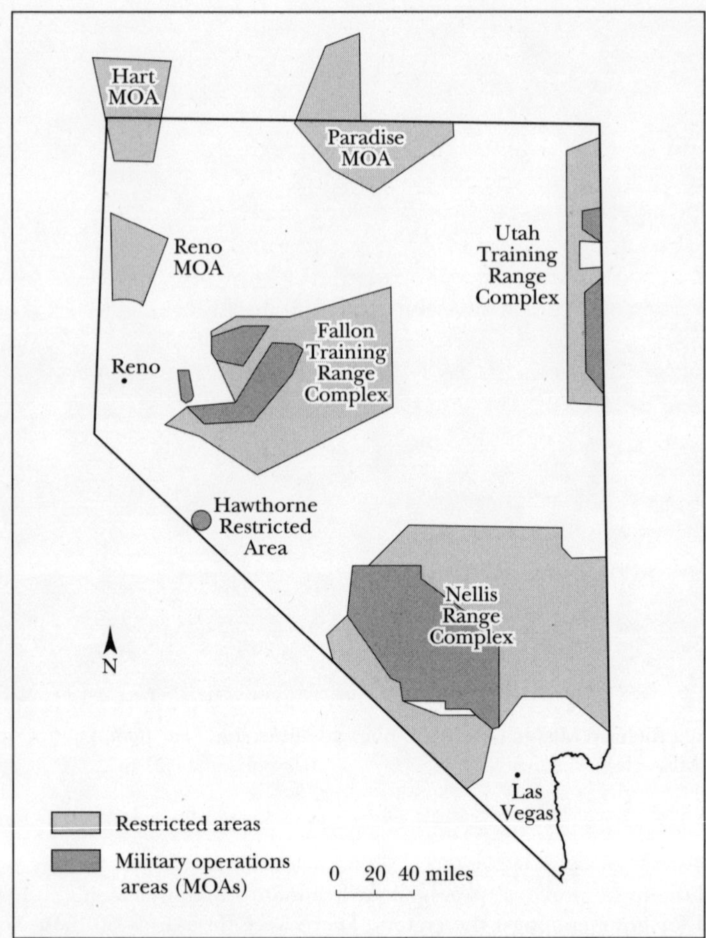

Map 19.1 Pentagon Nevada.

grids which, from space, must now look like a colossal Pentagon videogameboard.

In his most recent collection of cantos, *Violent Legacies* (which includes "The Pit"), Misrach offers a haunting, visual archeology of "Project W-47," the supersecret final assembly and flight testing of the bombs dropped on Hiroshima and Nagasaki. The hangar that housed the *Enola Gay* still stands (indeed, a sign warns: "Use of deadly force authorized") amidst the ruins of Wendover Air Base in the Great Salt Desert of Utah. In the context of incipient genocide, the fossil flight-crew humor of 1945 is unnerving. Thus a fading slogan over the A-bomb assembly building reads BLOOD, SWEAT AND BEERS, while graffiti on the administrative headquarters commands EAT MY

FALLOUT. The rest of the base complex, including the atomic bomb storage bunkers and loading pits, has eroded into megalithic abstractions that evoke the ground-zero helter-skelter of J. G. Ballard's famous short story "The Terminal Beach." Outlined against ochre desert mountains (the Newfoundland Range, I believe), the forgotten architecture and casual detritus of the first nuclear war are almost beautiful.[15]

In cultivating a neo-pictorialist style, Misrach plays subtle tricks on the sublime. He can look Kurtz's Horror straight in the face and make a picture postcard of it. This attention to the aesthetics of murder infuriates some partisans of traditional black-and-white political documentarism, but it also explains Misrach's extraordinary popularity. He reveals the terrible, hypnotizing beauty of Nature in its death throes, of Landscape as Inferno. We have no choice but to look.

If there is little precedent for this in previous photography of the American West, it has a rich resonance in contemporary—especially Latin American—political fiction. Discussing the role of folk apocalypticism in the novels of García Márquez and Carlos Fuentes, Lois Zamora inadvertently supplies an apt characterization of *Desert Cantos*:

> The literary devices of biblical apocalypse and magical realism coincide in their hyperbolic narration and in their *surreal images of utter chaos and unutterable perfection.* And in both cases, [this] surrealism is not principally conceived for psychological effect, as in earlier European examples of the mode, but is instead grounded in social and political realities and is designed to communicate the writers' objections to those realities.[16]

Resurveying the West

Just as Marquez and Fuentes, then, have led us through the hallucinatory labyrinth of modern Latin American history, so Misrach has become an indefatigable tour guide to the Apocalyptic Kingdom that the Department of Defense has built in the desert West. His vision is singular, yet, at the same time, *Desert Cantos* claims charter membership in a broader movement of politicized western landscape photography that has made the destruction of nature its dominant theme.

Its separate detachments over the last fifteen years have included, first, the so-called New Topographics in the mid-1970s (Lewis Baltz, Robert Adams, and Joel Deal),[17] closely followed by the Rephotographic Survey Project (Mark Klett and colleagues),[18] and, then, in 1987, by the explicitly activist Atomic Photographers Guild (Robert Del Tredici, Carole Gallagher, Peter Goin, Patrick Nagatani, and twelve others).[19] If each of these moments has had its own artistic virtue (and pretension), they share a common framework of revisionist principles.

Figure 19.3 Richard Misrach, *Princess of Plutonium, Nuclear Test Site, Nevada,* 1988. Copyright Richard Misrach.

In the first place, they have mounted a frontal attack on the hegemony of Ansel Adams, the dead pope of the "Sierra Club school" of Nature-as-God photography. Adams, if necessary, doctored his negatives to remove any evidence of human presence from his apotheosized wilderness vistas.[20] The new generation has rudely deconstructed this myth of a virginal, if imperilled nature. They have rejected Adams's Manichean division between "sacred" and "profane" landscape, which "leaves the already altered and inhabited parts of our environment dangerously open to uncontrolled exploitation."[21] Their West, by contrast, is an irrevocably social landscape, transformed by militarism, urbanization, the interstate highway, epidemic vandalism, mass tourism, and the extractive industries' boom-and-bust cycles. Even in the "last wild places," the remote ranges and lost box canyons, the Pentagon's jets are always overhead.

Secondly, the new generation has created an alternative iconography around such characteristic, but previously spurned or "unphotographable" objects as industrial debris, rock graffiti, mutilated saguaros, bulldozer tracks, discarded girlie magazines, military shrapnel, and dead animals.[22] Like the surrealists, they have recognized the oracular and critical potencies of the commonplace, the discarded, and the ugly.[23] But as environmentalists, they also understand the fate of the rural West as the national dumping ground.

Finally, their projects derive historical authority from a shared benchmark: the photographic archive of the great nineteenth-century scientific and topographic surveys of the intermontane West. Indeed, most of them have acknowledged the centrality of "resurvey" as strategy or metaphor. The New Topographers, by their very name, declared an allegiance to the scientific detachment and geological clarity of Timothy O'Sullivan (famed photographer for Clarence King's 1870s survey of the Great Basin), as they turned their cameras on the suburban wastelands of the New West. The Rephotographers "animated" the dislocations from past to present by painstakingly assuming the exact camera stances of their predecessors and producing the same scene a hundred years later. Meanwhile, the Atomic Photographers, in emulation of the old scientific surveys, have produced increasingly precise studies of the landscape tectonics of nuclear testing.

Resurvey, of course, presumes a crisis of definition, and it is interesting to speculate why the new photography, in its struggle to capture the meaning of the postmodern West, has been so obsessed with nineteenth-century images and canons. It is not because, as might otherwise be imagined, Timothy O'Sullivan and his colleagues were able to see the West pristine and unspoiled. As Klett's "rephotographs" startlingly demonstrate, the grubby hands of manifest destiny were already all over the landscape by 1870. What was more important was the exceptional scientific and artistic integrity with which the surveys confronted landscapes that, as Jan Zita Grover suggests, were culturally "unreadable."[24]

The regions that today constitute the Pentagon's "national sacrifice zone" (the Great Basin of eastern California, Nevada, and western Utah) and its "plutonium periphery" (the Columbia–Snake Plateau, the Wyoming Basin and the Colorado Plateau) have few landscape analogues anywhere else on earth.[25] Early accounts of the intermontane West in the 1840s and 1850s (John Fremont, Sir Richard Burton, the Pacific railroad surveys) chipped away eclectically, with little success, at the towering popular abstraction of "the Great American Desert." Nevada and Utah, for instance, were variously compared to Arabia, Turkestan, the Takla Makan, Timbuktu, Australia, and so on, but in reality, Victorian minds were travelling through an essentially extraterrestrial terrain, far outside their cultural experience.[26] (Perhaps literally so, since planetary geologists now study lunar and Martian landforms by analogy with strikingly similar landscapes in the Colorado and Columbia–Snake River plateaux.)[27]

The bold stance of the survey geologists, their artists and photographers, was to face this radical "Otherness" on its own terms.[28] Like Darwin in the Galapagos, John Wesley Powell and his colleagues (especially Clarence Dutton and the great Carl Grove Gilbert) eventually cast aside a trunkful of Victorian preconceptions in order to recognize novel forms and processes in nature. Thus Powell and Gilbert had to invent a new science, geomorphology, to explain the amazing landscape system of the Colorado Plateau where rivers were often "antecedent" to highlands and the "laccolithic" mountains were really impotent volcanoes. (Similarly, decades later, another quiet revolutionary in the survey tradition, Harlen Bretz, would jettison uniformitarian geological orthodoxy in order to show that cataclysmic ice-age floods were responsible for the strange "channeled scablands" carved into the lava of the Columbia Plateau.)[29]

If the surveys "brought the strange spires, majestic cliff facades, and fabulous canyons into the realm of scientific explanation," then (notes Gilbert's biographer), they "also gave them a critical aesthetic meaning" through the stunning photographs, drawings, and narratives that accompanied and expanded the technical reports.[30] Thus Timothy O'Sullivan (who with Mathew Brady had photographed the ranks of death at Gettysburg) abandoned the Ruskinian paradigms of nature representation to concentrate on naked, essential form in a way that presaged modernism. His "stark planes, the seemingly two-dimensional curtain walls, [had] no immediate parallel in the history of art and photography. . . . No one before had seen the wilderness in such abstract and architectural forms."[31] Similarly Clarence Dutton, "the *genius loci* of the Grand Canyon," created a new landscape language—also largely architectural, but sometimes phantasmagorical—to describe an unprecedented dialectics of rock, color and light. (Wallace Stegner says he "aestheticized geology"; perhaps, more accurately, he eroticized it.)[32]

But this convergence of science and sensibility (which has no real twentieth-century counterpart) also compelled a moral view of the environment as it was laid bare for exploitation. Setting a precedent which few of his modern descendants have had the guts to follow, Powell, the one-armed Civil War hero, laid out the political implications of the western surveys with exacting honesty in his famous 1877 *Report on the Lands of the Arid Region.* His message, which Stegner has called "revolutionary" (and others "socialistic"), was that the intermontane region's only salvation was Cooperativism based on the communal management and conservation of scarce pasture and water resources. Capitalism pure and simple, Powell implied, would destroy the West.[33]

The surveys, then, were not just another episode in measuring the West for conquest and pillage; they were, rather, an autonomous moment in the history of American science when radical new perceptions temporarily created a pathway for a utopian alternative to the future that became Project W-47 and The Pit. That vantage point is now extinct. In reclaiming this tradition, contemporary photographers have elected to fashion their own clarity without the aid of the Victorian optimism that led Powell into the chasms of the Colorado. But "Resurvey," if a resonant slogan, is a diffuse mandate. For some it has meant little more than checking to see if the boulders have moved after a hundred years. For others, however, it has entailed perilous moral journeys deep into the interior landscapes of the Bomb.

Jellyfish Babies

If Richard Misrach has seen "the heart of the apocalypse" at Bravo 20, Carole Gallagher has spent a decade at "American Ground Zero" (the title of her new book) in Nevada and southwestern Utah photographing and collecting the stories of its victims.[34] She is one of the founders of the Atomic Photographers Guild, arguably the most important social-documentary collaboration since the 1930s, when Roy Stryker's Farm Security Administration Photography Unit brought together the awesome lenses of Walker Evans, Dorothea Lange, Ben Shahn, Russell Lee, and Arthur Rothstein. Just as the FSA photographers dramatized the plight of the rural poor during the Depression, so the Guild has endeavored to document the human and ecological costs of the nuclear arms race. Its accomplishments include Peter Goin's revelatory *Nuclear Landscapes* (photographed at test-sites in the American West and the Marshall Islands) and Robert Del Tredici's biting exposé of nuclear manufacture, *At Work in the Fields of the Bomb.*[35]

But it is Gallagher's work that proclaims the most explicit continuity with the FSA tradition, particularly with Dorothea Lange's classical black-and-white portraiture. Indeed, she prefaces her book with a meditation on a Lange motto and incorporates some haunting Lange photographs of St. George, Utah, in 1953. There is no doubt that *American Ground Zero* is intended to stand on the same shelf with such New Deal–era classics as *An American Exodus, Let Us Now Praise Famous Men,* and *You Have Seen Their Faces.*[36] Hers, however, is a more painful book.

In the early 1980s, Gallagher moved from New York City to St. George to work full-time on her oral history of the casualties of the American nuclear test program. Beginning with its first nuclear detonation in 1951, this small

Figure 19.4 Carole Gallagher, *Ken Case, the "Atomic Cowboy," North Las Vegas.* Copyright Carole Gallagher.

Mormon city, due east of the Nevada Test Site, has been shrouded in radiation debris from scores of atmospheric and accidentally "ventilated" underground blasts. Each lethal cloud was the equivalent of billions of x-rays and contained more radiation than was released at Chernobyl in 1988. Moreover, the Atomic Energy Commission (AEC) in the 1950s had deliberately planned for fallout to blow over the St. George region in order to avoid Las Vegas and Los Angeles. In the icy, Himmlerian jargon of a secret AEC memo unearthed by Gallagher, the targeted communities were "a low-use segment of the population."[37]

As a direct result, this downwind population (exposed to the fallout equivalent of perhaps fifty Hiroshimas) is being eaten away by cumulative cancers, neurological disorders, and genetic defects. Gallagher, for instance, talks

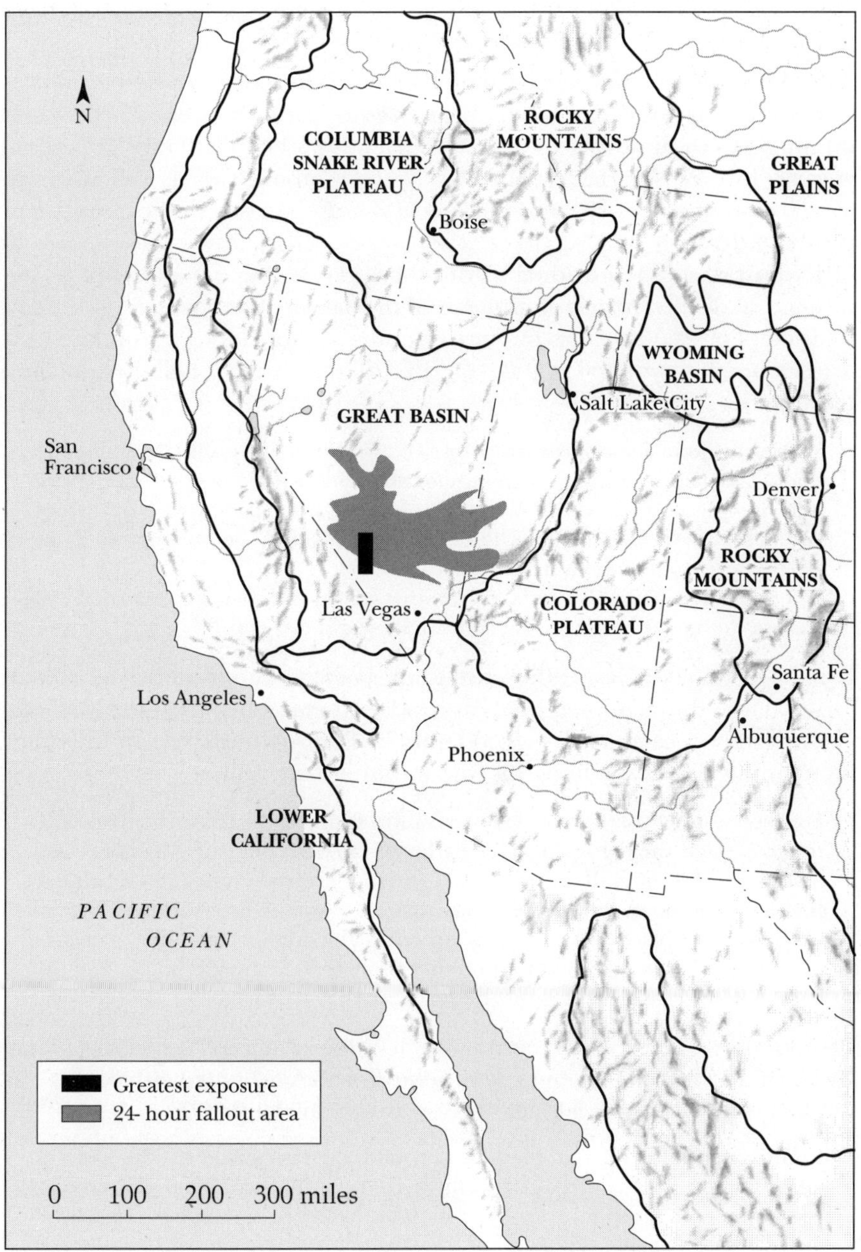

Map 19.2 Downwind.

about her quiet dread of going into the local K-Mart and "seeing four- and five-year-old children wearing wigs, deathly pale and obviously in chemotherapy."[38] But such horror has become routinized in a region where cancer is so densely clustered that virtually any resident can matter-of-factly rattle off long lists of tumorous or deceased friends and family. The eighty-some voices—former Nevada Test Site workers and "atomic GIs" as well as Downwinders—that comprise *American Ground Zero* are weary with the minutiae of pain and death.

In most of these individual stories there is one single moment of recognition that distills the terror and awe of the catastrophe that has enveloped their life. For example, two military veterans of shot Hood (a 74-kiloton hydrogen bomb detonated in July 1957) recall the vision of hell they encountered in the Nevada desert:

> We'd only gone a short way when one of my men said, "Jesus Christ, look at that!" I looked where he was pointing, and what I saw horrified me. There were people in a stockade—a chain-link fence with barbed wire on top of it. Their hair was falling out and their skin seemed to be peeling off. They were wearing blue denim trousers but no shirts. . . .
>
> I was happy, full of life before I saw that bomb, but then I understood evil and was never the same. . . . I seen how the world can end.[39]

For sheep ranchers it was the unsettling spectacle they watched season after season in their lambing sheds as irradiated ewes attempted to give birth: "Have you ever seen a five-legged lamb?"[40] For one husband, on the other hand, it was simply watching his wife wash her hair.

> Four weeks after that [the atomic test] I was sittin' in the front room reading the paper and she'd gone into the bathroom to wash her hair. All at once she let out the most ungodly scream, and I run in there and there's about half her hair layin' in the washbasin! You can imagine a woman with beautiful, raven-black hair, so black it would glint green in the sunlight just like a raven's wing, and it was long hair down onto her shoulders. There was half of it in the basin and she was as bald as old Yul Brynner.[41]

Perhaps most bone-chilling, even more than the anguished accounts of small children dying from leukemia, are the stories about the "jellyfish babies": irradiated fetuses that developed into grotesque hydatidiform moles.

> I remember being worried because they said the cows would eat the hay and all this fallout had covered it and through the milk they would get radioactive iodine. . . . From four to about six months I kept a-wondering because I hadn't felt any kicks. . . . I hadn't progressed to the size of a normal pregnancy and the doctor gave me a sonogram. He couldn't see any form of a baby. . . . He did a D and C. My husband was there and he showed him what he had taken out of my uterus. There were little grapelike cysts. My husband said it looked like a bunch of peeled grapes.[42]

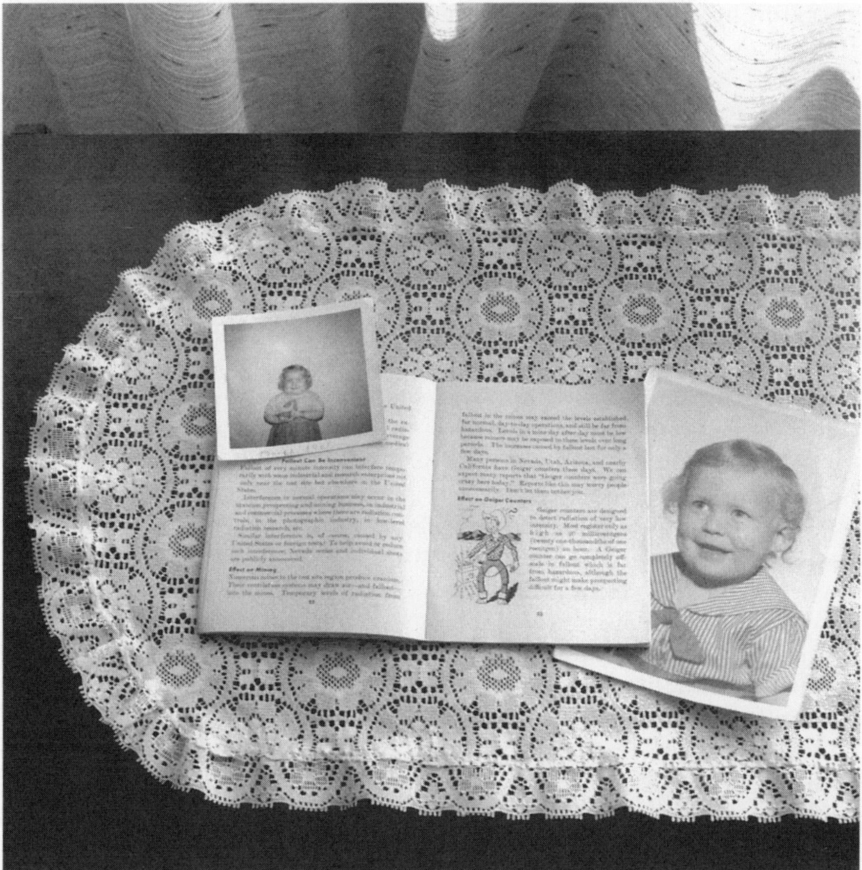

Figure 19.5 Carole Gallagher, Baby photographs of Sherry Millett, before and during the leukemia from which she died, with the 1957 Atomic Energy Commission propaganda booklet. Copyright Carole Gallagher.

The ordinary Americans who lived, and still live, these nightmares are rendered in great dignity in Gallagher's photographs. But she cannot suppress her frustration with the passivity of so many of the Mormon Downwinders. Their unquestioning submission to a Cold War government in Washington and an authoritarian church hierarchy in Salt Lake City disabled effective protest through the long decades of contamination. To the cynical atomocrats in the AEC, they were just gullible hicks in the sticks, suckers for soapy reassurances and idiot "the atom is your friend" propaganda films. As one subject recalled his Utah childhood: "I remember in school they showed a film once called *A is for Atom, B is for the Bomb.* I think most of us who grew up in that period . . . [have now] added *C is for Cancer. D is for Death.*"[43]

Indeed, most of the people interviewed by Gallagher seem to have had a harder time coming to grips with government deception than with cancer. Ironically, Washington waged its secret nuclear war against the most patriotic cross-section of the population imaginable, a virtual Norman Rockwell tapestry of Americana: gung-ho Marines, ultra-loyal Test Site workers, Nevada cowboys and tungsten miners, Mormon farmers, and freckle-faced Utah schoolchildren. For forty years the Atomic Energy Commission and its successor, the Department of Energy, have lied about exposure levels, covered up Chernobyl-sized accidents, suppressed research on the contamination of the milk supply, ruined the reputation of dissident scientists, abducted hundreds of body parts from victims, and conducted a ruthless legal war to deny compensation to the Downwinders.[44] A 1980 congressional study accused the agencies of "fraud upon the court," but Gallagher uses a stronger word—"genocide"—and reminds us that "lack of vigilance and control of the weaponeers" has morally and economically "played a large role in bankrupting . . . not just one superpower but two."[45]

And what has been the ultimate cost? For decades the AEC cover-up prevented the accumulation of statistics or the initiation of research that might provide some minimal parameters. However, an unpublished report by a Carter administration task force (quoted by Philip Fradkin) determined that 170,000 people had been exposed to contamination within a 250-mile radius of the Nevada Test Site. In addition, roughly 250,000 servicemen, some of them cowering in trenches a few thousand yards from ground zero, took part in atomic war games in Nevada and the Marshall Islands during the 1950s and early 1960s. Together with the Test Site workforce, then, it is reasonable to estimate that at least 500,000 people were exposed to intense, short-range effects of nuclear detonation. (For comparison, this is the *maximum* figure quoted by students of the fallout effects from tests at the Semipalatinsk Polygon.)[46]

But these figures are barely suggestive of the real scale of nuclear toxicity. Another million Americans have worked in nuclear weapons plants since 1945, and some of these plants, especially the giant Hanford complex in Washington, have contaminated their environments with secret, deadly emissions, including radioactive iodine.[47] Most of the urban Midwest and Northeast, moreover, was downwind of the 1950s atmospheric tests, and storm fronts frequently dumped carcinogenic, radioisotope "hot spots" as far east as New York City. As the commander of the elite Air Force squadron responsible for monitoring the nuclear test clouds during the 1950s told Gallagher (he was suffering from cancer): "There isn't anybody in the United States who isn't a downwinder. . . . When we followed the clouds, we went all over the United States from east to west. . . . Where are you going to draw the line?"[48]

Part Two: Healing Global Wounds

Yet, over the last decade, Native Americans, ranchers, peace activists, Downwinders, and even members of the normally conservative Mormon establishment have attempted to draw a firm line against further weapons' testing, radiation poisoning, and ecocide in the deserts of Nevada and Utah. The three short field reports that follow (written in 1992, 1993, and 1996–97) are snapshots of the most extraordinary social movement to emerge in the postwar West.

Humbling "Mighty Uncle"

Flash back to fall 1992. The (private) Wackenhut guards at the main gate of the Nevada Nuclear Test Site (NTS) nervously adjust the visors on their riot helmets and fidget with their batons. One block away, just beyond the permanent traffic sign that warns "Watch for Demonstrators!" a thousand anti-nuclear protestors, tie-dyed banners unfurled, are approaching at a funeral pace to the sombre beat of a drum.

The unlikely leader of this youthful army is a rugged-looking rancher from the Ruby Mountains named Raymond Yowell. With a barrel chest that strains against his pearl-button shirt, and calloused hands that have roped a thousand mustangs, he makes the Marlboro Man seem wimpy. But if you look closely, you will notice a sacred eagle feather in his Stetson. Mr. Yowell is chief of the Western Shoshone National Council.

When an official warns protestors that they will be arrested if they cross the cattleguard that demarcates the boundary of the Test Site, Chief Yowell scowls that it is the Department of Energy who is trespassing on sacred Shoshone land. "We would be obliged," he says firmly, "if *you* would leave. And please take your damn nuclear waste and rent-a-cops with you."

While Chief Yowell is being handcuffed at the main gate, scores of protestors are breaking through the perimeter fence and fanning out across the desert. They are chased like rabbits by armed Wackenhuts in fast, low-slung dune-buggies. Some try to hide behind Joshua trees, but all will be eventually caught and returned to the concrete-and-razor-wire compound that serves as the Test Site's hoosegow. It is October 11, the day before the quincentenary of Columbus's crash landing in the New World.

The U.S. nuclear test program has been under almost constant siege since the Las Vegas–based American Peace Test (a direct-action offshoot of the old Moratorium) first encamped outside the NTS's Mercury gate in

1987. Since then more than ten thousand people have been arrested at APT mass demonstrations or in smaller actions ranging from Quaker prayer vigils to Greenpeace commando raids on ground zero itself. (In *Violent Legacies* Misrach includes a wonderful photograph of the "Princesses Against Plutonium," attired in radiation suits and death masks, illegally camped inside the NTS perimeter.) Dodging the Wackenhuts in the Nevada desert has become the rite of passage for a new generation of peace activists.

The fall 1992 Test Site mobilization—"Healing Global Wounds"—was a watershed in the history of anti-nuclear protest. In the first place, the action coincided with Congress's nine-month moratorium on nuclear testing (postponing until this September a test blast codenamed "Mighty Uncle"). At long last, the movement's strategic goal, a comprehensive test ban treaty, seemed tantalizingly within grasp. Secondly, the leadership within the movement has begun to be assumed by the indigenous peoples whose lands have been poisoned by nearly a half century of nuclear testing.

These two developments have a fascinating international connection. Washington's moratorium was a grudging response to Moscow's earlier, unilateral cessation of testing, while the Russian initiative was coerced from Yeltsin by unprecedented popular pressure. The revelation of a major nuclear accident at the Polygon in February 1989 provoked a non-violent uprising in Kazakhstan. The famed writer Olzhas Suleimenov used a televised poetry reading to urge Kazakhs to emulate the example of the Nevada demonstrations. Tens of thousands of protestors, some brandishing photographs of family members killed by cancer, flooded the streets of Semipalatinsk and Alma-Ata, and within a year the "Nevada-Semipalatinsk Movement" had become "the largest and most influential public organization in Kazakhstan, drawing its support from a broad range of people—from the intelligentsia to the working class."[49] Two years later, the Kazakh Supreme Soviet, as part of its declaration of independence, banned nuclear testing forever.

It was the world's first successful anti-nuclear revolution, and its organizers tried to spread its spirit with the formation of the Global Anti-Nuclear Alliance (GANA). They specifically hoped to reach out to other indigenous nations and communities victimized by nuclear colonialism. The Western Shoshones were amongst the first to respond. Unlike many other western tribes, Chief Yowell's people have never conceded U.S. sovereignty in the Great Basin of Nevada and Utah, and even insist on carrying their own national passport when travelling abroad. In conversations with the Kazakhs and activists from the Pacific test sites, they discovered a poignant kinship that eventually led to the joint GANA-Shoshone sponsorship of "Healing Global Wounds" with its twin demands to end nuclear testing and restore native land rights.

In the past some participants had criticized the American Peace Test encampments for their overwhelmingly countercultural character. Indeed, last

October as usual, the bulletin board at the camp's entrance gave directions to affinity groups, massage tables, brown rice, and karmic enhancements. But the Grateful Dead ambience was leavened by the presence of an authentic Great Basin united front that included Mormon and Paiute Indian Downwinders from the St. George area, former GIs exposed to the 1950s atmospheric tests, Nevada ranchers struggling to demilitarize public land (Citizen Alert), a representative of workers poisoned by plutonium at the giant Hanford nuclear plant, and the Reese River Valley Rosses, a Shoshone country-western band. In addition there were friends from Kazakhstan and Mururoa, as well as a footsore regiment of European cross-continent peace marchers.

The defeat of George Bush a month after "Healing Global Wounds" solidified optimism in the peace movement that the congressional moratorium would become a permanent test ban. The days of the Nevada Test Site seemed numbered. Yet to the dismay of the Western Shoshones, the Downwinders and the rest of the peace community, the new Democratic administration evinced immodest enthusiasm for the ardent wooing of the powerful nuclear-industrial complex. Cheered on by the Tory regime in London, which was eager to test the nuclear warhead for the RAF's new "TASM" missile in the Nevada desert, the Pentagon and the three giant atomic labs (Livermore, Los Alamos, and Sandia) came within a hairsbreadth of convincing Clinton to resume "Mighty Uncle." Only a last-minute revolt by twenty-three senators—alarmed that further testing might undermine the U.S.-led crusade against incipient nuclear powers like Iraq and North Korea—forced the White House to extend the moratorium.

Although the ban has remained in force, there is some evidence that the Pentagon has participated in tests by proxy in French Polynesia. In 1995 the White House, breaking with the policy of the Bush years, allowed the French military to airlift H-bomb components to Mururoa through U.S. airspace, using LAX as a stop-over point. The British Labor Party, echoing accounts in the French press, charged that Washington and London were silent partners in the internationally denounced Mururoa test series, sharing French data while providing Paris with logistical and diplomatic support.[50]

More recently, the spotlight has shifted back to Nevada where peace activists in spring 1997 were preparing for protests against NTS's new program of "zero yield" tests. The Department of Energy is planning to use high explosives to compress "old" plutonium to the brink of chain reaction, an open violation of the Comprehensive Test Ban agreement, in order to generate data for a computer study of "the effects of age on nuclear weapons." This is part of the Clinton administration's science-based Stockpile Stewardship program, which, critics allege, has merely shifted the nuclear arms-race into high-tech labs like Livermore's $1 billion National Ignition Facility where super-lasers will produce miniature nuclear explosions that will in turn be studied by the next generation of "teraflop" (1 trillion calculations per second) supercomputers. Great Basin peace activists, like their Global Healing counterparts fear that such "virtual atomic tests," combined with data from "zero yield" blasts in Nevada, will encourage not only the maintenance, but the further development of strategic nuclear weapons. In the meantime, motorists will still have to "Stop for Demonstrators" at the Mercury exit.[51]

The Death Lab

January 1993. It has been one of the coldest winters in memory in the Great Basin. Truckers freeze in their stalled rigs on ice-bound Interstate 80 while flocks of sheep are swallowed whole by huge snow drifts. It is easy to miss the exit to Skull Valley.

An hour's drive west of Salt Lake City, Skull Valley is typical of the basin and range landscape that characterizes so much of the intermontane West. Ten thousand years ago it was an azure-blue fjord-arm of prehistoric Lake Bonneville (mother of the present Great Salt Lake), whose ancient shorelines are still etched across the face of the snow-capped Stansbury Mountains. Today the valley floor (when not snowed-in) is mostly given over to sagebrush, alkali dust, and the relics of the area's incomparably strange history.

A half-dozen abandoned ranch houses, now choked with tumbleweed, are all that remain of the immigrant British cottonmill workers—Engels's classic Lancashire proletariat—who were the Valley's first Mormon settlers in the late 1850s. The nearby ghost town of Iosepa testifies to the ordeal of several hundred native Hawaiian converts, arriving a generation later, who fought drought, homesickness, and leprosy. Their cemetery, with beautiful Polynesian names etched in Stansbury quartzite, is one of the most unexpected and poignant sites in the American West.[52]

Further south, a few surviving families of the Gosiute tribe—people of Utah's Dreamtime and first cousins to the Western Shoshone—operate the "Last Pony Express Station" (actually a convenience store) and lease the rest of their reservation to the Hercules Corporation for testing rockets and explosives. In 1918, after refusing to register for the draft, the Skull Valley and Deep Creek bands of the Gosiutes were rounded up by the Army in what Salt Lake City papers termed "the last Indian uprising."[53]

Finally, at the Valley's southern end, across from an incongruously large and solitary Mormon temple, a sign warns spies away from Dugway Proving Ground: since 1942, the primary test-site for U.S. chemical, biological, and incendiary weapons. Napalm was invented here and tried out on block-long replicas of German and Japanese workers' housing (parts of this eerie "doom city" still stand). Also tested here was the supersecret Anglo-American anthrax bomb (Project N) that Churchill, exasperated by the 1945 V-2 attacks on London, wanted to use to kill twelve million Germans. Project W-47—which did incinerate Hiroshima and Nagasaki—was based nearby, just on the other side of Granite Mountain.[54]

In the postwar years, the Pentagon carried out a nightmarish sequence of live-subject experiments at Dugway. In 1955, for example, a cloud generator was used to saturate thirty volunteers—all Seventh-Day Adventist conscientious objectors—with potentially deadly Q Fever. Then, between August and October 1959, the Air Force deliberately let nuclear reactors melt down on eight occasions and "used forced air to ensure that the resulting radiation would spread to the wind. Sensors were set up over a 210-mile area to track the radiation clouds. When last detected they were headed toward the old U.S. 40 (now Interstate 80)."[55]

Most notoriously, the Army conducted 1,635 field trials of nerve gas, involving at least 500,000 pounds of the deadly agent, over Dugway between 1951 and 1969. Open-air nerve-gas releases were finally halted after a haywire 1968 experiment asphyxiated six thousand sheep on the neighboring Gosiute Reservation. Although the Army paid $1 million in damages, it refused to acknowledge any responsibility. Shrouded in secrecy and financed by a huge black budget, Dugway continued to operate without public scrutiny.[56]

Then in 1985 Senator Jeremy Stasser and writer Jeremy Rifkin teamed up to expose Pentagon plans to use recombinant genetic engineering to create "Andromeda strains" of killer microorganisms. Despite the American signature on the 1972 Biological Weapons Convention that banned their development, the Army proposed to build a high-containment laboratory at Dugway to "defensively" test its new designer bugs.[57]

Opposition to the Death Lab was led by Downwinders, Inc., a Salt Lake City–based group that grew out of solidarity with the radiation victims in the St. George area. In addition to local ranchers and college students, the Downwinders were able to rally support from doctors at the Latter Day Saints (Mormon) Hospital and, eventually, from the entire Utah Medical Association. Local unease with Dugway was further aggravated by the Army's admission that ultra-toxic organisms were regularly shipped through the U.S. mail.

The Pentagon, accustomed to red-carpet treatment in super-patriotic Utah, was stunned by the ensuing storm of public hearings and protests, as well as the breadth of the opposition. In September 1988 the Army reluctantly cancelled plans for its new "BL-4" lab. In a recent interview, Downwinders organizer Steve Erickson pointed out that "this was the first grassroots victory anywhere, ever, over germ or chemical warfare testing." In 1990, however, the Dugway authorities unexpectedly resurrected their biowar lab scheme, although now restricting the range of proposed tests to "natural" lethal organisms rather than biotech mutants.[58]

A year later, while Downwinders and their allies were still skirmishing with the Army over the possible environmental impact of the new lab, Desert Shield suddenly turned into Desert Storm. Washington worried openly about Iraq's terrifying arsenal of biological and chemical agents, and Dugway launched a crash program of experiments with anthrax, botulism, bubonic plague, and other micro-toxins in a renovated 1950s facility called Baker Lab. Simulations of these organisms were also tested in the atmosphere.

The Downwinders, together with the Utah Medical Association (dominated by Mormon doctors), went to the U.S. District Court to challenge the resumption of tests at the veteran Baker Lab as well as the plan for a new "life sciences test facility." Their case was built around the Army's noncompliance with federal environmental regulations as well as its scandalous failure to provide local hospitals with the training and serums to cope with a major biowar accident at Dugway. The fantastically toxic botulism virus, for example, has been tested at Dugway for decades, but not a single dose of the anti-toxin was available in Utah (indeed in 1993, there were only twelve doses on the entire West Coast).[59]

In filing suit, the Downwinders also wanted to clarify the role of chemical and biological weapons in the Gulf War. In the first place, they hoped to force the Army to reveal why it vaccinated tens of thousands of its troops with an experimental, and possibly dangerous, anti-botulism serum. Were GIs once again being used as Pentagon guinea pigs? Was there any connection between the vaccinations and the strange sickness—the so-called "Gulf War Syndrome"—brought home by so many veterans?

Secondly, the Downwinders hoped to shed more light on why the Bush administration allowed the sales of potential biological agents in the months before the invasion of Kuwait. "If the Army's justification for resuming tests at Dugway was the imminent Iraqi biowar threat," said Erickson, "then why did the Commerce Department previously allow $20 million of dangerous 'dual-use' biological materials to be sold to Iraq's Atomic Energy Commission? Were we trying to defend our troops against our own renegade bugs?"[60]

In the event, the Pentagon refused to answer these questions and the Downwinders lost their lawsuit, although they remain convinced that bioagents are prime suspects in the Gulf War Syndrome. Meanwhile, the Army completed the controversial Life Sciences Test Facility, and rumors began to fly of research on super-lethal fibroviruses like Ebola Fever. Then, in 1994, Lee Davidson, a reporter for the Mormon *Deseret News,* used the Freedom of Information Act to excavate the details of human-subject experiments in Dugway during the 1950s and 1960s. Two years later, former Dugway employees complained publicly for the first time about cancers and other disabilities that they believe were caused by chemical and biological testing. The

Department of Defense, finally, admitted that clean-up of Dugway's 143 major toxic sites may cost billions and take generations, if ever, to complete.[61]

The Great "Waste" Basin?

Grassroots protest in the intermontane states has repeatedly upset the Pentagon's best-made plans. Echoing sentiments frequently expressed at "Healing Global Wounds," Steve Erickson of the Downwinders boasts of the peace movement's dramatic breakthrough in the West over the past decade. "We have managed to defeat the MX and Midgetman missile systems, scuttle the proposed Canyonlands Nuclear Waste Facility, stop construction of Dugway's BL-4, and impose a temporary nuclear test ban. That's not a bad record for a bunch of cowboys and Indians in Nevada and Utah: two supposedly bedrock pro-military states!"[62]

Yet the struggle continues. The Downwinders and other groups, including the Western Shoshones and Citizen Alert, see an ominous new environmental and public-health menace under the apparently benign slogan of "demilitarization." With the abrupt ending of the Cold War, millions of aging strategic and tactical weapons, as well as six tons of military plutonium (the most poisonous substance that has ever existed in the geological history of the earth), must somehow be disposed of. As Seth Schulman warns, "the nationwide military toxic waste problem is monumental—a nightmare of almost overwhelming proportion."[63]

The Department of Defense's reaction, not surprisingly, has been to dump most of its obsolete missiles, chemical weaponry, and nuclear waste into the thinly populated triangle between Reno, Salt Lake City, and Las Vegas: an area that already contains perhaps one thousand "highly contaminated" sites (the exact number is a secret) on sixteen military bases and Department of Energy facilities.[64] The Great Basin, as in 1942 and 1950, has again been nominated for sacrifice.

The Pentagon's apocalyptic detritus, however, is a new regional cornucopia—the equivalent of postmodern Comstock—for a handful of powerful defense contractors and waste-treatment firms. As environmental journalist Triana Silton warned a few years ago, "a full-fledged corporate war is shaping up as part of the old military-industrial complex transforms itself into a new toxic waste-disposal complex."[65]

There are huge profits to be made disposing of old ordnance, rocket engines, chemical weapons, uranium trailings, radioactive soil, and the like. And company bottom-lines look even better when military recycling is combined with the processing of imported urban solid waste, medical debris, industrial toxics, and non-military radioactive waste. The big problem has been to find compliant local governments willing to accept the poisoning of their natural and human landscapes.

No locality has been more eager to embrace the new political economy of toxic waste than Tooele County, just west of Salt Lake City. As one prominent activist complained to me, "the county commissioners have turned Tooele into the West's biggest economic red light district."[66] In addition to Dugway Proving Ground and the old Wendover and Deseret bombing ranges, the county is also home to the sprawling Tooele Army Depot, where nearly half of the Pentagon's chemical-weapons stockpile is awaiting incineration. Its non-military toxic assets include Magnesium Corporation of America's local smelter (the nation's leading producer of chlorine gas pollution) and the West Desert Hazardous Industry Area (WDHIA) (see map 19.3), which imports hazardous and radioactive waste from all over the country for burning in its two towering incinerators or burial in its three huge landfills.[67]

Most of these facilities have been embroiled in recent corruption or health-and-safety scandals. Utah's former state radiation-control director, for example, was accused in late December 1996 of extorting $600,000 ("in everything from cash to coins to condominiums") from Khosrow Semnani, the owner of Envirocare, the low-level radioactive waste dump in the WDHIA. Semnani has contributed heavily to local legislators in a successful attempt to keep state taxes and fees on Envirocare as low as possible. Whereas the two other states that license commercial sites for low-level waste, South Carolina and Washington, receive $235.00 and $13.75 per cubic foot respectively, Utah charges a negligible $.10 per cubic foot. As a result, radioactive waste has poured into the WDHIA from all over the country.[68]

Meanwhile, anxiety has soared over safety conditions at the half-billion-dollar chemical-weapons incinerator managed by EG&G Corporation at Tooele Army Depot. As the only operational incinerator in the continental United States (another, accident-ridden incinerator is located on isolated Johnson Atoll in the Pacific), the Depot is the key to the Pentagon's $31 billion chemical demilitarization program. Vehement public opposition has blocked incinerators originally planned for sites in seven other states. Only in job- and tax-hungry Tooele County, which has been promised $13 million "combat pay" over seven years, did the Army find a welcome mat.[69]

Yet as far back as 1989, reporters had obtained an internal report indicating that in a "worst case scenario" an accident at the plant could kill more than two thousand Tooele residents and spread nerve gas over the entire urbanized Wasatch Front. (The National Gulf War Resource Center in Washington, D.C. would later warn that "if there is a leak of sarin from the Tooele incinerator or one of the chemical warfare agent bunkers, residents of Salt Lake City may end up with Gulf War illness coming to a neighborhood near you.") Federal courts nonetheless rejected a last-minute suit by

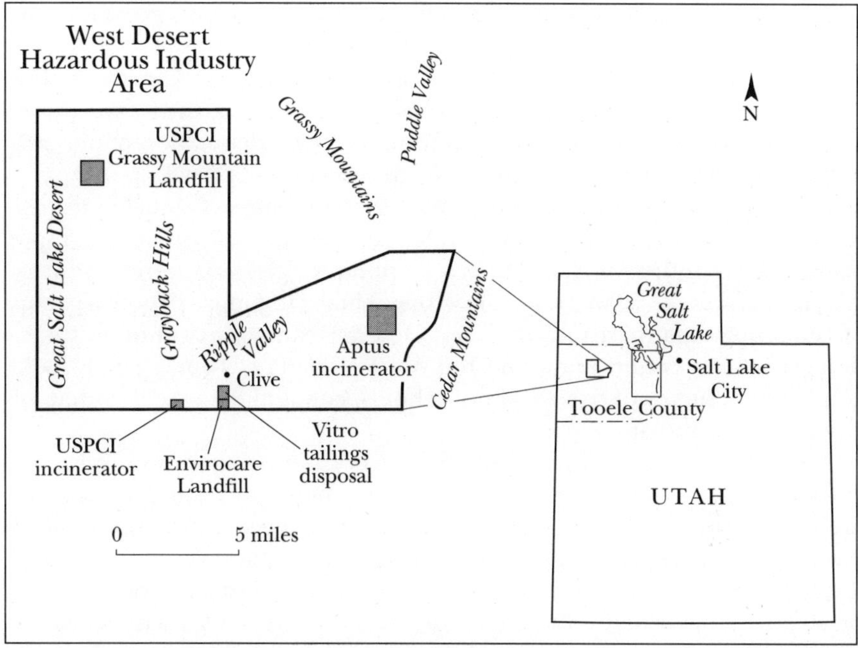

Map 19.3 Location map of Tooele Valley and the West Desert Hazardous Industry Area, Tooele County, Utah.

the Sierra Club and the Vietnam Veterans of America Foundation to prevent the opening of the incinerator in August 1996.[70]

Within seventy-two hours of ignition, however, a nerve gas leak forced operators to shut down the facility. Another serious leak occurred a few months later. Then, in November 1996, the plant's former director corroborated the testimony of earlier whistleblowers when he publicly warned EG&G officials that "300 safety, quality and operational deficiencies" still plagued the operation. He also complained that the "plan is run by former Army officers who disregard safety risks and are too focused on ambitious incineration schedules." Environmental groups, meanwhile, have raised fears that even "successful" operation of the incinerator might release dangerous quantities of carcinogenic dioxins into the local ecosystem.[71]

Indeed, there is disturbing evidence that a sinister synergy of toxic environments may already be creating a slow holocaust comparable to the ordeal of the fallout-poisoned communities chronicled by Carole Gallagher. At the northeastern end of Tooele Valley, for example, Grantsville (pop. 5,000) is currently under the shadow of the chlorine plume from Magnesium Corporation, the emissions from the hazmat incinerators in the WDHIA, and whatever is escaping from the Chemical Demilitarization Facility. In the past it has also been downwind of nuclear tests in Nevada and nerve-gas releases from Dugway, as well as clearly from the open detonation of old ordnance at the nearby but now closed North Area of the Army Depot.

For years Grantsville had lived under a growing sense of dread as cancer cases multiplied and the cemetery filled up with premature deaths, especially women in their thirties. As in a Stephen King novel, there was heavy gossip that something was radically wrong. Finally in January 1996, a group of residents, organized into the West Desert Healthy Environment Coalition (HEAL) by county librarian Chip Ward and councilwoman Janet Cook, conducted a survey of 650 local households, containing more than half of Grantsville's population.

To their horror, they discovered 201 cancer cases, 181 serious respiratory cases (not including bronchitis, allergies, or pneumonia), and 12 cases of multiple sclerosis. Although HEAL volunteers believe that majority Mormon residents reported only a fraction of their actual reproductive problems, they recorded 29 serious birth defects and 38 instances of major reproductive impairment. Two-thirds of the surveyed households, in other words, had cancer or a major disability in the family: many times the state and national averages. As Janet Cook told one journalist, "Southern Utah's got nothing on Grantsville."[72]

"Most remarkable," Ward observed, "was the way that cancer seemed to be concentrated among longtime residents." One source of historical exposure that Ward and others now think has been underestimated were the Dugway tests. "One respondent, for example, reported that she gave birth to seriously deformed twins several months after the infamous sheep kill in Skull Valley in 1968. Her doctor told her that he'd never seen so many birth defects as he did that year."[73]

But more than one incident is undoubtedly indicted in Grantsville's terrifying morbidity cluster. Environmental health experts have told HEAL that "cumulative, multiple exposures, with 'synergistic virulence' [the whole is greater than the sum of the parts]" best explain the local prevalence of cancers and lung diseases. In a downwind town where a majority of people work in hazardous occupations, including the Army Depot, Dugway, WDHIA, and the Magnesium Corporation, environmental exposure has been redoubled by occupational exposure, and vice versa.[74]

Consequently, West Desert HEAL, supported by Utah's Progressive Alliance of labor, environmental, and women's groups, has been demanding increased environmental monitoring, a moratorium on emissions and open detonation, complete documentation of past military testing, and a baseline regional health study with meaningful citizen participation. By early 1997 it had won legislative approval for the health survey and a radical reduction in Army detonations. The Magnesium Corporation, however, was still spewing chlorine and the Pentagon was still playing chicken with 13,616 tons of nerve gas.[75]

From a bar stool in the Dead Dog Saloon, Grantsville still seems like a living relic of that Old West of disenfranchised miners, cowboys, and Indians. Yet just a few miles down the road is the advance guard of approaching suburbia. Since 1995 metropolitan Salt Lake City has expanded, or, rather, exploded into northern Tooele Valley. The county seat, Tooele, has been featured in the *New York Times* as "one of the fastest-growing cities in the West," and a vast, billion-dollar planned suburb, Overlake, has been platted on its fringe.[76]

Although local developers deride the popular appeal of "tree-huggers" and anti-pollution groups, significant segments of the urban population will soon be in the toxic shadow of Tooele's nightmare industries. "When the new suburbanites wake up one morning and realize that they too are downwinders," Chip Ward predicts, "then environmental politics in Utah will really get interesting."[77]

Notes

An earlier version of this essay appeared in *New Left Review* no. 200 (July/August 1993): 49–73.

1. Although whale-hunting and sewerage are considered at length, the environmental impact of twentieth-century militarism is an inexplicably missing topic amongst the forty-two studies that comprise the landmark global audit: B. L. Turner et al. (eds.), *The Earth as Transformed by Human Action: Global and Regional Changes in the Biosphere over the Past 300 Years,* Cambridge 1990.

2. This is the term used by Michael Carricato, the Pentagon's former top environmental official. See Seth Shulman, *The Threat at Home: Confronting the Toxic Legacy of the U.S. Military,* Boston 1992, p. 8.

3. Nuclear landscapes, of course, also include parts of the Arctic (Novaya Zemlya and the Aleutians), Western Australia, and the Pacific (the Marshall Islands and Mururoa).

4. Zhores Medvedev, *Nuclear Disaster in the Urals,* New York 1979; and Boris Komarov, *The Destruction of Nature in the Soviet Union,* White Plains 1980.

5. See D. J. Peterson, *Troubled Lands: The Legacy of Soviet Environmental Destruction,* a Rand research study, Boulder 1993, pp. 7–10.

6. Ibid., p. 23.

7. Murray Feshbach and Alfred Friendly, Jr., *Ecocide in the USSR,* New York 1992, p. 1.

8. Peterson, p. 248. Peterson also quotes Russian fears that western joint ventures and multinational investment may only increase environmental destruction and accelerate the conversion of the ex-USSR, especially Siberia, into a vast "ecological colony" (pp. 254–257).

9. Feshbach and Friendly, pp. 11, 28, and 39.

10. Indeed, their sole citation of environmental degradation in the United States concerns the oyster beds of Chesapeake Bay (ibid., p. 49).

11. Richard Misrach, *Violent Legacies: Three Cantos,* New York 1992, pp. 38–59, 86. Misrach's interpretation of the pits is controversial. Officially, they are burial sites for animals infected with brucellosis and other stock diseases. Paiute ranchers that I interviewed, however, corroborated the prevalence of mystery deaths and grotesque births.

12. An Irish nationalist who sympathized with the struggle of the Plains Indians, Mooney risked professional ruin by including the Ogalala account of the massacre in his classic *The Ghost-Dance Religion and the Sioux Outbreak of 1890,* Fourteenth Annual Report of the Bureau of Ethnology, Washington 1896, pp. 843–886. The actual photographer was George Trager. See Richard Jensen et al., *Eyewitness at Wounded Knee,* Lincoln 1991.

13. Richard Misrach, *A Photographic Book,* San Francisco 1979; and *Desert Cantos,* Albuquerque 1987.

14. Richard Misrach (with Myriam Weisang Misrach), *Bravo 20: The Bombing of the American West,* Baltimore 1990, p. xiv.

15. Misrach, *Violent Legacies,* pp. 14–37, 83–86.

16. Lois Parkinson Zamora, *Writing the Apocalypse: Historical Vision in Contemporary U.S. and Latin American Fiction,* Cambridge 1989, p. 189 (my emphasis).

17. William Jenkins, *New Topographics: Photographs of a Man-Altered Landscape,* International Museum of Photography, Rochester 1975.

18. Mark Klett et al., *Second View: The Rephotographic Survey Project,* Albuquerque 1984.

19. San Francisco Camerawork, *Nuclear Matters,* San Francisco 1991.

20. See Adams's own account of how he retouched a famous photograph of Mount Whitney to eliminate a town name from a foreground hill: *Examples: The Making of Forty Photographs,* Boston 1983, p. 165.

21. Barry Lopez paraphrased by Thomas Southall, "I Wonder What He Saw," from Klett et al., p. 150.

22. Aside from Misrach, see especially Mark Klett, *Traces of Eden: Travels in the Desert Southwest,* Boston 1986; and *Revealing Territory,* Albuquerque 1992.

23. Revealingly, a decisive influence on the New Topographics was the surrealist photographer Frederick Sommer. His portraits of the Arizona desert were published in 1944 at the instigation of Max Ernst. See the essay by Mark Haworth-Booth in Lewis Baltz, *San Quentin Point,* New York 1986.

24. Jan Zita Gover, "Landscapes Ordinary and Extraordinary," *Afterimage,* December 1983, pp. 7–8.

25. The cold deserts and sagebrush (*Artemisia*) steppes of the Great Basin and the high plateaux are floristic colonies of Central Asia (see Neil West [ed.], *Ecosystems of the World 5: Temperate Deserts and Semi-Deserts,* Amsterdam 1983), but the physical landscapes are virtually unique (see Graf, W. L. [ed.], *Geomorphic Systems of North America,* Boulder 1987).

26. It is important to recall that the initial exploration of much of this "last West" occurred only 125 years ago. Cf. Gloria Cline, *Exploring the Great Basin,* Reno

1963; William Goetzmann, *Army Exploration in the American West, 1803–1863,* New Haven 1959; and *New Lands, New Men,* New York 1986.

27. The aeolian processes of the Colorado Plateau have provided valuable insights into the origin of certain Martian landscapes (Julie Laity, "The Colorado Plateau in Planetary Geology Studies," in Graf, pp. 288–297), while the Channeled Scablands of Washington are the closest terrestial equivalent to the great flood channels discovered on Mars in 1972. (See Baker et al., "Columbia and Snake River Plains," in Graf, pp. 403–468.) Finally, the basalt plains and calderas of the Snake River in Idaho are considered the best analogues to the lunar mare (ibid.).

28. There were four topographical and geological surveys afoot in the West between 1867 and 1879. The Survey of the Fortieth Parallel was led by Clarence King, the Survey West of the One Hundredth Meridian was under the command of Lieutenant George Wheeler, the Survey of the Territories was directed by Ferdinand Vandeveer Hayden, and the Survey of the Rocky Mountain Region was led by John Wesley Powell. They produced 116 scientific publications, including such masterpieces as Clarence Dutton, *Tertiary History of the Grand Canyon,* Washington 1873; Grove Karl Gilbert, *Report on the Geology of the Henry Mountains,* Washington 1877; and John Wesley Powell, *Exploration of the Colorado River of the West,* Washington 1873. John McPhee has recently repeated King's survey of the fortieth parallel (now Interstate 80) in his four-volume "cross-section of human and geological time": *Annals of the Former World,* New York, 1980–1993.

29. Cf. R. J. Chorley, A. J. Dunn and R. P. Beckinsale, *The History of the Study of Landforms, Volume 1: Geomorphology before Davis,* London 1964, pp. 469–621; and Baker et al.

30. Stephen Pyne, *Grove Karl Gilbert,* Austin 1980, p. 81. (He is referring specifically to the renowned geologist, Clarence Dutton, another member of the Powell survey.)

31. Ann-Sargent Wooster, "Reading the American Landscape," *Afterimage,* March 1982, pp. 6–8.

32. Consider "relapsing chasms," "wilted, drooping faces," "waving cones of the Uinkaret," and so on. See Wallace Stegner, *Beyond the Hundredth Meridian: John Wesley Powell and the Second Opening of the West,* Boston 1954, chapter 2.

33. Ibid., chapter 3. The ironic legacy of Powell's *Report* was the eventual formation of a federal Reclamation Agency that became the handmaiden of a western powerstructure commanded by the utility monopolies and corporate agriculture.

34. Carole Gallagher, *American Ground Zero: The Secret Nuclear War,* Boston 1993.

35. Peter Goin, *Nuclear Landscapes,* Baltimore 1991; and Robert Del Tredici, *At Work in the Fields of the Bomb,* New York 1987. See also Patrick Nagatani, *Nuclear Enchantment,* Albuquerque 1990; John Hooton, *Nuclear Heartlands,* 1988; and Jim Lerager, *In the Shadow of the Cloud,* 1988. Comparable work by independent filmmakers includes John Else, *The Day after Trinity* (1981); Dennis O'Rouke, *Half-Life* (1985); and Robert Stone, *Radio Bikini* (1988).

36. Dorothea Lange and Paul Taylor, *An American Exodus,* New York 1938; James Agee and Walker Evans, *Let Us Now Praise Famous Men,* Boston 1941; Erskine Caldwell and Margaret Bourke-White, *You Have Seen Their Faces,* New York 1937.

37. Gallagher, p. xxiii.

38. Ibid., p. xxxii.

39. Israel Torres and Robert Carter, quoted in ibid., pp. 61–62. Gallagher encountered the story about the charred human guinea pigs (prisoners?) "again and again from men who participated in shot Hood" (p. 62).

40. Delayne Evans, quoted in ibid., p. 275.

41. Issac Nelson, quoted in ibid., p. 134.

42. Ina Iverson, quoted in ibid., pp. 141–143. Gallagher points out that molar pregnancies are also "an all too common experience for the native women of the Marshall Islands in the pacific Testing Range after being exposed to the fallout from the detonations of hydrogen bombs" (p. 141).

43. Jay Truman, quoted in ibid., p. 308.

44. The literature is overwhelming. See House Subcommittee on Oversight and Investigations, *The Forgotten Guinea Pigs,* 96th Congress, 2nd session, August 1980; Thomas Saffer and Orville Kelly, *Countdown Zero,* New York 1982; John Fuller, *The Day We Bombed Utah: America's Most Lethal Secret,* New York 1984; Richard Miller, *Under the Cloud: The Decades of Nuclear Testing,* New York 1986; Howard Ball, *Justice Downwind: America's Atomic Testing Program in the 1950s,* New York 1986; A. Costandina Titus, *Bombs in the Backyard: Atomic Testing and Atomic Politics,* Reno 1986; and Philip Fradkin, *Fallout: An American Nuclear Tragedy,* Tucson 1989.

45. Gallagher, pp. xxxi–xxxii.

46. Fradkin, p. 57; Peterson, pp. 203 and 230 (fn. 49).

47. See "From the Editors," *The Bulletin of the Atomic Scientists,* September 1990, p. 2.

48. Colonel Langdon Harrison, quoted in Gallagher, p. 97.

49. Peterson, p. 204; see also Feshbach and Friendly, pp. 238–239.

50. See my "French Kisses and Virtual Nukes," in *Capitalism, Nature, Socialism,* 7(1), March 1996.

51. Cf. Kealy Davidson, "The Virtual Bomb," *Mother Jones,* March/April 1995; Jacqueline Cabasso and John Burroughs, "End run around the NPT," *The Bulletin of the Atomic Scientists,* September–October 1995; and Jonathan Weissman, "New Mission for the National Labs," *Science,* 6 October 1995. On protest plans: interview with Las Vegas Catholic workers, May 1997.

52. See Tracey Panek, "Life at Iosepa, Utah's Polynesian Colony," *Utah Historical Quarterly;* and Donald Rosenberg, "Iosepa," talk given on centennial, Salt Lake City, 27 August 1989 (special collections, University of Utah library).

53. Ronald Bateman, "Goshute Uprising of 1918," *Deep Creek Reflections,* pp. 367–370.

54. Barton Bernstein, "Churchill's Secret Biological Weapons," *Bulletin of the Atomic Scientists,* January–February 1987.

55. See Ann LoLordo, "Germ Warfare Test Subjects," (first appeared in *Baltimore Sun*), reprinted in *Las Vegas Review-Journal,* 29 August 1994; and Lee Davidson, "Cold War Weapons Testing," *Deseret News,* 22 December 1994.

56. Lee Davidson, "Lethal Breeze," *Deseret News,* 5 June 1994.

57. For fuller accounts, see Jeanne McDermott, *The Killing Winds,* New York 1987; and Charles Piller and Keith Yamamoto, *Gene Wars: Military Control over the New Genetic Technologies,* New York 1988.

58. Steve Erickson, Downwinders, Inc., interviewed September, November 1992 and January 1993.

59. *Downwinders, Inc. v. Cheney and Stone,* Civil No. 91-C-681j, United States Court, District of Utah, Central Division.

60. Erickson refers to information revealed in December 1990 by Ted Jacobs, chief counsel to the House Subcommittee on Commerce, Consumer and Monetary Affairs.

61. Interviews with Steve Erickson and Cindy King (Sierra Club), Salt Lake City, October 1996.

62. Ibid.

63. Schulman, p. 7.

64. The estimate is from figures in Schulman, appendix B.

65. Interview with Triana Silton, September 1992.

66. Interview with Chip Ward, Grantsville, Utah, October 1996.

67. For a description of the WDHIA and its natural setting, see Barry Wolomon, "Geologic Hazards and Land-use Planning for Tooele Valley and the Western Desert Hazardous Industrial Area," Utah Geological Survey, *Survey Notes,* November 1994.

68. Jim Wolf, "Does N-Waste Firm Pay Enough to Utah?" *Salt Lake Tribune,* 10 January 1997.

69. Ralph Vartabedian, "Start-Up of Incinerator is Assailed," *Los Angeles Times,* 4 March 1996.

70. Lee Davidson, "An Accident at TAD Could Be Lethal," *Deseret News,* 23 May 1989; and Lee Siegel, "Burn Foes Fear Outbreak of Gulf War Ills," *Salt Lake Tribune,* 12 January 1997.

71. Joseph Bauman, "Former Tooele Manager Calls Plant Unsafe," *Deseret News,* 26 November 1996.

72. West Desert Healthy Environment Alliance, *The Grantsville Community's Health: A Citizen Survey,* Grantsville 1996; Diane Rutter, "Healing Their Wounds," *Catalyst,* April 1996. See also "Listen to Cancer Concerns," editorial, *Salt Lake Tribune,* 6 April 1996.

73. Interview with Chip Ward, Grantsville, Utah, October 1996.

74. Ibid.

75. Interview with Chip Ward, January 1997.

76. James Brooke, "Next Door to Danger, a Booming City," *New York Times,* 6 October 1996.

77. Interview with Chip Ward, January 1997.

20

LA FRONTERA DEL NORTE

JESÚS MARTÍNEZ-SALDAÑA

This work analyzes aspects of the artistic production of Los Tigres del Norte, a Mexican immigrant *norteño* group with great appeal in the United States and Mexico. It examines themes in their songs relevant to the ongoing debate over immigration in contemporary American society. This study of popular cultural expressions of Mexican immigrants is part of a broader research effort that is focused on addressing a question rarely considered in the relevant scholarship: How does participation in the process of international migration influence the politics of the millions of Mexicans who cross, on a temporary or permanent basis, the border into the United States?

Today, a full century after Mexican migration to the United States began, the political experience of this social group remains virtually uncharted territory. Scholars have not managed to identify and document their historical trajectory in a satisfactory manner, and they have had even less success explaining the group's views and activities. A principal reason for this dismal state of affairs is the tendency to view Mexican immigrants in reductionist terms. This is evident in the immigration-related scholarship, which devotes much attention to the Mexican immigrants' linkages to the labor market and disregards their relations to the Mexican and U.S. national polities.

A major consequence of this conceptualization is the narrowing of the political rights and spaces for Mexican immigrants in the two national societies. In the contemporary United States, for example, it is once again popular to perceive and treat Mexican immigrants simply as a disposable labor force that should be imported and deported as the economic needs of the nation dictate. The passage of Proposition 187 in California and restrictive immigration laws by Congress reveal the unwillingness of the electorate and legislators to view as full members of their national community the economic immigrants who ensure the international competitiveness of the American economy.

Unfortunately, the circumscribed economic approach to Mexican immigration also prevails in Mexico, where the government has consistently excluded from the policymaking process the millions of citizens who participate in international migration flows. The nation's immigration-related policies reproduce the authoritarian character of the political system, as these are formulated and frequently imposed by the federal executive, without any semblance of democratic input by the immigrants themselves. Even when important reforms like the "dual nationality" and "right to vote" laws approved by the Mexican Congress in 1996 are discussed in the national legislature, no actual mechanisms are created or considered to foster formal, effective, and adequate immigrant input. It appears that, to the Mexican government, Mexican immigrants are simpleminded laborers who lack the capacity to identify and represent themselves.

The employment of this dominant approach to interpret Mexican immigration is lamentable for many other reasons. In particular, it is objectionable because it does not consider other roles Mexican transnational migrants play in the sending and receiving nations. Their treatment in purely working class terms does not permit us to appreciate in an adequate manner other aspects of their existence, nor the relations they develop with markets, administrative systems, or polities. Specifically, they are not seen as consumers who demand and receive goods and services, nor as clients of administrative systems who exchange taxes for public services, and certainly not as full and mature citizens of national polities who have the capacity to exchange loyalty and consent for favorable political decisions.[1]

Due to the weight of the dominant interpretation, we are unable to find in the existing literature on Mexican immigration a theoretical formulation which approximates the framework developed by Don T. Nakanishi to examine Asian American politics or the conceptualizations of international migrants made by scholars such as Yasemin Soysal.

Nakanishi presents a model which suggests that empirical and theoretical studies of the electoral politics of Asian American can best be conceptualized by integrating three distinct but interrelated approaches: the interplay between domestic and non-domestic activities, electoral and non-electoral behavior, and micro and macro lines of inquiry. In this model, Nakanishi calls attention to the significance of non-domestic affairs and processes which, at times, may prove to be more important in explaining developments within the Asian community. He identifies at least five major issues relevant to his model: the transnational activities of Asian Americans in relation to Asia; the transnational activities of Asian governments and quasi-governmental institutions in U.S. communities; the impact of bilateral relations on Asian

Americans; the attempts by Asian Americans to influence the relations between the United States and Asia; and the influence of international processes and policies dealing with the flow of people, capital, goods, and ideas on Asian American politics.[2]

In turn, Soysal argues that the relationship between international migrants and nation-states has undergone a recent transformation, deeply influenced by a shift in the global discourse and models of citizenship. What has emerged in regions such as Western Europe is a new model of membership which she calls "postnational," and which is characterized by the extension to noncitizens of rights that in earlier times were exclusively reserved for citizens. Moreover, she justifies this emerging model of incorporation by arguing that international migrants, such as the Turks in Germany, exercise in their daily praxis a membership "that is multiple in the sense of spanning local, regional, and global identities, and which accommodates intersecting complexes of rights, duties, and loyalties."[3]

By continuing to rely on the dominant approach to the study of Mexican immigrants, scholars remain unable to understand in a satisfactory manner issues as fundamental as the meaning of naturalization to Mexican immigrants in the United States or the group's preferences for Mexican political parties and presidential candidates. This leads us to a situation in which we are unable to explain how the individual and collective identities of Mexican transnational migrants are transformed by their participation in a process of migration that simultaneously links them with two distinct societies and their powerful national cultural myths, including the notions of the Raza Cosmica and the melting pot.

It is time to reconceptualize the Mexican immigrant political experience. I offer an alternative interpretation influenced by works such as Nakanishi's and Soysal's: the interpretation of Mexican immigrants as citizens of a binational system, with rights and responsibilities in the two republics to which they are linked by historical accident, social networks, and/or economic necessity.

Employing this approach would improve our current understanding of the migrants' relationship with both the sending and receiving nations. As Nakanishi and Soysal suggest, approaches which limit their scope to the established territorial boundary of a single nation are ill-suited for social groups with a transnational character. The migration process links Mexicans to (at least) two national economies, societies, and political systems. This reality may imply playing distinct roles in the two nations to which they are connected. For example, an individual migrant may hold a position of relative privilege in one society and a subordinate one in the second. Their character as transnational migrants may lead them to hold parallel identities/roles and contribute to the emergence of a binational or postnational consciousness.

Historically, Mexican immigrants have had low rates of naturalization in the United States, thereby making electoral politics a matter of secondary importance. While post–Proposition 187 reports indicate that the number of Mexican immigrant applications for naturalization has increased, it is not clear if this is a conjunctural phenomenon or a long-term trend. After all, the continuing economic crisis in Mexico has made the return to the home nation less attractive to individuals and families who may have originally intended to migrate temporarily. Needless to say, it is also unknown yet if the increased naturalization is mostly a response to the fear of denial of public services to non-citizens in the future, an actual desire to participate in the electoral process, a strategy of migrants to facilitate the legal migration of family members, or a combination of factors. In any event, for the purposes of this essay, I also argue that the political experiences of Mexican immigrants are better understood by adopting an expansive notion of politics in order to incorporate both electoral and non-electoral interests, concerns, and activities.

Similarly, the utilization of the concept of citizenship in the proposed approach is not intended to be limited to the legal definitions that center on the process of naturalization. Rather, I prefer to emphasize a definition that can link immigration to the discourse on democracy in nations as distinct as the United States and Mexico. Despite the existence of differences in the definitions of citizenship and democracy in the relevant literature, it is widely assumed democracies can only exist if the members of the polities have the power and means for effective participation in the transformation of their world. I do not believe that at present Mexican immigrants enjoy full citizenship in the United States or Mexico.

The issue would not be significant if the group in question consisted of a handful of individuals. However, Mexican immigrants number in the millions and their importance to the two nations grows as the process of economic integration proceeds with the approval and implementation of accords such as the North American Free Trade Agreement. If this is the case, what kinds of democracies are we creating in the two countries if present trends point toward the increasing exclusion of international migrants? Does it matter to the United States and Mexico what Mexican immigrants think or do?

A Collective Autobiography

Social groups excluded from national political systems eventually find ways of expressing their views and interests. One of the channels worth considering is popular culture. In the case of Mexican immigrants, we find that popular songs serve as an important outlet for individual and collective expressions. The topics of these expressions may range from the expected references to love and scorn commonly requested by callers to commercial radio stations to the more serious attempts at social commentary which rarely receive air time in an entertainment-oriented industry.

Nevertheless, it is precisely within this context that the work of commercially successful groups such as Los Tigres del Norte needs to be examined. Contributions by other scholars help us to understand the value of popular songs. For example, in his pioneer works on Mexican immigration, anthropologist Manuel Gamio considered the songs of Mexican immigrants "a sort of collective autobiography." According to the researcher, undeniably influenced by the male-centered approach to migration studies at the time of his research, the songs provide information "on his likes and his dislikes, his hopes and his disappointments."[4]

This discussion of Mexican immigrant interpretations of race relations in the United States follows this tradition by analyzing the songs of Los Tigres del Norte, one of the best known norteño groups in the United States and Mexico. The collective autobiographical approach proposed by Gamio is valuable for three basic reasons: the group members are Mexican immigrants who reside in California's Silicon Valley; they have developed a musical trajectory characterized until recently by a consistent production of immigration-related songs; and a majority of these were composed by Enrique Franco, also a Mexican immigrant living in Silicon Valley.

The site of residence of the group members and Enrique Franco is significant for another reason. As the most important center of high technology research and development in the world, Silicon Valley plays a symbolic role in the national imagination; it is the one location in the nation which best represents the mythical American pioneer spirit. In the national consciousness, Silicon Valley is perceived as the future, the region in which Americans push forward the contemporary frontiers of technology and capitalism. President Clinton's frequent visits to the region and his laudatory remarks about the achievements of the area's high technology scientists and entrepreneurs reinforces such an assessment.

Moreover, corroborating views of local residents are reflected in their public comments. A local executive who once held public office confirms the existence of such views when he highlights in a nationally distributed advertisement for the city of San Jose the qualities he considers unique to the region:

> What to us seems normal, starting new businesses, creating community projects . . . , taking risks, exploring new ways to do things, don't happen in many places. . . . We don't appreciate this until we go to other parts of the country where such approaches are not prevalent. In some parts of the country, if one leaves a strong, established company to go it on his own, he is considered some

> kind of maverick. Here, if you don't leave a strong, established company to start your own business, people wonder if you've got what it takes.[5]

In turn, an executive of an international firm combines social Darwinism and inspiration drawn from Hollywood films to assert: "Silicon Valley is the Wild West of private enterprise. . . . It's survival of the fittest."[6] In such a highly competitive society ruled by information-age cowboys and gunfighters, there is little room or tolerance for the weak, for the losers in this battleground of postindustrial capitalism.

The success of the high technology economy in Silicon Valley also influences the local political system, as well as the governing style and agendas of elected officials. According to the advertisement: "The same kind of innovation that characterizes Silicon Valley business management also applies to government. Public officials say they too have to be lean, creative and competitive."[7]

In this vision of Silicon Valley, market efficiency becomes more precious than democracy, and citizens are replaced by consumers, elected leaders by political entrepreneurs. Since Mexicans, native and foreign born, cannot compete successfully in the labor or political markets because they are presumed to lack a competitive spirit or other essential qualities possessed by William Hewlett, David Packard, and other high technology pioneers, one can surmise that the local hegemonic culture can only consider them losers in this competition for social supremacy.

To some social sectors, Mexicans also constitute an undesirable element. A November 1992 letter to the editor published in the *San Jose Mercury News* expresses these sentiments.

> The No. 1 issue bothering me in this election year is immigration. The voter pamphlet I received in Spanish was the last straw.
>
> I am confronted on a daily basis with the nightmare that has become my beloved California. Our state's population grew from 23 million to 30 million from 1980 to 1990! . . .
>
> Solutions: no new immigrants, unless they can prove they have a skill we need; much more intense work with Mexico and other countries on illegal immigration; beefed up border patrols; a scouring and subsequent booting-out of all illegal aliens; better interdiction of illegals as they enter the country.
>
> You can call me a racist, call me whatever you want. But I am tired of seeing my beloved state and country having certain areas (including the Bay Area) overrun with immigrants. The environment can't take the added people, nor can the economy, the schools, the government, the cities or taxpayers. I don't feel that I or other long time citizens should have to put up with this nightmare.[8]

The existence of these views raises the question I wish to address in the rest of this essay: How do Mexican immigrants, in this case Los Tigres del

Norte and Enrique Franco, interpret their experience in this Wild West of private enterprise?

El Norte

Before initiating my analysis, however, a clarification is in order.

The American West does not exist only in the collective consciousness of this country. It is also present in the imagination of people in other nations. For example, there are many manifestations of what is now the American West in the Mexican national consciousness. Two are rather easy to recognize. One is *el territorio perdido,* the unknown but much celebrated portion of the national territory lost through an unjust war to the aggressive forces driven by Manifest Destiny. And thanks to the Spanish-language versions of Hollywood films and Madison Avenue publications, the American West is also *el viejo oeste,* a site inhabited by fictitious blond-haired, blue-eyed cowboys, valiantly creating a society of law, order, and progress amidst the instability fomented by war-mongering, uncivilized *pieles rojas* ("red skins") and wicked outlaws.

A third conception of the American West exists and is now profoundly rooted in Mexican society. It is *el norte,* the temporary or permanent destination for millions of Mexicans who have been forced to cross the northern border into the United States, at times searching for political stability and refuge, but generally seeking better economic opportunities than those found in the nation of origin, *la patria.*

These and other visions are not necessarily exclusive of each other. They may co-exist and reinforce each other under the proper circumstances. For example, a child belonging to a family with a long history of international migration might learn about the "lost territory" in school textbooks, fantasize about the "Old West" while reading *vaquero* comic books or watching reruns of *Bonanza* on Mexican television, and imagine other features of the foreign land while hearing accounts of life in California from migrant relatives, friends, or neighbors.

Frontera, Frontera Internacional

In the songs of Los Tigres it is apparent that, despite the relatively familiar nature of el norte, Mexicans experience a disturbing encounter with social injustice upon arrival at *la frontera,* the international border shared by Mexico and the United States. In fact, the reality of the border begins to define the immigrants' relationship to the United States. According to the songs of Los Tigres, at this gateway there is no Statue of Liberty welcoming Mexican immigrants, only a border guarded by the hated *migra* (Immigration and Naturalization Service). To Mexicans intent on crossing into this country, the border represents an artificial sociopolitical trench which divides human beings along national and racial lines; it must be defied, whether to seek work, unify the family, or carry out other activities, including the smuggling of contraband.

Many Tigres del Norte songs focus on this space in which social and political frontiers coexist. In fact, the group members owe their rise in popularity to a mid-seventies recording, "Contrabando y Traición," a love and drug smuggling *corrido* (ballad) featuring the adventures of Emilio Varela and Camelia *la texana,* two fictional characters who are now as deeply ingrained in Mexican popular culture as the fabled corrido figures Juan Charrasqueado, Gabino Barrera, Simon Blanco, Valentina, Adelita, and Rosita Alvírez.

The principal virtue of Los Tigres del Norte is that in the years following their commercial success based on drug smuggling corridos they managed to distinguish themselves from competitors by recording dozens of songs that directly explored distinct aspects of the Mexican immigrant experience. This was most successfully carried out during the phase of their career when they established an artistic partnership with Enrique Franco. When Los Tigres and Franco joined forces in the late seventies and he became the group's principal composer, the content of the group's songs shifted from drug smuggling and crime to a direction characterized by an exceptional social awareness mirroring the concern of Mexican immigrants with the often hostile immigration debate that was engulfing the nation. The character of the songs and their accelerated production and commercialization during the first years of the decade of the eighties reflected in a unique manner the increasing anxieties found among Mexicans in the United States, particularly as the dates for the approval and implementation of the Immigration Reform and Control Act of 1986 approached. A clear pattern emerged in the artistic production of Los Tigres, linking the immigrant experience, specifically the concerns over immigration policies, and the thematic evolution of their songs.

By the mid-eighties, Los Tigres had already established themselves as exceptional articulators of the Mexican immigrant experience, with dozens of serious, insightful, and predominantly denunciatory songs on U.S. immigration policy. In this collective autobiography composed of largely original compositions, one finds a consistent defense of Mexican immigrants. The songs criticize the imposition of political borders which divide Mexicans and other peoples, espouse Latin American and universal brotherhood, and celebrate the Mexican racial miscegenation known as *mestizaje.*

From a broader perspective, the songs may be considered surprisingly consistent with the ideology of revolutionary nationalism that has prevailed in Mexico during the post-revolutionary era. As Roger Bartra has indicated, it is an official ideology which has been imposed on Mexican society by the state-party system first created by Plutarco Elias Calles in 1929.[9] It is an ideology that is also espoused and transmitted to the Mexican masses on a daily basis by Televisa, the media conglomerate which had a virtual monopoly over Mexican television for decades. Fonovisa, the group's recording label since the mid-eighties, is affiliated with Televisa. Thus, it is possible to argue that the artistic work of Los Tigres del Norte is simultaneously conventional, within the Mexican cultural discourse, and oppositional, or at least denunciatory, with respect to the United States. In the case of Los Tigres, popular music reproduces the dual roles individuals play once they begin participation in the process of transnational migration.

An important quality of the songs recorded by Los Tigres del Norte during the decade of the eighties is their refreshing and innovative approach to issues which are linked to a historical phenomenon a century old. An awareness of this context is essential to appreciate the significance of the songs. They are fully understood only if one associates them with the migratory experiences of the composer, musicians, and a consumer market which exists on both sides of the international border.

An extraordinary exposition of these ideas is presented in "Frontera Internacional," a melancholic appeal directed at the international border itself by a Mexican who lost a brother in an attempt to cross into the United States. The individual returns to the scene of the tragedy, driven by the same forces which have perpetuated migration from the traditional sending regions of Mexico. This time, he intends to cross the river with his loved woman, notwithstanding the potential risks involved.

"Frontera Internacional" informs us of the social repercussions of successful and unsuccessful migration, acknowledges the economic origins of this process, calls attention to the unfair social divisions found by Mexicans in the United States, and affirms the need for the receiving society to consider more tolerant and humane immigration policies.

Frontera, tú que ves hombres llorar sin abrigo y sin hogar por que dejáron su tierra	Border, you who see men cry without coat or home because they left their land
Quisiera que cuando pase mi amor en el nombre del señor esa puerta se cayera	I would like that when my love passes in the name of the Lord that door would fall
Frontera, dejo mi patria y mi hogar todo por querer ganar un poquito de dinero	Border, I leave my fatherland and home all in order to earn a little bit of money

Dinero,
esa es la causa fatal
de que mi hermano al pasar
haya muerto allá en el cerro

Money,
that is the fatal cause
that my brother upon passing
perished there at the hill

Frontera,
frontera internacional,
abre que voy a pasar
con el amor de mi vida

Border,
international border,
open because I am going to pass
with the love of my life

Frontera,
frontera internacional,
si somos hombres igual,
¿por qué divides la tierra?

Border,
international border,
if we are equal men,
why do you divide the land?

(Hablado)
¿Cuantas madres se han quedado
llorando aquel hijo amado
y muriendo de dolor?
Yo te pregunto, frontera,
¿por qué en lugar de trinchera
no eres la linea que uniera
sin importar el color?

(Spoken)
How many mothers have remained
crying that beloved son
and dying of pain?
I ask you, border,
why instead of a trench
are you not the line that would unite
without regard to color?

(Cantado)
Frontera,
frontera internacional,
abre que voy a pasar
con el amor de mi vida

(Sung)
Border,
international border,
open because I am going to pass
with the love of my life

Frontera,
frontera internacional,
si somos hombres igual,
¿por qué divides la tierra?

Border,
international border,
if we are equal men,
why do you divide the land?

In the songs of Los Tigres one finds danger permeating the border region. As reports by human rights organizations repeatedly indicate, death is not an entirely unfamiliar occurrence at the border. It can be the result of an accident, an inability to swim, suffocation in a sealed railroad car, a robbery or rape, a high-speed automobile persecution, or the aggression of a U.S. border patrol agent.

As expected, Los Tigres have captured the essence of this dangerous passage into the unknown in another song in which la frontera becomes "La Tumba del Mojado." This composition is a first-person account of the difficulties associated with border crossing, subsequent persecutions and arrest, and the national-origin-based discrimination experienced by Mexicans without documents.

No pude cruzar la raya	I could not cross the line
se me atravezo el Río Bravo	the Rio Bravo got in my way
me aprehendieron nuevamente	I was apprehended once again
cuando viví al otro lado	when I lived on the other side
los dolares son bonitos	the dollars are pretty
pero yo soy mexicano	but I am Mexican

The initiation of conflictive relations with U.S. authorities begins as soon as *la frontera internacional* is crossed and the immigrants encounter the gatekeepers of a nation which may offer economic opportunities but is nevertheless perceived as unfair and discriminatory. This is illustrated in an eloquent manner in "Los Hijos de Hernández," a composition which examines and describes a confrontation between a legal immigrant and a border official. The conflict is the consequence of anti-Mexican remarks made by the official while inspecting the Mexican's immigration documents. Charges that Mexican immigrants steal jobs from American citizens, an accusation frequently made by contemporary politicians, intellectuals, and nativist groups, does not go unanswered. The immigration official is startled to see "the Other" talking back, transmitting in a heartfelt and reasoned manner the ire Mexicans feel upon hearing offensive statements.

In "Los Hijos de Hernández" the common immigrant assumes a position of power and moral authority, based on the use of reason, to chastise the official for holding prejudicial views against Mexicans. The representative of the State is criticized by the apparently passive Mexican for dismissing the immigrants' economic and social contributions to the United States, and for not acknowledging the many military sacrifices generations of Mexican Americans have made on behalf of this country. A common immigrant questions the lack of respect for others like himself as well as their U.S.-born youth who, ignoring prejudice and discrimination, take up arms to defend their country, serve courageously, and even lose their lives or remain missing in action.

Despite the conflictive nature of the song, reason finally prevails at the end with the repentance of the authority figure, the recognition of legal permission to enter American territory, and the validation of the male immigrant's once questioned manhood. Vindication is achieved with the change in attitude of the authority figure.

Mientras ésto le gritaba	While I shouted this at him
el emigrante lloraba	the immigration official cried
y díjo con emoción:	and stated with emotion:
"Puedes cruzar la frontera	"You may cross the border
ésta y la veces que quieras	this and other times you like
tienes más valor que yo"	you have more valor than I"

"Sin Fronteras" reaffirms pride in the Mexican's national origin, way of life, cultural values, male world view, and mestizo heritage. However, it departs from other Mexican nationalist songs in a number of ways. In particular, it offers an interpretation of the immigrant identity that embraces the universality of life and liberty. The immigrant experience is compared to the life of an eagle in order to impress upon the audience the natural origin of freedom and the artificiality of earthly divisions.

Soy como el águila	I am like the eagle
que vuela por el cielo	that flies through the heavens
libre su vuelo	free its flight
por donde es amo y señor	where it is master and lord
Arriba no esta dividido	It is not divided up above
como el suelo	like the ground
que la maldad	that the evil
de algunos hombres dividió	of some men divided

Such expressions of universal ideals placed Los Tigres del Norte at a considerable distance from their competitors in Mexican popular music. Their uncommon exploration of these themes is found in works such as "Tres Veces Mojado," a well received composition that extends the scope of the group's subject matter (and potential market) by presenting a song dealing with Central American migration to the United States. This extension of the collective autobiography is the account of a Salvadoran who flees the violence and poverty of his country, crosses three international borders with respective rivers, and encounters hardships in the three foreign countries (Guatemala, Mexico, the United States) before obtaining legalization in this country and achieving a satisfying lifestyle that more than makes up for the suffering previously undergone.

In two other recordings, "América" and "El Sueño de Bolívar," composed by Franco, Los Tigres present songs which further examine identity terms that become particularly relevant to a Mexican only when the international border is crossed into the United States. "América" manifests a strong attachment to the migrant's Latin American heritage. It defies conventional wisdom in the United States by seeking to reappropriate a term, "American," which this country has sought to monopolize.

In turn, "El Sueño de Bolívar" appears to adopt a more conformist, perhaps assimilationist, position by suggesting that liberator Simón Bolívar's nineteenth-century dream of a united America could be materializing, of all places, in the United States, due to migration and the development of ties between the different national origin groups established here. Moreover, it calls for the acceptance of the "Hispanic" identity label, a term generally preferred by the more conservative sectors of the Mexican origin community and repudiated by others who view it as a governmental and corporate imposition. In an interview, Franco declared the song was primarily an idealistic call for unity among the Latin Americans who immigrate to the United States.[10]

Franco has also indicated the most important song produced during his association with Los Tigres del Norte was "Jaula de Oro." This 1985 song was released in an interesting historical period: at the height of the restrictionist anti-immigrant debate which culminated in the approval of the 1986 Immigration Reform and Control Act. "Jaula de Oro" presents the plight of an undocumented immigrant parent, alienated from society at large, haunted by the fear of persecution by the Immigration and Naturalization Service, and growing increasingly detached from children undergoing a process of socialization which makes them ashamed of their Mexican heritage. To individuals such as the principal character of the song, the United States constitutes a gold cage; salvation, as well as the restoration of his humanity, can only be obtained in the idealized home country. The land of the mythical American dream has become dystopia. The song has a predictable but nevertheless disturbing climax, as the U.S.-raised child refuses to return to Mexico and leaves the parent in a state of despair and frustration.

And They Keep Going . . . and Coming

The growing success of Los Tigres during the eighties led to an increased involvement in the Mexican movie industry. In the decade of the seventies the corridos recorded by the group were exploited and utilized as the basis of a thriving border film industry. In some of the films the musicians even appeared in minor roles performing their songs. By the mid-eighties they made a substantial jump to the level of stars and producers. The first film they co-produced was a cinematic version of "Jaula de Oro."

The film version differs from the song because it has a happy ending. The final moments of the film consists of two interchanging events: one consists of the father figure, played by well known Mexican actor Fernando Almada, who drives from Los Angeles to the Mexican border in the company of a young son; the second is that of Los Tigres del Norte, in the role of older children, who are performing at a dance-concert organized to raise funds for the legal defense of undocumented immigrants.

One of the group members pauses during the performance to inform the audience of his parent's departure and express support for the father's decision. The singer then proceeds to dedicate a potpourri of Mexican nationalist songs to his father and others like him.

The final image is that of the smiling father arriving at the border. As the credits roll and the film ends, a still image presents a border sign reading "Mexico" while Los Tigres play "Que Bonita Es Mi Tierra."

The film ends with the immigrant's return to the homeland. Yet, the camera ignores the Mexicans crossing la frontera in the opposite direction, leaving behind a nation that fails to provide them with an acceptable living standard.

A decade later, a different camera did capture the northward flow of Mexicans across the same border checkpoint. California Governor Pete Wilson's reelection campaign utilized video images of undocumented Mexicans running past la frontera and across a freeway to influence public opinion in support of the anti-immigrant measures known as Proposition 187. The successful initiative denies education, health, and other public services to undocumented immigrants in the state. In the much televised political advertisement, a narrator's divisive message warns the predominantly European-origin, conservative, and middle class electorate of Mexican immigrant hordes invading the state and the nation: "They keep coming."

To Governor Wilson, and the political forces who support measures such as Proposition 187 in the NAFTA era of liberalized transnational flow of goods and capital, "they" not only do not belong in California, but their presence and activities undermine national integrity, the rule of law, and the democratic political system.

Then again, even the Pete Wilson family has had the need to hire a good, cheap, and undocumented Mexican immigrant maid.

Notes

All of the songs quoted here recorded by Los Tigres del Norte are reprinted by permission of T. N. Ediciones Musicales.

1. These roles are derived from a model presented by Stephen K. White, *The Recent Work of Jurgen Habermas: Reason, Justice and Modernity* (Cambridge: Cambridge University Press, 1989), p. 109.

2. See Don T. Nakanishi, "Asian American Politics: An Agenda for Research," *Amerasia Journal* 12, no. 2 (1985–86), p. 3.

3. Yasemin Nuhoglu Soysal, *Limits of Citizenship: Migrants and Postnational Membership in Western Europe* (Chicago: University of Chicago Press, 1994), p. 166.

4. Manuel Gamio, *Mexican Immigration to the United States: A Study of Human Migration and Adjustment* (New York: Dover Publications, 1971), p. 84. For the relation between gender and migration, see Pierrette Hondagneu-Sotelo, *Gendered Transitions: Mexican Experiences of Migration* (Berkeley: University of California Press, 1994).

5. *Fortune San Jose,* special advertising section, 5 June 1989 edition of *Fortune* magazine.

6. Ibid.

7. Ibid.

8. *San Jose Mercury News,* 26 November 1992.

9. Roger Bartra, "Changes in Political Culture: The Crisis of Nationalism," in Wayne A. Cornelius, Judith Gentleman, and Peter H. Smith, eds., *Mexico's Alternative Political Futures* (San Diego: UCSD Center for U.S.-Mexican Studies, 1989), pp. 55–85.

10. See Jesús Martínez Saldaña, "Los Tigres del Norte en Silicon Valley," *Nexos,* November 1993, pp. 77–83.

Selected Tigres del Norte Recordings

Unidos Para Siempre. Musivisa TUR/1672, 1996.
El Ejemplo. Fonovisa SDCD-6030, 1995.
Los Dos Plebes. Fonovisa SDCD-6017, 1994.
La Garra de . . . Fonovisa FPCD-9085, 1993.
Con Sentimiento y Sabor. Fonovisa FPCD-9044, 1992.
Incansables. Fonovisa FPL-9013, 1991.
Para Adoloridos. Fonovisa FPL-9001, 1990.
Triunfo Solido. Musivisa KMUPR-8002, 1989.
Corridos Prohibidos. Fonovisa FPL-8815, 1989.
16 Superexitos. Fonovisa MPCD-5084, 1988.
Idolos del Pueblo. Fonovisa FPL-8800, 1988.
Gracias! . . . América . . . Sin Fronteras. Profono PRL-90499, 1986.
El Otro México. Profono MPC-5043, 1985.
Jaula de Oro. Emi Capitol POP-849, 1985.
16 Grandes Exitos. Profono TPL-90379.
Carrera Contra la Muerte. Profono MPC-5034, 1984.
Internacionalmente Norteños. Profono MPC-5003, 1984.
Exitos Para Siempre. Fama 624, 1983.
Un Día a la Vez. Fama 607, 1981.
En la Plaza Garibaldi. Fama 594, 1980.
El Tahur. Fama 577, 1979.
Número Ocho. Fama 564, 1978.
Vivan los Mojados. Fama 554, 1977. Also Profono PRL-90398, 1984.
Pueblo Querido. Fama 538.
La Banda del Carro Rojo. Fama 536. Also Profono PRL-90396, 1984.
Contrabando y Traición. Fama 528.
Sí, Sí, Sí/Chayo Chaires. Fama 519.
Sufro Porque Te Quiero/La Cochicuina. Fama 516.
Juana la Traicionera/Por Amor a Mis Hijos. Fama 507.

CONTRIBUTORS

Blake Allmendinger is an associate professor of English at the University of California, Los Angeles. He is the author of *The Cowboy: Representations of Labor in an American Work Culture* (Oxford, 1992) and *Ten Most Wanted: The New Western Literature* (Routledge, 1998).

Karen Anderson is a professor of history at the University of Arizona. Her publications include *Changing Woman: A History of Racial Ethnic Women in Modern America* (Oxford, 1996) and *Wartime Women: Sex Roles, Family Relations, and the Status of Women during World War II* (Greenwood, 1981).

Miroslava Chavez is a Ph.D. candidate in history at the University of California, Los Angeles. The essay in this book draws upon her dissertation, "Mexican Women and the American Conquest in Los Angeles, 1821–1870," which she is currently completing. Research grants from the Institute of American Cultures, UCLA, and fellowships from the Graduate Affirmative Affairs Office, UCLA, and the American Association of University Women have made her work possible.

Mike Davis wanders the West without premeditation. His most recent book is *The Ecology of Fear: Los Angeles and the Imagination of Disaster* (1998). He is also the co-editor (with Hal Rothman) of *The Grit beneath the Glitter: Tales from the Real Las Vegas* (California, 1998).

Arleen de Vera received the Alexander Saxton History Essay Award in 1992 for her M.A. research on labor organizing among Filipino immigrants in the 1950s. She is now a Ph.D. candidate in history at UCLA and completing a dissertation on the roles of nationalism, colonialism, and culture in the creation of Filipino identity, 1919 to 1946.

William Deverell is associate professor of history in the Division of the Humanities and Social Sciences at the California Institute of Technology. He is the author of *Railroad Crossing: Californians and the Railroad, 1850–1910* and co-editor (with Tom

Sitton) of *California Progressivism Revisited* (both California, 1994). His essay in this volume is drawn from an in-progress book on the history of Los Angeles, 1850–1940.

Douglas Flamming is assistant professor of history in the School of History, Technology, and Society at the Georgia Institute of Technology. His book *Creating the Modern South: Millhands and Managers in Dalton, Georgia, 1884–1984* won the Philip Taft Labor History Award. The essay included here stems from his current book project titled "A World to Gain: African Americans and the Making of Los Angeles, 1890–1940."

Chris Friday is an associate professor of history at Western Washington University, where he is director of the Center for Pacific Northwest History as well as director of the Asian American Studies Minor. His first book, *Organizing Asian American Labor* (Temple, 1994), won the 1995 Association for Asian American Studies National History Book Award. He is currently working on a two-volume study of American Indian life and art in the twentieth century and a book-length manuscript that examines the multiracial nature of Pacific maritime labor markets in the nineteenth and twentieth centuries. Friday's other publications and research continue to focus on Asian American history and interracial relations and racial formations in historical perspective.

Anne E. Goldman is assistant professor of English at Sonoma State University. She is the author of *Take My Word: Autobiographical Innovations of Ethnic American Working Women* (California, 1996). At present she is completing a manuscript on late-nineteenth-century fictions called "Racing Region: Toward a More Dialectical Model for American Studies."

Ramón A. Gutiérrez is the associate chancellor and professor of ethnic studies at the University of California, San Diego. He is the author of *When Jesus Came, the Corn Mothers Went Away: Marriage, Sexuality and Power in New Mexico, 1500–1848* (Stanford, 1991) and, with Richard Orsi, the editor of *Contested Eden: California before the Gold Rush* (California, 1998). Gutiérrez is currently at work on a history of the Chicano Movement in the United States.

Louise V. Jeffredo-Warden, a writer/folklorist/poet of mixed European and Native American descent (Island Gabrielino/Payomkawish [Luiseño]/Creek), is a doctoral candidate in the Department of Social and Cultural Anthropology at Stanford University. She is a member of the Temecula (Pechanga) Band of Luiseño Mission Indians.

Susan Lee Johnson is an assistant professor of history at the University of Colorado at Boulder, where she teaches courses in western history, gender history, and the history of sexuality. She has published in the *Western Historical Quarterly* and *Radical History Review,* and her book on gender, race, memory, and the California Gold Rush is forthcoming.

Patricia Nelson Limerick is a professor of history at the University of Colorado at Boulder, and the chair of the Board of the Center of the American West there. The author of *The Legacy of Conquest* (Norton, 1987), she has two books in progress, *Something in the Soil* and *The Atomic West* (both forthcoming from Norton).

Jesús Martínez-Saldaña is an assistant professor of political science at Santa Clara University. His primary area of research is Mexican immigration.

Valerie J. Matsumoto is an associate professor of history and Asian American studies at the University of California, Los Angeles. The author of *Farming the Home Place: A Japanese American Community in California, 1919-1982* (Cornell, 1993), she is working on a book about Nisei women and the creation of urban youth culture in the 1930s.

Melissa L. Meyer is a specialist in American Indian social history and interdisciplinary methods. She earned her Ph.D. in 1985 from the University of Minnesota. She published *The White Earth Tragedy: Ethnicity and Dispossession at a Minnesota Anishinaabe Reservation, 1887-1920* in 1994. Her articles have appeared in the *American Historical Review, Social Science History,* and elsewhere. Her current research focuses on the history of American Indian tribal enrollment with special emphasis on "blood quantum requirements."

Mary Murphy is an associate professor of history at Montana State University, Bozeman. She is the author of *Mining Cultures: Men, Women and Leisure in Butte, 1914–1941* (Illinois, 1997) and co-author of *Like a Family: The Making of a Southern Cotton Mill World* (1987).

Peggy Pascoe is an associate professor and Beekman Chair of Northwest and Pacific History at the University of Oregon. The author of *Relations of Rescue: The Search for Female Moral Authority in the American West, 1873–1939* (1990), she is at work on a book about the history of miscegenation laws in the U.S. from 1865 to the present.

Virginia Scharff, associate professor of history at the University of New Mexico, is the author of *Taking the Wheel: Women and the Coming of the Motor Age* (Free Press, 1991) and co-author of *Present Tense: The United States since 1945* (Houghton Mifflin, 1991; 2d ed., 1996) and *Coming of Age: America in the Twentieth Century* (Houghton Mifflin, 1998). She is working on a book about women's movements and the West.

Jill Watts is an associate professor of history at California State University, San Marcos. She is the author of *God, Harlem U.S.A.: The Father Divine Story* (California, 1992) and is currently working on an interpretative biography of the life and work of Mae West.

INDEX

Compositor: Prestige Typography
Text: 10/12 Baskerville
Display: Baskerville
Printer and binder: Edwards Brothers, Inc.